Implementing the IB Diploma Programme

Editor

Marc van Loo

Assistant editors

Kevin Morley (language chapters)
John Goodban (IBO matters)
Frans van Loo (IBO external review)

Contributing authors

Ellie Alchin
Nick Alchin
Jay Atwood
Robin Barton
Mark Beverley
Nick Cotton
Jeremy Craig
James Dalziel
Ian Deakin
Robert Friesen
John Goodban
Julie Hessler
Dave Hobman
Cameron Hunter
Sarah Jeyaram

Stuart Jones
Peter Joseph
Luke Lawson
Marc van Loo
Bruce Love
Mark McCallum
Matias de Menezes
Kevin Morley
Monica Mueller
Andy Payne
Anu Ruhil
Jill Rutherford
Robert Walker
Phil Woolrich

Implementing the IB Diploma Programme

A practical manual for principals, IB coordinators, heads of department and teachers

CAMBRIDGE
UNIVERSITY PRESS

CAMBRIDGE UNIVERSITY PRESS
Cambridge, New York, Melbourne, Madrid, Cape Town, Singapore, São Paulo

Cambridge University Press
The Edinburgh Building, Cambridge CB2 8RU, UK

www.cambridge.org
Information on this title: www.cambridge.org/9780521544870

First published 2004

A catalogue record for this publication is available from the British Library

ISBN 978-0-521-54487-0 paperback

Transferred to digital printing 2008

ACKNOWLEDGEMENTS
The publishers would like to thank the IBO for permission to use the following material in
this publication. All the material remains the copyright of the IBO.

p. 4: Fig 1.1 © IBO 2002; p. 147: adapted from *Creativity, Action, Service* guide © IBO 2001;
p. 148 (top): adapted from Diploma Programme Coordinator Notes, August 2002 © IBO
2002; p. 148 (bottom): adapted from *Diploma Programme Coordinator Notes,* April 2002
© IBO 2002; p. 170: *Theory of Knowledge* guide © IBO 2003; p. 172: Fig 10.3 adapted from
Theory of Knowledge guide © IBO 2003; p. 203: Fig 11.4 © IBO 1998; pp. 373, 375: Figs 15.6,
15.7 adapted from the experimental sciences guides © IBO 2001; p. 210 table © IBO;
p. 376–7: Figs 15.9, 15.10, 15.11 comments adapted from the experimental sciences
guides © IBO 2001; p. 378: Figs 15.12, 15.13, 15.14 adapted from the experimental
sciences guides © IBO 2001; p. 435: November 2000, MHL Paper 1 Q5 © IBO 2000,
November 2001, MHL Paper 1 Q14 © IBO 2001; p. 451: Task 5 adapted from *Teacher
Support Material, Mathematical Methods SL, The Portfolio* © IBO 1998; p. 463: November
2001, MMSL Paper 1 Q8 © IBO 2001; p. 464: May 2000, MHL Paper 2 Q3 © IBO 2000;
p. 465: November 2001, MHL Paper 2 Q1 © IBO 2001; p. 468: November 1999, MHL
Paper 2 Q3 © IBO 1999, May 1995, MHL Paper 2 Q2 (ii) © IBO 1995; p. 469: May 2001,
MHL Paper 2 Q5 © IBO 2001; p. 527: Fig 19.1 © IBO 2002.

Cover image by ingrampublishing.com

Every effort has been made to reach copyright holders. The publishers would be pleased to
hear from anyone whose rights they have unwittingly infringed.

Cambridge University Press has no responsibility for the persistence or accuracy of
URLs for external or third-party Internet websites referred to in this publication,
and does not guarantee that any content on such websites is, or will remain, accurate
or appropriate.

Dedication To Isa, Igor and Kilan

Contents

Preface

What is the purpose of this book?

The International Baccalaureate (IB) Diploma Programme is a two-year pre-university high school programme. Its international foundation allows schools anywhere in the world to apply for authorization to teach it. For many educators, the Diploma Programme (DP) marks the only truly international high school diploma, and a rapidly increasing number of top-ranking universities regard it as a preferred high school qualification. Perceived by some as elitist, its inherent qualities are nevertheless undisputed.

This explains why the DP has become the world's fastest-growing pre-university education programme. However, introduction of the DP comes at a cost, and schools contemplating its introduction will have to invest significant time, effort and funding to meet the requirements set by its governing body, the International Baccalaureate Organization (the IBO), whose headquarters are located in Geneva.

Schools interested in introducing the DP should contact their regional IBO office as a first step. At that stage, the school receives some documentation, including the guides to IB diploma authorization and an application form. After studying these, schools can ask the regional office for a visit. Based on the feedback this visit generates, schools will then work for, typically, a year or more to prepare for authorization. When they feel they are ready, they request an *authorization visit* – the success of which, it should be stressed, is by no means assured (as will be evident from some of the case studies featured in this book).

Until recently, feedback from newly authorized schools routinely referred to the rather concise and scattered nature of the IBO documentation, which at times left schools at a loss on how to proceed. The IBO responded to this feedback early in 2003, when it issued more detailed guides to the authorization process and accelerated the development of its website. There are still a great number of documents to go through, however, so suggestions from IB educators now tend to focus on requests for further centralization and organization of the official resources.

This is one area where this book aims to assist: it is a *one-point* information source on the *entire* DP, containing clear references to necessary and useful existing materials. While the collation of information from the perspective of a school is one aim, the twin aim is to provide a guide on how to use this information. It may well be completely clear *what* to do, but not necessarily *how* to do it. In other words, this book offers prospective schools a clear roadmap towards successful IB authorization and implementation.

This is not to say that we offer a prescriptive one-size-fits-all approach. The editors and contributors strongly share the IBO's conviction that standard approaches are counter to good education, especially in view of the diversity of profiles of the participating and prospective schools around the globe. Rather, we believe that educators will benefit from looking at examples of successful – and unsuccessful – IB practice. This book will allow those new to the IB to benefit from the experience of established practitioners and gain from that experience. By avoiding potential pitfalls, schools can concentrate on what matters: to take full benefit of the learning opportunities provided by the IB.

The case studies in Part Two of this book reveal that it is surprisingly easy for even the most committed and sincere schools to stumble during the authorization procedures and initial stages, leading to a loss both of credibility and of students. With the benefit of hindsight, such problems could have been avoided. This book aims to provide that hindsight – before the event.

Who is this book for?

Originally, when Kevin Morley first put forward the idea of this book, we envisaged that its target group would be almost exclusively the upper management and teachers of a prospective or a newly IB authorized school. However, by addressing this audience, we have found that the text simultaneously serves as an ideal introduction to the IB from the point of view of a teacher contemplating a career-move towards teaching it. This book will prepare teachers for their interviews and for the task of teaching the programme. Every chapter is readable by administrators and teachers alike, and the text therefore also allows interested parents to find the answers to the question: 'What is the IB and is it the best choice for my child?'

In summary, this book offers all stakeholders:

- a deep understanding of how the DP affects the overall operations of a school and its community
- a reliable and realistic assessment of the benefits and costs associated with introduction of the IB diploma
- a hands-on manual for authorization, from administration to department level
- case studies of a range of regions and recently authorized schools, highlighting the pitfalls and successes associated with introduction of the IB Diploma Programme
- detailed advice on teaching the individual subjects (including the IB core): content, methodology and assessment.

With clear and typically self-contained chapters, written by relevant personnel from newly authorized schools, expert colleagues from some of the world's foremost IB schools and former IBO top officials, this book delivers a realistic assessment of the expectation and the magnitude of the task ahead.

The editors and authors value feedback from you, our colleagues, to ensure this text remains relevant in this highly dynamic field that is the IB diploma, and we look forward to your emails to: editor@dp-help.com.

Marc van Loo

Introduction

How to use this book

The introductory section summarizes the answers to the main question on the list of prospective IB schools and parents: 'Why should we embrace the IB Diploma Programme (DP) and what should we be aware of?' This is followed by an overview of the IB DP. A glossary of IB terminology and abbreviations is included at the end of the book for easy reference.

Chapter 2 is by John Goodban, the long-serving regional director of IBO Asia-Pacific. It details the expectations the IBO has of an IB school, and how the IBO guards the integrity of its programme, and of itself as an organization. Having explained *what* to do as a prospective IB school, the next few chapters then turn to the question of *how* to do it. A hands-on authorization manual is followed by a series of case studies: of regions, of recently authorized schools, and of Malaysia's Mara College Banting, arguably one of the world's most successful IB schools. Taken together, the case studies paint a vivid picture of the IB diploma and its potential as perceived by different types of schools in different parts of the world.

Part Three of the book concerns the *IB hexagon* – the academic structure of the DP. The section opens with a discussion on how to set up the IB core, a topic that concerns all academic staff. Thus armed, the reader is presented with the essentials for preparing individual departments for the successful introduction of the DP. Leading teachers from some of the world's most successful IB schools have written individual chapters on each area of the diploma curriculum: core, first and second languages, humanities, sciences, mathematics and the arts as well as trans-disciplinary subjects close to the philosophy of the IB such as ecosystems and societies. Also included is a discussion on the merits and difficulties of the school based subjects.

In the final chapter, John Goodban outlines such issues as pre-IB preparation and likely future directions for the IBO.

Mindful of our readers' busy schedules, we have endeavoured to write chapters as stand-alone sections. Nevertheless, it is recommended that every reader who is interested in the IB reads the introduction and the first sections of the book (to the end of Part Two). Readers with more time could read the introductory sections of each chapter to get a broad overview of the IB. For easy reference within chapters, each chapter opens with its table of contents. A note on quoted material: when we quote from IB materials, we may have omitted, added to or summarized some of the materials – but any such editing is always done within the overall IB philosophy.

Certain details not covered in this book, such as detailed lesson plans, ready-to-use forms, additional subject chapters and so on, appear on the website that accompanies this book: www.dp-help.com.

Why adopt the IB diploma?

The holistic philosophy of the IB emphasizes high academic standards in the mandatory areas of first and second languages, mathematics, humanities and science. Academic excellence is coupled with emphasis on personal development in areas such as philosophy, social awareness and the arts. The IBO is an independent organization unfettered by individual national demands, which allows it to act as a powerful guarantor of unbiased assessment procedures. This explains why a growing number of universities in more than 100 countries hold IB graduates in high regard, and why a rapidly growing number of high schools are considering adopting the IB.

A school wishing to consider offering the IB diploma, however, needs to consider the impact such a decision has on all stakeholders: the students and their parents, the teachers, the school as a whole and the community at large (region, nation). To name some of the frequently encountered anxieties we mention here: fear of change in general, fear of being a guinea pig, fear of loss of national identity, fears associated with the IB's perceived elitist nature, fears relating to university recognition, and fear of examination in a language not your own (currently, in terms of documentation and examination, English, French and Spanish are the official DP languages). Furthermore, until recently the IBO did not wish to endorse subject textbooks of any kind. This, and the fact that the curriculum of the DP changes on a regular basis in response to feedback from schools, examiners and universities around the world, held publishers back from embarking on IB book projects. The IBO has begun to relax its opposition to textbooks, but it is fair to say that the current offering of course-specific textbooks is still poor compared with the offerings in other major examination programmes. Given the above list of concerns and further concerns addressed below, it is clear that all stakeholders need to be convinced that the advantages of adopting the IB outweigh the risks. Amongst all prerequisites for successful introduction of the IB, truthful communication surely ranks as the first priority.

Listed below are the key messages to be communicated to the stakeholder groups.

Key messages to students and parents

The DP provides enhanced learning opportunities for students. Along with these enhanced learning opportunities often (but not automatically) come expanded opportunities at tertiary institutions – including receiving significant transfer credits – for students achieving sufficiently high results. A universally recognized diploma and ranking, with an international perspective insisting on expertise in at least two languages and emphasizing areas of global concern, brings with it an increased adaptability and mobility, a major advantage in an increasingly globalized world. At the same time, the IBO's strong suggestion that students study their mother tongue as a first (A1) language ensures firm roots in the home culture. In line with university and job market demands, the mandatory IB core components emphasize personal growth through activities, through service, and through their insistence on reflection, on both an academic and a personal level.

Success in the IB is not determined by a final external examination alone; a substantial part of the assessment is internal (although typically externally moderated), and this affords students the opportunity to take a significant degree of ownership of their education, and be rewarded for their efforts in school. The perceptions on the elitist nature of the programme are to a large degree unjustified. While the demands of the programme are definitely greater than those of a typical US high school diploma, they are on a par with those of a typical AP programme (see Chapter 8). Turning to Britain, while it is harder to score highly in the IB diploma than in A-levels, the programmes are comparable on the pass level – in fact many students who pass the diploma with 24 points would have struggled gaining Ds and Cs at A-level (see Chapter 4). Furthermore, US inner city IB schools (many of whose students cannot cope with the full DP and obtain IB subject certificates instead) have reported an overall lift in student performance after introduction of the IB, and this experience is shared by international schools with a wide-range ability intake. (See the chapters in Part Two.)

On the other hand, as detailed in the first two case studies, parents need to ask the school hard and specific questions about university acceptance. While it is true that many top universities are well aware of the IB diploma and regard it highly, some admissions officers may be new to it and for some universities an IB diploma holder may actually be at a relative disadvantage compared with a national award holder. These problems can usually be overcome through hard work on the part of the school's tertiary advisers, who may have to canvass the typical target universities well before the IB programme is proposed to parents. (Naturally, the IBO is also working very hard – and with success – to address such recognition issues; refer to its website.) On another note of caution, students who are likely to move between schools should receive careful advice on their IB package choice lest they get stranded later at their new school.

Having noted that the IB programme is academically more accessible than is often believed, both students and their parents nevertheless need to realize that its rigorous standards and the substantial workload require a great deal of commitment, organization and initiative. Individual IB subject certificates enjoy less recognition at universities than the full IB diploma does, so students lacking sufficient drive may be better off in traditional national programmes, since partially completed programmes of national systems usually afford better recognition than those of the IB.

Key messages to teachers

Teachers will become members of a worldwide professional body, which offers opportunities for professional development. The DP affords them an international perspective on teaching and learning. The curriculum is clearly articulated but it allows and encourages teachers to experiment with ideas and practices, even to teach completely new courses such as the Theory of Knowledge. Introduction of the DP could potentially mean smaller class sizes, since the IBO strongly recommends a limit of 25 students per class. Being part of a school that is recognized as a good school is clearly an asset for those who work there.

The implementation of the DP does not mean that teachers have to start all over again. But the new curriculum coupled with the relative lack of good textbooks (see above) may well mean that teachers have to consider a wider range of resources and pick the best of each. While teaching the DP is initially more work, it clearly enhances teaching experience and confidence in the longer term.

In summary, implementation of the IB diploma will require commitment and a lot of work – but that hard work will be rewarded with better outcomes for students, international mobility, and potentially better remuneration packages. The increased marketability of teachers further provides a new IB school with an incentive to create an attractive working environment, as evidenced by the case studies.

Key messages to schools

The quality of learning for students is improved with the IB diploma; the opportunity for quality teacher professional development is enhanced; and the image and competitive position of the school will improve with successful implementation of the IB. Furthermore, the school will gain a sense of shared purpose and a mission – 'Education for life' – which boosts morale. The school will have a worldwide pool of teachers who can be contracted for service. Finally, introduction of the IB means a ready-made quality programme that can be integrated with feeder systems and with tertiary institutions.

On the side of caution, a school adopting the DP must prepare itself for significant investments in terms of time, effort and money. In the time leading up to IB authorization, a school will have to invest in professional development of its staff. Following this, teachers' salaries may well have to be revised upwards in order not to lose staff immediately after providing them with IB training; class size may have to shrink; and the IBO has strict requirements in terms of IT and library provision. As mentioned earlier, a school may have to invest significant efforts in 'clearing' the IB diploma with its target universities, well before proposing the IB to parents. While the authorization procedure typically takes less than two years, a school must allow up to five years for the IB diploma to fully embed itself in the school community: there will be no such thing as a 'quick-fix' here.

Since a number of schools will have the government represented as a stakeholder in one form or another, it may be important that a school can communicate on the regional/national level as well.

Key messages to the wider region and possibly the nation

Not only will the best and brightest students stay in their home country but foreigners may be attracted by the opportunity to study an internationally recognized programme. In well over 100 countries, the nation will benefit from the experience of others, thus placing the country squarely in the global community. Opportunities for exchange are vastly improved. Students will be taught the skills necessary to bring about change within their own society, while staying true to local values and customs. On the downside, when introducing the DP schools may also introduce the risk of the national school system being viewed as a second-tier system.

As a final point on the upside, all stakeholders will benefit from the new systems of learning associated with the IBO, as well as from access to its strong and developing research base which relies on input from dedicated schools and national curricula the world over.

In relation to this last point, the authors and editors of this book are delighted to point out that many of us gained new and often surprising insights into the IB by reading and editing each other's contributions. Some of our perceptions on the curriculum, academic accessibility, regional differences, attitudes of the IBO, and school marketing strategies needed adjustment. While all authors were positively inclined towards the IB from the start, it is fair to say that our collective regard for the IBO has grown. No organization is flawless, but our combined efforts revealed a clear pattern: the IBO does take criticism very seriously and responds to it in the spirit of its own philosophy. Since concerns may be raised anywhere around the world and at any time by force of the IBO's own constitution (see Chapter 2), the curriculum is by necessity dynamic and ever-changing. While this can be frustrating from the perspective of a single school trying to establish good routines, it is clear that any errors are quickly rectified and that long-term changes are invariably for the better.

One could argue that being small (slightly more than 40,000 students and 1,000 schools worldwide were involved in the May 2002 IB diploma examinations) makes it easier to retain such quality and flexibility, and that these virtues may diminish if the current annual growth of around 15% is maintained. But the IB diploma has been around for over 30 years, and 30 years of continual fine-tuning and a constitution assuring transparency and stakeholder sensitivity surely are powerful guarantors of continued success in the future.

In keeping with the dynamic nature of the DP, continuous updates at www.dp-help.com help ensure that this book will remain current. The DP changes typically do not affect the overall thrust of the chapters in this book, and can be digested quickly, either before or after reading each chapter. Nevertheless, the reader is strongly advised to download the latest update page to learn what has changed since publication of this book.

The editor would like to acknowledge the help of Ian Deakin in providing the basic framework of this introductory section.

This guide is not an IBO publication and is not endorsed by the IBO.

Part One

General Introduction to the IB Diploma Programme

Chapter 1
Overview of the Diploma Programme

Marc van Loo, MSc, PhD

Marc van Loo brought together the team of authors for this text and subsequently managed the project towards completion. He started teaching the International Baccalaureate (IB) Diploma Programme (DP) in 1995 in Singapore at the United World College of South East Asia, where he was in charge of further mathematics and where he taught all four IB mathematics courses as well as TOK. He went on to develop his passion for experiential learning, through an educational resort he set up in nearby Indonesia (LooLa Adventure Resort), by taking up the positions of coordinator of Critical Thinking at Nanyang Technological University, and of Professor of Mathematics and Physics at Overseas Family College, a college at the forefront of educational innovation in Singapore.

Marc conducts corporate training programmes as well as school trips for children of all ages, and taught adults at Singapore's Open University's BSc programme in Mathematics from 1996 to 2000.

This chapter features a brief overview of the IB DP curriculum and the way it is assessed. It establishes the terminology used freely in the rest of the book.

1 The IB diploma curriculum: the hexagon

The IB DP curriculum (offered in English, French and Spanish) is displayed in the IBO's trademark diagram, the hexagon (see figure 1.1).

Figure 1.1 The IB diploma hexagon

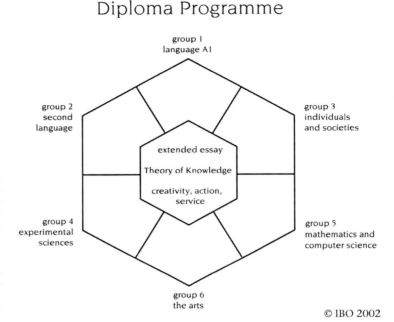

© IBO 2002

1.1 Constraints of the IB DP

All diploma students must complete the core programme (in the centre of the hexagon), and they must study six academic subjects – one subject from each corner of the hexagon (i.e. from each group). Of the six academic subjects, the IBO stipulates that at least three and no more than four subjects must be taken at Higher Level (HL), comprising 240 teacher–student contact hours; and the rest at Standard Level (SL), 150 contact hours. It is up to the student and the school advisers to determine which particular subjects are taken at HL.

The six subjects must be chosen subject to the following constraints.

First and second languages (groups 1 and 2)

The group 1 language is a literature course in the student's mother tongue or best language and is labelled A1. In Singapore, for example, this could be English A1 or Malay A1 or Chinese A1. A1 courses can be class-taught or, in the case of minority languages, self-taught. Forty-five A1 languages are offered, but other languages can be made available on request, given sufficient notice.

Group 2 is a second or foreign language programme that can be taken at *beginner's platform* (*ab initio*), *intermediate platform* (B), or *fluent platform* (A2, offered to bilingual students). Unlike A1, only the most common group 2 languages can be taken at all three levels, e.g. Spanish *ab initio*, Spanish B or Spanish A2. Other languages, for instance Hindi, can only be taken as language B but are not available at *ab initio* or A2 level. Schools wishing to teach group 2 courses other than those automatically available must make a special request to the IBO.

Both group 1 and 2 languages can be taken at either HL or SL, *except ab initio* and self-taught A1 languages, which are only available at SL. Note further that the IBO does not impose English as a mandatory language (unless it happens to be the student's first language). If this brief summary strikes the reader as somewhat bewildering, that is because it is so. Chapters 12 and 13 provide further details.

Individuals and societies (group 3)

History, economics and psychology enjoy great popularity; geography, business and management, and information technology in a global society (SL only) are also widely taken; also available are philosophy, anthropology and Islamic history.

Experimental sciences (group 4)

These are usually biology, chemistry or physics, but also available are design technology and environmental systems (SL only).

Mathematics and computer science (group 5)

Choice is between one HL course and two SL courses, one of which is fairly light, while the other is an introduction-to-calculus type course. The HL course is hard, covering more than a typical US college first-year mathematics offering.

The arts and free electives (group 6)

The arts subjects are visual arts, music and theatre arts. As free elective the student can choose a third language or one of the group 5 subjects computer science or further mathematics (further mathematics is an SL course equivalent in content to a typical first semester university pure mathematics course, and has no equivalent in any national system). Usually, however, students use the free elective option to choose another social study or science subject to allow them a degree of specialization necessary for university.

Students are allowed to take a seventh subject, from any group, at the discretion of the school.

1.2 A few details on the IB core programme

The heart of the IB DP is embodied in its three mandatory core components.

Creativity, action, service (CAS)

Students must show sustained and active participation in CAS. Typically this amounts to half a day per week over the two-year course, or 150 hours altogether, keeping in mind that CAS should not be approached as an hour-counting exercise. The goal of CAS is that students learn about themselves, about others, and about the wider community by *doing*, and that they learn to *reflect* on the knowledge thus acquired.

Theory of Knowledge (TOK)

This is a philosophical course that considers the ways in which people acquire knowledge as well as the typical strengths and weaknesses of each of these ways. Throughout, an awareness of the impact of culture on knowledge plays a key role. There is no equivalent of this course in any national education system, and the IBO prefers to see as many teachers as possible involved in the teaching of this inter-disciplinary course.

Extended essay (EE)

Students are required to write an extended essay of 4,000 words, for which there is again no equivalent in most traditional high school programmes. The extended essay is a research piece in an area of the student's choice (e.g. in mathematics, economics or language) which involves work outside the subject syllabus. University admissions officers often scrutinize this aspect of a student's work because the extended essay is typical of research work required at tertiary level.

1.3 School-based subjects and trans-disciplinary subjects

Within the hexagon, we finally briefly mention the role of the school-based subjects and the trans-disciplinary subjects, exciting courses that mark the future of the DP.

School-based subjects (SBS)

These are subjects developed by experienced IB schools in consultation with the IBO that typically meet a local need. About 20 such SBSs currently exist; they are only offered at SL.

Trans-disciplinary subjects (TDS)

These are subjects that satisfy the requirements of two hexagon corners at the same time, with a view to fostering cross-curricular understanding and to provide greater flexibility in package choice. These subjects are: text and performance (groups 1 and 6), ecosystems and societies (groups 3 and 4) and world cultures (groups 3 and 6). They can only be taken at SL and only at selected pilot schools, though once the courses have been tested and validated they will be on offer to all schools.

2 The assessment

The IB diploma subjects are examined by a combination of continuous coursework and external examinations at the end of the two-year programme. The exams are in the first three weeks of May, with resits in November. For most southern hemisphere schools the order is reversed, with students sitting examinations in November.

In each subject the student can gain a score of 1 (lowest) to 7 (highest). The maximum for the six subjects is thus $6 \times 7 = 42$ points. There are up to an extra 3 points – called *bonus points* – for both the TOK and extended essay together, but a student who fails both TOK and the EE or who fails to satisfy the requirements of the CAS programme will not be awarded a diploma.

The maximum score in a diploma is therefore 45 points (attained by about 0.2% of the worldwide cohort in May 2002). The minimum score needed to gain a diploma is 24 points (provided that all other requirements are fully satisfied). A good university will expect something like 28–36 points (about 4–6 points for each of the six subjects). Top universities might ask for 37–40 points.

Examination papers and syllabuses are written by teams of IB examiners and teachers comprising members from many continents and cultures. There is a five-year review cycle for all subjects which aims for continual improvement. Minor changes are introduced on a regular basis, and major changes every five years.

The IB diploma examination system is graded against absolute standards (with some mark adjustments if necessary) and so is not norm-referenced (i.e. there is no fixed percentage of each grade). This inevitably leads to a different grade distribution every year and for every subject (see section 2.1 below), but the IBO has made progress in moderating the differences. Grade inflation has not happened in the IB diploma. Since this sets the DP apart from many other examination systems, it is expected that the IBO is committed to keeping it that way.

All subjects in the hexagon, with the exception of the core, have a written examination, during a three-week interval at the end of the programme. Each exam consists typically of two or three papers, but the overall length is limited to a maximum of five hours per HL subject and three hours per SL subject. In addition, every subject has a coursework component, which may be internally assessed (and externally moderated by the IBO), or internally supervised but externally assessed. The assessment percentage contributed by the coursework varies, as illustrated in figure 1.2.

Oral and written communication is stressed, as are group work and analytical skills. The IBO encourages students and schools to take the initiative, and thus favours coursework as a means of assessment; it is held back from giving coursework greater weight by the entry requirements of many universities.

The system of assessment is recognizable to anyone familiar with US or UK examination board methods: there are standardization, moderation and grade award meetings. The whole assessment process is completed six weeks after the last examination, and results are given to students by a secure PIN number in the first week of July (or January for November candidates).

Figure 1.2 Assessment weight of coursework

Group	Coursework
Group 1: Language A1	30%
Group 2: Second language	30%
Group 3: Individuals and societies	20–30%
Group 4: Experimental sciences	24–36%
Group 5: Mathematics and computer science	20%
Group 6: The arts	30–50%
TOK	100%
Extended essay	100%

2.1 Statistical analysis of subject grade distributions

Figures 1.3 and 1.4 show a statistical analysis based on the IBO leaflet of raw data that goes under the name Statistical Bulletin (published twice a year after each examination). Figure 1.3 lists two important statistics. The *average grade* for each group indicates roughly how difficult the group is for the student. The *standard deviation* is a measure of the spread of the grades (i.e. the ability range of students) and thus roughly indicates how difficult the subject is for teachers to teach, especially for teachers who face the full ability range. The significant differences in these two numbers across the groups clearly demonstrate the absence of norm-referencing; figure 1.4 illustrates this visually.

Using these statistical interpretations, we see that sciences are somewhat tough on both student and teacher; arts grades are the toughest of all; the individuals and societies group is the 'model citizen' of the DP; while languages are somewhat gentler on both student and teacher.

Figure 1.3 Average grades and their standard deviations

May 2002	Average	S.d. (spread)
Overall	**4.8**	**1.5**
Group 1: Language A1	5.0	0.9
Group 2: Second language	5.3	1.2
Group 3: Individuals and societies	4.8	1.4
Group 4: Experimental sciences	4.6	1.8
Group 5: Mathematics and computer science	4.7	1.7
Group 6: The arts	4.4	1.7

Figure 1.4 Grade distribution per group, illustrating absence of norm-referencing

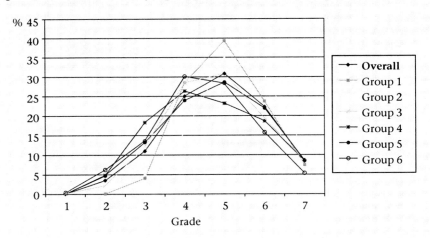

Chapter 2

Quality assurance and maintenance of the International Baccalaureate Diploma Programme

John Goodban, BA (Econ), Dip Ed

John Goodban was a founding member of staff of the United World College of South East Asia, Singapore where, between 1971 and 1991, he served at various times as head of the faculty of humanities, head of middle school, director of development and deputy headmaster. He taught IB geography Higher Level (HL), geology Standard Level (SL) and school-based subjects (SBS). He was for many years the Diploma Programme coordinator (DPC). From 1991 to 2002 he was IBO director for the Asia-Pacific region. To list just a few more achievements in his long career: member of the conceptual team for the development of the present IB Middle Years Programme (1984–92), chairman of the IBO creativity, action and service (CAS) committee (1990–97), member of the IBO Senior Management Team (1999–2002), coordinator of large-scale teacher-training workshop programmes – over 1,200 regional workshops arranged and conducted throughout the Asia-Pacific region (1991–2002) – author of the first IB diploma trans-disciplinary syllabus 'Science, technology and social change', and finally, author of the Longman geography series 'Living in Cities'.

In this chapter John Goodban provides a clear account of what the International Baccalaureate Organization (IBO) expects from schools that wish to introduce the IB Diploma Programme (DP). The emphasis throughout is on how the IBO guards and maintains the quality of its curriculum, its participating schools and itself as an organization. The next few chapters examine in detail the practical implications of this at the school level.

1 Introduction

Since its formal foundation in 1968, the IBO has made determined efforts to ensure that the quality of its various services to schools continues to meet the highest standards. The challenge of quality assurance in national education systems is a considerable task and, when applied to the complex diversity of the international arena, it is even more daunting. That so much has been achieved in the development of the DP during its relatively short existence owes much to the quality of its curriculum and its assessment. As a result, the diploma today is widely recognized and accepted by universities in more than 110 countries as a first-class qualification for entry to tertiary studies. Increasingly it is described as the gold standard in international education; a reputation that has been hard earned, is well deserved and is an ongoing challenge to maintain and to develop further.

Quality assurance and quality maintenance focus on both schools and the IBO. The overall quality of a school's DP and its delivery to students, and likewise that of the IBO, in terms of the curriculum, its assessment, corporate services and structures, are all vitally important. We all know the importance of quality maintenance of a new car to ensure that it continues to function efficiently or, in the case of a new house, to prevent it from falling into a state of disrepair and ruin. Not surprisingly, quality international education also requires quality maintenance. It is one thing to develop a new curriculum and innovative assessment methodologies, and to train teachers to teach them; it is quite another to ensure that standards do not decline, that development does not stagnate, that resources are restocked – and that the all-important teacher is not forgotten.

In this chapter, *quality assurance* is defined as being able to meet and adhere to certain prescribed IBO aims, objectives and requirements. It is measured against specific criteria and conditions that are applied fairly and equally to all schools that are preparing for authorization to teach the DP and to those that are authorized to teach it. However, not only are schools asked the questions: 'How good are you?' and 'Can you demonstrate how you meet our requirements?'; the IBO addresses similar questions to itself: 'How valid is the currency of the curriculum and its assessment, and is the organization responding appropriately to the needs of a rapidly changing, increasingly sophisticated adult world in which students will soon have to take their place?'

2 The authorization of schools

Arguably, the procedures governing the authorization of new schools to teach the DP represent the single most important of the IBO's quality assurance strategies. All schools are required to submit an application to the regional office, to be followed by an authorization visit and the approval of the application by the IBO director-general before teaching can begin. No school is permitted automatically to adopt the DP nor, for that matter, to purchase it by credit card payment or by any other financial transaction. In other words, it is not possible simply to buy your way into the IB and to become an IB world school.

In order to be eligible to teach the DP every school must first have its application approved by the IBO director-general. This approval will not be granted until the school has submitted a full application and required supporting documentation to the regional office, and has received a successful official authorization visit which this office will arrange and for which the school must pay the costs. However, no professional fees are paid to any members of the visiting authorization team. The team generally comprises a representative from the regional office plus one or two other members, usually an experienced DPC and a senior administrator from authorized schools situated within a reasonable distance but never from neighbouring institutions (this is to ensure a greater degree of objectivity).

The prime mover in the lead-up to the authorization visit and the visit itself is the IBO regional office. The coordination of the various procedures is the overall responsibility of the regional director or the regional DP manager. However, in a very large region, such as the Asia-Pacific, it is possible that the appropriate sub-regional representative would take on this particular responsibility.

The applicant or candidate schools should make every effort to familiarize themselves with all aspects of the DP. While a detailed internal school audit is of vital importance from the curriculum, resources, pedagogic and financial viewpoints, the staff designated to teach the IB should make every effort possible to visit nearby authorized IB schools that are already experienced in teaching the DP. Ideally, occasional future visits should also be arranged. A great deal can be learned through joint departmental staff meetings, sitting in on IB classes and talking with students.

The candidate school needs to give some serious thought early on as to when it intends to submit its application and when it will be ready for the official authorization visit. There is no fixed period that must separate the authorization visit and the time when a school first makes any serious move to go ahead and introduce the DP. Very few schools can be properly prepared in less than a year. Many schools need or prefer to take considerably longer, although a period of two years or more between the initial application and the authorization visit is exceptional and such an extended period of time may become unsettling for teachers and the rest of the school community. Most importantly, for all concerned, is that the school should be entirely prepared, as a premature visit will almost certainly be costly in terms of funding a repeat visit and will incur an extra delay of up to another year before authorization is granted.

A chronological overview of the whole authorization procedure is given in section 2.7.

2.1 The aims and objectives of the DP

In order to achieve authorization, every new school must be able to demonstrate that it has a good understanding of the IBO's overarching aims and objectives of the DP, which are to:

- provide an internationally acceptable qualification for entry into higher education
- promote international education and intercultural understanding
- develop a holistic view of knowledge that emphasizes the connections between the various fields of learning

- educate the whole person, emphasizing intellectual, personal, emotional and social growth in a student-centred philosophy
- develop enquiry and thinking skills, and the capacity to reflect upon and to evaluate actions critically.

Without exception, all DP schools must be fully committed to achieving these aims and objectives. Directly linked to them are the specific *criteria and conditions* for the admission of new DP schools and it is a strict IBO requirement that candidate schools must satisfy the demands of all of them. These are clearly set out in the application documents that schools receive from their particular regional office and to which every school must declare its full commitment. It is this commitment that bonds together all IB world schools.

2.2 Criteria and conditions for authorization

When a school expresses a serious interest in the DP, the ongoing process of quality measurement commences. Quality assurance for the DP is of paramount importance throughout the authorization procedures for new schools. As a not-for-profit organization, the IBO is not in the business of growing larger in terms of promoting the number of authorized schools, because growth alone is not a pre-eminent concern. But *quality* is.

First and foremost is the quality of every school that wishes to introduce the DP. The single most important aspect of the authorization visit is to determine whether the candidate school is able to demonstrate unequivocally that it has understood the import of the criteria and conditions for the authorization of new schools and that it is able to meet the demands of each one in practice.

The IBO's *Criteria and Conditions for Authorization* of new DP schools, as set out in the IBO's DP *School Guide to the Authorization Visit*, are standard worldwide. Similarly, the overall authorization procedures are globally common. These are enormously important in safeguarding the integrity of the quality of the new candidate schools that are approved by the IBO director-general. In recognition of the importance of well-defined global standards, the IBO has recently focused considerable attention on rewriting the authorization documents, including the production of new guidelines for the school and the authorization team on the actual visit. To be an authorized DP school is increasingly accepted around the world as being an internationally recognized statement of excellence.

The key criteria and conditions for authorization and their separate and conjoint significance will now be examined and explained in turn.

- ***IB DP candidate schools shall be committed to the promotion of international understanding through education as expressed by the objectives and practices of the IBO.***

This ideal, the promotion of international understanding along with intercultural awareness, connects directly to one of the four fundamental aims (to promote international education) of all IBO curricula and, possibly, is the most complex to achieve in many schools. The IBO requires all schools to embrace and to espouse the importance of developing certain international values in students, especially a strong sense of international awareness, intercultural understanding, tolerance and compassion. Candidate schools for the DP must recognize from the start that this goes far beyond holding the traditional annual United Nations Day celebrations, eminently worthy though these may be. In international schools, where there is significant advantage due to an omnipresent international milieu of students, international understanding and intercultural awareness are far easier to promote, especially in schools such as the United World Colleges. However, in national schools, which comprise nearly 50% of the DP schools' total constituency, where the everyday classes are often more likely to be monocultural or virtually so, no immediate sense of internationalism may exist.

To an extent, ready access in the library, classrooms and laboratories to the internet and the schoolwide use of IT, including IBNET and the IBO's Online Curriculum Centre (OCC), can improve this situation and offer some remedies to the problem, but these alone are insufficient. The whole school staff, from the senior administration to the most junior classroom teacher, must be encouraged to be fully committed to exploring and establishing a variety of ways in which the international is brought frequently to the forefront of everyday school life, not just in the assembly hall but particularly in the classroom, the laboratory, the workshop and during activities. The major player here must be the teacher. This is not to say or imply that internationalism is to be taught, since in its intrinsic sense this cannot be done effectively. The inherent *values* of international and intercultural understanding, respect and tolerance cannot be taught or learned directly as such. Like morals, they can only be absorbed organically by the student over a period of time, and certainly not through any radical, revolutionary form of instant enlightenment, but rather through example, argument and reflection. Thus teachers must endeavour to introduce regularly to their classes, in an uncontrived and relevant manner, international and intercultural issues for discussion that can be linked to their own subjects. There will be opportunities for teachers when participating in IBO-approved teacher-training workshops to discuss with and learn from colleagues in other schools proven ways in which the challenge of internationalism in schools has been successfully approached elsewhere. It is of paramount importance to note that the IBO expects DP students to learn to recognize that to be different, to look different, to think differently and to live differently is not wrong, that diversity is to be celebrated, not feared, and that the variety of cultures and attitudes that make for the richness of life should be respected.

However, it is certainly not only in the six subject areas of the DP hexagon that there is room for internationalism. The Theory of Knowledge (TOK), the catalyst of the DP, requires students to reflect on such directly related issues as bias, opinion and fact. A creativity, action, service (CAS) programme that encourages students to enrol in service activities that involve them in direct contact with people of the host country (in the case of international schools) and with minority communities (in national schools) can significantly enhance the international focus and understanding of the students.

A candidate school, when submitting its application to the IBO regional office and during the authorization visit, should be well prepared to demonstrate its commitment to internationalism and interculturalism and the ways in which these issues have been integrated across its entire DP.

- **Schools shall demonstrate to the IBO that they will have the required teaching faculty, administrative staff and other resources with which to implement the IB DP successfully.**

The IBO entrusts to all diploma schools worldwide the great responsibility for the quality of the delivery of its curriculum in the classroom. It is vital that candidate schools ensure that the quality of the DP staff-designate is the highest possible. Certainly, teachers must be university graduates and their professional qualifications must be appropriately geared for teaching their subjects at the two pre-university year levels occupied by the DP. It is also advantageous if a candidate school is able to recruit a few staff who are experienced DP teachers from other IB schools, particularly when they are skilled and knowledgeable in one of the more complex curriculum areas such as languages.

It is of utmost importance when staffing the DP to consider carefully class sizes. Although there is no absolute prescription for class size, it is imperative to bear in mind that the overall nature of the DP curriculum is fundamentally concept based and process led and, for the most part, absolute content has a much more subordinate role. The teacher has a significantly diminished didactic role to play and class discussion, general and detailed exchanges of opinion, the Socratic critical approach to learning and understanding and experiential discovery and research, are equally important and active. This can only work well when class sizes are reasonably restricted. Experience dictates that HL classes should not exceed a student population of 20 and SL classes should not rise above 25 students.

The emphasis placed on independent research and the students' growing responsibility for their own learning requires careful accommodation. Adequate research facilities and general study areas should be readily available, some of which should be in the library. The IBO places much emphasis on all IB schools having a high-quality library, and a candidate school must present a comprehensive budget for the library, focusing on the immediate future and forecasting its ongoing targets. It is strongly recommended to employ a fully trained and well-qualified librarian, ideally a teacher-librarian, to be responsible for the library. It is also expected that this important member of the staff will have a sound overall understanding of the DP curriculum and be sufficiently informed to be able to advise students on such important issues as resourcing their TOK assignment or researching the extended essay. Occasionally, regional offices organize librarians' conferences and workshops, which are highly recommended to candidate and authorized schools. There are a few associations of IB librarians scattered around the world that work closely with the regional offices and these help to play a very useful supportive role for librarians in DP schools.

It may be argued that the single most important investment any authorized school can make in its DP is in teacher-training. Such investment should be not only in initial training, but also in a carefully planned, budgeted and sequential development programme for all staff over a five-year cycle, which would fit closely with the IBO's own five-year curriculum review and development cycle. However, in terms of meeting the demands of the authorization visit, the IBO has made it very clear in its new application form, published at the end of 2002, that candidate schools must register *all* of their DP teachers-designate for IBO-approved teacher-training workshops before the visit takes place. Nevertheless, it must be emphasized that this is only the initial training stage and that the IBO expects to witness far more in the future as an ongoing commitment from all authorized schools to professional development and refreshment. The current and future school budget provisions for teacher-training should be presented with the other supporting application documentation.

Closely allied to workshops are conferences. All regions organize an annual conference for their schools. It is expected that authorized schools will give their full support to this event, as it provides an ideal opportunity not only to catch up with colleagues from other schools in the region but also to meet with IBO senior staff from the head office in Geneva, the IB Curriculum and Assessment (IBCA) office in Cardiff and the regional office in charge of the conference. Clearly, this needs to be factored into the budget as well.

It is unnecessary for schools to have extravagant resources to support the DP. In all regions where the programme is successfully taught there are many schools that have a limited budget, but they are all able to resource their programme satisfactorily. It is particularly advantageous for these schools that a substantial part of the curriculum is not content focused and, therefore, schools have a considerable freedom to select their own exemplar material, which often may be found locally and relatively inexpensively. As long as schools fully understand the specific resource requirements of the various subjects that they are planning to offer, there is no necessity for these to be expensive. Useful advice on means of acquiring resources at reasonable cost can be readily obtained at workshops, on visits to experienced schools and direct from the regional office.

- ***Schools shall formally agree to bind themselves to full acceptance of all IBO requirements encompassing the effective conduct of the DP, with particular attention to its student-centred philosophy, TOK and CAS. Schools shall appoint an IB DPC and a CAS coordinator.***

Schools must recognize that the DP has its own suite of specific requirements in order to satisfy fully the philosophy and teaching of the curriculum. While there must be a firm assurance that the quality of the designate IB staff is high, it is also important that a candidate school can clearly illustrate to the authorization visiting team, both in its documentation and during the visit, that the manner in which it intends to teach the DP will be in strict accordance with the IBO's requirements.

The construction of the school's timetable must provide a two-year programme of concurrent learning across the curriculum, with a balanced proportion of time allocated to each subject offered, that meets the IBO's minimum requirements at HL and SL. In addition, a minimum of 100 hours of teacher–student contact time must be provided for the TOK programme. A school should also demonstrate its understanding that the learning environment of the DP must demonstrate a recognition of the importance of the empowerment of the students for a significant degree of their learning, that students will be given ample opportunity for independent work and research, and that the time allocated per subject is teacher–student *contact* time which should not be dominated by formal didactic pedagogy. Schools must also recognize that all work produced as part of a subject course that is internally assessed by the teacher should always be viewed as an integral component of the work of a normal school day along with routine homework assignments. Every effort should be made not to add this on to the existing timetable. If this happens, it is likely to become a major cause of student overload.

Undoubtedly, the key administrative staff appointment in a DP school is the DPC, who is responsible for the general administration of the programme, for internal and external communications and for the control and security of the May or November examination sessions. The IBO channels all official communications through the DPC, apart from the statement of account for the annual subscription and the examination fees. These are sent direct to the head of school. The IBO regularly offers training workshops for new coordinators and there is an annual conference in every region for heads of schools and coordinators which schools are expected to support. The appointment of a DPC is a mandatory requirement of all schools.

New schools should also appoint a staff member to be responsible for the CAS programme. Although a student's CAS performance is not rewarded in the form of bonus points (as is done for high achievement in the TOK and extended essay), CAS is a vital element in the DP, with its own requirements which students must satisfy or risk not receiving the diploma even if all other requirements are in order.

Thus the qualities of the member of staff appointed to coordinate CAS must include a sincere commitment to and understanding of the aims and objectives of the programme and the administrative abilities to run it efficiently with an effective system for monitoring student performance.

- *The programmes of the IBO should not be marginal in 'IB world schools'; it is expected that they will positively influence those sections of a school not following an IB programme.*

The IBO certainly does not stipulate in any way that the DP must be the only curriculum offered in the senior high school. However, it must be made very clear that the programme does have a major role to play in the school and that the intrinsic values espoused by the IB DP are relevant to the whole school, are firmly embraced by the published school mission statement (or equivalent) and will have an influential role in any sections of the school that do not have an IB programme.

Another condition that is very closely allied to this is that all schools must be unequivocally committed to teaching the full DP and must recognize that certificate courses have secondary importance (in the past this was not always the case, especially in North America). *Certificate* students are not bound by the rules governing the diploma and are not required to take the TOK programme, write an extended essay or fulfil the CAS requirements. Nor are certificate students restricted in any way to the number of subjects that they take at HL or SL. Without a doubt, the all-important reason for teaching the IB is the DP and the benefits that are to be derived from it by diploma students.

Today, the IBO is much more stringent in its authorization of new schools in this area and it must be unquestionably shown that any certificate courses they may be intending to offer are subordinate to their DP, and will be specifically for students who are not intellectually or academically able to undertake the full diploma. As a consequence of this stricter policy, there has been a marked increase over the past few years in the proportion of diploma students who now comprise more than 50% of the total candidature for both the May and November examinations. There has also been a marked increase in the proportion of diploma students over certificate students in many well-established DP schools, where there is a greater awareness of the benefits and advantages that the diploma has to offer over certificate-only courses.

A closely allied issue to a school's commitment to the DP is *anticipated* subjects. The IBO permits diploma candidates to take up to a maximum of two SL subjects at the end of the first year. Originally, anticipation was to serve the interests of students who had very strong language Bs and were capable of achieving the highest grades at SL at the end of year 1 of the diploma. However, in some schools the policy has emerged of all students anticipating one or two subjects. The IBO frowns upon this system of getting two subjects 'out of the way', which it considers to be alien to the diploma aim of encouraging concurrent learning across the curriculum of a two-year programme.

While several other conditions for authorization are prescribed and strictly applied by the IBO, these are the main ones as far as assuring the basic qualities of the curriculum, resourcing, pedagogy and intrinsic values of all candidate schools are concerned, and their importance during the authorization procedures should never be underestimated. Nor, as will be seen, are they only of interest to the IBO during the initial authorization stage, since they continue to have undiminished importance for as long as a school is permitted to offer the IB DP.

2.3 Preparing the school's communities

Unsurprisingly, it has been the IBO's experience over the years that, as a general rule, the schools that progress the most smoothly and successfully through the implementation procedures of the DP are those that have fully informed their various communities from the beginning. By being an integral part of the decision-making processes and having a sense of being closely involved from the beginning with this major school development, the introduction of the DP should be welcomed by the whole school community and receive the full support of the school board, staff, parents and students.

In the great majority of cases it has been shown that this early support from the community has been readily sustained and has increased in strength as the programme has matured. As a consequence, the school's DP has been built on firm foundations where there have been little or no resentment or objections to its introduction. Thus school boards and administrators that are seriously considering the DP for their schools are urged to be as transparent as possible from the earliest stages. Experience has shown that if this is the school's policy, then the short-term and long-term support for the programme is strong from the time when the programme is first considered, from the whole teaching faculty (not only those colleagues who are designated to teach the programme), the parent body and the students, in particular those who would comprise the first cohorts of diploma students should its introduction proceed. Occasional meetings for parents and regular faculty meetings are essential in order to keep open all channels of communication. Such meetings will contribute enormously to avoiding any possible future grievances, suspicions or misunderstandings. It is also recommended that a representative from the IBO regional office be invited to speak at a parents meeting. Such a meeting offers an excellent opportunity for parental concerns to be raised, to discuss the DP in general and better to understand the advantages of the diploma as an entry qualification to higher education.

Schools that are prepared to invest significant time in introducing their communities to the IBO and the DP will not regret this. The outcome for most schools will be a strong support for the programme. In the case of a small minority of schools where such support is not forthcoming, there will still be savings benefits in the form of the probable avoidance of any future angst, programme collapse and the unnecessary acquisition of unwanted pedagogical and curricular resources. Because the IBO is not a profit-making foundation, schools are under no pressure from the organization to adopt the DP, or any of its other programmes, and they will certainly not be pressurized by the organization to become IB world schools, which would definitely not be in the interests of the IBO or of quality assurance.

2.4 Financial issues

Every school that is considering the introduction of the DP must give serious thought to all of the financial implications that will be involved both in the short term and the longer term. It is imperative, and wholly in the interests of the school's future DP, that there is a very clear understanding of what budget provisions must be made to meet the various costs.

Comments are sometimes made, incorrectly, to the effect that the diploma is a very expensive programme that only the richest selective schools can afford to implement and to maintain. Fortunately, today, this opinion is held far less widely, and there is an impressive range of schools now teaching the programme – rich, poor, large, small, independent, national, single-sex, coeducational, day and boarding. Nevertheless, it is a fact that an independent school in a developed world country is far more likely to be able to afford the programme than a national school in the developing world unless it receives some additional financial assistance from, for example, the state or local education authorities. Despite the financial challenges that the programme presents, there are still many schools throughout the world that have successfully implemented the DP and are certainly not considered to be rich in any financial sense.

In the earliest stages of considering the DP it is essential that a whole programme audit is carried out in which the costs are calculated within two distinct areas: the initial setting-up expenses leading to authorization, and the forecasted, ongoing expenses once the programme is up and running, including the examination fees over at least the subsequent four to five years. The most significant of these costs are undoubtedly the initial costs.

The initial costs

Purchase of official IBO publications
These may be ordered and paid for online from the IBO website: www.ibo.org. They are the curriculum documents including the subject guides (syllabuses), past examination papers and mark schemes. These are essential purchases for all schools very early on in the consideration stage.

Teacher-training
All DP teachers-designate need to be enrolled in introductory teacher-training

workshops that have been officially approved by the IBO. Staff who are being hired must have recent diploma teaching experience (i.e. they have been teaching a current DP subject syllabus); otherwise they, too, must be enrolled in relevant workshops. The DPC and CAS coordinator should also participate in introductory workshops. The head of school and DPC-designate should also attend their IBO regional conference, and the head of school is expected to participate in the biennial (or more frequent) heads of schools conference.

Contacts with experienced DP schools

The IBO does not enforce such contacts, but they are strongly recommended. They should involve at least one visit by key staff to an experienced IB diploma school, which it is valuable to reciprocate at a later date by a staff visit from that school. It is not uncommon for schools to forge lasting and mutually beneficial working relationships from such visits. In several parts of the world, particularly in larger urban areas, local associations of IB schools have been set up. One of the roles of these associations is to advise and support nearby schools that are in the process of introducing the DP. Another function may be to arrange job-alike seminars and discussion group sessions for subject specialists and programme coordinators, all of which could be of interest to new schools. It is probable that most schools will incur some travel costs if representatives attend these meetings.

Staffing

If senior class sizes are too large to satisfy the demands and expectations of the DP then the additional cost of hiring more staff must be assessed. Additional staffing may also include some secretarial assistance for the DPC and a coordinator for the TOK programme. Schools that have been teaching a more restricted curriculum model to their two pre-university year students, such as the English GCE A-level system with its narrower range of required subjects, may well have to hire more staff to teach some additional classes to ensure that the full six-subject range of the diploma hexagon is properly covered and that the students' interests at HL and SL are correctly served. Languages, in particular, often cause schools a significant amount of extra staffing and resourcing expenses.

Some saving may be possible in schools where the cost of putting on classes that are very small (e.g. fewer than 10 students) is prohibitively expensive. Several subjects in the first year of the programme can be combined at HL and SL. By allowing those students who are taking a subject at SL to *anticipate* it, only the HL students will need to continue with it on into the second year of teaching. However, as explained in section 2.2, it is the IBO's preference for concurrent learning across the curriculum for all subjects to be taught over two years.

Physical resources

A careful review must be made of existing resources matched against the demands of diploma courses. The review of physical resources should include the library; assessment of the adequacy of specialist teaching space; essential apparatus and equipment, including safety equipment; IT facilities for staff and students; and the availability of office space for additional administrative staff, especially the DPC.

Fees

There must be a budget provision for the payment of the application fee and the OCC fee, which is levied for all DP candidate schools.

The authorization visit

While no professional fees are paid, the school is required to pay in full all accommodation, travel and basic incidental expenses incurred during the authorization visit. Accommodation should be in a hotel of a reasonable standard and preferably one that is conveniently located near to the school. At least two nights' stay must be budgeted for each of the two or three members of the authorization team.

The ongoing costs

The annual basic fee

All authorized schools are required to pay this common annual fee to the head office in Geneva. No additional fee is charged to authorized schools for access to the OCC, unlike non-authorized schools which must pay an annual fee which has remained fairly stable over the last few years and was US$ 470 in 2003.

Examination fees

These include a candidate's per capita fee, plus fees in payment for the external assessment of a student's examination work, and for the external moderation of work internally assessed by the school. The fees for diploma students will be common irrespective of the subjects assessed. However, a certificate candidate's fees are totally dependent on the number of subjects that are examined. Directly related costs are the postal charges for the dispatch of examination scripts, samples of students' internally assessed work for external moderation and other substantial written assignments that are externally marked. Despite the much higher charges, it is always in the interests of security and speed that all examination materials are dispatched by courier service rather than by regular postal services.

It should be noted here that the majority of IB world schools pay the annual basic fee from the school budget but, in most schools, it is the parents who pay the examination fees. In national/state schools it is common practice for the state or local education authorities to pay these.

IBO's fees may change, and schools should contact their regional office to confirm what the current fees are, and when they are due.

Teacher-training workshops, regional and heads of schools conferences

The IBO views regular attendance of teachers at IBO-approved workshops as an ongoing, essential investment by authorized schools in their DP. The school should plan its professional development budget well ahead of time to ensure that funds are available for its teachers to participate in workshops that focus on the curriculum and assessment review developed by the IBO according to its five-year curriculum review calendar. As a rule of thumb, all teachers should attend a workshop at least every five years.

Resource development

A school must budget adequately to be able to acquire new resources, as required, to match curricular changes, in order to provide students and teachers with the necessary additional materials and equipment that they will need. It is recommended that every effort is made to ensure a generous annual provision for the library budget in order to purchase new books, IT hardware and software. The IBO is acutely conscious of the considerable cost that can be incurred with curriculum change, and it endeavours to gear changes to effect the minimum additional charges that may be considered reasonably possible.

Clearly, the initial and ongoing costs of implementing and operating a DP are a very serious issue. It is vital that a new school understands this, and the importance that it must give to appropriate financial investment and resourcing in its IB programme. Effectively done, this will contribute a great deal towards the establishment and further development of a strong DP, a well-informed staff, appropriate pedagogy, and high-quality student performance.

2.5 The school as a contributor to the IBO

Ultimately, the overwhelming justification for the existence of the IBO and its programmes is to be found in the IB world schools, in particular in the intellectual, emotional and social development of the students. The majority of schools would in all likelihood agree that the main reason for their original interest in introducing the DP was what it could do for them. The main attractions are the benefit of the experience of an international, balanced, liberal arts curriculum, the integrity of the assessment, the external award of the diploma and the advantage of the diploma as an international passport to university entrance virtually worldwide. Other considerations might include the opinion that as the IBO has no allegiance to any religious doctrine and as it is a non-governmental organization and in no way influenced by any government's policy, these facts augur well in terms of the future reliability and stability of the programme. All of these motivating factors for schools are, of course, of serious interest to the IBO. However, the IBO's interest extends well beyond what the school perceives that it will gain from authorization, teaching the DP and being an IB world school.

All IB world schools are enormously important to the IBO as potential contributors in various ways to the organization's own growth, development and quality. As a consequence, candidate schools should be prepared to discuss during their authorization visit how they might contribute in meaningful ways to the IBO in the future.

The range of possibilities is wide but the following are a few examples of particular opportunities that might be viable in newly authorized schools:

- to be prepared to open their doors to host training workshops and conferences
- to release expert teachers to lead workshops and to speak at conferences
- to release teachers to sit on curriculum review and development committees
- to release teachers to join authorization teams
- to assist regional offices in negotiating or improving diploma recognition agreements with local universities
- to assist regional offices in getting access to local and national government education offices and other education agencies.

2.6 Staffing

Without exception and regardless of the type of school that is offering the DP, the single most important player in the programme is the IB teacher, for it is to the teachers that the IBO entrusts the heavy responsibility of the delivery of the curriculum in the classroom and laboratory and the preparation of the students for examination.

The importance of teacher-training cannot be overestimated. However, closely allied to this is the tenure of contract by which teachers are hired. This, of course, largely applies to independent and international schools, although the contract system of teacher employment also exists in some national systems.

There is considerable benefit to be derived from developing a core of highly experienced, skilled DP teachers. While this may seem rather obvious it is surprising how many international schools in various regions offer only short-term contracts; one year is not uncommon. Others offer two-year non-renewable terms. Teaching in the DP is or should be very different from teaching a subject specialism and little else, as is the case in several national systems. The best IB teachers cover much more than their specialist subject and they have a thorough specialist knowledge and understanding, which has been built up over several years' experience of teaching, of the overall philosophy of a complex curriculum and of preparing candidates for diploma examinations comprising a wide range of different assessment methodologies. Continuity of a quality staffing core is in the interests of all schools and particularly those offering the DP.

2.7 Summary overview of the authorization procedure

The lead-up procedures to the authorization visit, and the criteria and conditions for the authorization of new schools, are all designed and rigorously enforced to give the IBO a detailed insight into each candidate school. In essence, does the school have a clear understanding of what it is trying to get itself accepted into, and of the IBO as an organization? And what does the IBO require and look for in the school, in terms of its commitment to providing a quality DP?

It is to be expected that, provided the criteria and conditions for authorization have been met in full and that the values espoused by the school are closely congruent with those of the IBO, the authorization visit will be successful and will result in the submission of a report, via the regional office, that recommends to the IBO director-general that the school's application be approved.

The following is a broad chronological summary of procedures leading to the authorization of a new DP school:

- First interests – talk widely, search the internet.
- Contact regional office.
- Purchase IBO curriculum and assessment publications.
- Conduct internal audit of human, physical and financial resources.
- Inform school communities – hold meetings.
- Visit experienced diploma schools and develop school contacts.
- Acquire application form and guidelines documents from regional office.
- Register all designated diploma teachers for approved IBO workshops.
- Submit application form and other required documentation.

- Negotiate authorization visit with regional office.
- Authorization visit.
- Approval from director-general.
- Teaching begins.

This list is not exhaustive but it does include all of the main procedures for the implementation of the DP in new schools. It is expected to span at least one year. However, under normal circumstances it is not expected to exceed far beyond two years. Furthermore, it should not be assumed that by following this list there is any guarantee of the director-general's approval being granted.

3 Quality assurance maintenance

The task of maintaining quality is crucial for both the current and future well-being of the constituency of IB world schools and the organization *per se*. It is a challenge that the IBO willingly shares with its major stakeholders, especially the authorized schools. By sharing this challenge, any unfortunate sense of imposition is avoided. It is not a top-down procedure, nor is it bottom-up. It is one that is a combined venture with all parties endeavouring to work together on the same level in sustaining, improving and assuring DP quality in its teaching by the schools and in its development and management by the IBO.

3.1 Quality assurance maintenance in schools

The granting of authorized status for a school to teach the DP is the recognition by the IBO that the school has the required qualities to be an IB world school. However, this recognition is based on the evidence witnessed by the authorization team at the application stage. It is, of course, vital that the school maintains and develops these qualities as its DP matures. In order to determine this, a number of checks and balances are employed by the regional office by which schools' programmes are monitored and reviewed.

The Five-Year Programme Review

The Five-Year Programme Review is a cyclical review carried out by the IBO regional offices at five-yearly intervals. It is not to be confused with the accreditation of schools system of the United States. The DP review is the *evaluation* of the quality of the current DP in a school that has been teaching the programme for five years or more.

The review strategy presently varies between regions. The IBO North America and Latin America regional offices conduct a more limited review to which the DPC is the major contributor. The Europe, Africa, Middle East and Asia-Pacific regional offices operate a far more detailed review system of questionnaires directed to all relevant sections of a school and its communities – the head of school, the DPC, the librarian(s), all IB diploma teaching staff, a selection of second-year diploma students, their parents, and the school board. The IBO is well aware of these inter-regional differences and is presently developing a single system that will work effectively globally. (The IBO brought out a new Five-Year

Programme Review system in March 2004. The format is more in keeping with the style of review in place for MYP and PYP.)

The review team will be made up of five or more members drawn from IBO regional staff and experienced DPCs from the region's schools. Significantly, the Five-Year Programme Review returns to the *Criteria and Conditions for Authorization* of new diploma schools and considers how well the school continues to remain as firmly committed to those requirements as it was when authorized to teach the programme. An analysis of the various completed questionnaires gives considerable insight into the well-being of the DP and affords an excellent opportunity to identify and commend the school on its strengths and, at the same time, to point out and explain areas of weakness that need improvement and the school's attention, either immediately or over the longer term.

The Five-Year Programme Review plays a major role in assuring and confirming the quality of the DP in all authorized schools.

Examination performance

When the Final Grade Award Committee has confirmed the examination results for each session, these are immediately dispatched to schools. In due course, a summary of the examination results by region is also sent by IBCA to the regional offices where they are carefully reviewed. When there are any concerns arising out of these results, the regional office may contact a school and endeavour to find out what has been the cause and to offer advice if something seems to have gone seriously wrong.

CAS records sampling

Annually, regional offices will sample 20% of their schools' CAS records. Schools are notified approximately six weeks ahead of time that they are required to submit to the regional office the complete set of CAS records of three randomly chosen diploma candidates. The records are carefully reviewed and a detailed report is sent to each school. It is important to note that it is not the students who are under review, as this is the responsibility of the school, but the quality of the school's CAS programme. This is an effective process of ensuring that the quality of a school's CAS programme meets the IBO's requirements.

3.2 Quality assurance maintenance in the IBO

The IBO is well aware that it must also maintain a high level of vigilance over its own business to ensure that its own quality is well maintained. There are certain key areas in which review, consultation and external advice operate and which are an integral part of this quality maintenance.

Examinations and grade awarding

Immediately after the completion of each examination paper in both examination sessions, all schools with candidates are encouraged to send in reports, critically appraising them, direct to IBCA. These reports are collated and then carefully analysed by IBCA subject experts and the relevant senior examiners. Teachers from authorized DP schools are invited, at the IBO's expense, to sit in as observers on the grade award meetings that are conducted for each subject at the end of the examinations. There are always teacher observers present at the Final Grade Award Committee Meeting. The observers are encouraged to critically appraise the meetings. In the event of a school disagreeing with a particular candidate's (or candidates') subject grade, this may be challenged and there will be a thorough reappraisal of the candidate's performance coordinated by IBCA. If necessary, a grade adjustment will be made but the candidate will not be downgraded.

Curriculum review

Curriculum and assessment in the DP are subjected to a review cycle that typically spans five years in most subjects (though during the writing of this book, this has changed to a seven-year cycle). The cycles do not all run at the same interval: each subject review has its own starting date. During the first two years of this cycle the subject syllabus is taught and it is not until the third year that review begins (hence the often-used name *2+3 curriculum review*). By the end of the fourth year or the beginning of the fifth, a final draft of the revised curriculum will be sent to schools for final comment. Outside of the five-year review cycle occasional minor amendments may be made to an existing curriculum, of which DPCs are informed by the IBO.

All schools are able to participate in the Five-Year Curriculum Review and cycle. There are two ways in which this happens. One is that teachers are invited, at the IBO's expense, to be members of the review committee, sitting equally alongside examiners, external advisers and IBCA senior staff. However, as this can only logistically involve a very few representatives from schools, there is also a second way in which all schools can take part. Reports summarizing each stage of the review committee's work and progress are sent to all authorized DP schools along with a questionnaire by which they are able to give their own feedback, and this will be circulated to the committee's members. The work of this review committee is considered to be a tripartite venture between the IBO, the board of examiners and the schools. It is disappointing to note that only a small minority of schools complete and submit these questionnaires, thus negating the opportunity to share with the IBO in curriculum development.

Governance and management

Governance of the IBO is in the hands of the Council of Foundation which is responsible for policy making. The new governance structure (since May 2001) is composed as following:

- *Officers:*
  President, vice-president, treasurer, secretary

- *Members:*
  One from each of the four regional advisory committees (RACs)
  One from each of the four regional heads of school representative committees (RHRCs)
  Three *ad personam*

- *Ex officio:*
  Director-general (non-voting chief executive officer (CEO); responsible for carrying out the council's policies)

Chair of the international heads of school representative committee (IHRC)
Chair of the examining board

There is a nominations committee comprising the president and elected representatives of each RAC. It helps with appointments to the council according to the Rules of Procedure of the Foundation.

- The president and treasurer are elected by the council, following consultation with the chairs of the RACs, IHRCs and any other persons the council deems appropriate to consult.
- The vice-president and secretary are elected among council members.
- The four RAC and four RHRC (subject to the consideration of the IHRC) members are nominated by their respective committees; nominations are then forwarded to the nominations committee, which in turn recommends to the council.
- The three *ad personam* members are proposed by the RACs and the IHRC or by at least five Council members; the nominations committee again recommends to the Council.

The overall quality of the organization worldwide, including the generation and integrity of its policies, the approval of the annual budget and the appointment of the director-general are under the aegis of the Council. The membership of the council ensures that the interests of the major stakeholders in the IBO (the schools) are well represented and the *ad personam* members add their vital input of external expertise and opinion, bringing appropriate balance to the governance of the organization.

Management and governance are entirely separate. Management is the responsibility of the Senior Management Team (SMT) that is chaired by the director-general who appoints all members of the SMT and acts as the CEO of the Council of Foundation. The SMT is composed of senior IBO staff, all of whom are directors and include the deputy director-general, the directors of the regions, curriculum and assessment, finance, ICT and human resources. The SMT is the committee responsible for the management of the IBO's various activities, which is mostly conducted from the central and regional offices, and for ensuring that policy decisions of council are put into action, as and when directed by the director-general.

4 Quality assurance and standardization

An all-important issue in the quality assurance of the DP and all the IBO's international education activities is that it is essential to ensure standardization. Simply expressed, this is to instil confidence worldwide that there is global uniformity in the procedures and conditions for the authorization of new schools, of the aims and objectives of the curriculum that is taught and in the integrity and methodologies by which the assessment of the students' work is designed, conducted and graded.

4.1 Assessment and grading

Examinations are held in May and November, and schools are, on authorization, approved for entering candidates for one of these as their main session. There is the opportunity to use the other session for resits.

All of the examination papers are set and approved by an independent, international board of examiners. The IBO does not undertake nor has the responsibility for assessing the candidates. After the May and November examination sessions the senior examining team for each subject appraises the effectiveness of each examination paper and the overall student performance on each and awards the grades. The examination papers used in each subject are identical in all regions. The conditions under which all candidates sit their examinations are prescribed and must be strictly respected. To ensure this, at every session, regional offices arrange for official representatives to make unheralded visits to 'live' examination halls to inspect these conditions and to submit a report to the regional office on each visit. In the event of the visit identifying any problems, the report would also be sent to IBCA.

The key players in the assessment arena are the chief and deputy chief examiners. These comprise a fully international body of recognized experts in their particular fields who have overall responsibility for the setting of examination papers, the construction of marking schemes and the marking of students' work. The normal maximum term of office for senior examiners is five years. This limited tenure is to ensure a regular flow of new blood into the assessment corpus.

A complex system of marking, moderating and final grade awarding has been established and carefully refined over time to ensure that all students are awarded the grades they have earned. Grades are not determined by norm-referencing (percentile grouping or grading on a Bell curve) but by measurement against specific performance criteria and grade descriptors. Grades are awarded for each student's final subject result by its measurement against a set of published performance criteria. Especially important to universities is the reliability of the grades achieved by the students. Universities have to be confident that a grade 6, for example, at HL in mathematics, achieved by students in London, New York and Singapore, is exactly the same. Schools, as well as universities, see this as being of paramount importance, as the achievements of a school's diploma students are, indirectly, an international statement of the success and quality of the school and its DP.

Internally assessed work that has been marked by the teachers, is moderated by the senior examiners. This is to ensure that there is no deviation from the marking guidelines provided to the teachers and that a common standard has been applied across all schools.

4.2 Authorization of new diploma schools

This has already been described and explained in detail. Nevertheless, it is well worth repeating, for emphasis of its importance, that the *Criteria and Conditions for Authorization* are equally applied to candidate schools in every region and that there are no officially approved regional variations, thus avoiding the emergence of any substandard grouping of DP schools.

5 Penalties

In a perfect world there would be no need for the IBO to have to resort to any form of penalties as a means to safeguard the integrity of the DP, the quality of its delivery and reliability of its assessment. Regrettably, we all live in an imperfect world. Consequently, in order for the IBO to remain at the cutting edge of international education, to strengthen further its professional relationships with governments, and to continue to earn and develop the highest respect by universities, it is necessary to have in place certain deterrents and penalties which can be applied in the event of any school or candidate failing to meet requirements or being guilty of deliberate delinquency. These are essential to ensure that these interests, which are as important to its authorized schools as they are to the IBO, are fully protected.

The main concerns of the IBO in this area are that the schools convincingly demonstrate that they remain fully committed to:

- the overarching aims and objectives of the DP
- the teaching of the full diploma as the prime focus
- the IBO's philosophy as being an integral part of the school's philosophy
- administering the diploma examinations strictly according to the IBO's guidelines as set out in its *Vade Mecum*.

In the event of a school failing to demonstrate convincingly its commitment to any of these major requirements, the regional office will be responsible for counselling the school in the short or longer term in an effort to resolve the problem. This may require a visit from a regional office staff member at the expense of the school.

However, if it is found in a school that the security of an examination session has been compromised or that there has been any form of deliberate malpractice, then the IBCA office will thoroughly investigate the situation, the outcome of which could be very serious and may lead to the invalidation of the examination and the withholding of diplomas.

In the case of a school that ignores the regional office's advice and remains unable to demonstrate a strong commitment to the DP's philosophy and its requirements, or when examination malpractice has been widespread or it is a repeat offence, a school may be asked by the director-general to withdraw from the IBO. In such a situation the IBO does all that it can to ensure that innocent students are not penalized in any way.

Fortunately, the withdrawal of schools at the organization's request is rare but, on occasions, it has been necessary for the IBO to take such action in all of the regions.

6 Professional training – training the trainers and the examiners

The professional development of teachers has already been recognized as an essential requirement to be an IB world school. Equally important is the training of experts of the highest quality possible to lead training workshops, to be examiners, to act as assessment moderators and to participate in authorization visits. Much of this training is a joint venture between the regional offices and IBCA, with the regional office assisting in the identification of the potential trainers and examiners, and with the training being largely organized and carried out by IBCA staff. This centralized system of training the experts is an effective way to maintain a parity of esteem in the standardization of the various DP training, assessment and authorization activities.

In the case of examiners, the IBCA office runs seminars and training specifically designed to provide the training for senior examiners but, in the case of assistant examiners, who number well over 3,600 and are spread widely throughout the world, this has not been possible. However, the great majority of assistant examiners or markers are experienced DP teachers and, therefore, have a good understanding of their subjects and their assessment. The regional offices are now endeavouring to include assistant examiner training within their regional workshop schedules.

In order to be appointed as an assistant examiner of diploma examinations, a formal application must first be submitted to IBCA and approved. Senior examiners, particularly chief examiners, are almost all in responsible positions in universities around the world, and are internationally recognized as being experts in their particular fields.

7 Conclusion

Reaching for quality, achieving it, ensuring that it is maintained and, if possible, to take it to even higher levels is an enormous challenge. This is a particular challenge to the IBO because it serves and operates in a highly complex, international education milieu of enormous diversity. When this challenge is compounded by the need to evince in all its activities a global uniformity, cynics might well observe that the IBO is trying to achieve the impossible.

Perhaps they are right. Certainly anyone who has grappled with the task of formally assessing students' knowledge, understanding and skills in ways that do not unfairly advantage or disadvantage any candidate, will be all too familiar with the problem of equal opportunity.

The assurance that all authorized schools have maintained a DP that closely adheres to those original tenets of authorization that were satisfied when the IBO approved their applications, is also very difficult. This difficulty has increased as the IBO constituency has grown. In the earlier days of the organization when the number of schools was much less, it was relatively easy to maintain a close working relationship with each school. Today this is virtually impossible, although it can be argued that new communication technologies have helped considerably to reduce the problem.

The IBO has come a long way in the development of an international curriculum of the highest quality, and in introducing various strategies that are successful in identifying schools that are committed to the values that it encourages students to understand, to care about and to nurture in their own lives. While it must probably always remain a moot point as to whether it will ever be possible to have an international programme that can unquestionably promise absolute quality assurance and global standardization, it is fair to say that the IB DP has come very close to achieving these goals.

Chapter 3
Implementing the Diploma Programme in school

Stuart Jones, BSc

Stuart Jones taught in schools in the UK and the Middle East before joining the International School of Singapore, where he took up the post of head of science and teacher of physics. He played a key role in the school's strategic planning and has worked for the Council of International Schools accrediting schools. Appointed as the school's Diploma Programme coordinator (DPC) in 1999, he successfully led the school through the IB diploma authorization (granted in 2000) and the programme's subsequent implementation. This chapter serves as a 'hands-on manual' for new DPCs, but school boards, too, will gain an invaluable insight into the practical advantages and challenges associated with the adoption of the IB DP. A careful study of this chapter will greatly enhance the likelihood of an informed board decision that can be executed smoothly and cost-effectively. This chapter also provides a unique chance for teachers and parents to understand how the philosophy of the programme links to its practicalities, and what role the parts play in the whole.

The author would like to thank and acknowledge Jill Rutherford and Ian Deakin for their contributions to this chapter.

1 General issues

1.1 The change process

It is not possible to provide a single-formula approach to implementing the IB DP since there is no such thing as a single profile of a prospective candidate school. Far from it: IB schools around the world exhibit enormous variety, as illustrated in the case studies set out in Part Two. What needs to be recognized, however, is the scale and scope of change that implementing the IB DP entails, and the major resource implications it has. It will also have an impact on teachers' traditional autonomy in the classroom and on middle-management's responsibilities and ways of working. In short, the change will require extremely careful forethought and management.

The following sets out the key issues that need to be addressed and some suggested approaches. As with most change processes, the sequential layout of what follows belies the true nature of the event. What to do and when, whom to appoint for what: these are matters for each school to decide.

The essential point to remember is that all stakeholder groups need to be extremely well informed about why the school is embarking on the IB and what it can bring (see the Introduction and Part Two). If people know why you are doing things and they have been honestly informed about the advantages as well as the challenges, they are much more likely to accept the inevitable errors made along the way. If, on the other hand, they are not sure about what is going on, any errors can develop disproportionately. An understanding and supportive community is the best environment for a smooth and successful implementation of the DP. Transparent communication not only makes sense from a management point of view, but the IBO explicitly requires it: the authorization teams will look for evidence that the whole community understands and supports the DP.

1.2 Authorization issues

As discussed in Chapter 2, the IBO has set standards for authorization, which are available from the regional office. The standards can loosely be grouped into three categories:

- commitment to the aims and philosophy of the IBO
- preparedness to deliver the curriculum
- community-wide understanding of the programme and general consensus.

The IBO has gone through distinct phases of growth and development over the years. Today the organization is clearly looking to manage quality growth and has recognized a need to review and further standardize its procedures in order to maintain quality control and a professional standard of service. Recently the IBO has made changes to its authorization, professional development and workshop quality assurance procedures. Consequently, candidate schools can expect to see a higher degree of transparency and uniformity in the authorization procedures across the regions. However, the authorization standards still require a degree of professional judgement on what is acceptable and the authorization team may come with perceptions about the candidate school. The candidate school needs to communicate effectively with the authorization team and help them to distinguish perception from fact. Since the team is often made up of an IBO representative and an experienced DPC, it can be very useful to find out what type of school that coordinator has experience with. It is even possible to ask for a coordinator from a successful IB school that is similar in nature to yours.

Several other points might be considered:

- Some of the practices and structures used by existing IB schools may not be fully consistent with the IBO regional office's standards, so be prudent in using existing IB schools as models.
- It is important to quickly establish and maintain good communications with the regional office. Get as much feedback on your progress as possible.
- The reality for many schools is that the DP will not be appropriate for all of its students, and will need to coexist alongside other programmes. It is important to explain early on what the school is about and how it can maintain the integrity of the DP. This is a particular issue for schools that are implementing the DP to drive academic improvement, or schools that have a very different structure from that of established IB schools in the area.

2 The groundwork

As part of the authorization process, the IBO regional office will look to confirm that the school has carried out a thorough self-study, and that there is broad support for and long-term commitment to the DP. Each school will have its own issues to face but many will find that costs, and building consensus, will feature prominently.

The following strategies have proved useful in laying the groundwork to implementation.

2.1 Contacting the IBO regional office

Contact the IBO regional office (www.ibo.org) to express an interest in the DP. The regional office will be able to:

- provide representatives to run an introductory information session
- visit your site to give you an indication of what work needs to be done
- inform you of upcoming conferences and regional training opportunities (this information is also available on www.ibo.org).

The regional office will also be responsible for running the (optional) pre-authorization visit and the eventual authorization visit.

2.2 Floating the idea

Run some introductory information sessions on the DP in your community. The regional office will probably be willing to visit the school to help with this. Additional materials are available via the IBO's public website, in the resources section on page 75 and elsewhere in this book. At this stage, the intention is just to get an overview. We recommend that you purchase the guides that describe subjects that your school currently offers, at the level you offer them. For mathematics it is advisable to have a look at all of the guides. It is further advisable to purchase the following items:

- The *Vade Mecum* – the IBO handbook of rules and regulations
- Creativity, Action and Service (CAS) Guide
- Theory of Knowledge (TOK) Guide
- Extended Essay (EE) Guide
- Examination papers and mark schemes for one session (available on CD-ROM). The IBO also produces a good series of PowerPoint presentations on CD-ROM.

A school that is expanding its middle-school operations to include the pre-university years will obviously need to consider more carefully what it wishes to offer. First-hand experience of a school with this scenario is described in the case study in Chapter 6.

As with any major change, school administrators should exercise discretion when floating the idea of implementing the DP. Several concerns inevitably surface which, if mismanaged, can foster strong opposition early on and lead to a loss of credibility. These concerns typically centre on:

- the cost of running the programme
- the market niche – Will the programme make the school more attractive to current students and new students? What competition is there locally?
- the suitability of the programme, especially if the school is non-selective or is moving away from a national matriculation system
- how standards in the IB diploma compare with other matriculation qualifications – can the students reach these standards?
- university recognition
- parents' fears that their children may be used as 'guinea pigs'.

The case studies in Part Two discuss these issues in depth, but some of the important points are reiterated here.

The DP is often viewed as being elitist and this impression can be exacerbated if there are highly selective schools in your region running the programme. There is no doubt that the DP is a challenging academic programme (for which the IBO makes no apology). The challenge comes from the breadth of the programme including its core areas (CAS, TOK and the extended essay) as well as the depth of the academic courses themselves. However, the DP is accessible to a wider range of students than is often perceived, and some of the IB diploma courses on their own are very accessible.

Many schools will offer students individual IB diploma courses ('IB certificates') as part of a package of matriculation qualifications. For example, a student may take IB certificates as part of a high school diploma, or a student in the UK may take an A-level, a GNVQ (vocational qualification) and a few certificates. However, schools need to be very careful how they sell such composite programmes (in addition to the full DP) as a matriculation qualification. The IBO has taken great efforts to explain the DP to universities and governments, but a 'certificate programme' is not formally recognized by the IBO, and many universities correspondingly accord such programmes less recognition.

The DP is widely accepted by universities around the world; top universities that have taken in many IB graduates over the years tend to appreciate the skills that the full programme fosters in its graduates. However, whilst the IB diploma, or a package of IB certificates, may offer a stronger education and better preparation for university and the world of work, it does not always have a correspondingly greater currency in university admission systems. Some parents and students will be very utilitarian when it comes to selecting matriculation courses and will weigh up the effort required with the currency of the qualification. Schools therefore need to do in-depth research on the universities that their students typically attend or, better still, invite representatives from key universities to outline their admissions policies with respect to the diploma or certificate programme.

Teachers will also make comparisons between the current courses offered and the DP courses. However, it is important that teachers (and all other stakeholders) do not compare courses on content only, but rather see the 'big picture': the strength of the DP lies in its breadth, skill development and assessment system. There is no reason, though, to worry about course content: years of experience have shown that Higher Level (HL) courses do prepare students well for specialist courses at top universities.

Some parents will be concerned about their children being 'guinea pigs' for the new programme. Here it can be useful to emphasize the school's investment in IB workshop training, the experience of the staff in teaching academic courses, and the track record of the DP which has been around for over 30 years.

2.3 Championing the DP

Ideally a school would be able to find champions in each area of its faculty and community, but in practice this is unlikely. However, we strongly recommend that the search is not limited to the administrative team only. Some teachers will have experience of the IB DP, having either taught it or experienced it as students. Some parents too will have experience of the DP. Getting a school governor or board member on side is also important. It can be a long process to convince the faculty and community that the IB DP really is the way to go. The more people you have who really know the programme and can actively support and explain it (especially to the community they represent), the better.

2.4 Conferences, workshops and visits to IB schools

The school should endeavour to send champions to conferences, workshops and established IB schools. The regional office will host an annual conference and a series of workshop sessions. Details of these are available on the IBO's public website or from the regional office.

Regional conferences

The conferences are ostensibly for heads of school and DPCs but they are not exclusive. At each conference there is a series of discussion sessions that are very relevant and useful to new schools. Some regional offices will run induction seminars for new schools prior to the conference. A conference is furthermore an excellent place to meet representatives of both established schools and schools going through the authorization process. Delegates from new schools will often stay on after the conference to visit established IB schools.

Workshops

In Europe and Asia-Pacific the main workshop sessions take place in July, with additional smaller sessions throughout the year. In North America they are more spread out, with the bulk of them between July and September. They are often based at existing IB schools, a different one each time, and typically last for two and a half to three days. However, those held in Eastern Europe in June/July run for five days and cost roughly the same. Understandably, these sessions are heavily subscribed and early booking is advisable. Details of workshop dates are available on the IBO website.

Prior to authorization most teachers will need to attend IB workshops. As early as possible, though, it would be very useful to send people to the following workshops:

- DPC
- CAS
- Theory of Knowledge
- A1 language
- The Regional Conference for Heads and Coordinators.

Visits to established IB schools

There is a very strong spirit of cooperation amongst IB teachers which is successfully fostered through the IBO's provision of workshops and its Online Curriculum Centre (OCC). IB teachers and coordinators are usually willing to share schemes of work and methods of organizing various aspects of the DP. These can provide a basis to build on and can save a great deal of planning time. It is a good idea to be as specific as possible about what you are looking for and to avoid the months of February and March (schools taking examinations in May) or August and September (November), as in these months schools are likely to be very busy with coursework.

2.5 The preliminary site visit

Schools should consider contacting the IBO regional office to arrange for a preliminary site visit. This may not be an easy or inexpensive matter depending on the location of the office, as the school will need to pay the travel and accommodation costs of the IBO representative. A visit from an experienced DPC in a nearby school may be just as useful and would be cheaper. The regional office should be asked to make recommendations. The school should weigh up its timeframe for implementation, the amount of work that it reckons needs to be done and the degree of support it needs in order to get things moving. A timely visit could help prioritize the areas that need to be worked on. As with every other aspect of the implementation process, it is important to make sure that everything is documented and filed.

2.6 The feasibility study committee

The school needs to establish a feasibility study committee. This group will be required to:

- carry out a position audit to identify the potential benefits of adopting the DP

- carry out a gap analysis to determine what work will need to be done
- analyse the potential costs of the DP
- plan a timeframe for implementation.

These four tasks of the feasibility study committee are discussed in sections 3–6 below.

3 The position audit

Some educators dislike the 'intrusion' of market economics into education but it is an everyday reality for most schools. Educationally the IB DP has great merit but it is more expensive to run than many other systems, including national examination systems, and all schools will need to ensure that they can generate sources of income to meet their needs. As part of the authorization process the IBO will be looking to see that schools have given due consideration to the costs of running the DP and are satisfied that it is a viable and long-term proposition. Schools are likely to engage in some form of strategic review, and there are many tools that can facilitate this, e.g. a SWOT analysis (Strengths, Weaknesses, Opportunities and Threats) which will help a school to focus on the key factors that are most pertinent to achieving its purpose and vision. When analysing markets and educational programmes, consider the following points (further highlighted in the case studies in Part Two):

- The IB diploma is an appropriate matriculation examination for most nationalities. In a few countries, though – Chile for example – the national system is required for university entry and so students may take this alongside their IB diploma. Details on such issues can be found in the university recognition section of the IBO website.
- It is important to market the DP well, but this may not be a simple matter. Schools will gain a certain advantage simply by being an authorized IB school, and some new students will find the school through searching the IBO's public website. At the same time, a new IB school may find that it has to work harder on its marketing to differentiate itself from the other IB schools in the area.
- The IB DP needs to be explained and promoted extensively over the first couple of years to parents, students and teachers. This may be perceived as a loss of status for the other programmes in the school, and deter non-IB students. At the same time, mistakes made with the IB implementation or over-optimistic claims regarding the IB programme can lead to a loss of credibility which can be costly for both the IB programme and the other school programmes.

4 Gap analysis

There will generally be differences between the existing situation and the IB situation in the areas of curriculum, staffing, facilities and timetable.

4.1 The curriculum

There are two important points to note here.

Determine the compatibility of currently offered courses and IB courses

Many schools will need to combine courses. In such cases, as part of the IBO authorization requirements, the IB course's subject guide and assessment scheme will take precedence. For instance, high school English (a creative writing course) and IB English A1 (a literature course) may be difficult to combine. With other subjects the IB course, although different in content, may be a suitable substitution for the current course. However, as the case study in Chapter 5 shows, this cannot be taken for granted and should be studied very carefully.

ESL (English as a second language) students can perform very well on the DP if appropriate strategies are adopted.

- The minimum level of English required (if the language of instruction is English) is around that required to study IB English B, i.e. three to five years' experience. There will need to be provision for these students to study their native language for language A1, but this could be on a supported 'self-taught' basis. Refer to section 7.4 below and Chapters 12 and 13 for more details.
- To cater for ESL students, some less language-intensive IB courses in groups 3, 4 and 6 (the humanities, sciences and arts subjects) need to be scheduled. Even in mathematics one has to be careful: see Chapter 16.
- If the student's native language is one of the IB response languages (English, French, Spanish), then the examinations in these subjects could be taken in this language. This is not automatically a benefit as some students will have difficulty translating the terminology back to their native language, so careful advice is needed.
- The faculty will need to move towards a more inclusive model of ESL teaching and teachers will need to be taught how to accommodate these students.

4.2 Staffing

A comparison of your school's current courses with the intended IB courses will highlight staffing needs. As discussed below, there can be issues of academic competence and literature competence, and each of the curriculum areas has specific issues. The new areas of TOK and CAS will also inevitably have an impact on staffing.

Academic. The HL courses prepare students to enrol for specialist courses at university. Staff teaching these courses need to be able to teach up to this level and they may be difficult to find. Also, students taking extended essays often need support from supervisors with an academic background in the subject.

Language. In languages, there are distinct needs for teachers of literature (language A1) and language (language B and language *ab initio*). Many but not all language teachers will be comfortable in all areas – see Chapters 12 and 13 for more details.

Science. In the sciences (group 4) there is a strong emphasis on practical science. Teachers will need to be able to create a student-centred, practical scheme of work that will allow students to hypothesize and investigate areas of the curriculum. There may be a substantial increase in the amount of practical work, as 25% of IB science courses should have a practical basis – see Chapter 15. Correspondingly, schools may have to hire extra technical support staff.

Mathematics. In the mathematics group (group 5) the mathematics HL course goes beyond what is expected in some national education systems for this age. The further mathematics course is only taken by a relative handful of candidates each year and schools may find it difficult to find high school teachers who are able to teach this course – see Chapter 16.

Arts. In *visual arts* (group 6) it is helpful if there are several specialists available. The course encourages a broad approach to art, and too narrow a focus can hinder students. In *theatre arts* there is a lot more focus on theatre production and play analysis, and less focus on acting, than in some drama courses. This may have staffing or staff development implications – see Chapter 17.

TOK. Staffing for the Theory of Knowledge course (TOK) needs to be considered early on. It is not a prerequisite that the TOK course be staffed with philosophy teachers but there are certain expectations (see Chapter 10 for more details). The TOK team should certainly not be decided on the basis of who is 'left over'.

CAS. Your school needs to appoint a CAS coordinator and many schools involve teaching staff actively in the CAS programme. One of the world's most successful IB schools, Mara College Banting in Malaysia, reserves a whole day in the week to do CAS – see the case study in Chapter 7.

IB coordinator. Your school needs to appoint a DP coordinator (DPC).

Secretarial support. The DPC will need secretarial support, typically for about one-third of a full-time position – see sections 5.11 and 5.12 below.

Library. The library plays a key function in the DP. Many schools rely on their librarians to teach research and referencing skills, and therefore employ teacher-librarians.

IT facilities. The syllabus (and particularly the coursework in mathematics) demands a commitment to IT, and a smooth internet connection is necessary. Extra technical staff may be needed to support this.

4.3 **The calendar/timetable**

A typical school year of around 180 contact days should be sufficient to meet the IBO's requirement of 240 hours of teacher–student contact time for HL courses and 150 hours of contact time for SL courses. However, late starting dates, examination weeks, and activity/camp weeks can quickly cut this short. The second year of the IB course will finish in early May (or November for southern hemisphere schools). For schools that work through until July, such as UK schools, this can make for a very short year. The situation may be even more pronounced for schools that teach courses on a semester basis, i.e. certain subjects are taught intensively in the first half of the year and other subjects in the second half. In this case, the courses running in the second semester of the final year may end up bearing the full brunt of the shortened session due to the examinations. Schools also need to consider the IB students' TOK and CAS programmes. They need to spend roughly half a day per week (in or outside timetable) on CAS activities, so a short and intensive school year may hinder students' participation in CAS. To get an idea of the scale of the problem you may face, perform a rough count of the number of contact hours for the courses that your school currently offers. The courses would have to finish in May (November), and you should exclude examination weeks and activity weeks and similar events.

In practice very few established IB schools report that they achieve the required 240/150 contact hours. The IBO, however, will expect to see a calendar and an analysis of contact time as part of the authorization process, and candidate schools are expected to get very close to this number of contact hours. Schools will probably need to explore the feasibility of:

- general timetable restructuring to increase the contact time throughout the year
- changing the length/dates of the school year
- changing the number and position of training days
- changing the length of the school day/length of lessons
- offering after-school/weekend sessions – although it is strongly recommended that this should only be an emergency measure.

The timetable should enable students to have access to courses from each of the DP's six groups (language A1, second language, individuals and societies, experimental sciences, mathematics and computer science, the arts and free electives). Many students will want to choose two or more sciences or humanities, so the timetable should make this possible (see section 7 below).

4.4 Facilities

Classrooms

The DP aims to place the student squarely at the centre of the learning process. Clearly this requires a fairly small class size, which is why the IBO strongly recommends a limit of 25 students per class. In our experience, an ideal class size is 15–20 students. For schools whose current class size exceeds 25, the impact of the DP constraints will be profound in terms of accommodation and staffing.

Library/media centre

The library is a major focus for authorization teams. It should provide access to high-quality reference materials, and it should be a spacious and inviting area conducive to study and research. The stock of reference materials, periodicals and literature should be representative of the nationalities in the school, in particular to support the language A1 courses that your students study. Reading material for the TOK course should be available. Most schools find that they need to spend some money on their libraries. Some schools have spent US$10–20,000 and more on their libraries for authorization, but a well-stocked library may not need that much initial expenditure.

Science laboratories

The science courses place a strong emphasis on practical work. The experiments are student-centred, often open-ended investigations, which call on students to demonstrate a range of practical skills. If the school is not already offering similarly practically based courses then there could be considerable start-up costs. Depending on what is already in place this could include provision for:

- suitably equipped science laboratories (benches, water, gas and electricity supplies, drainage, ventilation, emergency exit, blackout curtains, safety equipment, fume cupboard)
- suitable storage and preparation areas (prep rooms)
- sufficient equipment – student-centred practical courses are very equipment intensive
- lab technician(s)/lab manager
- the Group 4 Project (see Chapter 15) requires all students to carry out independent research over a period of several weeks. Resources and space need to be allocated to students to work at the same time over this period.

Music venues

There is a strong practical element in all IB arts courses and there needs to be enough space to accommodate the various activities. For music, in particular, there also needs to be a listening library with a good collection of recordings.

Visual arts studios

The studios will need to have good natural lighting. Students will build up a portfolio of all sorts of artwork, paintings, ceramics, three-dimensional work, sculpture, photography etc. and they could be working on some very large pieces. Workspace and storage space require careful consideration.

Theatre arts venues

If your school already offers a drama or theatre course it is likely to have the necessary equipment:

- staging
- scenery
- lighting/sound equipment
- props and storage.

The IB theatre arts course requires students to study a range of genres, for instance the Theatre of Noh, Kabuki theatre, Greek tragedy. This may necessitate the purchase of additional masks, props, costumes and texts.

IT

Many schools have already invested in IT infrastructure. For DP authorization four areas need to be considered.

- Students will need access to the internet, and very probably to online databases, in the library/media centre.
- The school must have a computer laboratory if it intends to run the IB computer science or information technology in a global society (ITGS) courses.
- The IB DP encourages the use of a wide range of learning tools and having computers in the classroom is obviously part of this. A display such as a TV monitor or an LCD hooked to the teacher's computer is highly recommended, especially for mathematics, where the use of IT is required by the

syllabus. It is hard to run good mathematics courses if there is not at least one room with computers and a printer where students can do coursework.

- The school should have a network to facilitate the sharing of resources. Teachers should have ready access to email and the internet. The IBO has put a large amount of its resources into electronic format. The DPC can carry out most administration tasks using email and the IBO's secure website, IBNET.

Athletics venues

There is as yet no IB physical education course, although it is something that the IBO is considering. However, access to good sports facilities will make creating a CAS programme much easier.

5 Cost analysis

5.1 IBO fees

The fees are listed in section H of the IBO's *Vade Mecum*. Fees have been fairly stable over the last couple of years. In the authorization year schools need to pay an application fee (currently around US$2,000). This covers the costs of the authorization visit but not the pre-authorization visits, should you decide to ask for these. It is also strongly recommended that schools sign up early for the Online Curriculum Centre (OCC), which currently costs around US$500 per year. There are many resources and discussions forums on this site that will assist with implementation and beyond. Visit the OCC at: online@ibo.org to request membership details.

Once the school is authorized it must pay an annual fee, the basic fee, of around US$8,000. This includes the OCC fee.

5.2 Curriculum documents

Curriculum documents and promotional materials are available from the IBO's publications department. A full list of the IBO's publications is available from their public website: www.ibo.org. Several hundred US dollars will be needed to buy the basic guides and several hundred more to buy the support materials, examination papers and marketing materials.

5.3 Examination and per capita fees

To give an idea of examination fees for a typical DP candidate taking three HL and three SL subjects, figures quoted in the 2003 *Vade Mecum* are displayed in figure 3.1.

In addition the school is charged (2003) a flat fee of US$326 for each examination round to cover the TOK course marking. Finally, there are penalty charges for late registration and amendments to registrations. The examination fees may not be a burden for schools since they are on a par with those charged by other examination boards; and many private schools will, in any case, bill the students for these costs.

Figure 3.1 Examination fees

Per capita fee:	US$ 137
Registration fee:	US$ 71
Subject fees:	US$ 318
Extended essay fee:	US$ 33
Total	US$ 559

Schools can ask for feedback on the examination performance of individual candidates. These reports are called 'Enquiry upon Results' and their cost should be built into the cost of running the programme; perhaps a few could be purchased each year on a rotation basis around the departments. Subject reports and extended essay reports are available free online.

5.4 IB workshops

IB workshops are run for both new and experienced teachers. They provide a lot of very useful information and they allow teachers to form networks and share resources. They do, however, constitute a major expense for the school. A typical IBO-approved workshop will cost (2003) around US$500 per participant, or around US$1,000 if accommodation and meals come as part of the package. On top of this the school needs to provide transportation and possibly substitute teacher cover. Depending on the location, the overall workshop expenses per participant can easily run up to US$1,500–2,000.

For authorization, the IBO requires a school to train all of its teachers unless they have already attended workshops elsewhere sometime in the previous three years. After authorization, the school needs to commit to ongoing professional development. IB curricula are reviewed and revised every five years, on a staggered basis (i.e. not all subjects at the same time), so there is a need to keep up to date with developments. The details of the curriculum review are listed on the back page of the *Coordinator Notes* – see the Resources section on page 75.

Established IB schools use various strategies to try to reduce these professional development costs. The regional office will be able to advise you about the options available, e.g.:

- If the department is large then it will be worth while inviting an IB workshop leader to your school. Note: this must be arranged in liaison with the regional office.
- Schools can send several people to a workshop and then use them to train others in their department.
- Schools can apply to host a workshop themselves for one or more subjects.

5.5 English as a second language (ESL)

The examinations must be taken in one of three official languages: English, French and Spanish. Of these, examinations in English are the most common, with English generally being the language of instruction. Competent bilingual or near-bilingual students should have little difficulty coping with the linguistic level of the DP. To successfully accommodate students who speak English as a second language, however, additional language lessons on their own are unlikely to be sufficient. ESL needs to be everyone's concern: all IB teachers and the ESL students themselves; it should not just be left up to ESL support staff. The type and scale of ESL training needed for staff will obviously depend on the profile of the school and the flexibility of the staff. The following are some possible strategies:

- A whole school workshop on 'ESL inclusion' (i.e. supporting ESL students in regular mainstream classes), followed by in-house training to develop and implement classroom strategies. Schools may wish to bring in a visiting expert to lead at least parts of this training.
- ESL or ESOL (English for speakers of other languages) teaching certification for key people in each department. Some of these qualifications can be obtained after a month's intensive course or after several months of part-time study. The key people would then coordinate teaching strategies and the development of teaching materials within their departments.
- Although the IBO does not formally require it, we strongly advise that schools insist that ESL students study the school's working language as language B. In fact, many schools go further and require the language B to be studied at HL. It is essential that such a course provides skills above and beyond the requirements of the language B syllabus so that the students learn practical cross-curricular literacy skills. See Chapter 13 for examples of suitable working practices.
- Schools may also wish to offer after-hours language support sessions so that students can get practical help with their work.

5.6 Departmental resources

For many departments the requirements will be limited to:

- textbooks
- reference materials for staff and students
- support materials.

From the DP subject guides or from this book, departments will be able to determine how suitable their current stock of textbooks is. Recommended texts can be found in Part Three of this book, on the IBO's OCC, through attendance at IB workshops, or via visiting IB schools. It is likely that the 'shopping list' that comes back from departments will give the school an upper limit of expenditure.

The language departments will need to purchase good-quality recording equipment if they don't already possess it. However, this equipment could be shared by theatre arts and music, which also need to submit oral assessments.

The music department will need to provide a comprehensive listening library for their course. Visual arts may need to expand its reference materials. These books and CDs can be very expensive.

Computing, ITGS, design technology and the sciences may also incur substantial additional costs in upgrading equipment and facilities.

5.7 Library

The library/media centre should play a central part in the discussions relating to purchases of all reference materials for the school, including those materials that departments wish to order for themselves. In addition, the library will need to consider the costs of purchasing or subscribing to:

- encyclopaedias, also available on CD-ROM or online, e.g. *Encyclopaedia Britannica*
- online databases such as Proquest, Xreferplus
- anti-plagiarism software services such as Turnitin.com
- periodicals for the key subject areas, including some foreign language periodicals to reflect the mix of nationalities in the DP cohort (some periodicals come included with the online databases)
- newspapers: some foreign language newspapers or different national English language papers should be available
- a variety of reference books and materials for the Theory of Knowledge course – recommended texts for this course can be found in Chapter 10
- foreign language sections containing language A1 texts, representative of your school's pre-IB diploma and IB diploma student base
- key foreign language textbooks for mathematics, science, humanities etc., again representative of the school's student base – parents can often help with this.

5.8 Facilities

Science laboratories

Equipping a science laboratory from scratch can easily cost US$10,000 just for the facility. Providing an adequate range of equipment will increase this initial cost considerably. Most schools will already have science laboratories but will need to consider what additional features and equipment need to be purchased and installed.

UK schools have a long history of student-centred practical science, and will recognize the format of the IB science courses. Consequently the UK-based Association for Science Education (www.ase.org.uk) is a good source of information on laboratory design, safety, and equipment suppliers. Membership is around US$75 per year. Another organization, CLEAPSS (www.cleapss.org), produces excellent safety information. Schools that have been accredited by the European Council of International Schools (ECIS) will also find that their health and safety measures are comparable to those required for IB authorization.

Equipment costs will depend on the style of science currently taught in your school. To estimate costs, the science department could obtain practical schemes of work (PSOWs) from established IB schools or at the IB workshops.

There are many school science equipment suppliers, which over the last few years seem to be merging and expanding their global presence. For example, the UK-based school science equipment suppliers (Unilab, Griffin and George, Findel, Philip Harris) have been catering to this style of science teaching for many years, and their catalogues give a good idea about the price and the type and quantity of equipment you will need. Ultimately, though, it will pay to shop around and source equipment locally where possible.

Fine and performing arts, library, IT, athletics venues

If your gap analysis has identified areas of concern relating to these facilities, it will be useful to visit established IB schools (recommended by the IB regional office) and/or to ask the regional office to make a site visit.

5.9 Support for the TOK course

Chapter 10 discusses in more detail some of the ways that this course can be run. Some suggested methods, which can have a cost implication, are:

- running a TOK camp, at the beginning of or at some point in the course, to set the tone, teach some of the basic ideas, and kick-start future discussions
- inviting guest speakers
- taking classes away on visits
- providing cover so that subject specialists can contribute to TOK lessons
- buying a textbook and/or producing in-house resources.

TOK can sometimes be forgotten on the normal department budget allocation. If TOK is not designated as a department, or assigned to one, then it will need access to some discretionary funds to purchase support materials.

5.10 Support for the CAS programme

It is of paramount importance to recognize from the start that the CAS programme should be allocated its own budget. Equally important, it should not be expected that students will run fund-raising events to support their CAS activities financially. Costs will vary widely for different schools. Students are encouraged to build their own individual CAS programme, but in many cases the school will find it necessary to provide opportunities or to facilitate attendance. This is likely to be the case for *service* and possibly also for *creativity* and *action*. Key factors will be how willing and able the students are to pay for these activities themselves, and what extra-curricular activities the school already offers.

The school's support for CAS may include:

- transportation
- school membership of various clubs/institutions
- paying for, or contributing to, the cost of external instructors, for karate and pottery for instance
- access to audio-visual and ICT facilities to assist students' record keeping
- organizing teachers to offer extra-curricular activities that meet the requirements and spirit of CAS.

The school will also need to consider the costs of monitoring the students' CAS programme. At the very least this will include stationery costs but the school could subscribe to an online tracking system, or use space on its server for students to upload information to their own web page. See Chapter 9 for more details.

5.11 Support for IB coordination

The DPC will need office space and enough storage space to have ready access to all the curriculum materials. Reliable internet access and email facilities are a must, as most of the administration of the DP is carried out via the IBO network, IBNET (soon to be redesigned and renamed as IBIS, or IB Information System). Email is also the preferred method of communication with the IBO. If the school is not already in a position to allocate a computer to each member of staff, the DPC at least should have one.

The DPC needs release time and must have some administrative support. The amount of release time will depend on the specific duties of the coordinator, which vary considerably from school to school. The IBO recommends that the DPC should only teach 50% of a full-time teaching load, though in many schools this figure is closer to 60%. Secretarial support of around one-third of a full-time position would be sufficient. These figures, perhaps surprisingly, are fairly independent of the size of the diploma cohort. They relate to the administrative workload connected directly to *external* agencies (the IBO, examiners and moderators), which varies little from small to large cohorts. The administrative workload relating to *internal* aspects of running the DP, such as counselling and scheduling students, marketing, supporting IB teachers, running examinations, and arranging professional development, varies considerably with the size of the cohort. However, these functions do not necessarily fall on the coordinator alone and would be incurred no matter what curriculum is taught. In many schools the DPC position is combined with other administrative positions, with adjustments made to the teaching load.

IB examination papers will need to be kept in a secure room. A safe or lockable filing cabinet in a room with additional locks and security would be suitable. A very few people at most should have access to this room.

The coordinator will need to produce and copy materials for the IB teachers and so will need a stationery and photocopy budget.

There are a few items such as examination packs and some promotional and support materials that do not really fall under any department's budget. In the implementation phase this could come to around US$1,000. Thereafter, around US$300 per year would be needed.

5.12 Administrative support

Secretarial support

Often the authorization team will require the secretarial support of around one-third of a full-time position to be put in place or to be planned before giving authorization. Secretarial support will be needed from the pre-authorization year onwards. It is better to have one dedicated individual than to share the support between several secretaries.

Postage

Examination scripts and internally assessed work need to be posted out to examiners and moderators all around the world. The IBO is working on a system where this work will be scanned locally and distributed electronically. However, for the next few years at least, schools will need to use a reliable system of distribution. It is worth while using a good courier service, which can be held directly accountable, rather than one that passes the responsibility to the receiving country's postal system and leaves you to track the package down. Around US$1,500 should be allowed for postage, although the final bill will be largely dependent on the number of candidates and how often courier services are used.

Invigilators/proctors

Schools may wish to hire people to invigilate the examinations. Often schools will use their own teachers. Note that teachers are not allowed to be in the examination room when their own class is being examined, and the DPC will need to start and finish examinations. The DPC may therefore need support for his/her classes during this period.

5.13 Salaries and allowances

The following positions should attract some time and/or monetary allowance.

IB coordinator. A stipend or responsibility allowance is common for this position.

CAS coordinator. Although CAS, at first sight, may look like an extension of the school's extra-curricular programme, the scale and breadth of the CAS programme should not be underestimated. Schools running the International Award or the Duke of Edinburgh's Award come closest to appreciating the degree of coordination required. The CAS coordinator position should have a time allowance and usually attracts a responsibility allowance.

TOK coordinator. There is a lot of preparatory work to be done for this course. Some time/monetary allowance in the implementation phase may therefore be appropriate. Once established, the degree of coordination will depend largely on the number of IB students enrolled and the style of TOK programme.

Key learning area coordinators. Schools may wish to alter or augment their middle-management structures, at least during the implementation phase, to ensure that there are key people in each subject area who can keep the developments on track and take on some leadership role.

5.14 Marketing

Accurate and effective marketing is very important and forms a key part of the communication that a school must have with its community. Several of the case studies in Part Two highlight specific considerations. The IBO produces some generic information brochures and PowerPoint presentations, which provide a good basis to build on and personalize. Once the school is authorized it will want to update its school brochure and advertising runs to reflect its new status.
Depending on what the school already has available, costs might include:

- audio-visual equipment
- disposable cameras (for general issue to staff to capture IB-style activities in classrooms or out of school), digital camera, video camera, LCD projector + laptop computer (more dynamic and much easier to update than overhead transparencies)

- film processing
- printing
- advertising
- room hire and catering for promotional events.

5.15 Sharing the additional expenses

It can be hard to justify sharing the extra administrative, annual subscription, examination fees (if paid by the school) and professional development costs across the whole school if the IB DP is just for a small group within a school. The costs of running the programme will dissuade some schools from adopting it, and persuade some others to rationalize their programmes to focus on it. Around half of all IB schools are in the state sector, and some enjoy government assistance with the IBO fees.

6 The timeframe for transition and DP introduction

A suggested timeframe towards the moment of authorization is one to two years. This will obviously depend on:

- the need for new facilities
- the budget for professional development
- what other development work is going on in the school.

It is not recommended that schools attempt to gain authorization too quickly. With a change of this magnitude, it is very difficult to bring the community along with you in less than a year. It also places an enormous demand on training and resource budgets. However, taking longer than two years is also inadvisable because it seems too distant a goal and momentum is lost.

It is very important that schools realize from the outset that the process of introducing the DP does not end with authorization. They will need to allow up to five years for the programme to fully embed itself in the school culture and environment. The case studies in Part Two give more details on this.

7 Guiding the school through the implementation process

Once the feasibility committee has concluded its gap and cost analysis and the school has decided to go ahead with the DP, a new phase begins: the implementation process. The impact of this process can be divided into two segments: the impact on the overall functioning of the school, and the impact on individual departments. Section 7 deals with the former while section 8 deals with the latter.

7.1 The implementation committee and the coordinators

Once the decision has been made to go ahead with the IB DP, the posts of the coordinators (DPC, CAS and TOK) should be settled. The DPC and CAS coordinator posts are mandatory, whilst the TOK post is usually recommended, depending on the size of the cohort. An implementation committee should be formed. This will probably consist of members of the senior academic team, a member of the board, the coordinators, the timetabler, the head of pastoral care, the head of languages, the head of ESL, the librarian, and the champions identified earlier in the process (see sections 2.3 and 2.4).

7.2 The action plan and the authorization file

A simple form based on the template in figure 3.2 can help in formulating your action plan for implementation.

The timeframe for introducing the DP will have been determined by the feasibility study and the board. The action plan should map out the implementation with the aim to almost finish it by the time of the pre-authorization visit. The pre-authorization visit is not a required part of the authorization, but it is something that we strongly recommend. The pre-authorization visit should take place three to six months prior to authorization. If the school believes – or thinks that the IB regional office believes – that it has a lot of work to do then it is possibly a good idea to request a pre-authorization visit six months prior to the authorization visit.

The school should aim to leave the visiting team with a clear impression that everything is on track to be completed by the time of the authorization visit, and ask for specific advice in the areas where the team feels more work needs to be done. If the pre-authorization visit is handled well, the authorization visit will be more like a final check.

We strongly recommend that you keep an *authorization file*. This could be in an electronic format during construction but it will need to be printed out for the authorization team later in the process. There are two reasons for this:

- as a check to ensure that the school has met all the criteria
- to show the regional office that the school has met the criteria.

This may seem overly cautious but we would argue that taking this stance from the outset is a small price to pay if it can help to ensure that authorization goes smoothly. Whilst some schools report that they found the authorization process professionally rewarding, others report that they found it frustrating or that the goalposts seemed to keep moving. This may simply be a matter of lack of preparedness on the school's part, or a matter of miscommunication. None the

Figure 3.2 Template form for an action plan

Action item	Action by whom	Reporting to	Deadline	Completed

less, it can be difficult to counter criticism such as '… inadequate resources in the science laboratories' or '… insufficient communication of the DP to all community members' unless the school has documented evidence to the contrary.

The authorization file should be compiled by a member of the implementation committee, and it should contain at least the items below:

1. The feasibility study
2. Agendas for meetings where the DP implementation is discussed, and minutes of those meetings:
   - board meetings
   - implementation committee meetings
   - whole faculty/department meetings
   - staff in-service training days/curriculum development days.
3. All internal correspondence relating to the DP: memos, emails, and so on. In particular there should be evidence that action items have been requested, approved, and completed or are in the process of being completed.
4. All external correspondence with the IBO regional office, especially feedback on progress to date.
5. Presentations made to each section of the school community. Photos of the event can be taken and included too.
6. Promotional materials: leaflets, handbooks, web pages, and so on.
7. Reports from colleagues that have visited other IB schools.
8. A list of the staff members who will be teaching the IB courses (see section 7.12).
9. Evidence of planning at the department level (see section 8.1).
10. Evidence of planning on a school-wide level (see sections 7.11 and 7.12).
11. Actual and planned developments in the pre-IB years to prepare students for the DP (see section 10).
12. Strategic plan for the position and role of the DP within the school.
13. Evidence of progress on each recommendation of the pre-authorization team.

7.3 The application form

The school should obtain the application form from the regional office. This will be submitted just prior to the authorization visit. The form requests information such as:

- school profile data
- expected DP enrolment
- how the costs of the DP will be met
- why the school wants to adopt the DP and the school mission statement
- how the school sees the development of the DP over the next five years – the strategic plan
- timetable, school policies, and a list of the teachers with their qualifications
- what the school can contribute to the programme.

Clearly, maintaining an authorization file as suggested above will help the school to complete the application form with confidence.

7.4 **The timetable: constraints**

The construction of the timetable is a pivotal and potentially complex task. The choice of subjects is crucial to the take-up of the IB DP. Offering too few subjects in the DP while offering a choice of alternative programmes could easily result in a non-starter in terms of DP uptake. On the other hand, offering many subjects could result in small class sizes that are not viable either economically or educationally. Many schools will want to combine or 'twin' the IB DP with programmes they currently offer, for example a high school diploma programme, or an A-level programme. The case studies in Part Two highlight some of the possibilities and challenges associated with these scenarios. If your school decides to twin, it is important to remember that the IBO expects to see evidence that the school can preserve the integrity of the DP within the twin scenario (see Chapter 2).

The courses currently offered in your school are likely to reflect student needs and can guide the school's initial subject choices. The range of IB subjects available is impressive, especially in the languages, and it can be tempting to select something 'exotic' to woo students. However, it is best to avoid creating 'one-teacher departments'. This can make moderating internal assessment work difficult, and it can pose difficulties for the school if that one teacher leaves. A full timetable can be constructed by the school in steps. First a simple timetable is created based on courses currently run by the school, taking careful note of the timetable constraints imposed by the DP. When this is up and running, you can think of refining it. This process is detailed below, beginning by listing the timetable constraints.

As an overall constraint, IB students must have access to courses in each group of the DP hexagon: three courses at HL and three at SL (see Chapter 1). Here, we discuss the further constraints faced within each hexagon corner.

Groups 1 and 2: Languages

Students must take a language A1 course (a literature course), and the IBO expects students to study their best language, normally their native language. Language A1 can be class-taught or, at SL only, self-taught. The latter is meant to support minority languages: any language for which you register more than five students (or six in 'special circumstances' according to the IBO) cannot be entered on a 'self-taught' basis.

It is strongly recommended that, in the first few years at least, the self-taught group is as small as possible – or there is none at all. Many schools offer taught language A1 courses in the dominant languages amongst students and require (or strongly suggest) that all students take one of these. Many schools report that they found the 'self-taught' course difficult to set up and that, for all but the most able and self-disciplined students, a good deal of support is necessary. However, experience shows that requiring ESL students to study English A1 is hard on them, and that their chance of failing is significant. As is argued in Chapters 12 and 13, the challenges of self-taught languages are not as insurmountable as is often believed. Once a school has found its feet after teaching the DP for a few years, exploring self-taught languages should be a priority. When the school is ready to offer self-taught languages, it really should appoint a self-taught language coordinator. Chapter 12 details the educational issues of running self-taught language A1, but for the benefit of the implementation committee, some of the administrative issues are set out here:

- *Success*. Students and their parents will be concerned about being able to succeed on the self-taught course (but they may also be concerned about doing a non-native A1 course too).

- *Fees*. Parents may question paying full school fees for effectively an 'incomplete' programme, especially if there is no self-taught coordinator or support class.

- *Tuition costs*. Schools and parents may wish these students to have private tuition.

- *Tutors*. Some parents will expect schools to be responsible for finding tutors. Schools will need to explain the A1 course to tutors to ensure that the tuition is focused.

- *Texts*. Without a self-taught coordinator it can be extremely difficult to source texts for some languages. (See Chapter 12 section 4.3 for advice on this matter.)

- *Tracking*. It can be difficult to keep track of self-taught students' progress and to determine whether they will pass the diploma or not.

As an alternative to providing self-taught language A1, many schools simply require all students to take a particular language A1, for instance English A1, and consequently only admit native or near-native English-speaking students into the DP. However, allowing non-native speakers onto an English A1 course requires the department to select texts carefully to accommodate the different cultural backgrounds and linguistic abilities in the group.

Students must take a second language. Usually, this is from group 2 (language A2, language B, language *ab initio*, described below) but students can also take another language A1, if the schedule permits. Schools need to study the language profile of their cohort (what are their potential first and second languages?) in order to determine what group 2 languages to offer. Here are some of the constraints:

- Allowing students access to two A1 courses complicates the timetable. This option requires the student to study a large amount of literature, and may only serve a minority of students.
- Language A2 is a language course for near-native speakers. The course is short on published resources and will therefore require a lot of preparation. However, Chapter 13 offers a great deal of practical advice on the setting up of an A2 course.
- Language B requires two to five years' experience with the language.
- Language *ab initio* courses are supposed to be for complete beginners only, i.e. those who have had no previous experience of the language.

In practice, this leaves a gap between the language B and the *ab initio* entry-level descriptors. The DPC and head of languages should select the appropriate level of languages for each student. Native speakers should not be put into language B courses and students with a background in a language should not be placed into *ab initio* classes. The real world of third culture students who have not maintained their mother tongue complicates matters, and schools need to use some discretion to determine what is best for the student (see the case study in

Chapter 6 for more details on this). The system is not actively policed and the IBO relies on the integrity of the school to enter students appropriately. However, the IBO does monitor the statistical data entered during candidate registration, and schools have been caught out, and increasingly will be.

The provision of languages in the IB DP can be complex, especially in schools that cater to many nationalities. Getting it right is crucial to the programme's success. Involving the head of languages in the implementation committee will allow the language department to see the bigger picture, which helps to construct an accessible and enriching languages programme. Refer to Chapters 12 and 13 for more details.

Group 3: Individuals and societies

The situation here is much more straightforward than in languages. There are nine group 3 subjects (business and management, economics, geography, history, Islamic history, information technology in a global society (ITGS), philosophy, psychology, and social and cultural anthropology). A school should offer several of these but not all. Group 3 is very accessible. Students do not need a specialized background in these subjects to do well, and those who demonstrate aptitude in pre-IB 'group 3 type' courses can access any group 3 subject. The school will want to strike a balance between the solid and familiar (e.g. an IB geography course following an existing pre-IB geography course), and the exotic or trendy. ITGS (at SL only) is worthy of serious consideration. It is a very accessible course and one to which all students might be usefully exposed. See Chapter 14 for details.

In group 3 subjects it is possible to combine HL and SL in one class for the first year, since both the HL and SL courses have a common core. However, in some group 3 subjects, the HL components comprise only a few additional statements in each topic in the subject guide, so when it comes to teaching the HL material the teaching can become very disjointed. In other subjects though, for example the sciences, the HL elements are more discrete units. How the HL material is arranged in the subject guide should be a factor in deciding whether to combine HL and SL classes, or at least a consideration when determining how to teach the HL material.

Schools will need to study the subject guides to determine to what extent there are connections with pre-IB courses. For example, IB business and management SL is very similar to the UK's business studies GCSE, a pre-IB course.

Group 4: Experimental sciences

The science subjects in group 4 (chemistry, physics, biology, environmental systems, and design technology) share a common framework. The slight exception is design technology, which has 36% of the grade determined by coursework as opposed to 24% for the other sciences. If necessary, it is relatively straightforward to combine HL and SL classes in the first year as they share a common core (see Chapter 15) but teaching needs to be carefully planned. Biology, chemistry and physics courses require a substantial background at pre-IB level. Environmental systems is often seen as a 'terminal science', for those who don't wish to study science any more. However, it is not an easy option, and is as rigorous as the other SL science courses. Although biology and environmental science have less mathematical content and students often perceive them as easier, ESL students tend to find them more difficult because of the substantial lexicon each one carries. As environmental systems has similar content to the biology SL course, students are not allowed to follow a DP that contains both environmental systems and biology SL.

An important point for schools wishing to accommodate future medicine students: *it is important to schedule biology, chemistry and physics so that all three courses can be taken*, since there are many medical faculties that advise students to do so. The IBO will allow students to take a non-standard DP if the university of their choice has particular requirements. This is true in general, not only for future doctors. Schools need to apply to the IBO for each individual case, but it is a routine matter. The timetable, however, needs to be able to accommodate this situation.

Group 5: Mathematics

Most schools choose to offer only mathematics HL (MHL), mathematics methods (MMSL) and mathematics studies (MSSL) in group 5. The fourth mathematics course, further mathematics, is difficult and has a very small candidature. Mathematics HL is similar in difficulty to a US-style AP mathematics programme or to a UK A-level course. It is meant for the very able mathematician who is aiming to study mathematics, engineering or physics at university. Students who need to study mechanics should take physics as mechanics is not part of the mathematics courses. The easiest mathematics course, MSSL, is aimed primarily at the arts student who ordinarily would not take mathematics further but needs to do so for the IB diploma. It is similar in content to a typical extended-level middle-school course, such as the UK's extended GCSE course. MMSL is much more demanding mathematically and is appropriate for those intending to study biology, medicine, or a business-related degree course. However, since it is much less demanding on lexicon than MSSL, some schools find themselves advising ESL students to take MMSL on the grounds of language alone.

Another drawback of MSSL is that some universities do not accept it, particularly universities in the Netherlands, Germany and Australia – refer to Chapter 16 for more details. It will be necessary to check the MSSL status explicitly with the typical target universities of your students.

Group 6: Arts and free electives

The arts courses are visual arts, theatre arts and music. Many schools, new and old, offer all three. It mostly depends on the commitment of the school to the arts and the number of DP students. It must further be kept in mind that most students take a free elective from groups 3 or 4 as their group 6 subject. The timetable should therefore have enough flexibility to allow students to take two group 3 subjects or two group 4 subjects or even a third language.

In addition to the constraints described above, there may be substantial additional constraints if your school aims to 'twin' the DP with other programmes – see the case studies in Part Two for more information on this.

7.5 The timetable: opportunities

Restrict the choice of SL subjects

Generally speaking, students will choose their HL subjects first (based on interest and aptitude), and then fill in their schedule with SL subjects according to the DP constraints. They are usually less concerned about the range of subjects offered at SL, enabling schools to restrict the SL course offering and thus ensuring viable class sizes.

Combine some HL and SL classes

The IBO recognizes that this will be necessary at times but schools need to consider carefully the impact on teaching and learning, and to use this option judiciously. Combining HL and SL is easier in some subjects than in others – refer to the subject chapters in Part Three for advice in this respect. Combining some classes, especially in the first year, can give the schedule a great deal of flexibility and much reduces the risk of inadvertently creating non-viable courses.

Anticipated subjects

In most subjects (except language *ab initio*) there is the option for a student to take the examination after the first year. The student is still required to have received the stipulated hours of tuition and to have completed all coursework requirements. This option is called *anticipating* a subject, and it is restricted to SL subjects only. Anticipating a subject can help with scheduling; and it also eases the pressure on students in the second year. Schools will need to weigh this, especially with the first cohort, against the confidence of teachers and students (and parents) in their ability to finish the course in just one year. Additionally, as is pointed out in Chapter 2, you will not win yourself friends on the authorization team by embracing anticipation too enthusiastically.

Allow the students access to four HL subjects

The DP requires students to study three HL and three SL subjects. However, students are allowed to study four subjects at HL. There will be a demand from able students to study four HLs even though HL and SL courses contribute equally to the final overall DP score. The IBO maintains that, in general, students are better advised to study three HLs and score well overall rather than take four HLs and score less well. Some students may benefit from four HLs, however, for example if their university of choice offers advanced placement or credit for subjects offered at HL. Taking four subjects at HL can be a lot of work and schools need to counsel students carefully to separate 'need' from 'ego' before requesting four HL subjects.

For the first few weeks or months, however, it can be very useful to schedule students into four HLs. If some of your courses are combined HL/SL in the first year then this is easily done. If students find an HL course difficult in the first few weeks then they can easily drop back to three HLs. If they start with only three HLs and they find, for example, that mathematics HL is difficult and need to change to mathematics methods SL, the timetable may well force major (unwanted) changes elsewhere in the schedule. Experienced schools can of course largely avoid these issues by carefully advising students but even then there will always be a few borderline cases where transfer is advisable. Usually, the requested transfers from HL to SL occur in mathematics and physics, and it is possible to construct your timetable so as to minimize schedule disruptions as a result of these transfers.

7.6 The timetable: creating the first draft and refining it

The school needs to create a timetable structure that will allow 240 hours for HL subjects and 150 hours for SL subjects over the two years. Schools will need to do the calculations themselves, and recall that the second year will end early at the start of the examination period.

As a general guide, for a 36-week year, HL classes will need 3 × 80-minute classes per week and SL will need 2 × 80-minute classes. Ideally, HL and SL classes are taught separately and the different classes are allocated a different number of periods per week. This system may be problematic in schools that have a standard blocking arrangement for all classes, or where teachers are teaching across grade levels and campuses and so on.

If some HL and SL classes need to be combined then teachers will need to carefully structure the teaching so that SL students are not overloaded. Consequently teachers' input is needed for the construction of the timetable. Some recommendations for a first edition of your timetable are summarized in figure 3.3.

Naturally, before deciding what courses you will offer exactly and when, it is

Figure 3.3 Recommendations for a first edition timetable

Group 1	Language A1: the native language of the majority of students. Other language A1: if a sufficiently large other language group exists. Language A1 self-taught: try to keep to a minimum or none initially.
Group 2	Language A2: if a clear bilingual population is present. Language B: modern foreign language with preparatory course in pre-IB years curriculum. Language *ab initio*: beginner language not taught in the pre-IB years.
Group 3	Follow the subjects currently offered in the school. ITGS is a course well worth considering. It is relatively accessible and provides a good background in the application of (internet) IT.
Group 4	Physics, chemistry, biology: it is difficult to avoid any of these if the school is to attract potential engineers and doctors to its DP. Design technology: large start-up costs. Environmental systems: since all the signs are that this course is about to be replaced by the new trans-disciplinary course 'ecosystems and society' (see Chapter 18) around 2005, it is probably best to wait for this.
Group 5	Mathematics HL, mathematics methods, and mathematics studies must all be offered. Don't include further mathematics initially. Mathematics studies is not an accepted course in some universities. Computer science could be offered as a free elective.
Group 6	Visual arts, theatre arts, music: offer one or two but not all initially. Make sure your timetable offers rich scope for students to take a second group 3 or group 4 subject as their group 6 choice.
TOK	Must be offered.

necessary that you profile your cohort's needs. The next section looks at ways of achieving this in some detail.

In later years, when your school has gained confidence in the teaching and administration of the DP, you could add more subjects. You could then also have a look at the trans-disciplinary and the school-based subjects – see Chapter 18 and the summary below.

Trans-disciplinary subjects

These relatively new subjects allow students to satisfy the requirements of two groups at once and thus free-up time for specialization in one area. See Chapter 18 for details.

School-based subjects

These are subjects created by established IB schools to meet a particular need. Other established IB schools can also subscribe to them. It is not recommended that new IB schools offer these courses. Again, Chapter 18 has the details.

7.7 Profiling the school cohort

Before asking students what courses they would like to study, they first need to be very well informed. You should run information sessions for all students, and teachers and homeroom teachers should follow these up. Most students start off not knowing what they want to do. It is much easier to eliminate what they do *not* want to do from a list of pure science, social sciences, service industry, engineering, business, law, medicine, and so on. Based on what they have left over, homeroom teachers could help by identifying courses suitable for them. Well before announcing the final timetable, you could ask your cohort to fill in a form like the one in figure 3.4.

The nationality and country of destination questions will help ensure that you don't build in problems from the start with your language schedule or by offering packages that are not suitable for universities (or schools) in the destination country. University and government acceptance policies for the IB diploma are available on the IBO's public website, and are further discussed in the case studies in Part Two.

There are a number of benefits of this whole profiling process:

- Student interest and motivation will be raised.
- The likely intake of students in the first few years becomes apparent, both for the full diploma and for certificates (students taking only some subjects).
- You will have an early warning of potential scheduling conflicts.

The process will need to be repeated later in the year but will probably only consist of modifications to some student schedules.

7.8 Communication to the community and marketing

This is a key concern for the authorization team. The school needs to run a series of information sessions and have a range of other media to explain the DP and its position in the school. The information sessions should target the whole

Figure 3.4 Draft schedule for the IB diploma/IB certificate programme

Name:

Nationality:
Country of destination for university:
Possible degree courses:

Group	First choice (subject/level)	Second choice (subject/level)	Teacher comment
1			
2			
3			
4			
5			
6			
	TOK	TOK	

Group	Courses on offer in this group (subject/level)
1	
2	
3	
4	
5	
6	(or another choice from groups 3 or 4).

Students wishing to take the full IB diploma must ensure that they take one subject from each group and that they have three subjects at HL and three at SL.

community and would naturally have a slightly different focus for each audience: teachers, students, parents and support faculty. Schools should also consider talking to feeder schools and selected universities. As implementation progresses schools will want to keep certain groups updated. These sessions should cover the following topics:

- Why consider the DP?
- The history/pedigree of the DP
- The DP's aims and philosophy
- The range of schools offering it and the range of possible student profiles
- The hexagon structure – the subject groups and the core areas
- The assessment
- University recognition.

Information brochures would typically range from general information about the DP on handouts, to more detailed information in the school handbook and specific information about courses in course handbooks. You must take care to distinguish the DP as a separate programme within the school even if many students are taking certificates only or are gaining dual certification.

The IBO produces a range of useful publicity materials, including PowerPoint presentations (see Resources on page 75). In many cases these will suffice, but the school will also want to personalize these so that its community can see what the programme would actually look like. A sample introductory letter used by Oakham School, in the UK, is set out in figure 3.5. An example of a more detailed information booklet which you could edit to adapt to your needs is Oakham's IB handbook, downloadable from www.oakham.org.uk. You are also most welcome to use the information in this book to construct similar materials (although a credit to this book would be appreciated in that case).

As the school prepares for authorization it will increasingly recognize areas where it exemplifies the spirit of the DP. This is likely to be seen first in its extra-curricular programme. Schools should plan to capture as much as possible of this on film and digital video so that it can be incorporated into presentations, promotional materials and websites.

The IBO has worked hard to promote the DP with universities. Amongst other things, it maintains a section on its public website that gives universities access to detailed information on course standards in the DP. However, some university admissions offices are more aware of the DP than others; some may not even be familiar with statements regarding the DP on their own website. It can be very useful to host a small university fair or to target those universities attending a local university fair, and ask them about their acceptance policies and required point scores for the diploma, as well as finding out their views on the certificate courses.

Marketing

Schools are advised to read the case studies in Part Two of this book in order to gain perspective on the issues that various schools have faced. With regard to the DP's 'currency' and 'mobility' in particular, schools need to be careful not to simply repeat the IBO's view. They must identify specifically the situation for their own graduates. Schools also need to be very careful not to claim prematurely that they are an authorized school. If you are unsure about your status, it is a simple matter to run any press release or publication past the regional office first.

The implementation committee will need to induct the marketing department into the programme and keep them abreast of changes.

Figure 3.5 is a slightly adapted version of the letter to parents of pupils at Oakham School, UK, referred to above.

7.9 Building up resources

A separate budget is likely to have been set up to purchase the necessary resources. It is recommended, during the implementation phase, to channel purchases of IB materials through the implementation committee, so that it has an overview of what is happening in each area and can monitor progress and costs.

Subject-specific resources

All teachers involved in selecting resources should realize that the IBO does not recommend any specific texts. The IBO is committed to curriculum develop-ment and continual review, which sits uneasily with the idea of set textbooks. None the less, an increasing number of publishers have texts aimed to support DP courses. Some of these are very good, and students certainly appreciate it if

Figure 3.5 Letter to parents

In September 2001, Oakham introduced the International Baccalaureate (IB) Diploma Programme as an alternative to AS/A2-levels in the upper school. Over a hundred students are currently studying the IB diploma at Oakham.

The IB diploma is a prestigious international pre-university qualification and is recognized by universities and governments throughout the world. It has been in existence for over 30 years and is now offered in more than 1,000 schools in 95 countries.

Within a well-established upper school, IB students study for their IB diploma. All students take six subjects across the disciplines in a manner that assures both breadth and depth of study. Usually, students take a literature course in their own language, another modern or classical language, a science and a mathematics course, a humanities and an arts course. These are at various levels and a wide choice of subjects is offered. In addition, all students complete a research paper on a topic of their choice (the extended essay), take a course in critical thinking (Theory of Knowledge) and complete a programme of creativity, action and service (CAS). The award of the diploma is recognition that students have completed all parts of the programme. It marks a high level of achievement.

Learning how to learn and how to evaluate information critically in a global world is an important part of the IB Diploma Programme. Personal growth alongside academic growth is another. Flexibility of choice allows students to follow their interests while the structure of the diploma safeguards the breadth of study. The deliberate combination of breadth and depth in both academic and personal areas equips students with the skills and attitudes they require for higher education or employment and engenders international understanding and responsible citizenship.

An international education does not replace a national one but refocuses it and adds to it. We live in a world of global economies and communications and Oakham School recognizes that students will be part of this world and need the education that allows them to live and to succeed in it.

In deciding to study the IB at Oakham School, students will take a fully integrated and active part in the life of the school. Academic classes are taught by specialist teachers and all sports and activities are undertaken as part of the wider school community.

---

the structure of the book mirrors that of the subject guide (but note that the latter are reviewed every five years). On the other hand some IB-specific textbooks are poorly written and contain many inaccuracies. Schools should therefore exercise the same careful review process they use when selecting any book. Part Three of this book and the IBO's OCC provide useful recommendations for texts.

Library resources

A visit to an established IB school can be very useful to determine what resources need to be purchased. There are also regional organizations of IB librarians, e.g. PALMS, and the IB regional office will be able to put schools in touch with these. The OCC has a resources section for librarians. If there are international students on the programme, then they and their parents can be brought in to help source copies of key subject texts in their native language.

Centralizing resources

It is common practice for departments to maintain their own mini reference libraries in a workroom or office. There is a lot to be said, however, for centralizing these resources in the library or at least cataloguing them centrally:

- The library becomes the focal point for students and staff who need to carry out research.
- Students are more able to study independently rather than relying on a teacher to suggest a text from a departmental collection.
- The system is a more efficient use of resources.

Departments should know what resources are available for their subjects in the library, and should work with the librarian to recommend reference texts. The same goes for TOK teachers and the TOK coordinator.

7.10 Preparing for changes at the philosophical level

Chapter 2 provides a good insight into the aims and philosophy of the IB DP. The DP can be a real leap of faith for some sections of the community, and the information sessions will only go so far in assisting with this transformation. A key strategy to combat a lingering lack of faith after the decision has been made to introduce the DP is to act confidently throughout as if you are already an established IB school. It is important to have the broad discussion on 'Why the IB?', but once the decision has been taken to introduce it there should be no looking back – just a steady execution of the measures needed to make it a success.

Students, teachers and parents need to appreciate the *holistic* nature of the programme. For students this means that they cannot work on one area to the detriment of others, and also that there is value to learning beyond the classroom. Parents also need to understand this so that they reinforce this message at home. This can be a big cultural shift for some families. Issues concerning teachers are discussed in greater detail in section 8 on page 70.

The aim of *intercultural understanding* can be developed through a Model United Nations (MUN) club, or a debating club. Schools can also run public forums and invite guest speakers from the community. Topical issues at the time of writing would be 'The nature of a just war' or 'The definition of terrorism'.

The DP's *assessment procedures* will also be unfamiliar to many people. Parents and students will want to make comparisons with the current grading system ('Does a diploma grade 6 equal a 3.2 in terms of GPA or a B at A-level?'), but schools should try to resist this. Instead they should explain the nature of criterion-referenced assessment in the DP, the different nature of skills required, and the fact that the DP must be seen as an overall package rather than as a collection of subjects. Instead of comparing subject grades, schools should compare university entrance requirements for key universities. For example, schools could demonstrate that a particular top university requires an IB diploma score of, say, 36, or AAB at A-level, or a GPA of 3.8 with a certain SAT score.

Creativity, action and service (CAS)

One cannot teach the values that the CAS programme aims to bring to students in the traditional sense of the word; rather schools will have to create the atmosphere and the infrastructure to facilitate this important learning. Schools will face difficulties in the early years persuading parents and students of the value of CAS. It is therefore important to have a strong CAS programme right from the start. See Chapter 9 for details.

Theory of Knowledge (TOK)

Students can begin to see the relevance of TOK fairly early on if the classes are taught with enthusiasm. Schools should also aim to demonstrate this to teachers and parents and use them as a resource: a strong TOK programme will extend beyond the classroom and involve the community. See Chapter 10 for details.

The extended essay

The extended essay is a key feature that sets the DP apart from other educational programmes. Through the extended essay students learn research, referencing and essay-writing skills. They also learn about themselves and how to study independently. All of these skills are extremely useful for university study, and indeed the student's extended essay will often be a focal point in university admission applications and interviews. The essay can give students a real sense of achievement and something to be proud of. These arguments need to be stressed regularly to counter the inevitable utilitarian arguments that the essay is only worth a couple of points on the diploma.

Academic honesty

There are several elements to this subject, such as cheating, unauthorized collaboration, and plagiarism. It is unwise to assume that students, or even teachers, understand or agree on these issues, and therefore an academic honesty policy as described in the next section should be created. Sessions explaining the nature of academic honesty need to be run and the message needs to be constantly reinforced so as to firmly embed itself in the school culture.

Some teachers utilize open-book examinations or allow students to bring in a page of notes. This may have great educational value but it is not allowed in diploma examinations. Teachers may encourage students to work in study groups, but this should not be permitted when the students are working on coursework. Teachers therefore need to be very clear with their instructions.

The issue of plagiarism highlights some academic, linguistic and cultural aspects of academic honesty. Students need to be taught how to reference their sources properly, and teachers will need to provide educational opportunities for students to practise these skills. Students working in their second language may be under greater time pressures from having to decode the material or may not have the necessary language skills to complete the assignment. Consequently, they are potentially more likely to deliberately plagiarize or may unintentionally plagiarize by 'patching' phrases together from several sources. Professor McKay, in her literature review of the cultural aspects of plagiarism (McKay 2001), argues that 'our *Western* view of plagiarism is culture specific – and it has developed and changed over time'. From her research McKay supports the view that the cultural background of students, in particular those from Confucian heritage countries such as Singapore, China, Taiwan, Vietnam and Korea, may be a factor in explaining incidences of plagiarism. She argues that in these countries 'originality has never been prized' and that 'students have been schooled into believing that by quoting excessively, they are honouring the authors'. Pennycook (1996 p.285) points out that memorization as a teaching and learning tool is fostered much more in these countries than elsewhere.

None of this is to suggest that a school should adopt different standards of academic honesty for different students, or that plagiarism by students from Confucian heritage countries is always unintentional or should be excused. Rather, it highlights that a school's academic honesty policy should be an active policy and should be as much about educating the desired standards as about punishing the undesired ones.

The OCC has a section on plagiarism that includes sample academic honesty policies. The February 2003 edition of *IB World* has many useful articles on the subject of plagiarism; news articles about the unacceptability of plagiarism in the world of work can particularly help reinforce the message.

7.11 Creating policies and procedures

Admissions

Schools will need to set entry criteria to their courses. They will find that the entry criteria they use for entry into US-style AP courses or UK-style A-level courses are generally appropriate. However, the DP is much broader and more demanding than a programme where the student just takes a few A-levels or AP courses. Overall academic ability, the ability to work independently, and good interpersonal and study skills are equally important predictors of success that schools should consider in their admissions policy.

The DPC needs to collate recommendations from teachers but should retain significant control over eventual admissions and the choice of DP package of the students. Due to the holistic nature of the programme, it may be necessary to go against the teacher-recommended courses in order for a student to meet the requirements of the overall programme. Also, it will take a couple of years for the faculty to see what factors are good predictors of success in the DP, and coordinators will learn faster if they are closely involved, at least initially, in all details of the admissions procedure.

Induction programme

The first couple of months of the programme can be very difficult for students who are not used to the style of learning. If they are to take responsibility for their learning and get the best out of the holistic programme they need to understand how it works as early as possible. An induction programme can help in this respect. On the most basic level, it could be used as reinforcement for all the information sessions the school has given on the DP and to forewarn and prepare students for the pressures they are likely to face. Students need to know that there will be some tough times ahead, what support is available, and what they can do to help themselves. It may be appropriate to run short courses on time management, goal-setting and learning strategies. The last can be particularly useful if students have had their instruction 'spoon-fed' up to this point. Leadership skills and team-building exercises are also very useful, particularly at this early stage, and can help liven up what might otherwise be a very dry induction programme. A well-designed school trip can do wonders in setting the right tone and expectations, and it would be possible to combine such an induction trip with the idea of a CAS camp – see Chapter 9.

The gap analysis, discussed earlier in section 4, should have identified potential areas of weakness or concern for new students. This may be within individual subjects or in the core areas of the curriculum. Depending on if and when the induction programme takes place, it may be possible for some subjects to run 'bridging courses' to help ease the transition of students. More generally, the impact of the transition to the DP can be eased by allowing students to work on aspects of the course during the long vacation prior to the first year. Language A1 classes could start on their reading lists during the vacation. Language A1 self-taught students can use holiday time to search for pre-selected texts and tutors. Although CAS hours cannot be counted prior to the start of the DP, students could spend time finding out what is available and start building their own CAS programme so that they are ready to start at the beginning of the year.

The extended essay

The extended essay programme will need considerable planning if the school's first DP cohort numbers more than a handful of students. Information sessions, monitoring procedures and the availability of suitable supervisors are all issues that need to be addressed. Chapter 11 discusses these issues in detail. These procedures do not need to be in place before authorization but schools would do well to familiarize themselves with the issues, and at least outline the steps they will need to take.

University counselling

An effective university counselling programme is a key element of a successful IB DP. To assist students with subject selection, it is important to talk with students in the pre-DP years and find out about their likely country of destination and preferred university course. University guidance counsellors may need to make links with key universities to reassure students and parents that the DP is an acceptable, or even desirable, matriculation examination. At the same time it is important for the integrity of the school that the counselling programme recognizes that the DP is not for everyone and that there are sometimes easier routes for students to get into their university of choice. These issues are discussed further in some of the case studies in Part Two.

Reporting and intervention

Students need to understand how they are assessed and their reports need to reflect the DP's grading structure. In schools where there is more than one programme running, this may mean that a separate or supplemental reporting system needs to be set up for the diploma students. Diploma students need to appreciate the holistic nature of the programme, so some form of summative report reflecting the overall performance within the DP is recommended.

The school will also need some form of transparent academic probation programme which can ultimately transfer students out of the full DP. A holistic view is again essential in order to make such transfer decisions.

Academic honesty

This is a crucial policy that will be examined closely by the IBO's visiting teams. Students need to be educated about the importance of academic honesty and what constitutes plagiarism. A whole-school research and referencing manual is useful here. The school should adopt a zero tolerance policy towards plagiarism and have clear procedures for reporting offenders. This policy should be enforced throughout the school and not just in the DP. The school should have procedures for checking if work is plagiarized, e.g. the requirement that electronic versions of coursework be submitted, so that they can be scanned using anti-plagiarism software such as Turnitin.com (www.turnitin.com). (But note that Google's free internet search engine at www.google.com is usually good enough to catch offenders: simply run a suspect sentence through Google and the original essay will come up!) Finally, there should be real consequences for persistent offenders, which should, at the very least, include a refusal for the school to submit the student's coursework to the IBO. Chapter 11 has more details on academic honesty policies.

Pastoral groups

In schools running several programmes, it is easy to develop an atmosphere where the DP is a school within a school (see the case studies in Part Two). Having pastoral groups that are composed of students taking different programmes can go some way to diminish this. This arrangement also helps to illustrate the nature of the DP to non-diploma students, particularly the CAS and TOK. Having first- and second-year DP students in the same pastoral group should help instil a healthy work ethic in first-year students early on. Pastoral care teachers or homeroom teachers can play an important role in helping students to manage their time effectively, in goal setting, and also in monitoring their CAS programmes.

Senior privileges

Schools may wish to grant their DP students certain privileges that could support them in their studies. This might include the ability to sign in and out of school so that they can attend CAS activities. The provision of common-room facilities, study rooms and better library access and lending privileges may also be appropriate.

English as a second language (ESL) inclusion

If there is an ESL population in the school, there should be procedures for including ESL students in the DP. ESL inclusion can be a very emotive issue for staff, and students will need to have realistic expectations. There are many tools available for assessing English language proficiency but these scores should be informative rather than rigidly binding. A positive assessment by the English B teacher plus evidence of overall academic achievement and commitment are equally good indicators. Some schools require ESL students to take intensive English classes in the holiday months prior to starting the DP. As we mentioned earlier, in sections 4.1 and 5.5, all subject departments will need ESL training and the school will need to set funds aside for this.

Training feedback

Workshop training sessions for the DP constitute a significant investment for IB schools. Many schools have put policies and procedures in place to maximize the benefit of this investment. This can take several forms, for example in the implementation phase feedback sessions will help the DPC and the subject teachers to understand the structure and requirements of each subject. Selective feedback to the whole faculty will help reinforce the philosophy and holistic approach of the DP.

Contractual obligations

Schools with high staff turnover rates in particular will want to consider their hiring practices, professional development policies, and possibly contracts to ensure that the school gets some return on its training investment. As indicated in the case studies in Chapters 5 and 6, the turnover problem can become acute for some newly authorized schools: freshly IB-trained teachers move out to better-paid jobs elsewhere, making use of the international mobility the DP affords them.

7.12 School-wide documentation for authorization

In general, any documentation that demonstrates the school's commitment to the DP and its aims and philosophy should be made available to the authorization team (for example the school handbook). Specifically, apart from the department-specific documentation (which is detailed in section 8), the authorization team requires the following documents.

Feasibility study – a summary

The authorization team needs to assure itself that the school has done the position and cost audits, sees the DP as a desirable and viable option, and is committed to it for the long term. The school should make available key findings from the feasibility study.

Mission statement

The authorization team would expect to see some congruence in the aims of the IB DP and the school's mission statement.

The IB DP teachers

A list of the staff members who will be teaching the IB courses should be included. The list should indicate their qualifications and experience, and specify when they attended or will attend an IB workshop. For those teachers who were trained in other IB regions it may be advisable to obtain confirmation of training from the respective regional office.

Procedures and policies (see section 7.11 above for details)
- The reporting system
- Academic honesty policy
- IB induction programme including entry criteria and guidance procedures

- University counselling procedures
- English as a second language provision

The school calendar and the timetable

The timetable is discussed in detail above, in section 4.3. The school calendar of internal and external IB deadlines for students, teachers and coordinator can be built on a sample general calendar printed in the IBO *Vade Mecum*. A schedule of IB DP faculty meetings with the DPC should also be included – it can simply give the names and dates of the meetings.

Evidence of school-wide involvement and support for the IB DP

Section 7.2 covered the 'authorization file', containing evidence of all the efforts the school has undertaken towards implementation of the DP. Parts of that file can be summarized, specifically relating to the points listed here:

- IB diploma information sessions
- composition of the feasibility study committee, dates of meetings and key agenda items
- meetings of the board, parent/teacher association, student council and faculty meetings where the implementation of the DP was scheduled for discussion
- outlines of in-service days set aside for implementing the IB DP
- materials used to market the DP: brochures, flyers, web pages etc.

This summary will normally suffice, but the authorization file should be available in case the authorization team has any further questions.

School-wide development plans

The school's strategic and development planning should reflect the aims of the DP. A development plan for the IB DP would highlight intended development in the range of courses to be offered, especially languages. It is also an appropriate document to show the school's commitment to developing infrastructure and resources, particularly those identified in the school's gap analysis.

Possible areas for attention in the development plan are as follows:

- changes to the extra-curricular programme towards CAS-type activities
- changes to the pastoral care model to foster better study skills or self-reflection
- changes to the structure of the ESL programme
- changes to the foreign language programme so that there is better continuity throughout the school, from the pre-IB DP years through to the DP
- support for foreign native language speakers
- integration of ICT into the curriculum
- development of a common research and referencing guide for the school
- development of the pre-DP curriculum (see section 10 below).

8 Preparing departments for the change

8.1 Departmental documentation for authorization

This section is intended to give the implementation committee an overview of the documentation that departments need to produce and the key issues that some subject areas will face. Much greater detail can be found in the subject chapters in Part Three.

In general, subject departments need to document:

- a scheme of work over the two years, such as those included in the subject chapters
- course booklets and outlines for students
- the recommended entry criteria for the subject at HL and SL
- the arrangements for internal assessment, including a calendar for the key assignments, sample assessments and arrangements for internal moderation of coursework
- transparent procedures for generating semester/term and predicted grades consistent with IB standards
- resource lists: equipment, textbooks and support materials
- an understanding of the extended essay and areas of investigation that can be supported by the department
- an indication of how the department can contribute to TOK
- a statement about how the department will introduce inter-cultural and global issues into the classroom.

More subject-specific issues are discussed below.

Languages

The department will spend some time putting together reading schemes suited to the profile of their cohort. If the school decides to offer self-taught languages, it should have made plans to support the work of the self-taught class. It is too late to start thinking about suitable texts and tutors at the start of the course, and the department should have procedures to counsel students and prepare them beforehand.

Group 3: Individuals and societies

These departments in particular will need to develop strategies to teach students about academic honesty and to combat plagiarism.

Group 4: Experimental sciences

The science department will need to structure its courses carefully, especially if SL and HL students are taught in the same class. Each science discipline should have a scheme of work showing where and when the core, additional HL material and options will be taught. In addition, each discipline needs to develop a practical scheme of work (PSOW). This scheme will consist of a list of practical exercises that cover the range of skills to be tested, and broadly cover the content in the subject guide. The practical exercises will need worksheets to support them. The department needs to have thought through the organization of the group 4 project and produced documentation to support this.

A complete stock list of the equipment in the department should be available.

The department should carry out a safety audit and upgrade its provision where necessary.

Group 5: Mathematics

The department will need to plan the coursework components of the courses. It should schedule a coursework calendar, and think how it will support the student. The integration of IT into the curriculum should be articulated.

Theory of Knowledge

The school needs to develop a teaching outline for TOK, including opportunities for visiting speakers, public forums and so on.

8.2 Seeing the big picture

It needs to be emphasized repeatedly that it is the DP package as a whole that is important rather than the individual subjects. Students will need to be told many times that they cannot afford to focus on just some subjects to the detriment of the others. All subjects count equally towards the diploma. Teachers must be fully aware of this too and avoid overloading their students. In particular, departments need to consider and re-consider the range of enrichment and reinforcement sessions they require students to attend. It is very easy for teachers to get lost in the 'nuts and bolts' of their own subject guides and lose sight of the 'big picture'. In some schools this insularity can result in academic departments becoming 'mini-empires'. The implementation committee and department heads need to counter this forcefully and ensure that teachers fully understand the role they can play to make the programme as a whole a success. Departments may need to embrace a shift in thinking to serve a wider variety of students than they have catered to traditionally. This is not to imply that standards should be lowered, but that there needs to be a different focus. For example, an English literature course serving a select few could be modified to include more texts from Commonwealth authors so as to open it up to the international population at the school.

The TOK coordinator should involve all subject teachers in a discussion on the TOK programme. Teachers may well have a background or a strong interest in this area and want to contribute. If teachers can see how their subject fits into the TOK programme then they are more likely to reinforce these ideas in their lessons.

Embracing the IBO philosophy

Teachers should appreciate what the DP is trying to achieve and must be well aware of its overall aims, as detailed in Chapter 2. The authorization team will look for evidence of such awareness in the department's documentation, in its schemes of work, and in discussions with the teachers. As detailed in Part Three, many of the central DP objectives find a natural place in the groups 1, 2, 3 and 6. However, the sciences and in particular mathematics departments have found it traditionally harder to address aims such as fostering a holistic outlook and developing inter-cultural awareness. The science chapter and in particular the mathematics chapter address this issue in great detail.

'IB Speak'

IB teachers need to know their PBLs from their PSOWs. The DP has its own acronyms and nomenclature. Using the correct terminology also creates a much better impression on the authorization team. Departments should make up a glossary of terms for their subjects, which also benefits the new students. Refer to the Glossary at the end of this book to aid this effort.

8.3 Getting used to a new way of working

In issues such as curriculum matters, scheduling students, setting department meeting agendas, assigning extended essay supervisors and internal moderation of coursework, the DPC and the implementation committee are going to be heavily involved in the work of the departments, especially in the implementation phase. There is the potential for a lot of tension to be created, emphasizing again the need for good communications in the school. Successful implementation of the DP will require a high degree of teamwork and cooperation from the teaching faculty. In the implementation phase, schools may find that a collegiate model is more efficient than a traditional hierarchical one. All teachers in the department may be new to the DP and working directly as a group with the implementation committee will improve communication. It will also help shape the required spirit of cooperation within each department, as teachers are expected to moderate each other's IB coursework marking.

8.4 Planning and documenting the change

It is important that department meetings are scheduled on a regular basis. Departments will need time to plan and prepare the necessary documentation. The implementation committee should help departments to map out what they need to do for authorization, and free-up meeting time and professional development days for this. Some time will be needed for whole-school meetings to discuss the overall progress with the implementation, the core areas and issues such as reporting and assessment. Although important, it is easy to let these issues take on too great a role, and schools should aim to ensure that departments are given enough quality planning time to work on their subject areas.

9 The authorization visits

The *pre-authorization visit* is not a standard part of the IBO's authorization process but it is frequently requested by schools. We strongly recommend that schools plan for one, three to six months before the authorization visit. A chance to demonstrate what the school is doing and to receive and act on feedback obviously improves the odds of a successful authorization visit (see the case study in Chapter 6 for an example of a school that could have avoided its initial failure to obtain authorization by doing so). The pre-authorization and authorization visits can follow a similar format. Schools should contact the IB regional office to request a visit and discuss the format. The visit usually takes two days, which will typically be arranged as follows.

Day 1
- Meetings with the community: board, senior academic team, coordinators, parents, students.
- Review of preparations for the DP: department documentation, CAS programme, TOK programme, school brochure, school newsletter, strategic plan, authorization file.
- Tour of the school's facilities: library, science laboratories, fine and performing arts venues, athletics venues.
- Visits to classrooms and informal discussions with teachers, students and support staff.
- Feedback and clarification sessions with senior academic team.

Day 2
- Meetings with individual departments.
- Writing time for the visiting team.
- Feedback to the senior academic team and the implementation committee.

A detailed report listing the team's comments and recommendations should follow.

The visiting team will need:

- an agenda for the visit
- private office space in which to discuss and write up sections of their report (team members will probably bring laptop computers; the school may wish to provide the team with access to the school's network)
- a meeting room in which to meet up with various members of the school community
- possibly a hall where the visiting team can hold a larger forum of students and parents, to help determine the degree of understanding and support for the DP.

The school will be required to pay for the travel, accommodation and reasonable incidental expenses of the team (which consists of a representative from the IBO regional office, typically the DP manager, and often an experienced DPC from a nearby school). The school will need to arrange the logistics for all the meetings. The DPC will want to be able to attend the department meetings. If the school has not invested a great deal of effort and time in promoting the DP and explaining itself to its community it will become apparent in these meetings.

The visiting team has only a short time in which to absorb a great deal of information. This pre-authorization visit should really set the tone and convince the team that the school will be ready by the time of the authorization visit.

The authorization visit

The visiting team by this time will already have a good impression of what the school has done and will primarily be looking to see that there has been sufficient progress on its recommendations. If there was no earlier pre-authorization visit, the visit will follow the format outlined above.

Schools need to prepare their community for the fact that the authorization team does not authorize schools and that the school will need to wait until the IBO head office in Geneva has had time to consider the team's report and recommendations before it can make a decision. Normally this process takes four weeks, but it is dependent on the director-general not being away for an extended period of travel at the time the application is sent to him for approval.

10 The pre-DP school programme

It is unlikely that the implementation committee will have time to change much in the pre-DP years. However, as the school works through the authorization process issues will come to light. The implementation committee will want to demonstrate to the IBO that it has recognized these issues and addressed them in the strategic plans for the development of the DP (see section 7.12 above). Typical issues might include:

- ensuring that there is a broad and appropriately balanced curriculum for the pre-DP years
- matching the pre-DP to DP courses, including possible bridging courses
- developing the spirit of the DP in the pre-DP years (presumably this is consistent with the school's mission statement anyway): inter-cultural awareness, developing the whole person, a culture of service
- skills and personal development: goal-setting, self-reflection, study skills, research and referencing skills, and a mother tongue maintenance policy: there is evidence to suggest that ESL students progress better if they continue to use their mother tongue; if the school is offering languages other than the language of instruction at language A1, then there is an even stronger rationale for maintaining one's mother tongue in the pre-DP years – the policy might include strategies such as:
  - encouraging parents to provide mother tongue tuition and recognizing the student's achievements in the final transcript
  - building mother tongue language sections in the library
  - providing mother tongue instruction.

11 Beyond authorization: maintaining momentum

After authorization it can be another three to five years before a school feels established as an IB diploma school. The first two years, as the first cohort goes through, will be the most challenging and public support may thinly veil persistent concerns. Some parents and students will naturally feel that they are guinea pigs – although the school should strive to have them view themselves as proud pioneers! Teachers too will have concerns about being able to prepare their students. These concerns will centre on:

- adequate time to prepare students
- the new assessment and grading procedures

- the structure of the courses, particularly if SL and HL classes have been combined
- the new support procedures, or lack of these.

It is important that the school prepares for this post-authorization phase, particularly the first three years. The implementation committee should remain active to monitor progress, listen to concerns, and put the strategic plan into effect. If authorization has been done quickly, in a year or less, then it is likely that some school-wide procedures are still being developed. Departments will also continue to work on developing schemes of work and support materials, and some time should be set aside for this.

The school newsletter and open days can be used to good effect to showcase the DP at the school, and its recognition by universities worldwide.

12 Resources

Academic honesty
www.online.ibo.org
Resources on this site will help schools develop their own academic honesty policy. The IBO also endorses turnitin.com (www.turnitin.com) which offers a discount to IB schools.

Addresses
www.ibo.org – shortcut menu to contacts section.
All the main and regional offices are listed here, as well as the regional representatives.

Coordinators' notes
www.online.ibo.org
Coordinators' notes list important amendments to the regulations for each subject area. The back page also lists the cycle of curriculum development and review. Candidate schools can therefore ensure that they order curriculum materials for the forthcoming subject guide rather than the existing (extant) one.

Discussion forums
www.online.ibo.org

European Council of International Schools/ Council of International Schools
www.ecis.org

IB schools directory
www.ibo.org – shortcut to schools

IB World
This is the IBO's quarterly magazine, which can be subscribed to through www.ibo.org

Library
www.online.ibo.org – the support area menu lists Library.

Marketing
The IBO website www.ibo.org can help a school to prepare its marketing materials for the IB DP. It contains links to a range of documents:
- the IBO's mission statement (link on home page)
- a basis for practice – the DP (Programmes menu)
- schools' guide to the DP (Programmes menu).

Online Curriculum Centre (OCC)
www.online.ibo.org – applications can be sent to online@ibo.org. The OCC is a substantial and very useful resource site.

Publications
www.ibo.org – shortcut menu to Publications section, or via Services menu. The website encompasses an online order form which calculates costs including shipping. The system is very efficient.

Recommended resources
- See the chapters in Part Three of this book.
- www.online.ibo.org – the subject sections of the OCC.

Special educational needs
www.ibo.org
The Programmes menu lists a link to DP – candidates with special assessment needs. The document lists what conditions can be accommodated and how to apply for special consideration.

Statistics
www.ibo.org – shortcut to publications.
The IBO's Statistical Bulletin lists a range of useful data, such as the number of IB schools, pass rates per region, etc. Schools will want to include some of this in their marketing materials.

Subject guides and teacher support materials
www.ibo.org – shortcut to publications.
www.online.ibo.org

University and government recognition policies
www.ibo.org – shortcut menu to universities and governments.
A search menu allows you to search through all the IB diploma recognition policies for universities and governments. The listing of universities that accept the diploma in each country is not comprehensive. However, a university's website will usually indicate its acceptance of the diploma in its section for international undergraduate admission.

Vade Mecum
www.ibo.org – shortcut to publications.
The essential handbook to the IB DP.

Workshops and conferences
www.ibo.org – shortcut to events calendar.
This page has a search function and region-specific calendars of workshops and conferences.

13 References

McKay, P. (2001) *Literature on Non-Deliberate Plagiarism: Current Directions*, Queensland University of Technology.
(Online: http://clb.ed.qut.edu.au/events/projects/ndp/)

Pennycook, A. (1996) 'Borrowing others' words: text, ownership, memory, and plagiarism', *TESOL Quarterly*, 30 (2), 201–230.

Part Two
Case Studies and Regional Perspectives

Chapter 4

View from the UK

Jill Rutherford, MA, DPhil (Oxon)

Jill Rutherford is highly regarded internationally for her enormous contribution to the Diploma Programme (DP) and for her considerable experience as a teacher, examiner and curriculum developer. Over the years, Jill has held significant positions in the IB which include the chief examiner for environmental systems, vice-chair of the International Baccalaureate Organization (IBO) examining board, group 4 representative on the diploma review committee, group 4 representative on the former Bureau of Chief Examiners, chair of the review committee for group 4, and on review committees for environmental systems and ecosystems and societies. She has also led many teacher-training workshops for environmental systems throughout the various IBO regions and served as an adviser to a number of schools in the UK (King Edward VII, Melton Mowbray, Prince William School, Oundle, Bedford School, St Helen's, Northwood). She is currently director of IB at Oakham School, UK where she initiated the IB DP.

This case study complements the previous chapter on how to implement the IB DP, providing more details on university recognition and 'twinning' the DP with existing curricula. While set in a UK context, care has been taken that all issues raised are relevant to IB schools around the world.

1 The IB in the UK

In the UK in 2002 it was difficult to go through a week without coming across an article about the IB diploma. The national daily papers have echoed the enthusiastic comments made in 1999 by former Minister for Education, David Blunkett: 'The IB is a deeply impressive qualification. I want to encourage schools and colleges to take it up as soon as possible. Eventually the IB could supplant A-levels altogether.' At the time the press used IB as a tool to criticize the national A-level system, which was going through a miserable year after the adoption in 2000 of two consecutive one-year courses, AS and A2. Clear academic endorsement of the IB by leading UK universities contributed to the volume of media support (see section 8 in this chapter).

While the newspapers were factually accurate, the message appeared to be that IB was the answer to all of the UK's educational difficulties and that schools should simply adopt the IB and so solve our problems. If ever it were that easy! The IB DP is a great educational philosophy but it is not designed for all students or all academic abilities. It is unashamedly academic and stretches even the most able students. It is possible for students to take the less demanding certificates programme. However, it does not offer vocational or other courses; nor does it intend to do so in the near future.

No matter how much we want educational reform, the IBO has no intention of taking over the 16–19 education system in England and Wales (director-general of the IBO, 2002). This would be contrary to its internationalist philosophy. Moreover, such a move would be out of step with the IBO's strategic plan to balance representation and increase school diversity in its four administrative regions.

Moreover, compared with the total UK number of 18/19 year-olds taking examinations, the IB DP candidature in the UK is small. In 2003, there were 50 schools and colleges offering the IB diploma in England and Wales. In line with global figures, about half of these UK IB schools and colleges are state-funded – the Learning and Skills Council (LSC) currently funds state-assisted schools and equates the IB diploma to 4.5 A-levels. In May 2002, English and Welsh diploma students made up about 2% of DP students worldwide.

Nevertheless, the IB carries disproportionate influence in certain sectors of the British educational establishment. The Headmasters' and Headmistresses' Conference has a membership of more than 240 UK single-sex and co-educational private schools and some 70 international schools. A survey taken in 2002 on their behalf reported that many of their members were looking at the IB diploma as an alternative to A-levels. Recently, the IB has grown at a rate of 10–15% a year in the UK. We will watch keenly to see how many more UK schools pursue their initial interest and adopt the DP in the years to come.

2 Which students should consider taking the IB?

Contrary to its popular elitist image, we have found that the DP's academic requirements are no more stringent than those for A-levels. In fact many students who pass the diploma with 24 points would have struggled to gain Ds and Cs at A-level. The difference is at the top end of the range: out of a maximum total of 45 points about 5% of the worldwide IB cohort attain 40+; 1% gain 42+; and only 0.2% achieve 45 (*IB Statistical Bulletin*, May 2002). By contrast, a whopping 19% of all UK A-level candidates obtained the highest possible grade (total grade A) in 2002. (On a side note, to illustrate the A-level grade inflation: that number has risen by about 0.5% every year since 1999. In mathematics, 36% scored an A in 2002, up from 29% in 2001; see the website of *The Guardian* for all these data.)

In view of the parity at the lower range, many UK IB schools have similar GCSE (a British middle-school certificate) entry requirements for the DP and A-level: typically a grade B or above for a Higher Level (HL) subject and a C or above for a Standard Level (SL) subject. A certain number of passes at grade C or above (five to eight of these) may also be required. Furthermore, students with learning difficulties or other special circumstances successfully participate in the DP. As with UK examination boards, the IBO allows up to 25% extra time in examinations and there are other special considerations for students with permanent or temporary disabilities. However, some dyslexic candidates may have difficulty with the second language requirement.

Prior to entry, schools may well want to test non-GCSE students, particularly for their abilities in oral and written English and mathematics as well as their knowledge in their intended HL subjects. Previous report grades are useful if these are based on a national system with standardized grading. Schools might also interview prospective students and may ask for further test papers to be taken for proposed Higher Level subjects. If English is not the first language of the student an additional test of competence is required. While schools could develop their own, we can recommend the Quick Placement Test (QPT) offered by Oxford University Press. It is quick and accurate; we suggest that a QPT level of proficiency of 3 or above ensures that the student can cope with any IB package in English.

Schools with overseas students who may return home would be advised to seek country-specific university entrance information on the IBO website. National IB requirements are changing rapidly so we strongly advise that schools check the website on a case-to-case basis. Things can be complicated, as we can see from the following example.

If German nationals take the IB diploma in the UK and then attend a UK university they can save up to four years of study (because of the difference in length of university study). Not surprisingly, there are many German students studying the DP in UK boarding schools. However, should students wish to return to a German university, the German Federal Ministry of Education imposes a number of restrictions on their IB packages. For example, German students studying in the UK must take an A1 and an A2 language in groups 1 and 2 (or both languages as A1 – see Chapter 12). In addition, the student must have studied a third language for at least four years, either within or outside the DP. For group 3 they must take either geography, economics or history. As a group 4 subject Germans must choose between biology, chemistry or physics and they must take mathematics HL or mathematics methods SL in group 5 (mathematics studies SL is not accepted) and at least one group 4 or group 5 subject must be at HL. In addition, the German states, or *Länder*, can impose further requirements!

3 Which schools are suitable?

There may be any number of reasons for schools to consider the DP: a stated preference for the IB philosophy and curriculum; disenchantment with A-levels; to improve their market position; to cater to an international audience; or to recruit boarders from overseas. There are two key factors for success, however: a genuine willingness to take on board the IBO's philosophy, and a long-term commitment to a consequent process of change.

During the authorization visit, the IBO team will examine management's strategic plan to embed the IB philosophy within the school and the community. Arguably, the greatest challenges national UK schools will face in this process will be:

- to adopt to a truly international education programme (see also Chapters 2 and 3); in particular, to widen the range of language courses offered (*ab initio*, B, A2, A1)
- to manage not only standard costs but also those that are specific to the administration of IB and those associated with running a parallel IB / A-level programme
- to manage the logistics of a timetable running an international and a national curriculum simultaneously
- to address the specific concerns of the community, especially those of parents.

4 What subjects should be offered?

In general, it is better to keep the initial IB package simple at first; more courses can always be offered in later years. In particular, in the first few years schools are advised to stay clear of non-traditional IB subjects. Financial constraints will limit the number of subjects. None the less, enough subjects must be offered to comprise a viable programme. As the IB Diploma has requirements across the groups, the students have less freedom of choice in the IB than they are used to. For example, unlike A-levels, students cannot take three sciences so careful counselling of students is essential to work out IB subject combinations that still keep the doors open to university degree courses.

It is safe to say that the following subjects are a typical practical minimum course offering for a UK-based school:

- Group 1: English A1 at both HL and SL caters for group 1 if students are native or near-native English speakers. If a school takes students who are not able to take English A1, it must offer English A2 and/or B *and* a range of other A1 languages. Unless students are self-taught, a suitably experienced native-speaker teacher of literature is strongly recommended for any A1 courses offered.
- Group 2: it is best to deploy native or near native-speaker teachers for A2 (language and literature) courses (not to be confused with A2 exams in England and Wales). As for foreign languages, SL and HL language B will be required for students who wish to continue GCSE languages, usually French, Spanish or German. Note that HL and SL Latin and Greek can also be taken as group 2. In addition schools may need to provide at least one *ab initio* programme.

- Group 3 subjects would probably include geography, history and economics.
- Group 4: biology, chemistry and physics.
- Group 5: mathematics HL and the two SL courses need to be offered.
- Group 6: at least two arts subjects out of theatre arts, visual arts and music should be available to balance the curriculum.

5 Staffing and staff training

The IB DP coordinator (DPC) needs to be appointed well before the authorization visit. For each DPC position advertised there will be strong competition from teachers overseas and within the UK. The question is whether to appoint an outsider to the school with IB experience elsewhere, or to promote an internal candidate who is keen to learn the ropes. An internal candidate knows the school, its students and staff. An outsider brings IB knowledge and perhaps a very different school culture. Both alternatives can work well.

For new schools the IBO's teacher workshops are essential but costly – even more so now that the IBO has made it mandatory that all teachers from new IB schools should attend workshops. There are, however, other workshops run by IB-experienced schools and approved by the IBO which may be closer to the school and cheaper to access. For example, in the UK, St Clare's College, Oxford runs teacher workshops each summer. The IBO offers workshops for experienced teachers every two years in most subjects in Europe – which means the opportunity should be seized whenever it arises. In addition, in July there are the annual workshops for new teachers in Eastern Europe. Whereas most IB teacher workshops are two and a half days long, the July workshops run from Monday to Friday but they cost the same! Not surprisingly they are over-subscribed and early booking is essential. Attending teachers can then cascade information amongst the faculty.

Alternatively, teachers can visit other regions' workshops (all advertised on the IBO websites). There are northern hemisphere summer workshops in New York, Florida and New Mexico. These naturally tend to concentrate on North American issues of IB teaching but give an insight into the challenges and differences facing colleagues in other systems. The largest 'summer' workshop series is conducted annually in early July in Australasia.

Schools should also consider bringing in an outside expert in the initial stages. This can be a cost-effective way of gaining expertise in a short time. In addition, casual networking between nearby schools means that subject staff can receive vital training and experience at very little expense.

Some government funding for staff training may be available. In the case of Oakham School, a 400-year-old private school, we have cooperated with King Edward VII School, a large state comprehensive, on a UK government-funded project entitled 'Building Bridges'. For this we hope to receive a joint state / independent school partnership grant from the Department for Education and Skills (DfES), worth £70,000. This would pay for the course costs and training for IB implementation. State-funded schools can apply for these grants from the DfES.

UK teachers should also be aware that the IBO is currently expanding its professional development arm at the IB Curriculum Assessment (IBCA) office in

Cardiff, UK, to help IB teachers to gain expertise. It is also developing online resources and improving workshop systems.

There are also initiatives, encouraged by the IBO, to franchise teacher-training workshops to IB-approved schools and colleges. In order to cope with the IB's rapid expansion, established IB schools are currently encouraged by the IBO to seek the organization's consent to conduct workshops. From the provider's point of view workshops help to raise a school's profile, even if they are not particularly financially profitable events.

6 Working with parallel systems: the IB, A-levels and other curricula

Within the UK, it is only Atlantic College (one of the United World Colleges) that offers only the IB diploma to students, and takes no other year-groups and offers no other programmes. Other schools and colleges will run a variety of courses including AS and A2, pre-IB courses, General National Vocational Qualifications (GNVQs) and Key Stage 4 GCSEs. Timetabling complexity increases annually with more and more layers added but none ever being removed. Schools and colleges must find time within the school day to prepare students for the Key Skills qualifications, offer general studies programmes, personal, health and social education (PHSE), careers guidance, citizenship, physical education – *and* fit in an academic programme. In adopting the IB diploma, the complexity increases again if no other course is dropped, as is typically the case in UK schools.

Unlike AS/A2, IB is not modular and the respective exams fall at different times (AS/A2 exams are in January and June whereas DP exams are in May and November). Effectively in the UK the IB DP is a five-term rather than a six-term programme, with final examinations starting in early May of the second year.

Examinations for the DP run for the first three weeks of May with the possibility of retakes in the November exam session of the same year. Students can retake individual examinations at the November session. The IBO is flexible with the internal assessment subject marks: these can be carried over (provided the subject has not changed its syllabus) to the November session and the IBO accepts the better score of each subject that is retaken. In this way, students can improve their total grade scores; however, they will be forced to delay their entry to university by one year because of the timing of the resits.

UK schools might find it useful to look at Oakham School's website: www.oakham.rutland.sch.uk to have a look at how the IB was timetabled together with A-level.

A school needs to consider carefully whether to offer students a free *choice* of A-levels or IB, or whether to *select* students for the IB. Schools that have set target numbers of IB students in the first cohort obviously prefer the guided selection route. Since the selection criteria are typically based on the GCSE grades, in effect the school takes an academic elite into its IB programme. This might create a 'them and us' situation where A-level students can see themselves as second-class students.

As we have seen, the IB diploma is suitable for students of a wide range of abilities and this skewing of the IB cohort is generally unhealthy for both the school and the students. Clear, detailed counselling and provision of reliable information should result in reasoned and informed choices from parents and students and give a more rational mix of IB/A-level students. The social disadvantages of a split in the school community introduced by offering the IB can be further minimized by school-wide strategies such as mixing tutor groups, taking all activities together and sharing talks with visiting speakers. The first IB cohort will inevitably feel special but the success of the programme within the school also lies in keeping everyone happy!

It is important to remember that whatever approach a school takes to these parallel curriculum issues, the IBO authorization team will not allow the IB diploma to be just tacked onto an existing curriculum (see previous Chapters 2 and 3).

7 Assessment comparison with A-levels

The IBO's assessment system is recognizable to anyone who is familiar with UK examination board methods. There are standardization meetings, moderation by tiers of team leaders and grade award meetings. The examination session is completed six weeks after the last examination in late mid-May and students receive results by a secure PIN number in the first week of July.

The IB diploma examination system is criterion-referenced, not norm-referenced. Grade inflation in the IB diploma has not occurred and a more or less constant pass rate of 80% has been maintained. An unofficial formula to transpose diploma grades to the A-level point score for league table purposes has operated for some years. This disappeared in 2003 as there is no official agreement on equivalence with A-levels, Scottish Highers or GNVQs. Moreover, the IBO is not currently part of the UK Universities and Colleges Admissions Service (UCAS)'s new tariff.

The UK IB community is glad to see the end of the attempts to compare grades between the IB and the national examination systems: the figures given in section 2, paragraph 1 demonstrate that this is a meaningless exercise. The DP must be seen as an entire package and not as a collection of subjects – a view increasingly accepted by UK universities.

8 University recognition

Universities around the world recognize that students who have completed the IB are well prepared for the world of study. The UCAS website at www.ucas.co.uk shows the diploma qualification requirements of British universities (but does not always clearly specify individual subject demands). Diploma students thinking of going to American universities might receive up to a year's credit; others may be awarded credits for individual courses taken (usually only for those taken at HL). Parents and counsellors would do well to go to the IBO's website for overseas university admissions policies or, better still, consult directly with the individual target university.

Quite rightly, parents and students want to know that universities know how to gauge their IB offers appropriately. Many UK admissions tutors prefer to consider the diploma holistically as a complete package and will give offers based on total point scores, including bonus points for TOK and the extended essay rather than individual subjects. A fairly typical UK university offer might be 28–36 points which is about 4–6 points for each of the six subjects. Oxbridge might ask for 37–40 IB points which they regard as equivalent to A-level grades of three As. However, Oxbridge engineering admissions tutors still like to see physics and/or mathematics at HL, so do check the details.

The IB headquarters in Geneva and the four regional offices have made, and continue to make, a huge effort to obtain recognition from universities. University departmental admissions tutors change regularly so, while the central admissions office of a university may be well acquainted with the IB diploma and its standards, there will always be tutors new to admissions who will have to be brought up to date.

9 Challenges from and responses to the community

On the financial side, governors and parents need to be convinced that costs will remain affordable (see Chapter 3).

Within the school, one must be prepared for different reactions to the IB. Some teachers, parents and students will naturally greet the innovation with enthusiasm and excitement. A minority may be cautious or even hostile. In our experience, opposition stops once teaching the DP starts and the educational process unfolds. Nevertheless, a school must allow at least a five-year period for the IB to embed itself within the institution. Anything shorter than this is not fair to the students or their parents. The time from the appointment of the DPC to the publishing of first results is three years. During this period, there will be uncertainty. Parents worry about their children being used as educational guinea pigs and it helps to remind them that up to 80% of the IB subject content overlaps with A-level in the same subject. Parents and students should also see that A-levels and GCSE courses have changed many times but the DP has maintained continuity. IB may be new to the school but is not new in the world of education. It has been around for over 30 years, which is longer than most home-grown exams.

In the early days of the IB, a school's every move will be scrutinized. Small errors in teaching or management can easily be blown out of proportion if the students or parents begin to lose confidence in the ability of the school to deliver the new programme. Uncertainty will also focus often on the assessment levels – are teachers being too harsh or too lenient? Only when a school has a proven IB pedigree will parents feel secure with teachers' assessments.

To allay parental fears about university admissions, we found it extremely useful to organize parents' meetings with academics from various universities as well as draw parents' attention to the many university quotes on the IBO website. For example:

> 'The IB is highly regarded by admissions tutors at Cambridge University for entry to all subjects. Candidates should expect to reach an overall score in the range 36–40 to stand a realistic chance of acceptance, normally with 6s and 7s in the Higher Level subjects.'

'The University of Edinburgh welcomes applications from candidates offering the IB … For the Faculty of Law, an overall minimum point score of 34 points is normally required, whilst in Medicine an overall points score of 35 is required with grades 6,6,7 at Higher Level, with chemistry or either physics or biology at Higher Level. For entry to courses in the faculty of social sciences 30/32 points is required.'

'The University of Sheffield regards the IB as a good preparation for university study and is pleased to consider candidates offering the IB diploma accordingly. Most departments are likely to make offers in the region of 28–33 points …'

As an important word of caution, it should be noted that these quotes do not always fully correspond to reality, and counsellors must obtain individual reassurances from the universities. For example, many counsellors report that – contrary to the claims above – Cambridge colleges do not usually invite a student for an interview unless 40–41 points are predicted, and that figure has been known to exclude bonus points. Edinburgh's threshold for all courses is now reported to be 36 points (although medicine would be higher, of course). In summary, the quotes on the website are somewhat on the optimistic side.

10 Authorization in the UK by IBAEM

If a UK school then decides to go down the IB route, requests for an authorization visit should go to the regional IBO office, IBAEM (IB Africa, Europe and Middle East) (ibaem@ibo.org) within the academic year before teaching of the DP is planned to start. The visits can be enjoyable events if they are well planned and if all staff are well briefed on the IB and what is expected of them. The following questions featured prominently during the authorization visit to our school:

- What language courses will we offer and how will these develop?
- How are we budgeting for the implementation of the DP and do we have a five-year plan?
- What training have teaching staff already received and what training will they have had before teaching commences?
- How do we plan to teach Theory of Knowledge?
- What provision for CAS activities is the school making?
- Which IB subjects will we offer?
- Will we teach SL and HL together, and will this work?
- How will we approach in concrete terms the requirement of internationality?

The authorization visit is not an inspection by Ofsted (UK Office for Standards in Education, the state-funded schools governmental inspectorate) or the Independent Schools Inspectorate (ISI, the private schools equivalent run on the same system). The IBO authorization team is looking for both knowledge of the practicalities of adopting the IB DP (What subjects? Why? Development?) and an acknowledgement of the IBO's philosophy within the various school communities. A school does not change overnight but an overt willingness to move towards internationalism over time or an increase in the choice of languages on offer is expected. Schools may be refused authorization or have authorization delayed until certain recommendations are implemented if the authorization team is unhappy. However, it is probably safe to say that UK schools are so accustomed to the national political input in education that they prepare the ground carefully for the adoption of the DP and know where the pitfalls may lie. For the vast majority of schools in the UK, therefore, the authorization visit is an encouraging event.

Chapter 5
Case study: a steep learning curve

Ian Deakin, MBA, MEd
James Dalziel, MEd

In Singapore's expatriate educational circles the Canadian International School (CIS) is often cited as a model for faculty-driven educational innovation. The CIS recently received authorization to teach the Diploma Programme (DP) as well as the Middle Years Programme. Ian Deakin, formerly chief executive officer and head principal of the CIS and currently deputy headmaster of Jakarta International School, was the main driver behind the change to DP, while James Dalziel, deputy principal at the CIS, led the efforts to introduce the Middle Years Programme. The editors of this book asked Ian and James to give a frank account of their school's process of change. Their analysis of what went right and what went wrong should be of value to any school starting the DP.

1 Background of the school

The Canadian International School (CIS) opened in 1990 to provide educational opportunities to members of the expatriate community living in Singapore. The high school grew quickly through the 1990s largely through the provision of high-quality learning opportunities for non-native English speakers. In 1996 an elementary programme was introduced which was again enthusiastically welcomed by the region's international clientele and subsequently enjoyed rapid expansion. The Canadian International School is known in Singapore's expatriate circles for its child-centred delivery, differentiated teaching and rich support programmes. At the time of writing, our student population stands at 1,080, with 200 students enrolled in the high school programme.

We first expressed an interest in the IB DP in September 2000. The pre-authorization visit by IB Asia-Pacific (IBAP) regional office, based in Singapore, was conducted in February 2001 followed by the authorization visit in September 2001. Authorization was granted on 1 January 2002 for teaching to commence in August 2002.

The introduction of the IB DP was expected to benefit the CIS community in four ways:

1. It would offer students and parents potentially greater programme choices, an international perspective and enhanced opportunities at tertiary institutions.
2. It would provide our teachers with a natural venue to connect with the world at large through regional workshops and conferences, and allow us to contract top teachers from a wider base.
3. Our school would benefit from the highly coveted accreditation from the IBO: it would improve our market position and was expected to be at least revenue-neutral. In particular, we believed the IB would better fit with our international and transient client base, and thus would slow and eventually stem the drift of students away from the CIS throughout the middle school years.
4. The international clientele we expected to attract with the IB would over time bring the high school's student demographics more closely in line with those in the elementary division.

It is difficult, after just nine months into the programme, to predict with accuracy how successful this initiative will be. Some of our expectations were not met as easily as we thought. However, we do still believe that the IB DP will, in time, deliver as expected to individual students and to the school community at large. Our confidence in the value of the IBO's programmes finds concrete expression in the fact that the CIS was recently also authorized to teach the IB Middle Years Programme, following a May 2003 authorization visit, and that we will implement the IB Primary Years Programme in August 2003 towards authorization in 2005.

The lessons we learned and the questions we faced, and continue to face, with the process of implementing the DP should be of interest to anyone engaged in school management or school leadership. They most certainly will be of value to administrators of schools similar to ours as they consider implementing the IB DP. We believe that most of our decisions involving the consideration, implementation and restructuring of the programme have followed good practice, and we hope that by sharing our reflections on the process we can help others avoid unnecessary pitfalls and contribute to a smooth and successful implementation of the DP.

2 Educational climate in the CIS before the IB

In 1998/99 the CIS embarked on a focused and aggressive plan to improve the pedagogical practices within our school. Driven initially by educational reforms in Ontario Canada (our original accreditation agency) we embraced the standards movement, using objectives, criterion-based assessment tools and teacher/learner strategies with a higher degree of professionalism. Likewise we considered and later institutionalized paradigms like teaching for understanding (Wiggins and McTighe, 1998), lateral and constructive thinking (De Bono, 1967) and metacognition (Flavell, Miller and Miller, 2001). We moved to a laptop-learning program and invested a great deal of our professional development time and money into information communication technology (ICT) skill development for our teachers. We identified ICT pioneers on the staff and encouraged them to lead the way. Students and teachers learned together how this new and powerful tool could assist the teaching and learning process and lead to higher-quality outcomes for students. We fostered a culture of sharing that is critical to any 'learning organization' (Senge, 1994). We succeeded in creating a culture of change within our school by focusing on the quality of teaching and learning. By 2001/02 we had met all the major objectives of the Ontario reform.

Our choice was to 'settle in' or to seek other opportunities to maintain our momentum and take our school to the next level. We chose the latter, and saw in the IB DP the opportunity to meet our next goal: to internationalize our programme and to achieve a better fit between our curriculum and our international and transient student population.

3 Consideration phase

This phase involved developing an understanding of what the IBO considers 'best practice'. We conducted a staff and student community audit to:

- gauge existing school and organizational culture, and the willingness of the stakeholders to embrace further reforms
- identify current student population needs and the benefit the IB DP could bring to this group
- identify curriculum gaps
- identify 'champions' on the staff.

We had previously developed a school culture that was eager for change for the sake of learning. Our model of educational reform relied heavily on both top-down and bottom-up (organic) elements. The head principal provided a framework, stimulated debate and often helped champion the cause. Faculty provided the curricular expertise, informed the process of change and determined the final outcome. Our philosophy and practices were closely aligned with the IBO's expectations and presented no barriers to implementation.

We began by building three IB diploma student profiles, one each for a fine arts, liberal arts, and science student respectively. These profiles were important in focusing our efforts and identifying specifically what and when courses needed to be offered, so that a 'typical' IB student could progress continually towards graduation.

We believed from the outset that the IB would not be for everyone, at least in the initial stages. We assumed that many of our students lacked the academic foundation and the discipline necessary for success in the IB DP. We estimated that 20% – about 40 students – of our high school population would enrol in the DP and another 30% or 60 students would take at least one certificate in a subject area. (However, for reasons detailed below, the actual numbers nine months into the programme are 10 and 5 respectively.) For many reasons, including familiarity, quality of graduates, and reputation among tertiary institutions, we decided to retain the Ontario Secondary Diploma (OSD) as the second programme.

With our low initial enrolment projections for the IB diploma, stand-alone IB classes were not an option so we tested the possibility of 'twinning' IB and OSD classes. Twinning would allow us to teach the IB courses in the same class with the corresponding Ontario courses. This approach was going to be problematic from the outset given the differences in instructional hours and in timing and emphasis of curriculum. The OSD strongly supports international values but in terms of content knowledge and references it is very much a national system. Our teachers studied the IB curriculum documents and compared them with our OSD course profiles to identify overlap and gaps. We had hoped that the overlaps would be significant so that very few 'extra hours' would be required for the IB curricula. The gaps proved to be surprisingly large in some subject areas and encouragingly small in others. In some courses the differences simply could not be reconciled and the option to offer the IB course was discarded. At the end of this process we decided that we could offer English, economics, history, chemistry, mathematics, music, drama and visual arts at Higher Level (HL) while offering *ab initio* Mandarin, geography, biology, mathematics methods, and mathematics studies at Standard Level (SL).

With a great deal of teacher input, the head principal, department chairs, IB diploma coordinator (DPC) and the student services coordinator bundled and sequenced courses and produced a timetable that provided for a continuous two-year IB programme and satisfied graduation requirements of both the IB and OSD.

4 Communication phase: getting all stakeholders on board

We held a series of 'courageous conversations' (Senge, 1994) with all stake-holders, and led through questions (Collins, 2001). These sessions were not about planning or timetabling, but were focused on having honest conversations in order to gain a deep *understanding* of the IB programme expectations and how to run these parallel with the OSD curriculum. Parents were pleased with the increased options presented for our students (OSD, OSD and certificates, or IB diploma). They appreciated the financial commitment to the programme expressed by the directors and were prepared to pay for the extra examination fees.

We finished this phase with a consensus and a school-wide commitment to implementation.

5 First experiences with running the programme

To make sure that the introduction of the IB was a school-wide affair we offered the opportunity to teach IB courses to all experienced teachers. Every high school teacher, even those without an IB assignment, was sent to subject workshops. This initiative proved successful in creating and maintaining enthusiasm for the programme with our staff.

On the more problematic side, we found that our IB/OSD twin timetable was complex and inflexible. Many excellent students who did not fit completely with our IB profiles opted for our OSD-with-IB-certificates programme instead of the full IB diploma. With the original timetable, students new to the CIS were required to attend at least one 'pre-DP' year to ensure a solid grounding for the programme. This proved to be very problematic for prospective students expecting to enrol in a two-year programme and led to loss of clientele. Further, we discovered the timetable was no longer flexible enough to meet the needs of students joining our OSD programme from outside our school or from our English second language (ESL) programme.

It also transpired that the gap between the OSD and IB curricula was larger than originally anticipated, and that teachers of IB students would be required to increase their contact time with students considerably. On average it appeared that an additional 40 hours a year would be required per course. We decided to compensate IB teachers on an hourly basis up to 40 hours per course at a rate commensurate with their annual salary. The magnitude of the curricular gaps came as a surprise and the incremental salary costs were never anticipated nor budgeted.

6 Reflective phase

Throughout the entire process of IB authorization, the CIS maintained a close and mutually supportive working relationship with the IBAP regional office, and believes this has contributed to a relatively smooth and swift authorization process. Convincing the IB, however, is only one part of the process. The other is to convince the school community.

We sold the IB DP to our students and parents on the two promises that it was transferable (between IB schools) and that diploma results of 33 or more points (out of a maximum of 45) would offer our students greater opportunities in choices of tertiary institutions.

We found instead that the IB diploma was highly *untransferable*. The difficulties of moving between our IB programme and one in another school were fraught with issues involving the sequencing of curriculum. One issue that is particularly problematic for students leaving the CIS for schools in Europe and North America is the continuation of our popular *ab initio* Mandarin course. We continue to struggle with transfer issues and have found that all we can do to alleviate our students' problems is to warn them of the risk of taking certain subjects, and to make our curriculum sequence available for students and other schools in order to minimize misunderstandings upon arrival at the new school. Unless IB diploma schools develop a common presentation sequence in subjects, problems with transferability will continue to be an issue.

Similarly, we discovered that our argument of improved university entry did not stand up to scrutiny. In our experience so far, universities' understanding of the IB programme is highly variable. In some cases universities do not provide advance placement or waive credit requirements for IB students. As a result, we had to intensify dramatically our efforts to gather information regarding tertiary advantages of the IB diploma for our graduates. In the meantime, many students concluded that the marginal and incremental tertiary opportunities of the IB diploma over the OSD curriculum did not justify the added workload.

In trying to create a timetable that met the needs of many we missed the mark. We should have realized that we would not get everything right the first time and built in some latitude for change. We did not. Nor did we communicate the possible need to revise the timetable to our community. When changes were made to the timetable for the following academic year (2003/04) we frustrated many and came away looking inexperienced. The most recent iteration of the timetable has been simplified and makes better accounting of the required instructional hours, but the choices available to our DP students were reduced quite dramatically, as we had to drop our economics, HL mathematics, music and drama courses.

Even though we pride ourselves on knowing our students well we most certainly overestimated their willingness to conform to a profile that was convenient for us to deliver but did not mesh perfectly with their interests or aptitudes. We similarly overestimated the value placed by our students on the learning *process*. Our students appear to be guided far more by the value of the final product in terms of initial university entry than by the benefits of a programme's learning process.

The non-transferability problems we encountered, the problems with the tertiary advantages over the OSD, and the poor fit between courses offered and personal interests all had major consequences on our IB diploma enrolment.

Clearly the costs in the initial years of running IB classes with few students must be weighed against the ability to attract students and nurture the programme. The CIS continues to ponder the questions concerning educationally and financially viable course offerings and class sizes.

Finally, addressing staffing issues, we have found that, despite having made great strides in bringing the compensation for our teachers to international standards, we continue to lose good teachers, as our pay packages are still not competitive enough. The loss of key faculty is a great concern. A human resource model that features high levels of annual staff turnover fits poorly indeed with the requirements of the IB world. Increasing salaries to attract and retain talented staff may be impossible for many schools, especially small schools, and particularly in prevailing market conditions. As we have found through our own experiences and those of other schools in a similar position, schools run a serious risk of ending up as a paying IB training centre, putting lots of resources into training staff for the IB, only to see the best ones take on better-paid jobs elsewhere as soon as they complete their training.

The need to engage universities much more actively has placed considerable strain on our student services personnel and was another unforeseen, but necessary, demand on our human resources.

In summary, we were interested in the curriculum, the assessment and the enhanced opportunity for our graduates that an IB diploma could offer. We were aware of what we could contribute to the IBO while it moved forward. In many ways ours was a model school: we had succeeded in creating a culture of change, we embraced uncertainty, we focused all reform on quality of programmes, we used student performance to inform change efforts and used technology to enhance our programmes but not to drive them. But in the end, we underesti- mated the amount of time that our IB DPC would be required to spend 'selling' the programme to students, to parents, and to universities, and we did not foresee the negative impact the IB would have on our ability to retain good staff.

With hindsight the implementation process was a difficult exercise but it provided meaningful reflection on curriculum issues and the process of creating effective change. We are better off for undertaking it, and remain confident that the lessons learned will stand us in a good position in the years to come.

7 **References**

Collins, J. (2001) *Good to Great: Why some companies make the leap ... and others do not*, HarperCollins.

De Bono, E. (1967) *The Use of Lateral Thinking*, Penguin Books.

Flavell, J.H., Miller, P.H. and Miller, S.A. (2001) *Cognitive Development*, 4th edition, Prentice Hall.

Senge, P.M. (1994) *The Fifth Discipline*, Doubleday.

Wiggins, G. and McTighe, J. (1998) *Understanding by Design*, Prentice Hall.

Appendix 1: Programme costs and financial responsibility

An overview of our initial and ongoing costs is set out below.

Implementation costs (US$):

Initial costs
Purchase of publications	$ 3,000
Teacher-training	$ 2,500 per session / teacher × 12
Library	$ 20,000
Authorization visit	$ 500

Total implementation costs in 2001 (approx.): $ 53,500

Ongoing:
Annual subscription	$ 1,400 p.a.
Publications	$ 1,000 p.a.
Staffing	$ 1,000 per IB section
Programme fees	$ 559 (registration, extended essay, exam fees, etc.)
Library	$ 5,000
Teacher-training	$ 2,500 per session
Head's and coordinator's	$ 2,500 per session

Total annual expenses directly related to the IB DP (approx.): $ 27,959

Appendix 2: Chronology of events (as told by Ian Deakin)

September 2000	Meet associate director of IBAP to express an interest in the IB DP.
October 2000	Attend the IBAP's Heads' and Coordinators' Conference in Singapore together with librarian, chair of the IB Implementation Committee, elementary principal.
January–September 2001	All teaching staff and teacher-librarian attend workshops in South East Asia, Adelaide, Florida, Atlanta, Toronto.
February 2001	Pre-authorization visit: IBAP associate director visits the CIS and meets staff to ascertain the school's readiness and to provide answers and guidance.
March 2001	IBAP associate director views a potential site for the relocation of the school's high school programme, to ensure that it can meet expectations as an IB site. She provides general advice and identifies contacts at established IB schools in Singapore that could provide guidance in classroom, laboratory and library design. She also suggests that we should postpone our authorization visit until after the move to the new campus. She comments on the absence of ongoing dialogue with parents.

April 2001	Communication plan created – monthly parents meetings started. Initial meeting to be introductory, subsequent meetings to focus on programme and individual course selections.
	Head principal and head of department for science visit United World College of South East Asia in Singapore, the Singapore American School, the German School and the Anglo-Chinese School to survey science laboratory designs and libraries to inform our renovation efforts.
	Librarian attends conference and joins Pan-Asian Librarians and Media Association (PALMS). Compiles a reading list/resource list for all IB courses under consideration. Contacts publishing houses and surveys book availability and delivery dates.
	Head of IB Committee orders materials from the IBO: • application guide • *Vade Mecum* • subject guides • examination packages.
	Subject area teachers begin conducting gap analysis between existing curriculum and IB HL and SL curricula. Discussions begin regarding how best to twin existing curriculum with IB curricula, the best sequencing of courses, how to codify courses, and what options/choices to provide.
	Staff work on student profiles for science student, fine arts student, arts and science (liberal arts) student.
	Head principal surveys staff support, appoints IB DPC and CAS coordinator.
June 2001	Head principal attends IB North America (IBNA) workshop at Ashbury College in Ottawa, Canada. Contact with IBNA schools used to source timetables for semester schools twinning IB and OSD curricula; examples gathered from public and private schools across Ontario.
	Courses scheduling for 2001/2002 commences.
	Draft a three-year timetable so that students can understand the consequences of choices made today, conflicts and future options.
August 2001	Occupy new high school campus and introduce technology on demand pedagogy.
Late September 2001	Authorization visit.
October 2001	Attend the Shanghai Heads and Coordinators Conference. Notified of concerns regarding authorization for a school operating with a semester timetable. A few days of intensive lobbying and convincing decision-makers of our understanding and ability to provide continuity in programming for DP candidates.

January 2002	Notification from the IBO of accreditation on 1 January 2002 for commencement of classes August 2002.
January–August 2002	Refine schedule, publish long-range plans and teaching units to meet curricular standards for the IB and OSD programmes. Recruit new staff.
	Create new marketing materials with IB World School logo.
	Examine Middle Years Programme and Primary Years Programme possibilities.

Chapter 6

Case study: view from the developing world

Julie Hessler

Julie Hessler's long IB experience includes two years at the Overseas Family School (Singapore), three years at the United World College of South East Asia (Singapore) as well as five years of work at IB schools in the developing world, notably in Ethiopia as head of the faculty of languages and Theory of Knowledge (TOK) coordinator, and now as IB coordinator and deputy principal at the International School, Brunei. The editors of this book asked her to share her views on the challenges that come with running the Diploma Programme (DP) in the developing world. She also reveals how it is possible to turn a bad start into a success story.

David Cox, an IB veteran and secondary principal of the ISB who prepared the school for its second (and successful) authorization attempt, contributed the section on authorization.

1 Introduction

1.1 Background of the International School, Brunei

The International School, Brunei (ISB) at inception in 1964 was named the 'Supervision School' and was attached to the South Australia Correspondence Scheme, organized from Adelaide. Worksheets were sent monthly to Australia to be marked and a new set dispatched to Brunei. However, with the advent of 40 expatriate teachers for the new Bruneian government college in Bandar Seri Begawan, the principal of the Supervision School, Mrs Bennett, realized there were enough trained, accompanying wives of the college teachers to staff a conventional school with teachers taking charge of and delivering the curriculum, and so was born 'The International School' in 1974 under her leadership.

The school established a strong community ethos from the beginning and for a considerable period of time resembled almost a home schooling environment. Initially the school buildings were large houses with extensions added as required, and eventually, with some government assistance, a purpose-built school was constructed for primary education. The school grew with the needs of the expatriate community in Brunei and by 1998 a secondary school had developed sufficiently to adopt the two-year British International General Certificate of Secondary Education (IGCSE) curriculum for 14–16 year-old students. The IGCSE examinations remained the most advanced course offered until the advent of the IB DP in August 2001.

1.2 Educational environment in which the school operates

Until 1997, the ISB was the only international school catering for expatriate children. However, an initiative by Prince Jeffrey, the Sultan of Brunei's brother, led to the construction of another custom-built international school offering the National Curriculum of England and Wales as well as the pre-university British A-levels. There are also several government-run A-level colleges. The Sultan, as well as the government of Brunei, maintains very close links with Britain in many areas, including defence and education. A significant number of scholarships to the UK are awarded each year and many of the office bearers in the government are UK trained.

Very few people in Brunei and Borneo knew about the DP when the ISB introduced it as its pre-university course. Fortunately for the ISB, one of these few was the chairman of the ISB board of directors, who had studied at an IB school himself. He was and continues to be a strong advocate of the programme at the ISB.

1.3 The first authorization attempt

The principal initiated the campaign to introduce the IB DP. Although he had never taught it, he had been head at other international schools and was familiar with the merits of the programme. The board of directors supported the initiative but there was some concern over expense, particularly the preparation and staffing costs in a school with modest fees and few avenues to raise significant sums of money. However, enthusiasm won the day, despite reservations.

The school hired an independent consultant at considerable cost to assist in introducing the programme. The management at the time was unaware that the relevant regional IBO office provides all the support necessary without charge. In fact formal application for IB diploma authorization was made very late in the process and this contributed to difficulties later experienced by the school. Meetings were held with parents and teachers and the announcement of the introduction of the DP appeared in the local press. Negotiations on government level commenced, but were not pursued to any significant degree at the time, as the school aimed for the greatest possible autonomy to run the programme.

The school actively campaigned to retain as many of its IGCSE students as possible, against parents' prevailing habit of sending their children outside the country for their final years of schooling. There was enough interest, however, to justify introducing the course, and one of the students who enrolled was a high-ranking member of the royal family. The initial visit by the IBO South East Asian regional representative, accompanied by a highly experienced DP coordinator (DPC), took place in February 2000 following a formal application for authorization.

The IBO representative made the following recommendations:

- Renovate poorly equipped science laboratories to ensure that they meet required safety standards.
- Increase the number of classrooms to meet the increase in roll resulting from the addition of an IB cohort.
- Reduce staff turnover.

The representative also expressed concern regarding the relationship between the board of directors and the senior management of the school, and the perceived lack of strength of the board's commitment to the introduction of IB DP.

By the second authorization visit in June 2000, the school had renovated two science laboratories and introduced new safety features. Plans were available for six new portakabin classrooms and a contractor had been appointed to carry out the work in the July/August 2000 vacation. The board of directors demonstrated a convincing unanimity in their commitment to the introduction of the IB programme. Teachers and subject coordinators interviewed by the IBO representative displayed appropriate knowledge of the relevant programmes and provided appropriate work schemes and teaching and learning strategies. Most teachers were optimistic that the school would gain IB diploma authorization.

As the end of the school year loomed closer without any word from the IBO, trepidation increased. In late July, a few days before the end of the academic year and seven weeks before the programme was due to start in the school, two letters, both dated 24 July 2000, arrived from George Walker, IB director-general in Geneva. One offered the school affiliated membership until July 2001. The other offered 'full participation' from July 2001 with certain conditions:

- All IB-designated staff should have contracts designed so as to ensure staffing stability during the first two teaching years.
- During the affiliate year, IB teachers yet to be trained should attend IBO teacher-training workshops.
- The building development work should be completed.

The letter also asked the school to seriously consider offering one arts subject.

Whatever promise lay in the future, in August 2000 the school was unable to offer the IB DP.

Morale in the school was already low. The principal had left abruptly in early July 2000 leaving the primary head in charge of the school. The new head of secondary arrived in June 2000 with a brief that included the task of ensuring the successful inception of the IB diploma into the school. Instead, he found himself acting as principal from August 2000 and faced with the task of holding together a school in crisis. Parents reacted with dismay to an institution unable to deliver the promised course and students went elsewhere, including our high-profile Bruneian prince, who had been a student at the school since kindergarten.

The following year the ISB struggled with a falling roll, and a large number of teachers left. The acting principal faced the major task of recruiting 27 new teachers across the primary and secondary schools. He accomplished this, and the school managed to meet the conditions set out by the IBO. A new principal was appointed in April 2001. In May 2001, following a visit by John Goodban, the IBO regional director, the school was finally granted IB authorization in a letter from George Walker dated 5 June 2001. The first cohort of 30 students began the DP in August 2001.

Looking back on those difficult times it is easy to see the mistakes. Approaching the IBO regional office in Singapore six months earlier would probably have created a more favourable impression and a willingness to accept at face value planned initiatives (some of the recommendations in George Walker's letter had in fact been met already by the time we received it). Secondly, all stakeholders need to be fully convinced of the decision to introduce the IB, and that includes the board and the senior management team. In short, as repeatedly stressed in this book, communication and commitment are key.

The ISB is now much stronger, with an increasing roll in the secondary school expected to reach over 400 in August 2003, recovering from a low of around 300 in 2001. The IB programme is well established with nearly 80 students enrolled overall. Section 2 describes in detail how the school managed to get back on track, and outlines some of the outstanding challenges. Many of the points made here will apply equally well to many a school operating in the developed world.

2 Communication and publicity

Clear and effective communication at all levels turned out to be of paramount importance. The following are the main communication issues with parents and students, staff, local universities and the national government.

2.1 Communication with parents and students

Personal interviews. Spending time with students and their parents on an individual basis contributes significantly to the successful implementation of the DP in schools in the developing world. One of the challenges faced at the ISB in terms of conveying the merits of the programme to parents from the local community was that many of the parents are financially successful but do not have advanced formal education and can sometimes feel out of their depth in an academic environment. Ensuring that the structure and benefits of the DP are explained in accessible English in a relaxed and friendly manner helps put parents at ease, encourages them to ask questions and gains their confidence that they will be valued members of the parent body should they choose to enrol their children at the school. To convince parents of the merits of the DP, it is essential to provide them with appropriate handbooks, brochures and newspaper articles relating both to the IB in general and to more specific 'local' IB issues such as the local language IB programme.

Presentations. In countries with little or no exposure to the IB programme and only limited exposure to international education, a significant degree of marketing is necessary, and frequent presentations about the IB held on school premises and advertisements in the local newspapers were important. The presentations seemed to work well when the presenters were formally dressed, but they adopted a relaxed presentation style and spoke in a clear, uncomplicated way, relating the presentation to local events and conditions wherever possible.

We highly recommend that schools offer high-profile presentations. We organized, and continue to organize, these in order to make the programme more familiar to influential bodies in Brunei. We hired a conference room at a good hotel to present the programme to, for example, heads of local schools in Brunei and various organizations representing the community. Section 2.4 details some of the windfalls that such presentations have brought us.

Publicity. The school has adopted a much more aggressive publicity campaign since the introduction of the DP, providing the local English newspaper with photographs and articles relating to the course on a regular basis. Articles have ranged from the visit of the IB Malay teachers from Mara College (see Chapter 7), who gave Malay in-service training to our Malay teachers, to creativity, action and service (CAS) projects, business management students' trips to companies and Model United Nations trips. CAS activities where the community benefits also served us well in terms of positive publicity for the school. Through the efforts of the CAS coordinator, many organizations have become aware of the IB DP at our school.

It is the view of the ISB that maximum attention must be paid to public relations to engender trust in the clientele during the establishment of a new programme, particularly one that is unknown to the community. For this reason, employing an experienced IB teacher who has a thorough knowledge of the programme, who is a confident, persuasive public speaker and who communicates effectively with parents and students as the DPC is pivotal in successfully introducing the programme into the community.

Surveying students' interest. As schools sometimes establish strengths in certain subjects, and regions can differ in their opinions about what subjects are important to take or to have on offer, carrying out a survey of students and parents is very useful for new schools. This can be done formally or, for example, in discussion form at parents' evenings. At the ISB, for instance, in the first year of the programme, we offered music and French B (and recruited new teachers for them), as both of those options are on offer at the school at IGCSE. However, not a single student chose either of these subjects. At the same time, we found ourselves hunting around for a Malay A1 teacher, which delayed the start of the Malay A1 course and led to the teacher and students having to put in many extra hours after the school day and at weekends to fulfil the course time requirements.

Regular assessment. Apart from a full report that goes out once a year (in May for the first year and in December for the second), students receive five other assessment documents: four interim reports which state attainment and effort grades and one exam report. To reduce the load on the teachers, these assessments contain only comments by the management. Parents have commented very favourably on receiving such regular feedback.

Follow-up with students. In the developing world, parents sometimes rely on the school to ensure that their children are performing academically. This can become increasingly the case as the children enter the higher levels of study. Parents may not have had the opportunity to complete a significant number of school years themselves, and their children sometimes adopt the attitude that the parents do not have the credentials to oversee their academic endeavours. Regular follow-up with students after each assessment, in terms of both praise and support, is pivotal in ensuring academic success in IB programmes in developing countries.

Newsletters. Students are notoriously bad at keeping their parents informed as to what they are doing at school. As noted above, this can be an even more pronounced problem in the developing world. To counter this, we recommend that regular newsletters be sent to the parents. At the ISB, an IB newsletter goes out at the end of every term covering CAS activities, programme information, university application details, dates of assessments, dates for the writing of the extended essay, and information from the IBO's website.

2.2 Communication with staff

Most new IB schools will begin with a number of teachers who have only workshop experience but no IB teaching experience. We have found that holding IB meetings regularly (twice a term) provides an important forum for dealing with IB issues and familiarizing teachers with the many aspects of the programme.

2.3 Local university recognition of the DP

New IB schools in developing countries often face the challenging task of getting the local universities to accept the IB as a valid entrance qualification. (However, it is a fact that DP students rarely enrol in universities in many developing world countries such as Ethiopia, Kenya, Cambodia, Vietnam, Laos.) It is important to start very early with this process as copious documentation is required, often more than once. Prepare a folder for the authority that is investigating university recognition of the IB, and present the IB material in a user-friendly way. Printing off information from websites of well-known universities to indicate the wide acceptance of the IB diploma is important. It is crucial for the head of school to make contact with the officials concerned and to maintain regular contact during the inspection of documents period. At the ISB, it is through the tenacity of our current director that Brunei's university recognition has now come through, about eighteen months into the programme.

2.4 Government recognition of the DP

Local university recognition was pivotal in gaining official government acceptance for the IB diploma as a basis for a scholarship award. In Brunei, the government awards a significant number of scholarships and these are highly prized by the local community. Apart from the obvious advantages of winning a scholarship, recipients who successfully complete their degree are guaranteed a job for life with superior remuneration with the government upon their return to Brunei. The director of the school has made several courtesy calls to the Ministry of Education and the ISB was invited by the ministry to do a presentation on the DP to its significant office bearers. We have been told that the ministry was so impressed by the presentation that they subsequently contacted the regional IB office. At our senior graduation ceremony, the deputy minister of education made the public announcement that the University of Brunei accepts the DP as an entry qualification and that the government recognizes it for scholarship award purposes. This was a major breakthrough for the school in terms of recognition of the IB programme by the Bruneian community. We are now in a position to attract the most academically promising local students.

3 Management issues

Apart from the usual procedures that are necessary to run the IB programme effectively, we have found that the following additional procedures have also contributed.

3.1 Establishing an academic board that includes teachers

As elsewhere in the developing world where educational opportunities may be limited, the ability range of applicants to the IB programme can be very wide. Students who would most likely be rejected out of hand by established IB schools in the developed world must sometimes be considered for a place, particularly if they are the children of expatriate workers who have limited options for the schooling of their children. Inevitably weaker students get admitted onto the programme. However, advice to schools in developing countries facing a similar situation is to ensure that they establish an academic board where all IB teachers can have an input. Our students gain admittance to the programme with certain conditions set out to parents in a letter of acceptance, so as to avoid complications at a later date. If a student's admission to the DP is a team decision, teachers cannot then feel that unsuitable candidates are being forced on them.

3.2 Financing the DP in a way that is acceptable to the community

Schools in developing countries often have a thriving primary school with waiting lists, and a small, but costly, senior school. The school board needs to decide whether they and the school community are prepared to subsidize the cost of running the DP, certainly in the early stages. There are a number of schools where the costs of running the DP have led to tensions among staff, managers, board members and in school relationships with parents because of concerns of unfair distribution of financial resources.

3.3 Scheduling the school calendar carefully

It is important to collaborate with IB teachers and to take note of key local festivals, holidays and so on, in order to produce a comprehensive calendar of dates for completion of IB internal assessment and assignments. This will help prevent student overload and alert parents to important deadlines. We have found, for example, that pleas to final-year DP students and parents not to go on holiday for Chinese New Year, have up to now not met with much success. Trying to minimize the workload over these times by advanced planning of the academic requirements calendar can reduce the damage of such undesired absences if your school cannot absorb major local cultural festivities into the holiday schedule.

Careful calendar scheduling can also be an important tool to prevent staff turnover, as explained towards the end of this chapter.

3.4 Planning a feasible timetable

Maximum and minimum class sizes have to be established beforehand, as well as the absolute core curriculum consisting of subjects that run regardless of uptake. For example, is physics an essential subject to offer even if only four students wish to study it in a particular year? Will you try to run set courses, or will you try to offer subjects that meet student needs (which may vary from year to year)? We would advise against the latter as it will create an inherent instability in the programme and in staffing. Our advice to developing schools, as stated earlier, is to do surveys among students and parents first, and aim to develop a good feel for trends. To give an example, the attitude among a significant sector of our local population is that visual arts is not a subject for higher levels of study, while music is. Business and management is a very popular option, and even in our first year of IB (which started with 34 students), we had to create two business classes. A complicating factor for small schools is that many students will often select subjects because of the popularity of the teacher. This can lead to the type of situation we experienced when we had two biology classes in one year with initial numbers of 26, and a single biology class with only 4 students the next. In view of all this, schools must prepare IB teachers, students and parents for the possibility of changes of courses on offer. If you don't do this, the disappointment of not being able to teach or take subjects originally on offer can be very demotivating.

3.5 HL and SL together?

For some schools new to the IB, particularly smaller schools, the only way to run the DP is to offer Higher Level (HL) and Standard Level (SL) together in subjects that attract few students. Teachers coming from larger schools who are used to separate HL and SL classes may find this arrangement unacceptable, so need to be forewarned before accepting a contract with the school.

3.6 Synchronizing the international and local school calendar

If your school operates according to the international school calendar (August until June) and local schools operate the southern hemisphere school year (from January until December), problems arise if local students are to participate in the IB DP. In order to help make the IB programme sustainable, we have had to find ways to attract local students despite incompatibility of school calendars. Local students take their O-level (more or less the equivalent of IGCSEs) in November. The ISB has introduced two ways of overcoming this problem:

1. We have devised a *late entry programme*, for high academic achievers from local schools. A late entry fee is charged to cover costs of producing catch-up manuals and to pay teachers for overtime. The students join straight after their O-level examinations and spend around three weeks at the ISB familiarizing themselves with the programme. Each IB teacher has produced a comprehensive catch-up manual for their subject, which takes the students through the seven weeks of the programme they have missed. Students are expected to work through the manuals during the lengthy December break (four to five weeks). After the December break, these students follow a scheduled catch-up timetable after normal school hours to ensure that they meet the hours requirement as laid down by the IBO. Teachers are paid well for these lessons, which helps sweeten the workload.

   The late entry programme at the ISB has been a resounding success, with most of our late entry students taking the lead in terms of academic achievement by May of the first year of the programme. We can strongly recommend this approach if your school finds itself in a similar position.

2. For less able local students, we offer a three-month *pre-Diploma course* which begins in May, at the time when IB year 2 students and IGCSE students are either on study leave or writing examinations. Teachers are then free to take on this teaching commitment. Once again, teachers are paid extra for teaching these classes, although not as generously as with the late entry programme (as their teaching loads have been significantly diminished at this time due to the examinations). The programme attracts students who, after completing their November O-level examinations, have not made up their minds about further study by January (when the local academic year starts). By the time May arrives, these students have been out of school for a few months, a cause of no small concern for many of their parents.

   To avoid awkward situations, the letter of offer of a place on the pre-Diploma programme must state that completing the pre-Diploma course does not mean automatic acceptance onto the full DP in August. Teachers of the pre-Diploma students have the challenge of providing an accessible introduction to the course, but also making the material challenging enough to try and establish whether the students will cope with the DP.

Through these two approaches, the ISB has managed to attract around 20 to 25 students, which makes a significant difference to financing the IB DP.

4 Curriculum issues

4.1 The mother tongue problem

A significant number of students in our cohort do not have mother tongue proficiency in any language. Most, if not all of them, speak three or four languages, but none of them in a way that enables them to comply with the demands of the IB A1 course. For all of their earlier schooling they had been placed in English as a second language (ESL) or English for speakers of other languages (ESOL) courses. This is a problem that is frequently faced in developing world schools, and of all the challenges we faced, this was one of the most serious in terms of putting together viable packages. As the IGCSE course had previously been the most advanced course on offer for the students at the ISB, the question of preparing the students for mother tongue proficiency in English was never perceived as important. English is commonly used as the language of communication in the home and with friends, but it is a form of English that has been adapted to regional conditions. While it adequately meets the needs of business and social interactions, adapting it to meet A1 require-ments is difficult. Most of the students referred to took English A1 SL. A very experienced IB teacher then faced one of the most difficult challenges in his career in trying to bring these students up to acceptable academic levels at A1. For the first six months, rudimentary work in both literature and language had to be undertaken through the texts under study, before any real critical analysis could be tackled. Consequently, we changed our language policy in the school to ensure that students have mother tongue proficiency in either English or Malay.

4.2 Teaching TOK

The major challenge we have faced in teaching Theory of Knowledge (TOK) is the underdeveloped abstract reasoning ability in a fairly significant number of students. The following reasons all seem to contribute to this problem:

- Lack of mother tongue proficiency in any language (a TOK issue in itself).
- The local community is for the most part concerned with the practical concern of conducting business successfully, and TOK is considered 'useless'. A common lack of formal education of parents reinforces this suspicion of TOK.
- For the most part, cultural activities in Brunei are few and far between. The significant contribution to the visual arts are several beautiful, world-renowned mosques, but apart from these, very little happens in the capital city with regards to aesthetics.
- Local education is still very traditional and students are required to be passive learners. Participative behaviour is considered disruptive. After many years of such training, it is difficult for students to become participative learners. This is a challenge in all areas of the curriculum.

In the early months of the course, students can sit dumbstruck, their faces registering mounting concern over the teacher's mental sanity. The good news is that after a few months, as long as the TOK material is presented in a practical hands-on way, and deals with issues that students find interesting or can relate to, most students can develop the necessary abstract reasoning skills as well as enthusiasm for the subject.

4.3 CAS

It is highly desirable to appoint a CAS coordinator who knows the region well and who has connections to the local community, preferably someone who is already active in a CAS sense. In most developing countries, there are good opportunities for CAS. When CAS is stressed in private interviews with parents, in IB presentations, and through press releases, it is often the case that members of the community start contacting the school with requests for help of IB students with events. One of the problems facing IB schools in some developing countries can be lack of adequate public transportation. If the school does not own buses, or the expense of hiring buses is too great for the school to bear, other ways of transporting students must be depended on. As in most traditional societies a significant number of mothers are still running their homes, and they can often be relied upon to give rides to other students. However, if a student is injured in a car accident, this can pose a legal problem that the school needs to address.

4.4 Extended essays

In small IB schools with limited resources in developing countries, finding some of the necessary equipment for students doing extended essays in groups 3 and 4 can be difficult. At the ISB, students have been successful in borrowing equipment from the university, the local hospital and the other international schools in the town. Depending on what is required, some businesses are also sometimes in a position to provide assistance with equipment. Providing students with letters of introduction, giving a brief outline of the IB diploma course and requesting assistance, has proved successful at the ISB. Advising the student to be appropriately dressed and to wear their school security tag also pays dividends. In terms of book resources, schools in developing countries with limited resources can usually get the cooperation of local universities or other organizations that have books available to the public for borrowing (some British Councils have book lending facilities). In order for cordial arrangements such as these to continue, students must obviously be scrupulous about returning the books borrowed.

5 Challenges

5.1 Finances

The single most challenging aspect of starting the IB programme in a small school or in a developing country is inevitably related to finance. In the case of the ISB, members of the board, some teachers and parents were concerned about the significant cost of the DP, particularly to set it up. New laboratories, extra classrooms, improved library resources, a study area with computer provision for senior students all had to be provided before the school could receive authorization. However, it should be noted that such expenditure directly or indirectly benefits the whole school.

Any new IB school should also try to recruit a number of highly experienced IB teachers so that guidance is available to staff who are new to the IB and to instil confidence in the community that the programme can be delivered effectively. However, experienced teachers obviously cost the school more money. The financial implications are far-reaching and a careful study must be undertaken by the school before it embarks on implementing the IB (see Chapter 3). The current director of the ISB feels that a proper feasibility study was not undertaken at the ISB and that we are lucky that all has turned out well. If the school had not attracted the fairly healthy numbers in the early years of offering the programme, we might well have had to abandon the IB. Our advice to new schools is not to rely on luck but to do your homework and to budget for a few expensive years in order for the programme to be established.

5.2 Staff turnover

We report exactly the same problem as the Canadian International School did in the previous case study (Chapter 5): financially constrained schools bear the cost of initiating a significant number of teachers into the IB programme by sending them on workshops, only to lose them at the end of the two-year contract period to better-paying institutions. The marketability of DP teachers seems virtually guaranteed given the DP's current growth rate. Worse still, some teachers break contract due to relatively low salaries and unattractive work scheduling. For reasons originating in the fact that we started as a primary school, school days are short without a significant lunch break. This leaves DP teachers with a lack of structured time to give individualized attention to struggling students or to supervise extended essays, and leaves both students and teachers feeling tired at the end of the school day. At the ISB, we attend school from Monday to Thursday, have Friday off, go to school on Saturday and have Sunday off. Suffice it to say that this is a major bone of contention for both students and teachers, and I would strongly advise schools to schedule two consecutive days off, no matter which two days. We try to accommodate both the wishes of the local community and the demands of following an international education. This leads to all sorts of compromises, such as a long December break that causes students to lose momentum, and a very uneven distribution of teachers' workload over the year. To reduce staff turnover, our advice is to offer a reasonably competitive package (higher salaries, bonus incentives and/or pension schemes). Also, a school needs to think very carefully what it can do to create an attractive working environment: spend time on designing a pleasant school day and timetable; you might be in a position to offer teachers and students a four-day working week (French schools, which have a tradition of catering to the social needs of their staff, often manage to do so).

In the final analysis, the ISB has faced and overcome many challenges in successfully implementing the IB programme. Despite the challenges that still remain, the general consensus is that it has been a worthwhile exercise and that the knock-on effect on the rest of the school and on the community at large has been overwhelmingly positive. In our case, even the early sceptics have become supporters.

Chapter 7

Mara College Banting: the dividends of a revolutionary vision

Matias de Menezes, BA, MA

One of the world's most successful IB schools in terms of academic results is a national school located in Malaysia: Mara College Banting (MCB). The editors of this book asked Matias de Menezes, long-time principal at MCB, to share with our readers the reasons for its success, for which he is widely considered the main architect. This study illustrates that it is possible to integrate the student-centred Diploma Programme (DP) within a traditionally rigorous Asian approach to education, a point of considerable satisfaction to the IBO. It also demonstrates that the IBO's call on schools to experiment can translate to success for those who are not afraid to try. Amongst other things, MCB sets aside a whole day a week for CAS, and reserves five weeks for study skills techniques.

The original text of this chapter as submitted to the editors was quite extensive and included detailed statistics. The full report can be viewed on www.dp-help.com. The author gratefully acknowledges the following people, who helped in production of the original report:

- Mr Azmi Mohamad, assistant principal of the MCB, for providing the MCB profile
- Ms Noraini Abdul Rahman, IB coordinator (DPC) of the MCB, for providing the DP results
- Ms Norlela Charom, chief intensive revision programme (IRP) coordinator of the MCB, for providing the IRP data
- Mr Abdul Latiff, CAS coordinator of the MCB, for providing the CAS data.

1 Background of the Mara College Banting

Mara College Banting (MCB) is part of the Mara College group, which operates 37 schools throughout Malaysia including four pre-university colleges. The umbrella organization, MARA (acronym in Malay for 'Council of Trust for the People'), was set up in 1968 to focus on the socio-economic and educational development of the indigenous people of Malaysia. Employing well over 5,000 people, MARA is a significant player in Malaysia's education field.

A multicultural, co-educational and fully residential school, MCB was founded in 1992, but started teaching the IB DP in 1991 at a previous temporary campus alongside the British-style A-level curriculum (which started in 1985). The MCB discontinued offering the A-levels in 1997 to become an IB diploma-only school in 1999. Located in a dynamic growth region close to Kuala Lumpur, the campus offers full residential and sports facilities for 900 students. Current enrolment is about 650 students, all aiming to study engineering or medicine in the UK, Ireland, Australia or New Zealand. There are 85 academic staff, most with masters degrees from leading universities, and 35 support staff. Due to the specific science focus of its students, the IB programme offered is equally focused: students take Malay A1 Standard Level (SL), English B (SL), business and management (SL), chemistry Higher Level (HL), choice of physics or biology (HL), and mathematics (HL). Traditionally, students undergo a selection process and are fully sponsored by MARA, the Public Services Division, the Ministry of Education and Malaysia's national petroleum corporation, Petronas. Enrolment is expected to reach the target of 900 students in 2004. Already one of the largest IB schools, an enrolment of 900 would make the MCB the world's largest IB diploma school.

More significantly, since 2000, Mara has also been one of the world's most successful IB schools in terms of diploma examination results. About 90% of the marks are 6 or higher. About 10% of individual marks are 5s (half of these are in business and management) and only 1% are 4s. In May 2002, almost half of the 126 students gained 40 points or more; over 99% gained more than 34 points and the overall average grade was 39. The precise grade distribution of the May 2002 results are summarized in figure 7.1.

Figure 7.1 Cumulative grade distribution for the MCB's May 2002 examinations

Grade	Number of students	Cumulative %	Grade	Number of students	Cumulative %
45	3	3	37	16	82
44	2	4	36	13	92
43	3	6	35	6	97
42	12	16	34	3	99
41	13	26	33	0	99
40	25	46	32	0	99
39	13	56	31	0	99
38	17	69	30	1	100

Percentages are rounded off to the nearest whole number.

2 Why the MCB discontinued A-levels in favour of the IB diploma

During the Asian economic crisis in 1997, many sponsorship programmes came under heavy pressure, prompting a profound re-evaluation of the MCB's position. For one, maintaining two academic programmes became too expensive, and the MCB had to decide which programme to continue: A-levels or the IB DP. The college settled on the IB for the following reasons:

- *Performance:* our DP students performed better academically at UK universities than our A-level students.
- *Curriculum:* we preferred the IB's broad-based approach to education.
- *International networking:* the IBO afforded the MCB a natural avenue to connect with the world at large through its regional workshops and conferences.
- *Assessment:* A-level was 100% examination based; the DP with its significant coursework component, presentations and pastoral programmes was superior in developing student confidence and hence academic results.
- *Pastoral:* the IB curriculum naturally stimulates close student–teacher contact through the internal assessment as well as the inherent pastoral aspects of TOK and CAS.
- *Student perceptions:* although the DP students looked with envy at the greater free time enjoyed by the A-level students, they felt more confident academically because of the significant weight of the internal assessment.
- *Business:* the A-level programme, while inexpensive to administer, could be offered by other schools in Malaysia, whereas the MCB's experience with the DP gave it a competitive advantage there.

3 Factors contributing to academic success

We introduced most factors contributing to the MCB's academic success after 1997. These factors are summarized here, and details follow in the rest of this chapter.

Financial and management support. The MCB has enjoyed the financial support of MARA, and a resolutely supportive management.

Focus on and within the DP. We offer only the DP and no other courses, and in view of our students' profile, we only offer seven academic subjects (see section 1). This focus is certainly not the only factor for academic success, however, since the MCB has had a science focus since its inception in 1990.

Raised selection criteria. In 1999 the MCB and the sponsors decided that students should have at least eight As on their Malaysian school certificates (SPM, the Malaysian equivalent of the British GCSE) as well as a good record of extra-curricular activities. This makes MARA very selective by the standards of government-supported schools and moderately selective compared with private institutions. To put it in numbers, 5–10% of the national SPM cohort satisfies our academic requirements. While selection contributes to success, it is certainly not the sole reason for it. Specifically, while raised selection criteria certainly raise the average grade, they will not ensure the narrow spread of marks we have achieved. Our statistical analyses show this narrow banding correlates strongly with the introduction of study groups and our intensive revision programme (IRP), discussed below.

Staff roles and staff development. Roles are clearly defined. New teachers familiarize themselves with the DP through a mentor system and induction programmes. Staff development comes in the form of internal training as well as external training through IB workshops. Very importantly, we are committed to retaining good staff: many teachers have been with us since the start of the programme and a great majority has been with us for longer than five years.

Development of subject course notes. All subject teachers are required to produce and continually update a *subject handbook* containing the outline of the syllabus, a summary of each topic, worksheets, exercises, additional reading material from other sources that are difficult to obtain, samples of past-year questions, and references and reading lists for each topic.

Intensive tracking of students' welfare and performance by the school. This comes in the form of bi-monthly one-on-one teacher–student consultations, after-school enrichment classes, and the IRP.

Student-centred learning. Classes are 20–25 students, and each class forms a coherent unit, taking the same courses with the possible exception of the electives biology and physics. Three months into the programme, students are organized into small groups of 4–6 students, so that each class typically consists of five groups. These groups work together and are the first point of contact for students and teachers should any problems arise. The study groups allow students to do more homework while reducing the teacher's marking load. In addition, there is a peer teaching system, whereby the school pays the better students a fee to help their struggling peers.

Institution of well-defined routines (protocols). The MCB has instituted daily, weekly, monthly and semesterly routines, providing stability and a sense of continuity.

Networking with target universities. The MCB has excellent contacts with our target universities in the UK, Ireland, New Zealand and Australia, who visit once a year to give presentations, which enthuse and motivate our students.

Emphasis on the DP core. Theory of Knowledge (TOK) develops thinking skills which are used and revisited in subject lessons, which habitually refer back to TOK. The extended essay is recognized by the students as advantageous for their university application and future work there, a point emphasized by the university representatives visiting our campus. Finally, our school sets the entire Wednesday aside for CAS alone – there are no regular classes scheduled then. Our students look forward to the CAS sessions, which are divided into internal activities (e.g. self-defence classes, fund-raising, tuition classes, organizing sports activities for primary schools, planning for external projects) and external activities (visits to hospitals, community development centres, and so on). As discussed in detail in section 4, the MCB has devoted considerable human resources to assist with the DP core.

4 Staff roles and staff development

Staff roles are clearly defined. The IB DP coordinator (DPC) is responsible for managing the academic programme, communication with the IBO and conducting the examinations. The core is very well staffed, with four full-time TOK teachers, two CAS supervisors (in addition each teacher supports one CAS activity in an advisory capacity) and a team of appointed teachers supervising the extended essay. The teachers, laboratory staff, library staff, residence halls wardens, dining-hall staff and the office staff are always fully up to date with the events happening in school. Coordination meetings are scheduled every Tuesday, chaired by the assistant principal and attended by the DPC, CAS coordinators, non-academic staff (including the IB secretary), the PA system man and the facilities coordinator. A schedule for the week is prepared two hours after this meeting by the secretary, and forwarded to the rest of the school. This whole-school approach is the main factor ensuring a smooth flow of the activities and of the school programme. The Students Representative Council is an official body elected by the students themselves. The council meets regularly and is a channel for students' requests, suggestions and dissatisfaction, if any. It also organizes school functions and oversees student activities.

Teachers and heads of department spend 15 and 12 hours a week respectively on teaching and CAS supervision, excluding consultation hours, mentoring sessions (see below), extended essay supervision and consultation, preparation and marking of papers. Teachers spend 1–2 hours a week at department meetings (agendas are discussed in section 8 of this chapter) and 2–3 hours a week if the department is responsible for a major function, such as graduation day or registration day. Furthermore, they spend about 1–2 hours in consultations with students and another 2–3 hours on CAS. Heads of department meetings may take up 3–4 hours a week. We actively strive to keep meetings to a minimum.

The schedule displayed in figure 7.2 is that of a typical teacher (note that Wednesday is CAS day for the whole school).

Mentor system and sharing of teaching material. All new teachers to the IB programme are placed on a one-year tutelage under a senior teacher. The mentor is responsible for guidance on subject content and provision of all teaching material for one year. The new teacher is expected to observe the mentor's classes throughout the year as necessary and the mentor is responsible for observing and coaching the new teacher.

The performance benchmark. This benchmark was developed over the years. Initially, teachers whose subjects scored above the overall world average were given rewards and incentives. As more teachers achieved the benchmark, the incentives were no longer necessary and it became a norm.

In-house teacher-training. Every year between the semester break and the new intake of students, a 3–4-day in-house training is conducted. Its focus is the dissemination of new teaching strategies, the consolidation of successful school programmes and the re-evaluation of programmes that have deviated from the desired outcome. The principal, assistant principal, DPC and teachers are assigned slots to share their expertise in areas such as:

- latest educational research, e.g. verbal skills appear to be decisive for effective teaching

Figure 7.2 Time schedule for a typical teacher at the MCB

TIME	MONDAY	TUESDAY	WEDNESDAY	THURSDAY	FRIDAY
8.00–8.50	CLASS 1		CAS		
8.50–9.40	CLASS 2		CAS	CLASS 1	CLASS 3
9.40–10.30		CLASS 4	CAS	CLASS 2	DEPT MEETING
11.00–11.50	CLASS 3		CAS		
11.50–12.40			CAS	CLASS 3	CLASS 1
12.40–1.30	CLASS 4	CLASS 2	CAS	CLASS 4	
1.30–2.20			CAS	MENTOR – MENTEE	
3.00–4.30	CONSULTATION				

- teaching methods: discussion of classroom management or theories and videos of master teachers, e.g. cooperative learning
- the IB curriculum: brainstorming and discussing new ways to implement aspects of the DP followed by coordination of resulting strategies
- school issues: suggestions and ideas, problems faced by teachers, and ways to deal with those.

The in-house training ensures that we share a common vision and perception of our entire programme.

IB workshops and other IBO organized activities. The IB workshops give our subject teachers the confidence to teach and interpret the subject correctly in line with the latest developments. This confidence manifests itself not only in the classroom, but also in the much-appreciated expert academic advice given to students. In addition, the subject workshops provide an added incentive and motivation to our teachers, as they offer them an opportunity to meet face to face other teachers from around the region. All our teachers are required to go at least once every three to five years, and a visit never fails to inspire, enthuse and motivate. Within two weeks of their return from a subject workshop, teachers have to conduct a sharing session with the rest of the subject teachers. This is done to update other teachers who have yet to attend and those who have not attended for the past two years.

Senior staff are encouraged to attend conferences and other IBO organized activities, specifically observation of the curriculum development and examination process at the IB Curriculum and Assessment (IBCA) office in Cardiff, UK (the IBO advertises for such observers and pays for all expenses of the selected teachers).

5 Subject course notes

All subject teachers are required to produce and update a *subject handbook* containing the outline of the syllabus, a summary of each topic, worksheets, exercises, additional reading material from other sources that are difficult to obtain, samples of past-year questions, and references and reading lists for each topic. The worksheets and exercises can be easily detached and handed up to the teacher on request (Note: the book is lightly gummed and the pages can be easily torn off much as you'd tear off the pages of a set of forms. There are two holes punched in the centre of the bound edge so that students can keep their book in a file, secured with a metal/plastic clip). The handbooks serve as guides for the students. They do not preclude teachers from developing and trying their own materials. In fact, they are encouraged to do so, and successful materials can then be included in the updates.

The system of institutionalizing handbooks has the following additional benefits:

- It allows teachers to tailor-make what they need, as no single textbook may suit their requirements.
- It ensures that the senior staff share the materials they have compiled over the years with the junior and new teachers.
- It ensures that preparation of teaching materials, especially worksheets, is done well ahead of time. This reduces haphazard and last-minute preparations and orders for printing at the office.
- It reduces the cost of printing and ordering textbooks. We noticed that after we introduced the subject handbooks, printing expenses went down by more than half.
- It serves as a guide for the students, allows them to work in advance if they wish to do so, and allows them to make up for lessons they have missed.

We require departments to update the master copy every year and to make modifications if there are changes in the syllabus. The printing is outsourced and ready at the beginning of each academic year.

Usually the handbooks are designed for the two-year course but for chemistry and biology, for instance, they come in two parts.

6 Student-centred learning and welfare

Three months into the DP, students are organized into small groups of 4–6 students, which means that each class typically consists of five groups. These groups help each other with homework, and are the first point of contact should any problem arise; only in the rare event that the group does not manage does the school step in. The institution of these groups significantly reduces the workload of teachers. In addition, there is a peer teaching system, whereby the school pays the better students a fee to help their struggling peers.

6.1 Peer tutoring

At the end of each semester, when the results are out, the principal and the DPC identify the weak students in each subject, select peers at the top end to provide peer-group tutoring or coaching, and match the two parties. Teachers are only expected to provide a list of topics to cover, and a timeframe.

The peer tutor sets the date and place for his or her tutees; the college provides for the resources needed. At the end of the timeframe, the peer tutor gives a report to the principal who then monitors the students' performance in the next examination. Struggling students have the option of rejecting the help but our students understand the purpose of this exercise and all happily accept it. In fact, without the teacher, students are more willing to ask questions, no matter how trivial. We have also found that having to explain the subject to others gives the peer tutors an even better grasp of the subject.

6.2 Study groups

The central idea behind these groups is that students look after their own affairs and take full ownership of their learning and lives.

The study groups become the first point of contact for a teacher if there are any problems. Key teachers monitor the groups to see that no problems develop within a group, and problems are quickly resolved through reshuffling if necessary.

The principal, with the help of key teachers, establishes the study groups three months into the course. By this stage, students will have had the chance to get acquainted. We have found that the following opening procedure, which can be completed in under two hours, allows for a smooth introduction of the concept:

- The principal, together with one or two non-academic staff, invites all year 1 students, dressed in sports attire, to sit on the floor of the hall, and introduces the concept and value of study groups.
- Students are given a rather controversial statement and are asked to agree or disagree. Those who agree form one group and those who disagree, another. The statement is simply an excuse to provide quick initial bonding. Within each class, each set of opinion-holders forms smaller groups of 4–6. Students continue to discuss the statement within their groups for five minutes.
- Each student is given a list of personal (but not too intimate) questions. Students then interview each other in pairs using the questions on the list. Students then take turns to speak about the person they have interviewed and this is when bonding begins. They enjoy this phase and are always fully engrossed during the whole session. They find it easier and less embarrassing to speak about someone else other than themselves.
- Non-verbal signals for communication within and between groups are developed.
- Individual groups establish an operating culture, rules, and roles for each group member. As a group, students are responsible for solving their own problems, consulting with other groups and teachers, keeping an eye on each other's personal well-being. As an individual, each student is responsible for making an effort, making enquiries, helping, and extending courtesy to their team-mates, classmates, teachers and the wider community. The individual roles

are: checker (for understanding, agreement); encourager (praising effort, ideas, roles); recorder (of ideas and decisions); task master; gate keeper (ensuring bully- and loafer-free participation); gofer (obtains materials); reporter (shares with other teams, class, teacher). These roles are allocated during the initial meeting (although changes can be introduced within the group later).

- Groups agree on a schedule for regular meetings. They meet at least once a week or more if required because of work assigned, outside school hours or during weekends. They also meet on Wednesdays if their internal CAS is scheduled for that afternoon.
- Details are logged and passed on to all teachers.

Subject teachers are encouraged to channel group work and class discussions using these study groups rather than setting up new ones. Students are encouraged to use their groups to discuss academic work. If a student has an academic problem, the study group is the first line of enquiry, especially outside the class, in the residence halls.

Study groups allow the teacher to set more problems while reducing the marking workload. If teachers would normally give 10 problems to a class to practise a new concept, now they can give 20 problems with instructions to a study group. The group must work out the problems together and in the process help strugglers. The next day the teacher can pick at random the exercises from just one member as representative of the whole group. The whole group will then discuss to make sure they understand the mistakes they've made. This approach reduces the total marking workload of the teachers while at the same time doubling the number of exercises. With each class typically consisting of five groups, teachers need to mark only five sets from each class, allowing for detailed and high-quality feedback.

Likewise, study groups can be used to cover more topics than otherwise would be possible: teachers can assign each group a topic to be researched and presented in class.

Students like the system, as it gives them a sense of ownership of their learning. The group widens their view of how others think about the same problems or issues and it provides them with a platform to test their ideas and articulate them. On the personal front, it presents an excellent opportunity to learn how to get along with other people and to function as a team player. In short, the study groups provide the students with enhanced academic and emotional confidence. As a result, students acquire those social skills essential for their future as adults in the working world.

7 Academic and pastoral support for students

This comes in the form of bi-monthly one-on-one consultations, enrichment classes after regular school time, and the IRP.

7.1 One-on-one consultations

All subject teachers are required to stay back in the afternoon at least once or twice a week for consultation with their students. They can do this either individually or on a study group basis. Students can see their own subject teacher or any other teacher who teaches the same subject. Teachers are expected to keep a log of the students they see and should, as a matter of habit, see each student at least twice a month either briefly or for a period of time depending on the student's needs. The log is simple and comprises the number of students seen and a summary of the meeting. If there are problematic students, more details are recorded. Teachers see the benefit of these consultations and have accepted them as part of their core business.

7.2 Enrichment and revision classes

These are scheduled by the subject teachers for the weaker students. The scheduling for enrichment classes is done at the end of each semester on the directive of the principal if the performance in any subject is not satisfactory. Teachers are also encouraged to schedule classes themselves if they feel the students are not coping.

7.3 The intensive revision programme

The intensive revision programme (IRP) is based on the premise that it takes two years to teach the syllabus but the examination for each subject lasts only a few hours, so students need systems and methods to prepare for the final examinations. The IRP was gradually developed by myself over a period of 18 years, first as a subject teacher and then as a principal in a number of schools; it was first introduced at the MCB in 1996, and we continue to develop it further. The IRP focuses on developing skills in: summarizing and note-taking; presentation; explanation and recall; and examination techniques. The programme has had a significant impact and reduces the spread of scores by creating a multiplier effect of 6s and 7s. Teacher-training is provided on how to implement the programme.

Summarizing and note-taking (continuous phase of IRP)

Each department prepares a master sheet detailing the different topics of the course. Subject teachers then assign specific topics to each study group, directing it to prepare *notes* on the topic meant for distribution to other groups. Groups receive a guide so as to ensure that their notes will be consistent across all topics and subjects, i.e. abbreviations, paper size and referencing are standardized and a maximum of six pages for notes is imposed. The groups are given a quite extended timeframe outside school time in which to complete the notes. On the appointed date, the subject teacher vets the notes, makes comments and gives feedback. When the notes are approved, the group is responsible for making copies for all other groups. In the process the individual groups become experts on their topic and as such are a reference point for other groups who struggle with the topic. So this phase not only develops note-taking and communication skills but also emphasizes the social responsibilities that each group has for the community as a whole.

Part 2 of the IRP, an intensive examination preparation scheduled by the DPC, usually starts four to five weeks before the final examination. All teachers are required to have finished teaching the syllabus beforehand. All resources at this stage are geared towards helping the students prepare for the final examination – even the food menu for the four to five weeks is redesigned – and teachers prepare all the material needed. Part 2 of the IRP consists of the following sequence of events.

Presentations

Presentations are usually done over four days about five weeks before the final examination. Each subject has a time slot; for example, physics on Monday between 8 am and 12.30 pm. *All* students taking the subject are present as well as the teachers teaching it. For each topic, the assigned group come forward, distribute their notes and are given 10 minutes to speak and answer questions. By 12.30 pm, all students will have seen all topics (around 20 for physics) and have received a complete set of notes for all topics. Since students know that getting these notes is very important, they remain motivated throughout.

The public presentation forces groups to be accountable for their research and produces quality revision notes. Knowing that they will be held accountable by the whole community motivates even the most reticent groups to do their best. Moreover, we find that each group takes natural pride in their work for the whole community.

All subjects get the same timeframe, except language B, as it is skills-based not content-based. In order to revise English, students do past papers as homework in groups. For text handling questions (Paper 1), students answer the questions within the time limit of each paper – they have to be honest about this – and discuss their answers with their teachers during the IRP slots. To revise text productions (Paper 2) they produce texts using input from all members of the group. These are also discussed during IRP slots.

Explanation and recall

This phase lasts uninterrupted for about two weeks. It entails a technique that enables each group to cover an entire subject in just 2–3 hours. That is achieved by giving each topic 5 minutes' *explanation* and 2 minutes of *recall*, i.e. 7 minutes per topic.

Each group is given 20–30 pieces of very large sheets of paper (one for each topic) and group members bring their own colour marker-pens to facilitate monitoring by the teachers.

The process begins with a group member reading and explaining topic 1 of, say, physics. Other members listen. When the 5 minutes are up, each student finds a section on the communal paper to write down as much as they can recall. Students often try to outdo each other in a friendly manner. When the 2 minutes are up, the next group member reads topic 2 and the process is repeated. If physics has 20 topics, it will take 20 × 7 minutes, i.e. about two and a half hours to complete one round. The next cycle for physics takes place over the next two or three days. The same duration of time is allocated and the students use the same big sheets of paper – this time merely adding what they left out during the first session. More paper might have to be used as the cycle is repeated. The cycle is repeated five or six times depending on how many members there are in each group so as to allow each member to read each topic once.

The explanation and recall process capitalizes on a natural learning process – repetition. It further enhances note-taking skills, and as an important by-product it develops students' ability to concentrate and work for 2–3 hours at a time, as is also required in a number of examinations.

Examination techniques

The last few weeks of the intensive Part 2 IRP are then dedicated to:

- past-year papers (study group based)
- examination simulation (mock examinations on an individual student basis)
- discussion of answers to past-year papers with answer guides provided by teachers (subject group based at a common venue for students taking the subject).

8 Institution of routines (protocols)

The MCB has instituted daily, weekly, monthly and semesterly routines, providing certainty, stability and a sense of continuity.

Staff meetings are scheduled at the beginning, middle and end of each semester. The principal, assistant principal and DPC are responsible for these sessions and the information to be disseminated. These sessions help to ensure that everyone knows what the others are doing and serve to keep rumours and assumptions to the minimum.

Daily routines
- Update the *master teaching plan*. This lesson plan is prepared by the whole subject department and contains the teaching materials, strategies to use, objectives, intended outcomes and evaluations. At the beginning of the year, the teacher will have the master plan for each topic. The daily updates then are: noting the amount of time taken to teach a topic, what worked and what did not, and adding new materials, if any.
- Check class attendance.

Weekly routines
- Consultation hours with individual students or groups – need to see each student at least twice a month.
- Conduct enrichment classes.
- Update the master teaching plan. This is mainly concerned with the distribution and sharing of newly added teaching materials, if there are any.
- Update the subject handbook if new materials have been tried and are confirmed.
- Department meetings (heads of department, subject coordinators, teachers).

Monthly routines
- Update records to ensure students have seen the teacher at least twice a month.
- Collect and check the topic notes prepared by assigned groups (see section 7.3, 'Summarizing and note-taking').
- Department academic meeting conducted by subject coordinators (heads of department, subject coordinators).

Semester routines

- Prepare material for the IRP.
- Prepare and mark semester examination papers.
- Prepare students' academic reports.
- Keep records of problem students and incidents, if any (a checklist is given).

A daily schedule for the academic year and the academic calendar are given at the beginning of each year.

Chapter 8
The Diploma Programme in North America

Jeremy Craig, BA, MA
Luke Lawson, MA, MEd

Luke Lawson was responsible for the introduction of the International Baccalaureate (IB) Diploma Programme (DP) at Halifax Grammar School, Nova Scotia, Canada, where, from 1993 to 2002, he was the DP coordinator (DPC) and for three years CAS coordinator. An experienced teacher of DP economics, he has also been an IBO economics examiner, participated in DP authorization visits, led IB North America (IBNA) teacher-training workshops, and attended various IB conferences in North America. Currently, Luke is the director of academics and university counsellor at Mulgrave School in Vancouver, which is in the early stage of introducing the DP. The editors of this book asked him to describe the DP in Canada, the country with the highest per capita participation in the IB DP.

Jeremy Craig gained his BA (East Asian Languages and Cultures) and MA (International Affairs) from Columbia University. He established an educational consulting company in Singapore and works as a consultant to US schools looking to increase their enrolment from South East Asia. The editors asked him to illustrate the US landscape for the benefit of our non-American readers, and to conduct a survey of the IB experience in the USA for the benefit of our US readership.

Jeremy Craig wishes to thank Lorrie Byrom, Northfield Mount Hermon School and James Dunaway, Kincaid School for input and guidance. A special thanks to George Burson at the Aspen High School for his kind assistance with the case study. The editor wishes to thank Suzanne Geimer, DPC George Washington High School, Denver, for helpful comments on the final draft of this chapter.

1 Introduction

North America has the largest number of IB diploma candidates worldwide, both in absolute and relative terms: more than 50% of all DP schools and students worldwide are from the region; Canada and the USA have the highest national uptake of the DP with about 3% and 1% respectively of their national high school cohorts sitting DP examinations, compared with about 0.25% in the next runner-up, the UK (figures based on the IBO *Statistical Bulletin* 2002). In response, the IBO has increased its staff levels serving the North America region. There are now six authorized teacher-training locations in New York, Georgia, Florida, New Mexico, California and Ontario, Canada while a new branches were recently opened in Vancouver, Washington DC and Texas.

North America also illustrates very clearly the inclusiveness of the IB: it leads the way in terms of school variety, from affluent private schools to poor inner-city schools where many students only sit IB certificates (meaning they take a number of subjects but often do not take the full diploma). Despite this enormous variety, pass rates are on a par with those of the rest of the world: about 80% of all diploma takers receive a diploma, comparable to 85% in the European zone and 90% in the Asian zone (figures again based on the IBO *Statistical Bulletin* 2002).

2 The US educational landscape

For the benefit of the reader who is not familiar with the US educational landscape, in this section we provide a quick overview.

2.1 Schools

Schools in the USA are of three types: *public* and *charter* (state funded), *private* and *parochial*, the last of which are normally supported by a combination of tuition fees and church funds. Since the curricula of parochial schools are sometimes incompatible with the IB curriculum, we restrict ourselves here to describing the private and public schools in greater detail.

Private schools

Private schools are schools fully funded by private money, either from sponsors or through tuition fees. Unlike private schools in most other countries, they are not bound by any governmental curriculum rules and can offer programmes and set entry criteria as they see fit although they still have to obtain a license. The top private schools are highly selective in their admissions and often act as 'feeders' to the top universities. They pride themselves on academic rigour, and the individuality of their programmes is steeped in history. They will typically offer a whole array of *Advanced Placement* courses, better known as APs, which, as the name suggests, offer direct credit towards university courses (see section 2.3). The established top private schools have naturally little to gain by adopting the IB as their profile is defined by their individual tradition. They may be inspired by certain aspects of the DP curriculum that they like, such as parts of the TOK, but will prefer to design their own courses rather than adopt existing ones. Interest in the IB by private schools is mainly expressed by the more newly established private schools that seek to establish immediate academic credibility or those that cater largely to international students. Broadly speaking, private schools seek to establish a clear identity, so when they adopt the IB it is typically for the majority of their students rather than as an 'honors program' for a chosen few, as is often the case with public schools.

Public schools

Public schools are state-funded schools, but unlike in most other nations, the funding and management are a local exercise at the state or municipal level, with no direct supervisory or financial involvement from the federal government in Washington. In most cases, the individual states' boards of education will set rough parameters of what topics need to be covered but then it is up to the local school boards at the municipal level to implement curricula and raise and allocate funding. All states have state-wide tests at the end of certain grades, but others leave it to the municipal boards to decide what constitutes satisfactory performance and who is eligible to earn a high school diploma.

Funding of public schools in some states is almost entirely from taxes levied at the local level, mainly from property tax. The result is that the more affluent towns have truly first-rate public schools thanks to a larger tax per household, while inner-city schools normally are chronically under-funded. Many families will move to a particular neighbourhood or town primarily because of the better schools there and then move to another place after their children have finished school to avoid paying the higher property taxes. Some states are moving towards a more progressive and socialist approach, with the public education funds being pooled centrally for the entire state and then disbursed in even allotments on a per-head basis to the municipal school boards. However, this is an exception to the rule and it is doubtful if this trend will continue beyond the most liberal states in the west and north-east.

A typical public high school diploma focuses on teaching the three 'Rs' (Reading, wRiting and aRithmetic); a highly content-driven curriculum leaving little room for individual expression on the part of the student. A school can decide whether it offers additional APs or the IB DP as either an honors program or a replacement programme.

2.2 Colleges and universities

In the US context, the terms *college* and *university* tend to be used interchangeably. Both colleges and universities teach similar programmes until the Bachelors level, but colleges typically stop at the Bachelors while universities also offer Masters degrees and post-doctorates. However, some of the colleges deliver highly prized Bachelors programmes, while the standards at some universities can be very low.

2.3 Advanced Placement

There are 23 Advanced Placement (AP) subjects available across the academic spectrum, examinations for which are administered on a nationwide scale by the College Board (the same board that also does the SAT tests). The AP courses are very much like typical first-year university courses and therefore often allow those who score highly to gain advanced credit and/or academic standing upon entry to college. (The same is true for IB subjects taken at HL.) However, the more selective tertiary institutions give less or sometimes even no credit for APs. A decade or so ago, able students would take one or two APs in addition to their high school certificates, but competition has driven schools to start teaching APs from the age of 16, and some students now finish high school with 10 or more APs. Similar to the IB DP, the AP system is valued because it has proved fairly immune to grade inflation, something that cannot be said of average school grades (the College Board's statistics show a clear decrease over the years in the SAT scores of students reporting an A average). Compared with the DP, the AP is much easier to implement – all it takes is time to fill out a form or two. The AP system, however, is more test-driven – there is no coursework, just a final exam and students could theoretically not even attend class – and it has a narrower focus, concentrating on academic rather than 'whole person' education (although this is changing).

3 The IB in the USA

Despite the relatively high uptake of the DP in the USA, the level of public awareness of it is rather low. National media interest is a far cry from what it is in the UK, for example, although things may change. *Newsweek*'s 26 May 2002 cover article 'The 100 Best High Schools in America' promotes AP and IB in one breath as tools to encourage educational excellence across the USA and to energize inner-city schools in particular. IBNA (the IBO North America regional office in New York) in turn has made great efforts to upgrade its regional page on the IBO website to share more information about the IBO as well as the activities of IB schools in the region.

American universities welcome IB diploma holders, and many award advanced credit and placement to students who achieve a 4, 5, 6 or 7 grade (out of a maximum of 7) for Higher Level (HL) subjects. The actual amount of credits awarded will vary among universities, with the more prestigious universities awarding fewer, if any, exemptions. American universities increasingly welcome IB applicants; many middle-ranking colleges have even gone so far as to have special scholarships available for IB students who obtain a certain IB score.

American schools generally recognize that the DP subjects are graded much more stringently, leading some schools to add an 'IB premium' (and, similarly, an 'AP premium') in their Grade Point Average (GPA) conversion of the DP grades. These premiums range from 0.2 to sometimes as high as 0.6 and can lead to technically impossible GPAs of 4.5 or higher.

As the *Newsweek* article indicated, the DP is often regarded as a European version of the AP. Timetabling the DP alongside existing AP programmes is often much less of a struggle than it is in other countries. Some AP schools introducing the DP will retrain the AP teachers in the DP and then slowly drop the AP subjects over the course of a year or two, replacing them with the DP classes – available either as the holistic diploma or as certificate subjects. This is especially true for smaller schools. Most schools running both programmes, however, continue to support both. Suzanne Geimer, DPC George Washington High School, Denver, reports that:

> Our school ran APs when we started the DP, and we have actually *added* AP courses as a result of DP students 'dropping down' from IB to AP. Many US schools encourage students to take both exams, even when they sit the DP classes. One reason for this is that schools get compensation for having students sit both exams. Another is that students may get more college credit this way, especially since Standard Level (SL) subjects are not always recognized by the receiving college (unlike APs). Many US high schools combine the AP and DP courses and teach them with a mix of both syllabi. When schools compare the DP with the AP, they find on the downside that the DP is more expensive than the AP. On the upside, they report that students taking the DP are frequently more committed to sitting the examinations since they have to follow classes, unlike with the AP where they can in principle just turn up for the exam (although this would cost them the arguably more important grade for the subject awarded by the school).

3.1 Why schools adopt the IB

Given the wide variety of schools in the USA at the secondary level, there is a wide variety in rationale and motivation for adopting the IB. Most of the IB schools are public schools, some of which are in affluent areas with the money and resources to try for IB adoption. One motivation behind adopting the IB is to help retain top students who might otherwise opt for private or parochial day schools in the area. Failing schoools can also be motivated to take up the IB in order to turn the school around; others may be seeking to attract a racial balance to the school. Another motivation is to make the region more attractive towards foreign investment by foreign companies. The usual reasons apply, such as attempting to attract an international clientele or gaining educational prestige and recognition. Inner-city schools like the IB because the DP curriculum – as opposed to the 'three Rs' high school curriculum – allows their culturally diverse students to analyse and express their own perceptions against those in the wider world. Says Brad Richardson, IBNA's director, in *IB World* (May 2003):

> Many schools now report that as many as 30 or more first languages are spoken at the home of their students. The public classrooms have become a cross current of cultural, linguistic, socio-economic and academic perspectives.

The feeling amongst schools that have adopted the IB, even if only in part, is that the IB diploma lifts the educational process even for those not enrolled in the programme. As the principal of Aspen High School, a recently authorized school featured in the case study in section 5, says: 'A rising tide raises all of the boats.' Nevertheless, the relatively low national awareness of the IB means that schools that wish to adopt the IB will generally have even more explaining to do to their communities than schools elsewhere in the world.

A severe challenge facing the DP in public high schools is salary constraints. Suzanne Geimer again:

Teacher salaries in the USA and Canada are negotiated by professional representation (sometimes unions) and are not dictated by programme adoption. In fact, most districts ask the question, 'How can I implement the DP without spending any extra?' As a rule, therefore, DP teachers are not given extra compensation for teaching IB classes and must consider teaching IB students a reward in itself. Public high schools thus face the challenge of getting teachers to work harder than their colleagues without being able to offer financial incentives.

4 The IB in Canada

Despite its relatively small population of 31 million, Canada has the second highest number of IB schools in the world and, as noted in the introduction, the highest per capita participation in the IB. There is no one single reason for the IB's popularity, but rather a variety of factors. While the IB enjoyed considerable growth in Canada throughout the 1980s and most of the 1990s, that growth has now slowed down.

4.1 The education system

The first important fact to point out is that, unlike in most other countries, there is no national system of education in Canada – in fact, there is no federal department of education. The original British North America Act of 1867 (now called the Canada Act of 1982) clearly states in section 93: 'In and for each province the Legislature may exclusively make laws in relation to education …'. This means that each of the current ten provincial legislatures has exclusive control over the education of its citizens. An outsider today would view this as somewhat bizarre and very confusing. Indeed it is. A person who moves from one province to another – say, Nova Scotia to British Columbia – would have to learn an entirely new system of provincial standards, curricula and methods. Some provinces, like British Columbia, have provincial examinations but most don't. Confusion and inconsistency are always apparent. For Canadian universities the admission process is very complex, as it must focus on ten educational jurisdictions and treat each one separately. It is in this light that the IB offers a considerable degree of continuity, predictability and an international standard of excellence which many parents, teachers, students and universities like. Many Canadian universities are now offering superb IB DP recognition policies.

The second important fact points to the notion that there is no 'typical' IB school in Canada. The vast geographical, cultural, political and religious diversities of this country make any attempt at painting the IB with a single stroke almost impossible. While the IB can be found mostly in public schools – some large, some small – some are Catholic, some are specific magnet schools while others are regular public high schools wanting to offer an alternative programme. The IB is also in place at some of the top private schools including the prestigious Upper Canada College in Toronto (now the largest IB school in the world on the basis of the number of examinations written), Strathcona-Tweedsmuir, just outside Calgary in Alberta, and the Halifax Grammar School in Halifax, Nova Scotia.

4.2 Why schools offer the DP

The motivation to offer the DP is also varied. Quite often the initiative comes from groups of parents, perhaps partly out of the frustration in the face of a myriad education systems, and the need (demand?) for a more standardized and challenging system. Some of these parents have been exposed to the IB, either in another part of Canada or somewhere else in the world. School boards tend to be enthusiastic about adopting the IB as this is expected to attract students and generate (hopefully) positive publicity. It is also worth noting that when asked the question, 'Why do you want the IB?' during the site authorization visits, the students' initial responses centred on the academic challenges, the internationalism and learning processes. When parents respond to the same question, their initial responses are usually 'It will help my child to get into university.' Students (at least in grades 8 and 9) and parents actually have differing views on why the school should have IB. Students focus more on the aesthetic and intrinsic value, parents more on the extrinsic and business value.

4.3 Different curricula

A big problem facing many schools is the interplay between the DP curriculum and that of the provincial curriculum. Some provinces, like British Columbia, actually recognize most IB subjects as provincial equivalents of their own. Notwithstanding some flexibility by some provincial governments, the overlap between the two curricula is sometimes quite minimal and hence very frustrating for teachers, students and parents. Another problem in recent years has been the very weak Canadian dollar, which has made it difficult for many public and some private schools to fund the DP. Coupled with government cutbacks and budget deficits in many public school boards, the IB has been close to extinction. Quite often the general public perceive the IB as an elitist programme and believe that only parents from the higher socio-economic segments support it. Because the latter group, according to the general public, generally has the means to pay for the costs, the feeling is that they should pay for the fees and that any IB-allocated money should be freed for special needs education and other urgent matters. As a result of this, in the near future the IB in some public schools will become a user-pay system. The AP (identical to that in the USA) is also becoming quite popular for some schools as it is easy to apply (a simple form is all that is required), it is somewhat cheaper, and it is easy to implement (one merely teaches to the examination since there is no internal assessment).

4.4 University recognition

University recognition at Canadian universities is varied. Thanks to the tremendous efforts at the IBNA offices in New York and Vancouver, many post-secondary institutions accept the DP on its own terms for admission – thus bypassing the schools' nightmare of somehow having to integrate the provincial curriculum and IB curriculum. When an IB student applies to practically any Canadian university (typically between December and February of the year of the student's graduation), the high school university counsellor will also send a list of all the DP courses taken or in progress along with the actual and/or anticipated grades. These anticipated grades are similar to the official predicted grades sent to the IBO by the schools in April. Most IB schools will place these scores either on their transcripts or on a separate page. Universities will then consider admission (and scholarships for that matter) based on the total score of these grades. Most universities will grant admission (as long as the prerequisites for a particular faculty are satisfied) with a minimum score of 24 to 28 points. For example, the University of British Columbia in Vancouver will give an unconditional letter of early admission acceptance with a total anticipated score of 32 (this includes Diploma Points). A total anticipated score of 35 or a final diploma score of 32 (including Diploma Points) will in addition secure a USP (undergraduate scholar programme) of CAN $2,500 per annum (a figure currently under review). The University of Calgary has recently announced a new DP recognition policy and many of the top universities in Ontario including Queen's, the University of Guelph and the University of Toronto will give credit/standing and scholarships based on anticipated scores. For many DP students applying to Canadian universities, all that is required to apply is an application and an IB anticipated grades form.

IB growth has slowed down in Canada – mostly for the reasons cited above. However, as parents become more demanding of the type of education that is offered, the IB in Canada may experience another surge. The growth of private and independent schools has exploded over the last few years and it is difficult to predict how many of these schools will seek the IB.

5 US case study: Aspen High School

Aspen High School is located in the picturesque Colorado ski-resort town of Aspen in the Rocky Mountains. The school is public and was established in 1886. It presently has an enrolment of 485, which makes it one of the smallest public high schools in the USA. As it is a resort town, the students' parents range from working-class to very wealthy, with a high degree of economic diversity. Located in an affluent region, the school enjoys public funding that is higher than average. About 10% of the students are in the school's ESL (English as a second language) programme. Prior to starting the IB diploma in the 2002–03 school year, it was an AP school (also offering the 'standard' American high school curriculum). About 80% of the students went on to higher education.

The school board first started to consider the DP in 1998 and then ordered the superintendent (who is responsible for all public schools in the school district) and the high school principal to take the necessary steps to implement the programme. The motivation behind the decision to move towards authorization was to increase the academic achievement of the school's students by providing the opportunity for them to earn the highly regarded IB diploma. It was known that not all of the students would be able to take up the programme but the expectation was that DP authorization would benefit the entire school. The internal timeline for expected approval at that time was towards the end of 2000.

5.1 Steps to authorization

The first step was to send the superintendent and principal to an IBNA heads of school workshop. After this, the principal held meetings with the faculty to inform them about the programme. Eight teachers were selected to visit an IB DP school about 300 km away and then the superintendent, principal and five teachers went to the 1999 IBNA Conference in Québec, Canada. The goals of these activities were to educate the faculty about the intricacies of the programme as well as to get the teachers excited about becoming an IB school. At the same time, the school worked with the middle school in the district to enable students in grades 7 and 8 to start taking algebra in grade 8 and foreign language in grade 7, to ensure that they would be prepared when authorization came through.

The principal invited teachers to apply for the post of DP coordinator (DPC). The early selection of a coordinator proved vital in communicating the programme effectively to other teachers, students, parents and the community at large. The coordinator was well respected in the community due to his long teaching experience and thus had the moral authority to convey the benefits of the IB versus the existing system. After attending a DPC introductory seminar organized by IBNA, the coordinator held numerous meetings with parents and prospective IB students. Additionally, the local media were employed to educate the community about the advantages of the programme, while memos and meetings helped to keep the faculty up to speed on developments and further familiarize them with the programme. We would like to stress the benefits of sending all of the prospective IB teachers to workshops, otherwise the non-trained teachers may feel overwhelmed during the application process, and they may believe that some teachers are favoured over others. Equal training also takes away the excuse that 'I couldn't do it because I wasn't adequately trained'.

During this time, the school contacted IBNA to ask for the application guidelines. There was intermittent contact with IBNA to clarify certain points, but the only visit by the IBO was the final authorization visit in November 2000. The IBO was very helpful when they were called upon and the teacher-training was excellent.

The biggest challenge in the application process was ensuring that all of the future teachers received sufficient training at the IBO seminars to enable them to transform their existing curricula to IB standards. To ensure that work was completed on time, the teachers were relieved from teaching for a day to participate in collaborative work on the curriculum. The authorization process itself was a very helpful exercise in self-assessment and was generally very constructive. It enabled all parts of the school (faculty, administration and school board) to fully understand the requirements of the programme. The final authorization team from IBNA was described as 'helpful, knowledgeable, friendly, and professional'. All in all the process involved in the application and final authorization was 'a good experience'.

After the November 2000 authorization visit, the school heard back from IBNA before the end of the school year (May 2001) that it was accepted as an IB school, with the authority to start IB classes in the 2002–03 school year.

5.2 Moving forward

The reaction among all parties has been excellent following the commencement of the programme and has actually had the happy result of an increase in enrolment, with growth to 500 students forecast for 2003–04 (from 400 when the school started the IB). Students in Colorado can choose to go to a school in a neighbouring district, and some students are using this freedom to choose Aspen High School over their closer options. The existing AP programme was dropped and students have the opportunity to take IB subjects for certificate credit. At present, over 50% of eligible students take at least one IB class. In the first year, 14% of the students in grade 11 started the DP, with 23% forecast for 2003–04.

There were several initial concerns that the school had to overcome.

- Teachers of the 'special' students (ESL, reading support, special education) worried that the 'trickle-down' effect of academic rigour would penalize their students with lower grades. This fear was not realized because classroom teachers understood the needs of these students and adjusted their grades accordingly. Worries that the cost of the IB would result in funding cuts for the special programmes were also quickly allayed.
- Another important issue was one of control. Who was going to implement the programme: the DPC and the teachers, or a small group of active parents (who wanted control)? Over the school year, as the programme was implemented successfully, parents came to recognize the professionalism of the staff, and there is now almost total trust in the school's implementation of the IB programme. This issue emphasizes the importance of training for teachers, as well as having a DPC who has a firm grasp of the philosophy and rules of the IB – knowledge and confidence are the best defence in control conflicts like this.
- Finally, to address concerns raised by students and parents regarding the impact of the IB subjects on students' GPAs, the school added an 'IB premium' of 0.2 to the grade (refer to section 1).

The DPC continues to meet with middle-school students and parents to describe the programme to them and to allow them the option of enrolling in the necessary pre-IB classes. The school counsellors and the DPC also meet regularly with students in grades 9 and 10. Every month an 'IB Coordinator's Newsletter' goes out to all high school parents. It is fully expected that the percentage as well as the total student number will continue to increase. All new teachers continue to be sent to IB teacher-training workshops and the new curriculum subject conferences which are held every five years.

The academic standards of the school district as a whole have increased thanks to the IB. Particularly notable is the number of students who are now able to think in the abstract. The single best thing about the programme for the school is its integrated nature, in particular the fact that the IB core components (CAS, extended essay and TOK) are so well married with a rigorous programme in the more traditional subjects. The one drawback present throughout the entire process was the cost, in terms of not only per student fees but also the added cost of teacher-training and travel.

Part Three
The Diploma Programme

Chapter 9
CAS: creativity, action and service

Mark McCallum, MEd, MBA, BA

Mark McCallum is CAS coordinator, Dean of Students, and Director of Corporate Relations at the International School Singapore (ISS), a recently authorized Diploma Programme (DP) school. He is credited with setting up, from scratch, one of this region's most acclaimed CAS programmes. Mark leads CAS workshops for the International Baccalaureate Organization (IBO) in the Asia-Pacific region.

CAS is one of the three core components of the IB DP that give the programme its heart and soul. In this chapter, Mark explains what CAS is, what it is not, and how to make it a success from the point of view of a CAS coordinator, a teacher and a student. The chapter also includes tips for seasoned practitioners and features two case studies contrasting two different approaches to CAS.

The author wishes to thank Ellie Alchin for major contributions to this chapter including the case studies in section 7. Special thanks also to Luke Lawson and Louise Favaro for their valuable input.

Note: all weblinks featured in this chapter can be accessed through our website: www.dp-help.com

1 Introduction

This chapter should help new CAS coordinators to get up and running as quickly as possible, while providing fresh insights and examples of best practice for seasoned practitioners. It supplements the IBO section E3 of the *Vade Mecum* and the IBO Creativity, Action and Service Guide (2001).

Clearly, schools will have to modify some suggestions to fit individual circumstances. One school may have vast financial resources, an established culture of staff support for sponsoring activities and a comprehensive activities programme. At the other end of the scale, a school could be starting a CAS programme with limited financial resources, in a politically volatile country and with no history of staff support for extra-curricular activities. School culture and environment also play their part. A large school in Tanzania and a small remote boarding school in New England will offer very different CAS activities. Ultimately, the style of programme adopted will depend on the cultural, contractual and practical contexts of the school environment. The IBO's compulsory workshops for CAS coordinators provide insight into the variety and practices of CAS programmes around the world. This chapter condenses the main generic insights and includes two case studies to illustrate actual CAS practices.

As a new CAS coordinator, it is important to realize that although the IBO CAS guidelines attempt to lay down specific regulations in black and white, there are bound to be grey areas. When in doubt, apply common sense. If you can justify your reasoning, you should be fine.

1.1 What is CAS?

The letters CAS form the acronym commonly used for the DP component 'creativity, action and service'. It is a non-examined component of the DP which emphasizes experiential learning. Over the full two-year programme all students must engage in activities outside the classroom, at least 50 hours in each of the three components: creativity, action and service. To give the students the opportunity to reflect, improve and develop over time, the activities must be spread regularly over the two years, amounting to approximately three to four hours per week according to the calculator, or half a day a week according to the CAS spirit. Typically therefore, one-off activities such as a weekend ski trip do not qualify as CAS (although a weekend clean-up of a pollution-threatened wetlands environment is well within the spirit of CAS). The three CAS components are not mutually exclusive; in fact it is fully within the spirit of CAS if an activity encompasses two or all three components, and the IBO actively encourages this. For example, students tutoring in a children's home for their service hours could also run basketball camps and log these hours wholly or in part as action or service hours, thus providing welcome 'CAS book-keeping' flexibility. However, hours can only be counted once, so the hours spent running basketball camps must eventually be logged as either action or service or split between the two.

Students must document their programme in a *CAS diary* (sometimes called the *CAS journal*), and hand it in to the CAS coordinator at the end of the diploma course. The primary objective of this document is to make the CAS programme a *reflective* process, and not merely a record of hours clocked – a very important distinction. Students must understand that CAS is the spirit of the IB diploma. It is about taking risks, exploring, challenging oneself, and personal development, and the diary must contain evidence of this. As spelled out in detail below (see sections 1.5 and 4), the diaries allow CAS coordinators to evaluate individual students, and the IBO to evaluate the school's CAS programme.

Creativity

Activities suitable for creativity are ideally imaginative and inspiring and can cover active participation in a wide range of artistic endeavours. Creative activities include dance, drama, theatre, music, painting, animation, school radio, video production, web design, pottery, cookery, calligraphy, dance choreography, debate, model United Nations, learning a new language, writing articles for a magazine or preparing posters to advertise upcoming charities. Note that any creative activity done for CAS must be separate from ordinary curriculum work, so it is not possible to claim work done in an IB arts class as a CAS activity.

Action

Action activities can involve team sports, individual sports, expeditions, camping trips, or participation in activities requiring physical exertion. Examples are martial arts, tennis, weightlifting, gymnastics, cross-country skiing and dance. Students can learn to participate, to perform and to instruct. Development assistance such as constructing homes for the poor with 'Habitat for Humanity' or digging water wells for a rural village in a developing country can count as action or as service.

Service

Service activities are predominantly defined as service to the *disadvantaged*, but a service to the school community at large and service in environmental projects are also considered appropriate. Service activities include working with the elderly, tutoring orphan children, writing letters for Amnesty International, working towards a school concert, constructing scenery for school drama performances, participating in a beach clean-up project or coaching a football team at a local community service centre. Where possible, service activities should focus on doing things *with* others, not just *for* others, and should focus on developing real ties of commitment to others. Service can also be carried out overseas; for example, participating in a group that is building a school in India.

Service activities are often the most resisted by students, but are equally often the most transformational. It should be noted that fund-raising *per se* is not considered to be a satisfactory service activity in itself. It should be clearly structured as a means to achieve a further aim, such as buying building materials for a local project or funding a part of the cost of an overseas service venture.

In general, for an activity to be considered appropriate for CAS, it should adhere to the spirit of the philosophy of CAS, captured in the following list of IBO guidelines:

- CAS activities should provide new roles for students. They should not be a continuation of an activity commenced long before the DP.

- CAS activities must be *meaningful* in some way, and not be artificially created for CAS or have no external purpose. For example, learning from watching television does not involve the student with others. On the other hand, making a short video does.
- CAS should have *consequences* for the student and for others. Visiting a museum does not have a real impact on others, but organizing a museum visit for a local youth home can have a significant effect on the children.
- Where directed at other people, the activity should bring real *benefits* to them.
- Students should have the opportunity to learn through the activity; everything that is done in CAS should be allied to experiential learning.
- CAS should offer the opportunity for reflection. This is absolutely essential. While a major feature of a student's CAS programme will be regular and consistent participation in the chosen activities, it is only through serious reflection that students can improve and learn from their experiences.

In contrast, *inappropriate* CAS activities include:

- paid work
- academic curriculum activities
- mindlessly repetitive activities offering no opportunities for learning or improvement
- community service activities aimed at people who are not disadvantaged (this is a somewhat grey area, but walking your elderly neighbour's dog could be considered appropriate if the neighbour was physically infirm)
- service within the family – filial duties are not CAS
- activities that are primarily religious in nature – see section 1.4 for details.

My favourite example of 'what CAS is not' comes from a student who spent two years supposedly helping disabled children ride horses for recreational and therapeutic reasons. As it turned out, he completely ignored the disabled children and worked only with the horses. In his video journal in answer to the question, 'What did you like most about the activity?' he replied, 'I liked walking the horses'. He completely missed the point.

The IBO guidelines above naturally leave some room for interpretation. For example, on the surface stacking books in the library seems a mindless activity (and indeed the IBO lists it as a poor activity choice). However, training in the cataloguing system and learning the Dewey decimal system could be of value to the student and the library. In view of the inevitable degree of subjective interpretation of the guidelines, I would recommend that coordinators communicate with the regional IB office to get a clear sense of what the office considers appropriate.

It is helpful to put the guidelines in question form on a form like the one in figure 9.1, so that students can check themselves before they start an activity, and so that the coordinator has an additional tracking tool.

1.2 What is the purpose of CAS?

Having described how to recognize *what* makes a CAS activity, we now turn to the somewhat less tangible but arguably more important issue of *why* we do CAS.

CAS is at the heart of the DP and sets it apart from other educational programmes. When properly implemented, the CAS programme should provide

Figure 9.1 Form for CAS activity authorization

CAS activity authorization worksheet (for students to complete)

Activity title: _____

This activity is **creativity**, **action** and/or **service** (delete as appropriate).

I will spend ____ hours on this activity per week during the next two years. I will gain approximately ____ hours on this main activity in total over two years. I realize the total for each of the creativity, action and service components must be at least 50 hours.

The Activity Supervisor is: _____
My Activity Supervisor may be contacted by email: _____
or at phone number: _____
My Activity Supervisor has agreed to be my supervisor for this activity. Yes ☐ No ☐

Detailed description of my activity (who, what, when, why, how)

Answer the following questions:
1. The activity is a new role / activity for me because:

2. The activity is meaningful for me because:

3. The activity has real consequences for me because:

4. I hope to learn:

5. What can I reflect on during this activity?

6. This activity benefits other people because:

My CAS coordinator has agreed that this is an appropriate CAS activity: Yes ☐ No ☐

---

the spirit and drive for the entire DP. The case study in Chapter 7 provides a radical example: Mara College Banting set the entire Wednesday aside for CAS alone.

Although my high school did not offer anything like CAS at the time, my experiences in the Boy Scouts had a profound effect on me. I was able to take physical and emotional risks that gave me tremendous personal satisfaction and a growth in self-esteem that I took back to the classroom. Similarly my brother, as a 13-year-old involved in scuba diving, learned study skills (to prepare for the diving exams), goal-setting skills and even financial management skills as he had to save for his training courses. The beauty of the CAS programme is that it provides the ideal venue for developing exactly these kinds of skills.

While classroom education focuses on cerebral learning, CAS focuses on the emotional growth and development of students. It is less about the activities themselves and more about what students learn about themselves and what they give to those whom they work with. The CAS programme focuses on the whole student, and gives students a chance to take risks in a safe environment, to explore the new, to stretch and to grow. Thus CAS brings together learning and character development.

The CAS programme is designed to complement the academic rigours of the IB DP, and to:

- help students develop an appreciation of the potential of the human mind and spirit, and realize the value of contribution
- help them develop new interests, knowledge, skills and understanding
- create opportunities for service, develop an awareness of humanitarian issues worldwide, and develop the recognition that education imposes lifelong ethical obligations and responsibilities
- extend self-discovery, self-reliance, self-reflection and self-esteem; develop goal-setting skills and help the student become a self-directed learner
- create challenges, and develop the confidence in the students' own ability to bring about positive change both within themselves and collaboratively
- enhance interpersonal communication skills.

Adapted from Creativity, Action, Service guide © IBO 2001

When you present CAS to your students, focus on these goals, and attempt as much as possible to change the mindset of students who see it only as 'clock watching' or as 'something we have to do for IB'. There is a real danger that students initially see and treat CAS as an add-on. Ideally, the students become aware of the values that underpin CAS and will come to value this part of the DP as central to it.

Some student quotes exemplify this:

> At first I thought CAS was all about doing the activities and getting sufficient hours in order to do the IB diploma. However, after doing a few activities I realized that I was completely wrong. I have learned [from this].
>
> Jason S, Indonesian, April 2002

> Initially, I knew CAS as one of the requirements that I needed to finish in order to attain the IB diploma … but now I now think of CAS as a very useful programme that can make a person independent. It forces people to be more active, and to interact within the community …
>
> Andre S, Indonesian, April 2002

> In the first year … I was thinking that CAS was just an obligatory thing to do, so I participated in activities just to meet the requirements, but towards the end of the year I realized that CAS was actually fun and interesting, and that is why I enrolled in so many more things in the second year.
>
> Mavis W, Portuguese, April 2002

1.3 Other awards programmes and other educational systems

Perhaps the largest comparable awards programmes are the International (or Duke of Edinburgh) Award and the Eagle Scouts Award (Boy Scouts). A student may work for CAS and another award, using the same activities. However, the reporting systems are different for each programme. Regardless of what other programme a student may be entered in, they must fully document their CAS programme to IBO standards.

The documentation of the other awards emphasizes what the student has done and how many hours it has taken. While this is an important part of CAS, the focus of the CAS diary is what the student became, learned, and how they grew. There is a fundamental difference that must not be underestimated. The International Award log, for example, is not suitable as a CAS diary.

According to the IBO, students may participate in another awards programme provided that:

- the awards programme is in the spirit of the CAS programme
- all the criteria for the CAS programme are still maintained
- students are still supervised in terms of the CAS performance criteria, regardless of the criteria of other awards programmes
- the activities are not part of the student's DP – these could be drama productions that are done after school (requiring a lot of extra work) but are part of your student's IB theatre arts class.

> Adapted from *Diploma Programme Coordinator Notes*, August 2002 © IBO 2002

Some CAS coordinators work in schools running the DP alongside other educational programmes where service of some kind is also a requirement. The question is then whether or not to run the CAS programme for the *entire* school in the last years of secondary school? If the school truly believes that CAS and its philosophy are important to the growth and development of its students, then requiring CAS from every student really makes sense (and this would certainly be appreciated by IBO authorization teams). However, this could generate a great deal of extra work for a new CAS coordinator. In some schools, where the academically stronger and more motivated students enter the DP, monitoring CAS for non-diploma students could be a lot of extra work.

1.4 Religion and CAS

The issue of CAS and religion is complicated, and the ultimate decision will come down to a school's individual interpretation of the guidelines. The IBO states that 'Religious devotion and any activity which can be interpreted as proselytizing' cannot count as CAS activities. It furthermore offers the following guiding principles to help determine whether or not a religious activity is suitable for CAS.

- The student can extend a community service to a religious community when the objective of the CAS activity is clearly secular.
- The student can team up with a religious group helping people in need in the larger community provided the group's activities are clearly secular.
- Observing the IBO's philosophy of promoting international understanding and developing attitudes and values which transcend race, religion, gender and politics, students who engage in activities intersecting with religion must show evidence of participation in all three areas of CAS outside their own religious community.

> Adapted from the *Diploma Programme Coordinator Notes*, April 2002 © IBO 2002

When in doubt, remember that the important thing is that the student and the coordinator can argue their case coherently within the CAS guidelines.

1.5 How to evaluate CAS – outline

The whole of section 4 of this chapter is devoted to the CAS evaluation issues; here we quickly summarize some of the main issues.

Students must complete the minimum CAS requirements of 50 hours of creativity, 50 hours of action and 50 hours of service to the standards as set out by the IBO and by the school, and must properly document their programme in their CAS diary. In particular, the IBO wants to see evidence of an equal and ongoing commitment to all three areas. Students are deemed to have finished their CAS programme upon handing in a diary at the end of the diploma course. While most schools encourage students to use a paper diary, the format is your choice (hard copy, soft copy, video, audio) so long as it meets the IBO documentation requirements (see section 3.4).

The diary serves two evaluation purposes: it enables the CAS coordinator to verify that a student has satisfied the CAS requirements, and it enables the IBO to verify (through a sample set of randomly selected diaries) that the school's CAS programme satisfies the IBO's requirements.

There are no diploma points or grades earned for the completion of CAS. However, the IBO will withhold an IB diploma, regardless of subject grades achieved, until the student has completed CAS to a satisfactory standard.

Near the end of a student's DP, coordinators will be required to send in a form CAS Programme Completion Form (PCF) to the IB regional office either stating that everyone has satisfactorily finished their CAS programme, or listing the student/s who have not satisfactorily completed it.

2 The role of the CAS coordinator

The CAS coordinator must personify the spirit of CAS within the school and thereby lead by example. The CAS coordinator develops and champions the programme and sets expectations. He or she must lead by example, from the front and not from behind the desk.

You are responsible for the quality and overall leadership of your school's CAS programme, and you should lead visibly at the beginning. However, once the programme is up and running, get out of the way and lead quietly behind the scenes. Let the students take a leadership role and, more importantly, make them feel they have done it themselves.

> A leader is best
> When people barely know that he exists,
> Not so good when people obey and acclaim him;
> Worse when they despise him.
> 'Fail to honour people,
> They fail to honour you.'
> But a good leader who talks little,
> When his work is done, his aim fulfilled
> They will all say, 'We did this ourselves.'
>
> Lao-Tzu, Chinese philosopher

The students will follow your lead. If you are passionate and enthusiastic about CAS, have high expectations and do not accept second best, your students too are more likely to adopt a constructive approach to CAS.

Spend time working with your students to tailor their activities to their personal interests. It will be two long years tracking your students if they undertake activities that they are not passionate about. Keep in mind that not every student will be keen to work with the elderly, with the frail or with children, and it is well worth taking the time to find out what your students are interested in before they start. If you work in a large school this may be harder to coordinate on a one-on-one basis with your students, but homeroom teachers and activity supervisors can help if you have properly informed them beforehand.

2.1 Monitoring

You are expected to monitor the progress of your students throughout their CAS programme. At the beginning, this involves monitoring the proposed activities and working with the students to ensure that the activities fit the IBO CAS requirements. While the student must think an activity through and explain why it fits the guidelines, your initial guidance is vital for success. If you monitor too many students to meet individually with each one, you may choose to have the students complete a form similar to that in figure 9.1, then meet individually or in small groups with students whose programmes do not meet the CAS programme criteria.

On an ongoing basis, you must make sure that students' diaries are up to date, and that CAS programmes are followed. This ongoing monitoring is important. As the academic pressure of the IB DP builds and homework increases, students can easily fall behind in their CAS programme and possibly stop participating in their individual activities. Also, when diaries are not maintained, students quickly forget their experiences, leaving them with little to say in their self-evaluation (section 4.2).

Monitoring your students is likely to be the most frustrating part of your CAS experience. Unless you are extraordinarily lucky, typically students will submit their diaries late and diary entries can be incomplete and not up to date, especially when other graded work is due. While CAS coordinators need to be aware of and sympathetic to the other demands of the IB diploma, they must persevere to ensure that completion of the CAS diary remains a regular part of students' IB programme.

There is no typical format for monitoring. It will depend on the culture within your school, the commitment of the students and your perception of their level of motivation. The IBO recommends that CAS programmes are monitored frequently in the first few months. Students need to know that they are being monitored, and that CAS is an essential part of the diploma.

2.2 Record keeping

First and foremost, you must ensure that the students keep their CAS diaries up to date. After students complete their CAS programmes, you must keep their diaries for another six months – including the CAS/AEF and CAS/SFS forms they have submitted (see section 4.2 for details on these forms).

To prevent students from saying 'I didn't know', or 'You didn't tell me that', and to remind yourself of events, keep track of correspondence that you pass to individual students regarding their CAS programmes. Secondly, keep a timed appointment calendar with brief notes on meetings you have held with the entire CAS cohort, with individual students, and with CAS activity supervisors; and keep a log of letters sent out to parents, students and the school community in general. Such logs become essential in case disputes arise as to whether a student has fulfilled the CAS requirements for the diploma (see section 4).

Formal student records also help in the writing of letters of reference for university applications or for transfer to another school.

2.3 Staffing the CAS programme

Many schools rely on the *homeroom* teachers for the timely collection of diaries as well as for some degree of monitoring, with early warnings to the CAS coordinator should any problems develop (see Appendix 2). Secondly, seemingly at odds with the idea that students take ownership of their CAS programmes, many schools ask teachers to act as *activity supervisors*, at least for some of the activities. The case studies in sections 7.1 and 7.2 explore in detail the pros and cons of having few or many teachers involved in the CAS programme. Note that however many staff you involve, you need to ensure that they fully understand what CAS is all about and what is expected from them.

2.4 Funding the CAS programme

The IBO expects that adequate funding will be secured for your school's CAS programme. Naturally, factors such as school size, number of DP students and available resources will determine the level of funding.

2.5 Promoting the CAS programme

The CAS coordinator is responsible for the promotion of the CAS programme within the school and outside the school to the community at large. The programme can be promoted through school newsletters, regular letters home, parents evenings, special guest presentations, and through a CAS website. Getting students to write the articles, do the presentations and set up the website is a great way to promote CAS. Students can even get CAS hours for it!

2.6 Programme authorization and evaluation

The IBO authorization team will interview the CAS coordinator about the school's proposed CAS programme through the CAS/PQ form (discussed in section 3.5).

On an ongoing basis, the IBO recommends an annual evaluation of your CAS programme. Questions you might want to consider include:

- What is working with the CAS programme at your school?
- What is not working? What needs improvement?
- What is the quality of your students' diary entries?
- What frustrations do you deal with in the administration of the CAS programme?

2.7 Time requirements of a CAS coordinator

The IBO recommends that a school provides the coordinator with adequate release time to coordinate the CAS programme. Many small to middle-sized schools provide one class allowance for CAS coordinators. This means that rather than teaching six classes (assuming this is a full teaching load in your school) a teacher would teach five classes, and use the sixth class as their CAS time. CAS coordination is often combined with responsibility for extra-curricular activities and/or field trips and/or overseas trips for the whole school – in which case more release time is needed.

3 Setting up the CAS programme

In setting up a CAS programme in my school, I found it helpful to go through the steps listed in sections 3.1–3.3.

3.1 Auditing existing activities and programmes

List every opportunity for activity available to students in your school. Break down your list into creativity only, action only and service only, and ask yourself what activities you need to add to balance the programme in your school. Most schools' extra-curricular activity programmes will already have sports-related activities, but not all will have service or creativity activities. You may need to find new sources of activities to enhance your list.

What organizations can you link with? Can you set up a formal arrangement with a nearby children's home to provide long-term (several year) support, and long-term spaces for your students to volunteer? What agencies need help near your school? What socio-economic problems are at your school's doorstep? How can you get the parents involved? Does your school have a parent-teacher association that can support you in some way?

3.2 Deciding on CAS camps and encompassing projects

There are several factors to consider in the creation of your school's CAS programme.

What is the duration of the CAS programme?

The CAS programme is a two-year programme. It typically runs from the first day of the DP to approximately a month before the final examination, although some schools permit their students to finish their CAS programme in the December of their second year. Students should normally not complete more than half of their programme in the first year. They may *not* count any activities done before the start of DP, but they may count those undertaken during the summer between years 1 and 2.

Should we offer CAS camps?

Running a CAS camp early on in the programme is a great way to build CAS enthusiasm and school spirit. They are also effective for team-building amongst your first-year DP class and can help significantly with information dissemination to new DP students. Camps could also be multi-day programmes mixing in some other elements of the DP such as TOK and the extended essay. In the long term such camps can save a great deal of time in the set-up of the programme. Depending on the number of students, you could schedule meetings with every student at the camp and set up their programmes.

Should we promote encompassing projects?

Popularly known as encompassing projects, these undertakings typically encompass two or all three CAS components and are designed to involve students in a big project that requires them to think through, plan and execute a major idea. Such an integrated approach is very much within the spirit of CAS, but as a general rule schools should attempt to spread the projects over a period of time, so that students' involvement is sustained, rather than a one-off event lasting, say, one whole week.

Encompassing projects are popular with schools, which may require their students to engage in at least one. Examples of encompassing projects could be:

- organizing a funfair or a winter carnival for a local children's charity
- organizing a blood donation drive
- organizing a major fund-raising event for charity
- participating in building sister schools in the developing world; pushing for exchanges, second-hand computer donations and internet connections to ensure sustained commitments
- raising money and building homes for disadvantaged families, e.g. with 'Habitat for Humanity', or in developing countries such as Cambodia.

Note that all of these projects offer plenty of scope to integrate all three CAS components, and that some could run over a long period of time.

3.3 Deciding on the overall CAS programme structure

There are several ways to structure your school's CAS programme. There is no strictly regulated format, but there seems to be a general preference for fewer activities that run over the full two-year period than a large list of activities run for short durations. However, this ideal scenario is difficult to implement, for various reasons (see below). The following are a few models for inspiration.

Model 1: many activities

The least preferred model is a CAS programme organized around a dozen or so seemingly random one-off (or short) activities over the two years. The IBO seems to be looking for long-term commitment, development and reflection, so may deem this unsuitable (please check with your regional office if in doubt).

Student example:
Robert's CAS programme consists of 14 activities (not all are listed here):
- six-week football training on Wednesday afternoons (action)
- weekend dance class (creativity or action)
- summer volunteer camp counsellor for disadvantaged children (service)
- beach volleyball workshop (weekend, action)
- 24-hour dance-a-thon (organizer and participant, service)
- environment club participation (three weeks, creativity)
- debate competition (creativity).

Robert starts his CAS programme with a six-week football camp. He then stops football because his interest falls and he sees a dance class that looks like fun. After attending the dance class, he realizes this is not for him and goes to another activity. Robert's CAS programme consists of many small and non-related activities. As a result, Robert has not been able to progress and develop – let alone reflect – in any.

Model 2: a few main activities

Alternatively consider a CAS programme using four main activities that the students follow over the two years. This makes tracking and coordination easier, but it is sometimes very difficult to limit students to just four activities in total.

> **Student example:**
> Jill's CAS programme consists of four activities:
> • weekly volunteering at the children's home (service)
> • weekly girls' rugby practice and games (action)
> • weekly Celtic Art club participation (creativity)
> • student council vice-president (more service).

The drawback of this model is that one or more of the activities may become unworkable for any reason: the children's home relocates, the CAS activity supervisor or coordinator changes job (for example, we had a teacher leading a Celtic Art activity who left, and we could not find anyone to continue the activity with the students in their second year) – and so on. In that case, Jill could end up missing an entire CAS area or missing the required number of hours for one. While model 2 may work for larger schools, it could prove more difficult for smaller schools with fewer resources.

Model 3: mix models 1 and 2

The most versatile model for your CAS programme is a combination of models 1 and 2. Students are expected to choose a few main activities that would fulfil the CAS requirements over two years, but would supplement these with mini-activities.

> **Student example:**
> Maria's CAS programme consists of the following main activities (running consistently over two years):
> • weekly volunteering at the children's home (service)
> • weekly girls' rugby practice and games (action)
> • yearbook committee member (creativity)
> and the following mini-activities (one-off activities or short duration):
> • weekend rock climbing course
> • helping at the school's environment conference
> • making food to sell at the PTA charity bake sale
> • week-long hiking trip (school sponsored)
> • cross-country ski trip (weekend)
> • tennis camp during spring break
> • speech competition.

Maria has a focused CAS programme addressing all three CAS areas, and these activities are enhanced with extra activities which range again across all three areas, providing back-up should any of the main activities fail.

This model is safe and it also encourages students to get involved in many different things and to take risks.

3.4 Deciding on a CAS diary format

The IBO offers considerable flexibility in the format of the diary. Whether you get your students to create a paper CAS diary or an online electronic manual is entirely your choice. While these are the most common, students can also record their activities and reflections wholly or in part on video, on a website, on tape, in drawings, or through other forms of communication.

If you are setting it up as a paper diary, it would be better to use a ring-binder or arch-file to keep everything together so that students can insert forms or new pages as needed. Scribbler format diaries are not recommended, as CAS forms tend to get lost if they are not secured between their covers.

You can ask your IT support to create an ftp site for your students to store their CAS diaries online. The advantage is that you can see at a glance when diaries are updated, and reminders could easily be sent by email.

3.5 Administration and CAS forms

The more prewritten forms and letters you create, the easier and less time-consuming the administration of a CAS programme will be; several are included in this chapter.

There are two types of official CAS form for the students to complete and submit to you: the *CAS/AEF form* and the *CAS/SFS form*, which are discussed in detail in section 4.2. There are two other forms for you to complete: the *CAS/PQ form*, to be completed prior to the approval of your CAS programme (see section 4.1), and the *CAS/PCF form*, to be submitted every year (see section 4.3). All four forms can be found in the *Vade Mecum* in section E3.

4 Evaluating CAS

Before DP authorization, the IBO team will interview the CAS coordinator, and evaluate proposed activities and the school's understanding of the aims and objectives of CAS through the CAS/PQ form (see section 4.1). For authorized schools, the IBO evaluates the school's CAS programme primarily through the students' CAS journals.

The CAS coordinator continually evaluates each student's overall programme through monitoring as outlined in section 2.1 and through the student's CAS diaries (section 4.4), while the activity supervisors monitor the individual activities.

While monitoring of CAS students is ongoing, formal evaluation occurs only near the end of the second year, when students must submit their diaries together with two specific CAS forms (see section 4.2). At that stage the CAS coordinator is required to write a formal evaluation for each student according to guidelines detailed in section 4.3. If students have submitted a poorly maintained diary or one that does not show personal reflection, it must be rejected and the student asked to resubmit it.

Technically speaking, a student cannot fail CAS, but there are consequences for poor or non-performance in the CAS programme. In the event that a student does not adequately complete their CAS programme, the IBO will not issue a diploma even if all other requirements have been satisfied. The student is allowed up to a maximum of a further year during which to satisfy the CAS requirements and, on doing so, the diploma will be issued. A diploma will not be given to any students who fail to meet the one-year deadline.

However, a CAS coordinator has the responsibility to communicate to students and parents any lack of progress in the CAS programme which might lead to the withholding of a diploma. This is why it was stressed in section 2.2 that it is wise to keep records of all formal correspondence with students and their parents. Through such records one can avoid difficult situations should there be any dispute regarding the facts.

4.1 Evaluation of a school's CAS programme by the IBO

Prior to authorization, the IBO team will evaluate your CAS programme through the *CAS/PQ: CAS Programme Questionnaire* (to be completed before authorization). This form is the IBO's main source of information about your CAS programme within your school's environment. Some questions are self-explanatory; the more ambiguous ones are set out here:

Question 3 asks for information about the social and physical environment of the community in your school's vicinity. Is your school in a developed or a developing country? Are you an international school in a foreign culture, or a state school in your home country? Is your school in a poor, middle-class or wealthy community? What are the security issues facing your school? What competition does your school face? Are you the only IB school or are there others nearby?

Question 5 asks about your CAS programme. What is your CAS policy? Do all students (IB or other) have to complete CAS? How is your CAS programme organized (see sections 3.2 and 3.3)? The question also requires information on the strengths and weaknesses in your CAS programme (see section 2.6).

Question 7 asks you to list every possible CAS activity in your school, activities available nearby in the community, and to identify whether they fit into creativity, action or service, or more than one category.

Question 8 asks how your school will evaluate your students' CAS programmes, and how your students will evaluate themselves. See section 4.3 for ideas on what you can do.

Post authorization, the IBO is primarily looking at your school's CAS programme through the diary of the student. Your regional IBO office will contact either the school's CAS coordinator or the DP coordinator (DPC) with a list of three randomly selected names of students whose diaries the CAS coordinator will be required to submit. These are due on the first day of the month of the final examinations, so all student evaluations (see section 4.2) must be done by this time.

Specifically the IBO could be looking for answers to these questions:

- What range and balance of activities are available at your school for CAS?
- What are accepted as appropriate CAS activities?
- What is the expectation for satisfactory diary entries?
- What level of supervision did the CAS coordinator give students over the two years?
- What quality of feedback did the CAS coordinator give students over the two years?
- What was the level of communication between the CAS coordinator and the student?

Note that the CAS coordinator is expected to hold on to the students' CAS diaries for six months after the students have finished their DP.

4.2 Formal obligations for students

Students should normally have finished their CAS programme about one or two months before the final exam. They will submit their CAS diary, together with the following IBO CAS forms (which can be modified to suit your school's requirements so long as the individual components are still present in your own version):

The CAS Activity Self-Evaluation Form (CAS/AEF) should be completed at the end of each activity or project and should be included in the diary.

The CAS Student Final Summary Form (CAS/SFS) is a list of the student's CAS activities, and a final self-reflection on the whole CAS programme. Some schools require students to complete a 500-word summative essay or do a final presentation (see section 4.5) as part of their evaluation instead of filling in the CAS/SFS form.

4.3 Final evaluation of students' work

The IBO outlines very specific criteria by which to evaluate students:

Personal achievement
- The student progressed in the new role and learned from the experience; learned to meet challenges while showing increased awareness of personal limitations; and helped to solve real community problems.

Personal skills
- The student demonstrated the ability to think creatively; to research community needs; to manage resources; to plan and organize and to identify a plan's successes and failures.

Personal qualities
- The student participated regularly, punctually, responsibly and reliably; and the student demonstrated commitment, initiative, perseverance, self-confidence and a degree of humility.

Interpersonal qualities
- The student demonstrated collaboration and adaptability as well as respect, empathy, and a sense of justice and fair play.

Awareness of global issues
- The student developed an appreciation of how humanitarian and environmental concerns can be addressed through action from a local, national and international perspective.

The CAS coordinator (or the CAS supervisors, in larger schools) must write a formal evaluation for each student, addressing each criterion listed above. The length of the report is not specified by the IBO, but in general CAS coordinators should focus on qualitative reports rather than quantitative reports. CAS coordinators are expected to provide insight into their students' performance over the two years, and not just check boxes on a standardized form. It can be very difficult to write meaningful comments for some criteria, which is why it is a great help to ask your activity supervisors to add some in their final evaluations.

This formal evaluation – together with a diary that includes the CAS forms specified in section 4.2 – completes the student evaluation.

Every year, before the first day of the month of the final examinations, the coordinator then submits the *CAS/PCF (CAS Programme Completion Form)* to the regional IBO office. In it you confirm which students have successfully met their CAS requirements and you list the students who have not. For such students an explanatory report outlining the specific circumstances must be submitted.

4.4 Helping students to write good diary entries

The CAS diary represents the proof that the student has done the work, and more importantly that they have reflected on their experiences and the manner in which they have matured. As discussed in section 3.4, while CAS diaries do not have to consist only of writing, writing will typically still be the most important tool to communicate reflections.

Writing good diary entries can be difficult, especially for those who have never written them before, or for students who are learning English. It is easy for students to write about what they did but hard to write about what they learned and what they have become. It is an arduous task moving students away from writing 'Today we …' to 'Today I learned …'. So the question is: how to focus students on producing quality diary entries rather than just keeping a log of their activities?

The IBO has outlined several guiding questions for students to answer when they are working on their diary entries.

- Describe the activity. What did you do at each stage? Include dates where relevant.
- What did you hope to accomplish by this activity? What did you actually accomplish?
- What difficulties did you encounter?
- Did you feel at any stage that you were failing to achieve what you wanted from this activity?
- What did you hope to learn and gain from this activity, about yourself, others, or academic subjects? (For example, self-confidence, modesty, respect, awareness, responsibility, curiosity, honesty, objectivity, commitment, initiative, determination, new skills and the ability to meet challenges.)
- Did anyone help you during this activity? If so, please describe.

- How did this activity benefit other people or institutions?
- What would you change if you did this same activity again?
- What would you like to do next if you could continue with this activity?

In my experience, stem sentences based on the above guidelines are a great way to lead students in the right direction with their diary entries. They force them to think, and take away the excuse 'But I don't know what to do!' and thus put the onus on the student, not the teacher, to come up with justifications and explanations.

Some sample stem sentences are listed below.

- In this activity, I did the following things at the following dates …
- I hope my programme …
- One thing I love about this activity is …
- During this activity, I feel really good when …
- One thing that frustrates me about my activity is …
- During this activity, I feel really sad when …
- One word that describes my CAS programme is …
- My CAS coordinator would describe my programme as …
- In this activity, I'd like to learn …
- When I disagree with my friends working with me in my activity, I …
- When my children get really angry, I …
- My friend would describe my commitment to CAS as …
- The children I work with would describe me as …
- One way I've tried to make my CAS programme better is …
- One way I've tried to make my CAS programme different is …
- One thing we do as a team to communicate better in the activities is …
- If I paid 5% more attention today in my activity I would have …
- If I spent 5% more time listening I would …

Naturally, one must take care to avoid such help sheets becoming a type of 'fill in the gaps' form – make sure that your students use the sheet to help them *reflect*.

4.5 An optional evaluation tool: presentations

Many schools require students to do a CAS presentation, but this is not an IBO requirement. Typically 5 to 10 minutes in length, these could be done at any time, but are most appropriate after the first year. A good approach might be for second-year DP students to do presentations for first-year DP students at the start of the school year. By doing this the students get a formal opportunity to express their involvement in and gains from their CAS programme. At the same time, and perhaps more importantly, presentations set standards for new students, and allow them to see the level of work required of them. They can also help in the CAS familiarization process, especially if your school is new to the DP.

The easiest way to make sure students make good presentations is to create a basic presentation outline for them. I get my students to print or video their presentation and to insert it in their CAS diaries.

5 Safety and liability issues

The IBO does not have specific requirements concerning safety and risk assessment nor liability but it is good practice to consider these issues carefully.

Safety and risk assessment is relevant to any sports or extra-curricular activity but also to expeditions, hikes and other activities that your CAS students might participate in. The Resources section 8 contains useful web links for risk assessment.

Investigate the liability of your CAS programme and the individual activities that are part of it. Does your school have insurance to cover injuries incurred during CAS activities? What if the activities are off the school campus? Do you have students working on projects without school supervision? What are the parents' expectations in terms of liability? Have the parents signed waivers? And so on.

6 Tips for developing and improving your CAS programme

The following are some ideas and suggestions for developing and improving the CAS programme based on personal experience.

- Get students to use journals for documenting extra-curricular activities before they start the DP. They can keep journals of field trips, camps and their activities. This develops the habit of writing diary entries early on, and makes the CAS coordinator's job much easier. The diaries need not be sophisticated but do need a structure that allows for easy monitoring by homeroom teachers.
- Request that students put their photos, personal and parental email addresses on the front pages of their CAS diaries. This helps with communication and learning names if you are in a big school.
- Create group email lists to broadcast messages to the whole DP CAS group.
- Hold after-school CAS 'boot camps' for students behind in CAS. This measure might be seen as running counter to the spirit of CAS, but some students simply will need the extra attention and structure to complete diaries and other paperwork.
- Have high expectations, and do not settle for less.
- Automate where possible. Standardize your forms/letters/email.
- Keep copies of your emails to students in a folder in your email program. This will help with documenting the monitoring of students.
- Keep good journal samples to show to new students.
- Be flexible. Use an alternative assessment system for students who are incapable of writing diaries. Could they produce a video diary instead?
- Help and encourage students to create a programme that hooks into their passions. Your life will be much easier, and they will enjoy it all the more!
- Set early deadlines. It usually takes forever to get students to hand in their diaries and to get signatures.
- Keep your own CAS journal. It could be a calendar where you just write what you did that day for CAS. It will help you see where you are spending your

time. Also document the work you have put into CAS for your head and for the IBO. In relation to this …

- Coordinating a CAS programme takes a huge amount of time and may go unnoticed. You may be able to argue for additional time or resources for your CAS programme if you have a well-documented case!

7 Case studies

There are many different ways in which to run a CAS programme. Here are two case studies of contrasting approaches listing advantages and shortcomings for each.

7.1 Case study A

The CAS programme in this large IB school in Asia is closely linked to a well-developed and extremely broad range of extra-curricular activities run by the school itself. All students take the DP and hence CAS is compulsory for this age group. The school ethos is that the role of the teacher extends well beyond the classroom and consequently there is a contractual expectation that teaching staff will be involved in a variety of extra-curricular activities. A teacher may for example coordinate the student newspaper; coach the under-14s basketball club; supervise weekly visits of DP students to a local care centre for the elderly; and participate on an annual trekking expedition to Nepal. In short, the expectation of teaching staff is that they will to some extent embody the spirit of CAS itself: that involvement in a variety of activities is both positive and important.

The practical benefits of such an approach are obvious: a range of CAS activities is on offer, costs to students are minimized, student attendance can be effectively monitored, and records easily kept. In the school, service projects within the local community are well established. At the start of the academic year the students choose their preferred service project: visiting an AIDS hospice, playing music to elderly people, assisting in a school for the deaf, and so on. Each week a bus takes them to their activity and the teacher who supervises them takes a register. In short the school makes it 'easy' for students to complete their CAS by providing the opportunities and administrative framework for them to do so.

There are additional pedagogical benefits of an in-house CAS activity programme: as we have seen, CAS is not simply about *doing* activities. It is about reflecting upon and learning from participation. When the activity supervisors are themselves teachers they are arguably more likely to be aware of and sympathetic to the underlying educational aims of CAS. They will therefore be more able to generate the sort of discussion and reflection that should be at the heart of a student's CAS experience. When all teachers are involved, CAS is more likely to play a central role in the educational ethos of the whole school. Thus long-standing students are likely to have been involved in extra-curricular activities from the start and will accept CAS without hesitation when they begin the DP.

An excellent example of a CAS project undertaken at this school is 'Cirque Attack'. This was set up by a group of teachers who had been running a circus skills club at the school for many years. One year they decided to run an actual circus. Students from all year groups were involved. The opportunities for CAS students were broad: they performed as clowns, jugglers, acrobats, developing their own routines and participating in others. They designed and set up the lighting and staging; they selected and performed the music; trained younger students in circus skills; choreographed acrobatic routines; designed posters; sold tickets and refreshments. The quality of the performance was outstanding, but it was the sense of shared student involvement in and ownership of a long-term project that made this an outstanding CAS project. Creativity, action and service activities were intermingled as students of all ages worked together. The number of hours did not matter to them. Making a success of their show was what counted. This is what CAS is all about.

Unfortunately an 'in-house' CAS programme of this kind is not without its problems. Clearly for such an approach to be effective, huge demands are made of teaching staff. Not only do they have to have the passion and energy to run all these activities, but they also need the time to do so. The CAS ethos needs to be a shared ethos, otherwise teachers and students end up paying lip service to contractual requirements. In addition the school needs to provide both the facilities and the practical back-up (buses, basketball courts, pottery kilns, big tops!) which may be expensive and impractical. The school, having taken responsibility for providing the CAS activities, will bear the brunt of these costs. Also, it is the CAS coordinator who must bear the burden of establishing and maintaining contacts and service activities with the local community.

Arguably making it 'easy' for students can lead to complacency on their part: little initiative is required other than simply showing up for the service bus. If an activity supervisor is taking an attendance list it is only a small step for the sense of responsibility to shift away from the student and onto the activity supervisor. CAS can come to be seen as simply an extension to school, or something in which the students are only passively involved.

The administrative system in this large school relies on whole-year group assemblies for the dissemination of information about practical administration and for the advertising and showcasing of different activities. With 600 students engaged in CAS in both year groups of the DP, the CAS coordinator cannot develop a personal connection with all students and so registration/homeroom tutors play an important role in mentoring students and monitoring records. The DPC has students use the IB CAS/AEF forms to record developments but these are sometimes inadequate to record reflective comments. Students who are involved intensively in a few activities may feel there is insufficient space to reflect properly on what they have done, whereas a student whose CAS activities have been more varied may be frustrated by having to respond to the same questions so many times.

7.2 Case study B

The profile of CAS programme in this smaller school in Europe is lower than in the previous example. Not all the students take the DP; about 10% take the Swiss Maturité and are not required to undertake CAS. The school does not follow the Middle Years Programme and so CAS is seen exclusively as something undertaken by diploma students. More time is therefore needed to introduce CAS to new DP students and to explain how the CAS differs in spirit from other extra-curricular activities done in the previous years. The CAS coordinator has prepared a comprehensive CAS guide and has developed 'An Introduction to CAS', an intensive two-day experience. Here students are presented with information about CAS and have the opportunity to try out new activities such as Japanese calligraphy and African drumming. At the expense of parents, outside experts are brought in to run these activities.

During the introductory CAS session, the CAS coordinator devotes considerable time to the process of reflective writing – a skill that needs practice and careful development. The students are introduced to examples of 'good' and 'poor' reflective writing and exposed to what makes a 'good' and 'poor' CAS activity. After discussions in groups they have an opportunity to try writing reflectively in response to the IBO's guiding questions, and to receive feedback. They also undertake a plan for their own CAS programme for the next two years.

Once the students begin the DP the onus is on them to sort out their own CAS programmes. There are of course some extra-curricular activities run by the school which are suitable for CAS, but there is an expectation that all students will have to organize some of their own service opportunities in the local community at local hospitals and through voluntary organizations.

With fewer assemblies and a more informal pastoral system, students are required to operate independently and so good communication and support are essential. Consequently, the CAS coordinator is kept fully occupied. A CAS bulletin is published every few weeks advertising possible contacts for activities, and provides reminders about deadlines and administration. New CAS forms were developed, both for students and for activity supervisors (who may not be familiar with the ideals of CAS). The forms encourage students to write longer reflective pieces about their activities, and are checked at regular intervals by the coordinator to ensure that everyone is on track.

With time students are able to write longer reflections on CAS, often more rewarding and closer in style to personal essays for university application. Therefore students take them more seriously, and for the CAS coordinator they are certainly more interesting to read than one-sentence responses!

The very structure of the CAS programme encourages independence and has clear pedagogical advantages. The students arguably feel a greater sense of ownership and responsibility for their CAS programmes. Students develop skills of communication and diplomacy and personal initiative as they arrange their own activities. As most activities are completed in conjunction with community centres and local voluntary organizations, students are more likely to meet and work with new people, undertake new roles and learn in the real world. Service can seem more meaningful when students have established links themselves and they may be able to volunteer for services appropriate to their career plans: for example, work in a cancer ward in a hospital or join an environmental group to do restoration work on mountain paths. This approach can be particularly successful when the parent community is willing to provide contacts and support and there are many active local organizations and institutions nearby (such as NGOs and the UN).

An excellent example of a CAS (action/creativity) project from this school was the trans-alpine hike. A group of six students decided they wanted to undertake a five-day hike. They planned the routes, prepared equipment, organized training walks, established safety guidelines with their parents, reserved campsites through National Park authorities, and whilst en route participated in other activities such as horse-riding and kayaking with established outdoor activity companies. They had a wonderful trip, and at the end worked together to produce an interactive CD of all their photos and reflections about the trip. The initiative for this trip had come from the students themselves. They planned it, organized it and felt enormous satisfaction as a result. They also learned a great deal about organization, working together, planning and safety.

The practical drawbacks of this school's approach are considerable, however. Many students find it very difficult if not impossible to arrange suitable CAS activities and consequently we are back to the unsuitable activities such as 'walking my friend's dog' or 'stacking shelves for free in my uncle's shop' mentioned at the beginning of this chapter. When these activities are disallowed it can lead to resentment and frustration. Monitoring the accuracy of time spent on activities is problematic, and students can find it hard to obtain confirmation from activity supervisors who are not in tune with IB demands. The DP students are already under pressure. Is it reasonable to expect them to spend time organizing and participating in CAS activities as well as reflecting on them? Less motivated and organized students certainly do not always make the most of the opportunities of such an approach.

Clearly there are strengths and weaknesses in both these approaches and there is no reason why a CAS programme cannot contain elements of both: a selection of in-house guided activities, but plenty of encouragement for students who want to develop their own CAS programme outside school.

8 Resources

All of the following weblinks can be found on the CAS page of: www.dp-help.com. Others will be added, and we appreciate your emails with any other links you can recommend.

International Award (Duke of Edinburgh Award): www.intaward.org

Eagle Scouts Award (US): www.scouting.org

Habitat for Humanity: www.habitat.org

Red Cross (US): www.redcross.org

Royal Geographic Society: www.rgs.org

Many resources (expeditions, risk assessment, guides) can be downloaded free of charge.

The Tabitha project is a Cambodian charity run by a Canadian. Many IB schools have linked with Tabitha to construct basic and simple one-room homes for Cambodian families. Some schools also help by selling crafts made by the families working with Tabitha. Details can be found at: www.tshooters.com/tab1.htm.

http://scoutdocs.ca/Documents/ contains links to varied resources that can be modified to help you in your planning. It also has equipment links, songs, sketches for download to help with the CAS camps.

Appendix 1: 'CAS concern' letter to parents

This form can be used to reduce the work of communicating concerns to parents. Be sure to keep a copy for your records.

CAS PROGRESS REPORT

Name: _____ Date: _____

Organization of diary
- ☐ Your name and grade are not clearly marked on front cover
- ☐ Pages are out of order
- ☐ Basic paperwork/forms not completed
- ☐ No photo on front page
- ☐ You have not got your activity supervisors to sign
- ☐ Not appropriate activity/permission not granted for activity
- ☐ Pre-approval not sought for activity

Diary entries
- ☐ Diary entries are sloppy, unprofessional, handwriting is hard to read
- ☐ Your diary entries do not follow proper guidelines
- ☐ Diary entries are not dated
- ☐ CAS activities are good but diary not complete
- ☐ Diary entries are not up to date
- ☐ Diary entries are not properly written and guidelines are not being followed
- ☐ Photo diary on activities is not up to date
- ☐ Diary entries appear to be done at the last minute
- ☐ Diary entries are not meeting expectations
- ☐ Pages not secured in the diary

CAS habits
- ☐ You have stopped attending a main activity
- ☐ There have been excessive absences from CAS activities
- ☐ Main activity has been dropped without permission/authorization
- ☐ Motivation/attitude appears to be below expectations

Overall
- ☐ Requests/suggestions made previously have not been corrected/improved upon in subsequent diary entries
- ☐ Previous suggestions have not been followed
- ☐ Will probably not be able to graduate with classmates should this continue
- ☐ Graduation will definitely be postponed/delayed due to unacceptable level of commitment
- ☐ Current level of effort is not at acceptable level for DP graduation requirement
- ☐ Participation level in CAS activities is not up to expected levels/standards
- ☐ CAS diary is long overdue
- ☐ Minimum number of hours is not being met
- ☐ Please contact me

Listed above is a summary of major problems with your CAS diary. It is very important that you take note of the issue and rectify the situation.

Signature: _____ Date: _____

Appendix 2: CAS calendar

This calendar can be used to help students and parents plan the CAS process. It is set up for students writing the May examinations, but can be adapted to fit your school's needs.

Date	Year One (Grade 11)	Year Two (Grade 12)
September (mid)	*Initial CAS programme planning* You should have read through the CAS book and have designed a CAS programme for yourself that you will follow for two years. This programme should be discussed with your homeroom teacher and your parents.	• Discuss your progress with your homeroom teacher at some point during the month.
September (end)	*CAS planning completed* You should have met with your CAS coordinator to discuss your programme. He/she must approve the programme. *Start your CAS programme* • You should start your programme. • You should discuss your progress with your homeroom teacher at some point during the month.	• Discuss your progress with your homeroom teacher at some point during the month.
October	*15th – Quarter review* • Discuss your progress with your homeroom teacher at some point during the month.	*15th – Quarter Review* Give your journal to your homeroom teacher.
November	• Discuss your progress with your homeroom teacher at some point during the month.	• Discuss your progress with your homeroom teacher at some point during the month.
December	*15th – Quarter review* Give your journal to your homeroom teacher, who will give it to the CAS coordinator. • Discuss your progress with your homeroom teacher at some point during the month.	*15th – Quarter review* Give your journal to your homeroom teacher. • Discuss your progress with your homeroom teacher at some point during the month.
January/ February	• Discuss your progress with your homeroom teacher at some point during the month.	• Discuss your progress with your homeroom teacher at some point during the month.
March	*15th – Quarter review* Give your journal to your homeroom teacher. • Discuss your progress with your homeroom teacher at some point during the month.	*You should be nearly done!* *15th – Quarter review* Give your journal to your homeroom teacher. • Discuss your progress with your homeroom teacher at some point during the month.
April	• Discuss your progress with your homeroom teacher at some point during the month.	*15th – DP students final journal due* Give your completed journal to your homeroom teacher.
May	*30th – Year One review* Give your journal to your homeroom teacher. You should have completed half of your CAS programme by this point.	*1st – Other students final journal due* Give your completed journal to your homeroom teacher.
June, July, August	*Summertime!* Continue your CAS programme during the summer. If you wish to, you may enhance your CAS programme by participating in 'other activities'. Perhaps you will take a sailing course, a karate course, singing lessons, or volunteer your time.	

Chapter 10
TOK: Theory of Knowledge

Nick Alchin

Nick Alchin was head of Theory of Knowledge (TOK) at the United World College of South East Asia for several years. After two years at the International School of Geneva he moved to Sevenoaks School, UK, where he is Head of Mathematics. He is the author of the widely acclaimed *The Theory of Knowledge* book for students and the companion *The Theory of Knowledge Teacher's Book* published by John Murray. He has examined TOK for several years, is a teacher-training workshop leader and has advised schools on various aspects of TOK. In this chapter, he introduces all aspects of this unique and central Diploma Programme (DP) course: what it is, what it is not, how to organize it, and how to teach it. An extensive guide to the use of resources is also included.

Note: all weblinks featured in this chapter can be accessed through our website: www.dp-help.com

1 Introduction

1.1 Summary of TOK

Theory of Knowledge (TOK) is a course unique to the IB diploma. As its place in the middle of the hexagon (see page 4) suggests, TOK is central to the educational philosophy of the IB curriculum. It is compulsory for all diploma students and the IBO looks for evidence that the school has made tangible efforts to integrate the course and its ideology within its overall DP.

There are probably few equivalent courses in current high school education systems and while TOK has some connection with philosophy and critical thinking it is different. The subject does not require the student to learn extra material. Instead TOK challenges students to reflect critically on the methodologies – their strengths and weaknesses – of the six curriculum areas. More generally, it challenges students to look at themselves and ask 'What do I believe in?', 'What are my reasons for believing?' and 'Are those reasons good ones?'

For almost all their lives diploma students will have been bombarded with 'facts' and many do not see 'knowledge' as a problematic term. TOK helps students to develop a more mature understanding about the nature of knowledge; to identify and compare different types of knowledge and ways of knowing and to develop their own judgement about what to believe and why to believe it – increasingly important in this electronic age of 'information overload'. Through TOK we ask students to question their preconceptions, not to attack them or prove them wrong, but so that they come to a better understanding of themselves as individuals and their beliefs. After six months of TOK at the International School of Geneva, TOK student Mattias Ivarsson (17) wrote:

> TOK is a subject where we as students can say what we really believe and is the first course where I have been taught to question just about everything I know. Paradoxically this has allowed me to feel that I know a large amount more about the world and about life than before. The course has stimulated me to think very carefully about everything I do and why I do it, and everything I think and why I think it. I also feel that it has greatly increased my tolerance and open-mindedness for different ways of thinking and different approaches to a particular problem. I also strongly believe that TOK is a subject where teacher–student relationships reach a new level; teachers and students together ask the questions, and we students then try to find the answers within ourselves.

It is worth stressing that TOK can, and should, be much more than 'just' another academic subject. With mounting academic and social pressures, IB students need hard-to-find space to stop, reflect and consider. We believe that TOK can both fulfil its academic aims and provide this space, thereby making a huge contribution to a school's pastoral programme. TOK is a focused forum that can be used to discuss ethics, religion, cultural differences, attitudes to war, sex, drugs and yes, even rock and roll. Students can explore contemporary topics that are important for them. For example, I have just read an essay in which one student explains how to be an ethical atheist, and another by a young woman who questions media representation of gender. By justifying a claim and analysing its possible consequences, students can develop a much better understanding of their values and, consequently, their personal identities. Thus one of the aims of TOK is to develop a tool with which to interpret everyday experience and make decisions. This is not at all pretentious. A successful TOK course is a journey of discovery, for students and teachers alike.

1.2 TOK, philosophy and critical thinking

Although there are many links between TOK and the group 3 subject course philosophy, there are also important distinctions. The latter is an optional course and deals with specific texts and thinkers. TOK, on the other hand, is a mandatory course that centres on posing questions. In keeping with this, the TOK guide is remarkable in that it consists largely of quotations and questions.

> Questions are the very essence of TOK, both ageless questions on which thinkers have been reflecting for centuries and new ones, often challenging to accepted beliefs, which are posed by contemporary life. Engaging with students in a critical examination of knowledge, teachers will foster an appreciation of the quest for knowledge, in particular its importance, its complexities and its human implications. A teacher may hope to bring alive … questions … for a new generation … and to encourage them to gain and apply their own knowledge with greater awareness and responsibility.
>
> *Theory of Knowledge* guide © IBO 2003

Some national curricula already place emphasis on critical thinking, often as a separate academic endeavour. Traditionally such a course has involved an evaluation of the nature of rational arguments. As such it emphasizes the importance of logical arguments, fallacies and the evaluation of evidence.

The following aims of TOK will also be found in the list of aims of a typical critical thinking course, and thus illustrate the overlap between the two subjects:

C1: Understand why a critical, analytical approach is important.
C2: Develop students' critical capacity to analyse claims from the various fields of knowledge.
C3: Develop a concern for rigour in formulating claims and for intellectual honesty.

While TOK probes less deep in the areas of overlap with critical thinking, the subject has a broader scope, as is illustrated by the following three 'TOK specific' aims:

T1: Make connections between different areas of knowledge.
T2: Understand that all individual and cultural perspectives may have strengths and weaknesses.
T3: Consider possible responsibilities that may come with knowledge.

For example, a critical thinking course could ask students to analyse statements such as the following:

> It is moral to save lives; by deterring murder the death penalty saves lives. Therefore we conclude the death penalty is moral.

> Research has shown that the death penalty does not act as a deterrent for crime. Therefore one should abolish the death penalty.

A critical thinker would carefully analyse the quality of the assumptions as well as the validity of the logical argument that builds on them. TOK students, however, in view of the aims T1, T2 and T3 stated above, would enquire on another level as well. Here are some of the questions that might arise from discussing either one of the statements about the death penalty.

- Is 'murder' always immoral? Is an execution really 'murder'? What do we mean by the word 'murder' exactly? Might the death penalty be wrong even if it saves lives? This links law, language and ethics (*aim T1*).
- Why do Americans and Europeans have such different views towards the death penalty? Actually, do they really – how do you know? How do cultural and religious backgrounds in these and other parts of the world influence specific moral positions? This explores connections with culture and religion and the strength of their influence (*aims T1 and T2*).
- Suppose we know the death penalty has no deterrent effect, do we still retain the right to be in favour of it? (*aim T3*).

Note that in each case an abstract problem of knowledge arises from the concrete example. Although both TOK and critical thinking are concerned with the logical consistency of the arguments, TOK also seeks to start a vibrant and lively conversation, connecting the religious, moral, cultural, legal and logical perspectives.

These examples illustrate one of TOK's main attractions: it allows the students to take the discussion in the directions they feel strongly about. As such, motivated students can take full ownership of the course. Of course, the associated risk is that the teacher could allow the discussion to degenerate into a whimsical exchange of unsubstantiated opinions. Therefore, the teacher and students must always keep in mind the central concerns of TOK. Which types of knowledge are we using, either implicitly or explicitly? How valid is each of these with respect to the topic discussed?

In terms of *attitude*, both critical thinking and TOK aim to guide the student away from two very unattractive poles, which we may loosely refer to as extremes of *prejudice* and *nihilism* (figure 10.1).

In my experience, of the two options, students have tended towards nihilism rather than prejudice. Very few of them realize that statements like those listed in figure 10.1 may actually be self-contradictory. If students leave the TOK course holding either of these positions then we have failed them. The central aim for teachers of TOK is therefore to try to move students on further. We are hoping that students will arrive at a balanced position, where they are sceptical, but their scepticism is not all-consuming.

Figure 10.1 Prejudice and nihilism

Prejudice	Nihilism
Obvious things must be true.	Certainty is impossible.
We can easily attain certainty.	Nothing is what it seems to be.
I know the truth.	There is no such thing as truth.
My culture is the best.	All cultural perspectives are equally valid.

A balanced scepticism
- Things are not always what they seem to be; we must examine and analyse.
- Certainty is very difficult to come by.
- Many standards are defensible; but many are not.
- I have considered several positions and can justify what I believe to be the most reasonable position.

1.3 Assessment overview

Note: The following details are currently under review and may change – see your DPC.

Figure 10.2 Assessment components for TOK

TOK assessment	
Internal component (33%)	One 10-minute presentation, possibly done in small groups, followed by a class discussion
External component (67%)	One essay, which is to be written in a student's own time, on a list of 10 titles known beforehand

Details about the assessment will feature in later sections of this chapter. Here we restrict ourselves to mentioning that focus on essay practice alone will *not* work, for reasons described in detail later in this chapter. Full engagement in wide-ranging class discussions and experimentation with their own and others' ideas is required to give students the confidence to tackle the essay at the highest level.

The grades for the presentation and the essay are combined to give a grade A–E for TOK. An A grade is difficult to achieve (historically around 10% of candidates or fewer are awarded it). It requires real sophistication and genuine insight into the problems of knowledge. It is also quite difficult to score an E grade, and even weak students usually achieve a D grade or higher if they have been well taught and have put some effort into their learning.

The TOK grade is then combined with the grade awarded for the extended essay (also A–E) to give an overall grade (referred to as *bonus points*, to be added to the overall total of the subject grades) according to figure 10.3.

Figure 10.3 Calculation of bonus points

		Theory of Knowledge					
		A	B	C	D	E	N
Extended essay	A	3	3	2	2	1	N
	B	3	2	1	1	0	N
	C	2	1	1	0	0	N
	D	2	1	0	0	0	N
	E	1	0	0	0	F	N
	N	N	N	N	N	N	N

Adapted from *Theory of Knowledge* guide © IBO 2003

Note that a student awarded either the F code (failure) or the N code (non-submission) will not be awarded a diploma!

2 Organizing the course

2.1 Ensuring TOK is taken seriously

The TOK course faces many disadvantages and schools may not be able to rectify them all. It is worth relatively little in terms of diploma points; it is new to students; it is difficult; it is compulsory; and it may be taught by teachers outside their speciality, perhaps against their will.

For these reasons, TOK is sometimes at the bottom of everyone's priorities. This naturally leads to a poor perception of the subject among students and staff and to an unsuccessful course. However, TOK is an essential component of the IB DP and should not be treated as an unimportant precondition of the programme. Schools and teachers should give it the respect it deserves, and a visiting IBO authorization team will look for evidence of this. The following suggestions may help new schools to formulate an appropriate policy.

- Do not schedule TOK at awkward times that would be unacceptable for other subjects (after school, lunchtimes, evenings, even weekends). If difficult timetabling needs to be done then share the 'problem slots' between all subjects fairly.
- Think carefully whether to schedule longer classes once a week or shorter classes twice a week. Once a week allows for a variety of activities and sustained debates; but twice a week could lead to pointed animated breaks from the ordinary school day.
- Do not have huge classes; certainly not more than 25 students.
- Allocate the required time (100 hours) spread over two years.
- Develop a team of teachers who want to and are able to teach TOK – just as for any other subject. Chopping and changing the teachers each year can be disastrous for curriculum development.
- Allocate funds to allow TOK teachers to attend workshops.
- Report to parents on TOK just as for the other subjects.
- Assign a TOK coordinator with specific responsibilities for developing the curriculum.
- Include evaluation of the TOK department and teachers in the regular school schedule.

A clear lead from the middle and senior management is essential.

2.2 Staffing the course

There are many views on this subject. It has been said that ideally there would be no separate TOK course and no TOK teachers – that TOK would be a part of each and every subject area and would 'just happen' naturally. I do not think this is correct; while each subject can and should touch on the strengths and weaknesses of its methodologies (see section 2.9), it is only in TOK that teachers can compare and contrast different areas of knowledge and spend time looking at common underlying themes.

There is no doubt that taking on TOK for the first time can be intimidating. One school which has recently done so is Oakham School (Rutland, UK) which has just dropped British A-levels in favour of the IB diploma. Jill Rutherford, the DP coordinator (DPC) says that:

... while schools are generally attracted by TOK, the lucky individuals asked to teach it are often horrified when they see the course! There is so much, and yet so little is familiar. Often the teacher is learning as much as the student. This is what makes TOK such a challenge to teach and to learn.

The choice of teacher is absolutely crucial. Usually one of the first requirements for teaching is the correct qualification – probably a degree in the subject taught, but there is no such thing as a degree in TOK and we have seen that philosophy is a very different thing. However, although some philosophical experience would certainly do no harm, background and qualifications are less important than certain personal qualities. The ideal TOK teacher will be:

- curious and keen to learn more about anything, from anywhere
- happy to run classes where the teacher is not the source of all wisdom
- willing to explore new ideas
- capable of seeing many different points of view
- a good listener
- intellectually rigorous and ruthless about quality of discussion
- keen to adopt a student-centred approach wherever possible
- willing to prepare lessons thoroughly and to read up on new subject matter
- widely read in literature, science, philosophy, current affairs.

Of course not all teachers meet all these criteria, and schools have other constraints. Good TOK teachers come from all subjects, from a range of backgrounds, and are willing to learn from each other. However, we must recognize that some people are simply not suited to teach TOK, not because of their background or intellect (this is a popular misconception), but because of their teaching style or temperament.

I should add from a personal perspective that teaching TOK has been probably the single most enriching professional experience that I have undertaken. I love my first subject – mathematics – but I feel that TOK is a chance to do something special with students, and it is still a privilege to be able to accompany them on the journey they make in this unique and wonderful course.

2.3 'When to teach?' and 'What lesson format?'

To meet IB requirements the course must be 100 hours long and the IBO strongly recommends that it also stretches over the two years of the DP (in some educational systems this may not be possible, which is why it is not a formal requirement). This offers scope for a number of possibilities (which can also be combined in various different ways).

The first question is 'When should we teach the course?'

Run the course for the full two years of the programme. This is in line with the 'TOK should be treated just like any other subject' approach, but there are two things to consider. First, TOK is examination-free, so it is the obvious course to drop as you get towards the end of the final diploma year. Second, both the essays and presentations must be completed two months before the actual IB examinations at the very latest, and it is hard to motivate students with so much else on when all the assessment is done with. For these reasons, many schools elect to end the course around the final assessment deadline.

Run the course for the second half of grade 11 and the first half of grade 12. This allows students to 'get into' their IB packages before starting TOK and also provides plenty of time afterwards to focus on subject examinations. The drawback would be that students always hate giving up time they see as 'free', and this might create negative feelings towards TOK. This unusual set-up might also cause some serious timetabling problems for staffing and students.

Whichever scenario you decide on, it can be a very good idea to follow the suggestion in Chapter 9 and have an (out-station) 'IB camp' early in the course, during which students are acquainted with core expectations of the IB, such as CAS, TOK, coursework, and academic honesty. Such camps can do wonders for morale, not only in terms of IB, but also in terms of team bonding.

A second question arises, 'Which lesson formats should be adopted?' Again, we can suggest some alternative approaches.

Spend all the time in regular lessons. This is the obvious approach to take – students spend all the course time in the classroom. It certainly keeps things simple.

Supplement the class-time with a range of other activities.
- Visit local events/places (e.g. an art gallery for aesthetics, a mosque for religion, a university psychology department for perception).
- Attend public lectures – these are available on a huge range of topics.
- Invite guest speakers to present ideas that can then be discussed later in class.

Fortnightly or monthly lectures can provide excellent material for lessons, and the topics can be fascinating. I have had doctors talk about the ethics of switching off a life-support machine, lawyers talking about reliability of witnesses in court, scientists speaking about scientific evidence for the existence of God, and traders talking about looking for patterns in stock-market chaos. Often the school community can provide an excellent source of speakers (especially for speakers from different religious faiths who are willing to share their beliefs with students). One piece of advice though (from past experience) – spend some time with guest speakers beforehand so that they understand what TOK is about; it is hard for non-educators to really grasp the thrust of the course immediately.

2.4 **TOK intensives**

I think there is a lot to be said for intensive educational experiences, and in the TOK context it can be a very positive thing to take a few days off the regular timetable and devote all the time to TOK. This may sound daunting, but with careful planning these intensives can be highly motivating and productive.

How intensive? One option is to have a number of TOK days spread throughout the course. The days can be focused around specific issues or around activities. Spreading the days out means that the 'intensive' is not quite so intensive and staff and students do not get so tired. Also, it can be a regular and eagerly anticipated break from a hectic schedule. On the downside, students do not get the buzz that comes from immersion and total involvement with a successful longer session.

What about a four- or five-day session all in one go, probably near or at the very end of the course? There are substantial administrative and curriculum issues here, but this can be a successful way of drawing the course to a close. If you do decide to include intensives, it is a good idea to put them just before a holiday so that pressure from other subjects is not a distraction for students. Intensives pull TOK teachers from their regular classes, which will need covering. In order to minimize lesson disruption it may be best to schedule intensives during periods where other year groups have examinations or are otherwise occupied. Schools that have problems with students leaving early for holidays may boost attendance by making the intensives compulsory and in order to fulfil TOK time requirements.

What to do during a TOK intensive? The day(s) need to have a variety of engaging, interesting and relevant stimuli. An assessment activity, especially one stretching over several days, at the end of the intensive, focuses students and maintains a desirable tension.

What about using outsiders? Getting all the TOK classes together for presentations by guest speakers or teachers can generate a real sense of fun and purpose, especially if you have a good auditorium and good speakers. While the odd lecture may work very well, you can get great mileage from more interactive things, such as:
- A (no-holds-barred) 30-minute debate between an atheist and a believer, followed by questions. This can be controversial but usually generates such a good response that it is well worth while.
- A 'beauty parade' where members of staff each spend a few minutes presenting something they (claim to) believe has some aesthetic quality (naturally, spoof entries are permitted, even encouraged). Afterwards the students discuss the presentations in groups and vote; the day can end with the results being made public and a 'prize-giving'.
- A carefully designed scientific experiment highlighting the hypothesis-test-refine-test-again scientific method. Follow up with a presentation from another discipline, e.g. business/economics, discussing the possible application and problems of the scientific method in this area.
- An analysis of a story/event covered in several newspapers/magazines/TV programmes. For example, most of President Bush's actions receive vastly different coverage inside and outside the USA. This analysis can be combined with a presentation from a journalist.

Sample timetable for four-day intensive. The sample timetable in figure 10.4 shows a possible schedule for a four-day intensive programme which might take place in the final week of the course. The activities are chosen to review and develop key aspects of the course and to assist in the essay-writing process. The final essay (see section 3.3) would be handed in on the Friday morning.

2.5 Two systems of organizing the staffing of the course

In smaller schools with one or two TOK classes this may not apply, but in larger schools there are different ways of organizing the staffing of the course.

Figure 10.4 Sample timetable for a four-day TOK intensive programme

Teaching periods	Mon	Tue	Wed	Thu
1,2	Introduction and 'beauty parade'	Debate on existence of God	Presentation on legal ethics by lawyer	Science experiment
Morning break				
3,4	Aesthetics discussion and voting	Meetings with believers	Discussion and case study on legal ethics	Presentation on truth and the media by journalist
5,6	Essay planning time	Religion discussion groups	Essay planning time	Essay planning time
Lunch				
7,8	Essay tips Results of 'beauty parade'	Essay planning time	Free time	Course feedback and finale

The rotation system

Usually each teacher takes responsibility for one particular area of the course and teaches this aspect to all the groups in turn.

Figure 10.5 displays an example schedule for six classes; the course has been divided into six modules, each module being taught by a different teacher and each class following a different schedule.

There are strengths to this system. Teachers need teach only one module (presumably the one they are most comfortable with) and students are exposed to a wide range of opinions, perspectives and (hopefully) teaching styles. Teachers often see a huge benefit of this arrangement as they are teaching within their 'comfort zone'.

There are, however, several disadvantages. From an administrative point of view, all the lessons have to be scheduled at the same time and all the modules have to be exactly the same length regardless of content. Also teachers, and hence students, may not develop a clear overview of the course, and may be unable to make appropriate links between the various TOK areas. This, in turn,

Figure 10.5 Example rotation schedule based on division in six modules

	Module 1	Module 2	Module 3	Module 4	Module 5	Module 6
	Natural science and perception	*The arts and emotions*	*History and social sciences*	*Religion and ethics*	*Maths and logic*	*Language*
1st rotation	Class A	Class B	Class C	Class D	Class E	Class F
2nd rotation	Class F	Class A	Class B	Class C	Class D	Class E
3rd rotation	Class E	Class F	Class A	Class B	Class C	Class D
4th rotation	Class D	Class E	Class F	Class A	Class B	Class C
5th rotation	Class C	Class D	Class E	Class F	Class A	Class B
6th rotation	Class B	Class C	Class D	Class E	Class F	Class A

may have a negative effect on student essays and presentations (under this system teachers may have to advise on essays on subjects that they have never taught). The order of units will be made random; this too presents serious drawbacks in terms of course coherence (see section 2.7 below). Arguably, though, the biggest drawback is psychological: when teachers are only delivering a small section of the course it is hard for them to really take responsibility for making the classes work. Similar remarks also apply to the students. When they know that in five weeks they are changing teacher it may give the course a disjointed feel and may lead to low motivation and commitment from both staff and students.

The class system

Under this system a group of students is assigned to a regular class and the teacher takes the students for the length of the course. The teacher must be able to lead classes and advise on the essays, presentations and overall assessments in all the TOK areas. This is both an exciting opportunity and an intimidating requirement, and how it is approached will depend on the attitudes of the teachers. With adequate support in the first few years I do not believe that it is asking too much of staff to become acquainted with all areas of the course. There is a wealth of resources available to help (see Resources section 4) and the teacher can always ask colleagues to do the odd guest presentation. That said, there is no doubt that teaching right across the TOK spectrum is a more demanding task than sticking to a narrower specialization, and resources must be devoted to staff development if schools intend to adopt this approach.

2.6 The flavour of TOK lessons

As has already been stated, TOK is not so much about the delivery of new content as it is about reflection on what students already know and on what they do in their six diploma subjects and beyond. Thoughtful reflection is the key and teaching methodology should be tailored to encourage this. Teacher talk, no matter how inspired, should not dominate the lesson.

So what should the lessons be like? There is no hard and fast rule; each teacher will develop his/her own style, but I think that we should, as a matter of course, be seeking *variety*. The IBO states in its TOK guide that 'teachers are encouraged to be adventurous' and as there is little content to deliver we can and should, over the length of the course, use games, puzzles, discussion, videos, quizzes, simulations, cartoons, presentations, research projects, essays, readings, and anything else you can think of that will engage the students. Lessons should be fun (without necessarily being funny); if introduced the right way students will find it interesting and rewarding to look anew at what they know and do.

Given the pressure on students, schools, and teachers to produce high results, it is worth stressing here that TOK is not about drilling in essays and presentations. To teach like this would not only be against the spirit of the course, but also counter-productive in that it would not lead to better grades. The assessment criteria (see section 3 of this chapter) award marks for what we call 'the voice of the knower' (that is, an ability to relate TOK to one's own experience) and this voice only develops through open and reflective class discussions. Essays derived from books and other thinkers tend to score poorly.

In short, there is no substitute for open and critical discussion – by all means follow up with written pieces but do not run the course with a focus on essays. It simply will not work.

2.7 Developing a scheme of work

Teachers have an enormous amount of freedom in teaching TOK. Though the course guide does detail the scope of the enquiry, there are no guidelines as to the time to be spent on the various areas of the course. There are, therefore, many approaches possible.

The first issue is content and the first port of call is, naturally, the *Subject Guide* which shows on page 5 a diagram containing:

Way of Knowing	*Areas of Knowledge*
Language	The Arts
Reason	Natural Sciences
Emotion	Social Science
Perception	History
	Ethics
	Mathematics

(You may wish to question this categorization. This is a perfectly valid exercise within the course.)

Though courses vary from school to school, these are the obvious elements to address in any scheme of work. A common theme of conversation at IB TOK workshops is exactly what each school does, and what emphasis it places on the different aspects. Three other themes that are often explicitly included in the course are 'The Nature of Truth', 'Paradigms' and 'Media'. Depending on the charter/mission statement of your school, there may be other aspects worth dedicating a unit of study to, such as 'Human Rights and Responsibilities', or 'The Role of Government'. Some teachers feel that TOK is the ideal vehicle for introducing students to important ideas that they would not meet elsewhere, thus moving the course towards a liberal arts conception of education. There is a lot to be said for this, as long as the approach remains a critical one and not focused on content, or 'delivery' of material.

A successful course does not need to include all the Ways of Knowing and the Areas of Knowledge. Arguably you could leave out any particular part and still do a great job, but the Ways of Knowing and the Areas of Knowledge are fairly 'core' topics and I would strongly recommend that you include all of them.

Once the core has been decided (and perhaps the decision will depend heavily on your staffing) you need to decide on the actual scheme of work. If you are operating a rotation scheme (see section 2.5) then this does not apply, but if you are operating a class system (again see section 2.5) then it is worth giving a good deal of attention to the order of topics. There are a myriad different approaches. Here are two:

The 'logical' order. It is sometimes said that you need to consider the Ways of Knowing first, before looking at how they operate within the Areas of Knowledge. Within the Ways of Knowing it can be argued that it makes sense to start with Language, as this is the medium through which the classes are held. So you work through the lists set out above, introducing individual topics as you wish.

The advantage of this system is clarity. The course outline is straightforward and is laid out in the subject guide. The disadvantage is that the scheme is not student-centred; it starts with the most theoretical themes (language, perception, reasoning, emotion) and then applies them to the specific areas from which they arise: the arts, natural sciences, human sciences, ethics, history and mathematics. I know that this approach is used successfully in many schools, but arguably students find it easier to do the reverse. This accords with the pedagogical approach of starting with concrete examples and developing abstract principles.

The next approach is rather more complex and needs more work to set up. However, I think it is a better system.

The narrative approach. The idea here is to develop a story that runs through the course and that ties all the disparate areas and themes together in a coherent manner. What follows here is one example of such a story. I use the metaphor of a journey in search of truth. At the start of the journey through IB we might ask the students 'What is knowledge?' and 'What is most certain?' In our technological world, the *natural sciences* may well appear to be the answer to both questions. Sciences have been incredibly successful in developing useful theories about the world around us and so their methodologies are well worth exploring. However, students are often surprised to find that there are significant issues that the so-called scientific method cannot address. TOK classes find that, despite its successes in uncovering certain kinds of knowledge, science leaves unanswered certain questions about our lives and the human condition. So our search continues and an obvious place to begin a search 'beyond' science is *the arts*. So we look at how the arts allow us to gain knowledge about ourselves, each other and our communities. However, students discover that subjective truth comes at a cost and we must sacrifice objectivity and certitude. So, returning to our search for certainty, how about $1 + 1 = 2$? TOK can then examine whether *mathematics* offers us absolutely certain knowledge. Mathematics naturally leads to general systems of *reasoning*, with all their strengths and limitations. Students can then ponder the limitations of applying reasoning to human endeavours – the *social sciences* and *history*. These disciplines attempt to combine the rigour of natural sciences with the insights and empathy developed in the arts but we find that trying to analyse humans introduces a whole raft of problems, not least those of individuality, bias and selection (some of which we will have encountered before in other contexts during the course).

This seems to be a fairly natural place to pause and take stock. By this stage a class will have covered several familiar areas of knowledge (natural sciences, arts, social sciences, history and mathematics) and one way of knowing (reasoning), but have we made much progress in our search for certainty? Student opinion varies, but discussion tends to highlight several themes/problems that will have arisen – perhaps *perception, culture, paradigms* and *language*. Now that they have been aired we can begin to look at these more abstract issues in their own right.

We will have come across the problems of perception several times. We can look at the practical problems (we can all think of times when our senses have failed us) and philosophical problems (could *the world* really be an illusion?) and this leads us nicely to paradigms as general problems of knowledge. The concept of paradigms reflects the fact that differing perspectives can result in radically different interpretations of the same information. As a simple example, the stars at night can be taken as 'evidence' either for the existence of God or for the meaninglessness of human existence! Students must come to understand that the biggest paradigm is background and culture. Our cultures strongly affect certain areas of knowledge (ethics is perhaps the most obvious example) and perhaps actually determine our belief systems. Subsequently, it is only natural to turn students' attention to language as a means of expressing cultural values and as a medium of communication. They will soon discover that language is not the ideal tool for the job that it first appears to be.

By this time we are approaching the end of the course, so it is natural to review our quest for certainty and apply the themes explored to areas of experience outside the school curriculum. I think it is always worth shifting the emphasis outward as we near the end of high school. After all, TOK is a tool for life so looking beyond the school walls is essential. *Ethics* and *religion* are the most obvious topics here and, taken together, these areas perhaps provide compelling reasons to go beyond the purely rational. This leads us to examine the nature of *feelings, emotion and intuition*. To end the course we ask how far we have come. Has our quest for certainty been successful? If so, how? If not, why not? Most importantly, where will our quest take us after the end of TOK?

I have put a fair bit of detail in here (far more can be found in my books – see section 4.3) because I think it is important to see that you can tell a story that includes all the elements of the course and from which the more abstract themes arise naturally. Having tried both methods (the 'logical' approach and the 'narrative' approach) I come down firmly on the side of the story. As long as there is a narrative that threads the whole thing together students will find it accessible and meaningful.

However you decide to plan your curriculum, IBO authorization teams will expect to see evidence that a school has developed its own schemes of work for TOK, which are suited to its particular students, timetable and teachers. We do not, therefore, include a scheme of work here. We hope that with the details in this chapter, in the subject guide and possibly from a good textbook, constructing such a scheme should be relatively straightforward.

2.8 Homework and class work

As you think about how much work to set each week during the course, it is important that you have the assessment model in mind (see section 1.3). That said, there is enormous variation in the amount of work given to students in different schools. While most schools do at least one practice essay and one practice presentation in addition to the actual assessed elements, others set multiple assignments and three or four practice essays. Deciding on the optimal amount of work requires some thought because of the IB workload and the very high demands of CAS on student time.

Written work

From the students' perspective, writing TOK pieces is very difficult. It's not just that the ideas are hard (which they are) but that structuring an original and complex argument is a real intellectual challenge. It is easy to spend a long time thinking hard but ending up very confused and even demoralized. This means that students need to be broken in gently, starting with shorter, more descriptive pieces and gradually moving into more analytic ones: in my experience, throwing them in at the deep end (i.e. with an IB essay title) is not a good approach. Since it is important to establish working expectations right from the start, I suggest that one written piece a week be the norm to start with – just one side of hand-written A4 or the equivalent. Assignments should be closely related to class work and 'easy' to get started on. For instance, start with 'Which of your six DP subjects do you think is the most reliable and why?' or 'Describe a time when your senses deceived you. Why do you think this happened?' or 'Why does the 21st century place so much trust in scientific results?' or 'What makes a great piece of art great?' As the course progresses and students become familiar with the focus of the work you can develop more difficult and longer essay-like assignments and allow them to set their own titles – and this is when their interest really takes off. Reading these journal entries can be a wonderful insight into the concerns and lives of the students, and I always make a point, when I mark them every few weeks, of writing detailed and personal responses. With classes of 20, all sorts of issues come to light and it is an excellent way of establishing a genuinely meaningful dialogue with each and every one of them. Once students have this personal engagement with the issues, writing the essays becomes less of a chore, more of a pleasure, and the grades are likely to improve significantly.

In general I would suggest that for most of the time the TOK workload should be light – certainly less than a standard level course. This is only realistic when the overall workload of the diploma is considered; many students will exceed the minimum requirements in any case.

Presentations

Again, I think the workload should be light and aimed at producing small amounts of quality reflection time. Some teachers use student presentations to introduce new topics in the TOK syllabus; some use them to break up the 'regular' lessons. Either way, it is important to let students have a trial run with feedback so that they know the standards that are expected. An important point is that the activity of presentations should be integral to the course and can be very short even if the assessed one has to be somewhat longer (see section 3.2 for more detail). For example, it would be perfectly possible to require members of the TOK class to bring in a piece of art (in the most general sense) and explain in three minutes each why it has aesthetic value to them.

2.9 Integrating TOK with other subjects

For TOK to be genuinely central to the diploma, it is vital that teachers draw attention to the TOK aspects of their own subject, and know how to lead a discussion on it. This is why the IBO advises that as many teachers as possible be involved in TOK. It is unhelpful for teachers outside TOK to say things like 'That's not on our syllabus' or, worse, 'We don't have time for that philosophical stuff'. TOK issues suffuse and permeate *all* subjects, and a successful programme will draw on subject teachers to complement (and sometimes disagree with) the TOK teachers' inputs to the students. A mathematics teacher might discuss the nature of mathematical truth and proof; a social scientist might address issues of modelling human behaviour; a linguist can talk (ironically) about the problems of meaning; an artist or musician can discuss what we can learn from the arts …

and so on. The input of specialists can enormously enrich the student experience of TOK, and significantly deepen their understanding.

If teachers are to contribute to TOK then they must have some idea of what TOK is about in general, as well as how it relates to their own subject. Both of these can be problematic and need careful consideration – though with the IBO decision to include a TOK session in every subject workshop, awareness will hopefully improve.

How to inform all teachers what TOK is about generally? This is ideally addressed by an in-service training session of at least half a day, led by an experienced TOK teacher who has been on IB TOK workshops. In this time one can cover the philosophy and aims, touch on major areas within TOK, and do a few practical activities.

How to ensure that all teachers are aware of the TOK issues within their own subject? One might think that this would not be an issue, but it certainly can be. TOK has a particular focus (knowledge issues) and even excellent subject teachers may simply be unaware of it. If the TOK teaching team has representatives from different departments in the school then these people can initiate discussions, lead a few sessions and otherwise raise the appropriate issues.

Whichever way your school decides to increase TOK awareness amongst teachers, the important thing is that the issue is not left to chance, but is consciously and carefully addressed.

3 Assessment

Note: The following details are currently under review – your DPC will have the latest information.

3.1 Overview

The TOK course is assessed via an externally marked essay which should be written in students' own time and an internally marked presentation. The assessment model and criteria for the essay and presentation are in the *Subject Guide* on pages 38–54. In section 3.5 below is a one-page summary of these criteria which staff and students have found useful. The grades for the presentation and the essay are combined to give grades A–E for TOK. Note that the essay is weighted twice as heavily as the presentation. This grade is then combined with the grade awarded for the extended essay (also A–E) to give bonus points as per figure 10.3.

Students awarded either the F code (failure) or the N code (non-submission) will fail the diploma.

3.2 When to assess?

We would always expect students to be producing their best work at the end of the course, but leaving all the assessment until then is not ideal for at least two reasons. Firstly, most other subjects may try and do the same, resulting in work overload, over-stressed students and poor-quality work (this problem can be alleviated if your school's DPC takes an overview of course works across the curriculum and negotiates a reasonable schedule). Secondly, the presentation is meant to be integral to the course; it is a formative as well as a summative assessment tool and the presentations should be done over a period of time. That said, spreading presentations over too long a time puts the earlier students at a disadvantage because of the lack of continuity. It seems to me that the right time is early in the second year of the programme, and to have the presentations fairly close to each other. The students enjoy hearing each other's ideas and I have found that they give the course a certain breadth of topics that is hard to come by otherwise. Certainly the lessons after the presentations always seem to have an energy and a willingness to engage with the outside world that was missing before.

However, finishing the assessment process too early is not conducive to motivating the students during the last few lessons; even the most motivated students find it difficult to concentrate on an area that is 'finished' in terms of assessment when there are so many other demands on their time. Retaining an assessed element until the end of the course maintains a certain healthy tension and these problems of motivation can be largely alleviated.

3.3 External assessment: the essay

The essay (1,200–1,600 words) must be written on one of ten prescribed titles, which the IBO distributes well over a year before the essay is due. Each essay must have a cover sheet, called the TK/CS, signed by student and teacher to say that the essay is the work of the student. This form can be found in the TOK section of the *Vade Mecum*. The essays are posted to external examiners, usually experienced TOK teachers, a few months before the examination date (the DPC will have the exact date).

Students find essays very hard to write; they need practice, time to discuss with the teacher and with each other and time to do a first draft. It is important to go over the differences between essays for assessment and other less formal written assignments that you might set over the duration of the course. Give students a reminder about general essay-writing skills. It is also useful to go over and mark sample essays as a class and to discuss the marking criteria in detail. It is also within IB guidelines to give detailed feedback on a draft, as long as you do not actually edit the draft or tell students what to write. As a practical measure I always insist on students handing in a first draft which I keep on file for submission in case a final version fails to appear.

Finally, the issue of plagiarism is increasingly a problem for all essay-based coursework. Some of it is inadvertent, and can be stopped by very clear instructions about referencing sources, but the only way to be sure about it in other cases is to be active in the drafting and revising process – that is, to prevent the problem from arising. If students know that their ideas are under scrutiny then they are very unlikely to copy from the internet or elsewhere (and you are almost certain to spot it if they do). If the essay is not submitted to the IB then a plagiarized essay is an internal matter for the school to deal with. If a plagiarized essay is identified as such by an IB examiner then the school will be contacted and asked to explain the circumstances under which the essay was verified as being the student's own work.

Your DPC will be able to supply you with current essay titles. Four recent titles are cited here:

- Should a knower's personal point of view be considered an asset in the pursuit of knowledge, or an obstacle to be overcome?
- 'What I tell you three times is true.' (Lewis Carroll) Might this formula – or a more sophisticated version of it – actually determine what we believe to be true?
- 'What distinguishes Areas of Knowledge from one another is not how ideas are generated, but how they are evaluated.' Do you agree?
- Evaluate the ways in which emotion might enhance and/or undermine reasoning as a Way of Knowing.

3.4 Internal assessment: the presentation

The presentation is a talk of around 10 minutes, but longer if done as a group activity, and may be done at any stage of the course (see section 3.2). Topics can be chosen by the students or assigned by the teacher but must not be one of the prescribed essay titles. The presentations should never be essays read out loud. In fact students should be encouraged to use imaginative forms such as poetry, little plays, simulations, games, dramatized readings, interviews or debates. They can use supporting material such as videos, posters, questionnaires, cassettes/CDs of songs or interviews, costumes or props. Some schools insist that students print an outline of their talk onto a single overhead transparency – this helps them focus on a proper structure to their talk and prevents rambling.

The teacher needs to help students with planning, to assist them with starter questions and ensure that they are focused on TOK material. It is also important to keep an eye on group presentations and to ensure that all students are contributing to the final result. This can be very hard to do if groups are bigger than two people. Remember that individual marks must be given and that each student has to fill in the TK/SER form in which they discuss some key points of their presentation (the form is in the *Vade Mecum*).

When scheduling the presentations, allow some time for class discussion afterwards; the topics chosen are usually quite interesting and it is certainly good for the students to get a chance to discuss informally. You can credit students for the content of their responses to questions, but remember that there are no marks for leading a discussion or arousing great interest in the rest of the class.

3.5 Mark schemes for essay and presentation

Figures 10.6 and 10.7 are condensed versions of the IB marking criteria, for both presentation and essay. It may be helpful for staff and students to see them all on one page. Notice that they are not official IB tables – the details in the TOK guide remain the definitive version.

Figure 10.6 TOK essay descriptors (current in 2004; likely to change to a 4-criteria system in future)

	Criterion A: Knowledge issues: Are problems of knowledge recognized, understood and addressed?					
	10	8	6	4	2	0
Recognition and understanding	excellent	good	satisfactory	poor	very poor	none
Relevance to TOK and writer	consistently relevant and purposeful; essay reflects voice of student	consistently relevant; essay reflects voice of student	generally relevant; essay mainly reflects voice of student	generally irrelevant	no relevance	no relevance

	Criterion B: Quality of analysis: Are problems of knowledge / counter claims handled critically and reflectively?					
	10	8	6	4	2	0
Critical reflection and insight	excellent critical reflection and insight	good critical reflection and insight	satisfactory critical reflection; some insight	poor level of critical reflection	very poor level of critical reflection	none
Recognition of counter claims	counter claims are identified and thoroughly evaluated	counter claims are identified and evaluated	counter claims are identified	none	none	none
Argument	detailed, cogent, valid discussion	detailed, valid discussion	adequate detail; generally valid	superficial or invalid arguments	entirely superficial or invalid arguments	none

	Criterion C: Breadth and links: Awareness of different ways of knowledge / areas of knowledge and links?					
	5	4	3	2	1	0
Awareness of ways/ areas of knowledge	excellent awareness; effective links and/or comparisons where appropriate	good awareness; appropriate links or comparisons	satisfactory awareness; appropriate links or comparisons	poor awareness; links or comparisons not always appropriate	very poor awareness; links or comparisons not appropriate	no awareness

	Criterion D: Structure, clarity, coherence: (linguistic skills are not assessed here)					
	5	4	3	2	1	0
Structure	excellently structured; concise introduction; effective conclusion	well structured; concise introduction; clear conclusion	satisfactorily structured; main points conveyed	poor in structure	very poor in structure	unstructured
Clarity and logical coherence	clear and logically coherent; concepts and distinctions succinctly defined and clarified	clear and logically coherent; concepts and distinctions are defined and clarified	satisfactory structure; adequately clear; main points conveyed	poor in structure and logical coherence	very poor in clarity and logical coherence	unclear or logically incoherent; no relevance to title

	Criterion E: Examples: Is the essay well supported by appropriate examples drawn from a variety of sources?					
	5	4	3	2	1	0
Quality	consistently succinct, appropriate and effective	consistently appropriate	generally appropriate	rarely appropriate	inappropriate	irrelevant
Range	wide variety; own experience; high degree of cultural diversity	good variety of examples; own experience; degree of cultural diversity	satisfactory variety of examples	limited variety of examples	narrow variety of examples	no relevant examples

	Criterion F: Factual accuracy and reliability: Are 'facts' accurate; were sources correctly cited?					
	NB total of strands used		3	2	1	0
Factual accuracy	–	–	no factual inaccuracy	little factual inaccuracy	some factual inaccuracy	extensive factual inaccuracy
Sources	–	–	–	all sources cited thoroughly and systematically, or no citation needed	most sources adequately cited	no workable information about sources given

Notes: For Criterion F, the sum of the two strands will be awarded. For Criterion F, 'fact' does not encompass definition or terminology.

Figure 10.7 TOK presentation descriptors

	Criterion A: Knowledge issues: Are problems of knowledge recognized and understood?					
	5	4	3	2	1	0
Recognition and understanding	excellent	good	satisfactory	poor	very poor	none
Relevance of ideas to TOK	consistently relevant	consistently relevant	generally relevant	generally irrelevant	no relevance	no relevance
Imagination and originality	high degree of both	evidence of both	some imagination	neither	neither	neither
	Criterion B: Quality of analysis: Are problems of knowledge / different views handled critically and reflectively?					
	5	4	3	2	1	0
Levels of critical reflection and insight	excellent critical reflection and insight	good critical reflection and insight	satisfactory critical reflection; some insight	poor level of critical reflection	very poor level of critical reflection	none
Engagement with issues	thorough engagement with issues	engages with issues in some depth	adequate engagement	generally superficial; inadequate engagement	entirely superficial; inadequate engagement	none
Recognition of multiple viewpoints	explicitly recognised; fully acknowledged	recognised and acknowledged in some depth	some recognition and some acknowledgement	little recognition	little awareness	no awareness
Logical rigour of arguments	logically valid; cogent justification	logically valid; coherent justification	generally valid and justified	may not be valid; main points may not be justified	no argument or completely invalid and unjustified	none
Concern with implications of main points	meticulous and thoughtful	thoughtful	some account	none	none	none
	Criterion C: Knowledge at work: To what extent does the presentation apply TOK to a contemporary issue?					
	5	4	3	2	1	0
Application to contemporary issue	excellent; explicit and successful application of abstract principles	good; explicit application of abstract principles	satisfactory; abstract principles related to issue	poor; some attempt to apply abstract principles to issue	very poor; very little attempt to apply abstract principles	no application of TOK to issue
	Criterion D: Clarity: Is the presentation clear and logically coherent? (linguistic skills are not essential here)					
	5	4	3	2	1	0
Clarity and logical coherence	excellent	good	satisfactory	poor	very poor	none

3.6 Marking and moderating the presentation

Since no TOK presentation exemplar material is currently available, schools will need to take a great deal of care marking and moderating the presentation. Here is some advice:

- Read the subject guide section in detail – there is a wealth of information there.
- Do not be afraid to award marks at both extremes of attainment.
- While there may be some correlation between essay and presentation scores, the skills for excellent presentations and excellent essays do not entirely overlap. Do not be surprised if the students do better in one component than in another.
- For criterion A, marks for 'imagination and originality' should be given if students are applying themselves in a thoughtful, personal and creative

manner. The descriptor should not be interpreted too strictly – after all, these are 17 and 18 year-olds dealing with issues that have troubled people over the centuries. They do not need to be producing groundbreaking philosophy!

- By the same token, do not be afraid to award full marks for criterion B which assesses the content of the presentation.
- The requirement in criterion C that students address a 'contemporary issue' can be interpreted broadly. They do not need to choose a topical issue, but neither should the subject be outside the students' experiences. Always avoid a theoretical perspective. We do not want a dry regurgitation of the thoughts of a philosopher on a particular problem. If a student argues a philosophical point it should be made relevant, perhaps by linking it to a current event.
- Assessment criterion D mentions 'clarity'. This refers to the logical structuring of ideas, not linguistic sophistication or pronunciation. These can be difficult to distinguish, but you must try to ensure that shy or non-native speakers are not disadvantaged here.

In schools with more than one TOK teacher it is important that grades are standardized. I would suggest that the best way of doing this is to have a standardization meeting before the bulk of the presentations are done. The TOK coordinator should video at least four presentations which should, ideally, reflect low, medium and high grades, and which offer a variety of approach: sketches, poems, talks. All TOK teachers can then meet to view and grade these presentations and compare marks.

In this way common standards develop. Discussions about grades and application of the specific assessment criteria benefit future marking, and increase teacher expertise.

If the presentations of a whole class are videoed as a matter of course then they can be used for the following year's standardization meeting. Once IB video exemplars are available the same moderation process can continue seamlessly.

3.7 Reporting on students' progress

In TOK the 'answers' are not really answers in the usual sense of the word, and so there are unusual problems in assessing student attainment. This applies both to feedback to students and to the more formal reporting procedures to parents or guardians.

In terms of feedback to students there are at least three traditional options – direct face-to-face feedback, grades, and comments – and teachers will need to make the usual professional judgements in determining exactly what mix they wish to use. For my part I avoid grades whenever I can; to emphasize that *the student* – and not an impersonal mark scheme – is at the centre of the course, I try to start a dialogue when marking written work in the first few weeks by giving lengthy written responses to students' work. It seems to me that this is in keeping with the spirit of TOK; in addition, when students realize that you will reply to their thoughts, and not just grade their work, their approach becomes far more open, thoughtful and sensitive. It is then possible to mould their efforts towards satisfying the more technical assessment criteria; eventually, practice essays and presentations should be marked according to the formal IB mark schemes in addition to comments.

In terms of reporting to parents and guardians, most schools employ a combination of comments and grades for effort and for attainment. In view of the above, some schools opt to give no attainment grades but only effort grades in the first few months, and perhaps even for the whole first year. Schools adopting this system will need to communicate carefully the reasons for this type of reporting lest students and parents think that attainment is unimportant or that in TOK all answers are equally good. If attainment grades are awarded then I suggest that they be done on a 1–7 scale (even though the diploma points awarded for TOK are not on this scale); to do anything else invites confusion and unnecessary anxiety from parents. I would also suggest that teachers err on the side of generosity in awarding grades; in TOK more than most subjects, self-fulfilling prophecies are easy to create.

Whatever schools decide, it is important that reporting be done seriously to communicate to the entire community that the school is fully committed to TOK and the central role it plays in the DP.

4 Resources

4.1 Staff development conferences

A school's best TOK resources are its teachers. Going on an IB workshop is, I would suggest, an absolute necessity for TOK beginners. For more experienced staff too, the workshops are an extremely valuable source of energy and ideas for teaching, texts to use, activities to try and books to read – well worth the money.

4.2 Using everyday resources

One of the many wonderful things about teaching TOK is that you can use so much everyday material. School issues are excellent – for example many senior students in a school will argue that they should have more privileges than they do; this is usually predicated on a certain moral position involving 'rights', and a close examination of their arguments can generate first-rate discussions and presentations. At time of writing we are four months into the US-led occupation of Iraq and the issues of 'just war' and 'truth in media' are highly topical. The start of a school art display provides aesthetics material; the religious festivals of the students can be an entry into religion; the multiple languages spoken in a class are a great asset in dealing with language … and on the list goes. The cliché that 'the students are the best resource' is not far wrong. In international and many local schools there is a wealth of different cultures and perspectives on which to draw, and in TOK we are extremely lucky that these perspectives form a vital part of the course. We can therefore let students speak, describe and analyse their own cultures and those of others; in this respect TOK is a wonderful vehicle to foster the IB goal of cross-cultural awareness and respect.

Newspapers are excellent sources of ideas. I recently saw an article on the failure of wine experts to distinguish a white wine that had a tasteless red dye in it from genuine red wine. When I asked students to discuss the article in small groups and report back to the class, issues of perception, language, social sciences and ethics arose in a very natural manner. Articles such as these generate a real sense of relevance and are not hard to find.

There are also several journals that provide excellent material for TOK.

Think – Philosophy for Everyone, published tri-annually by the British Royal Institute of Philosophy, is aimed squarely at those with no philosophical background – great for students and very accessible. See www.royalinstitutephilosophy.org/think.

Teaching Philosophy is a US publication aimed more at first-year undergraduates and university teachers than at high school students, but it still has lots of very useful ideas and articles. See www.pdcnet.org.

The Philosophers' Magazine, another British journal, is devoted to interesting issues within philosophy. Its scope is rather wider than Theory of Knowledge, though it is not an academic journal, and it is packed full of interesting and funny articles. See www.philosophers.co.uk (the interactive page www.philosophers.co.uk/games/games.htm is particularly fun and worth a visit). There are several possible class activities here.

Another magazine that is more general but regularly has excellent TOK resources is the British *Prospect* (www.prospect-magazine.co.uk). As an example, the April 2003 edition contains, among other things, articles on why art galleries should show copies of great works rather than originals; why the scientific community rejects controversial environmental findings; how Hollywood movies are in effect rewriting history for today's movie-going culture; and why a particular brand of relativism does not stand up to analysis. Some of these may be too difficult for the students, but most of them are very accessible.

Parabola Magazine (www.parabola.org) is published four times a year and is thematically based. The back issues on language, consciousness and several other issues are well worth ordering in. Highly accessible and stimulating, it draws from universal sources of all types.

The other main source of everyday resources is television and cinema. With NOVA, Horizon and other filmmakers producing documentaries like 'Who Shot JFK?', 'Kidnapped by UFOs?', and 'Fermat's Last Theorem' there is excellent material for detailed case studies. Short clips from movies and TV shows also break up a lesson and generate lively debate – 'Good Will Hunting', 'The Truman Show', 'Monty Python', '12 Angry Men', 'The Matrix', 'Memento' and even 'Friends' and 'Toy Story' all contain great 10-minute excerpts that can be used to make a specific point.

4.3 Textbooks

After staff development, and perhaps even before, this is the area that teachers like to spend money on. And unlike a few years ago, there are quite a few texts available these days (see below), some of them written specifically for the TOK course. Before mentioning any of them, however, it is worth addressing a concern often voiced at TOK conferences.

Some teachers feel that a textbook is inappropriate for the course; that it limits individual thought and is likely to lead to a uniform and standard response to the ideas. More than any other course, TOK is meant to be centred around the student, not an external body of knowledge, so surely a given text goes against this spirit?

I can totally understand this point of view – and if teachers have lessons designed so that students encounter books as texts to be 'worked through' and 'completed' then I think it is probably correct. TOK is meant to be taught and learned interactively and in an engaging manner, and no text can begin to make real the profound problems of knowledge; as always this responsibility and privilege remains with the teacher. But teachers often need support and a handy source of information, and so do students! Of course as the author of two of these texts it is clear what my view is: that the text can enormously enrich a course and actually free up a teacher to do more creative things. One can always use a text badly – but one doesn't have to.

Texts available at the moment are:

Abel, R. (1976) *Man is the Measure*, Free Press.

Alchin, N. (2003) *The Theory of Knowledge*, John Murray.

Alchin, N. (2003) *The Theory of Knowledge Teacher's Book*, John Murray.

Stuart, T. (2000) *Regarding the World: A Primer for ToK*, Tony Stuart.

Tomkinson, J. L. (1996) *The Enterprise of Knowledge*, Leader Books.

Woolman, M. (2000) *Ways of Knowing: An Introduction to Theory of Knowledge*, IBID Press Victoria.

4.4 **IB essentials**

The *Theory of Knowledge Subject Guide* (1999) is excellent and indispensable; it breaks the course into Ways of Knowing (perception, reason, language, emotion) and Areas of Knowledge (natural sciences, the arts, social sciences, history, mathematics, ethics) while always focusing on the role of the 'knower'. Under each of these ways and areas are listed many questions and quotations; and linking questions are provided to help move seamlessly between different aspects.

To a teacher new to TOK the sheer breadth of the guide is daunting. In addition to this, it has long lists of questions for which there appear to be no answers, which may be enough to deter the faint-hearted. For this reason it is important to look at the other resources and not at the guide in isolation.

Sections E and F of the *Vade Mecum* contain the necessary administrative details.

Lessons from Around the World is an IB publication with 20 examples of good TOK lessons – and the plan is that it grows over the years. It is an excellent resource to see that TOK is practical, student-centred, and perhaps not as abstract as it seems to be from the *Subject Guide*.

Marked Exemplar Essays are an excellent way of getting a feel for the standard of marking required. The pack contains several essays with grades for each criterion and a commentary from the senior examining team.

Forum is the official IB Theory of Knowledge magazine. Discussing assessment, lesson plans and activities, schemes of work and conferences, it is an extremely useful resource. The paper version is distributed free to all diploma schools; the online version is available at www.adastranet.net/forum.

The IB *Online Curriculum Centre* is a growing collection of links and resources. It contains a discussion forum, a resource centre, exemplar essays and the relevant chapters from the *Vade Mecum*. You need a password and user ID to log in – see your DPC if you do not have one.
See http://online.ibo.org/onlinecc/frontpage/index.cfm

4.5 Reading list

Apart from the texts already mentioned, I recommend the following:

Cade-Hetherington, S. (1996) *Knowledge Puzzles*, Westview Press.

Nagel, T. (1989) *What Does it All Mean?*, Oxford University Press.

Palmer, D. (1991) *Does the Centre Hold?*, Mayfield.

Pinker, S. (1998) *How the Mind Works*, Penguin.

Pinker, S. (1994) *The Language Instinct*, William Morrow and Co.

Russell, B. (1998) *The Problems of Philosophy*, reprinted by Oxford University Press.

Palmer's and Nagel's accounts are wonderful general material for staff and students alike. Many people feel that Pinker's two books present a one-sided case rather than a balanced argument – and he is certainly controversial – but both books cover so much ground that they are well worth reading even if you totally reject the arguments. Russell's and Cade-Hetherington's books are philosophy proper, and even though they are quite light they are generally too advanced for students.

More detailed reading lists for each topic area can be found in *The Theory of Knowledge* by Nicholas Alchin, listed above in section 4.3.

4.6 Web resources

I am reluctant to put more than a few links here, as any directory of online resources may quickly become out of date. You may be well advised to do a search on a popular engine, but be careful – as well as an IB course, 'Theory of Knowledge' is the casual name for *epistemology* – a fully-fledged branch of philosophy – and many results from a search may therefore be misleading. Nevertheless, at the time of writing, the following are a few sites that I have found especially useful.

www.amyscott.com/theory_of_knowledge.htm
This site is devoted to the IB Theory of Knowledge, providing links to all areas of the course – well worth perusing for background information and general reading material.

www.shef.ac.uk/uni/projects/ptpdlp/
This site is devoted to distance learning of philosophy. There are some very good e-books that you can download.

www.earlham.edu/~peters/philinks.htm#miscellany
This is an extraordinarily comprehensive guide to philosophy on the net. You can use it to find almost anything you want – probably in far more detail than you need.

http://home.swipnet.se/ulf_p/tok/tok.htm
This is a great little site with links to fascinating areas, all catalogued by TOK content.

Chapter 11
The extended essay

Stuart Jones, BSc

Stuart Jones, IB coordinator (DPC) and head of science at the International School of Singapore, is also the author of Chapter 3. In this chapter, he describes the third core component of the International Baccalaureate (IB) Diploma Programme (DP), the extended essay. He explains what it is, what the benefits are for both students and faculty, and how to successfully implement the programme.

Thanks are due to Simon Giddings for providing some of the tracking materials for this chapter.

Note: all weblinks featured in this chapter can be accessed through our website: www.dp-help.com

1 Nature of the extended essay

The extended essay is an academic research essay, and all Diploma Programme (DP) students must write one. More specifically, it is an in-depth research essay on a focused topic *within a single DP subject*. Not every diploma subject is acceptable but about 60 subjects are, including many languages (for the detailed list, see the extended essay subject guide). A group 1 or 2 language essay must be written in that language, while all others need to be written in English, French or Spanish. The upper limit on the word count is 4,000 words and the IBO recommends that students should spend around 40 hours in total on their extended essay. All work must be done *outside* regular class work, so students need to manage their time and work independently. This is not to say they must work unassisted: students must seek a *supervisor* (a teacher but not necessarily one who teaches the student) to guide them through the process.

Students must choose topics that require the gathering and analysis of information from a number of sources. The IBO expects that the content will present a genuine intellectual challenge. There is further a strong emphasis on the *process* of academic research, the level of analysis, the quality of argument, the coherence of communication, and the standards of formal presentation: the referencing, the bibliography and the abstract. As the IBO states in its literature, 'the essay requirement acquaints diploma candidates with the kind of independent research and writing skills expected by universities'.

The extended essay is externally assessed and is awarded a grade from A to E. This grade is then combined with the TOK grade to award up to a maximum of 3 bonus points (details in section 3 below). Note, however, that a student who receives an E grade for both the extended essay and Theory of Knowledge will fail the diploma, as will any student who fails to submit an extended essay.

2 Aims, objectives and educational benefits

The aims and objectives are listed in detail in the extended essay subject guide. In brief, they are to provide candidates with the opportunity to:

- choose and develop a focused topic for independent research that can be achieved within the word limit
- develop research skills and critical thinking skills
- practise the thesis approach to writing that will be required at university
- structure material from diverse sources in a coherent and logical manner according to recognized formats
- experience the excitement of intellectual challenge and discovery.

These objectives show that the extended essay is an ambitious undertaking for students – and for schools. While there are significant challenges to be addressed (see below), it is a fact that for many students the extended essay is a source of considerable academic pride and one of the highlights of their study. Furthermore, students returning from their first year at university frequently comment that the DP in general and the extended essay in particular prepared them very well for the work expected at university. The essay can also be put to good use in applications for scholarships, or as a topic for discussion at the university admissions interview. Discussing a topic that the student is passionate and knowledgeable about may well sway an admissions officer.

3 Assessment

The extended essay is assessed *externally* on a scale of 0–36. There are two sets of criteria: the general assessment criteria and the subject assessment criteria. The general assessment criteria (listed on pages 19–23 of the 1999 extended essay guide and summarized in figure 11.1 below) are worth 24 marks and concern general skills identical for all subject areas. The subject-specific assessment criteria (listed on pages 25–138 of the guide) are worth 12 marks and are specific to each subject (recall that the extended essay must be written in one of the DP subjects). The two marks are combined to give a score from 0 to 36, and on the basis of this score a grade A–E is awarded according to the conversion set out in figure 11.2. The resulting extended essay grade is then combined with the grade awarded for the TOK course (also A–E) to give up to a maximum of 3 *bonus points* (determined according to the assessment set out in figure 10.3, Chapter 10). An E grade for both, however, means the student will not receive a diploma. (Students who fail the extended essay, however, are allowed to submit another one at the next examination session.)

Although the supervising teachers do not mark the essays, they need to be very familiar with the grading criteria for two main reasons: first, to dispense sound advice to students; and second, to submit a *reliable* predicted grade for the extended essay to the IBO. Fortunately, this is not a difficult task; teachers will just have to avoid falling into some of the common traps, described in the sections below.

In general, the extended essay needs to involve the student in collecting data or analysing primary sources. Essays that are essentially literature reviews tend to do poorly. In the sciences, for instance, the best extended essays are those that involve the student in experimental design and execution. Supervisors need to help their students focus on the manageable and practical. This is of paramount importance and students must be dissuaded from embarking on grandiose projects more suitable for a PhD thesis. Remember that students are advised to spend only 40 hours on their extended essay including the research and writing stages. Whilst helping the student to keep the extended essay in perspective, be careful not to downgrade it. Especially for students who are struggling with TOK and risk an E grade there, the essay can be a lifeline: students who follow the guidelines and ensure they meet the general assessment criteria should be able to obtain a passing grade for the essay and thus avert diploma disqualification.

In fact, the grading criteria and the grade boundaries (see figures 11.1 and 11.2) reveal that a comfortable pass can be achieved by focusing on the general criteria and competently completing an exercise in academic writing. To gain a grade A or B, there must also be considerable subject academic merit to the essay. One of the most crucial mistakes supervisors and students sometimes make is to concentrate on the subject and the subject criteria, whereas this carries only one-third of the marks. More than anything else, the essay is an exercise in academic

Figure 11.1 Summary of general assessment criteria (with maximum marks for each)

A Focus (research question) of the essay is clearly expressed and specified?	2
B Chosen approach matches the research question?	3
C Materials, sources, data and evidence are properly considered?	4
D Argument and evaluation build on materials gathered and are relevant to title?	4
E Conclusion is consistent with arguments?	2
F Abstract includes research question, scope of investigation and conclusion?	2
G Formal presentation (content page, abstract diagrams, references, etc.) complete?	3
H Overall (holistic) assessment of engagement, initiative, insight and flair	4

Figure 11.2 Grade boundaries for the extended essay (May 2002)

Points awarded	Grade
30–36	A
25–29	B
17–24	C
9–16	D
0–8	E

writing and research; the specific subject acts more like a vehicle to make this happen, and allows the students to take some credit for deepening their understanding of an area of their interest. A general criteria checklist (based on a model by Ian Dorton, chief examiner for economics) is included in Appendix 3; this has proved excellent value to students.

4 Organization and administration of the extended essay programme

The DP coordinator (DPC) needs to maintain oversight on the extended essay programme, but should work in tandem with the teacher-librarian. Students should be encouraged (or required) to discuss their extended essay topic early on with the teacher-librarian. This will allow the librarian to source materials and provide better service. The coordinator and librarian should decide together on essay policies in particular with regard to plagiarism (see section 7), and subsequently clearly communicate those policies to both staff and students. They may well decide that it is in everyone's interest to run workshops (one for faculty and one for students) on available resources and research and referencing skills. Such workshops are in fact relevant to the whole school community because the school needs to develop these essential skills in the pre-IB years. In our experience, the consequence of such sessions is that students make better use of the library, and that the library will correspondingly find and acquire more resources to support the students. Without making firm and explicit links between the library, faculty and students, many students will never use the school library for their extended essay.

The responsibilities of the supervisors (according to the extended essay guide) are to:

- encourage and support students during the research and writing processes
- support students with the necessary research skills
- ensure that the essay is all the work of the student
- submit a predicted grade and complete a supervisor's report.

Clearly, some routines will need to be established in each school to ensure a consistent implementation of these rather broad guidelines. Such routines will naturally depend on the size of the school and the experience of the staff. In smaller schools the DPC is likely to play a key role to ensure consistency. In larger schools, the role of the DPC could be more that of an administrator, who ensures that every student hooks up with an extended essay supervisor on time and subsequently respects important deadlines (homeroom teachers and supervisors can of course help here).

Some schools tend to select the extended essay supervisors amongst their academically most qualified faculty, while other schools encourage *every* teacher to participate in a supervisory role. The first model may benefit the student in terms of professional advice, but the second approach allows teachers to grow professionally themselves; what teachers lack in experience they may make up for in terms of enthusiasm (teachers should always remember that they are not alone in this venture; the teacher-librarian's help can and should be engaged on issues dealing with research, referencing and essay structure). The DPC should draw up a list of teachers, the subjects they teach, their academic background, and their own research interests. This list can then be presented to the students. The list will inevitably unearth some useful surprises, such as an avid painter hiding in the mathematics department or a geography teacher with a background in teaching history. Naturally, publication of such a list needs to be carefully managed so as not to stir up ill-feelings by advertising some members of staff at the expense of others. Another problem with recruitment is that the DPC will need to explain the necessity of calling upon non-diploma teachers to act as supervisors. These problems can be alleviated if the school has invested sufficient effort in the 'whole-school approach' to the DP (as it should have, in order to be authorized as well as for its own well-being – see Chapter 3 and the case studies in Part Two).

Whichever supervisor model the school adopts, at the start of the extended essay schedule all staff should be informed about the procedures and the role of the supervisor. Next, to create a visible and well-defined start to the extended essay programme, it is helpful to hold a meeting between the students, DPC and librarian to go over procedures and expectations. During this meeting, support materials (see below) can be handed out and time can be spent clarifying and consolidating the advice therein. It is very useful to invite a few final-year diploma students to this meeting to talk about the need to meet deadlines and where to get assistance. Following quickly on from this introductory meeting, the students need to select a subject area and seek out a supervisor from the published list. The DPC will need to supervise this stage carefully, and set strict deadlines for students to find a supervisor and agree on a title.

The IBO advises that supervisors take on no more than four or five students. However, this figure should come with a health warning. Supervising five highly academic, motivated and independent students is very different from taking on five students who are struggling. Our recommendation is that the school should set a working limit of three students per supervisor, and increase this to no more than five students per supervisor at the teacher's and DPC's discretion. It is also evident that some subjects are more popular than others when it comes to the extended essay (see figure 11.3 for worldwide trends). The profile may well change from year to year; some subjects may get no takers at all, whereas 15 students are jockeying for one history teacher. Herein lies the need for the DPC to cast the net for extended essay supervisors as widely as possible, and to make sure that every department has a clear idea of suitable areas for research. Having to turn students away from their chosen subject defeats the purpose of the essay to some extent, so the alternatives need to be attractive. All departments outside group 3 (which attracts almost 50% of the extended essays), in particular the mathematics department, may have to be advised to explicitly advertise the essays in order to spread the supervision workload more evenly across the departments.

The IBO states that supervisors should normally spend between 2 and 3 hours in total with each student over the course of the extended essay, but they accept that this will vary according to the circumstances. In our experience we recommend that you set a working figure of between 3 and 5 hours' supervision time per student. Colleagues at workshops will privately state that a more realistic figure is two to three times this. Nevertheless, remember that the IBO requires the extended essay to be an independently researched and written piece of work and that it regards supervisors who offend this requirement as behaving professionally irresponsibly. In the opinion and experience of the authors of this book, 3–5 hours of support is indeed feasible provided the extended essay programme is well organized (with clear deadlines pertaining to well-defined outcomes) and supervisors have a bank of ideas for *viable* projects. Remember that supervisors should not be spending a great deal of time teaching and reinforcing the basic rules of referencing and essay structure. These are all matters that should be handled by the DPC and the teacher-librarian. Some supervisors get very involved with the student's extended essay and there is a danger that they can lose objectivity, focus too much on the subject specifics to the detriment of the whole process, or guide the student into areas of study that they are not capable of handling. Departments must realize that the extended essay is supposed to take 40 hours of work, and need to ensure they agree only to essay titles that can be completed within this time.

This begs the question of how a teacher or a school can do this without prior experience. The answer lies in the fact that libraries of IB schools usually keep a reference section of past extended essays (your school should do the same). The teacher-librarian can make contact with other IB school libraries and request copies of good extended essays. Should the teacher-librarian need assistance in

Figure 11.3 Percentage uptake (rounded off to one significant figure) of the extended essay per subject (IB *Statistical Bulletin*, 2002)

Languages	20%
Individuals and societies	50%
Sciences	20%
Mathematics	2%
Arts	10% (relatively speaking it is closer to 25% since less than one-third of the DP students study an arts subject)

this task, it is our experience that you will have little difficulty finding an experienced colleague from another IB school who can send you (by email or otherwise) examples of good essays. The relevant subject chapters of the IBO's *extended essay reports* also contain useful information about each subject area. The subject chapters in this book give further insightful comments. The DPC needs to engage department heads in the hunt for good resources.

The supervisor should not mark the essay in any way. On the completion of their extended essay students should submit an electronic copy of the final essay and an unbound copy so that the supervisor can carry out a final check for plagiarism. Assuming this is satisfactory I would suggest that the student should submit two or three bound copies of the essay (one for the IBO, one for retention by the DPC in case of loss, and one for the library – after the examination results are declared and assuming the student agrees). Printing and binding the essays can cause some students problems. By planning ahead it should be possible for the DPC to facilitate this. Either the school's reprographics department could assist or students could be told about the services of local copy shops. The supervisor will complete an official green IBO cover form (available from the DPC), and attach it to one copy of the essay. The cover form asks for a short comment from the supervisor about the context of the essay. The student and the supervisor need to sign the form and the supervisor indicates the number of hours spent with the student. The supervisor also needs to generate a predicted grade for the essay, using the general and subject-specific assessment criteria. Grade boundaries vary little year by year and those indicated in figure 11.2 are suitable for determining the overall letter grade. The DPC will then submit the extended essay with its completed cover form to the assigned examiner.

An extended essay schedule will typically run for seven to nine months, starting in the second half of the first year, and ending four to five months before the examinations. Delaying the start of the extended essay until the second half of the first year allows students time to learn new skills and mature academically; finishing it early means it does not clash with coursework deadlines and examination preparation. Most students have a substantial vacation between years 1 and 2, during which they can focus on the extended essay. Key dates in the schedule (such as 'finish first draft') can also be built around shorter breaks in the school calendar. Extended essays often naturally evolve from work the students are doing in class, and so informal discussion of the extended essay should begin very early on. At the start of the year it is useful to inform a new cohort – and remind the DP teachers – about what the essay involves. Teachers should draw attention in their regular classes to possible avenues for extended essays, and plant the idea early and firmly in students' heads.

On a final administrative note, we mention here the following. We believe it is more practical to give students and supervisors a full set of support materials at the outset, rather than customized versions piecemeal throughout the programme. There is some redundancy with this approach but it reduces the workload of the supervisors and also prevents any potential problems later on with students claiming that they were not informed about this or that. Suggested support materials are:

The school's guide to the extended essay programme. This would contain:
- a general overview of the extended essay and its place in the DP
- guidance on choosing a supervisor and topic

- a sign-up sheet to be submitted by a set date bearing the intended supervisor's signature – a school could also ask for the parent's signature to involve them in the process
- a calendar of key stages and dates due
- the tracking system you will use to support students with the deadlines
- a sample copy of the reports to parents (see section 7)
- guidance on any key events such as workshops, the presentation and the formal interview (see section 6)
- an overview of the *extended essay guide* and the school's *research and reference manual* (the next two items, below).

The IBO's extended essay guide. This guide is available from the IBO. The guide contains more detail on the extended essay, guidance for supervisors, an outline of the research process, and most importantly the general assessment criteria and each subject's specific criteria. The guide can be recycled for future students.

The school's research and reference manual. This manual details the research process and how to accurately reference a variety of sources. It should also point to useful resources in the school's library. This manual will form the basis of the workshops run by the teacher-librarian for students.

We mentioned in the introduction that students can choose to write an extended essay in any of the IB diploma subjects. This is in line with the IBO's philosophy to allow students to either deepen their knowledge of a subject they study in their package or add breadth to their academic experience by selecting a subject outside their subject package. Realistically, however, most students are best advised to write their essay in a subject they are studying, and preferably one they are studying at Higher Level and intend to major in at university. Some students will want to write the essay on a subject that they did not choose to study, or one that was not available but in which they have a strong interest. Too often, though, they underestimate the academic subject-specific requirements of the essay.

5 The supervisor and the student

Whereas the previous section concentrated on the overall organization and administration of the extended essay programme, this section concentrates on the interplay between supervisors and students. We have noted already that the extended essay can be a source of considerable pride to the student. Many teachers, likewise, value the opportunity it affords for guiding deeper research in their own subject area. In short, a good essay choice can be a joy to both teacher and student.

We also noted earlier that supervisors must have a good idea of the nature of viable and non-viable projects (having seen examples of both, and being aware of profitable areas for research, bearing in mind the resources available and the time allocated). Even with a viable essay, however, students may not put in enough work or, more often than not, get so carried away that they put in far too much work (much more than the required 40 hours). You need to prevent both scenarios, and the key tool for this is, naturally, a clear schedule of meetings with key dates. The first priority is to help the student to decide quickly on a clear title with a clear scope and well-defined focus of research. It is also useful to go over the stages of the research and writing processes (see Appendix 1 for a student version of these), subject-specific assessment criteria and, more importantly, the general assessment criteria. Many teachers have reported that a good, sharply defined title is half the way to a good essay. Experience shows that the best titles are those that can be phrased as clear *research questions*. Some sample titles are included in the subject sections in the IBO's *Extended Essay* guide (IBO 1998). This book's subject chapters feature more examples of good titles and a few are set out in figure 11.4. This is not to suggest that students should be simply handed a title, but rather that the supervisor should help the student formulate a title based on the interest of the student in the initial discussions.

Figure 11.4 Some sample extended essay titles

Subject	Title
English A1	Category 1 (based on the literature of countries where the language is spoken): *Clergymen in Jane Austen's novels* Category 2 (a comparison of works originally written in the A1 language with World Literature works): *The presentation of innocence in 'Joseph Andrews', 'Candide' and 'Wonderful Fool'*
English B	Category 1 (language based): *The use of language in the theatre of Noh* Category 2 (culture/society based): *Nuclear energy and national bias in the French press* Category 3 (literature based): *The relevance of 'The Crucible' by Arthur Miller to modern times*
Geography	*A study of the seasonal variation in the transport network of Jersey, UK*
History	*King Arthur: fact or myth?* *Cuba's changing view of the 1962 missile crisis*
Business and management	*New product /market development at XYZ (company)* *Comparing approaches to social responsibility in (companies) ABC and XYZ*
Economics	*Measuring the price elasticity of demand for products in the school shop* *The external costs of the Australian coal industry*
ITGS	*A study of the impact of virtual reality on people's leisure*
Physics	*Determining the mass of Jupiter from an analysis of satellite photographs of the motion of its moons* *Wind power: a clean source of energy?*
Chemistry	*Is it better to use dried animal manure as a fertilizer or as a fuel?* *The effects of sugar-free chewing gum on the pH in the mouth after a meal*
Biology	*A study of the effect of differing pH levels on the growth of Paseolus vulgaris* *A study of malnourished children in Indonesia and the extent of their recovery after a period of supervised improved nutrition*
Environmental systems	*Lead pollution: impacts and control in Toronto*
Design technology	*A study investigating the impact of computer-aided design on modelling techniques*
Mathematics	*The role of prime numbers in cryptography* *The Hausdorff dimension of fractal sets*
Computer science	*A computer simulation of a simple stock market* *Design and implementation of a database system for the school library*
Visual arts	*How did Wassily Kandinsky use colour?*
Theatre arts	*Contrasting female stereotypes in a selection of Brecht's plays*

The other area that is likely to produce problems is the process of academic writing. As we mentioned earlier, this should not be the focus of the supervisor's assistance. Rather, if you feel that things are not going as well as they should in this respect, alert and advise the student, and urge him or her to consult with the librarian.

The IBO's requirement that the extended essay is an independent piece of work has understandably led to some confusion. How can such a major task be independent if it is the student's first exposure to such work? The answer is that you can use 3–5 hours' time of assistance and that this is sufficient provided your advice is well structured. You can provide help with focusing, planning, methods, academic writing and identifying resources and mistakes, as long as the students do all the rest of the work by themselves. In our experience, such clear structural help need not be much more than 3 hours, and does not violate the hands-off approach for supervisors emphasized by the IBO. Any less assistance, on the other hand, is simply not realistic.

The supervisor must be careful not to let the students fall into the trap of concentrating all their efforts on hard subject-specific research. It should not be forgotten that subject-specific work carries only one-third of the overall mark; the rest goes towards general academic writing, research and reference skills that are virtually subject independent. On the notion of subject-specific efforts, we would also like to stress once again that the supervisor should take great care to focus the student's efforts strictly *within* one subject. Additionally, within language A1 and language B there are subcategories (see figure 11.4) and, in a further restriction of scope, students must focus on *one* such category. This is sometimes easier said than done. A common mistake is for essay titles to be too broad in nature and to range across several subjects. Classic examples of this are essays ostensibly in an A1 language that delve into psychology or philosophy, or an essay in biology which discusses a problem in biochemistry or medicine. Basing the essay on only one subject area obviously helps the IBO with assessment. It may even help some students to focus their research. In science, however, the distinction between subjects can often seem artificial as so many scientific fields are inter-disciplinary. It is common for science students to want to 'stray' into inter-disciplinary research but until the IBO revises its procedures this is something that students and supervisors must strongly guard against.

Supervisors of science-based extended essays will also need to watch out for safety and ethical considerations. Experiments that require the use of certain equipment or animals may well be standard practice in a university laboratory but not so in schools. Supervisors may need to submit a risk assessment to the school's safety officer. Essays involving survey work, for example in biology or geography, may also have inherent risks and the school administration and parents need to be aware of these. There can also be public relations (PR) considerations if students are interviewing, or more generally working with the general public, and supervisors need to advise students on acceptable practices and protocols. The subject-specific sections in Part Three of this book have more information on these issues.

6 Monitoring and reporting on progress

A tracking form which maps out key stages and due dates for the essay is very useful in helping students and supervisors maintain momentum (see Appendix 2). One system is to have the supervisor sign the student's form at each stage, after which it goes back to the DPC. The exact structure used will depend on the size of the cohort but it helps if the monitoring is external to the supervision meetings. Schools with a large cohort could assign groups of students to senior teachers.

As a second monitoring tool, you could ask your students to present a short PowerPoint presentation to a group of teachers and the student's classmates. Students are given a template of five or six slides (best designed by the individual subject departments) on which to outline their essay. For science subjects, for instance, the slides could follow the template outlined in figure 11.5.

This tool has proved very effective in focusing the students and ensuring that they can be productive over the long vacation. By inviting fellow students who write essays in similar fields to the presentation, all students can benefit from the collective feedback.

Another useful tool is a *formal interview* to discuss the first draft. It is a good idea to invite at least one other teacher or the DPC to create the sense of formality. The student's first draft of the essay, submitted a few days earlier, is discussed and students are encouraged to map out what they will do in the remaining couple of months to improve their work.

Parents will need to be kept informed of students' progress and provision should be made for some reporting procedures in the extended essay schedule. The page entitled 'The research and writing process' (page 9 in the *Extended Essay Guide* 1999) provides a useful outline against which to measure and report on a student's progress. The presentation and formal interview discussed above can also be used as the basis for an end-of-year report from the supervisor to parents.

Figure 11.5 Slide-show template for student presentation

Slide	Content
1	**Name:** **Title of your extended essay:**
2	**Area of investigation** State your research question and clarify each of the terms.
3	**Hypothesis** Make a prediction and give the scientific basis for it.
4	**Research methods 1** Outline the work that others have done in this field.
5	**Research methods 2** Indicate the data that you intend to collect. Outline your experiment. State the full scientific method.
6	**Summer work** Outline how you intend to proceed with your research over the summer. State the sources that you intend to use.

7 Academic honesty

Chapter 3 (in section 7.10) considers the issue of plagiarism and its complex cultural dimensions. Here we restrict ourselves to mentioning that it is in the very best interest of your students that the school guards strongly against plagiarism. If the IBO detects plagiarism the student may well be disqualified from the diploma. To drive this point home, it helps to highlight in a student assembly such cases in your own or neighbouring schools.

Another effective tool to combat plagiarism is provided by the company turnitin.com on the internet, discussed earlier in Chapter 3. You can send in manuscripts of a wide range of electronic formats (MS Word, WordPerfect, RTF, PS, html format). Turnitin will then produce a report highlighting suspected sources of plagiarism including the original source. Some schools decide to let the students submit their work to turnitin.com and hand in any drafts together with a turnitin report, while other schools submit the drafts on the student's behalf. A presentation to students with concrete examples can serve as a sobering reminder of the need for academic honesty. Finally, although there is no requirement from the IBO to do so, it can be a useful deterrent to make it a school policy to include a turnitin.com report with the submitted essay.

However, it must be noted that deterrent sessions alone can leave students scared and wary about using any sources. As we mentioned in Chapter 3, schools will need to educate students about the proper practices with regards to the use of sources, and the workshop led by the teacher-librarian, described in section 4, is a natural place to start.

Appendix 1: Sample extended essay schedule

The schedule set out below is an example of a possible timeline for a northern hemisphere school. Such a schedule would be included in a support booklet for students (see the last part of section 4 above).

Note: the three forms in this appendix can be downloaded from www.dp-help.com; please feel free to adapt them to your needs.

This extended essay schedule gives general dates.
Most of the meetings with your supervisor will be 20–30 minutes.
Specific dates for presentation and formal interview will be arranged nearer the time.

March week 1	Introduction to the extended essay Meeting with IB coordinator and the librarian
March week 2	Select a subject area and a supervisor. Complete the *Consent Form* and return it to the IB coordinator.
March week 4	**Meeting 1** with your supervisor Discuss suitable areas of research. Decide what you need to do over the spring break. During this time you should read the support booklets you have been given: *A Research Manual for Students* and *The IBO's Guide to the Extended Essay*.

April
week 3
	Meeting 2 with supervisor
	Your supervisor will review with you the following:
	• the subject-specific criteria and the general criteria from the IBO's
	  Guide to the Extended Essay
	• key points from the *Research Manual*
	• the reading/research that you did over the spring break.
	You should now:
	• refine your area of study
	• work out a reading bibliography/list of equipment required
	• set goals for the next meeting – this should include creating a skeleton
	  structure for your essay
	• talk to the librarian about finding resources.

April week 4	**Workshop** on research skills and referencing This is an additional workshop for those who feel they still need support in this area. The workshop will be held in the library and conducted by the librarian.
May week 2	**Meeting 3** with supervisor (progress and planning meeting) Decide on a title. Did you reach the goals set in the last meeting? Set new goals. These should include further reading/analysis/research/ experimentation. Outline your PowerPoint presentation to your supervisor. Plan what you need to do over the summer vacation.
May week 4	**Meeting 4** with supervisor, and **presentation** You will need to prepare a 5–10-minute PowerPoint presentation on your extended essay. Your presentation will be in front of other students, your supervisor, the IB coordinator and the librarian. Your presentation should include: your aim, hypothesis, sources of information/experiment details, areas of concern, a skeleton outline from title page to bibliography including chapter headings (this is like a roadmap and will be used to direct your work over the next five months). *Readers of this book:* refer to section 6 in this chapter for the presentation.
June week 2	**Report** home to parents from supervisor This report outlines the progress the student has made and what she or he needs to do over the summer vacation.
Summer vacation	**Complete first draft** by next meeting Your supervisor may ask you to keep in contact via email over the summer.
August week 4	**Submit first draft** (two hard copies and one soft copy on disc) to supervisor
September week 1	**Meeting 5** with supervisor and **formal interview**. *Readers of this book:* refer to section 6 in this chapter for the interview. Your supervisor will decide at this meeting whether she or he wishes to see a second draft of your essay in October.
September week 2	**Report** home to parent from supervisor Report highlights progress made and work still to be done.
October week 1	Complete second draft (optional) Your supervisor may request a last draft at this time, if he or she feels it is necessary.
November week 1	**Meeting 6** with supervisor. **Submit final draft**. Submit one soft copy to the librarian for a check on plagiarism.
December week 2	**Submit final copy** of your extended essay. You should give three bound copies of your essay to the supervisor and a soft copy on disk to the librarian.

Appendix 2: Sample progress tracking form

This form should be incorporated into the school's guide to the extended essay support booklet.

Use these pages to keep track of the compulsory meetings with your supervisor, questions you wish to raise, and tasks that you need to complete.

At each meeting ask your supervisor to sign and indicate how many minutes he or she has spent with you. In most cases you will also need to meet with the librarian. This is to support you with the research process and to assist you in referencing your work properly. In these cases, the librarian is also asked to sign but the time she or he spends with you is not counted in the total. **Please note: the amount of support given by the supervisor should not total more than 5 hours.**

If you need to have extra meetings with your supervisor, use the 'Notes' section at the end of this document to record information and how long the session lasted.

Meeting 1 (March, week 4)

Questions …

My tasks for the spring break are …

Supervisor's initials:	Date:	Time spent:	mins
Librarian's initials:	Noted area of research:		

Meeting 2 (April, week 3)

Questions …

My goals for the next meeting are …

Discuss resources with librarian

Supervisor's initials:	Date:	Time spent:	mins
Librarian's initials:			

Meeting 3 (May, week 2) progress and planning meeting

Questions …

My tasks for the summer vacation are …

Supervisor's initials:	Date:	Time spent:	mins
Librarian's initials:	Title:		

Meeting 4 (May, week 4): presentation

Feedback on my presentation ...

| Supervisor's initials: | Date: | Time spent: | mins |

Meeting 5 (September, week 1): formal interview

Feedback on my formal interview ...

| Supervisor's initials: | Date: | Time spent: | mins |

Supervisor requested to see a second draft in October? Yes/No

Meeting 6 (November, week 1)

Questions/concerns ...

| Supervisor's initials: | Final draft submitted: | Time spent: | mins |
| | Disk submitted: | | |

Librarian's initials:

Turnitin report to be forwarded to student and supervisor, so that student can rectify problems before submission.

Extended essay submitted

Notes:

Supervisor's initials:	Date:	Total time spent with supervisor:	hrs
Disk submitted	Final report from turnitin.com to be sent off together with essay to the IBO		
Librarian's initials:			

Appendix 3: An example of a general criteria checklist

(based on a version devised by Ian Dorton, chief examiner of economics for the IBO)

Note: Marks given for the general criteria constitute two-thirds of the total marks for the essay. Getting students to focus on the areas below is one of the easiest ways to improve their scores.

The majority of the points below are pertinent to all extended essay programmes. The IBO does not stipulate any one system of referencing sources. Points 6 and 9, however, have been included to reinforce the school's adopted common referencing system.

Point	Action	Check ✓
1	Is the essay within 4,000 words?	
2	Is there a Contents page?	
3	Are all pages numbered?	
4	Are all diagrams, charts and graphs indexed and labelled and sources referenced where applicable?	
5	Are all necessary terms defined/explained?	
6*	Is every reference cited in a footnote?	
7	Are your references cited consistently and correctly?	
8	Does the Bibliography include all and only the works of reference you have consulted?	
9*	Does the Bibliography specify author(s), title, date of publication and publisher for every reference?	
10	Are the Bibliography sources cited consistently and correctly?	
11	Does the Appendix contain only relevant information?	
12	Are all references to the Appendix clearly cross-referenced and labelled?	
13	Is your research question stated on the title page?	
14	Is your research question stated and in bold in the Introduction?	
15	Is your research question restated and in bold in the Conclusion?	
16	Does your Conclusion address unresolved questions?	
17	Does your Conclusion address new questions that have emerged?	
18	Are your Introduction and Conclusion titled?	
19	Is your Abstract within 300 words?	
20	Does your Abstract contain the research question (in bold), the scope of the investigation and the conclusion reached?	

* tailor according to the school's common referencing system

Chapter 12

Group 1: Language A1

Kevin Morley, BA, MEd, Mark Beverley, BA, MA and Anu Ruhil, PhD

Kevin Morley taught in a variety of schools in Germany and the UK before moving to United World College of South East Asia (UWCSEA) in 1992 where he has been Head of Department (English for speakers of other languages (ESOL) and A1 self-taught languages) since 1998. In this capacity Kevin has supervised over 150 self-taught students in 35 different A1 languages.

Mark Beverley taught in England for three years before coming to UWCSEA in 1997 where is currently Head of the English Department and a teacher of drama. Mark currently oversees the teaching of over 360 students taking English A1 in years 1 and 2 of the Diploma Programme (DP).

Anuradha Ruhil earned her doctorate from the University of Arizona, Tucson USA in Second Language Acquisition and Teaching. Her area of specialization is Pedagogy. She has been teaching IB English (English A2 and B courses) in the ESOL department at UWCSEA for the past four years. She has been responsible for the implementation and teaching of Hindi A1.

This chapter introduces the reader to group 1 literature courses in the student's mother tongue or first language (language A1). The authors provide an introduction to the aims of the group 1 courses and outline the common syllabus requirements. They also discuss course organization, choice of texts and assessment practice. In order to describe the diversity of group 1 there are three case studies. Mark Beverley gives practical advice for teaching in a school's majority language (English A1). Anu Ruhil discusses the challenges faced by those who will instruct A1 courses in minority languages (Hindi A1). In the section on self-taught A1 languages, Kevin Morley examines IBO's provision for individual students and gives advice to teachers and schools on running this unique educational programme. Information about language choices for the DP can be found in the appendix.

1 Literature studies in an international context

1.1 Languages available

One of the most imaginative aspects of the DP is the mandatory requirement of the study of mother tongue/first language (language A1) in a pre-university level literature course. In line with a commitment to a truly first-class international education for students from all over the world, the IBO does its utmost to ensure that all students may study their literary and cultural heritage in their own native tongue. This availability of a literature programme with a homogeneous structure and administration in a multitude of languages is unique. Thus, as well as providing an educational programme in one of the IBO's working languages – English, French and Spanish – schools are able to institute bilingual programmes which can include A1 courses in national or regional languages.

For example, a school in multiracial Singapore might offer the IB DP in English to teach the core programme and groups 3 to 6 (Individuals and societies, Experimental sciences, Mathematics and computer science, The arts). At the same time the school could offer its students a choice of Malay, English and Chinese as A1 languages. (The same languages could also be available as second language programmes in group 2.) In addition, the institution could also offer the minority national language, Tamil, as a special request A1 (see 1.4), as well as allow up to five students to study their mother tongue under the self-taught A1 programme. Such eclecticism gives schools unparalleled flexibility when it comes to choosing the optimum language programme for the student body.

Given that the IBO encourages international perspectives, currently about 80 languages are available for study. The sheer variety is best illustrated by listing here the A1 literature book lists currently available from the IBO: Afrikaans, Amharic, Arabic, Bosnian, Bulgarian, Catalan, Chinese, Croatian, Czech, Danish, Dutch, Filipino, Finnish, French, German, Greek (Modern), Hebrew, Hindi, Hungarian, Indonesian, Italian, Japanese, Korean, Latvian, Lithuanian, Macedonian, Malay, Nepali, Norwegian, Persian, Polish, Portuguese, Russian, Serbian, Sesotho, Sinhalese, Siswati, Slovak, Slovene, Spanish, Swahili, Swedish, Thai, Turkish and Welsh.

1.2 Aims and objectives

The aims of the language A1 programme at both Higher Level (HL) and Standard Level (SL) are the same. Briefly, the language A1 course is designed to hone students' writing and oral communication skills through a study of diverse literary texts. The flexibility and breadth of the course allow the teacher considerable freedom with regard to selecting texts and assigning written and oral work.

Students are encouraged to engage in rigorous literary criticism and to be concise, precise and clear in the written and oral expression of their ideas. Works are analysed together and comparison is a critical element in the study of literary works. Another central objective is to broaden students' global perspective by introducing them to literary works from other cultures/languages (see the discussion of world literature in section 1.6). In doing so, the A1 course subscribes to the internationalist philosophy of the DP. In addition to these objectives, the A1 course also encourages students to engage with literature on a personal level.

At HL the course is designed primarily for students who intend to study literature at university, whereas it is generally understood that students who study the subject at SL will not continue with it at university. Typically, HL meets three times a week, while SL meets twice a week; a sample two-year schedule for A1 is given in section 1.9. There are other differences between the HL and SL courses in terms of numbers of texts covered, assessment criteria and length of examination. Moreover, an ability to think imaginatively and to embrace abstract ideas, particularly in terms of the varying relationship between literature and life, will also help to ensure success at the upper levels of both SL and HL courses. However, in addition HL students need to sustain an enthusiasm for the independent reading of challenging texts and must demonstrate a willingness to engage in sustained class discussion.

1.3 Syllabus outline: required texts

At HL, students study 15 texts, and at SL 11 (self-taught candidates also study 11 texts). Texts must be selected from the IB Prescribed World Literature list (PWL) and the IB Prescribed Book List (PBL) for the specific language A1. The syllabus outline for both HL and SL is provided in figure 12.1. For all A1 languages, syllabuses are submitted early in year 2 of the DP (Form 1/A1AP – Advanced Notice of Programme).

The course has a requirement to study texts from at least four *genres* at HL and three at SL, two or three *periods* and at least two *places* in both courses. This constraint is bound to influence text choice, but some sections allow teachers to make 'free choice' of texts, not necessarily from the prescribed lists, that balance places or periods not covered elsewhere, or which focus attention on the literature of the region in which the school is located. In addition, the World Literature component is where much extension work can be done, and where significant opportunity is provided for tackling texts that raise social, cultural or political issues which might be relevant to particular individuals or groups of students. Indeed, given the wide scope for choice, the courses are ultimately as interesting and exciting as the teacher is inclined to design them.

One very confusing aspect of A1 courses is the IBO's numbering system. Each booklist is divided into four parts. There are, however, five assessment activities and the final written examination is divided into two papers.

Part 1: World Literature. Three texts are chosen from the Prescribed World Literature list (PWL). Students produce one 1,500-word essay at SL, and HL students produce an additional assignment.

Part 2: A detailed study. Two texts at SL (four at HL), each from different genres chosen from part 2 of the Prescribed Book List (PBL) for a given A1 language. This is assessed via an individual oral commentary.

Part 3: Groups of works. One World Literature text chosen freely plus two A1 texts at SL (three texts at HL) are chosen from Part 3 of the PBL. The texts must be linked by genre. Students write an essay under examination conditions. This essay is Paper 2.

Part 4: Schools' free choice. One text from the PWL plus two texts at SL (three texts at HL) are chosen freely. Students must give an individual oral presentation.

The fifth assessment component is Paper 1 of the final examination, the unseen commentary.

If student numbers only warrant a single class it may well be necessary to teach A1 (HL) and A1 (SL) together. Because of the structure of the course, the same 11 core SL texts can be used for both groups. In effect A1 (HL) must study two additional texts for Part 2 and two other A1 texts, one for Part 3 and one for Part 4. Like other diploma language programmes, both courses use the same assessment categories but employ differentiated levels of achievement. This makes assessment of a mixed class relatively straightforward. HL students will

Figure 12.1 Choice of A1 texts

Level	Part 1 World Literature (WL)	Part 2 Detailed Study	Part 3 Groups of Works	Part 4 School's Free Choice
Higher **Total number of texts =15**	Three works (linked by one or more aspects, e.g. genre, culture, period, theme, etc.)	Four language A1 works (each work from a different genre category on PBL) Each work by a different author	Four works: three language A1 and 1 WL (all from same genre category) All three language A1 from PBL WL work 'chosen freely'** and linked at least by genre to A1 works Each work by a different author	Four works: three language A1 and one WL (all four 'chosen freely'**) WL work linked to A1 texts by one or more aspects, e.g. genre, culture, theme, etc. Each work by a different author
Standard **Total number of texts =11**	Three works (linked by one or more aspects, e.g. genre, culture, period, theme, etc.)	Two language A1 works (linked by one or more aspects, e.g. genre, culture, theme, etc.)	Three works: two language A1 and one WL (all from same genre category) Both language A1 from PBL WL work 'chosen freely'** and linked at least by genre to A1 works Each work by a different author	Three works*: two language A1 and one WL (all three 'chosen freely')**

Note: Refer to *Language A1 subject guide* for definition of terms like author, genre, work, period.
Another often-overlooked anomaly is that it *is* possible to study a text originally written in the A1 language for Parts 3 & 4, provided the choice made is available in the relevant PBL and refers to a 'place' that is not covered elsewhere in the syllabus.
* Self-taught candidates' Parts 3 and 4 works must be selected from the PWL and PBL
** 'chosen freely' means from the PWL, PBL or elsewhere

receive extra teaching and can use the time to study the additional texts; they will also be expected to respond in much greater depth.

1.4 Special request languages

In certain instances schools may wish to take an A1 language for which there is no published PBL. In such instances schools may seek to teach the language as a special request A1. As with any SL A1, the school must provide a taught programme of 11 suitable texts. Six texts should be originally written in the relevant A1 language and should cover the same variety of genre as a taught A1. The remaining five texts should be World Literature texts in translation. However, IBO will waive this regulation if no suitable texts can be found. In this case the texts should be in the school's working language. These details must be submitted on form C2 for special request languages. On the form the DP coordinator (DPC) will also be expected to provide the IBO with a rationale explaining the student's need to study this language. The single most pressing reason is the student's requirement of an A1 language to complete a diploma package. In addition students must furnish the IBO with proof that they are linguistically capable of studying the language and DPCs are expected to provide the IBO with copies of school reports or other evidence, e.g. a letter from a *bona fide* tutor that the student is literate in the language.

In theory, students could study languages as diverse as Albanian, Bengali, Burmese, Dhivehi, Khmer, Oromic or Urdu as their first language. If a teacher is not available for a specific language, the student can study his/her language as a self-taught option (at SL level).

1.5 Assessment: a brief glance

The language A1 course may differ from other systems in that students' writing and speaking skills are assessed using a variety of assessment methods, which give a broad picture of the student's linguistic proficiency and ability to think critically. The allocation of 50% of the final mark to coursework activities means that a wide range of strengths, interests and abilities can be tested and students are able to demonstrate their skills to the best. The coursework also allows students to research and develop their ideas over a period of time. However, writing skills are also tested via traditional timed examinations. Thus the written component emphasizes writing both as a process and as a product. Two types of oral production task (the taped oral commentary and the oral presentation) measure speaking skills. The written component is assessed externally, whereas the oral component is moderated externally, but assessed internally by the teacher.

As with all the DP subjects, the *Vade Mecum* prescribes assessment procedures regarding both written and oral components. Each assessment method is discussed in some detail in the sections that follow. Moreover, an in-depth look at assessment and how it relates to practice is provided in the case study on English A1 (section 2).

1.6 Coursework: the World Literature assignment(s)

World Literature 1 is a comparative study in which the student finds a 'pertinent link' between two or three of the chosen texts. A total of three texts are read for this component at both HL and SL; one or more aspects, such as *theme* and *genre* to name two, must link all three. These texts should be written originally in a language different from the A1 language, and are selected from the PWL. The study is worth 20% of the final mark.

SL students complete one assignment which must be a comparative study between at least two of the three texts. HL students complete two, the second offering opportunity for an imaginative or creative response; this accordingly allows students to respond to the texts in a form other than the traditional essay. The length of assignment for both HL and SL is between 1,000 and 1,500 words and for A1 (HL) students completing a creative assignment for World Literature 2, this word count must include a statement of intent which outlines the thinking and the objectives behind the piece of work.

The *Language A1 Subject Guide* indicates that text choice should give students the opportunity to explore aspects of diversity in culture, politics and language and which at the same time draw attention to 'the underlying unity of human preoccupations' (*Language A1 Subject Guide*, page 16). In this way, much of the IBO's emphasis on international awareness and the promotion of a global perspective can here be realized.

The assessment rubric comprises four criteria:

A Selection of the aspect and its treatment
B Knowledge and understanding of work(s)
C Presentation
D Language.

Each criterion is marked out of 5, arriving at a final mark out of 20, and it is important to note that there is no difference between the criteria at HL or SL. Criterion A is wholly concerned with the choice of topic; B deals with knowledge of the texts; criteria C and D concentrate on standard aspects of presentation and language. It is worth noting that for specific mistakes, the assignment will usually be penalized in only one criteria band. Thus, an assignment on a poorly chosen topic could still, potentially, score a 5 in criteria C and D as these are more concerned with the mechanics of the writing rather than specific aspects of content.

Examples of types of successful titles are given in section 2.2.

1.7 Internal assessment: the orals

Figure 12.2 provides a quick look at internal assessment.

Figure 12.2 Internal assessment (orals)

Taped individual oral commentary (based on one of the Part 2 works)	Part 2 works HL = 4 SL = 2	20 minutes' preparation 15 minutes taped	15%
Individual oral presentation (based on Part 4 works)	Part 4 works HL = 4 SL = 3	10–15 minutes	15%

Oral communication skills comprise 30% of the student's grade. As we have seen, the oral component consists of two activities:

1. *The individual oral commentary*

   The individual oral commentary is based on an extract from one text studied as a Part 2 text (see figure 12.2 for number of texts read at each level). The teacher selects and prepares an extract, which should not exceed 40 lines. The extract is accompanied by two or three guiding questions, which help the candidate to structure the commentary.

   Candidates are also expected to be able to comment in detail on literary techniques and devices reflected in the extract. Although students are expected to know all Part 2 texts thoroughly, an individual student should not know the particular extract on which he/she will be tested during the oral examination. The student is allowed 20 minutes' preparation time plus 15 minutes for the actual taped commentary.

2. *The individual oral presentation*

   In contrast to the commentary, the second oral activity, the oral presentation, allows the student greater freedom to speak on a topic of individual choice. The student can select one or more texts from Part 4 of the syllabus (see figure 12.2 for number of texts read at each level). It is the teacher's responsibility to assist the student in selecting an appropriate topic. Total time given for the presentation is between 10 and 15 minutes. Each student's presentation is followed by a discussion, which allows students to exhibit their knowledge of the work(s) they have selected. The presentation can take place during class hours, enabling the entire class to participate in the discussion. Except in the case of self-taught candidates, the oral presentation is not recorded.

To obtain high scores for the oral presentation and commentary, the student has to structure the presentation/commentary in a logical and coherent manner, demonstrate thorough understanding of the text(s), use a formal register and sophisticated vocabulary, and provide an appropriate and interesting personal response to the text(s). The assessment rubric consists of four criteria at both HL and SL:

A Knowledge and understanding of extract or work(s)
B Interpretation and personal response
C Presentation
D Use of language

Criteria A and D receive up to 5 marks and criteria B and C up to 10 marks. Both the presentation and the commentary therefore end up with a mark out of 30.

Like other DP subjects, all A1 assessment is criterion-referenced and although there are no discernible differences in assessment criteria between HL and SL, HL candidates need to comment in detail on literary techniques in order to score a high mark. Of the two oral activities, the oral commentary is a greater challenge and since it is tape-recorded, students are understandably nervous during the examination. A possible way to reduce their anxiety is to conduct practice orals, which are taped (refer to section 2.3 for pointers).

Also worthy of note is a difference between HL and SL. The study of a World Literature text in Part 4 of the SL course is in fact optional and can be replaced by any A1 text from the PBL or elsewhere.

The oral assignments may be completed at any time, as per the guidelines in the *Language A1 Subject Guide*. However, one can safely assume that students should have reached a certain maturity and sophistication in their literary analysis by the second year of the DP. In addition, they will have had adequate practice in working with oral assignments. These two factors should enable them to score better in the second year. Once the oral assignments have been completed, the grades are submitted electronically, by email. Where there are fewer than 5 candidates all tapes should be submitted; if there are 20 candidates, centres submit 5; if there are up to 40 candidates, 8 recordings must be sent and above this number centres must send a maximum of 10 tapes for external moderation.

1.8 External assessment: the examinations

Figure 12.3 provides details regarding external assessment components.

Paper 1 tests the candidate's ability to write a commentary on an unseen extract from a literary text. The candidate can choose between a poem and a prose passage. Length of the text can vary; it could be a complete piece or an extract from a longer written text.

At SL the extract is accompanied by three or four guiding questions. For example:

• What do the details of the setting contribute to the atmosphere of the passage?
• What are the effects of the poem's form, e.g. stanza pattern, rhyme scheme, sentence structure?

Candidates are expected to write a literary analysis of the extract, commenting on content, author's purpose, literary devices and language. Candidates also need to quote from the extract in support of their observations.

Assessment criteria for Paper 1 are:

A Understanding of the text
B Interpretation of the text
C Appreciation of literary features

Figure 12.3 External assessment (final examinations)

Paper 1 Commentary	HL: 2 hours SL: 1 hour 30 minutes	a) Poem b) Prose text (select either a poem or prose passage)	25%
Paper 2 Essay/Part 3 works	HL: 2 hours SL: 1 hour 30 minutes	Two questions per genre Four general questions (select either one genre-specific question or one of the four general questions)	25%

Note: Split session self-taught candidates for southern hemisphere languages such as Afrikaans, Sesotho, Siswati and Zulu will take these two papers in November.

D Presentation
E Formal use of language

There are also differences between HL and SL in the phrasing of specific levels. For instance, to score a 5 for criterion B, HL students must demonstrate ideas that are 'convincing', whereas SL students need only be 'clearly relevant'.

Paper 2 examines the candidate's knowledge of texts studied as Part 3 texts. The texts must be of the same genre, which may be any of the following categories: short story, essay, novel, drama, poetry, etc. One must be a World Literature text, designed to offer a 'cross-cultural perspective', but this can be 'chosen freely' by the teacher and does not have to come from the PWL. One overlooked anomaly is that it is possible to study a text originally written in the A1 language for Parts 3 and 4, provided the choice made is available in the relevant PBL and refers to a 'place' that is not covered elsewhere in the syllabus.

As outlined in figure 12.3, students select either one of the two genre-specific questions, or one of the four general questions. In order to score well, students need to write an in-depth analysis. The essay should be conceived as an analytical exercise in which the most important skill is the formulating of a structured, detailed and cogent response. However, it is worth bearing in mind that the business of formulating a clear sense of argument and thesis, comparing elements of style and content and so on, must all be undertaken within the constraints of time. Therefore it is vital that students know the texts inside out. Moreover, the use of quotations and examples from the texts greatly strengthens a candidate's position to score highly.

Assessment criteria:

A Knowledge and understanding of works
B Response to the question
C Appreciation of literary features
D Presentation
E Formal use of language

As with the unseen commentary, there are differences between the HL and SL criteria, the former requiring for the higher grades more detailed knowledge of the texts and 'the subtleties of their meaning' as well as asking for 'independence of thought' on the part of the candidate. For each criterion (Papers 1 and 2) the student can score a maximum of 5 points, bringing the total to 25. For a detailed discussion of the assessment criteria, refer to the Appendix at the end of this chapter.

1.9 A sample timetable and course structure for A1

The order in which to deliver the various parts of the course is worthy of careful consideration. A number of approaches are feasible and each has strengths and weaknesses. The fundamental question is whether to divide up the various sections (the 'Parts') and pick and choose texts between them that offer variety in terms of genre and approach, or to teach each one in turn. For instance, it is possible to teach one or two texts for Part 3 (the written examination) in the first year and save the rest for year 2. Alternatively, the course can begin with two Part 4 texts (for the individual presentation), then switch to one or two from Part 2 (the oral commentary) in order to delay the formal oral assessments to the second year when the students will be more able.

Another solution is to teach all the texts from each particular part together before moving on to the next (see figure 12.4). In this structure, for instance, teachers can begin with Part 4, then move to Part 2, then Part 1 and end up with Part 3, each component being assessed on its completion. The disadvantage here, inevitably, is that students complete their oral assessments for Parts 2 and 4 in the first year of the course (although these could be treated as a 'practice' before the real thing in year 2).

The consensus of A1 teachers suggests the second approach is the most productive. The system avoids the fragmentation that could otherwise occur and also allows teachers to progress towards the assessment outcomes at the end of each particular section of the course. For instance, focusing much of the learning for Part 2 around oral activities is a practical way in which to develop the skills required of the final oral examination in that section.

Figure 12.4 is one model of the course based on a four-term school year. The following are some pointers:

- Beginning with Part 4 makes the most sense as there is a significant amount of creative breadth inherent in the section, enabling you to start off the course as dynamically as possible. Much can be made, for instance, of the opportunity it affords to give students 'tasters' of the kinds of activity they might select when it comes to the final examination. Possibilities for this include structured discussions, formal oral exposés, role play in the form of monologues or thought-tracking, and so on. Examples of the kinds of appropriate activities are given in later sections of this chapter and detailed information can be found on page 38 of the *English A1 Subject Guide*.
- The demands of the Part 2 individual oral commentary require more formal attention and my suggestion therefore is to begin the component in year 1 and complete a practice commentary before the end of the year, saving the real examination until just before or just after the mocks. The advantage here is that by this time the students' capacity for extended oral analysis should be about as developed as it is going to get. The disadvantage is that it will have been some time since the texts were taught, so it is essential to find the time for revision in preparation for the final examination. The official commentary must take place on an appointed day and it is the mark that must be sent off to the IBO, even if the student may have scored a higher mark in a previous practice.

Figure 12.4 A two-year timetable for teaching A1

Term	Texts	Outcome
One	Part 4	Individual oral presentation
Two	Part 4	
Three	Part 2	Practice oral commentary
Four	Part 1	Introduce World Literature
	Vacation	
Five	Part 1 Part 3 (Examination text 1)	Complete World Literature Final oral commentary (Part 2)
Six	Part 3 (Examination texts 2–3)	Mock examinations
Seven	Part 3 (A1 (HL) examination text 4) Revision	Final examinations

- Many schools will tend to set an internal examination at the end of year 1. The disadvantage of the above model is that students cannot gain experience of Paper 2 at that time because of course they have not yet completed any of the examination texts. Setting 'general' questions (of the type offered as an alternative to the genre-specific questions in the Part 3 examination) would allow students to answer on any of the texts they have so far studied from any section. However, the test here is to ascertain how far the students' analytical skills and their written abilities have developed. To this end, a practice Paper 1 (formal written commentary) is sufficient – and will, of course, be less of a burden in terms of marking!
- Setting up the World Literature might be appropriate over a long break between the first and second years of the course. Students can compile detailed notes and make constructive use of a journal in order to stimulate comparative thinking.
- Leaving the Part 3 texts until year 2 serves to enable examination skills to be fully addressed in the run-up to any internal examinations as well as the real thing. Some teachers feel nervous about this idea as the practice of formal examination skills is left until quite late in the course. However, I would further advise the setting of short formal essays from the beginning of the course on any of the texts. Ideally, this should encourage the development of the students' analytical ability and help them to develop their own methods of formulating successful examination responses.

2 Case study: English A1

In this section Mark Beverley discusses some practical methods of implementing and administering an A1 course when it is the majority language within a school. He looks at the practicalities of course organization and assessment. Given the homogeneous structure and administration of A1 courses, his advice is also relevant to teachers of all group 1 courses.

2.1 English A1: some guidelines

Like all A1 programmes of study, English A1 is a literature course and students must be able to demonstrate a fairly rigorous grasp of traditional critical technique as well as a high degree of personal engagement and individual 'voice' in their response to texts, especially at HL. That said, the course typically encourages a wide range of responses in the context of both written and oral coursework and formal examination, and a mixture of creative and analytical enquiry throughout its various components. It allows for much room in which to address the value of literature as a means of representing, shaping or challenging our sense of human experience and the world in general. In this way, English A1 relates particularly well to the core IB values and to TOK. For example, students should ideally see writing as an act of interpretation of the world around them. In addition, the study of literature emphasizes the different ways in which cultures represent their 'ways of seeing' through literature.

The strength of the course lies in its breadth and flexibility. As we have seen, A1 teachers are required to select authors or texts for most parts of the course from particular lists. For English A1 these are extremely broad – the only problem sometimes being to do with getting hold of copies of particular works that are still in print!

2.2 Coursework – World Literature

In common with all A1 programmes, teachers of both HL and SL must select three texts from a wide range originally written in languages other than English. These can be found in the PWL (see section 1.3). The *Language A1 Subject Guide* indicates that text choice should give students opportunity to explore aspects of diversity in culture, politics and language which represent the way in which 'cultures influence and shape the experiences of life common to all humanity' (*Subject Guide*, page 4). It is here then that much of the IBO's emphasis on international awareness and the promotion of a global perspective can be realized.

As far as the 1,500-word World Literature (1) essay is concerned, experience suggests that the choice of topic is integral to the success (or otherwise) of the final piece. The most common areas of enquiry are thematic or those that focus on character. However, it is always worth encouraging any student who can find a specifically 'literary' aspect (such as narrative technique) because these tend to be the most effective in preventing students from entering the most obvious danger zones. Whatever the focus, it is vital that students find a topic that is sufficiently narrow to allow for a high degree of focus and detail and to enable them to score well across the different criteria. These are often essays whose titles act almost as a thesis statement. For instance:

> The danger of obsession as presented through the mother figures in Esquivel's *Like Water for Chocolate* and Lorca's *Blood Wedding*.

> Idealism as a self-destructive impulse in the protagonists of *Antigone* and *Ghosts*.

> To what extent is art a source of both escape and destruction for the characters Emma in *Madame Bovary* and Molina in *Kiss of the Spiderwoman*?

Problematic assignments tend to occur when the aspect is too broad, or when it takes students away from the text into areas that are predominately sociological or philosophical. 'The portrayal of society in *The House of the Spirits* and *Like Water for Chocolate*' or 'The role of women in *Miss Julie* and *Blood Wedding*' are examples of very broad assignment titles which prevent students from making comment in any significant detail. Moreover, they are also titles that easily lead students into a speculative arena wherein the focus becomes not the text but life itself. Accordingly, the essay's central thesis too easily becomes wholly subjective or at best very generalized and simplistic.

HL students must complete the second assignment for their Part 1 coursework based on *any World Literature text from any part of the syllabus*. This means they can, if they wish, write on the World Literature text from Part 3 or 4. Once again, the assignment must fall into one of three categories:

1. A comparative study between one World Literature text and one language A1 text, e.g. 'The destructive impact of obsession in *Perfume* and *Enduring Love*'.
2. An imaginative or creative assignment plus statement of intent on one World Literature text, e.g. 'A suicide letter written from Emma Bovary to her daughter'.

3. Detailed study: based on an aspect of one World Literature text, such as a formal essay or analysis of one or two key passages, e.g. 'A comparative commentary on two extracts from *Love in the Time of Cholera*. In what ways do the passages explore the relationship between love and growth into old age?'

It is important to remember that students are not allowed to write on a text they have already covered in the first assignment, no matter how different the topic.

Students who have settled on the comparative or the detailed study (assignment 1 or 3) should ensure that the choice of topic or the passage(s) for commentary enables them to score well across all the criteria by retaining specificity of subject and scope for the development of a thesis. Note, for instance, in addition to achieving a healthy degree of focus, the above titles also suggest the nature of the argument the candidate intends to follow.

Students sometimes find themselves choosing the second, creative option simply to get away from the formal kinds of essay work that much of the syllabus demands, but any kind of assumption that a creative assignment will be somehow 'easier' should be quickly dispelled. It certainly does offer students the opportunity to reveal their understanding of a text(s) within a slightly freer format, but it can also lead to some inappropriate choices of assignment and a lack of formal control. The creative assignment must be accompanied by a statement of intent and this should also adhere to the concern for relevance and detail. Vague or generalized statements that do not refer pertinently to the candidate's work or to the original assignment will be penalized in criterion C (presentation).

Note that the statement of intent should immediately precede the assignment itself and should aim to offer critical reflection on such elements as the nature of the task, the aspects on which the candidate intends to focus and how he or she is going to explore those aspects. The subject guide suggests that the statement of intent should not exceed 500 words, unless the assignment itself is relatively short. See page 31 of the *Language A1 Subject Guide* for more information.

Ultimately, when selecting this assignment (and when preparing for the Part 4 presentation), students should first decide on a choice of topic that interests or motivates, and *then* consider the appropriate format in which to explore it. A series of letters, a monologue or additional scene might well be helpful as a context in which to demonstrate empathy and understanding of the complexities of a particular character or relationship, *but not necessarily*. A more formal essay might actually be more productive. Teacher advice is critical and helpful guidance and further examples of assignments are given in the subject guide.

The Part 1 World Literature texts can be chosen from anywhere in the PWL and may be any genre. Therefore, in effect, students could find themselves writing a comparative essay between a novel and a play. There are two schools of thought here: one suggests that mixing genres gives the students a greater breadth from which to select a topic, the other that comparing formal aspects such as language, structure and tone becomes more difficult when following this path. The latter approach has generally been more productive as it tends to lead to more subtle points of stylistic analysis.

The requirement to study texts from at least four genres at HL and three at SL, and two or three periods and at least two places in both courses, will be an influence on text choice. However, beyond this practical issue are more pedagogical considerations: the students in the class, their personal experience of different cultures and their particular strengths or limitations in their awareness of certain issues. For instance, classes with a number of students from developing countries might find Achebe's *Things Fall Apart* a text with direct relevant cultural experiences the students could share. Similarly, faced with a class with a very limited perspective on the culture and politics of countries in Asia, a teacher might wish to tackle relevant works such as *The Earth of Mankind* by Indonesian author Ananta Pramoedya or *The Wild Geese* by Japanese novelist Ogai Mori.

One golden rule can be made: it is best to select texts that can easily be related to each other, but which are also sufficiently 'broad' to allow for many different levels of comparison. A particularly successful combination for HL students could be *Madame Bovary, Kiss of the Spiderwoman* and *The Unbearable Lightness of Being*. Each text is weighty on its own terms and there is a multiplicity of ways in which students can discover a range of topics and points of comparison between each at the level of both form and content. The more conventional approach to structure, characterization, narrative voice and representation of theme in *Madame Bovary*, for instance, is dramatically contrasted with the effects produced by shifts in time and perspective in *Unbearable Lightness* and the variety of narrative forms in *Kiss of the Spiderwoman*.

'Independence of thought' is always an important factor in the achievement of the highest assessment grades. In the World Literature essay this descriptor is identified in criterion A. If students are to reach these upper echelons of achievement, teachers would do well to select texts that will stimulate students into examining a variety of aspects. This, in turn, will allow them to make imaginative leaps into various areas of similarity and difference. On the other hand, if the choice of text focuses narrowly or exclusively on particular key issues or themes, students often find it difficult to trace a more independent or original line of enquiry. An example of one problematic combination is *A Doll's House*, *Metamorphosis* and *The Outsider*. Such texts chosen together frequently limit the students' areas of interest to the significance of imprisonment or the question of existential freedom. The latter topic, in particular, frequently generates unhelpful responses as it is a type of philosophical enquiry. This reason alone makes it an inappropriate choice as the topic is non-literary. It is also worth remembering that the IBO stresses that students within a class should select topics that differ from each other and which allow scope for the discussion of literary features.

When preparing for the World Literature coursework assignment(s), as noted earlier, it is a requirement that students in any particular class all write their assignment in response to the same texts. However, it is sometimes useful to give them a range of more than three texts to read over their long vacation and encourage them to maintain a reading journal detailing their personal response to each. This nurtures autonomy on their part and when classes recommence the journals provide valuable grist for discussion about various points of connection between the texts.

Once the texts have been decided, the assignment should be the result of the student's *independent* research. Therefore, rather than comprehensively examining in class all the details of style and content, the teaching of this part should be an exercise in 'opening up' the texts and encouraging students to explore. As a result students should be able to find links and pursue individual areas of interest through the writing of their reading journals. Setting short assignments on each text that encourage independent thinking is crucial if students are to gain that vital need for ownership over the texts. The more likely they will then be to produce work that is successful in examination terms and the greater the chances of them enjoying their work. IBO regulations state that teachers can only offer help up to and including the first draft and comments should be given orally or on a separate sheet of paper, not written on the assignment itself. The consequence of this is that the research and planning stages are crucial and of necessity completed in as much detail as possible in order that the maximum amount of advice can be administered.

2.3 The oral commentary

For this assessment, we have seen that HL students must study four texts from different genres and SL candidates two. In English A1 Shakespeare is compulsory at both HL and SL and usually works very well. The richness of the language, the potential for comment on character, theme and relationship as well as the status of the text as *drama* give the students a great deal on which to focus. (Note that at HL it is possible to study two Shakespeare plays in Part 2.)

Another guiding principle is to find texts that are particularly rich in terms of their language. Students must be able to 'read' the extract in considerable detail and although they must of course be able to relate the passage to the work(s) as a whole, the majority of their commentary time should be spent in detailed discussion of the language features of the extract.

Students must have a specific date nominated when their examined commentary will take place and this is entirely at the teacher's discretion. The IBO advises that they are given an extract of 30–40 lines from one of the texts about which they must speak individually for about 12 minutes before being asked pertinent questions by the teacher within the allotted time of 15 minutes. Candidates are not allowed to know from which Part 2 text the extract will come up and they select a passage randomly from a range that the teacher has prepared. It is a good idea to prepare between five and six passages per text, make multiple copies and then place them in a series of unmarked plain envelopes. Having selected a passage, students then have 20 minutes in which to prepare by writing notes around the passage itself as well as on a separate piece of paper.

The formal assessment for Part 2 of the course tends to represent a source for considerable concern and anxiety among many students, largely because the skills it demands are fairly specific and not necessarily developed elsewhere in the syllabus. As noted earlier, the final outcome should inform the teaching of the texts; students should therefore have as much opportunity as possible for exploration of texts through formal oral activities. Therefore, classroom discussion and debate on the language and style in specific passages is invaluable before students hone their skills on the demanding commentary itself.

Students need to be able to examine an extract on different levels so that in the commentary they can analyse the different components of the text. When discussing the works, students should therefore have the opportunity to respond regularly to short extracts from the texts. It is also very helpful to give individuals or small groups of students specific targets to encourage them to think in an analytical way. One example of a system of 'reading' a literary text for different purposes is set out in figure 12.5.

These questions are of course by no means exhaustive, but they indicate the ways in which the act of critical reading should be seen as one of deconstruction – of both the text itself and the reader's response to it. For students new to literary criticism we can use the analogy of the art student in an art gallery. The purpose of the visit is to concentrate on different techniques: the ways in which eyes might be depicted in a variety of paintings – or buildings, trees, the impact of the colour blue, the use of different kinds of paint. Such an approach helps to develop sensitivity to the many and varied components that make up any particular image. In this way, attention is drawn to the specific details and the work of art is 'read' more subtly.

Figure 12.5 Stimulus questions for A1 commentaries

Reading	Purpose	Questions
1	Content and context	• Note the context of the extract. In what way does it relate to the rest of the work(s) or if it is a drama text, what has just happened and what is to follow? • Note the essential content of the extract. What is it, fundamentally, about? Or, who is on stage and what are they saying? • In what ways could it be considered an important passage?
2	Character or narrative voice	• What do we learn about the character(s) present? Which of their common characteristics do they here reveal? In what ways are they similar to or different from before or after? • Consider the narrative voice: Who is speaking the poem or prose extract? First or third person and what effect does this have? How would you describe the tone of voice and how is this achieved? Is there any kind of shift or development in the voice as the passage or poem develops?
3	Relationships	• If drama, who is on stage? How do the characters relate to each other? Who speaks more and why? • What is revealed about the relationship in the context of the work? • If there is more than one persona or voice in the poem, how do they relate to the other(s)?
4	Style and imagery	• What is significant about the vocabulary and syntax of the extract? • Does figurative language play any kind of role? • Look for strands of imagery. What do they contribute? • What can you say about the creation and the effect of tone and atmosphere? • In what ways does the language change and develop as the extract moves on – or does the difference in use of language between characters reveal something about them? • What is important about the way the passage is structured?
5	Theme	• What important issues or themes are revealed? • How does their representation here relate to the work as a whole?
6	Impact on audience/ reader	• How is the audience affected by the drama – evidence of kinds of dramatic tension or irony, for instance? • How is the reader's interest engaged? • In what ways, generally, are we manipulated by the language and content of the extract?

The criteria for formal assessment of the commentary in effect demand a combination of sustained critical insight and a more spontaneous degree of personal response. If students are productive in the note-making stage, they will be able to demonstrate significant 'knowledge and understanding' (criterion A) as well as a high degree of interpretive personal engagement and control over the direction of their argument (criteria B and C).

With this in mind, it is important that students are trained in using the 20 minutes of preparation time productively. Students are advised to make detailed annotations on the extract itself for 10–15 minutes before considering the structure for the commentary. One main reason for students dissolving into tears only minutes into the examination is often because they have written very little analytical material around the extract itself. This leads to a far too short, superficial presentation and consequently candidates finish prematurely before having managed to speak in any detail. It is far preferable to annotate the extract using the above methodology and have students produce a bullet-pointed structure that can then be written out on a separate sheet of blank paper in the minutes before the commentary begins. Marks are awarded for a sense of structure, so students should practise grouping points together under key headings. This helps to keep the structure of the presentation tight, and 'jumping between topics' is kept to a minimum. Less able students may adopt a 'talk-through' model but there is the danger here that they describe the content of the passage instead of analysing it.

The guiding questions provided at the end lend some further support, but the key to success, as stated above, is achieving the sense of genuine exploration and personal engagement. Significantly, some of the liveliest commentaries have emerged from the practice stage when students have been presented with an unseen poem or an extract. This suggests that the students who do best are those who can analyse clearly and yet retain a sense of spontaneity. Some students prepare for the examination by learning everything possible about a text and author (often from secondary sources); they end up trying to regurgitate a formulaic and rehearsed response which can lead to a very superficial analysis and which usually goes awry under the pressure of time.

Finally, the teacher-examiner can often end up playing an important part in helping the student to maximize their performance. We should remember, for instance, that students are obliged to respond to teachers' questions at the end of their commentary and if they 'dry up' relatively early on this interaction could take some time. On a personal note, I have sometimes heard tapes sent in for moderation on which some very misleading or frankly difficult questions have been posed to the students. Questions should be phrased in a helpful, open manner, and examiners should pick up on aspects the student may have missed out or failed to complete in enough detail. The examiner's questions are a compulsory element, as is the 15-minute time limit; a particularly loquacious student may have to be brought to a close after about 12 minutes in order to fulfil all the requirements of the oral.

2.4 The individual oral presentation

The key to this component of the course lies within its scope for 'free choice'. There is no requirement that texts are chosen from any of the prescribed lists so the teacher has absolute freedom to select literary texts from any source.

Consequently, it is here that teachers can look to expand the range of the students' reading, give them exposure to works they might otherwise not come across and generally tailor the nature of the work to the inclinations, interests and needs of their group. Part 4 is assessed through an individual oral presentation in which the student talks for up to 15 minutes, and as with the formal commentary, this includes a brief discussion with the teacher. Suggestions for the format of the presentation are provided by the IBO and these include structured discussions where the student takes the lead role, oral exposés on a particular theme, literary aspect or interpretation of a work, or a role play activity such as a monologue.

As with the formal commentary the criteria for assessing the Part 4 presentation differ between SL and HL, the latter requiring (amongst other things) evidence of understanding of 'the effects of the means' through which the respective author(s) have explored the particular aspect. HL students should be 'convincing and detailed' to score a top mark in criterion B (interpretation and personal response), whereas SL students need only offer an interpretation that is 'valid'. In basic terms, a good presentation will be detailed and thorough in its examination of a particular aspect, will show a strong sense of personal engagement and interpretation and be interesting and engaging for its audience. It is worth recording on video some successful presentations so that subsequent years can benefit from seeing the kind of thing that is expected.

Students complete an individual oral presentation that is based on one or more work(s) from the section. To this end, students should be encouraged first and foremost to select the topic before deciding on an activity or format. Decisions about the latter, of necessity, should derive from the most effective way in which a particular topic or interest can be best delivered, be it through structured discussion, oral exposé or expressive role play. The more the students are encouraged to actively reflect on the means as well as the content of their presentation, then the more likely they are to assume control over it and so to show greater assurance and confidence when presenting.

Beyond this, specificity and detail are once again important if students are to attain high marks across the range of criteria. Examples of the kinds of successful assignments are:

A formal presentation on 'the tick' as a symbol for Grenouille in Patrick Süskind's *Perfume*.

A monologue with rationale offering a psychoanalyst's perspective on Dr Frankenstein's rise and fall.

'Found' art work as a commentary on the theme of alienation in *Heart of Darkness* and the poetry of Grace Nichols.

Each of these presentations provide the student with the chance to show detailed understanding of the text as well as the opportunity for independent points of interpretation.

In the teaching of the various Part 4 texts, it is useful to give students exposure to the range of activities and types of eventual presentation they might eventually choose. Some students may be unused to this form of assessment and may find the notion of anything other than a straightforward formal presentation something of an anathema. Therefore, students need confidence-building practice to perform role plays and extracts of monologue, or take a key role in small group or whole class discussion. Furthermore, including reference to works of art, music and other alternative forms of expression in the teaching of the texts, can often provoke students into thinking about alternative means of responding that they might not otherwise have considered. There are some helpful suggestions along these lines on page 40 of the *Language A1 Subject Guide*. This area of the course is certainly one in which there is a little more room to breathe. There is less formality in terms of defining the final outcome and students can enjoy experimenting before arriving at a final choice of subject on which they would like to focus and find a forum for exploring it.

Ideally the individual presentation will take place in front of the other students in the group in order that the final product is as valuable to others as it is the presenting student. However, in very large classes it may not be possible to involve the whole class at once as it can eat away at valuable class time – especially at SL. For moderation, ideally two teachers should look at a number of presentations from different classes in order to arrive at a consensus; alternatively, have one or two presentations recorded and then marks can be awarded as part of a departmental training session.

Unlike the Part 2 formal commentary, there is no requirement to send recordings of individual presentations to the board, although you will need to record written details of each one on the form 1/IARF in case further evidence is requested.

2.5 Paper 1 Unseen commentary

Paper 1 of the final written examination is worth 25% of the student's final mark and as such demands a significant amount of attention throughout the course. Students have the option of choosing either a poem or extract of prose for the commentary and there are, inevitably, a range of ways in which it is possible to teach students an essential format for an appropriate approach and structure. This practice once again must be measured against the danger of over-teaching – in a prescriptive manner – a method that restricts students and renders their responses formulaic rather than independent and engaged.

Teachers need to encourage a range of response to the largest variety of texts available. The more students are asked to formulate a critique of as wide and as varied a number of texts as possible, then the more sensitive and discerning they will become. Bringing in short extracts of novels, plays or poems that are not necessarily part of the course, but for which the teacher has a particular enthusiasm, is a very good way of encouraging the development of critical autonomy. It is also a means of eliciting an enthusiasm for literature as a tool for responding generally to the world. The first year of the course should be seen as the place in which the students' independent critical ability is nurtured in a general sense; once this confidence is established, they can then move on to the practice of structuring their ideas in a formal commentary in the second year.

There are five strands of assessment criteria for the formal commentary. These are detailed in figure 12.6.

There are also differences between HL and SL in the phrasing of specific levels. For instance, to score a 5 for criterion B, HL students must demonstrate ideas that are 'convincing', whereas SL students need only be 'clearly relevant'. And in criterion C, HL students must be 'detailed and persuasive' in their 'appreciation

Figure 12.6 Interpretation of assessment criteria for the formal commentary

Criteria	Description	Interpretation
A	Understanding of the text	• How well has the candidate understood the thought and feeling expressed in the text?
B	Interpretation of the text	• How relevant are the candidate's ideas about the text? • How well has the candidate explored those ideas? • How well has the candidate illustrated claims? • To what extent has the candidate expressed a relevant personal response?
C	Appreciation of literary features	• To what extent is the candidate aware of the presence of literary features in the text such as diction, tone, structure, style and technique? • To what extent does the candidate appreciate the effect of the literary features? • How well has the candidate supported claims about the effects of literary techniques?
D	Presentation	• How well has the candidate organized the commentary? • How effectively have the candidate's ideas been presented? • To what extent are supporting examples integrated into the body of the commentary?
E	Formal use of language	• How accurate and precise is the language used by the candidate? • How appropriate is the candidate's choice of register for this task?

of the effects of literary features' to score a 5 whereas SL students must have '*clear* appreciation of the effects of *some* literary features' (author's italics). How these differences play out in practice is to some extent a matter of opinion, although HL students are expected to demonstrate a greater degree of depth and detail as well as a more developed ability to combine careful analytical awareness with a capacity for independent, personal engagement. For formally assessed pieces during the course, it is worth including the marks for each criterion at the bottom of a script in order that the students can see specifically how they performed in each strand.

When preparing students for the formal commentary examination, it is useful – as indicated in section 2.4 – to encourage students to use the preparation time to see the value of reading for different aspects. Breaking down the various components of which the text is made up, for instance at the level of *content*:

• narrative voice
• character/relationships
• plot/events
• setting

and *form*:

• diction/syntax
• figurative language

- structure
- imagery
- tone/atmosphere
- rhyme and rhythm

and making detailed and constructive annotations on each, the student is then free to structure the various notes into categories and so to begin the formulation of a plan. In order to arrive at a thesis, key questions on the extract provide the student with valuable critical tools:

- What is the subject or various concerns of the passage?
- What does the author seem to be saying *about* those particular concerns?
- Which of them stands out for you as the most important?
- Finally, what are the most prominent features of content and language?

In addition, students need to refer directly to the text as often as possible, keep to one topic per paragraph and ensure that their argument undergoes some kind of development as the commentary moves along.

2.6 Paper 2 The essay

In the introduction to this chapter we saw that teachers must select four texts at HL and three at SL for Part 3 from the relevant section in the PBL, and each work must come from the same genre category. One of the texts must be a World Literature text 'chosen freely'.

There is no reason to think that any one genre is likely to yield more profitable results than another. In view of the high degree of detailed work that is demanded by the examination, the best advice is simply to select both the genre and the individual works about which you are enthusiastic as you will need to spend a lot of time on close text study. Furthermore, selecting works that provide a range of points of similarity and difference, once again is an important factor in the drive towards imaginative thinking and independent analytical ability on the part of the students. Examples of helpful combinations are given in the Appendix at the end of this chapter.

One issue of note: for HL students it is very useful to find a more demanding or 'alternative' fourth text in order to really challenge and stretch the depth and degree of thinking as much as possible. Arguably, it is also worth choosing one that will offer a slightly different perspective from which to analyse more closely – or more subtly – the other three texts. Pinter's *The Caretaker*, for instance, serves as a very useful means of dissecting the more conventional forms of *Hedda Gabler*, *A Streetcar Named Desire* and *Master Harold and the Boys*. Because its more expressionistic, anti-naturalist format juxtaposes so forcibly with the 'realism' of the other three texts, students' understanding of each is increased. A similar method could equally be applied to novels or poetry and is an excellent technique for encouraging independent critical enquiry when preparing for the Part 3 examination.

Although students study three or four texts, it is advisable to choose two for detailed study in the examination, with perhaps a passing reference only to the others. This usually affords them much greater scope for the inclusion of sufficient detail and simplifies the kinds of comparative logic that would be required of writing successfully on three or more.

Whether to select the texts on the basis of the similarity or difference in the way they afford material from which to answer the question largely depends on the nature of what they are being asked. For this reason alone it is never a good idea to revise less than the total number of texts studied, as the question might well have suited discussion of the one or two texts the students omitted to include in their preparation. Remember that students have the option of answering a question from their specific genre category *or* one of four general questions, so they will need to have been given exposure to a range of different kinds of titles and model answers. The biggest danger, however, is to teach too prescriptively towards the examination and so to limit the degree of personal engagement and spirit of independent enquiry the students might otherwise show. Therefore, although they need to demonstrate their understanding of the texts in the form of a final, timed piece, try to keep the teaching as creative as possible and incorporate a variety of written and oral methods – both analytical and creative tasks.

3 Case study: Hindi A1

The internationalist nature of the IBO means that as well as English, Spanish and French there is an array of alternative languages available as A1. In theory schools may offer any language that has a corpus of written literature, and if there are six or more students taking an A1 language the centre should provide professional instruction. In this section Anu Ruhil discusses some of the challenges faced by teachers working with one of these minority A1 languages.

3.1 Introduction

As well as being a positive display of multicultural values, teaching an A1 course can be immensely rewarding and the students have the opportunity to examine the richness of their own cultural and literary heritage. Teaching a minority language also often means that the teacher will be in the driver's seat choosing texts, structuring the course in an effective manner and supervising assessment. If a teacher is new to the DP, this can be a daunting prospect. However, it is best to seek help and learn from the experience of other A1 teachers. This works well if there is an overall languages department which oversees other A1 languages.

In cases where the teacher is working alone it is best if the teacher is assigned an experienced 'buddy' who teaches A1 in the school's language of instruction. They can be consulted about worrisome issues such as suggestions for World Literature texts and coursework topics. It is also beneficial if the teacher can attend IBO teacher-training workshops and moderation sessions even if they are primarily concerned with other languages. As the procedures for all A1 languages are identical, the solo teacher can pick up a wealth of useful knowledge. Moreover, the IB specifies that all novice teachers should attend an IB A1 language workshop as soon as is practical.

Like all A1 languages, Hindi A1 is a course for students who have either native or near-native competence in that language. Our student profile for Hindi A1 comprises two groups of students:

- native-speakers of Hindi (Hindi as a home language)
- non-native speakers of Hindi who speak, but not necessarily write, another Indian language.

For example, in the current group of 18 students, about half are native-speakers of Hindi, and the other half are from the following language backgrounds: Bengali, Kannada, Marathi, Gujarati and Telugu. Most of these students have studied in an educational setting where English is the medium of instruction and Hindi the national language. In other words, the students from India typically have bilingual competence in English and Hindi, and in addition many use another language at home. However, it would be wrong to think that Hindi A1 is a catch-all subject for students from South Asia; the school additionally offers Bengali, Dhivehi, Gujarati, Punjabi, Sinhalese, Tamil and Urdu as self-taught A1 languages.

Some students have been in international schools outside of India for some time and may not have studied Hindi in a formal context after grade 7 or 8. In such cases, the students must demonstrate a sound grasp of grammar and vocabulary in order to opt for an A1 other than the school's language. A simple diagnostic test allows the teacher to assess whether a student is a suitable candidate for the A1 course. It is best to take an extract (preferably prose), provide two or three guiding questions that measure the student's comprehension of the content and ask the student to write a commentary. In effect this is similar to the kind of writing task required in Paper 1 of the A1 examination.

If a student is able to write a coherent analysis of the content, the chances of success in Hindi are high. Logically this scenario will apply to other languages too. However, expectations regarding the quality of the content should be realistic. It would be expecting too much to ask students to comment in detail on use of language, and literary devices. These skills are practised and developed over the course of two years of the DP. A practical suggestion to increase the confidence of students who may not have extensive exposure to Hindi literature is that they take additional lessons prior to starting the DP. Tutoring in the summer (prior to starting year 1) is an efficient and effective strategy for improving analytical skills.

However, good grades and results in Hindi do not come without work. As in the case of English, students are required to be autonomous learners – a learning style that is often new to many students from the national system in India. The delivery of the course requires them to learn to think independently, and synthesize ideas in a coherent manner. For example, right from selecting a topic for the World Literature essay and for their oral presentation, students are required to work independently with limited input from the teacher. In this, as well as requiring students to read literature from other cultures, the nature of the DP is different from that of national systems. Generally, oral assignments do not feature consistently within national educational systems due to financial and practical constraints. Thus for many students the oral component of the A1 course is an unfamiliar experience. Not only do students have to adapt to new material and testing formats, but they must also adapt to different teaching and learning styles. Group presentations and short written assignments allow students to gain confidence as they learn to adapt to IBO requirements.

Some parents are nervous at the prospect of their child studying an A1 language other than English, since they fear that grades may suffer. Their anxiety is understandable. However, a note of encouragement is in order here.

Well-motivated students, with limited formal instruction in Hindi, have succeeded at the DP. At the end of two years we have seen a significant increase in such students' written competence. Furthermore, results are usually very good; the majority receives either a 5 or a 6. Parents also need to see that earning a bilingual diploma also can enhance a student's profile when applying to universities. Finally, a less tangible but nonetheless equally important outcome is students' expressed appreciation for their literary heritage and culture by the end of the course.

3.2 World Literature for Hindi A1

As stated above, the availability of resources can be one of the first hurdles one encounters. It takes considerable time and groundwork to determine what texts are available and to order them well in advance. If interesting texts are not available in translation, the teacher may have to use the English originals. We have to read the World Literature texts in English and discuss them in Hindi (this scenario may also be valid for other A1 languages where texts are unavailable). When the course was first offered at our school, it was necessary for the DPC to seek the IBO's permission to offer a Part 1 component using texts in English.

Although working without Hindi translations is not ideal for students, particularly when it comes to writing about the texts, it can work. For example, while we are discussing the actual texts in class, students find it more natural to discuss them in English. This is less awkward than switching codes throughout a lesson. However, once the planning stage is in operation, all subsequent lessons are conducted in Hindi. Another problem with using the original texts is that students have to translate quotations into Hindi themselves. Not only is this additional work for them, it is also difficult and can result in awkward translations. However, it appears that examiners recognize the difficulty of the task for students and students do not appear to have been penalized.

Because of the similarities in aims and objectives, teaching strategies that work in one A1 language may also work with another. As has been suggested above, World Literature texts with cultural resonance for students work best as they are both interesting and motivating. For example, Indonesian and African texts that explore the colonial experience have particular relevance for students of Hindi. We also saw in section 2 that in order to score well students should steer clear of broad topics and work with a narrow focus instead. In addition, they need to think about the texts independently and should ideally explore an area that interests them. These strategies work equally well for Hindi. Here are some suggestions for World Literature texts:

- *Things Fall Apart* by Chinua Achebe
- *This Earth of Mankind* by Pramodya Ananta Toer
- *Heart of Darkness* by Joseph Conrad

Genre (novel) and theme (colonialism) are the links between these three texts. These three are germane for students of Hindi because of the parallels they can draw between the colonial experience in India and the experiences in Africa and Indonesia; they also work well because they can be compared on several levels.

3.3 The oral component

Figure 12.7 Part 2 texts for Hindi A1

Part 2: Taped oral commentary	Part 4: Oral presentation
1. *Dhruvswamini* (Jaishankar Prasad)	1. *23 Hindi Kahaniyan* (ed. Jainendra Kumar)
2. *Meri Priya Kahaniyan* (Mohan Rakesh)	2. *Meri Priya Kahaniyan* (Yashpal)
	3. *Ravindranath ki Kahaniyan*, Part 2 (trans. Kanika Tomar)

Texts that are rich in language as well as thematic content are particularly effective for the commentary. In our case, Prasad's *Dhruvswamini* is challenging linguistically and the topic of women's position and rights in society has particular relevance for current times. For instance, *Meri Priya Kahaniyan*, Rakesh's anthology of stories, explores different social issues such as political corruption, marital discord and alienation of the individual in urban settings. They also have certain stylistic features on which the students can comment. Thus content and style are the two most important issues when choosing texts for any A1 Part 2 component. Consequently, the task of culling suitable extracts for the commentary is both easy and interesting for the teacher. In the DP, all taped orals are difficult for students and Hindi is no different. Practice helps and allowing students to read an extract on different levels also enhances their chances of doing well. See section 2 for further discussion of commentary techniques.

Keeping the student profile in mind, I recommend the short story as a genre for Part 4, since it allows students greater choice for their presentations. The anthologies are also rich in material and ideas for students to draw upon; I encourage them to jot down key ideas/points that they can expand upon. It is useful to practise a couple of presentations in class so that students can think critically about this assignment and avoid simply regurgitating memorized material.

As far as moderation is concerned, the lone A1 teacher is out on a linguistic limb. However, if possible consult A1 colleagues in other departments about procedures and grade boundaries. Your DPC may also be able to track down other schools offering the same A1 language. Such long-distance connections may well prove to be a possible source of help and advice.

3.4 Written commentary

In order to do well in Paper 1 (the commentary) students should have adequate practice in working with a variety of texts. One obvious source is past papers but even here there are pitfalls. Teachers of Hindi will notice that past papers from the early to mid-1990s contained prose extracts that were non-literary. However, the IBO seems to have imposed a measure of standardization of the texts. Now, in line with other 'mainstream' A1 languages, prose extracts are literary in nature and explore some aspect of society, such as the tradition of arranged marriage, the generation gap, the abuse of political power, etc. These are the most useful texts to work with as they best reflect current practice. Over the past four or five years, prose extracts have become less dense linguistically. Texts also now contain dialogue, a feature that enlivens the text and also allows the student to comment on the relationship between characters as well as the use of language. However, teachers of A1 should take care: there is still great variation in the texts on Paper 1. In Hindi A1, for example, many extracts still contain dialectical variation and students need training to recognize it and comment on it in a meaningful manner. Examinations in other languages may have similar quirks.

3.5 The essay

Unlike English A1, for this part of the syllabus the novel has been selected as genre, since it gives my particular students better material for analysis. There are several reasons governing choice of Part 3 texts. Firstly, the novels are seminal works of Hindi literature and thus are known entities to the students. They are linked thematically, and have different narrative styles and language so that students can compare the texts on many levels. To this end, Premchand's *Nirmala* and Bharti's *Suraj ka Saatwan Ghoda* are very effective. In addition to two novels in Hindi, a World Literature text is mandatory for this section of the syllabus. It is essential that Part 3 books have thematic and stylistic similarities and, equally importantly, differences, so that the students can discuss these in detail and ultimately write about them.

In my view, texts that work well in this section must have cultural resonance and strong thematic links to the A1 texts as well as a distinctive narrative structure. Buchi Emecheta's *The Bride Price* is a good example. Ruth Prawer Jhabvala's *Heat and Dust* is also a good text, appropriate for a study of colonialism. Classics such as *Wuthering Heights* (one of those rare texts available in Hindi) are not as effective because the vocabulary is particularly difficult and that specific translation has very little cultural resonance for Hindi students.

4 Self-taught A1 languages

In line with the IBO philosophy of 'know yourself', students may opt to take their mother tongue/first language as a self-taught language. In this final case study Kevin Morley examines the case for introducing self-taught A1 languages into schools and discusses the advantages and the practicalities of running this unique feature of the DP.

4.1 Introduction and rationale

In the above case of Hindi there are enough students to form a teaching group and a suitably qualified teacher is available to the school. However, this is not always the case. Individuals may need or wish to take their first language and there are not always specialist teachers. In these cases, it is possible for a student or groups of up to five students (six in special circumstances such as the unavailability of a teacher) to take an A1 language as a self-taught option.

There are many academic advantages to this. As we have seen with the example of Hindi, many DP students have a mother tongue other than the working language of the school and can do well in an A1 other than English, French or Spanish. Students who are motivated and well organized can gain higher scores in self-taught A1 and, say, English A2 or B. For bilingual students this approach is both educationally and linguistically sound and is certainly more beneficial to those students, who would otherwise struggle with the school's majority A1 at HL or SL and a language B or *ab initio* programme. For example, Najada is Albanian and prior to the DP her education had been entirely in Albanian and had included the study of Albanian literature. She has had four years' experience of learning English as a foreign language. For her, self-taught Albanian A1 (special request) and English HL B represent a very valid and worthwhile educational experience. The only viable alternative would have been English A1 (including the in-depth study of a work of Shakespeare) and an *ab initio* language.

There are also other compelling practical and cultural reasons for allowing students to take the self-taught route. An A1 qualification may be a requirement or recommendation for university in the student's home country. Secondly, many parents of bilingual students have ensured that their children have remained literate in the mother tongue and welcome the opportunity for their children to continue to study that language and literature as part of the DP. Last but not least, taking self-taught A1 demonstrates a high degree of maturity and personal organization and can look very impressive on a student's university application.

4.2 Course administration for self-taught A1

A self-taught course is constructed in a broadly similar manner to any other A1 course. Students must study works divided into the same four parts and must undertake the same number of assessment activities. However, there are inevitably some differences. A self-taught course can only be taken at SL. The course has a requirement to study texts from three genres but the requirement to study texts from different periods and places is waived. All texts must be taken from the relevant part of the PBL. For example, even for self-taught, the Part 2 texts must be chosen from those Part 2 texts listed. There is no free choice from outside the prescribed syllabus. The administration is also similar and DPCs must also submit a form 1A/1AP containing the relevant syllabus details for each self-taught language.

As far as assessment is concerned, self-taught students must also complete the World Literature course and the written examinations Paper 1 (commentary) and Paper 2 (essay). These are the same as those for taught candidates. The assessment criteria are identical and there is no evidence that self-taught candidates are marked more leniently. The major difference lies in the absence of any internal assessment. The oral examinations for Parts 2 and 4 are externally set and assessed (see section 4.7 for details and procedures). From an administrative point of view the IBO will also require a centre to inform the relevant examiners of the students' choice of Part 2 and Part 4 works. These details are submitted on form 1A/1ST.

Teachers and DPCs who are familiar with self-taught programmes know that if things can go wrong, they do so. All concerned would do well to check that the books listed on the 1A/1ST match exactly those submitted on the form 1A/1AP. Like most 17 to 18 year-olds, self-taught students can be rather cavalier with apparently minor details like exact titles of works and the names of authors. Cross-checking is especially important when students are submitting information that is written in unfamiliar scripts. Both forms should be submitted to the IBO eight months before the final examinations.

Students may take any of the languages outlined in section 1 and other languages are available as special requests. In such instances the school must provide the IBO with evidence that the student is linguistically capable of the course. A school report or a letter from a recognized tutor will usually be sufficient. As with any SL A1, the school must provide a programme of 11 suitable texts subdivided into Parts 1–4. Six texts should be written originally in the relevant A1 language and must be in three different genres. However, special request language candidates must make sure that their chosen works are of literary merit, as the IBO takes a dim view of special request syllabuses that contain other genres such as anthologies of journalism or overtly political works. The remaining five texts should be World Literature texts in translation.

These details must be submitted on form C2 for special request languages. On the form, DPCs will also be expected to provide the IBO with a rationale explaining the student's need to study this language. The single most pressing reason is the student's requirement of an A1 language to complete a diploma package. A C2 should be submitted within the first month of the DP. On receipt of the C2 the IBO will contact, or if necessary locate, a suitable examiner for that subject. In instances where a language is to be requested but the student has been unable to provide a list of suitable texts, it is always better for the DPC to inform the IBO of the situation and seek advice on a case-by-case basis.

4.3 Choosing texts for self-taught A1

In cases where the A1 language is repeatedly requested, it is worth schools having a set syllabus for each language. Students can then take this up in successive years. This system reduces administrative headaches and also allows students in different years to discuss common texts and pass on notes and any available study guides from one to the other. It is also advisable, once a student has completed a self-taught A1 course, for the school to keep copies of books and other background material such as secondary sources. This can reduce the huge amount of time spent finding texts. It is also useful for students to collect suitable literature website addresses pertaining to their course that can be uploaded onto a departmental or college web page.

If the language is new to the school, the student's family should be asked to provide suitable texts from the PBL. At this point it is essential to check that the books conform to the relevant part of the PBL. If this is not the case, the submitted texts will be rejected by the IBO. On the other hand, students can construct self-taught courses using very user-friendly texts and there are no bonus points for choosing works of impenetrable complexity. When in doubt, students could be advised to go for works that are short, have contemporary relevance and which are widely available. This criterion is important because there is more chance that the students will find secondary source materials to assist their studies of the texts. However, most important of all is whether the student enjoys reading the works.

As we have seen in the introduction to this chapter, special request language candidates must make sure that their chosen works are of literary merit. An additional strategy is to ask the DPC to refer to the IBO to find which schools have previously offered the language. IB schools are generally very cooperative about providing syllabus details and once contact has been established it should be possible to make use of an existing and functioning syllabus. This system has the additional benefit of providing the school with an approved syllabus. This saves the frustration and inconvenience of submitting a book list that is subsequently pronounced unacceptable by the IB examiner for that language.

As far as the construction of the syllabus is concerned, the guidelines set out in figure 12.8 work well.

The rationale behind this programme is as follows:

- Popular novels for *World Literature* are easier to find in translation than other genres. It is also a good idea to select books that are relatively short and linguistically accessible, especially if the texts are to be used in a literature class where some of the students may still be learning English.
- For *Part 2* a drama and a set of short stories chosen from the relevant PBL allow the student to meet the genre requirements for the course. Both genres have a strong narrative structure and, therefore, are also relatively straightforward when it comes to preparing for commentary.
- For *Part 4* it is a good idea to include at least one set of poems. There are pragmatic reasons for this. In Paper 1 (commentary), students must choose between a poem and an extract of prose. Almost all self-taught candidates will go for the prose passage. If students have examined poetry as a genre it is somewhat easier to tackle a poem in the final examination and, consequently, this may give the students more options if the prose passage is not to their taste.
- For *Part 3* it is easier to choose the novel because it is the most popular literary form. If the students are taught as a class, it is easier for a teacher to examine one genre rather than several in preparation for the examination. This utilizes precious teaching time in the most efficient manner. Ideally the World Literature text chosen for Part 3 should also connect with the works chosen. In this instance, *Things Fall Apart* by Chinua Achebe is a very useful text.

Sets of past examination papers from 2001 are available on CD-ROM from the IBCA (IB Curriculum and Assessment) office in Cardiff, UK. Others can usually be obtained from colleagues in other schools. The format of Paper 2 changed in

Figure 12.8 Choice of texts for self-taught A1

Assessment method	Section of syllabus	Texts
Coursework	Part 1 World Literature	Three novels from PWL
Internal assessment	Part 2 Detailed study	Part 2: one play and one set of short stories by the same author
	Part 4 School's free choice	Part 4: one set of poems in A1, one free choice in A1 and one novel from PWL
Examination	Part 3 Groups of works	Two novels in A1 and one novel from PWL

2001 from a thematic to a genre-based approach to this part of the syllabus. Nevertheless, some of the questions from previous years can still be used. If there are no papers available, students can always make up their own examinations using extracts from their A1 texts as commentary material. This is a very useful exercise in its own right. Suitable questions can be translated from an English A1 paper.

4.4 Transparency

It is essential that self-taught students have a complete understanding of the aims and objectives of their chosen A1 course. Unfortunately, the IBO does not provide information regarding self-taught A1 in a single document, so it is worth putting together a handbook containing the following information:

- aims and objectives, assessment details and assessment criteria (all taken from the 2002 A1 guide)
- a course outline and timetable (see figure 12.9)
- forms 1A/1ST, 1A/1AP, C2 (special request) – students can fill these in so that they have a permanent record of their programme
- a sample Paper 1 and Paper 2 from English A1 SL
- a sample of World Literature assignments in English
- sample questions for Part 2 and Part 4 orals
- a copy of the procedures for the conduct of self-taught orals – this can be obtained from the *Vade Mecum*.

For the teacher it is also worth keeping files on each language. The file can contain a copy of the PBL, all available examination papers and photocopies of the completed forms 1A/1ST, 1A/1AP, C2 (special request). In addition it is also a logical repository for all miscellaneous correspondence, lists and addresses related to an individual language.

4.5 Encouraging study in A1

The IBO requires schools to provide self-taught students with a literature course. This can be as little as one lesson a week during the DP. Alternatively it can be timetabled as a regular standard A1 class over two years. The latter system has the advantage of giving the students adequate time and supervision to discuss content and acquire the skills of literary analysis. In addition some schools find tutors for their self-taught students. Tutors can help students to discuss individual works and comment on students' practice essays and commentaries. However, they cannot play a formal assessment or administrative role. Whatever system is adopted, students can study the five World Literature texts in English and learn literary analysis and commentary skills in the lessons provided by the school. The person teaching this class could also act as self-taught coordinator and liaise with the DPC.

There is never enough contact time, so teachers are advised to make extra study compulsory, but it should not be too much, and should not exceed the IBO's student–teacher time requirement of 150 hours, the same as for all taught A1 SL languages. Not all self-taught students have as many lessons as their counterparts, so have them learn the discipline of working in a designated space, such as the library, once a week. They can study texts and work on their written assignments for the term. Wherever possible, colleagues who know the A1 language can be recruited to look at students' work. In all other instances parents and guardians can also be encouraged to become involved, or to find tutors to assist with studies and comment on students' written work. Some schools agree to pay for suitably qualified teachers abroad, who can mark students' work and give feedback. Even if the language cannot be read, teachers can encourage good study habits by setting deadlines for assignments and insisting that all work is neatly presented and of appropriate length.

Figure 12.9 is an example of a scheme of work for self-taught A1, and in the next section there are some suggestions on a possible approach to assisting students with each component of the assessment.

4.6 A two-year teaching plan for self-taught A1 languages

Figure 12.9 A sample two-year timetable for self-taught A1 languages

Year 1	Administration	Class time	Non-teaching time
	GRADE 11		
1st Quarter	Submit special request forms C2 to IBO (September)	Part 1 World Literature texts 1	Practise WL writing tasks in A1
		December test 1 (in English) on texts for Part 3	Read both texts in A1 for detailed study (Part 3)
2nd Quarter		Part 1 World Literature texts 1	Practise WL writing tasks in A1
			Read both texts in A1 for detailed study (Part 3)
3rd Quarter	Registration of split session candidates	Part 1 World Literature text 3	Practise tasks on World Literature texts 1 or 2 and 3 leading to practice World Literature in A1 language
		Practice Part 3 Paper 1 commentary 1	
			Read both texts in A1 for detailed study (Part 3)
4th Quarter		April (internal examinations) Practice Part 3 Paper 1 commentary	Begin – 1st draft of World Literature essay in A1
		Read Part 3 World Literature text	Read texts 1 and 2 for orals (Part 4) Holiday work
		Set practice essay Part 3 Paper 2 (detailed study) on A1 texts	Hand in practice essay Part 3 on Paper 2 (detailed study)
		Practice Part 3 Paper 1 Commentary 2	

Year 1	Administration	Class time	Non-teaching time
	GRADE 12		
1st Quarter	1A/1ST oral IAI/1AP i.e. booklists to IB October	Read Part 4 World Literature text	1 September – hand in Part 1 World Literature essay (1st draft) in A1 language
		1 November test (in English) on Part 4 text	
		Practice Part 3 Paper 1 Commentary	Read A1 texts for Part 2
2nd Quarter	Circa 20 November split session candidates Part 3 examination (Papers 1 and 2)	Practice essay Part 3 Paper 2 (detailed study) on A1 texts	30 November – hand in Part 1 World Literature (students may submit improved versions until 30 January)
		Practice orals for Part 4	
3rd Quarter	Mock examinations on Part 3 Papers 1 and 2	Students prepare commentary passages on Part 2 texts	Practice Part 3 Paper 1 commentaries
			Practice Part 3 Paper 2 essays
		Students practise questions on Part 4 texts	Mock orals for Parts 2 and 4 (ongoing) in A1
4th Quarter	Oral examinations Part 2 and Part 4	Practice Part 3 Paper 1 commentaries	Practice Part 3 Paper 1 commentaries
	May – Part 3 examination	Practice Part 3 Paper 2 essays	Practice Part 3 Paper 2 essays

4.7 Preparing students for assessment

From the teacher/DPC's point of view, Part 1 World Literature is the most obvious place where students can be assisted to learn literary technique, albeit in English. For Part 1 the students themselves will limit the choice of text. If there is a Japanese student, none of the World Literature texts should be Japanese. Choosing works from the school's working language or other A1 languages taught in the school circumvents the problem entirely. It is also worth reiterating that some of the students will not have a totally fluent grasp of English and, therefore, it is best to teach books that are short and linguistically accessible. A useful homework exercise is to have students translate their lesson notes back into their A1 language. Students should also try to obtain translations of the works. If they cannot do so they should read the three texts in English but respond in A1, translating quotes where necessary.

Students need repeated writing practice in their A1: first to show understanding of the texts studied, and second to ensure that their written skills in the language do not atrophy. From the outset of the programme, students should write short assignments in A1 on different aspects of the World Literature works covered in class: character, theme, setting, narrative structure, symbolism. This can be done with each text studied. Afterwards the student can use these shorter tasks to help compose the World Literature coursework essay. It is advisable to commission two World Literature essays using two different pairs of Part 1 texts.

Students should complete this in year 1 so that they can present a completed version to the teacher/coordinator after the summer break.

Given the linguistic challenges they face, self-taught A1 candidates need to practice Paper 1 commentaries on a regular basis, at least one a term. Students should attempt both the prose and poetry passages, especially where resources are tight. It is a good idea to go through a couple of English A1 commentaries in class so that students know what to expect. As an additional study aid students can be given resources in English in order to help them to recognize certain literary features of the texts. They can translate the terminology. If students run out of material they should use extracts from their Part 2 A1 texts to create their own texts for commentary. This will also force them to recognize some of the stylistic features of the authors they have studied as well as give them practice at examining critically the very texts they have to study for the oral commentary.

One reason for setting Part 3 texts as the first reading assignment in the academic calendar is to prepare students for practising the essay skills required on Paper 2. A test can be set towards the end of the second quarter of the second year. This gives students plenty of time to obtain and read the texts. The test, in English, requires the students to give outline details of the plot, characters, source of conflict and endings. This can be an open book test. Students must have a grasp of the works that they are studying. It is not unknown for some unsupervised self-taught A1 students to read almost nothing until the final weeks before the examination.

Having completed their reading of the Part 3 texts it is possible to begin formal essay practice in the final quarter of the first year. If the Part 3 World Literature work is studied in term 3, students have a greater choice of material on which to base their essays. Regular examination practice can then commence in term 3 and continue throughout the second year of the course right up until the examinations. If students run out of essay titles (unlikely) they can always use questions from English A1. Using this schedule, students will have completed the Part 1 essay and the reading for Part 3 before the beginning of the second year.

The reading for the orals can commence in year 2. In term 1 much of the student's focus will naturally be on the final World Literature text for Part 4 and the reading of the other A1 Part 4 texts. The Part 4 questions are very general and should enable the student to make a spontaneous presentation lasting between 5 and 10 minutes. It is worth making a list of appropriate questions. These could include the significance of the title, the role of the protagonist, the significance of the setting, the main themes of the poet, etc. Students can write out their answers in A1. This helps them to practise both writing and preparing for the questions for the oral in April. They should do this for both the World Literature and the A1 Part 4 texts, including the selection of poetry. The Part 4 oral lasts only 5 to 10 minutes and it is worth 15%, the same as the much harder Part 2 commentary. Well-prepared candidates can score very highly here.

Once the students finish their World Literature programme, students will be able to turn to the two commentary elements of their syllabuses: Part 2 and Paper 1 of the final written examinations. As the Paper 2 passage is unseen, students can find suitable passages from their Part 2 texts, photocopy them and make up accompanying questions. This, in fact, mirrors the process that the examiner will undertake. Consequently, the students will have appropriate commentary material they can practise. If previous students have read the same texts the teacher may well have a bank of commentary materials for use with students in the current year.

Self-taught orals take place about one month before the final written examination. The procedures are very different to taught A1 internal assessments and warrant some explanation. Unlike other A1 languages, both the commentary and the presentation are taped. As we have seen, all schools must submit the form 1A/1ST for each candidate detailing the books to be examined for Part 2 and Part 4. It should be noted that where students have submitted a selection of poems or short stories from a larger body of work the specific titles must be listed on an accompanying sheet. Once received by the IBO, these will be passed on to the examiner for the A1 language who will set commentary questions for the Part 2 works and general questions for the Part 4 texts. These are then sent to the school approximately six weeks before the final examinations. Schools receive sealed envelopes containing two copies of the questions; one set for the student and the second for the teacher/supervisor. The contents of the envelopes may only be examined by the teacher/supervisor one hour before the oral is due to begin.

At the beginning of the oral the student opens the envelope containing the commentary on one of the Part 2 works and two general questions on the Part 4 texts, each one pertaining to a different text. The commentary question is compulsory but the candidate must answer only one of the two general questions for Part 4. There are 25 minutes available for the student to make notes. The student then records the commentary for a maximum of 15 minutes and, without pausing the tape, the candidate then presents the answer to the Part 4 question for a maximum of 10 minutes. On completion of the oral the tape and all questions and the candidates' notes should be sealed in the envelope and returned immediately to the DPC. At no time may the teacher/supervisor interfere or assist the candidate beyond silently indicating the time available for each portion of the recording.

As can be imagined the above procedure can be quite harrowing, especially given the length and importance of the recording. Fortunately there are a number of practical things that can be done to assist the self-taught student. Firstly, if possible recruit a colleague who understands the language to supervise the examination; this may put the candidate more at ease. Secondly, before the orals, students should learn the mantra 'Don't panic'. Students must learn that if there is still time to say something about the commentary they are advised to pause and re-examine the text to find additional features on which to comment. Finally, as we have said, the commentary presents far more of a challenge than the presentation. Students who are very well prepared for the Part 4 texts should need little time to prepare their ideas for the presentation. In effect this should give them much more time to analyse the commentary in the 25 minutes' preparation time available for both assessment activities.

5 Extended essay in group 1

Opting to complete an extended essay in English A1 represents an opportunity to explore a work or works in which a student has a particular interest. It is also an occasion for him or her to undertake research into cultural contexts and to locate helpful and relevant secondary sources. The most important key to success is to ensure that the student chooses a text or texts which they are particularly enthusiastic about and which enable them to engage in productive research because (as with any extended essay) many of the marks are awarded in this field rather than in the specific A1 content.

Students are allowed to choose any text 'of literary merit' from any era and the essay can be based on one or more. They can also, if they wish, include a text originally written in another language provided it is compared with one that *is* A1; and they are further allowed to write on a text they are actually studying as part of the A1 course.

The subject-specific criteria are as follows:

- knowledge and understanding of the literature studied and, where appropriate, reference to secondary sources
- personal response justified by literary judgement and/or analysis
- use of language appropriate to a literary essay.

In order to achieve the required degree of 'personal response', it is vital that students find texts and topics in which they are interested. Anything that is 'led' by the teacher can produce a rather 'forced' or formulaic response that will not gain good marks.

Finally, below are detailed some recent examples of successful A1 extended essay titles. Note that in nearly all there is scope for the discussion of literary features and evidence of original thinking in the selection of text and/or the choice of topic. As with the World Literature assignment(s), students will need careful advice at all stages of text and topic selection, research, phrasing of the title and essay planning and writing:

- An exploration of the Malabar Caves as a central symbol in E.M. Forster's *A Passage to India*.
- What is the function of setting in *The Fall of the House of Usher*, *Titus Groan* and *The Grotesque*?
- The Metaphor of Music: the use of music to express the paradox of love and war in the text and film versions of *Captain Corelli's Mandolin*.
- An exploration of Aristotle's tragic form in *Oedipus Rex* by Sophocles and *Death of a Salesman* by Arthur Miller.

6 Resources

Essential IBO documents

Language A1 Subject Guide (1999)

Prescribed World Literature list (PWL)

Published book lists (PBL); separate book lists are available for all of the languages mentioned in section 1.1

Vade Mecum

Diploma Programme Language A1 World Literature Support Material (IBO, 2002) is a very useful guide to this section of the course and offers sample material and examiners' comments.

Form 1/A1AP – Advanced notice of programme

Form 1/IARF – Internal assessment record form: language A1

Form 1/A1ST – Self-taught candidates – choice of authors and works: language A1 SL (titles of works studied for oral component)

Form C2 – Special request language A1: Justification and proposed

World Literature (Parts 1, 3, 4)

Bearing in mind the points made above about appropriate combinations and the selection of aspects on which to write, repeatedly successful assignments have come from combinations of the following texts:

The House of the Spirits, Isabel Allende
A Day in the life of Ivan Denisovich, Alexander Solzhenitsyn
Perfume, Patrick Süskind
Things Fall Apart, Chinua Achebe
Siddharta, Herman Hesse
Madame Bovary, Gustave Flaubert
The Unbearable Lightness of Being, Milan Kindera
Kiss of the Spiderwoman, Manuel Puig
Like Water for Chocolate, Laura Esquivel
Thousand Cranes, Yasunari Kawabata
The Wild Geese, Ogai Mori
Hedda Gabler or *Ghosts*, Henrik Ibsen
Three Sisters, Anton Chekov
Blood Wedding, Frederico Garcia Lorca
Miss Julie, August Strindberg
Oedipus the King, Sophocles
Antigone, Sophocles or Jean Anouilh.

Part 2 (detailed study) (English A1)

Productive Shakespeare texts for SL students include *Measure for Measure, Othello, The Merchant of Venice* and *Henry IV Part 1*. For HL, try *Hamlet, King Lear* or *Antony and Cleopatra*. Other texts that prove to be popular and seem to yield equally fruitful responses are *The Handmaid's Tale, Pride and Prejudice*, selected poems by Sylvia Plath, Kenneth Slessor, Ted Hughes or Judith Wright and essays, autobiography or travel narratives by Wole Soyinka, Vikram Seth, Janet Frame or George Orwell. Once again, choice will depend on requirements (in terms of 'balance') and constraints outlined above.

Part 3 (groups of works) (English A1)

A1 drama texts that are repeatedly successful include:

Master Harold and the Boys, Athol Fugard
Death of a Salesman, Arthur Miller
Cat on a Hot Tin Roof or *A Streetcar Named Desire*, Tennessee Williams
The Caretaker, Harold Pinter
Rosencrantz and Guildenstern are Dead, Tom Stoppard
Dr Faustus, Christopher Marlowe

Who's Afraid of Virginia Woolf, Edward Albee
The Caucasian Chalk Circle, Bertolt Brecht.

A few recommended novels are as follows:

Grapes of Wrath, John Steinbeck
Beloved, Toni Morrison
The Color Purple, Alice Walker
The Handmaid's Tale, Margaret Atwood
The Good Terrorist, Doris Lessing
Hard Times, Charles Dickens
The Quiet American, Graham Greene
Wuthering Heights, Emily Brontë.

Part 4 (school's free choice) (English A1)

Here you can of course exercise absolute freedom of choice, but the following have often proved helpful:

Gothic writing including *Frankenstein* and stories by Edgar Allen Poe.
Colonial short stories by Orwell and Theroux and *Heart of Darkness* by Joseph Conrad.
Poetry of Coleridge, Derek Walcott, Grace Nichols or Seamus Heaney.
The Handmaid's Tale or contemporary novels including *Enduring Love* by Ian McEwan, *Waterland* by Graham Swift and *The True History of the Kelly Gang* by Peter Carey.

For short stories that really inspire the students, try any from the Australian author, Tim Winton.

Figure 12.10 World Literature suggestions for self-taught A1 students

Work	Author	Original language
Kiss of the Spiderwoman	Manuel Puig	Spanish
Kitchen	Banana Yoshimoto	Japanese
Like Water for Chocolate	Laura Esquivel	Spanish
Lord of the Flies	William Golding	English
Metamorphosis	Franz Kafka	German
Of Mice and Men	John Steinbeck	English
The Old Man and the Sea	Ernest Hemingway	English
The Outsider	Albert Camus	French
The Bride Price	Buchi Emecheta	English
Things Fall Apart	Chinua Achebe	English

Appendix

Language choices for the DP – group 1 (literature) and group 2 (second languages)

One of the most complex issues for schools is language policy. Languages account for groups 1 and 2, a third of the entire DP. Because the IBO wishes to promote the use of languages as a tool for cultural awareness and understanding, it is intended for the widest variety of students to participate in the programme regardless of linguistic background. Therefore, the IBO's commitment to multicultural philosophies has created a set of innovative language policies without equal in their scope and breadth. However, one side-effect of this catholic language policy has been to create one of the most complex issues for potential IB schools to resolve.

Students must study two languages for the diploma: a group 1 language and a group 2 language.

Group 1
Mother tongue/best language
A1/STA1

Group 2
Additional/second/foreign/classical/language
A2/B/*ab initio*/Classics

Group 1 (literature)

A group 1 (A1) language is a best language/mother tongue. This is a literature course. In addition to Chinese, English, French and Spanish, the IBO currently offers over 80 different A1 mother tongues for examination. The course structure is identical in each case. If a student has a mother tongue not taught in school the student may take it as a self-taught language (STA1) at SL. Note: Students who cannot offer an A1 language do not meet the DP requirements.

Group 2 (language)

Group 2 offers three different programmes:

A2 is an additional language for functionally bilingual students. It contains literature but also teaches different skills and content from A1. Students investigate topic options, e.g. Language, Culture and Media. Much of the A2 course requires comparative textual skills. The course operates at a similar linguistic level to A1 but is assessed more leniently.

B is a second or a foreign language for students with some previous knowledge and experience of the target language but who are still at the stage of mastering the grammar and lexis of the target language. The focus of the course is language acquisition. Typical language B students would not succeed at A2.

Ab initio is a beginner's course. It is useful for students who wish to start a language afresh or have no previous experience of a foreign language. *Ab initio* may only be taken at SL.

Higher (HL) and Standard (SL)

All group 1 (except self-taught) and all group 2 languages (except *ab initio*) may be studied at either SL or HL. It is essential to clear up a common misconception here. Group 1 should not be confused with HL. By the same token group 2 does not equate with SL.

A few examples will illustrate the point.

Students may take a group 1 at SL and a group 2 at HL,
e.g. Jason takes English A1 (SL) and French B (HL).

Students may take a group 1 at SL and a group 2 at HL,
e.g. Ida takes Swedish A1 (SL) (self-taught) and English B (HL).

Students may choose to take both languages at SL,
e.g. Gururaj takes Hindi A1 (SL) and English A2 (SL).

Students can take two HL languages,
e.g. Chie takes Japanese A1 (HL) and English A2 (HL).

Which group 2?

In practice the school makes placement decisions regarding languages and levels and it is up to individual institutions to ensure that students take the appropriate courses. To a great extent many of the decisions will be based on availability of qualified language teachers and timetabling policies.

Other combinations

Students may take a third language as a sixth subject; Classical languages (Latin or Ancient Greek) are available at HL and SL in group 2. In theory, there is no compulsion to study the school's language of instruction so long as two languages are taken.

Students may also take two group 1 courses instead of a group 2. However, this would require the student to read 30 texts in two years if both languages are taken at HL (26 texts for A1 (HL) + A1 (SL) and 22 texts even if the student takes both at SL). A well-organized A2 course in the student's second language can often provide much greater variety of content and skills.

The bilingual diploma

This enhanced IB diploma will be awarded to all students who can offer an A1 language (mother tongue/first language) other than the school's working language. It is awarded in recognition of the fact that the student can communicate fluently and with the very highest degree of competence in two languages at IB level.

Students taking the bilingual diploma can take their second language as A2. Alternatively, the bilingual diploma is also open to students taking language B – if they take their mother tongue for A1 and their other subjects in the school's working language.

Chapter 13
Group 2: Second languages

Kevin Morley, BA, MEd

Kevin Morley taught in a variety of schools in Germany and the UK before coming to the United World College of South East Asia (UWCSEA) in Singapore in 1992 where he has been Head of Department (English A2/B and A1 self-taught languages) since 1998. He has been teaching English B since 1993 and A2 since 1995. In this chapter he introduces group 2 languages: A2, B and *ab initio*. Each section gives profiles of the intended students, and details of the course content and structure. In addition, there are many practical suggestions for course design. Each section concludes with advice on how to prepare students for assessment.

The author would like to thank colleagues at the UWCSEA for their advice and suggestions: Suzanne Mazeyrac (French B), Dr Anu Ruhil (English A2/B), Thea Birte-Skillicorn (German A2/B). Special thanks are extended to Esperenza Gutierrez (Spanish) for her invaluable input and advice on the writing of the section on *ab initio*.

Note: all weblinks featured in this chapter can be accessed through our website: www.dp-help.com

1 Introduction to group 2 languages

Group 2 encompasses the study of modern languages. Courses emphasize the development of the four skills – listening, speaking, reading and writing – and use communicative teaching methods. Modern language courses are offered at three different levels: language A2, language B and *ab initio*.

Language A2 is designed for bilingual students with a very high level of competence in the target language. Students are expected to enrich their linguistic skills through the detailed study of literature and topics such as media, global issues (for example poverty), or language issues (e.g. bilingualism).

In contrast, language B courses require students to have some knowledge of and experience with the language. Language B students are expected to hone their linguistic skills and to understand and use language in sophisticated ways. For example, language B students should be able to discuss abstract concepts and ideas in the target language.

The *ab initio* course is meant for beginners and is offered only at Standard Level (SL). No prerequisite knowledge of the language is necessary. *Ab initio* courses teach students to use the language for daily interaction.

Schools may also choose to offer Latin and Greek as group 2 languages.

A note on future trends: at the time of writing, group 2 languages are at the beginning of the IBO's five-year review programme with the first examination session of the new syllabuses due to take place in May 2004. All comments here relate to these courses.

2 A2 languages

A2 is a very advanced second language course for Diploma Programme (DP) students who have already achieved a large degree of proficiency in the target language or who are already effectively bilingual. Indeed, students who successfully complete their studies gain the bilingual diploma in recognition of their linguistic achievements. The advanced linguistic skill level makes A2 a unique secondary school language programme and the IBO should take a bow for producing this challenging and imaginative course, which is very popular with both students and teachers. A list of available A2 languages can be found in section C of the *Vade Mecum*.

2.1 A2 students

To understand the nature of A2, it helps to look first at the intended target student body for the course and examine some typical profiles. Firstly we have balanced bilingual students who take A2 in the school's language of instruction. For instance, Krishna has Indonesian as a home language but has been educated in English-medium secondary schools. He has remained perfectly literate in Indonesian. He takes Bahasa Indonesia A1 (group 1) and English A2 (group 2). On the other hand, we also have students who are still developing competence in English. Norwegian student Stine has only been educated in an English-medium school for the last three years, having previously learned English in Norway. She socializes in English, has an English language competence well beyond that of a language B candidate (foreign/second language learner) and yet she is not totally accurate. She writes better Norwegian than English and so she takes Norwegian A1 and English A2.

In addition, A2 also addresses the needs of a third group whose mother tongue is the weaker of their two languages. With such students an A2 teacher has to bear in mind that they may have left their A2 educational background a long time ago and now have to be brought into 'abstract thought mode' in that language. For example, Jeanne-Claire is French and was educated in the French primary system and has subsequently studied in an English-medium secondary school. She has retained some measure of written proficiency in French and her reading and spoken skills are well beyond the level of learners of French B. She takes English A1 and French A2.

2.2 A2 aims and linguistic levels

Language A2 courses require the study of both culture and literature. Therefore much of the teaching on the course will provide a rich and varied linguistic experience, so students become proficient in many different domains. To facilitate this, the IBO stipulates that students must take one of two modules: *Language and Culture* and *Media and Culture*. Additional modules may include *Future Studies, Social Studies* and *Global Studies*. Students are also expected to make detailed studies of up to nine texts of literary merit (see section 2.5 for organizational details).

Out of the study of this material, both Higher Level (HL) and Standard Level (SL) A2 students are expected to be able to produce fluent and coherent essays and comparative commentaries written in examination conditions. There are also two compulsory coursework elements. The first requires students to produce two fluent and convincing texts, one based on a topic option and the other based on a literature text. The final component is a pair of oral activities, one of which is a stylistic commentary. All assessment elements require the student to use the target language fluently and this leaves students with little margin for major linguistic errors.

A2 languages are offered at HL and SL. In practice, where A2 is the school's language of instruction, any student capable of studying A2 SL should be able to take the course at HL. However, students taking an A2 language used only in the classroom may have difficulty in meeting all the demands of an A2 HL course. For example, Frank came to Singapore from a bilingual (English/French) school system in Canada one year before starting the DP. English has always been his stronger language and, because he did not use French at home, he found that his written French skills deteriorated rapidly. For the DP he was advised to take A2 French at SL.

2.3 A2 assessment outline and criteria

Internal assessment
- Individual oral *(externally moderated)* 15%
  A commentary on an unseen passage from one of the student's set texts
- Interactive oral activity 15%
  A free choice, e.g. a presentation, or a speech in a debate, or participation in a discussion of a book or a topic.

External assessment
- Written coursework 20%
  Students produce two imaginative, journalistic or transactional texts with a maximum total word-count of 1,500 words. The student's own observations and comments will accompany each text.

Examination
- Paper 1 (comparative commentary) 25%
  A formal commentary based on two texts connected thematically but which may be from different genres.
- Paper 2 (essay) 25%
  This paper tests knowledge of course content, essay structure and linguistic expression.

(The assessment criteria for all of these activities can be examined in detail on pages 38–65 of the *Language A2* subject guide.)

The assessment activities are marked according to three criteria. Each criterion carries a maximum of 10 marks.

Criterion A – Task-specific criterion
- This assessment measures the student's ability to perform the assessment task.
- For A2 students these task-specific skills are a key to examination success. Therefore students should have opportunities to process a variety of assessment tasks in order to develop and practise those skills. This will ensure a high mark in criterion A.
- Criterion A varies according to the task – see figure 13.1.

Criterion B – Presentation (all assessment activities)
This refers to the student's ability to structure and organize texts in a logical and coherent manner on both the macro and micro levels. Students will need to learn drafting and text production skills in order to structure their work clearly and coherently. They need to use quotes in essays and commentaries and to write with a clear sense of audience and purpose.

Criterion C – Language (all assessment activities)
This refers to the students' linguistic performance in the above tasks. As we have seen from the student profiles in section 2.1, A2 students are expected to arrive at a level of linguistic competence and demonstrate fluent, articulate near-native speaker competence.

Differentiation between A2 SL and A2 HL lies in the reduced volume of work (three, not four, modules of study), a reduced number of lessons, and less stringent assessment material and criteria. Experience shows that by rule of thumb a student achieving a final grade of 5 at A2 HL would gain a 6 at A2 SL.

Figure 13.1 Criterion A task-specific descriptors for A2 assessments

• Orals	• Quality of ideas
• Written tasks	• Formal task requirements*
• Comparative commentary	• Understanding and comparison
• Essay	• Response to question

* Note that the formal task requirements for written coursework tasks are assessed on a scale of 0 to 5 only.

2.4 A2 course structure

A2 HL consists of four modules and A2 SL has three. One literature module is compulsory at both HL and SL. The IBO stipulates that a module consists of three texts of literary merit. Schools may opt for a maximum of three literature modules at HL and two at SL. In situations where student numbers do not warrant separate HL and SL classes, it is possible to organize the course so that the fourth module is taught when the SL students do not attend additional lessons for HL.

At HL the detailed study of literature texts is essential because, as we have seen in section 2.3, stylistic and literary analysis are key components of the assessment process and students must be able to handle them. However, in my opinion, an HL programme that utilizes three literature modules (nine texts) begins to look like an A1 course. Therefore a more balanced solution is to undertake two literary options and two cultural options. In addition, students benefit greatly from the unique opportunity to study topics such as media and language, as these are not covered elsewhere in the DP.

The approach to SL is somewhat different. Whereas most students take HL out of a genuine interest in developing their knowledge and use of English, A2 SL is a compulsory element of the DP. In A2 SL we find many students who take combinations of sciences, mathematics and computer science, and economics and business studies as HL subjects. Here the challenge is to prove to A2 SL students that the subject is a worthwhile area of study and one of potential benefit. To this end it is essential to find literature that is intellectually challenging. Therefore, teachers of A2 SL must decide whether to choose one literature option or two.

2.5 A2 literature texts

The free choice of literature texts means that books can be selected for their relevance to the students or contemporary political or social circumstances. For instance, in these times of increased international tension, the study of Kurt Vonnegut's pacifist novel *Slaughterhouse 5* can provoke impassioned discussion on the rights and wrongs of military action. Any book that stimulates students will make the job of teaching communication skills (which is, after all, a key aim of A2) a relatively easy task. Having said this, there are also linguistic and cultural considerations. It should be remembered that not all A2 students have a complete command of English and therefore the literature should be chosen with care. Dense pre-20th-century literature texts are less likely to speak to bilingual students or echo their personal concerns. In my experience texts that deal with personal struggle and conflicts of social identity are more likely to resonate with a bilingual and bicultural student body – hence Alice Walker's *The Color Purple,* or Maxine Hong Kingston's wonderful autobiography *The Woman Warrior.* In addition, in order to prepare for the essay question in the examination, students must be encouraged to compare the themes of the works and draw parallels between them. A2 students should also make some study of the formal literary elements – structure, narrative voice, symbolism and setting – as these can also be assessed in the essay and in the oral commentary. Figure 13.2 is a list of tried and tested texts for English A2.

Figure 13.2 Suggestions for literature texts in English A2

Themes	Book title	Author
Narrative technique	1. *The Great Gatsby*	F. Scott Fitzgerald
	2. *A Pale View of Hills*	Kazuo Ishiguro
	3. *Slaughterhouse 5*	Kurt Vonnegut
Women and society	1. *Pygmalion*	G. B. Shaw
	2. *The Color Purple*	Alice Walker
	3. *The Woman Warrior*	Maxine Hong Kingston
Social tensions	1. *The Bluest Eye*	Toni Morrison
	2. *Heat and Dust*	Ruth Prawer Jhabvala
	3. *Things Fall Apart*	Chinua Achebe
Childhood	1. *I Know why the Caged Bird Sings*	Maya Angelou
	2. *To Kill a Mocking Bird*	Harper Lee
	3. *Paddy Clarke Ha Ha Ha*	Roddy Doyle
Power and madness	1. *Macbeth*	William Shakespeare
	2. *Nineteen Eighty-Four*	George Orwell
	3. *Heart of Darkness*	Joseph Conrad

2.6 A2 topic options – some practical issues

As stated above, there are also two cultural topic options: *Language and Culture* and *Media and Culture*, one of which the IBO has made a compulsory study. Other available topic options are Future Studies, Social Studies and Global Studies.

One of the novel aspects of A2 languages is that although teachers must design the content according to the IBO's guidelines, they are at liberty to choose their own material. This intellectual freedom makes A2 such a pleasure to teach. Each course can be tailor-made to meet the needs and interests of the students. For example, personal growth and development are two of the key aims of the IBO and we can best engender them by providing pertinent content for intellectual stimulation and discussion. I would also emphasize that students are best motivated by subject matter that they can relate to. They are better able to internalize and to process the content and in doing so they acquire a great deal of abstract language. In addition, the study of bilingualism, as a component of Language and Culture, can become a voyage of self-discovery in which the students find out a great deal about themselves and their use of their languages. This self-knowledge is often the basis for stimulating and passionate discussion and writing.

However, the very freedom offered by the IBO in the choice of the material can also make it very hard for the A2 teacher to decide what to teach. One specific problem is that there are no textbooks written specifically with A2 in mind. Therefore it is not always straightforward to put the IBO guidelines into practice. Here let me use the example of the Media and Culture option to illustrate some of the difficulties faced by departments in designing a unit of work for A2.

In 2001 our department decided to introduce Media and Culture, firstly because the topic option had been elevated within the A2 syllabus, and secondly because there was growing student interest in media studies as a possible subject for study at tertiary level. According to the *A2 subject guide*, media topic areas can

Figure 13.3 Media and Culture: sample research questions

Concepts	Medium	Research question
Media audiences	Television	Are audiences affected by TV violence?
Representation and stereotypes	Advertising	What techniques do advertisers use to sell their products?
Institutions and censorship	Mass media	Do media giants have too much influence in English language media?

include: advertising, bias, censorship, film, the internet, media and government, news and public opinion, national security, popular novels, the press, propaganda, radio and television, sensationalism, stereotypes and tabloid journalism. However, we then realized that Media and Culture is amorphous in content and we found that none of the above topics could be studied in isolation. For example, where were we to begin (and end) with the study of 'radio and television'?

A second issue is the published material available. Media books produced for the 14–16 age group are conceptually unsuitable for the needs of DP students. This problem is then compounded by the fact that even most media studies textbooks tend to be very culture-specific and therefore either irrelevant or unsuitable for use outside the country of publication. What to do? We saw that pre-university media studies courses are arranged around concepts such as Audience, Representation, Institutions, Language, Genre, Narrative and Ideologies. Therefore we decided to veer away from the A2 list of media topics and came up with our own, based on commercially produced material. This then enabled students to grapple with the content and abstract concepts within each topic by allowing them to work from media studies books. Secondly we related specific concepts to specific media. This avoided the problem of looking at, say, 'Television' in a decontextualized manner. Thirdly, each concept was related to a specific research question, which could then be studied. The research questions set out in figure 13.3 were extrapolated from A2 media questions in Paper 2.

These issues of course design will also crop up with the other A2 topic options and teachers must find imaginative ways in which make each topic a coherent whole and relevant to the examination. Figure 13.3 demonstrates how topic options and literature modules can be given a clear focus.

2.7 Case study – exploiting a language topic

As we have seen, A2 is a curious hybrid. Students have to learn a body of knowledge as well as reach specific language targets. At first glance A2 seems to be a content-driven course similar to a first language examination. And indeed, we have seen that the course content requires a very high standard of linguistic and conceptual understanding. Moreover, A2 students are expected to respond to the material in a number of linguistically sophisticated ways. However, as developing bilinguals, many A2 students have different language needs to native speakers (as the latter can be expected to function with almost total linguistic accuracy). We know that linguistic performance in A2 is not always free from error and teachers must have two strategies in mind to help their students:
1. improve communicative performance
2. help them deal with the understanding of content.

In order for the course to meet this double objective, students must have ample opportunity to explore topics via oral and written assignments. Therefore class reading and discussion, group reading, debate, analysis and student presentation are the routine modes of learning. In the first year of the course, and even for the first term of the second year, many A2 students have still not mastered either the linguistic skills or the analytical tools to make a huge success of the assessment activities. Therefore, much of the time will have to be spent developing focused communication skills. This can be illustrated by examining the topic 'Language variety' within the topic option Language and Culture.

In the first year of the course, in order to boost students' spoken confidence and performance, it is essential that A2 students *talk*. They need to share ideas and discuss them with the rest of the group. In order to facilitate this I briefly introduce the concepts of language variety (global languages, dialect and accent, pidgins and creolization) using PowerPoint. Firstly the students have to come to a consensus in terminology. Then, using a handbook put together on the controversial topic of Singapore English ('Singlish') in local schools, the A2 class is free to discuss the (perceived) rights and wrongs of using dialect (this being a matter of heated debate in our local press). The handbook contains a variety of appropriate texts, including articles and editorials from the local newspapers, poems and short stories by Singaporean writers, extracts from autobiographies and academic works on language. While discussing the texts, students very soon become strongly partisan in their opinions, either championing the right of the individual to self-expression or defending the role and necessity of Standard English in a modern industrialized society. Either way, the students are soon engaged in unselfconscious discussion and debate within the topic.

However, to ensure that the discussions have a direction, three research questions are introduced:

- Why do new languages develop?
- Should Singlish (Singapore English) be recognized as an official language in Singapore?
- Should Singlish be a language of instruction in Singapore schools?

It is important that A2 students develop discussion skills and make presentations frequently. Therefore the more students are able to present course content in a non-threatening class environment, the more likely they are to feel comfortable and confident when formal assessment comes round. Using the research questions for a focus, groups of students now design a presentation, complete with handouts, worksheets and tests, which they then present to the class. Each student's contribution to the group presentation can be assessed formally as an oral activity according to the A2 oral assessment criteria.

Next there is writing to consider. Students can first write up their presentations in the form of essays using their particular research question as a stimulus. It is important that essay practice is given regularly, so they are spaced throughout the two years. Each essay will be a summation of ideas learned in the literature and topic options.

For coursework, students can analyse the nature of different text types. As we have seen, the handbook contains a number of texts from different sources: literature texts, a wide variety of magazine and newspaper articles, and extracts from textbooks – all related to the theme of speaking dialects. By examining the texts, students can ask questions: 'What kind of text is this?', 'What is the purpose of the text?', 'Who was the intended audience?', 'What are the special stylistic and structural details of the texts?'. By examining and then imitating the examples before them, for instance, A2 students are able to produce their own coursework texts on the theme of Singlish which look and sound reasonably authentic. Some choose to write letters to the local newspapers; some write speeches defending, or opposing, existing government language policy; others write newspaper articles based on fictitious events described in one of the short stories. Alternatively, others may produce reports of opinion polls based on the work carried out in class. In all instances, the students are fulfilling the coursework requirements, i.e. writing in a variety of styles and genres, to a variety of audiences, and for a variety of purposes. In doing so the A2 students are becoming truly creative users of the target language.

At this point we must mention the comparative commentary (Paper 1 of the final written examination). This element does not fit easily into the content of the course and A2 teachers tend to treat it as a separate task to be taught apart. It is also a most complex skill and all A2 teachers recognize that this test is the most difficult part of the course. This is also borne out by examination results. We look at an approach to the commentary below in section 2.16. In terms of written examination practice, it is recommended that comparative commentaries should be attempted throughout the two years at, say, one per quarter year. Work on the commentary needs to start early and students should go through this exercise at least eight to ten times before sitting the examination.

2.8 Working with literature texts in A2

However many literary topic options are chosen, in practice all A2 students should study at least two (preferably three) literary works in great detail. This means that much class time will be spent reading and analysing these texts. It is very rewarding to take a detailed approach, as it can be very beneficial for many A2 students, particularly those who have never studied literature before. As teacher of A2 it is a terrific experience to see students become aware that *The Great Gatsby* is an intricately structured work of art with layer upon layer of symbolic meaning. This can only be done if we take time to look at aspects of a work in great detail, both to explain and discuss with the students the meaning of the language before us. In doing so we provide students with analytical skills and open up to them the pleasures of reading. Moreover, such close textual analysis can easily be exploited for assessment practice purposes, either in the form of essays, or oral commentaries, or as a stimulus for an imaginative coursework.

Whatever books are chosen there should be cross-referencing within the course. In the final examination (Paper 2) students are always asked to compare two or more texts. Figure 13.4 is an outline of a unit of work comparing power relationships in *The Color Purple* and *Pygmalion*. This approach allows groups of students to conduct independent research and at the same time practise certain skills that will be tested as part of the final examination. Both books will have already been discussed and examined extensively in class.

In groups, students use the worksheets to discuss one of the four listed research topics. Each topic requires close reading of the relevant passages and scenes. They are given these instructions.

Figure 13.4 Sample worksheet for comparing texts in English A2

	The Color Purple	Pygmalion
A Physical and mental abuse		
	Alphonso and Mister ___	Higgins and Doolittle
In each text why are the men capable of physical and psychological abuse of women? How do the men abuse their strength: • physically? • sexually? • verbally? • emotionally?		
	Celie	Eliza
How do the women overcome abuse and empower themselves?		
B Economic power		
	Alphonso and Mister ___	Higgins and Doolittle
How much economic power do the men possess compared with the women? How do the men abuse their economic power?		
	Celie	Eliza
How do the women gain economic independence? Do the two women gain the same measure of economic independence from men?		
C Social equality		
	Alphonso and Mister ___	Higgins and Doolittle
How do the men abuse their social standing?		
	Celie	Eliza
How do the women achieve social equality? Do both women gain the same measure of social independence?		
D Education and information		
	Alphonso and Mister ___	Higgins and Doolittle
In what ways have the men better access to education and information? How do Mister ___ and Higgins use and abuse their knowledge?		
	Celie	Eliza
How do the women gain knowledge and education? To what use do the women put the knowledge they have gained?		

- Discuss each question and come up with a satisfactory justification for your ideas.
- Find evidence and quotes in the texts to back up your claims. You may use secondary sources.
- For each section decide on similarities and differences between the characters. Use quotes extensively to back up your ideas.
- What conclusions do you draw about the characters' motives? Are they similar or different?

As a result of these highly structured tasks the students can participate in the following activities which will ultimately be assessed.

Orals: group discussion and formally assessed presentation (as in the previous example on Singlish).

Essay: comparison of the two texts by looking at one specific aspect of the novels – plot, characterization, themes – *or*
'How do men abuse their power over women in *The Color Purple* and *Pygmalion*?'

Coursework: imaginative assignments which can be submitted as coursework (as in the previous example).

2.9 Example syllabus English A2 (HL) and A2 (SL)

In the manner described above, the topic options *Media and Culture*, *Language and Culture* as well as two literature modules can be integrated to produce a coherent and focused A2 syllabus.

Figure 13.5 Example syllabus English A2 HL and SL

Module 1: Language and Culture Topic	Research questions
Bilingualism and translation	• What kind of bilingual am I? • How do I translate between my A1 and A2 languages?
Language variety – English in Singapore (Singlish)	• What are accents and dialects? • Why do new languages develop? • Should Singlish be given official status in Singapore?
Language and identity	• How do bilingualism and diglossia affect my sense of identity?
English as a world language	• What impact has English had on my own national culture?
Module 2: Media and Culture (not A2 SL) Topic	Research questions
Audiences and television	• To what extent are audiences affected by television violence?
Institutions and mass media	• Do too few people control the media?
Language and print journalism	• How do different genres use language to communicate their messages?

Figure 13.5 Example syllabus English A2 HL and SL (continued)

Module 3 Literature: Identity and Social Change	
Social issues	Texts
Bi-culturalism, gender, class, education, personal development and empowerment	*The Color Purple* – Alice Walker *Pygmalion* – George Bernard Shaw *The Woman Warrior* – Maxine Hong Kingston

Module 4: Literature: Narrative and Style	
Literary techniques	Texts
Narrative voice, narrative structure, symbolism and imagery	*The Great Gatsby* – F. Scott Fitzgerald *A Pale View of Hills* – Kazuo Ishiguro *Slaughterhouse 5* – Kurt Vonnegut

*For A2 SL remove module 2 Media (or alternatively one of the literature modules)

2.10 A two-year A2 programme

In order to see how the disparate elements of the A2 course – literature, topic options, coursework, examination practice and revision – fit together, figure 13.6 is a working model to show how the English A2 courses function at UWCSEA.

As can be seen, there are many opportunities throughout the year to discuss content, develop skills and practise A2 assessment activities, either in class, as homework or in formal practice examination conditions in the manner described above. In section 2.11 we look at the practicalities of preparing students for the final stages of the assessment in the latter half of the course.

2.11 Internal assessment orals in A2

Students engage in a free range of interactive exchanges and student work is assessed as a matter of course, even when the results are below par. I use the oral criteria (pages 49–51 [HL] and 61–63 [SL] in the Language A2 subject guide) as the benchmark for assessing students throughout the course. For the sake of transparency it is recommended that after each assessed oral activity students be given their marks. In this way they learn their strengths and weaknesses, especially if teachers make time to go over individual marks and performance. In practical terms the reverse side of the oral assessment record form 2/A1 is useful to keep individual records. Logically, as the course progresses, so the students' performances will become stronger.

In theory, the later marks should be higher as the students' ability to cope with abstract language increases. However, one word of caution is required here. A2 students of a language that is not the school's medium of instruction, such as German, may feel that their linguistic ability deteriorates because of the influence of English. Therefore, A2 teachers of other languages might need to take account of this by having such students take their orals at the most appropriate time, for example after a holiday in the home country in which the student has spent time practising the language on a daily basis.

Either way, A2 students have two oral components to complete.

Figure 13.6 Sample A2 schedule

YEAR 1			
Term 1	**Assessment**	**Content**	**Exam practice**
August		*Pygmalion*	Introduce comparative commentary
September	• Introduce oral assessment • *Pygmalion* oral	*Pygmalion* Language Unit 1 Singlish	*Pygmalion* essay
October	• Introduce written tasks • Practise written tasks on language	*The Great Gatsby*	Language essay Comparative commentary II
November	• Student presentations on Gatsby	*The Great Gatsby*	*The Great Gatsby* essay
December	• Introduce written tasks II • Practise written tasks on literature	*A Pale View of Hills*	Final drafts of term 1 assignments
Term 2	**Assessment**	**Content**	**Exam practice**
January	• Student presentations on *A Pale View of Hills*	*A Pale View of Hills*	Comparative commentary III
February	• Written tasks on *A Pale View of Hills*	*A Pale View of Hills* Language Unit 2 Bilingualism and translation	Practice literature essay on *A Pale View of Hills*
March	• Presentation on bilingualism	Language Unit 3 Bilingualism and translation (contd)	Practice essays Language Comparative commentary
Term 3	**Assessment**	**Content**	**Exam practice**
April	• Internal exams	Exam autopsy Language Unit 4 English as a world language	
May	• Oral presentation on comparison of *Pygmalion* and *The Woman Warrior*	*The Woman Warrior*: 'White Tigers'	Essay English as a world language
June	• Written tasks on world language and *The Woman Warrior*	*The Woman Warrior*: 'No Name Woman'	Comparative commentary IV
YEAR 2			
Term 1	**Assessment**	**Content**	**Exam practice**
August	• S/A2 (HL) coursework 1 complete	*The Color Purple*	Comparative commentary V
September Internal assessment	• *The Color Purple* oral	*The Color Purple* Media Unit 1 Representation	*The Color Purple* vs *Pygmalion* essay
October	• 12 A2 (SL) All coursework completed by end of month	Media Unit 2 Audience	Comparative commentary VI
November	• 12 A2 (HL) coursework completed • H/A2 (SL) orals	Media Unit 3 Mass media *Slaughterhouse 5*	Media essay Practice orals *Slaughterhouse 5* essay

Figure 13.6 Sample A2 schedule (continued)

YEAR 2			
Term 1	**Assessment**	**Content**	**Exam practice**
December	• H/A2 (SL) coursework completed (final pieces)	*Slaughterhouse 5*	Practice Papers 1 & 2 (H/W)
Term 2	**Assessment**	**Content**	**Exam practice**
January Extended essay to sponsor second week	• Mock exams • Moderate exams	Exam autopsy	
February A2 (HL) Extended essay to DPC complete	• Moderation and submission of S/A2 (HL) • Oral tapes • Exam grades • A2 coursework to DPC	Revision *The Great Gatsby* and *Slaughterhouse 5* *A Pale View of Hills* Revision *The Color Purple* *The Woman Warrior* *Pygmalion*	Practice literature essay I Comparative commentary VII
March	• Tapes to DPC • Predicted grades	Revise Language and Media	Practice essays Media and Language
Term 3	**Assessment**	**Content**	**Exam practice**
April		Revision	Essay and comparative commentary
May	• IB exams		

2.12 The interactive oral activity in A2

This is a free choice activity to be chosen by the teacher. The Language A2 guide (pages 36–37) gives a very detailed exposition of suitable activities. It is best if assessed activities arise naturally out of class work such as a student presentation or a debate. Ultimately, only one activity needs to be assessed and that should always be the student's best performance regardless of when the activity was carried out. However, if the teacher has undertaken several assessments in the course of the second year there will be much greater variety to choose from.

2.13 The individual oral in A2

The individual oral (15%) is a commentary on a passage from one of the syllabus texts. Details of the oral and the kinds of questions can be found on pages 34–36 of the A2 guide. Information about the conduct of the oral can be found in group 2 sections 2a.5 and 2a.6 of the *Vade Mecum*. Most importantly: preparation time is 20 minutes and the recording time is 15 minutes maximum; the student commentary should last about 10 minutes and the remaining time should be given over to teacher questions on the passage.

The individual oral is potentially the most time-consuming and for the student it is often the most stressful element of the entire A2 course. Because the commentary is recorded, students find the experience stressful and often underperform. Therefore I would suggest that they prepare as much as possible. It is for this reason that we spend so much of the early part of the course going through the works of literature in such painstaking detail. Such experience will allow them to understand abstract literary concepts and also the language of literary criticism.

In terms of the actual oral itself much can be done to make sure that students perform to the best of their ability on the day. For example, they can listen to previous performances. Firstly this is much more beneficial than explaining the structure of the commentary. Secondly they can assess these previous performances using the A2 oral criteria. This will quickly give a feel for the level of performance required. It is also advisable that students begin to practise the skills of commentary early on in the course. For example, it can be done as a group activity, in which students analyse commentary passages and then present the final product collectively. Such a gradualist approach enables students to gain confidence in commentary skills without feeling vulnerable.

The time factor is another very important consideration. In an ideal world each student should have at least one opportunity to do a practice commentary. However, this depends greatly on the number of students. Our department deals with about 60 English A2 students per year. In order to complete the marathon task we already have to set aside a weekend for recording. This weekend usually takes place at least two months before the external deadlines. This allows time for moderation and administration of the final entries.

For the recorded commentary itself students may choose two texts to prepare. It is pot-luck which one comes up. IBO regulations state that the passages chosen should be about 40 lines long and should be typical of the book. When devising questions we have found it useful to use three broad categories:

1. *Context* – in which students identify the significance of the passage in the context of the overall plot and narrative structure.
2. *Content* – in which students give a detailed analysis of the passage itself, such as relationships and themes.
3. *Language and style* – students discuss the use of specific stylistic devices and the writer's creation of mood and atmosphere.

See section 3.15 for additional advice on the conduct of group 2 orals.

2.14 Internal assessment, moderation and submission of predicted grades

As the commentary is internally assessed but externally moderated, A2 teachers need to complete the recording process at least one month before the submission deadline (usually two months before the final written examinations). Internal and cross-moderation is an invaluable method of achieving consensus about assessment. The IBO requires that a centre's marks be accurate. In cases where a teacher has made an inflated assessment of student performance, the IBO has deflated both individual students' marks and also that of the entire class. As well as the internal assessment, all group 2 teachers have to submit a predicted grade. This should be an accurate assessment of a student's overall level of achievement and not just oral skills. Both the predicted grade (1–7) and the internal assessment (out of 30) have to be submitted to the IBO about two months prior to the final written examinations. Once the IB coordinator (DPC) has submitted details to the IBO, the latter will inform the centre of the names of students whose tapes and internal assessment record forms (2/RF) are to be submitted for external moderation.

Note: the procedures described here also pertain to other group 2 courses: language B and *ab initio*.

2.15 A2 coursework

This assessment activity consists of two written tasks totalling 1,500 words and is worth 20% of the overall mark. We have seen that the purpose of the coursework is to allow students to develop a practical repertoire of writing styles beyond the essay and the literary commentary. The IBO guidelines also state that one text production must be related to literature and the second to a cultural topic. In addition each text must be in a different genre/text type. A list of text types can be found on pages 15–17 of the A2 subject guide and details of the nature of the written task can be found on pages 31–33 of the guide. As the final coursework must be the students' independent work, for the A2 teacher the practical concern is how to help the students acquire the writing skills. Two sets of strategies are available.

The A2 guidelines require the student to be familiar with a range of genres and material. In the handbook these are classified as poetic (i.e. literary), mass and professional communication modes (see page 16 of the A2 subject guide). We have seen in sections 2.7 and 2.8 that there are countless opportunities to practise coursework assignments. These occasions can be used as opportunities for students to practise a variety of different writing styles. Teachers are at liberty to discuss the style and content of a student's list with a student as long as there is a clear understanding that this particular assignment is inadmissible as coursework.

Such an approach allows A2 students to experiment with different genres, receive advice about format and stylistic nuances, and then produce a new piece of writing in the same genre. In this manner they can learn about genre and style and still submit coursework samples free of teacher input. For each piece of coursework students must fill in form 2/WTRF. This allows the student to define the nature of the writing task and provide a set of objectives and examples and an analysis of the success of the task. As this form is new it is difficult to predict how successful students will be in achieving this level of self-analysis. Coursework should be submitted to the DPC two months before the final examination.

2.16 Examination Paper 1 (comparative commentary)

Emphasis here is on analytical response. The comparative commentary is an opportunity to demonstrate an understanding of context, content and style of two disparate texts linked by a common theme. From 2004 onwards there will be guiding questions at SL. On each examination paper students choose to write about one of two pairs of texts.

As stated, the comparative commentary is the least integrated element of the A2 course and almost all A2 students find it a complex skill to master. To complicate the matter further, there are, to my knowledge, no commercially produced materials that teach this particular skill at this level. The examiners' reports for English on Paper 1 tend not to prescribe methods of approach. However, amongst A2 teachers there is a great deal of consensus that it is best to go from general comments to specific statements about the two texts. Consequently, the following example is offered as a point of departure.

In November 2002, A2 HL students were asked to compare a dialogue taken from the historical novel *Lonesome Dove* by Larry McMurty and an extract taken from *The National Geographic*. Both texts describe the approach to the Yellowstone River. In order to structure the commentary, students would do well to start with generalizations about the two texts. For example, they can identify and compare the common themes and, in the case of the magazine article, speculate on the potential audience for the text. Students might also like to consider the different purpose of each text. For instance, whereas the novel is concerned with the development of character and atmosphere as the cowboys/frontiersmen approach the unknown river, the magazine article is much more prosaic, being a warning to visitors and potential anglers on the dangers of the waters.

As a next stage, students need to show a clear understanding of the similarities in the content of the texts, in this case the potential threat the river poses. In the literary text, students should observe the subtleties in the cowboys' reactions to the unknown. In the journalistic piece, students can look at each paragraph and discuss the development of the theme of danger. Having convinced the examiner that they are able to compare the content, students can now discuss the stylistic devices that make each text so individual. This is the place for a detailed discussion of imagery and tone as well as specific detail about the narrative and organizational devices found in each text. At all stages of the commentary students should be comparing and contrasting the texts in order to find similarities and differences in content and approach.

Students are advised to quote extensively, explaining which elements of the quotes illustrate their point. In addition, A2 examiners stress that the comparative commentary is not an essay and should not be referred to as such. The following is some general advice for students:

- Write about the texts, not your opinions of the subject matter.
- Don't write long and irrelevant introductory paragraphs.
- Start with general comments about audience, purpose, theme and basic content. Then move on to a discussion of structure, style and effects.
- Remember to compare and contrast and provide quotes.
- Don't just list stylistic devices. Show to what effect they are used.
- Don't speculate about what might be. Stick to the texts.

See section 2.3 for the assesment criteria.

2.17 Examination Paper 2 (essay)

The A2 guide states that the aim of the assessment for students is 'to demonstrate critical thinking by constructing a relevant, organized and well-supported discussion or argument about a given topic or issue' (page 30).

A2 examiners are impressed by well-researched, technically well-organized and well-written essays. Students who wish to write in an inspired but unstructured manner may have to be discouraged from doing so. As we have seen, essay practice will be a major component of the writing element of the A2 course. The individual skills within the essay will have to be honed and polished until the student is able to write independently. Only at that point will they be ready to sit the examination. When practising examination technique it is essential to remember that there are three key requirements.

1. Firstly the *Response to the Question* criterion requires that the students are able to demonstrate knowledge of the subject matter. For instance, the well-prepared student will be able to set out clearly the relative merits of monolingualism and bilingualism, or analyse the reasons why Ishiguro and Fitzgerald make use of unreliable narrators in their respective novels *A Pale View of Hills* and *The Great Gatsby*.
2. Secondly, students must also score well in the *Presentation* criterion. To achieve this students need to recognize the value of an overall structure to the essay. Time should also be spent on the development of the thesis, a structured argument and a logical and consistent conclusion. Further time should be spent on learning the use of the paragraph and, at a micro level, the use of topic sentences, connecting devices and logical cohesion between paragraphs.
3. Finally there is the criterion *Language*. As we would expect at this level, grammatical accuracy and appropriate use of vocabulary, idiom and register are the main concerns of the examiners. In short the nearer the student is to a native-like control of language the better.

In order that students score highly in all three criteria, it is vital that they adopt a process approach to writing. In the lead-up practice over the two years of the course, writing process skills such as planning, drafting and redrafting form a major part in this development and this should be done each time a student writes an essay.

3 Language B

Language B is the second tier of group 2 languages and sits between A2 courses for bilingual students and *ab initio*, the beginners' programme. SL B is an intermediate-level course for students, while HL B is an upper intermediate programme. Because of the international character of the DP there is an impressively wide range of B languages available (a full list is published in the *Vade Mecum*, section C).

3.1 Aims and target students

Language B measures students' ability to communicate in a second or a foreign language. To pass the examination students must become fluent in the target language. They should speak clearly and accurately and, by the end of the programme, students should be able to use a range of tenses, vocabulary and registers in spontaneous formal and informal conversation. They should also be able to make structured classroom presentations using a full range of cohesive and persuasive devices. Although listening is not tested as a separate skill, language B students must be able to understand a native speaker, and for examination purposes, they must be able to respond spontaneously to a wide variety of questions in an interview situation. When reading, B students need to interpret a variety of authentic texts, extract specific details and show understanding of specific language items, e.g. via gap-filling exercises. In addition, language B students must be able to understand the overall meaning of texts, e.g. by writing a letter in response to a given text. In short, language B students have to perform communicative tasks fluently and successfully in the target language B. In addition, in line with the internationalist aims of the IBO, students should also gain an insight into and an appreciation of the target culture.

A good number of SL students will fare indifferently or worse at HL. Consequently, it may be necessary to give new students a linguistic and a writing test (possibly a past SL B Paper 2) prior to course entry to decide which level a student can take. My own test consists of 20 multiple-choice mixed grammar sentences, 40 open cloze items in two separate passages, and an essay. As a minimum requirement, SL B students must show that they are able to write sentences clearly, use basic tense markers, and demonstrate an adequate knowledge of vocabulary to express themselves on the specific writing topic.

HL students would be expected to have a range, linguistic depth and control beyond the level for SL. They should already be able to write complex sentences using a variety of connecting devices. In addition they must show a depth and breadth of lexis, which would enable them to communicate fairly sophisticated and abstract ideas in the correct genre, i.e. they should have some idea how to use the linguistic and cultural conventions in a letter. At HL students must be able to answer interpretative questions; they must be able to separate fact from opinion and distinguish key points from detail. As far as the writing is concerned, HL students must be able to convey ideas clearly, grammatically and coherently. They also need to be able to write in specific genres and address an audience using the correct register.

Further differentiation between HL and SL B lies in the assessment criteria (see pages 43–62 of the Language B subject guide) and in the volume of output required in the examinations themselves. SL students must achieve a large degree of communicative competence but in assessment their writing and spoken output is marked less stringently and the reading tasks are less demanding.

Language B covers the needs of two distinct target groups. The first consists of students with several years' experience learning a *foreign* language. For example, Chantal studied German as a foreign language for five years in middle school in her IB school in the UK. She now takes German B in group 2.

The second client group takes a language B in the school's working language. Therefore language B also doubles as an *additional* or *second* language course. For example, Roxana came directly to an English-medium IB school from a local school in Romania, where she had studied English for five years. Because of her weak entry level of English, it was entirely appropriate that she studied English B (and not A2). Such students also gain a bilingual diploma in recognition of the fact that they are able to use two languages for academic purposes. Students such as Roxana might need additional language support coping with the DP. See Chapter 5 for further discussion of this point.

If student numbers are relatively small it may well be possible to teach HL and SL together. Because of the communicative nature of the course, the same authentic texts can be used to teach the target language to SL and HL students. Both courses use the same assessment categories but employ differentiated levels of achievement. Therefore HL candidates might be expected to respond at greater length or in greater depth. I do not wish to underestimate the work necessary, but at least joint classes are a workable option. All extension work for HL can be done when SL students do not attend. This extension work could take the form of additional topic modules or literature.

3.2 Assessment outline and tasks

Figure 13.7 is an overview of the assessment model for language B. The interactive oral can be based on any suitable oral activity. The individual oral is a recorded presentation and interview. We look at the practicalities of oral assessment in section 3.13.

For language B the assessment of reading takes the form of text handling. The four individual texts in the examination are each on average about 200 to 400 words in length. Both SL and HL students have to employ a variety of strategies to understand implied as well as surface meaning. Three of the texts require a variable number of specific responses. One text requires an extended 100-word written response.

Note that in many language B examinations the text handling paper is notoriously unpredictable in format and, therefore, students must also be exposed to a wide spectrum of assessment material if they are not going to be taken by surprise.

In Paper 2 students are expected to respond to one of six stimuli. Students are asked to write in a certain genre and to a specified audience. SL and HL students must be able to produce these specific text types: instructions, factual and

Figure 13.7 Language B assessments model

a Language B internal assessment, externally moderated (orals)

Assessment activity	Length	Mark	%
Interactive oral activity	(no time limit)	30 (HL & SL)	15
Individual oral	(10 minutes)	30 (HL & SL)	15
Total			**30**

b Language B external assessments (text handling)

Assessment activity	Length	Mark	%
Section A	(1 hour*)	40 (HL)	27
Reading	(1 hour*)	30 (SL)	30
Section B	(30 minutes*)	20 (HL)	13
Written response	(30 minutes*)	10 (SL)	10
Total	(1 hour 30 minutes)		**40**

*recommended proportion of available examination time given by the IBO

c Language B external assessments (written production)
Paper Two written production

Answer 1 of 6 HL	(1 hour 30 minutes)	30 (HL & SL)
Answer 1 of 4 SL	(1 hour 30 minutes)	30 (HL & SL)
Total		**30**

imaginative narratives, formal and informal letters, reports, speeches and other persuasive texts, book and film reviews. Certain IBO group 2 examiners seem obsessed by police reports (they occur with unnatural frequency in lists of IB group 2 writing tasks). In addition, HL students are required by the syllabus to write persuasive brochures and pamphlets, reported conversations, proposals for a plan of action, and last but not least, essays.

SL writing is principally concerned with accuracy and clarity, and the minimum word count is 250. HL Paper 2 puts great emphasis on the students' abilities to construct persuasive and effective texts with clearly constructed lines of argument. The HL minimum word count is 400. Better students will exceed these limits but language B examiners are more impressed by the quality of the language and the accuracy of the message than by the sheer quantity of writing.

3.3 Language B assessment criteria

Teachers new to the DP should note that speaking and writing are marked differently from reading. Three criteria – Language, Cultural Awareness and Task/Message – are used to assess both oral and written production (Paper 2). Each criterion is marked out of 10, giving a top mark of 30.

1. *Language* relates to features such as grammatical accuracy, use of vocabulary and accurate pronunciation and writing. At the top end of the scale HL students should be able to produce accurate, clear communication in the language B, although there is no expectation that the writing will be error-free. SL candidates should be able to communicate a message clearly, but there is an acceptance that their grammar, vocabulary and spelling may suffer when attempting more complex sentences.
2. The second assessment criterion is *Cultural Awareness*. This criterion measures the language learner's ability to understand and use the cultural conventions of the target language, such as the different levels of formality. For example, students of French B must be able to distinguish between *tu* and *vous*. Students must be able to write in formal as well as informal modes using appropriate connecting and rhetorical devices.
3. The final category, *Task/Message*, relates to the quality of the written content and measures how well the student has been able to complete the given task. For instance, students might be asked to write a speech on the subject of 'team versus individual sports'. In this case they will be marked on whether they have managed to write on the subject and in the format required (a speech and not, say, an essay), and whether the message is relevant, and clear.

The texts for text handling are each accompanied by approximately 10 questions or test items; each correct answer is usually worth one mark. In addition, there is a short writing response worth 10 marks. In the past the number of individual comprehension questions and marks has varied. In this instance, the final total must then be adjusted to a mark of 40%.

3.4 Organizing and teaching a language B course

In this section we look at the IBO guidelines for language B and see how they can be translated into practical schemes of work. My comments are based on experience of teaching English B in an English-medium school. To this extent the course provides skills above and beyond the requirements of the language B syllabus so that the students learn practical cross-curricular literacy skills. However, it is to be hoped that the reader finds that many of the practices are equally applicable to teaching foreign languages.

3.5 Course development for language B

In line with all IBO philosophy, schools new to the DP will have to create their own language courses. To some language departments used to working within the confines of a set syllabus it can come as a shock to find that for language B there is no rigidly prescribed syllabus. Moreover, there are no checklists of grammar or vocabulary, no set texts, no compulsory topics. As we have seen in the other parts of the DP, the IBO wishes teachers to take responsibility and ownership of their courses. In practice, each IB school needs to build a unique language B course designed to meet the specific needs of its students. To facilitate this, the IBO language B guide advises teachers to organize the syllabus around three concepts: *Language, Texts,* and *Cultural Awareness*. These concepts dictate the character of the language programme and the IBO has a clear expectation that students will develop the four communication skills and gain insight into the target culture through the exploitation of these three concepts.

In essence, *Language* describes a communicative approach to teaching. This, in turn, implies that all teaching will be carried out in the target language. Teachers and students are expected to communicate in the target language all the time (in practice some explanation in the school's language is inevitable, especially at SL level). It is also essential that students are exposed to a very wide variety of *Texts* from a variety of sources, including audio and audio-visual material. Language B teachers will see that there are four types of text with which the student needs to be familiar: informative texts, literary texts, mass communication texts e.g. advertisements and brochures, and journalistic texts. Departments and libraries should subscribe to a number of magazines in the target language. As the text handling paper uses real texts, it is vital that students are familiar with such material. As a consequence, it will fall to the language B teacher to find suitable material for classroom use. This will be a major chore. *Cultural Awareness* is the third concept, stipulating that material studied should bring insights into the target culture. It is self-evident that given the communicative nature of the course, grammar translation methods of teaching language B will not work and students would be very badly prepared for the assessment tasks. Moreover it follows that language B teachers must be fluent readers and writers and speakers of the target language.

If communicative teaching using real texts is to be made really effective, teachers need to provide students with reference and study tools with which they can carry out tasks. It is for this reason that I have developed a Language B Student Handbook. As we shall see in the next sections, such a tool enables me to assign reading and writing tasks knowing that students have suitable reference material to complete and evaluate their work.

3.6 A student handbook for language B

One of the IBO aims is for teachers to ensure transparency at all times. This handbook containing these items is given to all language B students at the outset of the course.

In the handbook students are given the items presented in figure 13.8.

Figure 13.8 Sections in student handbook

Section 1 The course outline
English B at UWCSEA: an introduction, aims and objectives and B syllabus (see figure 13.10)

Section 2 The assessment
Assessment outline
Assessment criteria (oral component)
Assessment criteria (Paper 2 – written production)
(All from Language B guide)

Section 3 The exams
Paper 1 – Text handling
(sample paper)
Paper 2 – Written production
(sample paper)
Oral guidelines
(in-house produced materials)

Section 4 Essay-writing skills
Persuasive skills
Introduction to the essay
The thesis statement
The introduction
The developmental paragraphs
The conclusion
(in-house produced materials)

Section 5 Composition skills – writing texts
Personal/formal letters
Magazine/newspaper articles
Reports
Sets of instructions
Diary entries
Advertisements
Brochures, handouts, leaflets, pamphlets
Conversations, speeches
(in-house produced materials)

Section 6 Linking ideas
Useful phrases for essays
Linking and organizing vocabulary
(in-house produced materials)

Section 7 The extended essay
Scope and subject-specific marking criteria
(IBO materials)
Application form
(in-house produced materials)

Appendix A: A mark scheme for error analysis
(in-house produced materials)

Appendix B: A note on homework
(in-house produced materials)

In addition, standards of work, i.e. deadlines, homework policy, strategies for dealing with unacceptable behaviour, are stated in the handbook.

Sections 1 to 3 give the student an outline course (see below) and the IBO marking criteria and sample past Papers 1 and 2. By discussing these items in class, language B candidates know what is expected and, consequently, all students automatically know the aims and objectives of the course. In addition, sections 4 to 6 (Essay-writing skills, Composition skills, Linking ideas) provide the student with the linguistic and organizational reference tools to undertake the writing tasks required by the course. I would strongly suggest that teachers develop their own handbooks for their individual languages. As a photocopiable resource it can be updated every year.

It is also worth emphasizing that good classroom work habits lead to positive outcomes. Students need to bring the handbook to lessons and be prepared to use it when doing assignments. I also include a clearly defined and consistent marking system, which I use when reading student papers.

3.7 Modules

Given the communicative nature of the course I have found that language B is most successful when the course is built around a series of modules. One of the problems with using authentic texts is that there is often a lack of overall continuity, especially if teachers use materials that are not thematically linked in any way. By using a series of topic headings and grouping sets of materials under those headings, teachers can give much more substance to a seemingly fragmented course (see figure 13.10 for an example scheme of work). As with A2, a module consists of a set of authentic materials based around a common topic or theme. The material then provides a series of oral and writing outcomes. The difference between A2 and B is the level of response expected of the students: whereas A2 students are expected to react holistically to texts, language B students need to perform more specific language tasks, such as answering questions or identifying specific vocabulary. Language B learners will need linguistic help with individual tasks and, as we shall see below, this is how a language B handbook can be used to great effect.

For instance, we have a module *Educational hot-housing – a case study: Should children attend university?* The module consists of a series of newspaper articles reporting first the disappearance and then the re-emergence of a 14 year-old student who is already attending university. In the first reading students are directed to pick out and comment on unknown vocabulary in the first two articles. In class a quick question-and-answer session soon establishes an understanding of the two texts. As each article tells a different version of the events, groups of students then work out a coherent narrative sequence. This sequence can be written up as a simple past tense narrative, or with more sophisticated learners as a report or as a diary entry or letter. At this point it is possible to interject material from section 5 of the student handbook, Composition skills, to help students to write in the appropriate form. This gives students specific help with writing in certain genres and contains vocabulary hints, notes on structure, and ideas to help with content.

The later material in the module *Educational hot-housing* consists of a series of tabloid newspaper articles which debate the wisdom of allowing a young person to attend university. Included here are a series of profiles and case studies concerning so-called child geniuses. These texts lend themselves to more complex information gathering in which students pick out evidence from the newspaper articles both supporting and opposing the concept of educational hot-housing. Such focused reading activities are always excellent practice for Paper 1 (text handling) as the student must focus on extracting both explicit and implicit meanings from a given text. Once this information has been gathered, students are asked to refine the information collected, in this instance to distinguish between personal and academic reasons for opposing/supporting hot-housing.

At this point students can be asked to speculate on how they personally would cope with such a situation. This usually leads to a lively informal debate on the subject. As we have seen with A2, such extended exchanges can easily be assessed as a free choice oral. As I have indicated above, once students are involved in the material they become less self-conscious about using the target language and they are more likely to do well.

As a follow-up students can write up their opinions in the form of an essay. From the reading of the newspaper articles and additional ideas gained from the debate and discussion, students already have a set of notes/ideas/jottings. See figure 13.9.

Using section 4 of the handbook, Essay-writing skills, and section 6, Linking ideas, students should now be in a position to attempt a first draft of the essay. The essay is a practice for the written tasks required by Paper 2. And in this way all the assessment elements of the language B course are covered.

In terms of the IBO aims I feel this is the most beneficial method of teaching language B. Home-made modules deliver the teacher from a prescriptive syllabus with a rigid structure. It allows language departments to construct imaginative syllabuses (time and finances allowing). Some departments make such material as a matter of course but for some schools considering the DP this may present novel challenges. Any modular syllabus should cover a wide variety of text types, as students need to handle many kinds of text handling/reading activities. Topics and texts should also give rise to assessable oral activities, for example by provoking debates and discussions. Students will also need to practise writing in

Figure 13.9 Language B educational hot-housing essay plan

	Advantages	Disadvantages
Academic		
Social		
Others		

This table can be used as the basis of the following essay plan.

Part 1
Definitions, examples and thesis statement

Part 2
Academic advantages and disadvantages

Part 3
Social advantages and disadvantages

Part 4
Other advantages and disadvantages

Part 5
Conclusions and proof of thesis

a variety of genres and for a variety of purposes and therefore the written outcomes should be varied. Section 5 of the handbook, Composition skills – writing texts, also acts as a handy reminder of the kind of written outcomes students are expected to produce.

One obvious drawback with this process is the amount of time needed to produce such material. For this reason it is best to have all teachers working cooperatively to produce a common fund of materials. Another problem is the relatively short shelf-life of some of the material. Articles that are topical in 2003 can seem old hat by 2004. Such rapid obsolescence can be particularly frustrating if the said article has taken hours to find and to prepare as teaching material.

3.8 Outline syllabus for HL English B

Figure 13.10 sets out the current English B syllabus in use at UWCSEA in Singapore.

The first set of modules, *Personal and social change,* reflects the need for students to examine and improve their study skills and explore their own identity. The modules also provide the students with valuable practical information, which they can use in their search for a suitable course at a suitable university. The second group of modules, entitled *Language matters,* enables the student to reflect on such issues as the nature of the English language abroad and in Singapore. Moreover, by looking at bilingualism as an issue, language B students can come to understand their own linguistic abilities. The third group

Figure 13.10 Sample syllabus for English B

Personal and social change	Language matters	Culture, politics and society
World of learning and education University education systems in UK and USA	**Bilingualism** Types of bilingualism Bilingualism and me	**Multiculturalism and national identity** Immigration and Australia The American ideal
Educational hot-housing case study: Should children attend university?	**English as a world language** The origins of English, English as a global language	**Global concerns** AIDS awareness Recycling
Personal change and development Self-esteem and self-image Motivation, learning styles Study skills	**English in Singapore*** Government language policy on Singapore English (Singlish)	**Ethics and human rights*** *Animal Farm* – George Orwell (video and text) *The Enemy of the People* – Arthur Miller (video)
Personality Personality types Personality tests and their uses Describing myself and others	**Bi-culturalism and identity*** *A Pale View of Hills* – Kazuo Ishiguro Interview with author (video)	**Morality and technology** Biotechnology Xenotransplantation
College applications Choosing courses Writing applications and essays		**Relationships** Teenage pregnancy: *The Catcher in the Rye* – J. D. Salinger*

* These modules are not taught at SL.

of modules, *Culture, politics and society*, asks students to reflect on contemporary issues in the outside world. I should also remind readers that these modules are vehicles for teaching language. Each one will contain a variety of text handling, speaking and writing activities to bolster students' communicative abilities. However, subject matter that is intrinsically interesting best motivates students to learn language.

3.9 Literature

Although students are not assessed on literary terminology, it is clearly to the advantage for all concerned to undertake some literary study in language B, particularly for HL. Moreover, a question requiring a response to literature is frequently found in Paper 2. As in A2, literature works best when it is done as a shared reading activity. Unlike A2, there is no need for language B students to study the literary techniques; it is perfectly valid to study the plot, the characters and the themes of a text. Literature lends itself to any number of communicative reading, writing and speaking skills. Well-chosen texts will always motivate discussion and thereby generate language learning. For example, Holden Cauldfield's motives and personality in *The Catcher in the Rye* can spark heated classroom discussion. Such lively interchanges can help students to express themselves unselfconsciously in the target language. Because of the catholic nature of the course, any text that grabs the students' attention can be used for language B.

Literature is also a great way of introducing the target culture to the students and can be a very effective method of introducing them to creative writing. To this end film and television can also be of great use. However, the value of the audio-visual input is directly proportional to the language acquired by the student as a result of the activity. Thus the use of film and TV should always be related to information-gathering tasks which, in turn, should lead to written or oral outcomes.

3.10 Commercially produced language courses

The autonomy offered to teachers by the language B course is liberating but commercially produced material can be of great boon to a language B teacher. For language departments moving to the DP it is worth running an inventory on existing material, as much of the existing materials within a department can be adapted for the DP with little difficulty. When evaluating commercial material it is worth posing a few questions. Some questions are true for any language course. Is the text at the right linguistic level? (By and large all material should be at upper/intermediate and advanced levels.) When analysing existing texts, or when thinking of ordering new ones, language B teachers must also think of the requirements of the B syllabus. To this end certain specific questions come to mind. Are the exercises communicative in nature? This is essential. Comprehension activities based on question-and-answer exercises will not cultivate the text handling skills required by Paper 1. Is there a writing reference section in the book? Does it cover the kinds of writing required in Paper 2? Can each unit stand on its own and so make it possible for teachers (and students) to decide which sections they would like to study? Can they decide what they need to know? Some other pointers relate to general IBO aims. Do books represent gender and ethnic minorities fairly and avoid stereotyping?

The language B teacher's reliance on commercially produced material will be in direct proportion to the amount of authentic material available. For schools starting the DP or for departments starting new languages, commercial material can prove a very valuable stop-gap on the way to achieving ownership of a language B course.

3.11 Grammar and vocabulary exercises

The presentation, development and review of appropriate grammatical structures and vocabulary will have to be built into the structure of the course. Most language B students have a love–hate relationship with grammar. On the one hand they see it as a chore. On the other hand they see that grammar can be a shortcut to understanding and mastering areas of language that they are unable to use successfully. On HL language B courses there are two ways that grammar exercises can be incorporated and work reasonably well. Firstly, relevant grammar exercises can be used as a quick 'warm-up' at the beginning or end of a lesson. Secondly, grammar can be used diagnostically. Thus when it becomes apparent that an individual student has a specific problem then there should be a homework opportunity of reviewing and practising that particular item. Teachers of foreign languages should note that explicit knowledge of grammar rules is essential for text handling. For example, in a text handling exercise German B students might be asked to decline articles and adjectives according to whether the word takes an accusative or a dative case.

3.12 A two-year SL/HL schedule for English B

Language B students need to internalize a corpus of language in order to arrive at the appropriate level during the course. They will also need to practise speaking, reading and writing. However, it is probably more appropriate to wait until the second year of the course to begin using text handling past papers in earnest. Students can easily become disheartened if they find the level too hard in the first year. Even in the second year of the course, over-reliance on past papers and assessment activities would soon lead to boredom and have a negative effect on student motivation. In the timetable set out below (figure 13.11) we can see that there is plenty of time to include new material and topics as well as prepare students for the examination without overkill.

In the first year of the course, students' language skills can be developed through the use of home-made modules, the analysis of literature texts, commercial material and, when necessary, grammar. In terms of writing practice (Paper 2) it is a simple procedure to produce appropriate writing activities that relate to the tasks being undertaken. In addition students can attempt four practice Paper 2s in the first year in order to practise writing in a spontaneous manner about an unseen subject. Text handling can also be systematically built into each task given to the student. There is a general consensus amongst language B teachers that Paper 1 (text handling) has been of variable quality and format and students have found some of the tasks depressingly difficult. This is partly because of the examinations and partly due to the level of English of the

Figure 13.11 English B timetable, year 2

Term 1	Required assessment activities	Topics	Exam practice
August	Interactive oral activities	Module A	Text handling Paper 1 Text production
September Extended essay review with sponsor	Interactive oral activities	Module B	Text handling Paper 2 Text production
October	Interactive oral activities	Module C	Text handling Paper 3 Text production
November Internal deadline for extended essay	Interactive oral activities	Module D	Text handling Paper 4 Text production
December		Module E	Individual oral practice
Term 2	**Required assessment activities**	**Topics**	**Exam practice**
January	B orals	Exam autopsy	Mock exams Papers 1 & 2
February Exam grades Internal assessments Extended essay to DPC complete	Moderation and submission of B oral tapes Final interactive oral activities	Module F	Text handling Paper 4 Individual oral practice Text production
March IBO request for taped orals B tapes to DPC + predicted grades		Exam practice	Text handling Paper 5 Practice Text production
Term 3	**Required assessment activities**	**Topics**	**Exam practice**
April			Text handling Paper 6 Individual oral practice Text production
May	IB exams		

students. Consequently, two or three suffice in the first year of the course. Even in this case, examination of the past paper is probably best done as a class activity, with the exception of the paper given as an internal examination.

Figure 13.11 is a timetable for the second year. The modules refer to items from the syllabus outline in section 3.8. As we can see, the volume of direct examination work increases but there is still plenty of time to introduce new material and new language to the students (especially if much of the text handling is done for homework). Once again the interactive oral activities will all occur as a result of students' involvement with one of the modules. Text productions can result either as part of a module or from a past Paper 2. Details about specific examination preparation are given in section 2.16.

In the following section we look at the assessment and also look at what is useful by way of preparation for the examinations themselves.

3.13 Internal assessment (oral component)

As stated earlier, the orals are assessed using three equally weighted criteria – *Language*, *Cultural interaction* and *Message* – and each category has a maximum of 10 marks. We have seen that the oral component is worth 30% of the final grade although any amount of practice is both permissible and indeed is recommended. It should be noted that for some students elocution and clarity of speech are issues (language B HL students are penalized for unclear pronunciation). Therefore some students need plenty of time to practise speaking at a normal pace without hesitancy or gabbling. In such instances, a large amount of teacher modelling, and patience, is required. As with all group 2 orals, teachers should keep individual records of all assessed orals on the form 2/A1 as these will have to be submitted along with sample taped oral material demanded by the IBO.

3.14 Interactive oral activity

One activity is the school's free choice. Like A2 this may take the form of a discussion or a debate or presentation. In fact any sustained activity that requires little or no input from the teacher may be used. Students should be familiar with the type of tasks and assessments in the first year of the course. They should be aware that tasks are marked according to the three criteria. All potential assessed activities should take place in the final year of the syllabus. There are so many possible opportunities for oral work that the individual teacher should assess several, and then choose the best. There is no onus on the teacher to take the student's last oral piece.

3.15 Individual oral

The language B guide gives the details of the three-part oral:

Part 1: Presentation
3–4 minutes: a presentation based on support material chosen by the candidate

Part 2: Interview
3–4 minutes' follow-up questions and discussion on the student's presentation

Part 3: Discussion
3–4 minutes' general discussion between the teacher and the candidate

This activity is compulsory. It is recorded and internally assessed. The tape is externally moderated (see the *Vade Mecum* for the exact details). Sample tapes and moderation exercises can be obtained from the Publications Department at the IB Curriculum and Assessment office in Cardiff, UK. All teachers must participate in the trial moderation process (see section 2.14 for more details).

It is very useful for students to go through a moderation exercise with other students listening to tapes. If the school is new to the DP, the sample material can be obtained from the IBO. Let students mark using HL language B criteria. In the course of the two years students should practise individual elements of the oral and feel confident when tackling oral tasks. In this respect if students record their oral scores it gives them a clear perspective on the level of proficiency required. Whenever possible teachers should give language B students opportunities for public speaking outside class as this is an excellent method of improving student confidence. For example, when I give presentations on English B to groups in middle school, each student has to give a 1-minute presentation of the course outlining the course structure and giving his or her perspectives on the value of English B.

As with A2, it is worth remembering that students consider the recorded orals as the single most stressful activity in the entire IB assessment process. Make sure that the students plan well ahead. Publish dates of orals in advance. Both the stimulus text and the student prompt cards (maximum of 10 bullet points) should be prepared about a month in advance. In this way the material can be well rehearsed, but not learned by heart, for the day of the oral. A sympathetic approach by the teacher-examiner is essential. During the presentation section of the oral the teacher-examiner should facilitate the flow of information without being intrusive. If a student dries up during a recording a gentle prod in the right direction is usually sufficient to remove any mental block. During the second and third parts of the interview it is essential to remember that the oral is an opportunity for the student to display his or her abilities. Therefore prompts should be related to facilitating communication. It is never the role of the language B oral supervisor to corner individuals on a point of logic, or to test knowledge. Such an unsympathetic approach has been known to reduce a student to tears.

In order to help the student perform, it is a very useful stratagem to plan questions during the presentation phase of the oral. For example, if the student is presenting a short talk on the problems faced by returning students who have had an education abroad, I can jot down a few notes: 'personal experience of this?', 'solutions?' This helps to avoid surprise questions or sudden changes away from the topic as this can unsettle the student. If supervisors use open and 'either … or' questions, this will give the student an opportunity to respond. On the other hand if a particular student's turn is going on too long or straying from topic, it is valid to interrupt gently and move on to the next phase. Examiners would do well to silently indicate to the student when one minute remains for each part of the activity.

One problem with all group 2 orals is that the interviewer must be simultaneously interlocutor and assessor. The teacher must ensure the flow, direction and structure of the oral and also simultaneously make judgements on the student's linguistic performance. In order to achieve this I have modified the IB descriptors for use as a formative mark sheet. As performance will tend to vary within the interview, this time-tested method allows teachers to assess formatively the range of skills shown within each oral criterion. As the oral progresses, impressions about the student's overall performance can be adjusted during the 12-minute interview (these changes in student performance are represented by the x's on the mark sheet, figure 13.12). Consequently, individual criteria scores can be adjusted as the student progresses. As we can see from the example, a student's performance can vary within the oral itself. The score sheet

Figure 13.12 Language B commentary mark sheet with criteria

Name _____   Student No _____

Extract No (A2 only) _____   Theme _____

Time started _____   Date _____

Score	A Language	B Interaction	C Message
1 & 2	Very limited? Production Grammar and vocabulary Intonation	Limited? Appropriate response? Contribution? Appropriate formality?	Simple ideas with difficulty? Coherent ideas? Relevance? Coherent flow?
3 & 4	Limited? Production Grammar and vocabulary Intonation	Basic? Appropriate response? Contribution? Appropriate formality?	Simple ideas/some difficulty? Coherent ideas? Relevance? Coherent flow?
5 & 6	Fairly good? Production Grammar and vocabulary Intonation	Quite successful? Appropriate response? Contribution? Appropriate formality?	Simple ideas fairly well? Coherent ideas? Relevance? Coherent flow?
7 & 8	Good? Production ✗ Grammar and vocabulary ✗ Intonation ✗	Successful? Appropriate response? Contribution? Appropriate formality?	Complex ideas well? Coherent ideas? ✗✗ Relevance? ✗ Coherent flow? ✗
9 & 10	Very good? Production ✗✗ Grammar and vocabulary ✗✗ Intonation ✗	Very successful? Appropriate response? ✗✗ Contribution? ✗✗ Appropriate formality? ✗✗	Complex ideas very well? Coherent ideas? Relevance? ✗ Coherent flow? ✗

Note that in criterion B Interaction, I have used 'formality' not 'language' to distinguish this descriptor from category A (also called language).

showing the variations in performance can then be used to reach a summative conclusion about a student's overall marks in each criterion. Additional space on the sheet can be used for noting other comments and administrative notes, e.g. time spent on presentation and questions asked.

In the example in figure 13.12, the student's mark for *Language* has moved between the ranges 7–8 and 9–10 in the course of the performance. As I feel this student's overall performance on individual criteria is more towards 9 than 8 I would award the student the higher mark. In the case of *Interaction,* this student is clearly at the 9–10 boundary, and in this instance if I feel that the student's contributions have been totally appropriate and the student has used the correct level of formality/register throughout so I would award 10 for this category. In the case of *Message* the student is clearly more in the lower 7–8 range than the top 9–10 bracket, so the student receives 8 for Message.

This would give the student an overall oral score of:

Language	9
Interaction	10
Message	8
Total	27/30

Note this format could also be adapted for all group 2 orals by using the relevant criterion and descriptors. For comments about moderation and predicted grades, see section 2.14, as the procedures for language B are identical to those for A2.

3.16 Paper 1: text handling

The text handling paper lasts for 90 minutes and consists of two sections. It is worth 40% of the final mark. In the first part we find a variety of reading and comprehension tests designed to test surface and implied meaning. These may take a variety of communicative forms: multiple choice cloze exercises, matching exercises, rearranging sentences, short comprehension questions, labelling diagrams.

Of all the language B assessments the text handling is the most problematic and has come in for a great deal of justifiable criticism. In the past these have included:

• unpredictable format and assessment activities which make it very difficult for students to anticipate or to practise and apply specific examination techniques
• overlong texts which require an inordinate amount of reading
• inappropriate literary texts which are stylistically and lexically too difficult for language B students
• ambiguously worded questions which baffle even first language speakers
• questionable or subjective answers.

As has already been suggested, language B teachers would do well to prepare students by making their own text handling material. Much of this will arise naturally from the exploitation of topic-based texts but teachers should take care to design response material so that students encounter a variety of text handling strategies. This is essential. For instance, if students have done question-and-answer comprehension exercises, they will be ill-prepared for other types of assessment. Page 34 of the Language B subject guide provides a list of suitable activities.

Students should be encouraged to use the 5 minutes' reading time usefully, noting the difficulty of each text and the attendant activities and devising a strategy for the paper. Firstly students must be taught to read the questions very carefully to make sure they respond correctly. In addition texts are not always in order of difficulty. It is perhaps wise to tell students to scan for easier texts and to do them first. Alternatively they should use the 5 minutes to get on with rehearsing answers to the first question. In the course of the year students must practise speed reading/timed reading activities in order to make sure they cover the material in the time available (90 minutes). It should be noted that in 2004 there will also be a written response to the final question. As yet a sample paper has not been published.

3.17 Paper 2: written response

Like Paper 1, this examination also lasts for 90 minutes. Students choose one written task from a list of six. This task may be a formal essay or may take another form, for example a letter or a brochure or an advertisement. It is important that students write in the appropriate genre. Paper 2 is marked according to the three criteria: Message/Task, Cultural interaction and Language.

There is a minimum of 400 words (250 words at SL). There is no recommended upper limit but I feel students should not exceed 750 (450 SL) as they must give themselves time to re-read and check their work before submitting it. If language B students are to do well on the writing paper they must see that their work is always capable of further linguistic refinement and organization.

Examination practice is essential and therefore writing should form a substantial amount of the student work in language B courses. During the B course it is vital that students practise writing in different genres and are able to use the appropriate style (although it is not necessary to be able to reproduce the format). As part of pre-examination training, check that students understand what text type they are supposed to write, e.g. letter, speech, brochure, diary entry. They must learn to be consistent in the use of register and not use an idiosyncratic mix of formal and informal language.

In order to stress the interdisciplinary nature of the DP some language B questions now reflect IB experience (CAS etc.). Therefore during the two years students should be encouraged to write about such issues. In addition it is perfectly valid to use examples from other subjects in writing the Paper 2 essay. In terms of transparency of aims it is essential that students should be marked according to the IB criteria. At HL upper descriptors include words such as 'clear', 'comprehensible', 'logical' and 'accurate'. The students would do well to adopt these adjectives as bywords for their own personal writing targets.

3.18 Mixed A2 and B classes

At the lower end of the ability range there will be a very fine line between A2 and B. However, by rule of thumb we can say that those students who display very little grammatical and formal control over the target language would be better advised to take language B.

In some schools, setting separate A2 and B classes may well be impractical or economically impossible. In this case the teacher is recommended to choose the same three literature texts for both groups. This simplifies issues tremendously. Teachers of mixed classes can also make the A2 topic options *Language and Culture* or *Media and Culture* a focus for some of the language B content. In this way A2 students cover their compulsory content requirements. For a third module I would choose *Society* as a theme. This fits both the requirements of A2 and is a useful catch-all category for organizing material about the target culture for language B. In this way it is possible to cover both the content requirements of B (HL) and A2 (SL) syllabuses. However, teachers with A2 (HL) and B (HL) students may need A2 (HL) candidates to attend an extra lesson to deal with an additional literature or topic option.

In Year 1 of the DP a mixed group can work reasonably well. However, in the second year there will be some divergence of interest and the teacher will have to meet the assessment needs of both groups. Essays and writing tasks can be set for both groups. A2 students will need additional material and ideas to produce coursework text productions. Orals can also be undertaken at the same time and in fact the language B students may well benefit from the presence of a number of fluent speakers in the class. Note that the individual recorded oral will follow a different format and cover different content. The real problems come with the massive differences in the format of Paper 1 which for B consists of text handling and comprehension and for A2 requires the completely separate skill of comparative commentary. In this instance the teacher can only alleviate the problem by using two separate sets of materials and groupwork activities.

4 *Ab initio*

Ab initio (literally 'from the beginning') is the third tier of examinations available within group 2. In addition to providing a beginners-level language course, the IBO encourages students to see *ab initio* as a way of promoting internationalism. A full list of languages can be found in the *Vade Mecum*, section C – note that *ab initio* English is not available. Students with very low levels of English must be capable of a minimum of Standard B. Because of the great differences in the languages available in this section, this part of the chapter focuses on making general observations about *ab initio* practice common to all languages taught at this level.

Like A2 and language B, the *ab initio* course is designed around communicative principles and aims to promote language competence and an awareness of and sensitivity to the target culture. To this end students are expected to reach a competent understanding of surface meaning in authentic texts. In addition they are expected to use a range of language functions to narrate, describe and instruct. They are also expected to be able to express past and future events. As we can see below, the final assessments test the ability to use the language in everyday circumstances, rather than abstract knowledge of grammar and vocabulary. The course is only available at SL and is suitable for students who have not previously learned a foreign language, or those who wish to start a new language, and need a group 2 language to complete their DP package.

Although *ab initio* operates at beginners' level it is not a soft option and the learning curve is steep. By the end of the course, students are expected to have achieved real levels of fluency and literacy, and this will require a real commitment on their part. Good grades have to be achieved through a great deal of hard work. Because of the rigorous nature of the course, some *ab initio* candidates do score badly and there seems little point in herding them towards the course if the students have a viable language B, or an alternative group 1 (A1 mother tongue/best language) and English A2 or B.

Although students start at the same level it is usual to find them progressing at different rates. If numbers warrant two classes, it is a good idea to split the students into two groups: those who have some linguistic ability or motivation, and those that do not. This should be fairly clear after the first term. If classes are taught at the same time, class sets should be easy to manipulate.

4.1 Assessment outline

Like language B, there are two written papers externally set and externally assessed.

Like language B, *ab initio* assesses communication skills and so all tests and instructions are in the target language. Moreover, students may not use

Figure 13.13 *Ab initio* assessments

Paper 1: Text handling 1 hour 30 minutes	
Text handling exercises based on four written texts	32%
A short writing exercise in response to the fourth text	8%
Total	40%

Paper 2: Written production 1 hour 30 minutes	
Section A: Short writing task One writing task from a choice of two	
Section B: Extended writing task One writing task from a choice of three	
Total	30%

Internal assessment: oral component	
Two oral activities to be internally assessed by the teacher and externally moderated by the IBO	
Interactive oral activity	15%
Individual oral. Short interview with the teacher	15%
Total	30%

dictionaries. Therefore, the examinations are a real test of memory and linguistic skills and, consequently, material should have been thoroughly practised and internalized before the students sit their examinations.

4.2 Assessment criteria for *ab initio*

Like A2 and B, *ab initio* oral and written tasks are marked according to three criteria: Language, Communication skills, and Interaction. Each is marked out of 10 and the total of 30 reflects the percentage weighting in the final assessment.

For text handling, 1 mark is awarded for each individual answer or response. Students gain marks for the idea rather than the grammatical accuracy of the answer itself. The response question is marked out of 10 but it is worth only 8% of the total mark. (The assessment criteria can be found on pages 38 and 39 of the *ab initio* subject guide.) Students have to write a minimum of 40 words (48 Mandarin characters or 80 characters in Japanese). Examples (in English) can be found on page 27 of the *ab initio* subject guide.

4.3 Organizing an *ab initio* course

Ab initio teachers say that there are two fundamental problems with *ab initio*: there is too much to do, and too little time in which to do it. As with all other DP group 2 courses, teachers are responsible for course design as well as assessment. The core syllabus must be the foundation for any *ab initio* course, which is divided into the following topics: The individual, Education and work, Transport, Shopping, Food and drink, Leisure, The environment, Emergencies. However, there is a problem with this arrangement. These topic areas are too big to be covered. For example, how does a student learn all the vocabulary associated with 'Education and work'? It would therefore seem preferable to use the subtopics (listed in the *ab initio* subject guide) to structure the course. In this instance 'Education and work' is subdivided into 'School life' and 'Plans for the future'. In this way teachers can ensure that associated vocabulary can be learned in manageable quantities. In time departments usually add vocabulary lists related to each subtopic for students to learn.

As well as the wide range of topics, there are a large number of communication activities to be covered. For example, like language B, it is vital to ensure that students can handle a variety of text handling tasks. If the range is limited to, say, question and answer, then students will find it very difficult to carry out all the assessment tasks on Paper 1. Similarly, students will have to carry out a variety of writing tasks and be able to manipulate past, present and future tenses. All this has to be done in the limited time available. In effect teachers have 20 months to bring students up to speed in a language.

4.4 Commercially produced language courses and *ab initio*

Because of the time available to teachers for the development of materials, textbooks will have to be used on this course. Therefore, schools should think twice about putting on *ab initio* for languages where there are no supplies available of suitable commercial material. Pointers for assessing the usefulness of commercially produced language courses can be found above, section 3.10.

An additional consideration for *ab initio* is the huge gap between receptive skills and productive skills. In the final analysis the students' writing and spoken output is assessed at a much lower linguistic level than the reading component of *ab initio*. One textbook will have to cover the basic structures and functions of the target language, as well as allow students to practise simple writing tasks. In addition, any textbook purchased should contain a variety of topics and domains similar to those outlined in the *ab initio* guide. This is essential as the students have to learn vocabulary that is specifically related to the said topics and domains.

Reading, however, is another matter entirely. *Ab initio* students will need to undertake comprehension and text handling tasks at a much higher linguistic level. Paper 1 (text handling) uses quasi-authentic materials and the students are expected to achieve a level of understanding far greater than their productive abilities. In some Paper 1s over 50% of the vocabulary may be unknown to the candidates in the examination. So preparation for the examination will involve the use of suitable reading material at intermediate level. Consequently, a second book of commercially produced material may well be necessary to practise these reading skills.

Like language B, the course should also explore some aspects of the target culture. To this end, a few audio-visual materials might provide a quick shortcut and prove a useful diversion at the end of a hectic term. In practice the shortage of time will limit this to one or two videos a year.

One important difference between language B and *ab initio* worth noting is the fact that the IBO does give *ab initio* teachers specific lists of core vocabulary and grammar items which must be learned as part of each course. They are available in the Language Specific Syllabi available from the IBO. A word of warning: the lists provide core language and are not exclusive; *ab initio* students must expect to encounter vocabulary not included in the lexicon and will need the strategies to cope with unfamiliar lexis. (Note that Chinese and Japanese are largely an exception to this rule. Only 20% of the material in Paper 1 (text handling) should come from outside the given lists in these languages.) The IBO also suggests that grammar and vocabulary be taught in the target language. However, this is clearly impractical. It is preferable that students use grammar books which utilize explanations and illustrations in specific language points in the target language.

Like other group 2 courses, no single textbook will cover the needs of an *ab initio* course and teachers will have to supplement courses and fill gaps. Such material will have to come from newspapers, magazines and from the internet.

As with language B, departments may wish to give students a handbook. Such a document could also contain the appropriate lexicons and an overview of the content of the overall course (see language B subject guide section 8.4 for an outline of possible content).

4.5 A two-year schedule for *ab initio*

Figure 13.14 is an outline model for an *ab initio* course.

Figure 13.14 *Ab initio* years 1 and 2

YEAR 1			
Term 1	Formal assessment	Topics	Exam practice
August		Myself	
		Nationalities	
		Personal information	
		The family	September/October
		Physical descriptions	Internal assessment 1
		Personality	
		Hobbies and sport	
		Things I like	December
		Time	Internal assessment 2
Term 2			
January		School	
		Uniforms and clothes	
		The city	March
		Home	Internal assessment 3
Term 3			
April		Exam autopsy	Internal exams
		Routines and diaries	Papers 1 & 2
		Reflexive verbs	
		Holidays	
		Past tense	
		Future tense	
		Food	

(continued)

Figure 13.14 *Ab initio* years 1 and 2 (continued)

	YEAR 2		
Term 1	**Formal assessment**	**Topics**	**Exam practice**
August		Work Future plans Shopping Food and recipes The imperfect tense Lost and found Accidents and emergencies Car repairs	Paper 2 practice 1 September/October Text handling practice 1 Practice for individual orals Paper 2 practice 2 November/December Text handling practice 2
Term 2			
January	Preparation for orals Oral exams February Moderation by beginning of March	Exam autopsy Environment Transport Public services	Mock examination January Text handling 3 Paper 2 practice 3
Term 3			
April May	 Exam Papers 1 & 2		Past papers

4.6 Integrating assessment practice into an *ab initio* course

As stated earlier, all classroom activities apart from explanations of grammar are best conducted in the target language. At the end of the day, 30% of the final grade is for an oral activity conducted in the *ab initio* language. Students will need as much practice as possible. In the individual oral the student must be able to understand the teacher, and familiarity will only come with time. In theory students are expected to listen to a variety of aural material and various accents. From a practical standpoint, this is unnecessary and, given the time constraint, impractical. Listening is not assessed.

Teachers can make the individual oral very predictable in format. It is very important that the students are able to talk about key topics such as themselves, their family, their home and holidays. Make sure that students are able to talk about themselves in the present (self and daily routines), the past (last holiday) and future (future plans). It might be a good idea to start this at the beginning of the second year as the grammar will have been covered and first year topics can be revised. Students can also write this information and this will also give them practice for Paper 2.

Text handling practice can be done throughout the course. Prior to year 2 students will not have enough linguistic knowledge to cope with the authentic texts of Paper 1. Therefore in the first year it is a good idea only to give practice material in the form of internal assessments. One idea to circumvent this difficulty would be to use texts already covered and to doctor them by adding an element of manipulation: cloze exercises, matching definitions, re-organizing texts, etc.

Only in the second year of the course can most students be let loose on the real thing. In the course of the first year students need to be familiar with two essential techniques. Firstly, they should learn to recognize question words and the various instructions associated with the examination. Secondly, it is a good idea if they can recognize the meaning of conjunctions and cohesive devices in texts in order to work out internal structure and logic of a text.

The final element of assessment practice is writing. This also should feature throughout the course and students will have to be able to use first and third person present tense description, produce simple accounts of daily routines and give clear, simple instructions. These language functions are best practised within the topics being studied as this will reinforce the vocabulary. For example, within the topic 'Education and work', students should be able to write about the organization of their school day, their daily timetable and the subjects they study. As the course progresses, students can acquire more complex writing skills. Again the use of conjunctions and other structural devices will lend organization and coherence to the students' writing.

4.7 Assessment in *ab initio*

The main reason for students not doing well is insufficient ability to use the target language. The reasons are equally unsurprising: lack of vocabulary, poor use of grammatical structures, poor use of cohesion, inability to construct basic sentences and poor examination technique. Therefore the question is how to anticipate these problems and solve them.

4.8 Oral assessment in *ab initio*

Here an individual presentation of a picture is followed by a question-and-answer session in which general conversation is compulsory. The oral is recorded and internally assessed. The tape is externally moderated. Like language B, other activities are the school's free choice. All activities should take place in the final year of the syllabus. Both tasks are marked according to three criteria: Language, Communication skills, and Interaction. Each is worth 15% of the final overall mark.

For the individual oral, it is obvious that the more the student has prepared, the better the presentation. However, students should be penalized for reading pre-prepared presentations. The taped oral should sound natural. The most successful orals are those in which the examiner encourages the student, and gives helpful prompts which allow the student to respond in the target language. To this end it is very helpful if the students are thoroughly familiar with question words and know how to respond to them. Another useful strategy is clarification. Learning to say 'Excuse me, could you repeat that?' enables the student to continue in the conversation rather than simply suffering a communication breakdown. As a standby, students should make sure they are able to talk about certain stock topics with which they are most familiar: home and family, their future, and holidays.

It is possible for a good examiner to help the students. Here are some general tips:

- Ensure that candidates are thoroughly familiar with the oral procedures in order to reduce stress.
- Avoid long, rambling questions.

- Work out in advance questions on the topics presented.
- Look interested at all times.

4.9 Examination Paper 1 (text handling)

Paper 1 (text handling) is worth 40% of the final grade. Here students need to show an understanding of a short text by responding to it in an appropriate manner. Examples can be found in the *ab initio* subject guide. As we have seen for language B, the text handling paper uses a number of different reading assessment strategies designed to test surface comprehension. As well as short comprehension questions, *ab initio* examinations include multiple choice, vocabulary matching, cloze exercises and the labelling of diagrams. Like Language B, there is little consistency in the format (for example there is no guarantee that there will be a gap-filling exercise). This makes it difficult to prepare students for this assessment paper. As we have seen, the issue is further complicated by the fact that the vocabulary used often greatly exceeds the list used in lexicon 1. This leads to great differences in the linguistic density of the assessment material. Therefore students have to be able to deal with new vocabulary and be taught reading strategies for doing so. It is essential that candidates are able to differentiate between tenses and to recognize features such as basic word order and cohesive devices. Knowing cognates is also a valuable tool. Students should also take care to differentiate between similar common words with very different meanings. Going through a vocabulary list containing these commonly confused items before an examination or even an internal test can be a great help.

4.10 Examination Paper 2 (text production)

This examination is in two sections. In section A students must complete one of two tasks using a minimum of 60 words. In section B students must complete one task of minimum 120 words from a choice of three. It is important that the student writes in the style appropriate to the text. For instance, a letter should sound like a letter. Therefore it is important that students are able to use both formal and informal registers of the target language. Both tasks are marked according to the same criteria: Language, Communication skills and Presentation.

By the end of the course students are expected to be able to function for day-to-day purposes in the target language. Therefore upper descriptors include words such as 'clear', 'comprehensible', 'logical' and 'accurate'. The material is based around the eight topics outlined in the *ab initio* subject guide, so it is very important that students know how to write a variety of written tasks within each topic area. These include:

- giving reasons and explanations
- describing people and places
- giving instructions
- narrating using past tense markers
- writing the same information equally well in both familiar and formal forms of address
- using formal and informal greetings and closes.

However, planning skills are also important. As well as being accurate, student responses should be relevant and coherently sequenced. Students need to use connecting devices within sentences and paragraphs. It should also be noted that all written work has the additional benefit of helping students to prepare for the oral assignments.

5 The extended essay in group 2

A group 2 extended essay is referred to as a language B extended essay. Broadly speaking, there are two basic purposes behind writing an extended essay. First, it gives students the opportunity to research a topic in the target language. Secondly, like extended essays in other parts of the IB hexagon, it introduces them to the type of work required at university. In my experience, only HL students of languages A2 and B should attempt an extended essay in group 2.

Group 2 extended essays must fall into one of the following three categories:

Category 1: Language (analysis of a sociolinguistic aspect of language)
Category 2: Culture and society (analysis of the impact of culture on language)
Category 3: Literature (literary analysis of target language texts).

Examples of suitable topics for each category are available in the subject guide, which also gives students guidelines for conducting and writing up their research. In addition to the general criteria for assessing the extended essay (criteria A–I), there are three subject-specific criteria (J–L). Each criterion is described in the subject guide:

J: Knowledge and understanding of the language/culture/literature studied
K: Point of view on the topic studied
L: Communication and use of an appropriate register and style.

Examples of successful (i.e. they received either an A or a B grade) extended essay titles are:

1. English as a global language: Will the spread of English cause death to the mother tongue in Swaziland?
2. What have been the consequences of forced adoptions within the Australian Aboriginal community?
3. Why and how did English become an official language in Singapore?
4. To what extent are the female protagonists in *The Woman Warrior* by Maxine Hong Kingston and *Wild Meat and the Bully Burgers* by Lois-Ann Yamanaka able to find a balance between the differing Asian and American cultures and, thus, ascertain their identities?
5. How does a Freudian psychological analysis assist an understanding of Kazuo Ishiguro's novels *A Pale View of Hills* and *The Remains of the Day*?
6. What effects are achieved by the imagery used in editorials from the *Washington Post* and *The Nation* discussing the events in the United States on September 11th, 2001?

6 Resources

Essential IBO documents

Vade Mecum sections 2 and 3
IB A2 Guide (2002)
IB Language B Guide (2002)
IB Language ab initio Guide (2002). In addition there is a Language Specific
Syllabus for each *ab initio* language (2002).
Form for oral coursework 2/A1
Form for A2 written text productions 2/WTRF
Language A2: Written Assignment Cover Sheet (Note: only issued in
February/August of final year of the course.)
Examination papers (Note: A2 (HL and SL) Paper 2, language B, and *ab initio*
Paper 1 will all change format for the first examination in 2004.)
A2 Listening moderation, IBO 2003

A2 specific material

Language texts can be obtained from a variety of academic sources. However,
many tend to be above the level of the student and are too dry for use in the
classroom. David Crystal's *Encyclopaedia of Language* is an excellent introduction
to the subject. In many multilingual societies, such as Singapore and Malaysia,
bilingual language policies are the subject of ongoing discussion within the local
media and so the local press is always an excellent source of topical information.

Two books that can be heartily recommended are David Crystal's *English as a
Global Language* and Bill Bryson's *The Mother Tongue*. The latter performs the feat
of being both richly informative and immensely amusing. For questions on
dialect and identity one text is very insightful: Lois-Ann Yamanaka's semi-
autobiographical novel *Wild Meat and the Bully Burgers* vividly describes the
humiliation of Hawaiian Pidgin speakers forced to communicate in Standard
English. Singaporean writer, Catherine Lim, has a book of short stories *Little
Ironies* which offers some well-observed comments on local language issues.

Two texts provide a sufficiently broad approach to media studies. *An
Introduction to Media Studies* by Ziauddin Saddar and Borin van Loon (Icon Books,
1999) is an excellent and amusing illustrated guide to the big ideas. *The Media
Student's Book* (Routledge, 3rd edition, 2003) provides more than enough
material for A2 students and their teachers.

Schools putting together an A2 course will be very hard-pressed to find single
sources of materials for any of the cultural topic options and the photocopier
will be the A2 teacher's best friend.

Course materials for English B

For English B it is possible to make use of materials designed for the Cambridge
Certificate in Advanced English (CAE) examination. Over the years I have found
that *Focus on CAE* by Sue O'Connell (Longman, 1999) provides a very easy-to-use
format, with systematic language development, text handling and writing
activities. Moreover, by allowing students to decide on the relevance of a
particular chapter, they are able to establish a measure of autonomy in the way

that the material in the book is delivered and processed. There is also an excellent writing reference section in the middle of the book with a very useful list of connective devices. This provides very useful skills and language revision for writing Paper 2 type tasks. This can be supplemented with other CAE material. As far as grammar books are concerned there is plenty of commercial material available, but no single text stands out as exceptional.

Literature for English B

One valuable source of reading material is young adult fiction. Much of the material reflects contemporary issues in the target culture and has the double bonus of being written in a style that is linguistically rich and yet accessible. However, a word of caution is required. Not all texts speak to 16–17 year-olds and the subject matter can be patronizing. In English B, contemporary texts that work are *Make Lemonade* by Virginia Ewer Wolff, *Holes* by Louis Sachar and *A Step from Heaven* by An Na. By the final year of a language B course, students may well be ready for more substantial literature. For English B I can heartily endorse Kazuo Ishiguro's *A Pale View of Hills*, John Steinbeck's *Red Pony*, and the perennial favourite, J. D. Salinger's *The Catcher in the Rye*.

Text handling

Text handling is a reading and response examination. It is Paper 1 of the language B and *ab initio* external assessment.

For teachers new to language B I would suggest looking at page 34 of the subject guide for a useful list of possible text handling tasks. These are valuable suggestions as to how authentic material might be adapted for the classroom. In addition, Elfreda Hedger's *English B* (from Ibid Press, 1999) is also a possible source of practice and revision material, especially for homework. Finally there are the past examination papers themselves. However, these have proven to be of such variable quality that many students find doing them a very depressing activity. Until the IBO comes out with a more standardized format, students will always be anxiously wondering what text handling activities the IBO will ask them to deal with.

www.english-to-go.com is an excellent commercial site for text handling materials. It is linked to Reuters press.

Chapter 14
Group 3: Individuals and societies

Phil Woolrich, with Jay Atwood, Robin Barton, Nick Cotton, Robert Friesen, Sarah Jeyaram and Monica Mueller

Group 3 is a special section within the IB Diploma Programme (DP) curriculum in the sense that its subjects do not follow a common curriculum structure. The chapter therefore opens with a general introduction to group 3, and then continues with individual subject specialist sections on business, economics, information technology in a global society (ITGS), psychology, geography and history. These are the six subjects in group 3 which each attract at least 5% of the group 3 student population.

The authors of the individual sections are as follows:

Sections 1–5 (introduction, economics, and business and management): *Phil Woolrich, BA*
Phil Woolrich, who is also the editor of this chapter, spent four years as a teacher of IB economics and business at the United World College of South East Asia (UWCSEA) in Singapore, then took up the post of head of department at St Andrew's Scots School in Argentina, where he set up the business DP in a bilingual (Spanish and English) school environment. Phil returned to UWCSEA in 2001. He is an assistant examiner for the IBO, which invited him to take part in the curriculum review committee for business in 2003 and to set examination questions for the DP business and management programme.

Section 6 (ITGS): *Monica Mueller, BA, BEd, MEd*
Monica Mueller has taught in Toronto, Hamburg, Curaçao and Singapore. She began teaching the ITGS programme in 1997 at the International School of Curaçao, and became an assistant moderator for the project portion of the ITGS internal assessment in 2000. Since 2001, she has assisted with the implementation of the IBO's Middle Years Programme and Primary Years Programme at the International School of Singapore, where she is currently IT instructional leader. She gives an overview of the ITGS course, and draws on her classroom experience to share her thoughts on effective classroom management of the subject. Monica was assisted in this section by Barbara Stefanics, ICT Head at Vienna International School and ITGS Senior Examiner, IBO.

Section 7 (psychology): *Jay Atwood, MA, BA*
Jay Atwood is a deputy chief examiner for IB psychology. He taught IB psychology at the American International School in Cairo (where he was also IB coordinator) and at the Taipei American School (where he also taught ITGS and where he is currently the webmaster and the upper school information technology coordinator). He has been a senior examiner and/or principal examiner for all three externally assessed papers, a senior moderator and principal moderator for HL internal assessment, and an assessor and team leader for extended essays. Jay has led IB workshops in three of the IB regions: Asia-Pacific, Africa-Europe-Middle East and North America. He has served as the psychology faculty member for the Online Curriculum Centre (OCC) and was involved in the curriculum review and development committees that worked toward publishing the course guide for first examinations in May 2003. In this section, he shares his insights to focus on the areas of concern for both new and experienced teachers. He was assisted in this section by Wally Hobbs, IB psychology teacher at the Taipei American School, and by Jim Wong.

Section 8 (geography): *Nick Cotton, BA*
Nick Cotton is a teacher of geography and outdoor education manager at UWCSEA. He also teaches ecosystems and societies and has previously held the post of coordinator of science, technology and society (see Chapter 18). As a head of grade he advised students on their IB package options and requirements. He gives an overview of DP geography, provides practical tips on how to organize and teach the course, and shares a list of internet resources that are good starting points to resource the course.

Section 9 (history): *Sarah Jeyaram, Robin Barton and Robert Friesen*
Sarah Jeyaram has taught in England and Singapore. She began teaching the IB history as well as business and management programmes in 2000 at the International School of Singapore. Since 2001 she has assisted with the implementation of the IB Middle Years Programme.

Both Robin Barton and Robert Friesen have taught in Canada and Singapore. They both began teaching IB history as well as Theory of Knowledge in 2001 at the Overseas Family School in Singapore. Robin has conducted workshops about the IB to Singaporean principals and heads of departments. Since 2002, he has been the academic adviser at the Overseas Family School. Robert is the curriculum area leader for humanities, and has been involved in various IB workshops and training sessions.

These three authors join forces to provide a brief overview of the history curriculum and assessment structure and offer advice on how to interpret and apply the wide curriculum choice.

Note: all weblinks featured in this chapter can be accessed through our website www.dp-help.com

1 Introduction

With nine subjects, group 3 is, apart from languages, the largest and most diverse group of subjects in the hexagon. Centres are not expected to cover all of these subjects and typically choose options that best fit their own demographic situation. What do other rival schools offer? What constraints are imposed by national requirements? What resources are necessary? These are often the driving forces behind programme choice.

It may be helpful to divide group 3 into three distinct subgroups. The first set of subjects represent the traditional face of societal studies:

- economics
- geography
- history (with a number of regional specializations)
- Islamic history.

The next set is slightly different in that they have no direct connection to any middle school curriculum, but are found in the general studies unit of a typical US college curriculum:

- philosophy
- psychology
- social and cultural anthropology.

Then there is a final pairing of subjects that one would perhaps not expect to see in a group called 'Individuals and societies', but which earn their place here because of the IBO's emphasis on their interaction with society. They are the most recent subjects in group 3:

- business and management
- information technology in a global society (ITGS, at SL only).

The IBO takes pride in being open to new ideas and is committed to developing its group 3 programme further. Individual schools have created innovative and imaginative SBS (school based subject) courses such as 'World Studies' and 'Political Awareness' which in time may also become accepted subjects within group 3. Other co-habitants of group 3 are trans-disciplinary (TD) subjects. These simultaneously satisfy the requirements of two segments of the hexagon and thus allow for greater DP package flexibility. (See Chapter 18 for a detailed discussion on SBS and TD subjects.)

There are two interesting features of group 3 that set it apart from the science and the mathematics groups. The first is that all subjects are *ab initio*, i.e. they require no previous instruction in the subject. The second is that in general the Standard Level (SL) subjects can be as intellectually demanding as Higher Level (HL). If a student is deemed capable of taking the former they should be able to take the latter provided they have a genuine motivation to do so. The difference is mainly in content, not in skills. In general, HL students do a slightly more in-depth piece of coursework although the actual structure in both cases is often similar. The HL courses cover more modules and the DP requires a minimum of 240 hours contact time versus 150 hours for SL. It is quite possible to teach both sets of students in the same class.

The accessibility and variety of subjects on offer in group 3 explains the popularity of group 3 subjects as free electives.

1.1 Prerequisites and language issues

As a basic requirement, both HL and SL students need to be sufficiently numerate to deal with relatively straightforward statistical, mathematical and financial calculations. Moreover, they need to be able to express themselves both fluently and cogently in their language of examination. This is a problem area in group 3. Often the examination questions in group 3 put a lot of pressure on the non-native speakers to write at length but offer too little time to do so. If students have acceptable grades in the school's working language (English, French, Spanish), together with mathematics from recognized pre-DP programmes, they should be able to cope with group 3 courses. However, students struggling with the working language may have difficulties with certain language-heavy subjects such as history, which requires a lot of reading of sources with, at times, difficult language.

1.2 The central aims of the DP and the group 3 curriculum

Many of the central aims of the DP (internationalism, cultural sensitivity, student-centred learning, holistic outlook) should be familiar to teachers in group 3. Consequently, whereas the central aims have had a remarkable impact on the curricula of groups 4, 5 and 6, experienced teachers new to the DP in group 3 will encounter relatively few surprises. Many humanities teachers are used to taking a student-centred approach to deliver their lessons and to meet their objectives. A historian presenting the neo-imperialism of the 1870s, or a geographer discussing global warming, will often naturally adopt an international and holistic viewpoint because these topics demand it.

Group 3's internationalism manifests itself in two important ways. On the one hand, students in all subjects are expected to gain an understanding of situations and views around the globe. The IBO's global perspective is further evident in subjects such as economics, which emphasizes *development economics*, not always a focus for the national syllabuses. On the other hand, the IBO recognizes that many students will need to learn about their own regional culture. Therefore many syllabuses such as history and geography feature regional options. This elegant solution enables students to place their own culture within the context of a global environment.

Student-centred learning allows students to determine and develop their own views and ideas, and manifests itself in the *coursework component* in the assessment. This coursework is again no great departure from established procedures for teachers experienced in these fields, so their transition to the DP should be relatively straightforward. Group 3 syllabuses allow schools the freedom to design their own curriculum in order to deliver the central aims. Therefore in order to pass on specific skills, teachers can use any topics they deem suitable. This too will be a familiar strategy.

While the central aims do not introduce unexpected changes in perspective for group 3 subjects, they have given birth to an entirely new subject. Quick to recognize the impact of the internet on society, the IBO introduced ITGS as an embodiment of its approach to education. Science, technology, culture, global society, and the role of the individual all come together in this course.

Schools and universities increasingly endorse the IBO's perspective, and consider the IB courses excellent preparation for tertiary study.

1.3 What courses to offer?

For schools new to the IB, it is wise to begin by offering a selection of courses they are familiar with, both from an educational and financial point of view. Many North American schools that are competing with the AP system, for instance, limit themselves to economics, history or psychology. European or British schools that are competing with the British A-level, German *Abitur* or the French *baccalauréat* tend to concentrate on economics, history and geography. Centres in either case with enough resources can extend the range by offering increasingly popular courses such as psychology, business and management, and ITGS.

Figure 14.1 shows the percentage uptake of individual subject examinations within group 3 as of May 2002; total percentage uptake in 1998 and 2002; and the difference between these two numbers (the table is adapted from the IB's *Statistical Bulletin* May 1998 to May 2002; figures are rounded to one significant figure).

Figure 14.1 demonstrates that history and psychology managed to hold the fort and keep up with the general growth of the DP, but that the new subjects ITGS and business and management are making gains at the expense of the other subjects. Students often perceive business as easier than economics, but the statistics do not support this perception (see section 2). History is fairly literature intensive, so schools with many non-native English speakers need to keep this in mind. Geography is a very practical course with lots of fieldwork and is well liked by the students. Prospective and established IB schools should certainly have a look at section 6 in this chapter to understand why ITGS is growing so fast – it is an accessible, exciting, and highly topical course.

Figure 14.1 Relative popularity within group 3 and relative growth since 1998

	HL % uptake May 2002	SL % uptake May 2002	Total % uptake May 1998	Total % uptake May 2002	Difference (relative growth)
History Africa	0.2				
History Americas	24				
History Asia/Middle east	0.2				
History Asia/South east and Oceania	0.7				
History Europe	16				
History total	**41**	**7**	**47**	**48**	**+ 1**
Economics	8	8	19	16	− 3
Psychology	3	10	13	13	0
Geography	4	3	8	7	− 1
Business and management	3	3	3	6	+ 3
ITGS	−	5	−	5	+ 5
Philosophy	1.5	2	6	3	− 3
Social and cultural anthropology	0.5	2	3	2	− 1
Islamic World studies	0.03	0.03	0.3	0.1	0

1.4 Assessment overview of group 3

Unlike with the sciences, it is impossible to find a common assessment structure for the different subjects in group 3. However, the IBO could do a better job with its question labels, which seem needlessly confusing. Not only do the examination teams each employ their own terminology, they also assign different meanings to the same terminology. Figure 14.2 is the author's interpretation of the terms.

Figure 14.2 An explanation/interpretation of IBO terms

Essay question	Questions requiring a detailed and lengthy response. The student is expected to take up to an hour per question.
Structured question	Questions that have a series of linked questions based on a stimulus passage or a set of data. The student should take up to 45 minutes per question.
Data response question	Same as structured question.
Extended response question	a) Economics, history – an essay question broken down into two or more sections. Takes an hour to do. b) Business and management – a longer version of the structured question. It takes up to an hour to complete. c) Psychology – an essay question that may require either a detailed and lengthy response or one broken down into two or more sections.
Short answer/structured question	Short technical questions taking approximately 15–20 minutes each.
Seen case study question	Questions related to a case study shown to the students at least one month before the examination. The questions are unseen until the examination. They cover the full range of the course, and the student has to answer all.
Free response question	Answers are required to meet a given set of assessment criteria but the exact structure of the answer is left to the student. It should take the student up to an hour to answer each question.

Figure 14.3 and 14.4 (next two pages) summarize the assessment components for the different subjects at HL and at SL.

Figure 14.3 Assessment overview of group 3 – HL

HL	External assessment			Internal assessment
Subject	Paper 1	Paper 2	Paper 3	
History (1st exam 2003)	Four short structured questions	Two extended response questions	Three extended response questions	Historical investigation 1,500–2,000 words
	1 hr	1 hr 30	2 hrs 30	20 hrs
	20%	25%	35%	20%
Geography (1st exam 2003)	Two structured questions	Four questions – essay or structured		Two pieces – either fieldwork reports or research assignments
	1 hr 30	2 hrs 30		30 hrs
	25%	50%		25%
Economics (1st exam 2005)	One extended response question	Three short answer questions	Three structured data response questions	Four commentaries each 650–750 words
	1 hr	1 hr	2 hrs	20 hrs
	20%	20%	40%	20%
Philosophy (1st exam 2002)	One compulsory structured question and two essay questions	Two essay questions		Two philosophical exercises each 1,000–1,200 words
	2 hrs 30	2 hrs		20 hrs
	40%	40%		20%
Psychology (1st exam 2003)	Short answer and extended response questions	Two extended response questions	Short answer questions	Experimental study 1,500–2,000 words
	2 hrs	2 hrs	1 hr	25 hrs
	30%	30%	20%	20%
Social and cultural anthropology (1st exam 2002)	Three compulsory short answer questions	Two free response questions	One essay question	Field research max. 2,000 words
	1 hr	2 hrs	1 hr	N/A
	20%	30%	20%	30%
Business and management (1st exam 2002)	Seen case study – four compulsory +1 extended response questions	Four data response questions		Business report 2,000–2,300 words
	2 hrs	2 hrs 30		30 hrs
	40%	35%		25%
Islamic world history (1st exam 2003)	Four short structured questions	Three extended response questions	Two extended response questions	Islamic historical study 1,200–1,500 words
	1 hr	2 hrs	1 hr 30	25 hrs
	20%	35%	20%	25%

Figure 14.4 Assessment overview of group 3 – SL

SL	External assessment		Internal assessment	
Subject	Paper 1	Paper 2		
History (1st exam 2003)	Four short structured questions	Two extended response questions	Historical investigation 1,500–2,000 words	
	1 hr	1 hr 30	20 hrs	
	30%	45%	25%	
Geography (1st exam 2003)	Two structured questions	Two questions – essay or structured	Fieldwork with two reports or research assignments	
	1 hr 30	1 hr 30	integrated in course	
	40%	40%	20%	
Economics (1st exam 2005)	One extended response question	Three structured data response questions	Four commentaries each 650–750 words	
	1 hr	2 hrs	20 hrs	
	25%	50%	25%	
Philosophy (1st exam 2002)	One structured question and one essay question	One essay question	Two philosophical exercises each 1,000–1,200 words	
	1 hr 30	1 hr	20 hrs	
	50%	30%	20%	
Psychology (1st exam 2003)	Short answer and extended response questions	Extended response question	Simple experimental study 1,000–1,500 words	
	2 hrs	1 hr	15 hrs	
	50%	30%	20%	
Social and cultural anthropology (1st exam 2002)	Three compulsory short answer questions	Two free response questions	Observation and criticism exercise Observation of 500–600 words and report of 600–700 words	
	1 hr	2 hrs	N/A	
	30%	40%	30%	
Business and management (1st exam 2002)	Seen case study – four compulsory questions	Three data response questions	Business report 1,000–1,500 words	
	1 hr 30	1 hr 30	15 hrs	
	40%	40%	20%	
Islamic world history (1st exam 2003)	Four short structured questions	Three extended response questions	Islamic historical study 1,200–1,500 words	
	1 hr	2 hrs	25 hrs	
	25%	50%	25%	
ITGS (1st exam 2004)	Four short answer questions	Three structured answer questions	Portfolio Three pieces of work 800–1,000 words	Project Log book, product and report
	1 hr	2 hrs	20 hrs	20 hrs
	25%	35%	20%	20%

2 Facts and fables about economics and business

The special relationship between business and economics courses is interpreted in different ways by different centres. Some schools offer only one of the courses, others offer one course at HL and the other at SL. I recently taught both courses at HL to the same students in Argentina in order to meet national requirements. Before deciding on what your school will offer, it is wise to conduct a survey amongst students and parents first (as stressed forcefully in the case studies of this book). This section, as well as the next two, aims to help you disseminate factual information about the courses in such surveys.

Economics is a popular choice amongst the group 3 subjects on offer. The perception of administrators and students is that it is a rigorous 'academic' course. Therefore economics classes tend to get a large proportion of 'strong' students. Especially at SL, classes can be made up of students with 'strong' packages (such as physics and/or mathematics at HL). Many students, parents and administrators perceive business as less academically challenging than economics, and as a result weaker students are often encouraged to choose business. On a more positive note, many students and parents consider business as a more practical introduction to the realities of the commercial world. In international schools, many students choose to do business because their parents are in business, often as owners or executives. Certainly, successful economists acting as role models for their children are in short supply! The net effect is that IB students – just as students in national curricula – are continuing to move away from economics and towards business.

While the proportion of group 3 students taking economics between 1998 and 2002 fell from 19% to 16%, economics is still about three times bigger than business, so economics is still going to be the big player for a little while to come. For those familiar with the Boston Matrix, economics is the 'cash cow' and business the 'problem child'!

From an educational point of view, economics is easier to teach and assess. The course is more content-driven and fairly prescriptive, which allows teachers to teach towards the examination. It is certainly much more difficult to 'spot' an examination question in business than in economics. This suggests that it may be meaningless to compare the subjects in terms of academic difficulty, a view supported by the similar grade distributions. In May 2002, business had a pass rate of 90% and 89% for HL and SL respectively, whereas economics had 88% at both levels. The numbers of students who achieve the top grades are also not significantly different: 9% at HL and SL business and 12% at HL and SL economics. Not only are grades similar, but the entry requirements for students are identical as well. Both are *ab initio* subjects (IB terminology for beginner subjects), so students do not need any previous experience (although it obviously helps). What they do need is numeric skills and an ability to express themselves in the language of instruction. They will need the confidence to discuss and evaluate a series of options. Analysis and interpretation are skills that will be developed over the duration of the course at both HL and SL.

This chapter now proceeds with separate accounts of the two subjects, followed by a common resources section.

3 Business and management

3.1 Resources

Resourcing the IB business courses should follow the same patterns as for other similar business courses. There are no textbooks specific to the DP. There are excellent textbooks that cover most of the ground (see section 5 below) but there is no one textbook that has all of the material needed. Most departments can choose between a multitude of national high school or even first year university textbooks. However, the variety can appear somewhat daunting to the students who prefer the comfort of the 'one book covers it all' approach.

Four elements need to be considered when choosing resources:

- curriculum content
- case study approach
- language
- internationalism.

In terms of the curriculum the DP is broadly similar to the British A-level courses and so a textbook such as Chambers' *Business Studies* will be sufficient in most cases.

The case study is an integral part of the IB business programme. It represents 40% (see figure 14.5) of the externally assessed marks. Therefore it is essential that the IB student has the ability to absorb and analyse a large body of information about a specific company and develop answers on a range of questions about that company.

Language is a key issue for many students in two ways. Firstly, although the IB is committed to producing examinations in Spanish and French, these may be translations from the English. Direct translations can have different interpretations. My Argentine students would regularly be confused by examination questions – not in terms of the content but simply with the language. For example, 'redundancy' was a term that lost its meaning in the translation in Argentine labour laws! The second area of concern is the range of terminology used in textbooks. This is particularly a problem in dealing with accounts when there are different methods of presenting the same accounts as well as different phrases to describe the same concept.

Teachers should use local or national examples and resources wherever possible to help the students understand the theoretical issues. At the same time, to meet the global and international emphasis of the course it is good to try to develop concepts from an international point of view. To give some examples: business organizational structures will include MNCs (TNCs) or joint ventures, marketing must have an international marketing section, corporate cultures take on a different meaning when you move beyond national boundaries, and of course a large part of the module 'the external environment' (see section 3.2) depends on the interaction of regional businesses and economies.

IT and its availability are important but not a prerequisite for this syllabus. However, judicious use of the material available can provide topical and fun lessons. There are some excellent sites on the internet such as www.bized.ac.uk. Although few are geared solely for the IB they can be extremely useful when trying to put matters into an international perspective.

Videos/DVDs can also become an important part of the course. There are numerous business programmes on TV and these can afford wonderful opportunities to reinforce or bolster differing points of view. Similarly, the written media (newspapers, magazines) can be a great support tool. See section 5 for specific items.

3.2 Curriculum for HL and SL

The HL syllabus comprises six modules:

- *Introduction to organizations* (types of organization, growth and evolution, organizational and ethical objectives, decision making, and management of change).
- *Accounts and finance* (final accounts, working capital, ratio analysis, sources and applications of funds, investment appraisal, budgets and cash flows, costs and costing, and break-even analysis).
- *Marketing* (the role of marketing, market research, the marketing mix, marketing theories, marketing plans and international marketing).
- *Human resources* (organizational structure and communication, motivation and leadership, human resource planning, conflict resolution, and corporate and organizational culture).
- *The external environment* (the legal, social, cultural, technological, ecological, economic and political environment).
- *Operations management* (production, new product development, production planning, quality and location of production).

The SL does not include the last module and the external environment is included – in a reduced form – in the first module. In addition, the remaining first four modules lose some elements, for example the accounts module has a reduced investment appraisal element in it. The result is that the SL syllabus is similar to the HL option with less of the more technical topics. The modular nature of the courses makes it possible to teach the two levels in the same class. The depth of teaching can be the same in the areas of overlap.

3.3 Assessment overview

Both the HL and SL business and management courses are externally assessed by two examination papers. They more or less follow the same format. The only major difference is that HL students have an extra section with additional information (and questions) in Paper 1 (the case study). In Paper 2 the HL students have slightly more time to produce their answers (about 40 minutes per question versus 30). Figure 14.5 shows the respective exam details, including the coursework components.

In the sections below, we will address each of the assessment components in turn.

3.4 External assessment: Paper 1 (the seen case study)

The case study material is presented to the students at least one month before their examination (the students will see the questions about it only at the time they sit the examination paper). In fact, the same case study is presented to HL and SL and both the May and November examinations. Since there is a lot of

Figure 14.5 Business assessment outline

	HL		
Exam	Context	Time	Content
Paper 1 40%	Seen case study	2 hours	Section A: up to four compulsory questions. Section B: one question to be answered from a choice of two.
Paper 2 35%	Data response	2 hrs 30	Four questions to be answered from a choice of six.
Coursework 25%	Business project	30 hrs	*Research proposal* (300 words) and a 1,800–2,000 word *report* on an ongoing business decision, taking place in a real world situation.

	SL		
Exam	Context	Time	Content
Paper 1 40%	Seen case study	1 hr 30	Four compulsory questions.
Paper 2 40%	Data response	1 hr 30	Three questions to be answered from a choice of five.
Coursework 20%	Written assignment	15 hrs	1,000–1,500 word written assignment on an ongoing business decision, taking place in a real world situation.

information to absorb in the case material, students – especially those for whom English (or French or Spanish) is not their native language – will appreciate this welcome innovation introduced in the current syllabus (previously, students saw the materials only at the time of the examination).

The material is normally presented in a short piece of approximately 300 words and including three or more sets of figures. It will include company history, current problems (there will be some!) and future options. The range of material is really quite wide and there are many possible areas of study that could be used. The only distinction between SL and HL is that the HL students have a wider range of questions and have an additional section B where they respond to extra information about the case only provided in the examination.

Departments will have different approaches to working through the case study material with their students. There is no set way, although the IBO recommends not more than four weeks' work on the case study. Even this may prove too much for many students, and they could become over-familiar and jaded by the time of the examination. As a minimum, it is a good idea to get an initial impression, work through a more detailed reading of the case study with reference to the syllabus modules and then leave time for students to come up with their own problems and solutions.

Section B (for HL students) seems to follow the pattern of the Paper 2 data response questions – perhaps with a little more detail and related specifically to the case study. The students will receive some new information during the examination and they will have to deal with this. One would expect technical questions such as critical path or decision trees to be favoured here, since section B deals with the part of the additional HL syllabus not covered in SL.

3.5 External assessment: Paper 2 (data response)

The data response questions are straightforward. They tend to fall into one of two categories – numerical or written. This is not to say that they are mutually exclusive; the IB does like to tack onto the end of a 'decision tree' question, say, a short qualitative point. Moreover, since the business and management programme is considered to be an integrated course, there is a degree of overlap in the questions set. It would therefore be foolish for students to revise only a limited number of topics and pin all their hopes on these coming up, and they should be warned against this. Also, the sheer breadth of the course means that any attempt to second-guess what will appear on Paper 2 is a risky strategy.

An interesting point to note is that for the first time for a while, the November 2002 (and May 2003) Paper 2 actually included questions set on real companies. Before this, the IB had relied on self-created circumstances. It may be too soon to say whether this is a new direction or just a one-off.

3.6 Judging the holistic assessment levels

The business and management examinations are marked in a holistic manner, which inevitably leaves room for interpretation with the marking. In my experience as a teacher and assistant examiner for the IBO, the IB recognizes three levels of response demanding increasing levels of sophistication, and if a student can recognize the required level it helps them to target the answer. As a guide, I would suggest the descriptors and examination question 'trigger' words for the three levels as outlined in figure 14.6.

To achieve a level 3 response, students would have to produce a level 1 and 2 response and then build on that by adding the evaluation or opinion. Note that pure rote learning, or use of pre-learned responses, can only achieve level 1 or 2 marks. For a response to qualify as a level 3 response, the student should produce a balanced and effective argument.

Figure 14.7 is a general guide as to how many marks each level gains. The 'total marks' displayed refers to the maximum marks allocated for (a part of) an examination question, so figure 14.7 suggests for instance that to gain at least 8 marks for a question worth 10 marks, the students should have demonstrated level 1 and 2 quality answers, and at least certain facets of a level 3 response. It also shows that questions worth 5 marks or less do not require level 3 responses.

Figure 14.6 Examination question key commands

Level	Descriptor	Exam 'trigger words'
Level 1	*Limited* understanding, knowledge and organization	*describe, list, outline, calculate*
Level 2	*Reasonable* understanding, knowledge and organization (analysis may be incomplete and/or contain errors or irrelevancies)	*analyse, explain, prepare, produce*
Level 3	*Thorough* understanding, knowledge and organization	*evaluate, justify, examine, discuss, assess*

Figure 14.7 Examination questions marks versus level

Level	Maximum marks for question							
	12	10	8	7	6	5–3	1–2	
3	9–12	8–10	7–8	6–7	5–6	–	–	marks awarded
2	5–8	4–7	3–6	3–5	3–4	3–5	–	marks awarded
1	0–4	0–3	0–2	0–2	0–2	0–2	0–2	marks awarded

3.7 Internal assessment

HL students have to produce a business project, which comprises two parts: the *research proposal* and the *business report*.

The *research proposal* is a 200–300 word summary of the process. This is really only a necessary logistical exercise. I begin and finish off the project with this but during the times in between I let the students get on with the business report.

The research proposal comprises four elements, outlined in figure 14.8.

As an initial exercise, I get my students to create a presentation to the rest of the class outlining these points. We keep records of this and this provides a basis for the final proposal that is attached to the business report.

The *business report* is a 1,800–2,000 word report on an ongoing business decision, taking place in a real world situation. For example 'Should company X redesign the layout of their office space by introducing open plan and desk sharing?' The report may also be written as a research issue involving the company. For example, 'How important is the layout of the office space for company Y?'

The student is expected to use a standard business report-writing format as seen in the subject IA guide. They must apply a variety of concepts covered in the course in order to provide a recommendation to the business about their decision or research. There are many possibilities for the student to choose from but given the relatively low word limit they should seek to restrict themselves to three or four concepts at the most. In addition, a student should try to combine numerical/technical ideas with more abstract or theoretical notions. In the above example, the student may wish to consider the following concepts:

- motivational theory
- communication theory
- organization of production
- budgeting.

Of course, there are many other possibilities but the student should be wary of choosing either too ambitious a concept or one that is too simplistic. For

Figure 14.8 Elements of the IA research proposal

IB term	My interpretation
The research question	What is the student going to do?
The theoretical framework	Why is the issue so important?
Methodology	How will the student do what they said they would?
The action plan	When will the student do what they said they would?

instance, many students would do well to avoid *SWOT* or *PEST/SLEPT* analyses as these are too often used inappropriately and send a signal to the examiner that the coursework has been dealt with superficially.

Turning now to the coursework for SL, we note that SL students have to produce a less taxing written assignment of 1,000–1,500 words based on the same concept of a real, current business problem.

There are two differences between the HL business project and the SL written assignment. Firstly, the SL student does not have to do the research proposal. Secondly, they have fewer words to complete their task. Otherwise, the pieces of coursework are similar and can be treated as such. In fact, I always ask my SL students to do the same as the HL students and start the process off with a presentation based on a research proposal. As a means of focusing their minds, this works well.

An important issue that should be dealt with is the timing of the internal assessment. Obviously, the students cannot make a start on the job until they have covered sufficient material. Leaving it too late also creates problems, especially if we bear in mind that the student will have other deadlines and commitments outside the business classroom. Assuming we have a 35-week timetable per year and that we are teaching the course over two years then I would begin the work around week 25 in the first year. This has the advantage that the student can start the process and use the long holiday between years 1 and 2 to do the research and collect their data. I would ask students to hand in their final draft after 10 weeks of the second year.

How much guidance should a teacher give? Definitely more than for a typical piece of class work, but very few teachers will give as much guidance as they do for the extended essay (for which 3 hours' contact time is considered reasonable). The IBO does not encourage the student to produce endless drafts of work in progress, but I do discuss with the student on a regular basis how far they have got.

3.8 Moderation

This should be straightforward. The marking criteria are easy to follow and the IBO does have an internal assessment booklet with exemplars for the centres to use. One of the few areas of concern is the word limit, which is not specifically mentioned in the marking criteria, and is really a bit too tight. So how much leeway should be given to the students is a question that departments need to address. I work on a basis of 10% more than the upper limit but even at that extended limit, students are pushed to squeeze in an excellent report/assignment. Needless to say, though, you follow my methods at your own peril!

3.9 The extended essay

Students like to do extended essays in business and management. This popularity can create problems for a department as it is likely to become overloaded relative to other subject departments. Issues that need to be considered could therefore include the following:

• Selection of students – the extended essay is popular in this subject so departments may need to set policies to decide which candidates to accept.

- Timing – when to do the extended essay, keeping in mind other DP deadlines.
- Choice of topic – making sure that the topic is appropriate for the assessment criteria.
- Writing style – stress that the business extended essay is very different from a business report!

It is worth while elaborating on the last point, which is a particular problem for business and will only become more pronounced in view of the subject's increasing popularity. A look at the subject-specific assessment criteria will show that the main problem is getting the student to treat the extended essay *differently* from their business coursework. The current business-specific extended essay assessment criteria are very similar to the previous set used for internal assessment in business. For example, 25% of the marks are related to a 'decision making framework', an assessment criterion shared by the essay and the coursework. Many students then take this similarity further and produce an extended essay that reads rather like a business report. To compound this problem, students writing a business extended essay often want to use the same company for both pieces of work. The IBO allows this as long as the student answers two identifiably different questions using separate sets of data. However, the student who is keen to economize on effort too easily falls into the trap of using the same style to answer each question.

3.10 Future developments

Business and management is just about to begin its next curriculum review. Compared with economics there is more potential for change within the business programme. In some ways the course reflects the changing fashions of management theory. For example, management of change (a popular idea in the 1990s) now seems to have had its moment in the sun. Also, in recent examinations there seems to have been more emphasis on general 'economic' issues and the use of real world examples. Whether these trends will continue is harder to predict. Whatever the changes, these will not have an impact until 2005 at the earliest.

4 Economics

4.1 Resources

Textbooks will be the mainstay of any classroom resource and here again there is a multitude of fine books targeted at the high school market. There is an IB specific textbook produced by an ex deputy chief examiner (Glanville, see section 5.2) which strictly adheres to the syllabus and is therefore of interest.

Perhaps the key to choosing a textbook is to consider how much content is devoted to development issues. If this is limited then a textbook specifically devoted to development economics will be important. A good example is the Australian textbook *Economic Development* by Michael P. Todaro (see section 5.2).

One way of bridging the gap between national-based textbooks and development issues is to use such excellent sites such as www.bized.ac.uk or http://hdr.undp.org

With the introduction of the portfolio coursework, students and staff should be familiar with the process of following economic events in the media. Once again, there is a variety of possible sources for inspiration. Section 5 of this chapter has more details.

4.2 Curriculum for HL and SL

The HL course comprises five modules:

- *Introduction to economics* – foundation of economics, definitions of growth and development, scarcity, choice, rationing systems.
- *Microeconomics* – demand, supply and elasticity, the theory of the firm, market failure.
- *Macroeconomics* – national income, introduction to development, macro-economic models, demand side and supply side policies, unemployment and inflation, distribution of income.
- *International issues* – reasons for trade, protectionism, economic integration, WTO, balance of payments, exchange rates, balance of payments problems, terms of trade.
- *Development economics* – sources of economic growth and development, consequences of growth, barriers to growth and/or development, growth and development strategies, evaluation of growth and development strategies.

The SL course is not that much different from the HL course. Students do cover the five modules listed above with a few minor differences, particularly in the second module (microeconomics), which is shortened. On the whole, the difference in the course is one of depth and content rather than skills: whilst an HL student may spend two months going through the different theoretical market structures, the SL students would really only gloss over this material. Similarly, whilst the HL student may discuss the national income determination model, the SL student would only briefly touch upon this.

In August 2003, a new economics syllabus was introduced. The content has not have changed much. It is more a case of rearranging the existing concepts into a more practical manner. For example, it is noticeable that 'development' is being given even more emphasis; in some ways, the IBO is reacting to the good practice of many economics teachers who already introduce this concept early and refer to it continually as the course progresses. The IBO is acknowledging this fact by explicitly highlighting this in the new syllabus.

4.3 Assessment overview

Figure 14.9 outlines all the assessment components at HL and SL. The individual components are discussed one by one in the sections that follow.

4.4 External assessment

While the curriculum did not change much in the syllabus for first examinations in 2005, there were major changes in the way the course is assessed. An old favourite – the multiple-choice examination – was removed, because of its failure to provide suitable questions on the development section of the course.

Figure 14.9 Economics assessment outline

	HL		
Exam	Context	Time	Content
Paper 1 20%	Extended response	1 hr	One (two-part) essay question from a choice of four
Paper 2 20%	Short answer	1 hr	Three questions from a choice of six
Paper 3 40%	Data response	2 hrs	Three questions from a choice of five
Coursework 20%	Portfolio	20 hrs	Four commentaries of between 650 and 750 words

	SL		
Exam	Context	Time	Content
Paper 1 25%	Extended response	1 hr	One (two-part) essay question from a choice of four
Paper 2 50%	Data response	2 hrs	Three questions from a choice of five
Coursework 25%	Portfolio	20 hrs	Four commentaries of between 650 and 750 words

The removal of multiple-choice questions was a contentious issue, with the IBO rather than teachers calling for a change. Dropping the multiple-choice paper, however, has made it easier to rearrange the examinations to separate the essay and data response papers. What is left is an abbreviated set of examinations that will be easier to administer. The administration is further facilitated by the fact that the assessment criteria for Papers 1 and 2 for the HL are the same.

Paper 1 – extended response

Paper 1 comprises four questions (from which the students must choose one) taken from all parts of the syllabus, both for HL and SL. The paper follows the same format (often even the same questions) for HL and SL. The questions are set in two parts, the first part typically determining knowledge, the second part typically testing the student's ability to apply this knowledge, often in another field of economics. For example, the first part of a question may deal with an issue such as market failure whilst the second part asks the student to apply this knowledge in the context of a development issue. Development economics is part of many questions. The two-part structure of the questions typically ensures that every module of the syllabus features in at least one of the questions. The fair (and predictable) choice of questions and the amount of time available make this a relatively straightforward examination.

Paper 2 (HL) – short answer questions

These questions are for HL only. They come from the areas of the syllabus that deal with technical questions. The students are asked to recall their theory and apply the knowledge in a limited (20 minutes) manner. The questions are content-driven and examination preparation should be relatively straight-forward for experienced economics teachers.

Paper 3 (HL) and Paper 2 (SL) – data response

These papers are designed to test the students' ability to respond to a given set of information, both in written and in statistical format. The examinations are set on average two years in advance. Consequently the information may have been topical at the time of writing but by examination time it may have become an issue that will have been covered (with a bit of luck) by teachers in their lessons. The questions are not as content driven as for Paper 2 (HL) since they require a base knowledge level that can be applied to a real situation.

It is still straightforward examination preparation for experienced teachers, although students tend to find this the most difficult paper.

4.5 Internal assessment

The internal assessment has also been modified. The number of commentaries has been reduced but the word limit for each has been increased. Also, the oral component has been removed. The concept (of coursework) is not in question; the IBO still believes in asking the students to build up a portfolio of commentaries on media articles during their course. This process begins in the first year of the course and continues into the second. It is expected to be an integral part of the course, making up for the lost immediacy resulting from setting the examinations in advance. The HL portfolio is a smaller proportion of the final grade – 20% as opposed to 25% for the SL.

Both HL and SL students have to complete four commentaries of between 650 and 750 words. There is no difference between an HL and an SL response. Each has to show that the student can absorb economic knowledge and apply their theory to a given situation. Typical articles to base the commentary on could be any of the following:

- 'Banana war leaves the Caribbean a casualty' (*The Observer*, UK, 24/11/02)
- 'PM confident of better times ahead' (*The Straits Times*, Singapore 09/08/03)
- 'Las privatizadas ganaron $ 3171 millones' (*La Nación*, Argentina, 08/08/03)

The trick is to choose an appropriate article or cartoon (although I have yet to see a student try the latter): one that is not too long, or too technical, or too shallow. Students do have to be steered away from choosing articles based on stock prices or other 'sexy' topics that have limited economics content in terms of the syllabus.

A key issue will be when to introduce the portfolio coursework: too early and the student may not have covered the right material; too late and there may well be a rush towards the end. Also, the IBO does make it clear that the portfolio should be an integral part of the course to be run as part of the overall programme. It is not permissible to wait until the very last few weeks and produce four articles one after the other. In my experience, I prefer to wait until the student has completed module 1 and then start the process, beginning with two practice pieces. I treat them the same as the rest and they stay in the portfolio. When it comes to choosing the final four articles to be handed in, the student can then choose the best four out of six (which may not necessarily be the last four).

The portfolios are marked towards the end of the course. The assessment criteria are clear and uncontroversial. The marking should take into account the ability of the student to synthesize information and produce a balanced understanding of economic issues. The portfolio itself is treated as a complete piece and although each commentary does not receive an individual grade, failure by a student to meet any of the assessment criteria in one or more of the individual articles will harm the student's overall mark. Of course, the reality for most schools is that each individual commentary is an important indicator of the student's ability, and they will therefore be used for internal school assessment. As long as the internal school marks and the final overall IB mark are kept separate, there should be no problem employing dual grading practices.

As a result of the very recent set of changes, the marking no longer takes into account natural progression. Failure to meet some assessment criteria in just one piece implies a reduction in the grade awarded to the whole portfolio. This is a shame, as it seems a step backwards from an educational point of view.

A final point may be that one of the major changes as a result of the last curriculum review is that the IBO no longer requires the student to be assessed orally. This is a sad but understandable development. Given the difficulties of moderating unsubstantiated oral contributions, the IBO has chosen to remove the issue from the current assessment structure. However, either in the form of class discussion or presentation, I feel that oral assessment is still a valid educational exercise and I will continue to use the procedure as part of my normal classroom activities.

Overall, experienced teachers will have few problems teaching the portfolio, as the concept of a commentary as well as the tone of the assessment criteria are commonplace in many national curricula.

4.6 Moderation

This should be straightforward as the marking criteria are easy to follow and the IBO does have an internal assessment booklet with exemplars for the centres to use. It will be interesting to see how students respond to the changes in format for the internal assessment in the coming examination cohorts. However, from a moderation point of view these changes should not cause any heartache – and indeed the removal of the oral component will make the job easier for centres.

4.7 Teaching and organizing the course

The IBO gives a relatively free hand to individual departments as how to run the course. As long as the syllabus is covered, questions of timing and delivery are left up to the centres to decide. I have taught the whole material to one HL class as a single teacher; I have taught classes with HL and SL combined; and I have even taught in a 'one class two teachers' system (teacher 1 did modules 1, 2 and 5; teacher 2 did modules 3 and 4). No one way is best and it really depends on local circumstances. For example, if one teacher takes the microeconomics element of the course and the other does the macroeconomics during the same time period, this has the advantage of covering a lot of related material at the same time and with possibly different points of view. On the other hand, administratively and financially the 'one class two teachers' system may be a more difficult option.

It is pleasing to see the IBO respond to good teaching practice in the latest economics curriculum review. By introducing the students to a taster of the central issue of development issues at the start of the course in module 1, the

IBO encourages weaving this module throughout the course. For example, if the teacher is taking a lesson on market failure then the destruction of natural habitats in Indonesia could be a way of applying the material.

The method or style of teaching the course will again vary depending on local circumstances. However, you need to make sure that you take note of the IBO global perspective. Also, excessive note-taking and rote learning will fail to give the student the necessary breadth of opinion that is needed in the final examination. Naturally, use of past questions and examination material will still help the student gauge what is to be expected in the final examination. Economics papers tend to be more standardized than their business counterparts, and students may well be able to pick up certain patterns more easily than their business colleagues.

4.8 The extended essay

An economics extended essay is a popular option. However, popularity can create problems of overwork for the economics teacher. I am adamant that a teacher should not take on more than is recommended (five students) by the IBO. Having taken nine students in one session, I know that more does not mean better.

The examiners seem to expect standard formulaic responses, and a thorough read of the examiners' report and the IB extended essay documentation provides huge dividends and will show the correct approach to take.

The issues that need to be considered are broadly similar to those facing the business teacher. However, perhaps because economics students are trained to write essays they do not fall into the trap discussed earlier for business students, and style tends not to be a problem here. To repeat the remaining points (identical to those for business), set department policies for:

- selection of students – the extended essay is popular in this subject so departments may need to set policies to decide which candidates to accept
- timing – when to do the extended essay, keeping in mind other DP deadlines
- choice of topic – making sure that the topic is appropriate for the assessment criteria.

4.9 Future developments

At the time of writing, the IB economics team have just gone through the latest review process. The first examination cohort using the new syllabus started in August 2003 (and take their examination in May 2005). The latest review process is now complete and we should not expect to see any further changes until 2008, as part of the next cycle.

5 Resources for business and economics

In this section, I list textbooks that I have found useful in one way or another, separately for business and economics. This is followed by a list of useful internet sites.

5.1 **Business textbooks**

There is no one book that covers the whole DP business and management syllabus but the pick of the bunch would appear to be as listed here:

Chambers, Ian (ed.) (1999) *Business Studies*, 2nd edition, Causeway Press Ltd. I think this is the textbook that best suits the DP. The majority of the course is covered, the layout is good and interesting, and although it is a British textbook it does consider business in a international context.

Jewell, Bruce (2000) *An Integrated Approach to Business Studies*, 4th edition, Pearson Longman.
Similar to Chambers except a little more terse. Pretty good value.

Marcousé, Ian *et al* (1999) *Business Studies*, Hodder and Stoughton.
The list of authors reads like a list of top examiners. As you would expect, very comprehensive and full of ideas … and there is a teacher's workbook.

A variety of other general textbooks have proved useful at times:

Dyer, David *et al* (2000) *Business Studies for AS*, Cambridge University Press.
A book designed for AS-level business and so a bit lacking in depth even for SL. Otherwise a fair choice.

Dyer, David and Simpson, Peter (2001) *Business Strategy for A2*, Cambridge University Press.
A book written for A-level students, which focuses on the formulation and review of business strategies. The text is supported by a range of case studies based on real-world business strategies.

Dyson, J. R. (1997) *Accounting for Non-Accounting Students*, 4th edition, M and E Pitman Publishing.
For a non-accountant like myself, this was a godsend. However, be wary about using too much of it as it is for accounting students in further education!

Hodgets, Richard and Luthans, Fred (1991) *International Management*, McGraw Hill.
There are newer versions of this book and related ones but this is a good reference book for the teacher.

Marcousé, Ian (1998) *Business Calculations and Statistics*, Longman.
Great little book for those unsure about moving averages and the like. Good teacher reference.

Marcousé, Ian and Lines, David (1997) *Business Case Studies*, 2nd edition, Longman.
Excellent variety, if a little dated by now – and, oh yes, British.

Myddleton, David (1992) *Accounting and Financial Decisions*, Longman.
A bit dated but very thorough – a good teacher reference book.

Powell, John (1992) *Quantitative Decision Making*, Longman.
A bit dated but very thorough – a good teacher reference book.

Stimpson, Peter (2002) *Business Studies: AS Level and A Level*, Cambridge University Press.
This book covers both AS and A-Level and has been written specifically for an international audience. There are activities to test understanding, tasks to encourage exploration of issues highlighted, and case studies from a variety of countries and industries. Examination practice questions are also included.

Wall, Nancy *et al* (2000) *The Complete A–Z Business Studies*, 2nd edition, Hodder and Stoughton.
An excellent business dictionary. A really good buy, especially with ESOL students in mind.

It seems that every time I go into a bookstore there are hundreds more guru guides to be the best manager, the star, the ace, and what not. However, careful use of some of the big names such as Tom Peters or Peter Druckner can be rewarding. An interesting and useful resource that takes a different point of view to the guru approach of business consultancy firms is a TV programme in the 'Dangerous Company' series (BBC), which looked at the effects that tapping into the latest fashions put forward by management consultants such as McKinsey had on the Cadbury-Schweppes company.

There are too many books to list here but as an example when I have taught 'corporate culture' I have used the following two books with great effect as they are fun – and accessible.

Handy, Charles (1995) *The Gods of Management*, Oxford University Press.

Trompenaar, Fons (1997) *Riding the Waves of Culture*, McGraw Hill.

5.2 Economics textbooks

For standard classroom use, being British I have relied on A-level textbooks from the UK but there are a variety of non-British texts that cover the same ground. However, from my point of view the following has proved to be the best:

Anderton, Alain (2001) *Economics*, 3rd edition, Causeway.
Of all the British A-level textbooks this is my favourite; it is well designed and quite detailed, with a better than normal amount on international and development economics.

These have also proved invaluable at times too:

Begg, D., Fischer, S. and Dornbusch, R. (2000) *Economics*, 6th edition, McGraw-Hill Education.
A standard textbook – perhaps a little too complex for the DP but a useful reference.

Glanville, Alan (2003) *Economics From a Global Perspective*, 2nd edition, Alan Glanville.
A great idea and the student (and teacher!) in search of the 'all in one' book will love this one. It is written by an ex deputy chief examiner in economics for the IB, and so religiously follows the (new) syllabus. No thrills, but a good safe bet. Caters for both HL and SL. This is a brand-new edition with some excellent ideas such as great lists of useful websites.

Maunder, Peter *et al* (2000) *Economics Explained*, 3rd edition, Collins Educational.
A standard A-level textbook.

Ransom, David (2001) *The No Nonsense Guide to Fair Trade*, Verso.
One of a series from *The New Internationalist* (others include 'Globalisation' for instance), so a little one-sided but a good source. Excellent value with figures and other stimulus material. There are also BBC videos on development such as

'Bananas Unpeeled' which can be used together with this book.

Sloman, John (2002) *Economics*, 5th edition, Financial Times/Pearson Educational Books.
Pitched a little bit higher than DP (first year undergraduate) but this is very thorough and a useful reference. A bonus here is that there is a linked set of PowerPoint presentations on the Bized website.

Sloman, John (2003) *Essentials of Economics*, 3rd edition, Pearson Educational Books.
A slimmed-down version of the previous book. A safer bet for the students, especially at SL.

Todaro, M. P. (2000) *Economic Development*, Longman.
The saving grace for development. Again pitched a little bit higher than is necessary but a useful reference.

Wall, Nancy *et al* (2000) *The Complete A–Z Economics and Business Studies*, 2nd edition, Hodder and Stoughton.
One of the many A–Z guides on the market. A good source for definitions, especially useful for ESOL students.

I have also used a variety of general economics books when dealing with various sections. A favourite, although I suspect it is now out of print, is:

Stewart, Michael (1991) *Keynes and After*, Penguin.
A very readable overview of Keynes, his theory and its impact on economic thought.

More up to date but just as readable is:

Smith, David (2003) *Free Lunch*, Profile Books.
A fresh and enjoyable look at economic theories.

There are a number of very accessible general economics books in the shops now. Probably the most popular author is Paul Krugman (*Return of the Accidental Theorist; Peddling Prosperity*, etc.) who seems to be like a modern-day Galbraith. Then there are Naomi Klein (*No Logo*) and Eric Schlosser (*Fast Food Nation*) with their fascinating and provocative views on the modern business practice that can provide excellent stimulus material. Of special mention is the video by John Pilger 'The New Rulers of the World', a brilliant attack on the leading institutions of our global village. David Shipman (*Globalisation*) provides the opposite point of view.

5.3 Useful websites

Note: all weblinks featured in this chapter can be accessed through our website www.dp-help.com

There are simply thousands of sites on the web that can be used by business/economics teachers. Those listed in figure 14.10 may be a useful starting point. I have used all of them at one time or another. For example, I do not think you can do better than the first site, Bized, which from its 'virtual economy' or 'Cameron's Balloon – a virtual factory' to its revision material and its web links is a fantastic way into discovering what there is out there.

Figure 14.10 Websites for business and economics

Name	Address
Bized	www.bized.ac.uk/
Advertising Standards Authority	www.asa.org.uk
Asian Development Bank	www.adb.org/default.asp
Business Review Weekly	http://brw.com.au/
Consumer Jungle	www.consumerjungle.org/
Economic Commission for LA and Caribbean	www.eclac.cl/default.asp?idioma=IN
Economic Statistics UK	www.nationalstatistics.gov.uk/
Great Ideas ...	www.swcollege.com/marketing/gitm/gitm.html
Keynes	www.jobsletter.org.nz/jbl04610.htm
Latin Focus	www.latin-focus.com/
Onepine	www.onepine.info
S-Cool	http://s-cool.co.uk/
The Economist	www.economist.com
The Times	www.thetimes100.co.uk/
Tutor2u	www.tutor2u.net/
UN Development Programme	http://hdr.undp.org/default.cfm
Woodgreen	http://test.woodgreen.oxon.sch.uk/

6 Information technology in a global society (ITGS)

The ITGS course (presently offered only at SL) incorporates the integrated study of information technology (IT) and the social and ethical issues connected to it. Throughout the course and through the internal and external assessments, students are invited to examine, analyse and evaluate the local and global impacts of IT on our society.

Depending on the school's size, student population and interest, schools could offer either ITGS or computer science or both. Computer science tends to attract students who enjoy programming and have a higher degree of mathematical skills, whereas ITGS attracts students who have an affinity for the typical group 3 issues and skills.

The ITGS subject guide has recently been changed for first examinations in 2004. Both in terms of content and format, it now offers a more integrated approach. Some changes to the internal and external assessments have also been made. The comments offered in this section are based on the recent guide.

6.1 Requirements

It is expected that students have had some previous experience with using a variety of application software packages. Students who have taken an IT course in their pre-DP years will have a better understanding of the various IT systems and how they function. The IBO's Middle Years Programme (MYP) technology programme, for instance, presents a good basis for further study in ITGS. Section 6.7 offers suggestions on how best to assist students with minimal IT experience or with gaps in their skills.

6.2 Course outline

The ITGS subject guide incorporates three sections (see figure 14.11), which are covered simultaneously in an integrated approach. Section 1 examines the social and ethical issues related to a variety of IT systems (listed in Section 2) as they have an impact on specific societal areas (listed in Section 3). There is no prescribed order of and within the sections: teachers decide what they think works best.

Figure 14.11 ITGS course outline

Section	Details
Section 1 Social and ethical issues	Reliability, integrity, security, privacy and anonymity, authenticity, intellectual property, equality of access, control, globalization and diversity, policy and standards, and people and machines
Section 2 IT systems in a social context	• Hardware and networks: systems fundamentals • Applications: software fundamentals, databases and spreadsheets, word processing, desktop publishing, images, sound and presentations, modelling and simulations, tutorials, training and wizards (assistants) • Communications systems: the internet, and personal and public communications • Integrated systems: robotics, artificial intelligence and expert systems
Section 3 Areas of impact	**Part A:** Business and employment (compulsory area of study) **Part B:** Choose three of the following five areas: education; health; arts, entertainment and leisure; science and the environment; politics and government (but note that students are examined on only two areas – see figure 14.12.

6.3 Assessment overview

The assessment objectives may be summarized as follows (for the original text, see the *ITGS Curriculum Guide* for first examinations in 2004).

1. *External assessment:* demonstrate *knowledge* and *understanding* of, and the ability to *critically examine, analyse,* and *evaluate* the social and ethical impact and implications of IT systems and developments, at the local, national and global levels.
2. *Portfolio:* analyse and evaluate relevant examples of the global impact of IT in a portfolio of individually researched studies.
3. *Project:* design and apply IT solutions to a problem set in a social context through a project.
4. *Assessed throughout* (in internal and external assessments): express ideas clearly and coherently with supporting arguments and examples.

The overall assessment structure for the SL course is displayed in figure 14.12.

We proceed now with a discussion of the individual assessment components.

Figure 14.12 ITGS assessment outline

External	**Paper 1** *Short answer questions* on Sections 1 and 2 of the syllabus 25%	1 hr	Four compulsory questions based on scenarios and/or information in some form (text, table, graphic or a chart), with subsections requiring short answer responses. A specimen Paper 1 (exam and mark scheme) is available.
	Paper 2 *Structured questions,* integrated approach of all three sections of the syllabus with a focus on Section 3 35%	2 hrs	*Part A:* One compulsory question focused on business and employment (syllabus Section 3, part A, see figure 14.11) with subsections involving both short answer and extended response questions. *Part B:* Five questions focused on the other five areas of impact (syllabus Section 3, part B, see figure 14.11) with subsections involving both short answer and extended response. Candidates must choose two of the five questions in this section (although they study three areas from part B throughout the two-year period). A specimen Paper 2 (exam and mark scheme) is available.
Internal	**Portfolio** 20%	20 hrs	Three pieces of work of 800–1,000 words each, based on three different areas of impact.
	Project 20%	20 hrs	Log book, product, and a 2,000–2,500-word report.

6.4 External assessment

For both papers, it is very important that students are familiar with the 'Glossary of command terms' (or key terms), which can be found in the back of the ITGS subject guide. To give an idea, some of these terms are: *outline, identify, describe, explain* and *discuss.* Other key terms may also be used to ask candidates to present an answer in a specific way. Each 'key term' defined in the glossary requires a different level of response. For example, having to *outline* an answer does not require the same depth of response as a *discussion* would. Students will be expected to construct their answers in an integrated way, using all three sections of the syllabus in their answers. Critical thinking, analysis, organization and supporting arguments and examples are expected in the responses.

6.5 Internal assessment: the portfolio

The portfolio consists of three research assignments, which count for 20% of the overall assessment. Each of the portfolio pieces focuses on a different news item, which the candidate selects. Teachers can help by directing them to appropriate sources. The news item could be taken from any published source (newspaper, journal, the internet) but it must be *recent* (published no earlier than six months before the student started the ITGS course). For each portfolio piece, the news item must focus on an IT issue related to a different area of impact: three different areas of impact (out of the five mentioned in figure 14.11) to be covered in total, one per portfolio piece. Each portfolio piece should then expand on the news item, and explore in depth how the IT issue affects that one specific area of impact. Students must conduct additional research in order to provide supporting arguments for the topic of the portfolio piece. At least three additional resources, other than the news item, are recommended as supporting research in the syllabus. More thoroughly researched portfolio pieces use between eight and ten resources.

To give an idea of suitable portfolio topics, we print a list of titles here (the first three of which are suggested by the IBO, and the latter three by my students).

- E-voting: what are the issues?
- Workers, use and abuse of company email
- The effects of virtual reality games on children
- Can electronic waste be eliminated?
- Is a techno-office a healthy and safe environment?
- Can robotics improve surgery in the medical field?

The first three IBO portfolio topics listed above, along with the evaluator's comments, are provided in the *ITGS Teacher Support Materials*, which can be ordered from the IBO.

It is very important to guide students through the selection of an appropriate portfolio topic. Topics that are too broad in nature usually achieve lower marks than more specific topics. Teachers should practise with students how to analyse an article for appropriateness, identify an issue from the article, and ensure that a specific area of impact is addressed. A good way of doing this is to introduce new topics in class using news articles. Class discussion is an integral part of the process as well. Based on my personal experience, I would recommend introducing a portfolio piece after studying an area of impact. This gives students the basis upon which to build a well-developed piece.

To assist students throughout the entire process, I have them submit an outline of their portfolio piece, based on the criteria headings, with point-form notes written under each criterion. The criteria headings are:

Criterion A – Presentation of the issue
Criterion B – The IT background of the issue
Criterion C – The impact of the issue
Criterion D – Solutions to problems arising from the issue
Criterion E – Selection and use of sources.

There is a sixth criterion, which is not included as a separate criteria heading in the portfolio piece. Criterion F – Expression of ideas relevant to the social issue – is an evaluation by the teacher of the student's ability to express ideas coherently with arguments and examples throughout the portfolio piece.

Having students submit an outline gives me the opportunity to examine the portfolio issue as well as some of the main thoughts or ideas, and to ensure that appropriate resources are being used. Once I have approved their topic, I ask students to submit a first draft of the portfolio piece. I provide feedback in the form of general comments and questions which students can use to improve their draft. The resulting final copy is then submitted for formal evaluation.

To avoid plagiarism, teachers should train students to cite references properly, both in the body of the portfolio piece and in the bibliography. A useful website for students to create properly formated bibliographies is www.easybib.com. In order to check that students have cited their sources correctly, the IBO recommends that you submit a soft copy of the students' papers to http://turnitin.com, which will analyse the document for plagiarism. There is a small fee involved, but it is worth it. You could also run suspect sentences quickly through the Google search engine at www.google.com.

When providing the overall assessment for the portfolio, the levels of achievement of the portfolios *are not averaged together*. Instead, for each portfolio piece the teacher determines the achievement level for each criterion (based on the descriptions provided in the ITGS guide), and then awards an overall mark for that criterion that is *most consistent* with the mark for each of the three pieces. For example, say the student's first portfolio piece is awarded a level 2, whereas the other two pieces are awarded a level 4 for criterion A. The teacher would then assign a level 4 final grade for criterion A, since that is the most consistent level of achievement for that criterion. A score of 2, 2, 4 would not necessarily mean an overall 2, however. In cases like this, or when there is no consistent level of achievement, the teacher must decide which level of achievement *best reflects* the student's overall capabilities, and justify this mark with supporting comments. This illustrates that it is important to guide the students through the portfolio so as to minimize inconsistent mark distributions. Teachers can access the Online Curriculum Centre (OCC) forums in order to discuss such assessment matters further. Once the overall mark for each criterion is established, these are then added together to total a grade out of 25. The IBO will then request some student samples for external moderation. In order to assist the external moderator with how the marks were determined, it is necessary for the teacher to write comments (in pencil) in the right-hand margin of the portfolio piece, that explain how that level was awarded. It is also very helpful for the moderator if you include an overall comment sheet (also for the project, discussed below) to justify your overall mark for each criterion.

It is very helpful to space out the portfolio pieces throughout the two-year period, but be careful not to leave everything for the second year, as the students will need to complete the ITGS project (discussed below) as well as other IB requirements such as the extended essay. I recommend completing two portfolio pieces in the second half of the first year and one portfolio piece in the second year, along with the project.

6.6 Internal assessment: the project

The project can gain a maximum of 35 marks, which are scaled to contribute 20% of the student's overall assessment. The project consists of a *product* (the IT solution the student creates, integrating several different IT skills or applications), a 2,000–2,500-word *report*, and a *log book*. Students are required to identify a 'real life' problem or need, set within a social context. There are various project ideas outlined in the IBO *ITGS Teacher Support Materials*. Additional examples of some projects undertaken by my students include:

- the creation of a university counselling website for the counsellor in order to keep students and parents better informed of university-related information
- the creation of a spreadsheet system for coaches to gather and analyse players' statistics, in order to identify areas for improvement
- the creation of a database system to help dive masters and marine biologists record and organize marine life data/information, used to help track population growth/decline.

Each one of these projects was generated through discussions conducted between the student and the *client* and/or *end users*, in order to identify a real life problem/need. The client is the person who is directly affected by this problem. For example: if a student discovers that the CAS coordinator is having difficulty tracking the CAS hours of the DP students effectively, the student will want to sit down with the CAS coordinator to find out what exactly his/her needs are. The CAS coordinator is then considered to be the client and the DP students are considered end users, as they could be the people who will use the system to record their hours.

There are many ways in which these problems or needs can be identified. One way is through classroom discussions, where examples of problems/needs are identified within the school setting. Students may then pursue one of those examples by further discussions with the people (client/end users) who are directly affected by this problem/need. Through students' day-to-day school experiences, personal interactions with family and friends, or their involvement in the outside community (sports, cultural clubs, personal interests), they may come across situations where the present system (paper-based or electronic) is inefficient or absent. The students are only limited by their imagination. I have even had students create systems for people with a problem/need in other countries.

Product (6 out of 35 marks)
Students are required to integrate a minimum of three different IT skills while creating the product (for example: using a scanner, using website development software, and using graphics editing software for creating a website). Since the projects students undertake can be very different in nature, the IT skills that students acquire will be varied. The outline in Section 2 of figure 14.11 gives some idea of the various IT skills that students could incorporate into the project; the subject guide description of Section 2 provides detailed information. Students are expected to undertake a challenging task that addresses a real problem, then design, create, test and implement the solution. Through the development of the product, the students will further their understanding of the impact the solution will have for their client and end users. As with portfolios, projects that are too simple or too complex for the students' skill level, usually achieve lower marks. A copy of the product must be submitted to the IBO for moderation. The product is worth 6 out of the total of 35 marks assigned to the project, and is evaluated based on its design, functionality and complexity.

Report (26 out of 35 marks)
The report is a document that describes the entire process, from start to finish, and must be written using the project criteria headings (Criterion G – Identifying the problem within a social context, Criterion H – Analysis and feasibility study, Criterion I – Planning the chosen IT solution, Criterion J – Testing and evaluating the solution, and Criterion K – Assessing the social

significance of the product). The report is worth 26 marks out of the total of 35 marks. At the end of each stage of the process, I have the students write a draft copy of that particular section of the report, while the process is still fresh in their minds. That way, the students are not faced with writing the entire report at the end of the process. It is important for students to use the log book (see below) as a basis for writing their reports. Constant referral to the assessment criteria listed above throughout the process and during the final stages is vital to produce a quality report. Visual evidence of the entire process must be included throughout the body of the report (by scanning in documents or sections of the log book, or by including screenshots of the product as it is being designed, created, tested and refined). The visual evidence included in the report must be referred to in the text, not just simply inserted.

Log book (3 out of 35 marks)
The log book is a very important document for the student. Not assessed in the previous curriculum guide, now it is awarded up to 3 marks, based on evidence recorded at each stage of the development process. The log book is a journal of the tasks undertaken, progress at each stage and the student's reactions throughout the entire process. Each entry must be dated and the organization of the log book must appear in chronological order. Assigning log book entries for homework and collecting log books on a regular basis will ensure that the teacher is aware of the student's progress and can identify and assist students with any difficulties they may be having.

Students should write everything related to the project in the log book. Visual evidence should also be included. Providing examples of sample log book pages from the *ITGS Teacher Support Materials* to the students will help ensure proper documentation. Students who choose to create an electronic log book usually produce a higher-quality report. Typically, log books are paper-based notebooks with handwritten entries and sketches, with screenshots and other evidence glued in. I would advise against digital log books because they do not generally contain the same depth and detail characteristics of the paper-based log books. In my experience, students who choose to create an electronic log book either do not spend enough time documenting the process, or spend too much time and energy scanning-in images and visual evidence and formating the document, instead of investing their energy on properly documenting the process and improving the quality of the report.

Teachers need to make sure that students have ample time in order to complete the entire process and the product. I introduce the project towards the end of the first year, so that students have time to find a 'real life' problem within either the school or the local community. We brainstorm in class possible real clients' and end users' problems/needs, which are set in a social context, and examine projects previous students have undertaken. While examining the projects, we discuss in class how the former students identified the need as well as the social context in which the project was set. Having students identify a real client will provide the necessary content, as well as assistance in the design, development and testing of the product, which is vital to the project and to producing a quality report. The concept of working closely with a client is an important one and simulates real world IT solution development.

When identifying a project, a variety of questions need to be addressed, so that the student can understand the full scope of the problem. Using the key questions outlined in the ITGS guide will help direct students towards an appropriate project. Some of the key questions to be considered are: 'What is the present system? How does it work? What are the limitations of the current system? What is the problem? Who will benefit from an IT solution? Has the need been determined through discussions with relevant people and end users?' (ITGS Guides)

In some cases, students like to choose projects they are interested in, which do not necessarily have a 'real need' or address a 'real problem'. They then try to find a need for the project. This, however, doesn't allow them to work through the project following the guidelines. It is important that the problem/need and client/end users are identified *first*, before any possible project solutions are discussed. The student cannot begin to create the actual product until the need has been identified, the problem has been analysed, and the feasibility of alternative IT solutions (two different approaches) have been considered. Once one of the solutions has been chosen, the student can begin the process of collecting content information, designing, creating, testing and evaluating the product.

During the main holidays between the first and second year of the DP, I have students outline three possible 'real life' problems with clients and end users, so that when they return at the beginning of the second year, they have some options from which to choose. Their options are reviewed and the most appropriate need (set in some specific social context) is chosen, for which a project proposal is submitted and approved by me before the next stage is undertaken. During the first half of the second year, the students complete the product and the entire process. They are then allotted ample time to revise their project report and hand it in for evaluation. This also gives me enough time to thoroughly evaluate the product, report and log book based on the assessment criteria before they are submitted to the IBO for moderation towards the end of March (for May examinations, or September for November examinations).

6.7 IT skills

The objective of this course is to integrate the concepts included in all three sections of the guide (social and ethical issues, IT systems in a social context, and areas of impact). It is not the intent of this course to cover the practical skills associated with IT systems; in fact, it is expected that students have had some previous experience with using a variety of application software packages such as those outlined in Section 2 of the syllabus (see figure 14.11). However, there are cases where students begin the course with some gaps in these skills. In order to help students bridge these gaps, IT skills can be developed automatically while teaching the syllabus. For example, students may be assigned a homework task to create electronic presentations based on networking concepts (Section 2) and their corresponding social and ethical issues (Section 1), with the focus on health (Section 3), and present their findings to the class. Such a homework assignment will give students the opportunity to develop their skills in using IT applications.

In the past, I have found that students are not fully conversant with the use of some standard IT systems, as those required in Section 2. However, it is important for them to have first-hand experience with using the various systems in different contexts in order to understand the related social and ethical issues, and to get a feeling for how the application is used in various situations. For example, having students create and manipulate databases, as well as use databases in various contexts (such as the school's electronic card catalogue system), will help to build a competent level of understanding of databases. Moreover, it lays the groundwork for understanding how businesses use databases and how the privacy of individuals can be invaded.

In order to provide students with resources to increase their level of IT competency, I have found Lawrenceville Press, www.lawrencevillepress.com, to be particularly useful for this purpose. The publisher offers texts and teacher resources based on MS-Office applications, as well as other application software packages. Students may have access to these texts when completing assignments so that they can independently further their level of competency with the particular software application.

Another resource is the Atomic Learning website (www.atomiclearning.com). Purchasing a site licence for your school will allow students, teachers and parents the opportunity to learn a wide variety of software packages. The website currently offers more than 3,000 tutorials, with regular updates and new tutorials. Subscribing to an online tutorial system allows for easier updating of resources, rather than relying on having to purchase textbooks of this nature every year.

It is also recommended that students be encouraged to further their IT skills development by building and incorporating IT systems throughout other DP courses. In the biology course, for example, they may be given opportunities to collect and analyse data. This could be done through the use of a spreadsheet or database. Students also have ample opportunities to incorporate electronic presentations into topics covered in various courses. Chapter 16 in this book, for instance, offers plenty of suggestions for the use of IT in mathematics courses. When working on the extended essay, the use of the internet for research purposes is vital for gathering information. Having students use the variety of research tools available will help to expand their knowledge of the internet.

6.8 The extended essay

The intent of the extended essay is to thoroughly research an appropriate ITGS research question and the related social and ethical issues and solutions. It is important that the general assessment criteria and the specific ITGS subject criteria are closely followed. Students are expected to be enthusiastically engaged in their research by thoroughly investigating both primary and secondary resources. ITGS extended essays that focus on the technological aspects of a topic, rather than have an ITGS orientation, tend to achieve low marks.

In my experience, students who have a keen interest in IT choose to undertake their extended essay in ITGS. Students must not use their extended essay as an extension of a portfolio piece and it cannot be related to the project in any way. Students who do not take ITGS may still choose ITGS for their extended essay. This is to be discouraged, however, because experience shows that non-ITGS students do not have the background experience in identifying social and ethical issues in IT.

6.9 Future developments

Higher Level (HL) will begin in August 2004 with first examinations in May 2006.

6.10 Resources

IBO (2002) *The ITGS Teacher Support Material: Internal Assessment August 2002*, IBO.

IBO (2002) *Information Technology in a Global Society (Curriculum Guide), for first examinations in 2004*, IBO.

IBO, *Group 3 ITGS Subject Report* (November and May sessions), IBO.

The *ITGS Subject Report*, published after the November and May sessions of each year, contains external examiner feedback on the type of responses the students have given for the internal and external assessments, and suggestions to instructors for future practice (such subject reports are provided for each DP subject). It is a very important reference, which can aid the teacher with anticipating any difficulties the students may encounter. Problems identified in all assessment components from the previous session and suggestions for further improvements are included in these reports.

The Online Curriculum Centre (OCC) is also an invaluable resource, where ITGS teachers can take part in the online discussion of any issues related to the ITGS course and the internal assessments. Teachers are encouraged to share and access resources, which are linked to specific topics in the ITGS guide. Access to the OCC is now free for IB schools. It is located at http://online.ibo.org. You can obtain your school's code, your user name and password from your DP coordinator (DPC).

A text that I have found to be quite comprehensive, covering most topics listed under Section 2, is *Computer Confluence* by George Beekman. The textbook incorporates the use of a CD-ROM with supporting materials for each chapter, as well as a website of resources for both students and faculty (www.computerconfluence.com). A variety of editions is offered by Prentice Hall/Pearson Education. One of the latest editions, *Computer Confluence, IT,* 5th edition, by George Beekman and Eugene Rathswohl, covers more information as it relates to business, which is a compulsory area of impact in Section 3 (see figure 14.11). There is a teacher's resource package as well, which can be ordered separately. The level of language in the text can be quite challenging at times for ESL students. So it is important to review with the students the information covered in each chapter, to ensure that they understand it.

One of the best textbooks for providing students with an overview of social and ethical issues is *Gift of Fire – Social, Legal, and Ethical Issues in Computing* by Sara Baase, which is published by Pearson Higher Education. It is also accompanied by a website www-rohan.sdsu.edu/faculty/giftfire.

In order for students to gain first-hand experience and a clearer understanding of the impact of IT on society, it is quite helpful to compile a varied list of resources upon which to draw. Some suggested resources are:

- computer ethics books (for high school students), which are made available to students from the library

- local and international paper-based newspapers
- IT magazines (*PC World*, *PC Magazine*, etc.)
- IT topic-related websites
- electronic newspapers and magazines
- electronic journals
- topic-related video clips
- topic-related movies
- scenarios and case studies based on current issues.

Utilizing community resources such as local companies, organizations and institutions will give students first-hand experience and a clearer understanding of how IT systems affect our society. For example, I have taken my students to a local hospital to see a demonstration of how virtual reality (VR) is used in helping to train doctors for very complex operations. Students were given the opportunity to actually use the VR system, in order for them to fully understand its capabilities and limitations. Social and ethical issues surrounding the use of VR in the medical field were discussed as a follow-up to the visit.

7 Psychology

7.1 Introduction

Within the Diploma Programme (DP), psychology is defined as the systematic study of behaviour and experience. The DP psychology course introduces candidates to a variety of topics within the discipline and aims to develop skills that will allow them to be well versed in psychology content, issues and evaluative commentary. While much of the content that a teacher includes in this course may be very similar to that of other national programmes, the IBO's course focuses on a holistic view of the subject and aims to integrate the topics. Additionally, students have the opportunity to specialize in some of the more current issues that affect the discipline of psychology. Exposure to various research methodologies, ethical issues, gender considerations and cultural factors helps to develop critical thinking so that candidates are better able to understand psychology as more than a set of seemingly disjointed bits of information.

One of the unique aspects of DP psychology as compared to A-level or AP psychology is the IBO's focus on psychological perspectives (also known as 'approaches' or 'schools of thought') as the core of the course, especially at Standard Level (SL). Other boards may have a unit about psychological perspectives, but none of them makes this the central and most heavily weighted component. The aim is to develop the student's ability to interpret a wide range of psychological issues from multiple points of view.

The options available for study represent a variety of specializations within the broader discipline of psychology. Students must choose one option at SL and two at Higher Level (HL). The options section of the syllabus is not designed to be a broad overview of all topics within psychology, but rather provides more opportunity for the focused, in-depth study referred to above.

The research methodology component of the course allows candidates the opportunity to learn the basic concepts of experimental research methodology and to design and then apply these concepts and skills in practical work. The HL course also includes a component on qualitative research methodology, including interviews, questionnaires/surveys, observations, content analysis, case studies and the concept of triangulation. This section is new to the DP as of the May 2003 examination session. It is seen as a step to make the DP psychology course more current, as much of the research that psychologists are now undertaking has some degree of qualitative data gathering and analysis.

There are no prerequisite courses for candidates taking DP psychology. While it might be beneficial for students to have some background in psychology prior to the course, it is generally accepted that most candidates will not have had any exposure to the discipline.

7.2 Course outline

An outline of the courses at HL and SL is shown in figure 14.13.

Figure 14.13 Psychology course outline

	Perspectives	Options	Research methodology	Internal assessment
SL	• Biological • Cognitive • Learning	Choose one • Comparative psychology • Cultural psychology • The psychology of dysfunctional behaviour • Health psychology • Lifespan psychology • Psychodynamic psychology • Social psychology	• Ethics • Quantitative research methods	Experimental study (simple)
HL	Additional perspective: • Humanistic	Choose two of list above	Additional: • Inferential statistics • Qualitative research methods	Experimental study (extended)

7.3 Distinction between HL and SL

The distinguishing characteristics between the HL and SL are found in four main areas:

1. Number of required perspectives
2. Research methodology
3. Number of options the student must study
4. Internal assessment (or the experimental study).

A unifying characteristic of the three required perspectives at SL is that they have historical foundations in experimental research methodology. While some psychologists within each perspective now also use some degree of qualitative research methodology, the experimental method was the method of choice early in each perspective's development. The HL course adds the humanistic perspective, to which qualitative research methods are more amenable. It is true that there have been attempts to experimentally validate concepts and theories of this perspective; however its foundation is in qualitative methods.

This difference in the focus on methodology also has an impact on the externally assessed component on research methodology. HL has an additional paper (Paper 3) that focuses solely on qualitative research methods. The experimental research method, both at SL and at HL, is assessed through the internal assessment (in the experimental study).

The options offered are identical for SL and HL, also at the examination level; the difference is simply that HL students study two while SL students study one.

7.4 Assessment outline

Figures 14.14 and 14.15 outline the assessment components at SL and HL respectively.

Figure 14.14 Psychology SL assessment outline

External assessment		Internal assessment
Paper 1	Paper 2	
Perspectives (3)	Option (1)	Quantitative research methodology
Short answer and extended response questions	Extended response question	Simple experimental study 1,000–1,500 words
2 hrs	1 hr	15 hrs
50%	30%	20%

Figure 14.15 Psychology HL assessment outline

External assessment			Internal assessment
Paper 1	Paper 2	Paper 3	
Perspectives (4)	Options (2)	Qualitative research methodology	Quantitative research methodology
Short answer and extended response questions	Extended response questions	Short answer questions	Experimental study 1,500–2,000 words
2 hrs	2 hrs	1 hr	25 hrs
30%	30%	20%	20%

7.5 Teaching and organization

Each perspectives section of the course is divided into four broad elements: development and cultural context, framework, methodologies, and applications. These four elements provide common threads across all of the perspectives and can form the basis of comparison across them, as illustrated on figure 14.16. The study of the *development and cultural context* gives the students an understanding

Figure 14.16 Perspectives and elements

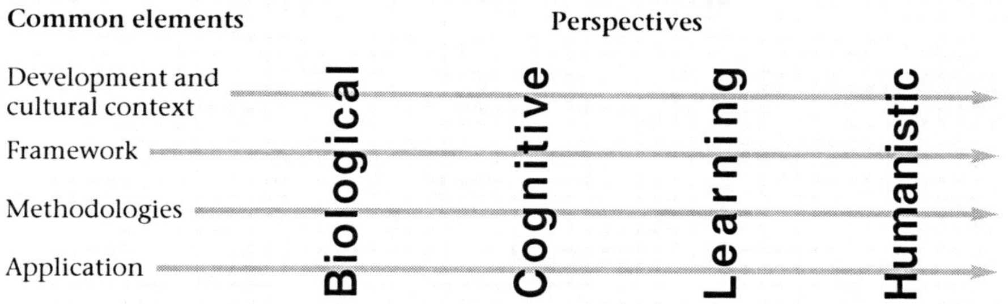

of how historical events and cultural norms of the region in which the perspective developed affected each. The *framework* includes common beliefs or assumptions about behaviour within each perspective, as well as theories and theorists who generally follow those common beliefs. Each perspective also has a foundation in the use of particular research *methodologies* appropriate for the study of their concepts and theories. Finally, students should be able to use the assumptions, concepts and theories to interpret a variety of issues, such as aggression, gender role development or education (*application*). Teachers are free to choose issues they feel are appropriate and are not bound to any particular application. Additional information on the structure of the syllabus and its relation to assessment are noted later in this section.

A special note here about the learning perspective, as this terminology may be new to some teachers. The previous version of the IB psychology course guide included the behavioural perspective, which was limited to traditional behaviourism and did not take into account more recent advances in the field. While the learning perspective has its roots in traditional behaviourism, it has been expanded beyond the simple environmental, stimulus–response model. It now includes the study of how biological factors (such as Seligman's concept of preparedness and Lorenz's imprinting) and cognitive factors (such as Tolman's latent learning and Bandura's observational learning) can affect behaviour. Traditional behaviourism does not offer good explanations for the influence these factors might have on learning.

There are seven options available in the DP psychology course as outlined in figure 14.13. SL students study one option while HL students study two. Each of these represents an area of study within the broad field of psychology. Within each option there are generally three major topics listed in the content column in the course guide and each topic has two or three subtopics. These subtopics are limited in scope to allow for more in-depth study. It should be noted once again that the 'suggestions for detailed study' in the right-hand column of the course guide are just examples devised to give teachers an indication of what could be used to cover the topics and subtopics listed in the content column on the left. Teachers are not required to teach these examples; they should tailor the content to match their needs.

The choice of which option(s) to cover is left to the teacher. Considerations such as teacher expertise and experience, availability of resources, areas of student interest and possible interconnection with other topics all come into play. I taught in an international setting with students who had lived all over the world. For my situation, doing the cultural psychology option was logical and interesting for my students, as they had personally experienced some of the issues within the option. The most popular options tend to be the psychology of dysfunctional behaviour, psychodynamic psychology and social psychology.

Quantitative (i.e. experimental) research methodology is included at both SL and HL. The course guide provides a listing of the topics with which students should be familiar. There is no formal external assessment of these topics; however, they are assessed through the experimental study done for the internal assessment. Students should fully understand these topics and be able to demonstrate this knowledge as they design, conduct and report on an experimental study. There are more details on internal assessment in section 7.8.

HL students are required to study qualitative research methods. The course guide outlines the major topics, including interviews, questionnaires and surveys, observations, content analysis, and case studies. With each of these methodologies, candidates should be able to explain each method and its use, compare various methodologies, and discuss their relative strengths and weaknesses. Additionally, the concept of triangulation (or the multi-method approach) is important. Section 7.11 lists some books that have been recommended by experienced teachers.

Teaching students about quantitative and qualitative methods can take on various formats. Some teachers like to begin the course with a brief introduction to the various methods. Then the concepts of each method are reinforced as students cover the other topics of the syllabus. For example, to learn more about behaviour, early learning theorists relied on the experimental method, some cognitive psychologists have used verbal protocols (or think-aloud protocols), and some biological psychologists have used the case study method. When teachers get to these points in the syllabus they could review the research methods used. This approach of introducing research methods early and then reviewing them throughout the rest of the course has been adopted by many DP psychology teachers.

A hands-on approach has also proved to be an effective way for students to learn not only what each method was about, but also to see it in action. I used to have my students do a series of 'quick studies' throughout the year in which they would take a topic (such as short-term memory capacity) and use 20 minutes of our class time to go out and gather data from students around the school. This type of exposure helped them not only to understand what to do when collecting data, but also (and possibly more importantly) what not to do. We discussed the problems they encountered and how to remedy them. The students felt very confident when the time came to do the internal assessment as they had some experience with data collection and analysis.

The order in which the different sections of the psychology course are taught varies among teachers around the world. Probably the most common order of instruction is to start with a short, general introduction on the history of psychology, then to cover the perspectives, research methods and internal assessment, and end with the options. Other teachers choose to start with the options, as the topics could grab their students' interest. More recently some teachers have decided to make the *application* element of the perspectives (as discussed above) the central issue of the course. For example, an issue such as gender identity or aggression could be generally introduced first, after which students learn about the perspectives throughout the course by learning how each deals with that issue. Student knowledge of each perspective comes from the application to a particular issue.

Teachers also have a choice of which order they teach the perspectives. Some teachers take a chronological approach following the timeline of when each perspective had the greatest following, for example, learning, cognitive, humanistic (HL only) and biological. Others may start with biological as they see the biological basis of our behaviour as being the most important. Each of these orders of delivery has been effective in its own right and the choice is purely up to the individual teacher.

7.6 Skills

In addition to the content that is included in the course outline, there are also many skills that students must develop throughout the course, since for most students this will be their first exposure to the systematic study of psychology.

The ability to critically evaluate psychological theories and studies is probably the most important skill in terms of the assessment and development of well-rounded students of psychology. The assessment descriptors outlined in the psychology guide specifically state that students will be assessed on their ability to evaluate issues by taking into account cultural, ethical, gender and methodological considerations, as appropriate. This is not to say that students have to use all of these considerations with every piece of evidence they provide, but rather that they should apply only those that are most appropriate. For example, Seligman's studies on learned helplessness used dogs as participants. Pain was inflicted on the animals. This raises ethical issues and, for some, the application of findings from studies using animals might be methodologically contentious. Additionally, students should be able to evaluate a theory and/or study by providing an alternative which holds a different belief or interpretation. For example, both Bowlby and Fromm challenged Freud's interpretation of Little Hans's behaviour.

Teachers might also have to teach students how to read a psychology resource, both a psychology textbook and primary source documentation. Exposing students to full-text, published research helps them to better understand the study and the implications of its results, and it informs them of the structure of a psychological write-up. In turn, the skills they pick up this way will assist them in doing their internal assessment.

7.7 External assessment

The external assessment for the DP psychology course takes the form of examinations based on short answer and extended response questions, as summarized in figures 14.14 and 14.15. Based on this format of assessment, there are some key skills in addition to detailed content knowledge that students need to develop in order to do well in the examinations, including 'unpacking the question' (explained below), structuring an essay, writing concisely, managing their examination time, and using evaluation techniques.

'Unpacking the question' refers to the students' ability to read, interpret and understand what the particular examination question asks them to do. Questions are set using specific terms from the course guide – found in the introduction and learning outcomes sections along with the content column in each part of the syllabus. The command terms found at the end of the course guide published by the IBO indicate how students are to use their knowledge and give them direction in answering the question appropriately. For example, there is a difference in the type of answer required by students if the command term is *compare* versus *identify*. Each of the possible terms to be used is defined and an example is given of a question using each term. Students should be given a copy of this section of the course guide so that they can familiarize themselves with the terms and what each requires. One way to teach this skill is to give students questions from past examinations and 'unpack' them, or to have students write their own questions based on the terms from the syllabus and the command terms. In either of these teaching strategies students could work individually, in small groups, or as a whole class.

Short answer questions are used on Paper 1 for both SL and HL and on the whole of Paper 3 (for HL only). Paper 1 assesses the perspectives for both SL and HL. At both levels, Paper 1 covers the biological, cognitive and learning perspectives; HL also includes the humanistic perspective. Section A of Paper 1 has short answer questions, one for each perspective, and all questions must be answered by the student. Students must therefore have a solid foundation in all of the required perspectives.

A key to success on the short answer questions in both section A of Paper 1 and all of Paper 3 is the candidate's ability to write an appropriate answer within the time limit, which calls for concise answers. Each question has mark allocations written next to it from which the student can infer the amount of writing necessary. Students should not spend inordinate amounts of time answering questions that are worth fewer marks than others. For all short answer questions the same recommendations apply: be concise, be accurate and budget your time.

Section B of Paper 1 and the whole of Paper 2 use extended response questions (or essays) for external assessment, one for each perspective. Both HL and SL students choose one question out of several questions for section B of Paper 1. HL students choose one from a list of four possible questions about the perspectives while SL students are given three from which to choose. Questions in this section might cover just one perspective or they may ask students to discuss more than one perspective. For example, there could be a question asking students to compare the methodologies used by the learning and biological perspectives.

Paper 2 is divided into seven sections, one for each of the options available in the course. Each option has three questions from which students choose one to answer. SL students select one option to write about, while HL students write about two options, corresponding to the one(s) they have studied. Teachers should remind students to choose only from the option(s) that they have studied. Sometimes students are attracted to a question from an option the teacher has not taught but this invariably leads to lower-scoring essays.

A special note should be made about SL Paper 2. In this paper, students answer only one question from one option, so a lot rides on that one essay. If students were to answer this question inaccurately or imprecisely it could have a negative impact on their final result, as this is their only chance to earn marks on this paper. HL Paper 2 has a bit more leeway as students answer two questions, so if they were to misunderstand one question, the second could still afford them some marks. This reliance on just one question for SL seems to be an unfortunate consequence of the structure of the paper and teachers should therefore help students avoid the most common pitfalls by teaching them some skills that are seen in very good essays, described below.

There are several characteristics commonly found in the best essays. First and foremost, the candidate must write a response that answers the question. This may seem an odd thing to say, but it is a problem that is prevalent and has been noted in many of the examiners' reports written after each examination session for the past few years. Sometimes students will write answers that are full of detailed psychological knowledge, but fail to specifically address the question as it is written. An example of such an error might be in response to a question about the current developments in psychodynamic psychology. If a student were to answer with an 'everything I know about Freud' response, they would not be specifically answering the question. The response may be full of accurate and valid points, but if it does not answer the question then it will attract very low marks. One tactic that helps students stay focused is to use the specific terms from the question throughout their essay. Using the example above, a student might write something like, 'Some of the current developments in psychodynamic psychology include ...' and then go on to describe and evaluate some of these current developments without relying completely on Freud.

Another common characteristic of good essays is the ability to use relevant description of specific studies and/or theories, including detailed evaluation. By linking the evaluative comments they make to the specific question, candidates are pointing out possible errors, confounding variables or alternative explanations that should be taken into account. Giving an alternative explanation shows depth of understanding beyond the simplistic memorization of studies, concepts and/or theories; it demonstrates understanding that not all research is carried out perfectly and that not all theories or conclusions are applicable to all people. When citing studies and theories, students should focus on the bits that are directly relevant to the question rather than give every detail from the study.

I have found it beneficial to students if the teacher tries to mirror the time constraints, assessment format and criteria in the assessments they give students throughout the course. If the daily timetable of the course allows for 60 minutes of assessment time, time management skills can be practised throughout the year. The use of questions from previous examinations or creation of questions similar to exam questions helps to familiarize students with the terminology and the 'unpacking' of questions. The mark bands and mark schemes from previous examinations can be used to assess student work and give them feedback. Each of these techniques will help to better prepare students for external assessment.

7.8 Internal assessment

The internal assessment (IA) is designed to assess knowledge and skills related to experimental research methodology and design. At SL, candidates are required to design, conduct and report on a simple experimental study. They can conduct a partial replication of a published experimental study; they do not have to create their own, completely novel research aim. Instead, it is perfectly acceptable, and recommended by many experienced teachers, that students base their study on a previously published experiment. Some examples could include Stroop's experiment on visual interference and mental processing; Craik and Lockart's studies on memory and levels of processing; White, Fishbein and Rutstein's studies of heart rate arousal and perception; or Zajonc's studies on familiarity and perceptions. Many appropriate experimental studies are cited in most general psychology texts and can be used to generate ideas about the topic to be investigated.

The purpose of the IA is not to establish a new, ground-breaking psychological theory, but rather to give the students the experience and opportunity to conduct a well-designed experiment. Many students want to do their IA on some topic that has either never been researched before or do a study that is not truly experimental (e.g. comparing gender, culture or age differences). The pitfall with doing novel research is that students have a hard time finding background studies to justify their aim or hypothesis. Studies that do not explicitly identify and manipulate an independent variable do not meet the requirements for IA. It is the teacher's responsibility to ensure that students do not fall into these common traps.

HL internal assessment is a little more involved and requires a more thorough foundation in published research to justify the aim. Additionally, HL students are required to report not only on descriptive statistics, but also to analyse their results with inferential statistics. The use of inferential statistics may sound daunting to inexperienced teachers but a good research methods book (such as the one listed in section 7.11 by Hugh Coolican) will help.

Some other key points to remember when designing the IA include the need for explicit manipulation of one independent variable (such as, in Stroop's studies, the colour of the ink in which words are written and how it compares to the actual word itself) and the measurement of one dependent variable (such as the amount of time it takes a participant to read through the list of congruent words versus the incongruent words in the Stroop example), the appropriate use of random selection and random allocation techniques, and appropriate, documented consideration of ethical guidelines. It is the teacher's responsibility to ensure that all experimental studies conducted by students adhere to published ethical guidelines, such as those developed by the American Psychological Association, the British Psychological Society or local or national guidelines.

The DP psychology guide explicitly states that the process of doing the IA must be integrated into the contact course time that teachers spend with students. Teachers should remember that most students will have had no previous experience in designing and conducting experimental studies. This contact should include time spent finding background studies, design, write-ups, and discussion. Experienced teachers recommend that the topics chosen for investigation in the IA be closely tied to other course topics. Some areas that lend themselves well to experimental investigation include concepts in the cognitive perspective (e.g. the effect of interference on short-term memory retention), biological perspective (e.g. physical arousal and perception) and social psychology (e.g. the effect of style of clothes on impression formation).

All teachers should have a copy of the *Teacher Support Material* that the IBO published in 2002. This document includes information on the report format, ethics, examples of assessed IAs with commentary, and a recommended process of delivery for the IA. The process includes writing a research proposal, how to set up a student-run ethics and review committee, doing an annotated references project, using peer review and holding individual conferences with students to discuss their unique project. Note that students may work in small groups and they are allowed one draft on which the teachers can provide general feedback. Nevertheless, the final papers must be the individual work of each candidate; collaboration, collusion and plagiarism are not allowed.

Additional information and support can be found on the Online Curriculum Centre (OCC) website (http://online.ibo.org) and in the subject guide. The OCC has a forum on which teachers can exchange ideas and there are many experienced teachers who follow the threads of discussion. The subject guide also lists some additional ideas for topics that could be appropriate. Section 7.11 has some references that have reportedly proved very helpful to teachers.

The assessment criteria were modified for the first examinations in May 2003. These revised criteria now provide more structured descriptions that will help teachers to apply them appropriately. They also follow more closely the required format outlined in both the course guide and the *Teacher Support Material* (TSM). The TSM includes five exemplar IAs that have been marked using the assessment criteria, as well as commentary on why each mark was awarded. Teachers should read through these exemplars to better understand the assessment criteria.

7.9 Moderation

Internal assessment work is assessed by the teacher based on published criteria provided by the IBO. The moderation process for internal assessment happens a month or two before formal examinations (May or November) and its purpose is to ensure that the teachers are interpreting and applying the assessment criteria appropriately and consistently. A sample of five to ten IAs is sent to a moderator who then attempts to confirm the marks awarded by the teacher. A mathematical moderation factor might be applied if the teacher's marks are inappropriate. This moderation factor would then be applied to all of the IAs from the school. It is very important that teachers apply the assessment criteria consistently across the work of all of their students. If the teacher is too inconsistent, a larger sample might be requested by the IBO for further moderation. Moderators also fill out a feedback form that is returned to school a few months after the examination session.

7.10 Extended essay

Psychology tends to be popular for many students when they choose their topic for the extended essay (EE). The most important point to make to students is that the EE has very different requirements to the internal assessment. The most noticeable difference is that the EE does not require any sort of data gathering that would be done in a psychological research study. In the IA, students design and conduct an experimental study that is based on previous research. In the EE, students develop a focused research question and then use primary and secondary resources to develop the issues in the question and arrive at a focused answer to the research question. It might be helpful to think of a psychology EE as more of a 'library research' project than a psychological study, experiment, survey or observation.

The EE is centred on a specific research question – quite often phrased as a question rather than a statement. Phrasing the research question as a question helps focus the students as it reminds them that they have to specifically answer that question. For example: 'To what extent does divorce have an impact on the educational development of adolescents?' is better than 'Divorce and adolescence'. The first question can elicit a specific answer while the second lends itself to the broad, general coverage of the topic. Students do not have to select a topic from the DP psychology syllabus for their EE. In fact, some of the best EEs have come from topics completely outside of the course. (I once had a student write an amazing EE on psychological stress in airline pilots. He had done an internship with an international airline over the summer and then based his EE on his own experience and on journal articles he had found. In this case the student had an intense connection with the topic.) Students can combine their own personal interests in life with psychological research – athletes might want to investigate sport psychology, musicians might be interested in the effect of music on psychological functioning, students who travel frequently could look into the impact of tourism on developing cultures or the effects of jetlag. One of the great characteristics of psychology is that it can be combined with just about any area of interest. Generally, the more personal interest the student has in the topic, the better the EE will be.

It is best if students use primary source documents as the main basis of the EE. Articles from published, peer-reviewed psychological journals form the basis of some of the best papers. Other sources, such as internet websites, popular magazines and newspapers, should be carefully evaluated for accuracy and authority before being used. In any case, these other types of source should not form the majority of the research base.

Students should apply the skills they have learned in the course to their EEs. They should be well-versed in psychological terminology and its appropriate use, show an ability to integrate theory and concepts from the sources they use, and apply the evaluative skills and critical thinking processes used throughout the course. Cultural, ethical, gender and/or methodological considerations should be taken into account as appropriate.

7.11 Resources

General texts based on the perspectives

Glassman, W. (2000). *Approaches to Psychology*, 3rd edition, Open University Press.

Jarvis, M. (2000) *Angles on Psychology*, Nelson Thornes.

Keegan, G. (2002) *Higher Psychology: Approaches & Methods*, Hodder and Stoughton Educational.

Tavris, C. and Wade, C. (2000) *Psychology in Perspective*, 3rd edition, Prentice Hall College Division.

Internal assessment

IBO (2002) *Psychology Teacher Support Material*.

Coolican, H. (1996) *Introduction to Research Methods and Statistics in Psychology*, 2nd edition, Hodder and Stoughton Educational.

Flanagan, C. (1998) *Practicals for Psychology: A Student Workbook*, Routledge, an imprint of Taylor & Francis Books Ltd.

Flanagan, C. with Cliff, N. *Resource Pack for AS/A level Psychology Practicals (AQA B)*, Hartshill Press.

Qualitative research methods

Robson, C. (2001) *Real World Research*, Blackwell Publishers.

Wilig, C. (2001) *Introducing Qualitative Research in Psychology: Adventures in Theory and Method*, Open University Press.

General psychology textbooks

Eysenck, M. (2000) *Psychology: A Student's Handbook*, Psychology Press.

Hayes, N. (2001) *Foundations of Psychology*, Thomson Learning.

Hill, G. (2001), *Psychology A Level through Diagrams*, Oxford University Press.

Revision books and key studies

Banyard, P. and Grayson, A. (eds) (1996) *Introducing Psychological Research: Sixty Studies That Shaped Psychology*, Palgrave Macmillan.

Gross, R. (2003) *Key Studies in Psychology*, Hodder and Stoughton Educational.

Cross-cultural readings

Price, W. and Crapo, R. (2001) *Cross Cultural Perspectives in Psychology*, 4th edition, Brooks Cole.

8 Geography

8.1 Course overview

The current syllabus was introduced for first examinations in 2003, and as such is likely to remain stable for at least the next five years apart from minor changes. The syllabus comprises three parts plus fieldwork, as outlined in figure 14.17.

The first part, 'Geographical skills', should not be considered to be a distinct unit of the syllabus, as these skills should be developed throughout the course as part of the delivery of the subject material. The prescribed skills list (which is the same for HL and SL) requires students to show competency in the interpretation and construction of maps, basic numerical skills such as the interpretation and construction of graphical data, some basic geographical statistical techniques (such as Spearman's rank correlation coefficient), data collection and handling and academic writing skills. These skills are not exceptional and any competent teacher of the subject should have little difficulty incorporating them into classroom activities during the course. For example, an exercise designed to illustrate spatial differences in development may start with various development data and expect students to identify trends in the data and then map the spatial patterns; hence this one exercise has accounted for a good number of the required skills. The skills cannot be ignored, as they will play an integral part in examination questions. Because these skills are developed throughout the course, geography is available as an *ab initio* subject (just like all group 3 subjects). Obviously, those students who enter the course with a good grounding of skills are at a distinct advantage.

Figure 14.17 Geography content and assessment

	Comments	Assessment
Geographical skills (HL, SL)	A standard set of geographical skills which should be integrated into the teaching of the course (identical for HL and SL)	No specific exam paper: candidates should be able to display competency throughout all exam papers and coursework
Core theme (HL, SL: 90 hrs)	Integrates human geography topics into one broad theme (identical for HL and SL)	Paper 1 (same paper for HL and SL, 1.5 hrs): two structured questions involving stimulus material Assessment weight: HL 25%, SL 40%
Optional themes (30 hrs per theme)	A choice of four (HL) or two (SL) themes from a list covering a broad range of physical and human topics	Paper 2 (HL 2.5 hrs, SL 1.5 hrs): candidates are offered the choice between a structured question and an essay question for every theme they studied Assessment weight: HL 50%, SL 40%
Fieldwork (HL: 30 hrs)	HL students must complete 30 hrs of field study. SL students can opt to complete fieldwork although it is not compulsory (details below)	HL: two reports based on fieldwork SL: two investigations based on fieldwork or research assignments or both (integrated in course) Assessment weight: HL 25%, SL 20%

The second unit is the 'Core theme – population, resources and development' and is an attempt by the IBO to encourage an integrated approach to the more traditional 'human geography' topics. It should be allocated 90 hours of teaching time both in HL and in SL. The IBO goes to great lengths to stress the 'integrated' nature of this theme – it is not enough to study demographics in isolation, for example, but this should be put into the context of development, trade, resources, sustainability and so on. In my opinion, this is a strength of the syllabus as it allows students to see the relevance of the material they are studying. This process may take some time, however, and it may not be until quite late on in the course that it all comes together in the student's mind. It may also require a shift in the approach of the teacher who is used to delivering the information as distinct topics.

The third part of the subject comprises 11 optional themes, with HL students required to study four and SL students two (figure 14.18). Each theme requires 30 hours of contact time. These units provide a school with the flexibility to choose the most appropriate course, allowing them to take into consideration the background of the teachers, the geographical location of the school (studying arid environments is likely to be more relevant – and interesting! – in a North African school than in an urban European one), the resources that are available, and the strengths and interests of the students. The ideal situation would be one where students were able to choose their own themes (modules) of study – just as they would at university – although this would only be possible in the very large and well resourced schools. The themes are grouped into three sections, outlined in figure 14.18.

HL and SL students share a common core syllabus; the difference between HL and SL is mainly the number of hours rather than academic ability. Therefore it is quite straightforward to teach HL and SL in the same classroom. Clearly

Figure 14.18 Geography optional themes (sorted by sections)

Section A: Physical themes	Section B: Human themes	Section C
• Drainage basins and their management • Coasts and their management • Arid environments and their management • Lithospheric processes and their management • Ecosystems and human activity • Climatic hazards and change	• Contemporary issues in geographical regions • Settlements • Productive activities: aspects of change • Globalization	• Topographic mapping

While SL students have open choice of any two optional themes from the list, HL students' choice of four themes must include at least two from section A and one from section B (and one free choice), thus ensuring that the balance between the physical and human elements of the subject is maintained.

allowance will have to be made for the slightly different internal assessment procedures as well as the extra time required by HL students.

8.2 External assessment

As summarized in figure 14.17, SL and HL students sit two papers.

Paper 1
HL and SL sit the same paper. Candidates answer two questions from a choice of three structured questions. These questions refer to some stimulus material such as graphical or spatial data, and will usually start by asking the student to describe the significant trends illustrated, moving on to related analysis of the information, with the concluding section requiring students to bring in related knowledge from the core theme and possibly exemplars. For example, a question that begins by requiring a student to be capable of handling data in the form of an age–sex pyramid in South Africa, may conclude by demanding a discussion of the influence of disease – such as AIDS – on a country's development. This underlines the necessity of dealing with the core theme as an integrated unit rather than as distinct subject areas.

Paper 2
In accordance with the options in figure 14.18, Paper 2 is broken into sections A, B and C. HL students are required to answer two questions from section A (which will always address some aspect of management or impact on society), one from section B, and a fourth of their choice; SL students can choose any two questions. In each section, students are presented with two different questions relating to the given subject, an essay question and a structured response (similar in structure to those found in Paper 1), and the students can choose to answer either one. For example, students attempting the 'Drainage basins and their management' option in section A might be presented with the following two questions (of which they would be required to answer only one):

Essay question:

For a drainage basin that you have studied, show how human activity can increase the impact of floods.

Structured question:

a) Using [some pictorial data] above, describe the differences in the discharge of the two drainage basins throughout the storm event.
b) Explain the possible reasons why these differences may occur.
c) Suggest some of the disadvantages of human management of a drainage basin system. You should illustrate your answer with relevant examples that you have studied.

Whilst this is a welcome attempt by the IBO to allow students to choose the question that meets their strengths (e.g. ESL students may prefer the structured question), experience shows that candidates tend to opt for the question which they are most able to deal with in terms of subject matter, only considering style if they are in the luxurious position of being able to deal equally well with either question. Nevertheless, students appreciate the choice of question format.

We finish this external assessment section with a note on the optional question from section C (the topographic mapping question that tests the range of mapping skills). Whilst this theme fills some students with dread (because it is skills-based and they often enter the course with little or no foundation in these), it is quite possible to thoroughly prepare students and give them the opportunity to score highly. Some schools teach this theme throughout the course (either integrating it within other topics, or using up 'spare' weeks within the year), effectively giving students who feel capable an extra choice. In that case, HL students would in effect have prepared for five instead of the obligatory four themes and SL students for three instead of two by the time of the examination.

8.3 Teaching and organizing the course

Given the fact that the external assessment is very straightforward, there is no 'right' way to teach the course and as such teachers are able to adopt the approach that they are most comfortable with. However, there are certain issues of paramount importance to be borne in mind when you plan your course.

The subject aims of the geography syllabus are closely linked to the central aims of the DP. For example, a teacher who discusses climate change (one of the optional themes) would as a matter of course introduce the interrelationship between physical and social environments. The study would also identify the diversity of opinion depending on level of development, political and cultural background etc. as well as the notion that the data are contestable and uncertain. It would also be necessary to interrogate data and synthesize various ideas into a conclusion, thus addressing some of the geographical skills that are so central to the course. Thus, the stated aims of the course need not be at the forefront of the teacher's mind – by teaching the course, one is automatically addressing the aims directly. However, once a department has become fully conversant with the syllabus, it would be a shame if the holistic, global and cultural aspects of the course, which make it so vibrant and relevant to the DP, were not developed further and overtly addressed.

Students are expected to be able to apply the concepts that they study in the context of actual examples by using case studies. This may be done by looking first at the concepts and then investigating how they apply to a suitable example, or, alternatively, looking at the issues that arise in a particular case (geographical location) and then identifying the relevant theories that apply to it (the factors that helped to shape it). The second approach is probably more demanding as it requires good resources and more flexibility (you may have to talk about various concepts at the same time rather than introducing them one at a time), but it has the virtue of ensuring that students have a realistic understanding of case studies rather than thinking of them as examples of one particular concept. The second approach to case studies is also particularly relevant in view of the core theme, which stresses the integrated nature of the course. Finally, it also allows teachers to introduce and develop the geographical skills more naturally.

To give an example of the two approaches, it would be possible to introduce the theories of economic development to students by discussing first the role of development indicators, second the models of development, and finally looking at the factors that influence levels of development. These students could now be given a case study – that of Uganda, for example – in order to identify how these classroom theories combine to explain the development of a country. Or the teacher may choose to use Uganda as a vehicle for highlighting the various theories. This approach may start with some data relating to Uganda, leading on to a discussion of possible problems with the data and then identifying the possible causes of the level of economic development. Models of development could be woven into this analysis and students asked to critically assess their relevance to the country. The chosen approach will be dependent upon the individual's experience and preference.

There has been some discussion surrounding what constitutes a suitable case study, and in the past some examination questions have stated that only recent examples are acceptable. This is an understandable attempt to ensure that teachers discuss contemporary issues, although it would be acceptable to select an older example if it was considered a defining example. In reality, there are so many contemporary examples that there should be no problem in providing up-to-date examples. Nonetheless, it would be helpful if the IBO would define more clearly what they mean by 'contemporary' – say within 5, 10 or 15 years.

There is no correct order in which the course must be taught. Perhaps the biggest consideration is the timing of the fieldwork. Clearly if it is done too soon then students may not have developed the necessary foundation of skills and knowledge, but if done too late then it may clash with other demands such as internal examinations and extended essays, etc. The course is flexible enough to be able to fit around the individual demands of schools. Some schools are able to timetable two teachers to teach an HL set so that one may be responsible for the core theme while the other deals with the optional themes and perhaps fieldwork preparation. This way of timetabling clearly depends on the resources available but is worth considering as it would increase flexibility and expose students to a range of teaching methods.

8.4 Internal assessment: fieldwork

HL students are required to spend 30 hours of the course on fieldwork and writing two reports discussing the processes, observations and results. Obviously, the subjects covered should be taken from the syllabus, although it is possible, and highly effective, to use the fieldwork to further develop some of the material that has already been studied. Fieldwork can be completed in any suitable location – ranging from studies on campus through to adventurous foreign trips. Experience shows that students respond very positively to the opportunity to experience working in a new environment and can focus on the study if they are removed from their day-to-day environment. I strongly recommend that students be given the opportunity to experience a residential trip; this is also good for the image of the subject within the school. Obviously, the organization of a successful residential field course requires greater planning and preparation, but this is justified by the benefits. Safety of students is a major consideration, and staff should not be tempted to go beyond the realms of their own experience and expertise. This is not the place to enter into an in-depth discussion of fieldwork safety, but it should be in the forefront of the department's – and management's – thoughts.

The topic of fieldwork study should be very carefully chosen so as to allow students the opportunity to complete a suitably detailed report, without attempting to write an academic report that rivals the extended essay, and consequently over-burdens students. Given the fact that students are required to write two reports, two distinct areas of study should be provided – if possible one of physical geography and the other of human geography (if not, then two areas of either should be assigned). These reports are marked as a whole, i.e. each of the skills that is assessed should be present somewhere in the two reports, rather than marking each of the pieces and then submitting the average.

The fieldwork reports are excellent preparation for the extended essay, which follows the same structure. This familiarity with the process of data collection and report production means that geography extended essay candidates can be more efficient, and if they follow the guidelines, have the potential to do well.

At SL, candidates are required to submit two pieces which can be either fieldwork reports, i.e. their own analysis of primary data collected in the field – meaning that they can be included in the arrangements for HL students – or research assignments (an activity completed in class or for homework, not based on data collected by the student) or one of each. These assignments are designed to give the students the opportunity to display a range of skills, and should be arranged accordingly.

There is no specific time set aside for SL coursework; the idea is to integrate it in the lessons.

The material provided by the IBO in the internal assessment teacher-support material for both HL and SL is very helpful and provides a good starting point for inexperienced departments.

8.5 Resources

Resourcing a geography course has become considerably easier in the last decade. The quality of some of the material on the internet is so good one can base a course upon it. It is possible to provide notes, diagrams, animations, statistics, video and audio, as well as superb images, all with the use of a classroom projector. (However, it is worth remembering that these resources are also available to students and plagiarism can be a problem.) So if a teacher is prepared to spend the time finding good web materials and putting them into a student-friendly format with some suitable tasks, very few published resources need to be purchased. In addition, many websites – far more than we can mention here – provide a department with general support. This can take the form of resources (such as lesson plans, activities or images), discussions of relevant events, glossaries, course notes for students, and revision help.

Some of the sites that I have found useful are listed in figure 14.19; and many of these provide links to the more topic specific sites.

Note: all weblinks featured in this chapter can be accessed through our website www.dp-help.com

Given the amount of excellent information available on the web, the importance of textbooks in the subject is diminishing. However, textbooks are

Figure 14.19 Suggested geography websites

www.internetgeography.co.uk/
A support site with subject information that can be used in lessons: case studies, etc. It is a British site so not IB specific, but easily transferable.

www.gtasa.asn.au/index.htm
Geography Teacher's Association of South Australia (Inc.). This site contains support material such as a glossary, image bank and links to IB notes and IB revision notes (although these are links to other sites and the quality is not as good as it could be, and naturally not necessarily specific to what is taught by each centre).

www.ibgeog.com
Published by the Geography Department of the International School of Toulouse. Contains a selection of information that is directly relevant to both students and teachers of IB, including list of skills, assessment criteria, coursework information and so on. Also has a course outline with some links for some of the topics, which can be used to build activities around. Very clear – especially useful for schools just starting the IB as it includes outline of assessment process and skills required by students.

www.spartacus.schoolnet.co.uk/REVgeography.htm
A list of links which relate to all parts of the syllabus.

www.geocities.com/ibrevise/geography.html
A comprehensive source of IB revision notes.

www.geoworld.co.uk/
This site provides excellent ideas and activities designed to encourage students to develop their thinking skills. Suitable across the age range but many are suitable or adaptable to IB.

www.pupilvision.com/mainframe.htm
Pupilvision teachers' resources – site as a whole has won many awards and has information relevant to any geography course. It is aimed at teachers rather than students.

www.geographyinthenews.rgs.org/
A Royal Geographical Society site which selects news stories related to geography. A great way to illustrate a topic with contemporary material or to start a discussion.

www.nationmaster.com/
A great resource that allows a wide range of statistics to be compared.

www.geog.ouc.bc.ca/physgeog/contents/table.html
A general introduction to physical geography – contains some useful notes and glossary of terms relating to some of the optional themes.

http://geoimages.berkeley.edu/PhysicalGeography.html
A bank of images which can be used to illustrate a range of physical geography topics.

www.georesources.co.uk/
Although designed for the British National Curriculum, this site has a whole range of relevant pages – photos, case studies, teacher resources, outline maps, etc.

www.geographypages.co.uk/
Although based around UK examinations, this list of links would be useful to any teacher of the subject. Very comprehensive.

plentiful, often very good, and very easily found. The most relevant, perhaps, is *Planet Geography* (Stephen Codrington, Solid Star Press), which is written specifically to support the IB course. Students appreciate the fact that its layout closely follows that of the syllabus. In general, they also feel more confident if they have a course text to which they can refer.

9 History

IB history teaches students how to evaluate and integrate source material and how to analyse, compare and explain historical events and their different interpretations. A striking feature of the curriculum is the wide range of topics, particularly at HL, covering many geographical regions. This range of choices can be exploited to offer the students an interesting and stimulating curriculum that excels in both breadth and depth.

Close to 50% of all group 3 students choose history, and most of your students are likely to be HL. In May 2002, more than 80% of the history candidates were HL students (*IBO Statistical Bulletin*), which makes history a unique subject in the IB Diploma Programme (DP): all other DP subjects offered at both Standard Level (SL) and Higher Level (HL) tend to be fairly evenly split between the two levels.

History is traditionally a difficult subject for ESL students, as it requires extensive regular and independent reading, particularly at HL. Realistically, students should be able to cope at least with English language B (see Chapter 13) to succeed with history.

9.1 Course content overview

Figure 14.20 History course outline

HL and SL should only study one prescribed subject from section A and at least two topics from section B below. The difference between HL and SL is that HL studies in addition one region from section C.	
A Prescribed subjects HL and SL choose one topic **Examined in Paper 1**	Only **one** prescribed subject should be chosen.
1. The USSR under Stalin, 1924–41 *2. The emergence and development of the People's Republic of China (PRC), 1946–64* *3. The Cold War, 1960–79*	
B 20th century world history topics HL and SL choose at least two topics **Examined in Paper 2**	At least one of the two topics chosen should relate to the prescribed subject (section A). Case studies should be drawn from different regions and studied and explained from an international perspective, covering political, social, economic, cultural and gender issues, although it should be noted that Papers 2 and 3 strongly emphasize *political* issues.

Figure 14.20 History course outline (continued)

1. *Causes, practices and effects of war*
   (Arab-Israeli, Chinese civil war, First and Second World Wars, Korean War, Mexican Revolution, Nigerian civil war, Russian revolutions and civil war, Spanish civil war, Vietnam War)

2. *Nationalist and independence movements, decolonization and challenges facing new states* (Algeria, the Caribbean, Ghana, South Asia, Indo-China, Indonesia, Kenya)

3. *The rise and rule of single party states* – from two regions
   (Perón, Mao, Castro, Nasser, Hitler, Mussolini, Nyerere, Lenin, Stalin)

4. *Peace and cooperation: international organizations and multiparty states* – from two regions
   (League of Nations, United Nations, Argentina, Nehru and India, Japan, South Africa, F. D. Roosevelt and the USA and Spain – specific dates given)

5. *The Cold War*
   (War-time conferences, developments in Europe, especially Berlin, Truman Doctrine, Marshall Plan, NATO, USSR policies, east European satellites, COMECON, Warsaw Pact, containment, China, Cuba, Korea, Vietnam, Middle East, non-alignment, arms race, arms control, détente)

6. *The state and its relationship with religion and with minorities*
   (Buddhism in Indo-China, Christianity in Europe and Latin America, Hinduism in South Asia, Islam in Africa and Asia, Judaism in Europe and the Middle East, Aborigines in Australia, Asians in East Africa, Chinese in Malaysia, Kurds in Europe and the Middle East, Native and African-Americans, Québécois in Canada)

Note: Not all subtopics listed above need to be covered within each topic, but teachers will need to cover a few, as examination questions ask students to compare issues using examples from the five geographical regions (identified in a map given in the history subject guide). Consider for example the following, quite typical, examination question on topic 3, requiring knowledge of two regions:
   'In what ways, and for what reasons, did two rulers of single-party states, each chosen from a different region, fail to achieve their objectives?' (May 2002)

C Regional options	There are five regional options, each with its own
(Only) HL choose one	time period. Within each option there are 22
Examined in Paper 3	subtopics. A period of approximately 100 years
	should be studied for an in-depth study. Only **one**
1. Africa	regional option must be selected by the school
2. Americas	and the IBO recommends the selection of 6–8
3. East and South East Asia	subtopics within the chosen option.
and Oceania	
4. Europe	
5. South Asia, the Middle East	
and North Africa	

9.2 How to structure and organize the course?

There is obviously a lot of scope for what the student can study, more so than in a typical national curriculum. The five regional options for Paper 3 are particularly broad and can accommodate the international make-up of a history class. Easily accessible resources from the school's local environment are likely to be relevant to at least one of the regional options and such an option is obviously a good one to select.

The course requires both depth and breadth in its assessment. The individual examination questions require depth, while the structure of the syllabus and the structure of the examinations require breadth. The selection of topics and the way you structure your course are crucial to meet both requirements. It should be noted that the course should not be taught chronologically but instead should be taught thematically or topically as displayed in the syllabus outline. You could for instance spend a semester around single-party states focusing specifically on the rise and rule of Stalin, Mussolini and Mao. A study of these leaders covers the required different regions, and it obviously allows the teacher to compare and contrast between them.

As mentioned earlier, the syllabus requires the study of a variety of regions, so it is not possible to focus the course on only one region. One can achieve cohesion by selecting a prescribed subject (section A) and a world history topic (section B) that complement each other. This affirms the in-depth coverage the curriculum demands without sacrificing breadth. Either of the examples in figure 14.21 would adequately prepare the students for all three papers. It should be noted that the two examples given in no way exhaust the possible combinations.

To narrow down the scope and to understand what the emphasis may be in the examinations, teachers should acquire as many past examination papers as possible. You will find new ways of looking at a topic with each different examination.

The structure of the course allows HL and SL to be taught in the same class but, as always, this will require careful planning. In many schools there are so few SL students that they are scheduled for the same time slots as the HL students. You could use the resulting spare time for SL students to let them work on homework assignments, internal assessment, and source evaluation practice for their two papers. An alternative is to have the SL students learn the regional option along with the HL students. This will give the SL students greater depth and in no way compromises their ability to handle their examination questions; in fact, it provides a wider historical knowledge base for the SL students. For example, if SL and HL students were covering topic 1 (causes, practices and effects of war) with a focus on the Russian Revolution (1917), then the HL regional option of Europe would provide greater historical knowledge of the background to the Russian Revolution. Naturally, this teaching model makes planning and delivery a lot easier for the teacher. A possible drawback of this approach is that SL students are not formally assessed on the regional option and therefore may question the need for this extra coverage.

Figure 14.21 Sample course syllabuses

Example one	Example two
Prescribed subject 1 (Stalin) complements world history topics 3 (single-party states) and 5 (Cold War) which complement the European region (HL)	**Prescribed subject 3 (Cold War, 1960–79)** complements world history topics 1 (causes of war) and 5 (Cold War) which complement the East and South East Asia region (HL)
Note: It would be unwise to do the African region as it would not complement Stalin. If the African region is desired, it would be wise to use prescribed subject 3 (Cold War) which would complement better.	

9.3 Assessment outline

Figure 14.22 outlines all the assessment components at HL and SL.

Figure 14.22 History assessment outline

External	**Paper 1** (section A) Structured questions, source evaluation	HL 20% SL 30% 1 hr	Choose one of the three prescribed subjects (PS) of section A (see figure 14.20). Each PS has five sources and four questions. Answer four questions on five of the sources.
	Paper 2 (section B) Essay writing	HL 25% SL 45% 1 hr 30	Choose a total of two essays, each from a different topic section. Six topic sections from section B (see figure 14.20), five essay questions per topic, total 30 essay choices.
	Paper 3 (section C) (HL only) Essay writing	HL 35% 2 hrs 30	Choose three essay questions out of a total of 25. The school will select one of the five regional options and will receive that paper.

Internal	**Coursework** Internally marked but externally moderated	HL 20% SL 25% 20 hrs	One historical investigation 1,500–2,000 words, 20 marks		
			A Outline plan	100–150 words	2 marks
			B Summary of evidence	500–600 words	5 marks
			C Evaluation of sources	250–400 words	4 marks
			D Analysis	500–650 words	5 marks
			E Conclusion	150–200 words	2 marks
			F List of sources	No word count	2 marks

9.4 Teaching the course

Some teachers allow student input into the selection of prescribed subjects and historical topics; others prefer to keep the decision to themselves. Whichever model you follow, the examinations require so much depth that we strongly counsel against experimenting with topics you are not familiar with.

Figure 14.22 highlights that the focus in history is on evaluation of evidence and writing essays. Therefore regular essay-writing (at least one every two weeks) and source evaluation are necessary to ensure that the students are well prepared for both internal and external assessment, in particular to achieve the required depth of response.

To achieve a sound knowledge base, the familiar technique of regular tests applies. Many teachers make it a habit to take all their test questions from past examinations or to closely model them on past examination papers.

In order to increase depth of knowledge and correct use of terminology, students need to learn how to create and maintain their own glossary of key terms for each topic, for example 'sphere of influence' or 'Truman Doctrine' during the Cold War topic. Teachers should encourage the use of a consistent school-wide method of referencing from the first essay onwards as students *must* reference all their sources in both the internal assessment and the extended essay (should they elect to do one in history).

We have found that it helps students to work together in class and discuss amongst themselves, especially on how to extract relevant quotations. Some teachers report good results from regularly running classes on a seminar basis, with students being responsible for leading some of the seminars.

We believe it is a fair expectation to have students read around 20–30 pages of academic text during any one week. With such a large amount of reading, students' enjoyment of and motivation for the topics is obviously important.

The large amount of reading and writing tends to discourage ESL students from choosing IB history but occasionally some do wish to take the course. In that case, reading and writing skills may well require explicit teaching time. We have found the following tools useful to help the ESL students:

- *Dictionary of 20th Century World History* (1997) Oxford University Press (paperback reference series)
- explicit notes on terms and concepts
- use of simpler texts as an introduction to new topics, followed by more appropriate academic texts (some lower high school texts are a good place to start)
- (teacher assisted) explicit note-taking exercises in class as well as class reading of texts.

In our experience, using the teaching techniques above in a class of committed and motivated students who are able to cope with English language B will be able to overcome both the language and history-specific difficulties.

9.5 External assessment

Students must be given frequent opportunities to practise for all three papers. To develop students' understanding of the demands of the examination questions, we believe it is essential that you give detailed feedback after each test. Mark test papers according to the IB marking schemes whenever possible. The IBO has made it possible to order past papers and marking schemes.

Paper 1
This examination paper has set question types. For example, question 3 has consistently had the following format:

'With reference to their **origin** and **purpose**, assess the **value** and **limitations** of [the following] documents …'. (authors' emphasis).

By using such questions, the teacher can then explicitly draw the student's attention to the key words and concepts for each of the questions.

Paper 2 and Paper 3 (the essay papers)
Students need practice at writing essays. Each essay should be completed in approximately 40 minutes in order to cope with the demands of the two essays in Paper 2 (90 minutes) and three essays in Paper 3 (150 minutes). Some teachers feel that it is useful to explicitly outline the basic essay structure on the board whilst reviewing a topic for weaker students. Following the structure on the board, the students then provide the detailed information to write the model essay.

A frequent comment in IB subject reports is that students often give the right answer to the wrong question, because the students fail to understand the demands of the essay question. The IBO recognizes this problem and has given a list, along with explanations, of key words and terms used in IB history examinations in the older subject guides. Unfortunately, they do not appear in the newer subject guides. The older subject guides also provide the mark bands for Paper 2 and Paper 3. We have found it helpful to use these for the marking of all essays to make sure students understand what is required in a good history essay.

The subject reports stress that students must demonstrate depth of analytical knowledge and not simply breadth of narrative knowledge:

> Able candidates usually structured their answers and focused on the set questions in an analytical manner. However, some obviously able and very knowledgeable candidates adopted a narrative or descriptive approach, which was disappointing …
>
> Subject reports, May 2000

9.6 Internal assessment

The internal assessment (IA) is a historical investigation of the student's choice whereby the student will apply the skills of a historian, which are to evaluate, analyse and organize evidence. Examples include: 'How successfully did Hitler promote the ideal of the family in the Third Reich?', 'How did newspaper reports on the death of Kennedy vary, and how reliable were they?' and 'To what extent was the defeat of the British Army by the Zulu at Isandlwana in 1879 due to the mistakes made by Lord Chelmsford?'. It is very useful for teachers to have the 'assessed examples' published by the IBO, which show the marks the students gain against each criterion.

The internal assessment is different from the traditional essay structure such as required in the extended essay. A close examination of the criteria used to assess the IA will demonstrate that it is not an expository essay. For the IA, the section headers are effectively provided by the IBO, and the students must execute each step in sequence (what is my plan of investigation, how do I summarize the evidence, evaluation of sources, and so on). Please refer to the subject guide, which offers clear guidelines.

The internal assessment criteria and requirements are identical for HL and SL. The IBO recommends 20 hours of work on the investigation and this includes both class time and homework. We would suggest you allocate about 1 hour in class for discussing the criteria, about 8 hours for researching and writing in class, particularly the plan/section A, and about half an hour to two hours for one-to-one discussion with each student, depending on how many students you teach. Initial teacher assistance with finding resources and in formulating relevant, focused investigations is crucial. Teachers could make a point of taking the students to the local university library to give them access to appropriate academic sources and documents. Such visits cater to the IB demand for depth while they can also be used to teach research skills. Teachers can give advice on the first draft but should not heavily annotate or edit it. The student's second draft is the final one. To combat plagiarism, references must be checked, as should the style of writing compared with the student's other work.

For both the IA and the extended essay (should the student elect to do one in history), a 'quote-finding' exercise initiated by the teacher in class is useful: the resulting quotes often form an excellent basis for coursework or essays. To give an example, Vietnamese General Giap said to the Americans, 'You can kill ten of my men, for every one I will kill of yours. But even at those odds, you will lose and I will win.' Based on this quote, a student could then research the question of to what extent this attitude was a reason for the 'victory' of North Vietnam and the Vietcong in the war against the USA.

The concept of the historical investigation will be reasonably familiar to history teachers. It is the assessment that may well be different from what many teachers are used to. Sarah Jeyaram reports: 'From my own teaching of the British A-level, for instance, evaluating sources was more of an implicit requirement whereas the IB history makes it explicit.' The same is true for the 'plan of the investigation'. The IBO's assessed examples referred to above, however, spell out the differences quite clearly.

We would recommend that the student chooses a topic based on:

- what has been studied already in class (especially for weaker students, either academically or in their level of English) – strong and well-organized students may choose a topic not within the school's chosen syllabus
- the likelihood that it will create a greater depth of knowledge that may possibly assist in some examination questions, for example, an in-depth study of Vietnamese nationalism could possibly provide an opportunity for doing well in an examination question provided that the topic has been supported by in-class teaching
- the time period restrictions imposed by the IBO – the event needs to have occurred at least 10 years ago to be classified as 'history' and not 'current affairs'
- resources likely to be available
- the student's interest and motivation
- the teacher's confidence in supervising the chosen topic.

Some teachers are comfortable developing an IA from one element or subtopic of the extended essay question. One student, for instance, focused her IA on how much influence the defeat of the French at Dien Bien Phu had on their withdrawal from Vietnam. Her extended essay then considered the question of to what extent Vietnamese sacrifice and nationalist feeling led to the American defeat. This approach can work well provided the student has a very clear understanding of the very different criteria used to assess the IA and the extended essay. Other teachers consider this approach somewhat risky, as students could be tempted to mix the assessment criteria, and they prefer to keep the IA and extended essay completely separate. The differences in assessment between the IA and the extended essay are discussed in section 9.7.

One of the three authors of this history section prefers to let students choose their IA topic at the same time as they begin their extended essay research, two months before the end of the first year (approximately April if the examination is in the following May). This provides them with plenty of time to ask questions and receive feedback before the long holiday begins, during which time they should complete their research for both tasks. The long holiday between the first and second year of the DP is crucial for the student to do research, so a timeline of deadlines should be given before the holiday begins. Students should finish the historical investigation before the middle of the second year, before the mock and actual examinations. Sarah Jeyaram reports: 'My students have always expressed relief that their internal assessment was completed before their mocks, since this frees up their time for other subjects' coursework and for revision preparation during the pre-examination holidays.' The other two authors of this section prefer to complete the IA in the first year, but give the students the opportunity to review the IA in the second year. The extended essay is planned in the first year and the first draft is written over the summer break. The final draft of the extended essay is refined in subsequent drafts in the second year.

The IBO will send to the teacher an IA feedback form (3/IAF) on IAs submitted for that year. It discusses the suitability or relevance of the investigations, the relevance and use of research materials, referencing and acknowledgement of sources, application of the assessment criteria, compliance with the requirements (format, length) and general comments. It is not pupil specific but is still very useful.

As always, internal moderation is important, and departments should coordinate such efforts. At the Overseas Family School, the teachers meet to discuss the criteria and how they should be applied. Informal meetings are held regularly during the IA marking process to discuss application of the criteria to specific IAs. After IA marking by the individual teachers, IAs are exchanged and re-marked without teachers being aware of the marks given by the others. Meetings are then held to discuss any discrepancies. The process takes a lot of time but the advantage is that a clear and consistent marking of the IAs is achieved.

9.7 Extended essay

It must be noted that students and teachers should be careful not to produce very similar extended essays and IAs. A good place to start to learn about the differences is the IBO Online Curriculum Centre (OCC), which allows teachers to contact IB officials and other DP history teachers.

The links with the IA have already been discussed, and all recommendations we have made for the IA in section 9.6 apply equally to the extended essay. To facilitate smooth classroom management, teachers may find it useful to restrict the subject choice to an area from the IBO syllabus. Any such restrictions could be stipulated before accepting a student for an extended essay. Whatever you do, it is worth your while to set 'extended essay rules' for your department (see also the comments in section 3.9 of this chapter, and in Chapter 11).

9.8 Future directions

The DP history course is stable in that only recently (fairly minor) changes were made to the prescribed subjects and phrasing of questions in Paper 1. The structure of the IA has likewise changed a little. All in all, there is no reason to expect major changes anytime soon.

9.9 Resources

Note: in the list below we use the following abbreviations:
S = student text   TR = reference or teacher reference

Cold War

Rayner, E. G. (1992) *The Cold War* (History at Source), Hodder and Stoughton. (S) This has an excellent range of sources with comprehensive narrative for each set of sources. The questions are too difficult for some students and may need to be interpreted or rewritten.

McCauley, M. (2003) *Origins of the Cold War*, 3rd edition, Longman. (S) This has some useful sources and detailed narrative with references to other sources. An excellent overview of Cold War histography.

Dockrill, M. (1988) *The Cold War 1945–63*, Humanity Books. (S) Detailed narrative; useful for essays and to practise and develop note-taking and reading skills for HL.

McCauley, M. (1982) *The Soviet Union Since 1917*, Longman. (S and/or TR) A detailed analysis of Russia with good sections on foreign policy.

Judge, E. H. and Langdon, J. W. (1998) *The Cold War: A history through documents*, Prentice Hall. (TR) Comprehensive notes with some useful sources.

Gaddis, J. L. (1998) *We now know: Rethinking the Cold War*, reprint edition, Oxford Press. (S and/or TR) This offers an excellent overview of Cold War historiography.

China, Korea, Vietnam

Bailey, P. J. (1988) *China in the Twentieth Century*, Blackwell Publishers. (S) Very detailed narrative that needs to be worked through with the students in small bite-size chunks. The language can be very challenging but very useful for developing reading and note-taking skills needed particularly at HL.

Brooman, J. (1990) *China Since 1900*, Addison-Wesley. (S) A good starter for students studying China although it is GCSE level.

Lynch, M. (1998) *The People's Republic of China since 1949* (Access to History), Hodder and Stoughton. (S) This is a small, quite detailed text that has some useful summaries and questions.

Spence, J. D. (2001) *The Search for Modern China*, W.W. Norton & Company. (TR) An excellent detailed book that will 'frighten' the students but they should use it as a source for their essays.

Ebrey, P. B. (1999) *China* (Cambridge Illustrated History), Cambridge University Press. (S) Detailed narrative and photographs, which the students like.

Burke, P. (1999) *Studies of Asia* (Heinemann Outcomes), Heinemann. (S) A comprehensive guide but quite general in its coverage. Students find this a good place to start.

Karnow, S. (1997) *Vietnam: A History*, Penguin USA. (TR) Excellent source but too detailed. Students are encouraged to use this so as to become familiar with a detailed, reputable text.

Sandler, S. (1999) *The Korean War: No Victors, No Vanquished*, University Press of Kentucky. (TR) Detailed text with useful introduction and conclusions about the Korean War.

Fall, B. (2002). *Hell in a Very Small Place*, DaCapo Press. (TR) Detailed look at the French defeat (useful for the American defeat also), increasing US involvement and the rise of nationalism in Vietnam.

Duiker, W. J. (2001) *Ho Chi Minh: A Life*, Hyperion. (S) Has excellent level of research detail for the influence of Minh and the rise of nationalism.

Maga, T. (2000) *The Complete Idiot's Guide to the Vietnam War*, Alpha Books. (S) A good place to start, especially with weaker students.

USA – civil rights, domestic and foreign policy

Paterson, D., Willoughby, D. and Willoughby, S. (2001) *Civil Rights in the USA, 1863–1980*, Heinemann Educational Secondary Division. (S) Very student-friendly book with detail, summary questions and very well-organized crucial information on individuals, organizations and laws.

Vick, J. (1988) *Modern America*, Irwin Publishers. (S) A sound basis for American history although this is more a pre-DP text. Always a good place to start!

Cuba, Mexico and Latin America

Williamson, E. (1993) *The Penguin History of Latin America*, Penguin USA. (TR) Detailed relevant sections.

Rogozinski, J. (2000) *A Brief History of the Caribbean*, Plume. (S) Very good section on Cuba.

First World War

Pope, G. *The Origins of the First World War*, IBID Press. (S) Specifically designed for the DP history course. A useful source for topic 1 (Causes, practices and effects of war). Pope has been teaching IB history for many years.

Single Party States

Bullock, A. (1993) *Hitler and Stalin: Parallel Lives*, Vintage Books. (TR) Good source for the teacher.

Lee, S. (1987) *European Dictatorships*, Routledge. (S and/or TR) Excellent source offering a comparative analysis of the following people: Franco, Stalin, Hitler, Mussolini.

Todd, A. (2002) *The European Dictatorships: Hitler, Stalin, Mussolini*, Cambridge University Press. (S and TR) A good account of the three leaders with in-depth topical studies.

General texts

Traynor, J. (1993) *Europe 1890–1990*, Nelson. (S) This covers the World Wars and is a broad summary of the Cold War with some useful sources. Well-presented and good for students to do background reading.

Farmer, A. (2000) *An Introduction to Modern European History 1890–1990*, Hodder and Stoughton. (S) As above – similar style.

Farmer, A. (2001) *Nineteenth Century European History 1815–1914*, Hodder and Stoughton. (S) As above – similar style.

Periodicals

Modern History Review

New Perspectives

Series

Access to History (Hodder and Stoughton). (S and TR) Excellent chapter summaries and good overview with interpretation and some good source documents.

Perspectives in History (Cambridge University Press). (S and TR) A focus on a number of major periods of British and European history. It has theme texts on some topics for greater depth.

Seminar Studies in History (Longman). (S and TR) Though pitched at a higher level, this series offers the students various interpretations of events.

Videos

The Chinese Revolution (Films for the Humanities and Sciences (FH)). Succinct overview.

CNN Perspectives Cold War Series (Turner Original Productions) with accompanying books. Excellent source for the Cold War with lots of interviews from both sides and very well-organized in bite-size chunks.

Inside the Cold War – Superpowers Collide (David Paradine Television, Inc). A good short summary.

The Life and Times of Joseph Stalin (FH). Provides depth on Stalin even if only using for Russian background to the Cold War.

Gorbachev and the Fall of the Soviet Union (FH). Relevant to the fall of the Soviet Union.

War and Peace in the Middle East (MIA Video). Relevance to Suez, Non-Aligned Movement and Nasser, part of the Cold War and useful in its own right.

The Fateful Decade: From Little Rock to the Civil Rights Bill (FH). Clear summary but limited time period.

Martin Luther King 'I have a dream' (Home Video). Very specific to the ideals of the Civil Rights movement and King.

That War Korea (Time Life). Used mainly for its bias and therefore the evaluation of historical evidence.

No Man's Land: The Fall (The Century FH). Vietnam.

The World At War Part 4 (Thames Video). Popular and well produced but not a lot of depth.

Websites

Note: all weblinks featured in this chapter can be accessed through our website www.dp-help.com

http://cnn.com/SPECIALS/cold.war – the website that accompanies the video series

www.historylearningsite.co.uk – a website that gives a general overview but lacking in detail

http://online.ibo.org – teachers should use this recently revamped site as it provides forum discussions from around the world along with teaching strategies and resource materials (TR)

www.ihffilm.com/ – this website offers military, political and social historical films of the 20th century

Chapter 15

Group 4: Experimental sciences

Cameron Hunter, with Andy Payne and David Hobman

Cameron Hunter is one of the most experienced chemistry teachers at United World College of South East Asia (UWCSEA) in Singapore, and is known for his innovative, engaging and successful teaching style. In this chapter, he and his co-author team provide a full description of all the IB Diploma Programme (DP) science subjects, emphasizing the area where DP science departs from national curricula: the internal coursework.

Section 6 (design technology): *Andy Payne and David Hobman*
Andy Payne is head of design technology (DT) at UWCSEA, and is currently the faculty member responsible for the DT section of the IB Online Curriculum Centre and an assistant moderator for practical work.

David Hobman was a founder member of the steering committee that started IB DT and he is currently an IB assistant examiner and a DT workshop leader.

Cameron Hunter wishes to thank all of the staff of the science department of UWCSEA, in particular David Allan, Tony Bleasdale, Andy Cockburn, Shaun Hanley, Martin Lyon and Gary McKnight.

1 Introduction

This section introduces the reader to the science subjects of the IB Diploma Programme (the DP), highlighting the areas where the curriculum differs from that of traditional systems. It provides details on areas relevant to school administrators and a summary of the points of interest to teachers (which are subsequently discussed in greater detail in the rest of the chapter). Many of the ideas and practices included in this chapter have been adapted from those utilized by the science department of United World College of South East Asia.

1.1 Summary of group 4

The subjects available in group 4 are biology, chemistry, physics, environmental systems, and design technology (DT). A common curriculum model applies to all the DP group 4 subjects, with some exceptions in DT (see section 6 for details). All subjects are available at Standard Level (SL) and Higher Level (HL) except environmental systems (only at SL). Both SL and HL students study the same *core* material, and both include the study of two *option topics* from a range of topics. On top of this, HL students also study the so-called *additional higher level* (AHL) material.

The IB sciences place a great emphasis on practical work and students must complete a minimum of 60 experimental hours for HL courses and 40 hours for SL courses. A unique and exciting feature of the IB DP science practical curriculum is the group 4 project (discussed in detail in section 4), which aims to demonstrate the interconnectedness of the sciences and of science with the rest of the world. The practical work is ultimately rewarding in terms of educational outcome but is also the biggest challenge that a teacher new to the IB will encounter; this consequently takes up most of this chapter.

The group 4 common curriculum model (except DT), including number of contact hours recommended by the IBO, is summarized in figure 15.1. The curriculum model shows the recommended teaching time in hours for group 4 subjects. This includes the compulsory experimental work for 60 hours at HL and 40 hours at SL *inclusive* of the group 4 project referred to above. This experimental work is known as *internal assessment* (IA).

Figure 15.1 Curriculum framework (teaching hours)

Curriculum framework (HL)	240	Curriculum framework (SL)	150
Theory	180	Theory	110
Core	80	Core	80
Additional Higher Level (AHL)	55		
Options (choose two)	45	Options (choose two)	30
Internal assessment (IA)	**60**	**Internal assessment (IA)**	**40**
Investigations and practical work	45–50	Investigations and practical work	25–30
Group 4 project	10–15	Group 4 project	10–15

The group 4 assessment (valid for all subjects except DT) is summarized in figure 15.2.

Figure 15.2 Group 4 assessment

Assessment summary	SL		HL	
External assessment – 76%				
Paper 1 – multiple choice, no calculators	45 min	20%	1hr	20%
Paper 2 – shorter and longer data response questions	1hr 15	32%	2hr 15	36%
Paper 3 – questions on options	1hr	24%	1hr 15	20%
Internal assessment (IA) – 24%				
All experimental investigations and the group 4 project together count for 24%; details in sections 3 and 4.				

1.2 Course content: chemistry, physics, biology

In general, the DP core and AHL material will not throw up any great surprises for teachers used to other pre-university systems. As the subject outlines in figures 15.3–15.5 demonstrate, the majority of core and AHL material is fairly standard for any pre-university course. The main differences lie in the option modules offered, and in the internal assessment. Design technology and environmental systems are covered separately in sections 6 and 7.

Figure 15.3 Chemistry course content

SL	HL
Core	All core topics and the following advanced higher level (AHL) material
1. Stoichiometry	12. Atomic theory
2. Atomic theory	13. Periodicity
3. Periodicity	14. Bonding
4. Bonding	15. Energetics
5. States of matter	16. Kinetics
6. Energetics	17. Equilibrium
7. Kinetics	18. Acids and bases
8. Equilibrium	19. Oxidation and reduction
9. Acids and bases	20. Organic chemistry
10. Oxidation and reduction	
11. Organic chemistry	
Options. Select two from A–F	**Options. Select two from B–H**
A. Higher physical organic chemistry	B. Medicines and drugs
B. Medicines and drugs	C. Human biochemistry
C. Human biochemistry	D. Environmental chemistry
D. Environmental chemistry	E. Chemical industries
E. Chemical industries	F. Fuels and energy
F. Fuels and energy	G. Modern analytical chemistry
	H. Further organic chemistry

In chemistry options B–F, SL students study the core of the option only while HL students study the whole option. Each option accounts for 15 hours of teaching time for SL and 22 hours for HL.

Figure 15.4 Physics course content

SL	HL
Core	All core topics and the following advanced higher level (AHL) material
1. Physics and physical measurement 2. Mechanics 3. Thermal physics 4. Waves 5. Electricity and magnetism 6. Atomic and nuclear physics	7. Measurement and uncertainties 8. Mechanics 9. Thermal physics 10. Wave phenomena 11. Electromagnetism 12. Quantum physics and nuclear physics
Options. Select two from A–H A. Mechanics extension B. Quantum physics and nuclear physics C. Energy extension D. Biomedical physics E. The history and development of physics F. Astrophysics G. Relativity H. Optics	Options. Select two from D–H D. Biomedical physics E. The history and development of physics F. Astrophysics G. Relativity H. Optics

In physics options D–H, SL students study the core of the option only while HL students study the whole option. Each option accounts for 15 hours of teaching time for SL and 22 hours for HL.

Figure 15.5 Biology course content

SL	HL
Core	All core topics and the following advanced higher level (AHL) material
1. Cells 2. The chemistry of life 3. Genetics 4. Ecology and evolution 5. Human health and physiology	6. Nucleic acids and proteins 7. Cell respiration and photosynthesis 8. Genetics 9. Human reproduction 10. Defence against infectious diseases 11. Nerves, muscles and movement 12. Excretion 13. Plant science
Options. Select two from A–G A. Diet and human nutrition B. Physiology of exercise C. Cells and energy D. Evolution E. Neurobiology and behaviour F. Applied plant and animal science G. Ecology and conservation	Options. Select two from D–H D. Evolution E. Neurobiology and behaviour F. Applied plant and animal science G. Ecology and conservation H. Further human physiology

In biology options D–G, SL students study the core of the option only while HL students study the whole option. Each option accounts for 15 hours of teaching time for SL and 22 hours for HL.

1.3 General notes on the options

The options are varied and interesting. Some are specific to SL or HL (see figures 15.3–15.5) but many share a common core of SL material with extension material for HL, similar to the structure of the main syllabus. Depending on the teacher's background, these options can be somewhat of a challenge, especially since it is likely that a teacher new to the IB DP will have to prepare for at least one non-familiar option. Overall, the options allow schools to investigate areas that hold the interest of the majority of students or fit the particular expertise of a teacher. They also allow schools to promote areas close to their ethos or mission statement – such as *Ecology and conservation* in biology or *Environmental chemistry* in chemistry.

In chemistry, *Medicines and drugs* is an appealing topic and, for many educators, a refreshing break from traditional chemistry. This option is also highly relevant and gets a great response, particularly from the many students who are studying chemistry with a view to studying medicine at university. The most popular topics in HL tend to be *Modern analytical chemistry*, *Chemical industries* and *Further organic chemistry*. *Modern analytical chemistry* goes into more detail than most national curricula and provides ample scope for intelligent digression in the classroom. *Further organic* also connects well with the non-option material at HL. The *Chemical industries* topic is considered dull but undemanding but unlike the other two topics, it cannot be easily integrated into the non-option syllabus for HL. Such integration is not so easy to accomplish for any option topic in SL, where the options tend to stand alone more. Consequently, option take-up at SL is often more diverse and is usually dependent on teacher preference and sometimes student choice (see 'Managing the options', below).

The biology options provide the potential for stimulating in-depth study. For instance, for those more interested in the human body, the *Physiology of exercise* and *Diet and human nutrition* options for SL students are popular. They take students away from the more traditional areas of biology and allow some interesting hands-on experiences. HL students intending to study medicine or related subjects at university may prefer the challenging *Neurobiology and behaviour* or *Further human physiology*, which study very specific areas in much greater depth. The latter also ties in neatly with the non-option material at HL. *Evolution* offers a more detailed study of our place in history and *Ecology and conservation* provides insight into the wider problems associated with humans and their impact on the environment.

In physics, the contemporary nature of the *Astrophysics* and *Relativity* options makes them popular choices. Latest developments and discoveries in astrophysics are well covered in the media and are useful in provoking interest, discussion and debate. Some schools teach the *History* option as this connects with related topics in the core syllabus. At SL level, the more traditional options of *Mechanics* and *Optics* often prove the most popular.

Managing the options

The choice of option topic can be critical in a student's overall performance, although the 'correct' option to choose will be unique to each combination of teacher expertise and student preference. Many students prefer topics that include some overlap with other science topics they are studying; certainly this can improve the attainment of some students. For example, students studying chemistry and biology often select the chemistry option of *Human biochemistry*. Teachers also often prefer options that fit in with the non-option material as this gives continuity to the subject, which explains the above mentioned popularity of *Mechanics* in SL physics, *Further organic* in HL chemistry and *Further human physiology* in HL biology.

Some schools rely on independent study of the options by students, with teacher guidance given to individual students during class time. This can prove successful provided the students are given good study materials and the teacher is experienced enough to give instruction and explanation when necessary. However, for even the best and most skilled educator, it will be extremely stressful if students are given a free choice of options. As a result, most teachers dictate the choice, based on personal preference or the perceived difficulty of examination questions. Of course, students are perfectly at will to simply ignore your advice (and your teaching) and study their own preferred option. Intelligent students will always do well, but you should attempt to dissuade even the most able from this independent venture.

A final point worth mentioning is that students occasionally accidentally answer the wrong option, either by poor preparation or nerves or simple folly. To prevent this, include a full set of options in your final practice examination to ensure that students are used to the DP's examination format.

1.4 Internal assessment: the great challenge of group 4

The following quote by a teacher new to the IB highlights a common experience.

> I started teaching IB chemistry last September. The school I worked at before had always opted for the practical examination and not for the continuous assessment. As reference materials I was using the *ILPAC Advanced* practical chemistry package, the *Chemistry in Context Laboratory Manual* and past papers. I now have the feeling that the whole practical course should come from the top of my head! Any advice, guidance, support would be greatly appreciated.

Practical assessment is based on eight different criteria: Planning (a), Planning (b), Data collection, Data processing and presentation, Conclusion and evaluation, Manipulation skills, Personal skills (a), and Personal skills (b) (discussed in detail in section 3). The problem for teachers new to the IB is to devise a practical programme that addresses all these criteria and conforms to all the assessment conditions set out by the IBO.

Most established national curricula are supported by a vast array of commercial, off-the-shelf practical handbooks. However, at the present time there are few, if any, similar practical guides for the DP. The IBO, on its part, is not keen on any form of standardization (through off-the-shelf books or otherwise) of the internal assessment programme, as this would stifle its treasured values of educational freedom and expressions of cultural diversity, and because a standard system would disadvantage less affluent schools. Publishers, on their part, have been wary of investing in the DP's rapidly evolving curriculum. Nevertheless, attitudes may be changing as more schools start to implement the IB: certainly, more resources have become available recently – see section 10 for more details in this area.

In view of the difficulties described above, sections 3 and 4 of this chapter concentrate entirely on the internal assessment.

1.5 What courses to offer and how to offer them?

Ask IB diploma students which subject they find the most difficult and the answer is likely to be their group 4 course. This response to the sciences is not unique to the IB curriculum and is heard in school systems all over the world, contributing to a worrying slide in the number of science students in many countries. None the less, the DP compels all students to undertake a science course. In addition to this the student is expected to reflect on the nature of science and compare it with other areas of knowledge in Theory of Knowledge (TOK).

While many high school educators and universities regard the policy of science-for-all as a very positive aspect of the IB curriculum, it also poses problems. Keeping an eye on their budgets, administrators must provide HL courses that go deep enough to satisfy the university requirements for medicine, and science and engineering. In particular, schools that wish to cater to potential medicine students must take note of the fact that most medicine faculties require students to study two science subjects, usually a combination of chemistry and physics or biology, although a few go further and advise students to study all three sciences. (This is a rare combination; students can apply for exceptional permission to study these three sciences if necessary to gain admission to medical school – see Chapter 11.) At the same time a school has to offer SL science courses that are accessible to students whose natural inclinations lie elsewhere.

To facilitate the course selection process, all SL science courses are designed to be introductory courses that require no background in the subject. There is no doubt that previous knowledge of a science subject will allow for more rapid comprehension of that subject at SL. Although this may influence the diploma package negotiated between the student and the school, it should not be used to prohibit an enthusiastic beginner student from studying a particular science at SL. On the other hand, the HL courses require a good scientific background in the subject area – typically a minimum of one year's exposure – before entering the DP. Almost 50% of all diploma students study biology. It is popular because of the current excitement regarding genetics and biochemistry and because it is often perceived as an easier option. Physics and chemistry attract about 20% each, leaving 5–10% for design technology and environmental systems together. The worldwide figures show that SL and HL attract roughly the same number of students in each subject.

In a move to address the package concerns of schools and students, a new trans-disciplinary course, *Ecosystems and societies*, is currently being piloted in a number of schools (see Chapter 18 for more details). This course fulfils both group 3 and group 4 requirements, and attempts to place equal emphasis on the sciences and their impact on societies. *Ecosystems and societies*, generally expected to be available for examination around 2008, is almost certain to replace the current group 4 subject *Environmental systems*; it is for this reason that we mention *Environmental systems* only briefly in this chapter.

SL and HL together in one class?

While the IBO does not encourage teaching SL and HL courses in one class, it can be done thanks to the shared common core. Small schools just starting to develop the DP, or schools running the DP in conjunction with a national programme, will inevitably have little choice but to combine both sets of students. The accepted practice is to cover the core for all students together and quickly move on to the AHL material when only the HL students are present. Option choice is also generally dictated by the constraints of combining SL and HL on the basis of their having a common SL core (as most options have), or by selecting an extension option for SL which is mainly AHL material, for example mechanics in SL physics. There is no problem in combining both sets of students in your practical programme, as long as it is demanding enough to be acceptable for HL work; see sections 3 and 4 for further details. In the past some schools have elected to finish the SL course in the first year and enter the SL students in early examinations as so-called *anticipated* students. This is a practice the IBO would prefer to phase out, and schools wishing to receive favourable reports during authorization would do well to make efforts to stay clear of this course.

Internet assistance

If schools are only able to offer very few science subjects, as many schools new to the DP are, the group 4 inter-disciplinary project (see section 4) may force them to cooperate with other schools in the region, a move that would in itself be welcomed by the IBO. If a school is particularly isolated, the use of email and web-based interactive forums can be used to great effect to enable schools in different parts of the world to collaborate directly with each other. A small school in Zagreb which only supports chemistry in their DP can cooperate with another school in Venezuela, which only includes biology and physics, on the group 4 project. Departments comprising single teachers only could also use this technology to moderate internal assessment with solo colleagues elsewhere. The IB online forum enables groups wishing to cooperate in this manner to find like-minded schools.

Having listed here some of the concerns and constraints, we should make it clear that the IB DP science curriculum offers educators plenty of opportunities to allow the students to enjoy the courses. One of my current students commented: 'It's not easy but I feel that I've achieved a lot since I started chemistry HL. I feel like I'm being challenged to think constantly, especially when writing (lab) reports.' This point of view is further corroborated by comments from ex-students after their first year of university science courses: 'I definitely had a head start on others [non-IB students]. The practical work was a really good experience and I had no difficulty writing reports.' Many students come back to get their old lab books from my classroom shelves, and they seem to serve more than a purely sentimental purpose!

1.6 Group 4 and the overall DP aims

The DP's central aims (see Chapter 2) include the promotion of international-ism, intercultural understanding, student-centred learning, and the delivery of a holistic education. While the option modules in group 4 feature efforts to translate these general aims into the actual curriculum (as discussed in section 1.3), we have noted already that the core syllabus contents of DP sciences do not differ markedly from those of other mainstream science curricula. In this respect, we feel the IBO could do more to promote its values. For example, a small external assessment section on ethical implications would ensure that schools and students consider seriously the profound impact of science on society.

Although not externally assessed, the IB DP's objectives can and should be addressed in the teaching of the course. Biology discusses in depth the important issues surrounding the powerful but controversial new technologies involving genetic engineering. The study of genetics itself teaches much about internationalism. Debate about genetics and the nature–nurture issue is encouraged, as is discussion of the historical outcomes of the Eugenics movement and Social Darwinism, although the last two connected areas are not strictly part of the syllabus. Another area that discusses world issues is the ecology option, where experiences from around the world can be drawn upon to increase the relevance and interest of the topic. Plant science also encourages the use of examples from around the world, such as how certain types of plant adapt to different environmental conditions. In chemistry and physics, most of the materials directly relevant to internationalism are to be found in the option topics. The cross-border consequences of pollution are discussed in several topics (fuels and energy, chemical industries, environmental chemistry) and problems associated with power generation are discussed in the physics SL energy extension. Nevertheless, the IBO could make these issues more specific and relevant to students by direct requirements in the main syllabus.

Generally there is scope for further alignment of the group 4 syllabuses and the IBO's overall aims. At the very least, more reference to environmental chemistry should be emphasized in the non-option syllabus. Some teachers new to the IB have felt distinctly let down by the lack of direct syllabus reference to important areas of global concern and see this as a missed educational opportunity. They claim that, although the organization's aims are different from national systems, the actual syllabus contents are hardly different from those of other systems. This is an issue that the IBO may wish to consider more closely in future reviews.

The overall aims have had a more marked impact on the internal assessment. The 'Personal skills' and 'Planning' criteria of the internal assessment, and the cross-curricular teamwork required in the group 4 project, place the student squarely at the centre, and have proved innovative and successful features of the DP's sciences.

2 External assessment

All group 4 subjects share a common format for examination or external assessment. The variations with regard to design technology are discussed in section 6.

The external assessment for group 4 subjects consists of three papers:

Paper 1
Multiple choice (MC). 30 questions at SL, 40 at HL. A calculator is not allowed for this paper, although students will be expected to carry out basic arithmetical calculations. SL questions come from the core; HL questions contain a mix of

core and additional HL (AHL) material. Negative marking (removing marks for answering incorrectly) is *not* employed in this paper. As in most MC papers, the style of questioning becomes fairly predictable throughout the years and students can prepare well for this paper; access to questions from past papers is all the teacher needs (see section 10).

Paper 2
This is a written paper with two sections. Calculators are required. Section A is made up of short answer response questions and also includes a data response question. Section B gives students a choice of extended response questions. These questions are more open-ended and require longer analysis and extended writing. SL students must answer one question from a choice of three (core material only). HL students must answer two questions from a choice of four (core and AHL material combined).

Paper 3
Paper 3 focuses entirely on the option material. Two option questions must be attempted from a choice of between five and eight, depending on the course and level – see figures 15.3–15.5. SL option questions consist of short answer response questions, whereas HL options consist of short answer response questions plus one extended response question. In biology, a data response section is also included in both option questions. Calculators are required for this paper.

The option Paper 3 is an excellent opportunity for students to score highly. The questions are not always easy, but students can only be asked questions on the area of the syllabus pertaining to option topics, as opposed to Papers 1 and 2 where the whole range of the syllabus, excluding the options, is assessed.

3 Internal assessment

3.1 Introduction

The group 4 experimental sciences are based around a rigorous, experimentally based core. The practical work that is the internal assessment (IA) generally takes up about one-quarter of teaching time and counts for 24% of the final examination marks. Furthermore, there is no external practical examination as in many other pre-university courses because all practical work is internally assessed. This is a challenging area of the IB diploma, both for students and for the educators who spend a lot of time preparing and assessing this area of the course. The reward is that properly prepared students learn more key techniques and have more practical experience than students in other science programmes. As a consequence, IB students cope very well with the demands of first year university science courses.

Any IA course needs to be sufficiently demanding and experiments should be included to cover the range of the syllabus studied (core, AHL if an HL course, and options). As we have seen, it should be 40 hours for SL and 60 hours for HL. This can include 10–15 hours for the group 4 project (see section 4). The time that is allocated for each practical is for student experimental work only and should not include teacher demonstrations or time spent writing the report at home, though time spent designing plans is accepted as part of a student's 'experimental work'. A simple experiment could be complete in 1–1.5 hours, although a full investigation could last maybe 3 hours or even longer, particularly in biology, where extended practical sessions form a large element of the experimental work. Obviously, these times are just guidelines but they should give an idea of the number of practical lessons needed in a course. Sample schedules are included towards the end of this chapter, and these include possible investigation titles which are appropriate for this level of study (see section 8).

There are eight criteria for practicals that must be assessed on *at least two occasions* during the course. They are: Planning (a) (Pl (a), Planning (b) (Pl (b)), Data collection (DC), Data processing and presentation (DPP), Conclusion and evaluation (CE), Manipulative skills (MS), Personal skills (a), (PS (a)) and Personal skills (b) (PS (b)) (see section 3.2 for details). All eight criteria should be internally moderated and the first five will be externally moderated by the IBO. (Moderation is covered in sections 3.7 and 3.8.)

How does this grading work? The highest mark available for each of the eight criteria is 3. As the students proceed throughout the course, they will complete a range of experimental investigations which can be assessed with respect to one or more of the eight criteria. For each student, overall grading in IA is obtained by taking the two highest grades that the student has attained in that particular criterion throughout the IA course. This process is repeated for all criteria. The internal assessment grade is thus marked out of a total of 48 ($8\times3\times2 = 48$), which is reduced to 24% for the final examination mark. The IBO requires schools to send samples of their students' work, which will be checked and moderated to ensure that the school's lab programme and IA marking are in agreement with their criteria. This is a controversial area of group 4 assessment as many schools have had their IA marks moderated down, some quite drastically. If you are starting the DP for the first time you'll want to make sure you get this part of your work correct from the start. The following section aims to help in this respect.

3.2 The assessment criteria

Issues relating to marking, moderating and the delivery of sample material to the IBO are common to all group 4 subjects. The IBO common group 4 assessment criteria are listed and discussed in this section. Remember that each of the eight criteria needs to be assessed at least twice and the maximum score for each criterion is 3.

Each criterion has either two or three 'aspects' and each aspect is graded either 'complete'(c), 'partial' (p) or 'not at all' (n). The grade of 0, 1, 2 or 3 is then awarded according to a simple marking grid – see figures 15.15 and 15.16.

Guidelines are included for each criterion to show how it should be interpreted. Readers should note that this commentary is based on my personal experience as an IB teacher and is not the voice of the IBO.

The planning criteria, and in particular planning (a), tend to be the criteria that teachers who are new to the IB find most difficult to come to terms with. We will therefore spend some time reviewing this important area.

The planning criteria Pl (a) and Pl (b)

In planning (a) (see figure 15.6) the first aspect concerns the research question or aim of the experiment. Students should never simply repeat the general aim or

Figure 15.6 Assessment of planning PI (a)

LEVELS	ASPECTS		
	Defining the problem or research question	Formulating a hypothesis or prediction	Selecting variables
Complete	Identifies a focused problem or research question.	Relates the hypothesis or prediction directly to the research question and explains it, quantitatively where appropriate.	Selects the relevant independent and controlled variable(s).
Partial	States the problem or research question, but it is unclear or incomplete.	States the hypothesis or prediction but does not explain it.	Selects some relevant variables.
Not at all	Does not state the problem or research question **or** repeats the general aim provided by the teacher.	Does not state a hypothesis or prediction.	Does not select any relevant variables.

title supplied by the teacher. The IBO advises, on the Online Curriculum Centre (OCC), that your teacher title should be 'sufficiently specific to give candidates a sense of direction, but not sufficiently specific to serve as a research question'. For example, 'Investigate projectiles' is good, but 'Investigate the effect of the angle of firing on projectile range' is not. 'Investigate the voltage of a cell' is good, but 'Investigate the effect of varying concentration of metal ions on the voltage of a cell' is not. The second title in each case in effect specifies the research question that the students themselves should identify in aspect 1. As a consequence, you take away any chance that they could score a 'c' for aspect 1. In addition, you have made it too easy for them to identify the variables (see aspect 3, also below), and therefore made it impossible for them to score a grade 3 for this criterion. If students simply use your title as a research question they will be awarded 'n' (not at all) for the first aspect.

For the second aspect, the student is required to state what possible outcome they feel will occur and then explain fully their scientific reasoning, employing calculations to justify this where necessary. For example, in the physics example above the student may state, 'The projectile range will be at a maximum between the angles of 30° and 40°'. A prediction or hypothesis has now been stated and the student will be awarded at least 'p' for aspect 2. To gain a 'c' the student would then have to explain this logically, with reference to any equations or concepts. A good student would also attempt to draw a sketch graph of their predicted results, if appropriate. Note that the prediction and consequentially the explanation need not necessarily be correct, but must be logical and based on sound scientific principles.

The third aspect requires the student to clearly outline the variables involved. *Controlled* variables are those variables that the scientists can control, and they will remain the same throughout the entire experiment. In the above chemistry example, the student could realistically be expected to control the surface area of the metal electrodes exposed, the temperature of the solutions, and the apparatus used. The *independent* variable is the variable that the student changes or manipulates in the investigation. In this example they will vary the concentration of metal ions. The *dependent* (responding) variables are those that depend on the independent variables, and which are typically the responses that the student measures, such as voltage in this case. In the projectile example, the variables could be listed as:

- independent variable – angle
- dependent variable – range
- controlled variables – initial velocity, height, mass of object and shape of object.

Note that any of the controlled variables in this example could have been used as independent variables by other students, giving rise to a variety of possible investigations.

It will come as no surprise that there has been substantial debate regarding the amount of detail you can provide in the assignment or title, both on the online forums and at IB workshops. However, when assessing Pl (a), it is best to avoid any possible ambiguity by only supplying a dependent variable in your title or, in the case of 'investigate projectiles' (replace projectiles with photosynthesis or osmosis, etc. for other investigations), providing no variable at all. Either is acceptable. The more general titles will provide for interesting projects, but will be more difficult to manage in the lab, although it should be noted that there is no requirement for a student to actually carry out the experiment to gain marks for Pl (a). (Students prefer to carry out their plans, however, and this can sometimes lead to an interesting extended essay for initial plans that are too ambitious for normal class time.)

The important point is that students come up themselves with a research question that includes the relevant controlled and independent variables. It helps to train them into the habit of phrasing their research questions along the lines of 'How does this (independent) affect that (dependent)?' Another important point to note is that the Pl (a) criterion does not lend itself very well to titles that aim to prove existing scientific laws. For example, a teacher title such as 'Justify Hess's Law', or, 'Find *g* by throwing things out of the window', has already implied the hypothesis or prediction. These experiments are best left to planning (b) (see below), where a wide variety of different experimental techniques can be used to investigate the given research question. As a final example, we include one more practical activity that is assessable under Pl (a).

Teacher title: 'What affects the speed of waves?' (Note that the dependent variable, speed, is given.)

Students have lots of possible investigations here. They could look at water, sound, light, slinkys, waves on strings, etc. Once they isolate their area of study, they then decide which variable to investigate. Possible student research questions include:

- How does the tension in a slinky affect the speed?
- How does the depth of water affect the speed?
- How does the concentration of sugar solution affect the speed of light through it?

Notice the phrasing of the questions, utilizing the 'How does this (independent) affect that (dependent)?' approach. Students then state the necessary controlled variables and move on to explaining how to carry out the investigation – the area that is assessed in planning (b) (see figue 15.7).

Figure 15.7 Assessment of planning Pl (b)

LEVELS	ASPECTS		
	Selecting appropriate apparatus or materials	Designing a method for the control of variables	Designing a method for the collection of sufficient relevant data
Complete	Selects appropriate apparatus or materials.	Describes a method that allows for the control of the variables.	Describes a method that allows for the collection of sufficient relevant data.
Partial	Selects some appropriate apparatus or materials.	Describes a method that makes some attempt to control the variables.	Describes a method that allows for the collection of insufficient relevant data.
Not at all	Does not select any apparatus or materials.	Describes a method that does not allow for the control of the variables.	Describes a method that does not allow any relevant data to be collected.

For the first aspect, the student should list all appropriate apparatus, materials and reagents. They should include all details such as timing devices, distance measuring devices, volumes, concentrations, sizes and even uncertainties. A clearly labelled diagram is acceptable. Do not give the student an apparatus list or diagram or experimental method. If you do, all aspects in this section could be marked down. If students simply copy this then they will be awarded 'n' for the apparatus aspect. If students select additional apparatus, then they may be given credit for those but will only gain a maximum of 'p' (partial), and consequently will be unable to gain a 3.

You should never give out step-wise methods for instructions when assessing this criterion as methodology is assessed in aspects 2 and 3. The student's method must clearly detail how the variables stated in Pl (a) will be controlled or measured. The method must also show how all relevant data required to fulfil the research question will be generated in the investigation.

Planning experiments that do not fulfil the requirements of Pl (a) can still be used to good effect in Pl (b). Titles such as 'Determine *g* experimentally' will still enable students to come up with many different experimental approaches and are therefore suitable for this criterion. The same cannot be said for a title such as 'Justify Hooke's Law', as students will effectively perform the same old textbook 'mass on springs' experiment.

The planning criteria are challenging and can be rather frustrating when first implementing the IA. However, this is clearly an area that offers students the opportunity to think for themselves and indeed think in a truly scientific manner. Furthermore the open-ended approach to investigations makes a refreshing change, for both teachers and students, from standard experimental work.

Figure 15.8 is a condensed version of a form that is passed to the students by the physics department of UWCSEA when the planning skills are being assessed (naturally, the space available for student answers needs to be considerably expanded if you decide to use such a form).

Figure 15.8 Planning help sheet

Planning A

Aim:

Hypothesis:

Why do you believe your hypothesis is true?

Explain what pattern you expect to see in your results, and justify this, quantitatively where appropriate.

Independent (manipulated) variable	Dependent (responding) variable	Controlled variables

Planning B

Draw a diagram of your equipment.

Explain how you will keep the controlled variables constant.

Draw a table that can be used to record your results. (How many readings will you take?)

Say how you will make each of these measurements.

The criteria DC, DPP and CE

Figure 15.9 Assessment of data collection (DC)

	ASPECTS	
LEVELS	**Collecting and recording raw data**	**Organizing and presenting raw data**
Complete	Records appropriate raw data (qualitative and/or quantitative), including units and uncertainties where necessary.	Presents raw data clearly, allowing for easy interpretation.
Partial	Records some appropriate raw data.	Presents raw data but does not allow for easy interpretation.
Not at all	Does not record any appropriate raw data.	Does not present raw data **or** presents it incomprehensibly.

Aspect 1 concerns the recording of raw data such as observations and/or measurements. Observations should be recorded in detail, not simply final colours. Data must be to correct significant figures, and must include units and uncertainties. If an experiment includes qualitative and quantitative data, then *both* must be included. For example, a titration should include indicator colour changes in addition to all standard quantitative recordings.

Aspect 2 assesses how clear and easy it is to understand the collected data. This invariably means a well-designed results table with *all* relevant information. Do not give a results table that needs to be filled in or explicitly tell the students what data to collect.

Figure 15.9 Data collection (continued)

Example: Your instruction sheet provides a table with units and headings. The student copies this table and accurately fills in data. Some teachers would give 'c,c' (complete, complete) and therefore award a 3 for this criterion. However, for the first aspect the student cannot be awarded a 'complete' as you have already indicated to the student what units to use, which the students should obviously decide themselves to get a 'complete' mark. For the second aspect the student will be penalized heavily as well since they have not designed their own presentation format, only copied yours. So since you have already given both units and a presentation format, the IBO will moderate this as 'p, n' and award 0!

Figure 15.10 Assessment of data processing and presentation (DPP)

LEVELS	ASPECTS	
	Processing raw data	Presenting processed data
Complete	Processes the raw data correctly.	Presents processed data appropriately to aid interpretation and, where relevant, takes into account errors and uncertainties.
Partial	Some raw data is processed correctly.	Presents processed data appropriately but with some errors and/or omissions.
Not at all	No processing of raw data is carried out **or** major errors are made in processing.	Presents processed data inappropriately **or** incomprehensibly.

The first aspect is very clear with calculations but becomes more ambiguous with qualitative data. How should observations be processed? Well, students can propose deductions and conclusions, can write equations and explain trends. However, be aware that in this type of qualitative data processing, your grade will be open to more interpretation by the IBO moderator than with numerical data work.

For the second aspect, calculations should be easy to follow and clear. Ensure that HL students process random errors in calculations. Any qualitative deductions should be expressed clearly, perhaps with a summary table, and graphs should be correctly labelled, designed and executed. Do not provide students with sample calculations or explicitly tell them which axes to plot when graphing. *Example:* Your instructions include 'plot a graph from raw data' and indicate which variables to plot. The maximum the IBO will award is 'c, n', giving a grade 1 maximum.

Figure 15.11 Assessment of conclusion and evaluation (CE)

LEVELS	ASPECTS		
	Drawing conclusions	Evaluating procedure(s) and results	Improving the investigation
Complete	Gives a valid conclusion, based on the correct interpretation of the results, with an explanation and, where appropriate, compares results with literature values.	Evaluates procedure(s) and results including limitations, weaknesses or errors.	Identifies weaknesses and states realistic suggestions to improve the investigation.
Partial	States a conclusion that has some validity.	Evaluates procedure(s) and results but misses some obvious limitations or errors.	Suggests only simplistic improvements.

(continues overleaf)

Figure 15.11 Assessment of conclusion and evaluation (CE) (continued)

LEVELS	ASPECTS		
	Drawing conclusions	Evaluating procedure(s) and results	Improving the investigation
Not at all	Draws a conclusion that misinterprets the results.	The evaluation is superficial or irrelevant.	Suggests unrealistic improvements.

Investigations that are well suited to this criterion tend to include previous processing of numerical data. In aspect 1, the student's processed data leads to a conclusion which the student then proceeds to fully justify scientifically. The processed data is compared with a sourced literature value, if available, which then allows students to determine how accurate their experiment may have been, speculate or identify systematic errors, and generally evaluate and improve on their experiments in aspects 2 and 3. HL candidates, who will have calculated error boundaries in their processed data, should be able to demonstrate if their answer is consistent with the literature value, hence giving an approximate value of systematic errors in the experimental design. Make sure that students provide realistic improvements (aspect 3) for all errors identified in their evaluations (aspect 2). Again, you should avoid using leading questions specific to the investigation that could assist the students in their conclusion and evaluation, although using general questions which restate the above criteria, so as to remind the student what to do, is fine. For example; 'Evaluate the experimental procedure and suggest appropriate improvements' is fine, but 'What would be the effect of using a poorly calibrated ammeter and how could you correct this problem?' is too specific.

The comments in figures 15.9, 15.10 and 15.11 are adapted from the experimental sciences guides © IBO 2001

The criteria MS, PS(a) and PS(b)

Figure 15.12 Assessment of manipulative skills (MS)

LEVELS	ASPECTS	
	Carrying out techniques safely	Following a variety of instructions
Complete	Is competent and methodical in the use of the technique(s) and the equipment, and pays attention to safety issues.	Follows the instructions accurately, adapting to new circumstances (seeking assistance when required).
Partial	Requires assistance in the use of a routine technique. Works in a safe manner with occasional prompting.	Follows the instructions but requires assistance.
Not at all	Does not carry out the techniques(s) or misuses the equipment, showing no regard for safety.	Does not follow the instructions or requires constant supervision.

Comments for this criterion and the next two are to be found in section 3.7.

Figure 15.13 Assessment of personal skills (a) (PS (a))

	ASPECTS		
LEVELS	Working within a team	Recognizing the contributions of others	Exchanging and integrating ideas
Complete	Collaborates with others, recognizing their needs, in order to complete the task.	Expects, actively seeks and acknowledges the views of others.	Exchanges ideas with others, integrating them into the task.
Partial	Requires guidance to collaborate with others.	Acknowledges some views.	Exchanges ideas with others but requires guidance in integrating them into the task.
Not at all	Is unsuccessful when working with others.	Disregards views of others.	Does not contribute.

Figure 15.14 Assessment of personal skills (b) (PS (b))

	ASPECTS		
LEVELS	Approaching scientific investigations with self-motivation and perseverance	Working in an ethical manner	Paying attention to environmental impact
Complete	Approaches the investigation with self-motivation and follows it through to completion.	Pays considerable attention to the authenticity of the data and information, and the approach to materials (living or non-living).	Pays considerable attention to the environmental impact of the investigation.
Partial	Approaches the investigation with self-motivation or follows it through to completion.	Pays some attention to the authenticity of the data and information, and the approach to materials (living or non-living).	Pays some attention to the environmental impact of the investigation.
Not at all	Lacks perseverance and motivation.	Pays little attention to the authenticity of the data and information, and the approach to materials (living or non-living).	Pays little attention to the environmental impact of the investigation.

Awarding grades

After assessing each aspect as either c, p, or n the teacher then awards a grade of 0, 1, 2 or 3 for that criterion as follows:

(a) For those criteria with three aspects, figure 15.15 details the final score calculation.

Figure 15.15 Final numerical score calculation for criteria with three aspects

Levels	3	2	2	2	1	1	1	1	0	0
Completely (c)										
Partially (p)										
Not at all (n)										

To give an example, there are three ways a student can score a 2 for PS (b) (the last listed criterion): he/she needs to have scored the combination 'c, c, p' or 'c, c, n' or 'c, p, p' for the three aspects of PS (b).

(b) For criteria with only two aspects (such as MS), grades are awarded according to figure 15.16.

Figure 15.16 Final numerical score calculation for criteria with two aspects

Levels	3	2	1	1	0	0
Completely (c)						
Partially (p)						
Not at all (n)						

(The mathematically inclined may notice that the same grade can be obtained by equating $c = 1$ ($c = 1.5$ if there are only two aspects), $p = 0.5$, and $n = 0$ and then adding up and *rounding down*, but the IBO insists on using the letter system.)

3.3 IA support from the IBO, and a sample investigation

The IBO have produced sample IA material which is available for viewing and subsequent download from the Online Curriculum Centre (OCC). Once registered, view the files from your subject homepage by accessing 'teacher support material phase 1 and phase 2'.

Teacher support material phase 1 covers three main areas:

1. The planning criteria (Pl (a) and Pl (b)).
2. Uncertainties and errors relevant to criteria DC, DPP and CE.
3. Manipulative and personal skills (MS, PS (a) and PS (b)).

Teacher support material phase 2 contains sample investigations which have been marked and assessed by IBO moderators. All material in phase 1 and phase 2 is subject-specific. By checking with these examples, you should be able to ensure that your IA programme is in line with the standards expected by the IBO.

You may also find it helpful to look at the sample schemes of work in section 8 of this chapter, which contain the titles for a full IA programme for biology, chemistry and physics.

In order to demonstrate the application of the assessment criteria, we have included an example of a marked student's investigation in figure 15.17. The student's work has been retyped for ease of reading, but is essentially unaltered. Although the work is in chemistry, and physics and biology teachers may not be interested in the details of this student's work, the gist of the work and the nature of my comments should be clear to science teachers of all subjects. The investigation under consideration was entitled 'Investigate heat of neutralization' by the teacher, a chemistry planning practical. The heat of neutralization is the heat released when an acid neutralizes a base (thereby forming water) and can be easily measured by recording the temperature rise when the two reactants are mixed and using some simple thermal physics to gain an approximate value. The units are standardized in $kJ\,mol^{-1}$. No direct instructions are given to the student who is assessed on the first five criteria: Pl (a), Pl (b), DC, DPP and CE. The student's work is shown in italics. My comments regarding assessment are in boxes (note that this is my own marking and not that of an IBO moderator). You should refer to the IA criteria (see section 3.2) when viewing these comments.

Figure 15.17 A sample investigation

<u>Investigate heat of neutralization</u>

<u>Research question</u>
How will varying the type of acid affect the heat of neutralization?

<u>Hypothesis</u>
I believe that the use of a stronger acid will increase the heat of neutralization.

<u>Variables</u>
Independent variable: Type of acid used
Dependent variable: Temperature released in reaction (This, of course means that the heat of neutralization is actually the dependent variable as well.)
Controlled variables: Type of base used, concentration and volume of acid and base, type of calorimeter, initial temperature of both solutions, amount of stirring, lab temperature.

Pl (a) assessment
The student uses a focused and specific research question which is not simply a copy of the title given. 'Complete' (c) awarded for first aspect. The hypothesis is stated, but not explained in any way, hence 'partial' (p) awarded for second aspect. To gain 'complete' the student would have to have supplied a logical, though not necessarily correct, explanation of the hypothesis, and in this case would also have been required to display how he would work through the problem quantitatively. The variables section is excellent – 'complete' (c) awarded. The student therefore gains c, p, c, i.e. a grade 2 for Pl (a).

<u>Apparatus and reagents</u>
1. Two polystyrene calorimeters and one foil lid with small hole for thermometer.
2. Thermometer, $-10\,°C$ to $60\,°C$, $+/-0.25\,°C$.
3. Two $50\,cm^3$ beakers.
4. Two $25\,cm^3$ pipettes, grade A, $+/-0.03\,cm^3$.
5. Standardized 1M NaOH – exact concentration in data collection.
6. Standardized 1M HCl, CH_3COOH, $CH_2ClCOOH$ – exact concentration in data collection.
7. Distilled water for washing.

<u>Method</u>
1. Measure the room temperature.
2. Pipette $25\,cm^3$ of standardized 2M HCl and place in first calorimeter. Record temperature.
3. Pipette $25\,cm^3$ of standardized 2M NaOH and place in second calorimeter. Record temperature.
4. Rapidly mix contents of first calorimeter to second, secure lid and quickly insert thermometer. Stir three times with thermometer. Measure highest temperature rise.
5. Repeat steps 1 to 4 to gain second reading.
6. Rinse calorimeter, thermometer and acid pipette thoroughly.
7. Repeat steps 1 to 6 for the other two acids.   (continues overleaf)

Figure 15.17 A sample investigation (continued)

<u>Pl (b) assessment</u>
Student selects appropriate apparatus and is awarded a 'c' for the first aspect. Note that a well-labelled diagram would also have been fine. You could argue that the thermometer is lacking in accuracy and penalize accordingly here, but I feel this would be over-zealous. However, this is something that I would penalize if it was not noted in the student's subsequent evaluation. At UWCSEA we also encourage students to include uncertainty and range with all apparatus. The exact concentration of solutions is left until later since in this case, the students would not know the exact value until they arrived in the lab, though it is important that the student has noted that the solutions should be standardized (of accurate concentration). The method controls the previously stated variables and will give sufficient relevant data. Note that this is not the most accurate method possible; a thermometric titration would probably be better, but the award of 'complete' does not have to mean absolutely perfect work; 'c, c' awarded for aspects 2 and 3. The student therefore gains c, c, c, i.e. a grade 3 for Pl (b).

<u>Data collection</u>

Recorded data for heat of neutralization investigation			
All volumes +/−0.03 cm³	25 cm³ 0.997M HCl and 25 cm³ 1.007M NaOH	25 cm³ 0.999M CH_3COOH and 25 cm³ 1.007M NaOH	25 cm³ 1.005M $CH_2ClCOOH$ and 25 cm³ 1.007M NaOH
Max. temp. rise run 1 (+/−0.5°C)	6.5	6.0	6.0
Max. temp. rise run 2 (+/−0.5°C)	7.0	6.0	6.5
Average max. temp. rise (+/−0.5°C)	6.75	6.0	6.25
	Room temperature during all experiments = 24.0 +/−0.25 °C No uncertainty was provided with the given solutions		

<u>DC assessment</u>
In the first aspect the student must record all raw data including units and uncertainties. There are no qualitative observations, but in this case, there would be none of note anyway. However, the student has not included initial or final temperatures, though he has added the errors in measuring these together to give the overall error of (+/−0.5°C). Some raw data is included (room temperature, exact concentrations) so 'p' is awarded. The second aspect focuses on presentation and this table provides for easy interpretation. A 'c' is awarded. Note that SL students only need to list uncertainty values; they would not need to combine them in any way, even simply by adding two together to get a single uncertainty. The student therefore gains p, c, i.e. a grade 2 for DC.

<u>Calculations</u>
$\Delta E = mc\Delta T$, where ΔE = the energy released by the reaction in kJ, m = mass of solution in kg, ΔT = the temperature rise in °C and c = the specific heat capacity of water = 4.2 kJ kg^{-1}°C^{-1}.

<u>Assumptions</u>
1. As the solutions are dilute, the volume used is assumed to be water. Water has a density of 1 g per cm³. As 50 cm³ is used in all experiments, the mass used is assumed to be 0.050 kg in all cases.
2. As the solution is approximated to be water, the specific heat capacity of water is used.
3. All heat released in the reaction is transferred to the solutions.
4. Since the alkali is slightly in excess in all reactions, the limiting reactant will be the acid and this will govern the amount of water formed.

Figure 15.17 A sample investigation (continued)

Calculations for neutralization of HCl and NaOH
$\Delta E = mc\Delta T$
   $= (0.050)(4.2)(6.75)$
   $= \underline{1.42\,kJ}$
Number of moles = volume $\times$ molarity
         $= (0.0250)(0.0997)$
         $= \underline{0.0249\,mols}$ *water formed releasing 1.42 kJ*
Therefore, 1 mole will release 1.42/0.0249 = 57.0 kJ mol^{-1}
Errors: pipette = (0.03/25)100 = 0.12%, pipette used twice, therefore pipette error = 0.24%
Thermometer = (0.5/6.75)100 = 7.4%   overall error = 7.4 + 0.24 = 7.64%
         Therefore heat of neutralization (HCl and NaOH) = 57.0 +/−7.64%
                          $= \underline{-57.0 +/-4\,kJ\,mol^{-1}}$

Calculations for neutralization of CH$_3$COOH and NaOH
$\Delta E = mc\Delta T$
   $= (0.050)(4.2)(6.0)$
   $= \underline{1.26\,kJ}$
Number of moles = volume $\times$ molarity
         $= 0.0250 \times 0.0999$
         $= \underline{0.0250\,mols}$ *water formed releasing 1.26 kJ*
Therefore, 1 mole will release 1.26/0.0250 = $\underline{50.4\,kJ\,mol^{-1}}$
Errors: pipette = (0.03/25)100 = 0.12%, pipette used twice, therefore pipette error = 0.24%
Thermometer = (0.5/6)100 = 8.3%   overall error = 8.3 + 0.24 = 8.54%
         Therefore heat of neutralization (CH$_3$COOH and NaOH) = 50.4 +/−8.54%
                          $= \underline{-50.4 +/-4\,kJ\,mol^{-1}}$

Calculations for neutralization of CH$_2$ClCOOH and NaOH
$\Delta E = mc\Delta T$
   $= (0.050)(4.2)(6.25)$
   $= \underline{1.31\,kJ}$
Number of moles = volume $\times$ molarity
         $= 0.025 \times 1.005$
         $= \underline{0.0251\,mols}$ *water formed releasing 1.31 kJ*
Therefore, 1 mole will release 1.31/0.0251 = $\underline{52.2\,kJ\,mol^{-1}}$
Errors: pipette = (0.03/25)100 = 0.12%, pipette used twice, therefore pipette error = 0.24%
Thermometer = (0.5/6.25)100 = 8.0%   overall error = 8.0 + 0.24 = 8.24%
         Therefore heat of neutralization (CH$_2$ClCOOH and NaOH) = 52.2 +/−8.24%
                          $= \underline{-52.2 +/-4\,kJ\,mol^{-1}}$

DPP assessment
The data is processed correctly, therefore 'c' awarded for the first aspect. The
calculations make for easy interpretation and errors are processed fully, giving a 'c'
for the second aspect. Note that SL students need not process errors at all. The
student therefore gains c, c, i.e. a grade 3 for DPP. It could be argued that the
student's work contains errors with respect to significant figures, though I don't
believe this would justify a p grade for either criterion.

Conclusion and evaluation
Final results

Experiment	Experimental value (kJ mol^{-1})
HCl and NaOH	−57.0 +/−4
CH$_3$COOH and NaOH	−50.4 +/−4
CH$_2$ClCOOH and NaOH	−52.2 +/−4

The trend displayed above confirms my original hypothesis that the use of a stronger acid
will increase the heat of neutralization, since HCl is the strongest acid, followed by
CH$_2$ClCOOH (pKa = 2.86*) then CH$_3$COOH (pKa = 4.76*). Weak acids, unlike strong acids
like HCl, do not dissociate completely into ions and stay mainly in molecular form. In order

Figure 15.17 A sample investigation (continued)

to release H⁺ ions, bonds must be broken within the molecule. This takes energy and the energy released from neutralization is therefore reduced. As the acid becomes weaker the effect becomes more marked, hence the trend observed above.

A comparison of my experimental values with data book values is shown below.

	Experimental value (kJmol⁻¹)	*Data book value* (kJmol⁻¹)*
HCl and NaOH	−57.0 +/−4	−57.1
CH₃COOH and NaOH	−50.4 +/−4	−55.2
CH₂ClCOOH and NaOH	−52.2 +/−4	*unavailable*

*Chemistry Data Book, 2nd edition.
I could not find an entry for the combination of CH₂ClCOOH and NaOH. My value for the heat of neutralization of HCl and NaOH is within the range of uncertainty of the accepted data book value; however, the result for CH₃COOH and NaOH is not within the accepted range and there must be systematic errors affecting the experiment in addition to the calculated random errors.

Evaluation and improvements
There are obvious sources of error in this experiment. The thermometer scale was very inaccurate and led to a large random error. An experiment which allowed for a higher temperature rise would have reduced the error in this reading. Heat loss to the surroundings was also unavoidable. The assumption that the solutions were mainly water could also have been a cause of error, both in the mass used and the value of the specific heat capacity. To improve this experiment, I would use a far more accurate thermometer, possibly a digital one reading to two decimal places. I would use double the concentration of the reagents used in order to increase the temperature rise and hence reduce the error in this reading. I would use a tight-fitting lid instead of a foil top and insulate the calorimeter by using a double cup. I would also try and gain a more accurate reading for the specific heat capacity of the resulting solution.

CE assessment
The conclusion is based on the processed results and, though rather brief, the explanation of the trend is logical and appropriate. The results are also compared with available literature values; hence a 'c' is awarded for the first aspect. There is a good evaluation of the experiment and realistic improvements are proposed. Note again, that it's not perfect work; the student could have noted that the experiment could have been made more accurate by performing a thermometric titration, but I believe it would be rather pedantic not to award 'c' for both the second and third aspects.
The student therefore gains c, c, c, i.e. a grade 3 for CE.

3.4 Practical Scheme of Work (4/PSOW) sample forms

The selected IA programme is known as the Practical Scheme of Work (4/PSOW). As stated above, the IBO gives some guidelines for investigative practicals but you are given full creative freedom to design your own programme.

Although it is a substantial amount of work, it would be advisable to prepare an electronic *4/PSOW cover sheet* as well as a *4/PSOW detail sheet* which lists all your intended investigations, *before* you start the course. This will help you to prepare for the number and range of practicals you will need to cover. Sample PSOW cover and detail sheets are reproduced as figures 15.18 and 15.19. These have been slightly amended from the IBO originals to fit my own preferences. They are downloadable as Word files from our website: www.dp-help.com.

Figure 15.18 Sample 4/PSOW (Practical Scheme of Work) cover sheet

International Baccalaureate
Form 4/PSOW
Internal assessment cover sheet : Group 4

School Name:			School code:	
Candidate Code:	Subject:	HL	SL	Session: May / Nov 2005 (choose one)
Candidate Name:	Teacher Name:		Is this student in the moderation sample? (tick box):	YES NO
Teacher's Signature:	Date:			

- *Type or write legibly using black ink and retain a copy of this form.*

Total lab hours:				SKILLS ASSESSED						
	PI (a)	PI (b)	DC	DPP	CE	MS	PS (a)	PS (b)
BEST TWO GRADES FOR EACH CRITERION (MAX 3 EACH):								
TOTAL FOR EACH CRITERION (MAX 6 EACH):								
OVERALL TOTAL (OUT OF 48):								

This total must also appear on the IA/PG mark sheet

Figure 15.19 Sample PSOW (Practical Scheme of Work) detail sheet

Candidate Code:			Subject:		Session:	May / Nov 2004 (choose one)
Candidate Name:			Teacher Name:	HL	SL	
				Is this student in the moderation sample? (tick box)		YES □ NO □

SKILLS ASSESSED

Date(s)	Outline of Experiment / Investigation / Project Title and brief description (If you coded investigations then please include the coding here)	Topic/ Option	Time (h)	PI (a)	PI (b)	DC	DPP	CE	MS	PS (a)	PS (b)
	P1 INTRODUCTION TO LAB TECHNIQUES	1	1.25								
	P2 DETERMINATION OF THE AVOGADRO CONSTANT	1	1.25								
	P3 FORMULA OF A HYDRATED SALT	1	1.25								
	P4 STANDARDIZING SODIUM HYDROXIDE SOLUTION	1	2.5								
	P5 PERCENTAGE OF IRON IN AN IRON TABLET	1	1.25								
	P6 DETERMINING THE FORMULA OF A METAL HYDROXIDE BY TITRATION	1+10/19	1.25								
	P7 ANALYSIS OF SUPERMARKET VINEGAR BY TITRATION	1	1.25								
	P8 WHAT'S AN EGGSHELL MADE OF?	1	2.5								
	P9 INVESTIGATE THE DECOMPOSITION OF HYDROGEN PEROXIDE	1+10/19	1.25								
	P10 INVESTIGATING FLAME COLOURS	2/12	1								
	P11 WAVELENGTHS OF Na AND Li EMISSIONS	2/12	1.25								

Enter topic/option areas from the syllabus as numbered by the IBO[2], time spent on lab work[3], and grade awarded if assessed.[4]

PSOW detail contains date, code[1] and title of practical.

[1]Code refers to a simple numbering, such as P1, P2, P3, for the tasks you've set; not strictly necessary but helpful and recommended.
[2]Labs do not have to cover specific syllabus topic/options, but should show a good range. Labs can, of course, cover additional "extra-syllabus" worthwhile work.
[3]Does not include time spent writing reports after experimental work, but can include some time, maybe 1 or 1.25 hrs for planning preparation.
[4]Remember that you can assess all or any criteria you wish, assuming the investigation is suitable for it. However, you do not need to assess an investigation: the only IBO requirement is that you assess each criterion at least twice.

If you decide that you don't want to do certain practicals or if you have spent more time on an investigation than planned, you can edit these sheets.

In addition to this you need to produce a *lab cover sheet* for each practical, to be given to your students beforehand, or you may wish to put them onto your school website. Whatever you do, you also need to reproduce them for the IBO at the end of the course when you send example work to be moderated. A sample of a lab cover sheet is shown in figure 15.20.

Figure 15.20 Sample lab cover sheet

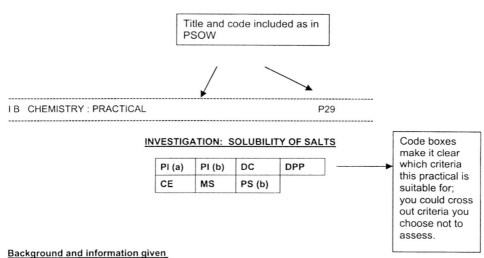

Background and information given
Students were asked to investigate the solubility of salts in water.

Investigation

Design an experiment that allows you investigate the solubility of salts in water. You will have to do some research regarding solubility. Ensure that your experiment is safe by consulting the safety notes concerning your chosen salts in the CLEAPSS manual in your chemistry lab.

You will be assessed on the criteria indicated in the boxes above. Structure your plan with the headings below.

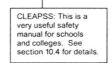

Research Question:

This must be focused and specific and must enable you to carry out the experiment safely.

Hypothesis:

Must be detailed, include all the chemistry involved and be quantitative where appropriate.

Practical sheets must include all information given to students. But as this particular example is an investigation which will assess planning skills, very little information should be given.

3.5 Do's and don'ts

Teachers are free to construct their own IA programme, but they must ensure that all practicals are suitable for the criteria which are being assessed. 'Suitable' means that practicals should be *'sufficiently' challenging*, and that the teacher *should not* provide the students with crucial information offering specific assistance for any assessed criterion (see the comments in figures 15.6–15.7, 15.9–15.14 and 15.21). To avoid this, teachers may well need to revamp their existing lab programme to fit the IB criteria by removing advice in the existing instructions which relates to the criterion you are assessing.

For easy reference in the construction of your IA, we print a checklist in figure 15.21.

How does one know if set investigations are sufficiently challenging? Historically, this was always a difficult area, so teachers tended to set their practical work towards the more challenging end of the pre-university spectrum to be sure. As mentioned earlier, the complexity of the IA programme prompted the IBO to post sample practical material on their website and this material should help you gauge the appropriate standard of work to set. Titles of appropriate investigations are also included in the sample schemes of work in section 8 and should give new IB teachers a good idea of what is required. (Additionally, we aim to put a full range of good sample practicals on our website (www.dp-help.com) for easy download, and you are invited to send in your best materials for inclusion.) Generally speaking, the system is based on a good deal of trust between teachers and the IBO, and this has worked well on the whole. Should your programme be deemed to be too simplistic, you will be informed after the IBO has moderated your work, enabling you to improve upon it for next year.

Figure 15.21 Points to remember when constructing a new IA programme

Length	60 hrs HL, 40 hrs SL, inclusive of the group 4 project.
Content range	A range covering most aspects of syllabus content, including options.
Assessment	Each criterion assessed twice, at the very least.

	Lab cover sheets for students
Pl (a)	**Planning.** Only include a general title, without independent or controlled variables which students expand upon.
Pl (b)	**Planning.** This could be the same as Pl (a), or could be far more specific, if Pl (a) is not assessed. Do not include a method, or a diagram or an apparatus list.
DC	**Data collection.** Could be part of a single investigation including above criteria, or could be part of a far more descriptive practical which includes a stepwise method and other assistance. Do not, however, include a results table or inform students which specific data to collect.
DPP	**Data processing and presentation.** Could be part of a single investigation including above criteria, or could be part of a far more descriptive practical which includes a stepwise method and other assistance. Do not include sample calculations or assist in how to process data. Do not include graphs to be filled in or inform the student which axes to plot in a graph.
CE	**Conclusion and evaluation.** Could be part of a single investigation including above criteria, or could be part of a far more descriptive practical which includes a stepwise method and other assistance. Avoid leading questions which help the student to complete their conclusion.

3.6 Preparing the students for IA

Having stressed in the previous section that assessment of IA criteria has to take place without any specific assistance for that criterion during that practical, the obvious question is: How are students supposed to learn?

The answer is not by drilling by rote learning, but by undertaking practicals – which you may decide to grade or not. Theoretically, you could complete the lab programme by only *assessing* two investigations which cover all criteria (though you would still have to complete 60 hours of IA work and document this on your PSOW). However, it is not easy to score maximum marks in IA and your students will require many attempts to get their work up to or close to a grade 3. This means you will need to give a lot of feedback on the students' work before they are able to attain this high level. Clearly, it is in a student's best interest to undertake as many graded tasks as possible, but obviously the student's interest needs to be balanced against the workload this imposes on the teacher. A good IA programme will assess the more difficult criteria, such as the two planning skills and conclusion and evaluation, about five or six times. However, this is left entirely to the teacher's discretion and many courses do not come close to this 'ideal' figure, particularly in SL where time is restricted.

How often should you mark practical work according to the IB criteria? There are many possible ways to approach this but the overall outcome should be the same in all cases: by the end of the course students should be able to gain good grades in the majority of the criteria. Two alternatives are outlined below.

1. *Formal assessment of a limited number of practicals*
   In this approach, the bulk of your IA is used for training without any formal assessment. A small number of investigations are chosen to formally assess all criteria; the absolute minimum would be two practicals, each of which assesses all skills. The advantage here is that you will be far more familiar with the particular requirements of a few investigations, and of course you will have fewer assessments to complete in a formal manner. The downside is the lack of opportunity for students to score well in IA. In addition, it is not easy to find investigations that lend themselves to assessment on every criterion.
2. *Formal assessment throughout the course*
   Here, assessment and feedback provide the training essentials for your students. Most practicals are assessed against one or more criteria and as the course progresses students become more proficient in all skill areas.

For example, you could begin with a training practical which you do not assess but where you include all the necessary teaching information relating to the criteria DC (data collection), DPP (data processing and presentation), MS (manipulative skills) and CE (conclusion and evaluation). You could do this by including instruction sheets containing the following information:

- DC tables with units and uncertainty
- sample calculations for DPP (error analysis required for HL)
- guidelines for students on what to focus on in their conclusion and evaluation (CE)
- a full review of the manipulative skills required to complete this experiment.

Next, you could target the criterion DC, probably the easiest of all criteria. Ensure that no results tables are given in the student's lab sheets for your next practical, while still giving advice (training) for DPP and CE. In the third step, you could remove advice for DPP and CE as well and assess in all or some of these areas. Then you could start looking at the conceptually harder planning criteria using a similar technique.

> *For chemists only:* Referring to the PSOW above (figure 15.19), you could use P2 as the first trainer. P3 assesses DC, P4 assesses DC and DPP, although it would be advisable to use it as a titration 'trainer' allowing the students to be well prepared for P5, P6 and P7 with which you could assess DC, DPP and CE if you wish. P8 and P9 provide the opportunity to introduce Pl (b), so you could use P8 as a trainer and help the students work through the planning work together in class before formally assessing Pl (b) and other relevant criteria in P9. For the P8 trainer, since it is group work you could probably assess PS (a), making full use of student contact time. Note that P9 could also be used to introduce Pl (a). All these investigations are, of course, suitable for the assessment of MS (manipulative skills).

Peer evaluation

Self-evaluation and peer evaluation can be employed to great effect in the IA programme. I find that self-evaluation works best in the group 4 project (see section 4) while peer evaluation (where one student assesses another) works best at the beginning of the IA programme. Peer evaluation is a very useful technique and one that can be extremely successful in getting your class to adapt quickly to the criteria. The idea is simple: students mark a colleague's work and have to justify the mark awarded. Motivated students are often extraordinarily critical of other students' work and this enables them to fully understand the rigours of the IA programme, often resulting in rapid progress. However, you should manage this process very carefully to avoid creating bitterness between students. Pairing up existing friendships has worked very well for me. If you choose to implement some form of self- or peer evaluation, remember that you will still have to assess this work yourself if you intend to use it as part of the student's final IA score.

Safety

An issue central to all science departments is safety (see section 4.4). Self-evaluation forms, such as the risk assessment form shown in figure 15.28, help to foster a more mature and responsible attitude towards safety amongst your students. Strict marking in the MS criterion will likewise prove beneficial.

Student handbook

It is a good idea to compile an IA student handbook for each IB DP science. This should include all the IBO guidelines and relevant subject-specific advice to make it clear to your students exactly how you want them to approach each criterion. Teachers could include sample reports as in section 3.3 or include IB exemplar material from the website. You may want to devise 'hypothetical' reports yourself to illustrate certain points. Include good and poor examples and display how a grade is awarded using the IB criteria. This provides students with confidence from the very start of the practical course. You could even include the 4/PSOW forms and all of the investigation cover sheets, making a single IA course book.

Internal assessment and plagiarism

Although it is a good idea to update your practical programme regularly by removing investigations that don't work or don't fit the criteria well, and adding new ideas that you pick up, there will probably be little change to the bulk of your material from year to year. This raises the possibility of cheating, as students could copy work from elder colleagues or siblings. The IBO takes a strong, principled stance against plagiarism. In this case, as in several others, however, they have to rely on trusting the teachers involved to be vigilant. The work of students who copy from their peers can easily be recognized, but not so if they have copied it from previous students. For this reason, it is a good idea to keep your IA marking secure in your possession, as opposed to using lab books which the students keep themselves. A paper wallet with an individual 4/PSOW form can be used to keep the student's whole personal IA portfolio which they can check each time you return marked work.

3.7 Preparing for internal moderation

This takes two forms:

1. Ensuring that all members of your department are completely familiar with the marking criteria.
2. Formally re-marking samples of work. This is particularly important with the higher-end marks as these will be exposed to the greatest scrutiny during moderation.

To implement effective moderation:

- Discuss IA at every meeting. Pass round practicals, checking, discussing and verifying marking. This is particularly important at the start of the course, when people may interpret criteria differently.
- Formally moderate, particularly higher-end marks. A good idea is to have two extended sessions, one in year 1 and one in year 2, where you formally re-mark colleagues' work. If you have practice examination sessions, then it would make sense to do it before these. This way, you can combine the IA score (24%) with the examination score (76%), as is done in the final IB examinations, to give the overall student grade. Any students working under the impression that the IA 'doesn't count' will soon see the light.
- You could assign staff to moderate particular practicals for formal assessment. This is a good option if you want to rely on only a select set of investigations.
- Assign staff to moderate particular criteria, enabling them to become 'expert' in that area. Initially, you could use a system where all '3' grades are re-marked and each teacher becomes responsible for the moderation of a single criterion. This is a good option if you have a large department but may prove too time-consuming for some. When the marking within the department becomes more consistent and in line with that expected by the IBO, sample frequently as opposed to re-marking.
- Many schools have only one member of staff for each subject. This teacher should still look over their work periodically, as understanding and interpretation of the criteria will vary with time. That mark of 3 you gave so easily at the start of your course may not match up to your exacting standards by the end of the two-year course. It would also be a good idea to use IB

conferences to meet with other teachers in the same situation, and of course to seek advice from IBO representatives. Visit the IB Online Curriculum Centre (OCC), as it contains some very active forums where you can seek advice on IA from other teachers, in addition to sample material posted by the IBO. Solo subject teachers have also taken to moderating each other's work by email.

- As the IB course is dynamic in nature, with regular syllabus reviews, you'll have to keep in touch with all the changes. Check the OCC regularly. Even midway through the course, certain aspects of the programme may be clarified.

You certainly do not want be in a situation where you have awarded several 3 grades only to find at the end of the course that you have been too lenient (especially after you have sent off your IA marks to the IBO), because it will be too late to change by this point. Moderation is absolutely vital and does not take too much time once you are familiar with the criteria. The consequences of poor moderation for your final grades are discussed in section 3.8.

A tricky issue: how to moderate MS, PS (a) and PS (b)?

The only grades that are externally assessed by the IBO are Pl (a), Pl (b), DC, DPP and CE. The nature of the other three criteria – MS, PS (a) and PS (b) (manipulation of apparatus and personal skills) – really makes it impossible for the IBO to assess your grades, so they are moderated only relative to the five that you send in. For example, you send in a maximum score of 48 for all eight criteria ($8 \times 3 \times 2 = 48$). The IBO moderates the material in the first five criteria and decides that you have been too lenient in each case: each 3 sample is judged to be a 2. The remaining three criteria of MS, PS (a) and PS (b) will then, similarly, also be moderated down.

If the IBO does not actually look at these criteria, then obviously the situation arises where teachers could abuse this system, and simply give a 3 for each grade in these criteria. The IBO places a substantial amount of trust in teachers not to abuse the system. Your approach to these grades should not be superficial; they can really act as motivators for students to work safely, responsibly and cooperatively, and you should assess them as regularly as the others. Moreover, the IBO may decide in the future to start to ask for evidence of your assessment in these areas – probably not grades, but at least an outline of what you are doing to get your actual grades – so it is a good idea to be prepared for that. Simple checklists like the one shown in figure 15.22 for MS, amended from one used by the chemistry department of UWCSEA, can be used to quickly assess these criteria for the entire class and you can easily construct checklists for the personal skills areas as well. The IBO again produces some assistance for this in the OCC (access 'teacher support material phase 1') which has plenty of ideas for assessing these three criteria in an easy checklist manner. The group 4 project is perfect for assessing personal skills, particularly PS (a), and any extended investigation can be used to assess PS (b) ('a' is effectively teamwork and 'b' covers motivation, scientific ethics and respect for the environment). If different teachers in the same school use the same checklists, this will enable a measure of internal moderation which should be more than satisfactory.

Figure 15.22 Manipulative skills checklist

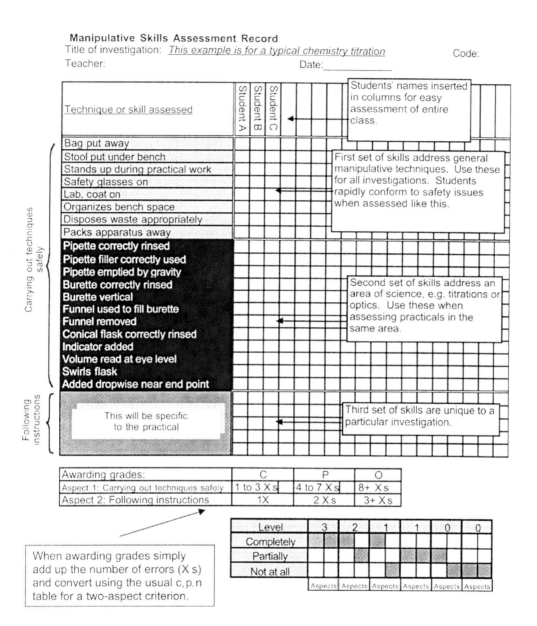

Manipulative Skills Assessment Record
Title of investigation: *This example is for a typical chemistry titration*   Code:
Teacher: Date:_____

Technique or skill assessed	Student A	Student B	Student C									
Bag put away												
Stool put under bench												
Stands up during practical work												
Safety glasses on												
Lab. coat on												
Organizes bench space												
Disposes waste appropriately												
Packs apparatus away												
Pipette correctly rinsed												
Pipette filler correctly used												
Pipette emptied by gravity												
Burette correctly rinsed												
Burette vertical												
Funnel used to fill burette												
Funnel removed												
Conical flask correctly rinsed												
Indicator added												
Volume read at eye level												
Swirls flask												
Added dropwise near end point												

Carrying out techniques safely { (first two sets of rows)
Following instructions { (last set)

Students' names inserted in columns for easy assessment of entire class.

First set of skills address general manipulative techniques. Use these for all investigations. Students rapidly conform to safety issues when assessed like this.

Second set of skills address an area of science, e.g. titrations or optics. Use these when assessing practicals in the same area.

This will be specific to the practical

Third set of skills are unique to a particular investigation.

Awarding grades:	C	P	O
Aspect 1: Carrying out techniques safely	1 to 3 X s	4 to 7 X s	8+ X s
Aspect 2: Following instructions	1X	2 X s	3+ X s

When awarding grades simply add up the number of errors (X s) and convert using the usual c,p,n table for a two-aspect criterion.

Level	3	2	1	1	0	0
Completely						
Partially						
Not at all						
	Aspects	Aspects	Aspects	Aspects	Aspects	Aspects

3.8 Preparing for external moderation

Towards the end of the course your DP coordinator (DPC) will give you an IA/PG form for all science candidates. You include the IA marks and a predicted grade. It is a requirement for schools to subscribe to IBnet and at this stage a list of students for sampling is selected automatically. The number of students selected depends on your candidate entry numbers but will always be between 5 and 10.

What do you need to include in your sample selection?

For each student selected, you must include the following:

- A detailed and accurate 4/PSOW detail form (see figure 15.19), with completed 4/PSOW cover sheet (see figure 15.18).
- The 4/PSOW detail form should have all criteria assessed at least twice.
- The 4/PSOW detail form must highlight the top two grades for the five criteria Pl (a), Pl (b), DC, DPP and CE. The three other criteria, MS, PS (a), PS (b), do not need the top two grades highlighted as these criteria are not directly moderated by the IBO, as discussed in section 3.7.
- For each grade highlighted: legible photocopies or originals of student's work, annotated clearly by yourself and/or an internal moderator as to why the marks awarded are justified.
- For each grade highlighted: practical instruction sheet for the corresponding investigation.
- Evidence of the group 4 project – see section 4 below for details on this.

Make it user-friendly for the IBO moderator and annotate your marking as much as possible. The IBO realizes that exact objectivity with regard to the criteria will not always be possible. If you justify your marking logically, clearly and consistently, using the c, p, n notation throughout, moderators will be much more sympathetic than if they have to search through vast folders of poor photocopies with one-word feedback from teachers. Many schools running parallel examination systems such as DP and AP together might be tempted to leave the numerical mark used for AP and not use the IB c, p, n system. As a consequence, their grading is inappropriate and will inevitably be disregarded.

How does the IBO implement external moderation?

The IBO employs a team to re-mark the sample work your school has been asked to send in. As explained at the end of section 3.7, the eventual moderation of the eight criteria is based on the actual moderation of only the first five, with MS, PS (a) and PS (b) grades being moderated accordingly. Suppose that as a result of this moderation the IBO marks your 47 points down to 34 (13 points difference). The result will be that *all* student marks in the same range will be moderated down, by about 13 points! Obviously a change of $+/-1$ out of 48 will not make a huge difference but a large disagreement in scores definitely will. It is not necessarily true that all marks across the board will go down by 13 points. IBO moderating teams differentiate between high-end, average, and low-end achievers, so that could mean that while your high-end grades go down by 13 points, your low-end grades go down by only 7 points or none at all. However, care will be taken that the grade moderation will not alter the rank *order* of your candidates.

In view of this, it is imperative that teachers try to get a feel for the IBO's standards and that departments are *consistent* with their internal moderation, so as not to penalize students unfairly.

3.9 Summary: IA checklists

Figures 15.23 and 15.24 are two final checklists for the IA.

Figure 15.23 Checklist (a): before completing the course

Procedure	Check
Read the section on IA at the start of all group 4 subject guides	
Read section 4 and section F in the current edition of the *Vade Mecum*	
Amend existing practical to fit the DP's internal assessment criteria	
Ensure students are fully aware of the nature of the new practical programme	
Ensure your programme has a *wide range* of investigations from across the subject syllabus (core, AHL if an HL course, and options)	
Implement internal moderation procedures	
Ensure time allocation of *at least* 60 hrs for HL and 40 hrs for SL	
Ensure all candidates have completed their group 4 project – see section 4.5	
Ensure that you have assessed all criteria *at least* twice	

Figure 15.24 Checklist (b): before sending in samples

Procedure	Check
4/PSOW is detailed and accurate (investigation titles, dates, names, grades, cover sheet, hours, total marks)	
4/PSOW has best two grades in Pl (a), Pl (b), DC, DPP, CE clearly highlighted	
Student reports of highlighted work are included, are legible and clear	
Teacher and/or internal moderator has annotated this work to clearly justify given mark	
Instruction sheets are included for practicals of highlighted work	
Evidence of group 4 project is included	

4 The group 4 project

4.1 What is it, who does it, and when to do it?

What is the group 4 project?

The collaborative, inter-disciplinary group 4 project is a unique and exciting feature of the DP. The idea is to try and recreate a real problem-solving situation in a similar manner to that which could take place in industry or the 'real world' – different members of the same team working together to resolve a problem or discover something novel. There are many different ways to approach the project but a possible outline would be as follows. First a general *title* is identified either by the teacher or by student consensus, for example 'The science of sport'. A group of about 10 students from different scientific disciplines identify and then pursue a more specific hypothesis or investigation, say 'Improving aspects of soccer'. After a series of brainstorming sessions and animated discussions involving the whole group of students, individual students proceed to investigate a particular area of the hypothesis. In this example, the biologists could investigate the effect of a closed roof on turf growth, design technologists could investigate modern boot design, and physicists could look at the mechanics of David Beckham's free kicks. In the same manner students of chemistry and environmental systems would investigate a particular area and report their results back to the whole group before finally presenting the project as a whole to a larger audience. The real beauty of this innovative venture is the manner in which students collaborate with each other, handling the demands of group dynamics and, possibly for the one and only time in school science, finding out what the real scientific method is all about.

However, there has been some criticism of the project due to the low level of science achieved. This is, of course, hardly surprising, given the short amount of time devoted to the project (students can claim 10 to 15 hours of IA time for it). Nevertheless, some impressive material can be produced. Moreover, it is important to remember that the process is more important than the science. The students get quite excited with the collaborative nature of the project, as they get to work with new colleagues in a fresh and very different environment. However, it needs careful monitoring by staff, discreetly in the early, formative stages and proactively with regard to safety in the experimental stages. Teachers frequently identify hidden talents in students, who often respond impressively when given this unique opportunity to shine. The 10–15 hours of IA allocated to the group 4 project come within the IA assessment structure outlined earlier. Details are in section 4.5.

Who needs to complete the group 4 project?

All DP students must study a group 4 subject and, whether this is at HL or SL level, they must, therefore, complete a group 4 project. Students enrolled in two science courses will have to complete two experimental investigations, one in each subject, even though the initial discussion and final reflection phases will be common stages.

When should the project be carried out?

This really depends on the way in which teachers implement it (see section 4.3). Some educators feel that it should be left until year 2 of the diploma course, so that students have a greater mastery of the subject matter and are therefore able to take a more 'academic' approach. However, bear in mind that it is the collaborative process that is the most important reason for doing the group 4 project and that the project lends itself most naturally to assessment of MS, PS (a) and PS (b) (many schools assess the group 4 project only on these criteria). As a consequence, the project could be carried out any time up until about two months before the final examination, but not any later because IA samples will need to be sent to the IBO at this time and evidence of the project is required in these samples.

Can you do the whole project in year 1?

There are good reasons for doing the project close to the beginning of year 1 – enthusiastic students and a relatively free academic calendar being only two of them. However, one should avoid doing the project at the *very* beginning as students may not have mastered basic experimental techniques and will be unfamiliar with the IA criteria. In this regard about 10 weeks into the course is an appropriate time to implement the project, but do remember that at that stage the students would be armed with only a limited academic background. The rest of the first year could also work well, but make sure you avoid the time when your school is busy with field trips.

If your school teaches SL and HL in one class with SL anticipated students (i.e. students who will sit their examination at the end of year 1) then you will have no choice but to complete the project in the first year.

Spread the project out over two years

Discussion and planning could take place at the end of year 1 with experimental work occurring in year 2, giving ample time for reflection during the long vacation. Some impetus would undoubtedly, however, be lost over the long break.

Do the project in year 2

The beginning of this year would also be appropriate, but the second year soon becomes a very busy time for both teachers and students. It is advisable, therefore, to avoid doing the project any time after 10 weeks into the second year, when extended essays and world literature demands become intense. Neither is the period before examinations particularly suitable. On the other hand, a few teachers claim that these intense times of the year are exactly when the project *should* be done, as the project provides a welcome respite from the never-ending cycle of reports and coursework deadlines. This is a valid point, but if the project is to be done well (and if you want to justifiably claim 15 IA hours for it), it should be demanding and challenging for students and staff alike. Bear in mind that if you portray the project as 'light relief', then the performance of the students will reflect this.

4.2 Sample project themes

How do I choose a theme?

The main criterion for selecting a theme for investigation is its potential application to all the group 4 sciences. You should, for example, avoid themes that are great for biology and chemistry but hopeless for physics. The topic should of course be sufficiently interesting to maintain the students' motivation. This is often achieved by making the theme contemporary or related to your specific environment or both. Figure 15.25 features a few examples to get you started. The best projects are generated from the students themselves, but remember to keep their expectations realistic and keep a keen eye on safety (discussed in detail in section 4.4).

Figure 15.25 Sample themes for a group 4 project

Theme: The science of sport – the Olympics, World Cup, etc.	
Biology	Physiology. O_2 uptake, blood pressure and heart rate variations. Lots of obvious possibilities. Turf growth.
Chemistry	Not so easy here. Main investigations surround materials use and wear. Exposure to chemicals in the environment. If you have access to a friendly local university, you could do GC/MS (gas chromatography/mass spectroscopy) work on doping.
Physics	A mechanics specialist's dream! Javelin trajectory, the physics of a spinning cricket ball, golf ball, etc. Lots of possibilities.
Environmental systems	An environmental impact assessment of new stadium building.
DT	Design factors inherent in manufacture of sporting equipment and even stadiums – this worked very well in the year of the soccer World Cup in Korea/Japan.
Theme: Can we improve the environment in our school?	
Biology	Effect of pollutants on plant growth and effect of plants on pollutant removal (CO_2 and respiration).
Chemistry	Estimation of pollutants from exhausts by lab simulation. Exposure to chemicals in the environment. Could alkali beds remove CO_2? Lots of possibilities with recycling.
Physics	More difficult. Experiments with air flow, light absorption and energy-saving devices.
Environmental systems	Pollution monitoring within the school. Analysis of pollutants in surface run-off.
DT	Design of building and work spaces – can it be improved to let in more/less heat and light? Passive solar heating.
Theme: Science and art – fashion, dance, visual arts, theatre, etc.	
Biology	Perception experiments. Colour and sight. Perfume and smell. Physiological responses to art stimulation.
Chemistry	The chemistry of pigments and paints. Chemistry of cosmetics. Lots of opportunities for good lab work.
Physics	The physics of dancing. Visual effects in the theatre – shadows, use of filters. Jewellery and optics.
Environmental systems	Measurement of environmental impacts of heavy metals in paints. Impacts of new theatre construction on local ecosystem.
DT	Seat ergonomics, designing a new artist's easel.

Figure 15.25 Sample themes for a group 4 project (continued)

Theme: Transport – could be local transport, school buses, global transport, etc.	
Biology	Effects of pollution on immediate environment. Cycling and walking: physiological investigations.
Chemistry	Comparative lab work on fuels: energy content, pollutant index.
Physics	Power output from different engine types or different transport modes. Efficiency rating. Investigate physics of new rapid transit train systems versus more traditional means. Is new really more efficient?
Environmental systems	Measurement and detection of transport pollution. Analysis of increasing transport on local ecosystem and resources.
DT	Seat ergonomics, cabin design, station design. Lots of design investigations possible here.

4.3 How to implement the project

General points regarding implementation

The IBO allows a lot of creativity for this project, which is only to be expected given the range of resources available to different schools throughout the world and the huge difference in school sizes. There are lots of different possible approaches and, before finalizing an implementation plan, many factors will have to be considered:

- The *number of students*.
- The *school calendar*: will it be possible to have the students out of class for several days to complete the entire project or will you have to complete it in normal syllabus time?
- *Location*: whether or not the school wishes to collaborate with neighbouring schools.
- Involving *non-IB students*. Schools running dual systems, for example AP and DP, may find that the project will apply equally well to investigative work in the non-IB system. This will save on resources and could be a crucial factor in management permitting off-syllabus time for the venture.
- The *number of sciences offered*. If only one is offered then you will have to make this a collaborative venture with another school or non-IB students of science within your school. As mentioned in section 1.5, collaborative ventures are becoming much easier with the use of web-based chat and interactive forums, and this would be an excellent way for two small schools, each offering only one science, say physics or chemistry, to coordinate a group 4 project. There is no problem with this type of electronic collaboration. Indeed, in many ways it encompasses the international ideals of the IBO's aims.

Two possible implementation schemes for the 'science of sport' project described in section 4.1 and featured in figure 15.26 are outlined below.

Scheme 1

For schools that cannot take time out from regular lessons, the experimental phase of the scheme is completed in normal curriculum time.

Figure 15.26 The several stages of the group 4 project

Stage	Comment
1. Introduction and launch	A member of staff introduces and explains the nature of the project to all students. An overall title *could* be given here, e.g. 'The science of sport', or students could propose titles and then vote for them. An overall title does not actually have to be used – students could work on completely different titles from the next stage onwards. However, it does give the school a sense of collective teamwork and tends to make the final presentation more of an event. Students then split into inter-disciplinary groups. The group size will depend on school size, but 10 is a good number. Ensure you have a good mix of science subjects in the group and appoint a member of staff to oversee each group.
2. Formulation of theme	Within the overall title each group should now focus on a particular theme, chosen by consensus within the group and based upon its suitability for experimentation with all sciences involved. The group should brainstorm possible areas of investigation for all scientific disciplines present in the group. Let's say the group focuses on soccer and decides on 'Improving aspects of soccer' as their theme. Can all scientists carry out lab work particular to that science? Can experimental work in each discipline be carried out with a view to fulfilling an objective? The biologists, for example, can investigate turf growth under covered and low-light conditions to assess the effect of playing under a closed stadium roof and how this could possibly be improved. The DT students could look at improving boot design, physicists look at the angular momentum of a ball during a free kick, and a similar process is carried out for all science disciplines. For this topic there is a good range of possible study areas for all the sciences. All group members are given tasks. Two students of the same discipline can work on the same area; any more than that and you should assign a new project area for that discipline, so you may have to find a new biology area besides turf growth if there are more than two biologists.
3. Planning	Students plan experiments to perform in individual subject classes. This needs to be done well in advance in order to give staff time to arrange apparatus and, very importantly, so that you check the safety and viability of their proposal – some students may want to blow up the turf with TNT! In the biologists' example, they will need to think of a way to recreate the conditions of the stadium, what variables they will investigate and what they will change, and what apparatus they will need.
4. Experimental work with intermittent discussion	Students carry out experiments under the supervision of their science teachers during normal subject time. The original inter-disciplinary group meets intermittently at lunch or after school to discuss progress: the biologists report their progress with the turf, the physicists with the free kicks, and the DT students report on their revolutionary new shoe design. Students of other science disciplines report back likewise. The use of email or electronic chat between students is of use at this stage if it is available to all.
5. Final group discussion / conclusion	Students write final reports. Group meets again, collates data and agrees on their final conclusion on 'Improving aspects of soccer'. Tasks are set for presentation.
6. Presentation	Students present project and findings to interested staff, students and possibly parents. If the project has a local theme, possibly environmental, it would be good to invite the local press.

This whole process could take between 3 and 5 weeks, depending on your theme and the number of IA hours you wish to include in your 4/PSOW for each student. From the recommended 10–15 project hours, possible timings could be:

- 2–4 hours for planning: this stage is crucial to the whole exercise
- 6–8 hours' experimental work
- 2–3 hours' evaluation and presentation of results.

In this scheme, the experimental work would have to be completed in normal subject time but there would still be a degree of flexibility regarding how this is carried out. Some schools complete the exercise with 2 weeks' lab time, some reserve 1–2 hours' lab time a week for several weeks and continue to teach as normal in the remainder of the time. The latter schedule has the advantage that students are able to carry out longer-term investigations, although some teachers feel that momentum is lost and the students lose interest.

Scheme 2

Set aside curriculum time for the project. The format is the same as for the scheme above except that stages 3, 4 and 5 are completed in 2–3 intense days during which normal lesson time is suspended. Note that the planning phase must still be at least a week to ten days in advance to allow sufficient preparation time. This scheme has the advantage of focusing the students on the problem on hand, but is unsuitable for investigations such as certain environmental projects, which take several weeks to complete.

A summary of the whole process, with *possible* times at each stage, is set out in figure 15.27.

Figure 15.27 Summary of the group 4 project

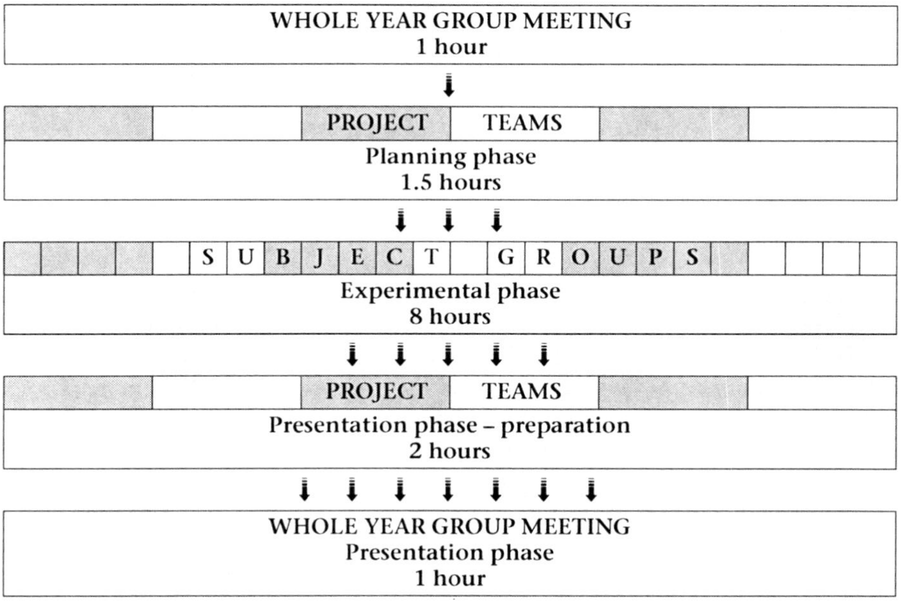

4.4 Safety considerations

Students should be encouraged to monitor the safety of all their experiments. It is good practice to get all students to complete a safety form for all investigations in IA including the group 4 project. You must, of course, rigorously check the validity of their assessment and the viability of their experiments. Generally they respond well. Good safety practice forces students to be aware of the risks inherent in laboratory work, and self-assessment fosters a more mature and responsible approach to safety.

Getting students to be more aware of safety issues is also an excellent preparation for tertiary science education. Students should complete a form like figure 15.28 and then hand it in with their plan for you to check before they start the investigation. It is a good idea to leave copies of relevant safety data books in the lab for the students to refer to. See section 10, Resources, for an appropriate book to use.

Figure 15.28 Risk assessment form

Chemicals or materials you intend to use. State name, concentration, quantity and nature of use.	Apparatus you intend to use.	Hazards as listed in data. Possible side reactions. Hazards associated with apparatus and set-up.	Steps taken to reduce hazards.

Student name	
Supervisor's name	
Student's signature	
Supervisor's signature	
Date:	Approved: Yes/No

4.5 Assessment

All IA samples sent to the IBO must contain evidence of the group 4 project, although this can take a variety of forms: individual lab reports, students' self-assessment or peer assessments. You could include pictures of final presentations, printouts of web pages designed for the project, or a combination of some of these. Note that there is no requirement for you to formally assess the project in any way, although it would be unusual for a school not to assess at least the personal skills. Although not impossible, it is difficult to formally assess the other criteria, since these other criteria assess individual achievement. The main objective of the IBO with regard to the project is that students *experience* a cross-disciplinary group project, and it will ask schools for evidence that this has happened. Teachers *can* assess the project on selected criteria, but the project lends itself most easily to assessment in the three criteria not directly moderated by the IBO: personal and manipulative skills.

Figure 15.29 Group 4 project self-evaluation sheet (PS (a) and PS (b))

	Student assessment	Supervisor assessment or comment
Student name:	**Project supervisor:**	
Title of project:	**Subject:**	
Time spent on planning phase. Include all planning meetings.		
Time spent on experimental phase for this subject (chem/bio/phys etc.) only. Do not include time for report writing.		
Time spent on actual presentation phase.		
Total time spent on group 4 project for this subject. (Sum of all times above)		
Personal skills (a)		
Do you think you were an active member of the group; did you work well within the team?		
Were you willing to listen to the views of others? Did you seek the opinion of other people in your group?		
Did you contribute ideas to the group? Were you willing to exchange and consider the ideas of others within the group?		
Supervisor only: Grade awarded for personal skills (a)		
Personal skills (b)		
How motivated do you think you were with this project? Did you follow the project through to completion?		
Did you source any ideas or information for this project? If so, did you use a citation to credit the author appropriately? Did you work in an ethical manner with respect to materials, living or non-living, used in the project?		
In what way did you consider the effects of your project on the environment?		
Supervisor only: Grade awarded for personal skills (b)		
Project assessment		
How could the introduction and planning phase of the project be improved for next year's group?		
How could the experimental phase of the project be improved for next year's group?		
How could the presentation phase of the project be improved for next year's group?		
Any other comments?		

The personal and manipulative skills lend themselves very well to self-assessment and peer assessment. Figure 15.22 is a self-assessment form for MS (manipulative skills). Figure 15.29 is a copy of the self-assessment form used at UWCSEA to measure PS (a) and PS (b).

5 Extended essay

5.1 Subject-specific assessment criteria and choice of title

In addition to the eight general criteria for assessment of the extended essay discussed in Chapter 11, which are common to all extended essays, there are three additional subject-specific criteria for the group 4 sciences, with the exception of DT, which has four. In all cases the subject-specific criteria amount to 12 marks compared with 24 for the general criteria. For exact details of subject assessment criteria, you should refer to the appropriate subject in the extended essay guide (for first examinations in 1999), available from the extended essay section of the OCC. Although not exactly identical for each subject, the criteria for the majority of group 4 sciences are similar and can be roughly approximated to those set out in figure 15.30.

Theoretically, students do not actually have to study a subject to undertake an essay in it, although for obvious reasons this is not recommended. Most extended essay candidates tend to take science as an HL subject but SL students are also permitted as candidates, and many produce good essays.

Many DP science teachers believe that it is difficult to gain a high grade with an extended essay in a group 4 subject and they often voice this complaint at group 4 workshops. The statistics provided by the IBO do not fully support this. Science average grades are close to the overall average DP grade; 'C' grades amount to 37%, which is equal to the total percentage of 'C' grades; 'A' grades do seem to be slightly more difficult to obtain – only about 10% 'A's in the sciences compared with an overall total of 15% 'A's (May 2002 IB *Statistical Bulletin*).

While it may not be so difficult to score well, writing a science extended essay may well prove more *time-consuming* due to both the experimental nature of most science essays and the need for vigilance with regard to safety. Nevertheless, although students and teachers spend a great deal of lab time on the extended essay there is a reward: the awakening of intellectual curiosity. Extended essays in science can also be a valuable experience for the student who intends to pursue a science-based university course in the future.

Figure 15.30 Group 4 subject-specific assessment criteria for the extended essay (biology, chemistry, physics)

Note: each of the three criteria is worth between 0 and 4 marks.	
Criterion J	Understanding of the science
Criterion K	Appropriate use of scientific methods and literature research
Criterion L	Evaluation of the research and investigation

Although the essay does not necessarily have to be laboratory based, it is difficult to score high marks for criterion K (see figure 15.30), and in some respects for criterion L, if the essay is not based on an experimental investigation, since these criteria are particularly suited to the assessment of scientific methodology. It is also important that the essay has a very definite personal input from the student – something that is easy to achieve if students do their own experiments but difficult to achieve with a scientific literature search.

As explained in Chapter 11, choice of title is paramount for success, and titles should be sharply focused. The following examples of titles for extended essays are intended as guidance only. The pairings illustrate that focused topics (indicated by the first title) should be encouraged rather than broad topics (indicated by the second title).

Biology
- The effect of detergent toxicity on certain bacterial strains *is better than* Detergents in the environment.
- A study of malnourished children in Indonesia and the extent of their recovery after a period of supervised improved nutrition *is better than* Malnutrition in children.
- A study of the effect of differing pH levels on the growth of *Phaseolus vulgaris is better than* The effect of acidity on plant growth.
- The competitive and evolutionary nature of the symbiotic relationship in *Paramecium vusaria is better than* Symbiosis in animals.
- The effect of banana peel on seed germination *is better than* Factors that affect the germination of seeds.

Physics
- How does the intensity of sunlight affect the efficiency of (a specific type) of solar cell? *is better than* Power from the sun.
- How effective are different golf ball designs in increasing spin? *is better than* The physics of golf. (Note that sports make for truly excellent extended essays in physics, providing that the student has ensured that they can gain sufficient data to fulfil the investigation. In practice, it will be difficult to get data for this experiment due to the high speeds and small size of the ball. The use of digital video will help, but you may need to focus on a larger ball, say a soccer ball.)
- Determination of the mass of Jupiter by direct observation and analysis *is better than* Investigating astrophysics.
- An analysis of the relative amplitude of overtones in a traditional Philippino guitar and a contemporary electric guitar *is better than* The physics of sound waves. (Sound analysis is a good topic as there is lots of available software to assist with the analysis.)

Three of the four physics examples above exploit the obvious interest that young people have in sports, music and astronomy. Physics extended essays never need to be dull.

Chemistry
- TLC analysis of sugars in fruit juice under different storage conditions *is better than* Analysis of fruit juice.
- Can polarimetry be used to analyse the purity of sugars? *is better than* An investigation of polarimetry and sugars.

- In the chemiluminescence of luminol, what is the order of reaction with respect to hydroxide ions? *is better than* An investigation of reaction rate in chemiluminescence. Extended essays investigating kinetics contain the potential for the student to cover lots of good chemistry that is both challenging yet achievable. Choose a reaction which can be monitored easily in the lab by, say, gas evolution or colour change if you have a colorimeter or spectrophotometer. The student can investigate the order with respect to one reactant or, better still, if the reaction can be monitored with respect to all reactants then the student can propose a possible mechanistic pathway – a very focused and satisfying extended essay. Students can choose a fun reaction like that used above with luminol or something else that has captured their imagination, but it should not be a standard reaction for which they can look up appropriate techniques and data.

Further examples of extended essay titles in all group 4 sciences can be found in the extended essay guide, available for download from the OCC, by accessing 'diploma programme', then 'extended essay'. This site also contains examiner reports for extended essays in every subject, which make useful reading for teachers.

The science extended essay must also be:

- *Achievable*. The aim of the investigation must be attainable given the academic inexperience of the candidate and limited laboratory apparatus.
- *Subject specific*. The question must be answerable within the confines of a single subject. Candidates are not to be encouraged to stray into other subject areas. Questions with substantial overlap of, say, chemistry and physics, should be amended to be more specific. Some very good essays have lost marks because the science involved has straddled two subject areas. Students are penalized in criteria J and K in this respect, so until the IBO resolves this situation – as it should in view of its overall aims – you must ensure that the essays are specific to a single science throughout.

Some teachers have a bank of ideas and questions, like the examples given above, which they then recommend to students. It is definitely wise to point the students in meaningful directions, particularly if you have only certain lab techniques available. However, this is not to say you should simply provide the research question, since this is not really in line with the spirit of independent learning that the essay promotes. Furthermore, the best and most rewarding ideas do come from the students and they should be encouraged to think creatively in this respect. It is best, therefore, to give the students a list of your available scientific techniques, and ask them to fit a research question to the techniques.

Although not compulsory, it is recommended that the investigation be carried out within the school lab or environment. This ensures a more personal input to the project, and from the teacher's point of view, creates fewer problems with regard to plagiarism.

5.2 Subject-specific guidance for students

Once the research question has been agreed upon, an experimental plan is devised to answer it. When enough data has been collected, the student can proceed to write the essay. Group 4 essays follow the same general guidelines as all essays, so it is essential that the criteria are fulfilled as the essay proceeds. A common difficulty here is the fact that the general criteria are assessing essay writing, whereas the student tends to complete an extended lab report. The trick is to merge the two by using the same, precise experimental skills learned in IA (experimental details, results tables, uncertainty, errors, etc.) yet allowing the essay to flow freely. If data collection is excessive then the bulk of it can be moved to the appendix and replaced with more concise presentation tables, allowing the reader to grasp the main points of the scientific investigation without being distracted; tables of results should not interrupt the flow of continuous prose but must be clearly presented. This is, after all, a science essay and the students' results should be as obviously displayed as those normally presented in the internal assessment.

Role of the supervisor

In addition to the requirements of the supervisor set out in Chapter 11, a science supervisor must ensure that the essay work is safe. Make students carry out a risk assessment using a form like the one in figure 15.28. Check this thoroughly before the experimental phase begins. The nature of the investigation will determine the extent of direct hands-on supervision that you need to give. Chemistry essays, for example, will need to be completely supervised in the lab, but some environmental investigations could be carried out without any direct supervision. If supervision is necessary, then you can consolidate staff time in this respect by having scheduled extended essay times for all students in one lab at specific points in the day, or after school.

6 Design technology

For many teachers who are more familiar with their own national systems, it might come as a surprise to see design technology (henceforth, DT) included as part of the group 4 experimental sciences. The information in this section is intended to outline what the subject involves (after all, it is a fledgling subject within the DP and is probably unfamiliar to many curriculum planners) and what its place is within the IB sciences. While all of the science subjects conform to a similar curriculum and assessment model, there are a number of differences between DT and the other sciences; in the interests of saving space, discussion here is limited to those differences.

A possible way of understanding design is to think of DT as 'using materials, tools and systems so that people can intervene to modify and improve their environment and technology'. DT is a subject that can be studied successfully in conjunction with another group 4 science for students considering a career in science and engineering, or on its own for a prospective arts or humanities student. The subject is heavily dependent on problem solving and it is not solely about understanding a fixed body of knowledge.

6.1 Curriculum framework and assessment model

The common curriculum model discussed in the previous sections of this chapter applies as much to DT as to other subjects within group 4. However, one key difference is that DT students must complete an additional compulsory design project (see section 6.4) as part of their course. This contributes up to 12% of the final grade and constitutes 19 and 31 hours of the internal assessment time allocation at SL and HL respectively. However, to accommodate this element of the course some adjustment has had to be made to the common curriculum model in terms of the time devoted to each element of the scheme and to the assessment in terms of the relative weightings of each element. The curriculum framework sees slightly reduced time allocations for the core and AHL material and for the investigations to compensate for the time added by the design project. The group 4 project and options remain consistent with the other sciences. The DT-specific framework is summarized in figure 15.31.

Figure 15.31 Design technology curriculum outline

	Hours		Hours
Curriculum framework (HL)	240	Curriculum framework (SL)	150
Theory	159	Theory	95
Core	65	Core	65
Additional Higher Level (AHL)	49		
Options (choose two)	45	Options (choose two)	30
Internal assessment (IA)	81	Internal assessment (IA)	55
Investigations and practical work	35–40	Investigations and practical work	21–26
Design project	31	Design project	19
Group 4 project	10–15	Group 4 project	10–15

External assessment

The external assessment weighting is slightly different in DT to compensate for the increased allocation of marks in IA from 24% in other sciences to 36% in DT. The types of question and the material on which they are based remain consistent with the other sciences although at both SL and HL, students answer only one question from three in section B of Paper 2, again to reflect the slightly shorter paper and lower weighting in DT.

Figure 15.32 Design technology assessment outline

Assessment summary	SL		HL	
External assessment – 64%				
Paper 1 – multiple choice, no calculators	45 min	20%	1hr	20%
Paper 2 – shorter and longer data response questions. One extended response question	1 hr	24%	1hr 45	24%
Paper 3 – questions on options	1 hr	20%	1hr 15	20%

Internal assessment (IA) – 36%
All experimental investigations and the group 4 project together count for 24%.
A further 12% is awarded for the design project.

6.2 Course content

SL	HL
Core	**Core**
1. Designers and the design cycle	1. Designers and the design cycle
2. The responsibility of the designer	2. The responsibility of the designer
3. Materials	3. Materials
4. Manufacturing processes and techniques	4. Manufacturing processes and techniques
5. Production systems	5. Production systems
6. Clean technology and green design	6. Clean technology and green design
	AHL
	7. Raw material to final product
	8. Microstructures and macrostructures
	9. Appropriate technologies
Options (choose two)	**Options (choose two)**
Available SL options are the three AHL components, as well as the core of the options for HL.	D. Food technology
	E. Computer-aided design, manufacture and production
	F. Invention, innovation and design
	G. Health by design
	H. Electronic products

As with the other sciences, it is highly likely that the vast majority of DT teachers will be familiar with the core of the course which delves, among other things, into the role and responsibility of a designer, the design process, materials and manufacturing techniques and other issues. A recent addition, and a major emphasis, is the section on 'Clean technology and green design', a highly topical issue and one that should be at the forefront of any designer's activity. This topic should not present any difficulties to the teacher who is well informed on the international developments to help preserve the planet. The AHL material builds on the issues raised in the core, adding the detail and body required at HL although still keeping the material applied as much as possible. The options are interesting and take account of the varying expertise and facilities available in schools around the globe.

6.3 Internal assessment

DT students spend slightly more time on internally assessed coursework than their peers in the other sciences, as shown in the curriculum framework, figure 15.31. The coursework consists of a series of short-term or long-term investigations that would be a mixture of experimental and design exercises, a design project and the group 4 project. A sample 4/PSOW form is shown in figure 15.34 and includes some appropriate investigation titles. This is for an HL course and has been adapted from the IBO original to reflect the DT requirements. Note that each assignment addresses certain criteria. Only one assignment and the design project address *all* eight criteria (the design project *must* assess all criteria). However, taking a holistic view of the practical scheme of work (PSOW), it can be clearly seen that students have a number of opportunities to achieve a good grade in each category. Given that the IBO requires a design project score and

Figure 15.34 Form 4/PSOW internal assessment: group 4

Form 4/PSOW
Cover sheet

SUBMIT TO:	MODERATOR	ARRIVAL DATE:	20 APRIL (20 OCT)	SESSION:	MAY 2003
SCHOOL CODE :		SCHOOL NAME:			

- *Type or write legibly using black ink and retain a copy of this form.*

SUBJECT: **Design Technology** | LEVEL : **HIGHER** | CAND. NAME: | CAND. NO:

Date(s)	Outline of experimental / investigations / projects (include title, a brief description and internal school coding if used)	Topic /option number	Time (hrs)	PI (a)	PI (b)	DC	DPP	CE	MS	PS (a)	PS (b)
								Levels awarded			
	Product design and development – case study	1.1/1.4/ 2.3/ 5.1	3	-	-			-	-	-	
	Product evaluation	2.2/2.3	4		-				-		
	Ergonomic audit	2.1	4	-	-				-		
	Design and make an ice-cream cone holder for a fast food restaurant	2.1/3/4	8								
	Radio construction kit		1	-	-	-	-	-		-	
	Design and make a radio	3/4/7/A	12	-	-	-	-	-		-	

PROJECT

INVESTIGATIONS

Total for project and investigations, both out of 24, go here.

→

*Design technology : the highest level attained in each criterion in investigations and the level attained in each criterion for the design project.

Both totals must also appear on the IA/PG marksheet

To be completed by teacher   Name: Signature :   Date :

Figure 15.34 Form 4/PSOW internal assessment: group 4 (continued)

Form 4/PSOW (reverse)

SCHOOL NAME :

SUBJECT: Design Technology	LEVEL : HIGHER	CAND. NAME:			CAND. NO:						

	Outline of experimental / investigations / projects (include title, a brief description and internal school coding if used)	Topic/option	Time (hrs)	Levels awarded							
Date(s)				PI (a)	PI (b)	DC	DPP	CE	MS	PS (a)	PS (b)
	Reuse of a plastic bottle	9/C	2	-	-	-		-		-	
	Fuel efficient stove	6	5	-	-	-					
	Use CADCAM to design and make a three-dimensional toy from two-dimensional shapes	E	4	-	-	-		-		-	-
	Redesigning a microwave control panel for the blind	F	6								
	Group 4 project	-	10								
	Design project	-	35								

This is merely an example practical scheme of work. It uses more than the 81 hours required at HL but is broad and touches on a wide variety of core, AHL and optional material.

one other in each category, arguably a school could operate a PSOW consisting of just two projects: the design project and one other (this could even be the group 4 project). However, schools should be encouraged to construct a PSOW with a few more projects for three key reasons:

1. A PSOW should be varied and reflect the elements of the course; core, options and, in the case of HL, the AHL material.
2. Students should have the opportunity to hone their skills through a progression of ever more challenging assignments rather than being given a one-shot chance to gain a grade.
3. Investigation work should be seen as the preparation for the design project. Again, the more opportunities to practise before embarking on the design project, the better.

Investigations may vary in length. As in the other sciences, investigations must be designed to fulfil the requirements of the criteria that are assessed, and it is important that students receive adequate feedback after each assignment is marked. The 'c, p, n' scheme should be used and feedback to students should justify the grades awarded. During moderation, this same information helps the moderator tremendously, especially where the evidence for the grade awarded might not be explicit.

Differences in IA between DT and other sciences

The coursework produced by DT students can be assessed against the same eight criteria (planning (a), planning (b), data collection and so on) that are used in the other group 4 sciences. If students undertake experimental work as part of the practical scheme of work, then the same descriptors for each aspect may be used to arrive at a grade for each criterion using the 'c, p, n' system – see section 3.2. However, in DT it is more likely that students will be involved in 'design and make' activities or in applying some element of the design process (for example, the evaluation of an existing product), as opposed to 'scientific' experimental work. Where this is the case then it is more appropriate to use the assessment scheme that has been formulated specifically for DT. This can be viewed in the DT subject guide, obtainable from the Online Curriculum Centre (OCC). *This effectively means that there are two sets of IA criteria available to be used in DT.* When assessing standard experimental work, follow the guidelines for all group 4 sciences as outlined in section 3. When assessing the elements of the design process, as in the design project, use the unique DT criteria. Figure 15.35 contains some useful advice to bear in mind when employing the unique DT criteria.

Once each aspect of each criterion has been assessed, the grade awarded (out of 3) is arrived at using the 'c, p, n' science marking grids shown in figures 15.15 and 15.16. Where students have worked in teams it is absolutely essential that their individual contributions are recorded to gain marks for Pl (a), Pl (b), DC, DPP and CE. The best approach is an individual 'write-up', where each student determines the way in which material is communicated. Work that has been produced and photocopied for each student's folio is not acceptable.

Figure 15.35 Comments on DT-specific internal assessment criteria

Pl (a)	Students must identify their own research problem and formulate their own *brief* and *design specification* to gain full marks for this criterion. If a problem or brief is set then the student should be expected to expand considerably on that provided if this criterion is assessed as part of a practical. Schools frequently fall into the trap of providing too much information and then awarding high-end marks. One strategy might be to provide a rigid problem and brief in early exercises and then provide progressively less information in subsequent assignments. This is good preparation for the design project where students must identify their own problem to solve. See section 6.4 for further details.
Pl (b)	Students frequently fail to include an estimate of time for each stage of their production plan. This is an important element of production planning and useful at the evaluation (CE) stage when comparing the planned and actual courses of action. Students should be encouraged to keep a photographic record of their work. This allows them to quickly, easily and effectively communicate problems/design changes as well as to illustrate the quality of workmanship for the award of a grade for 'manipulative skills'. As in planning (a), schools should avoid providing too much information. A student who has been given a list of equipment and a plan to follow will not gain any credit. It should also be noted that production plans should not be retrospective accounts.
DC	There is a tendency for students to rely on secondary data (e.g. books, magazines, websites and so on). They should be encouraged to exploit a wide range of sources of data of both a primary nature (e.g. user questionnaires, expert opinion and an exploration of existing solutions) and a secondary nature. The gathering of user and expert opinion also helps the teacher to assess PS (a). Students should determine their own sources of data and their own methods of presentation if they are to be awarded full marks for DC.
DPP	Schools equipped with the facilities for computer-aided design are encouraged to use it wherever appropriate as a tool to help students develop and communicate their ideas. Very often students jump from a concept to a working drawing with no development in between and you should ensure that this important area is not omitted.
CE	Students should be encouraged to thoroughly test and evaluate their solution against the specification using a variety of sources of data. They should employ performance testing, user feedback, expert opinion and so on as well as their own observations. In evaluating procedures, students tend to focus on the manufacturing stage. They should take a more holistic view of the design process, focusing on the strengths and weaknesses of each and every stage they have worked through. In suggesting improvements to the product, students must provide detail and show changes in the form of drawings where appropriate. Comments such as 'make bigger' or 'use a different material' will not score highly!
MS	Students should be well practised in safely handling apparatus, tools, equipment and resources and skilled in relevant techniques. This can be assessed by observation of their performance and the final product. Awareness of health and safety issues is important here, as is the ability to safely follow any instructions or guidance given by the teacher.
PS (a)	Personal skills (a) revolves around the performance of a student as part of a team. This can be judged very easily by using one or more group projects as part of a practical scheme of work and then observing the student in that situation. The group 4 project is ideal, of course, since it shows the student collaborating not only with other students but with students from disciplines other than DT. To assess a student in a team project, apply the group 4 science criteria for PS (a) given in section 3. The design project, however, tends to be tackled individually but you still need to assess PS (a). See the DT-specific assessment details in the subject guide to see how PS (a) might be assessed in the design project.
PS (b)	Issues related to ethics and the environment should feature in the students' documentation through such areas as the specification and the evaluation. This criterion also assesses other factors, details of which can be found in the subject guide.

6.4 **The design project**

A key difference between DT and the other group 4 sciences is the requirement for students to complete the design project. This is worth 12% of the 36% allocated to coursework and is assessed separately from the other coursework, as described in section 6.3. SL students should spend at least 19 hours and HL students 31 hours completing the project. As with all coursework, these times reflect the time set aside in school for the completion of the design project, and they exclude 'homework'.

The design project is compulsory and must be assessed against *all* eight criteria. It is a chance for students to apply what they have learned to one unified project that addresses all aspects of the design process.

The project consists of a *project summary report* and a *log book*. The work submitted by a student will also feature the intended outcome and this will vary according to the project title. The final outcome may be a fully functional prototype or a scale model, two-dimensional or three-dimensional, and so on.

The *log book* is an ongoing record, a sort of diary of how the design project has progressed. It should contain notes and sketches, design ideas, research material, laboratory practicals, details of decisions taken at various stages, and so on. Work will be dated and entered chronologically and in this respect will reflect the nature of the design process, where the reality is that the designer jumps from one activity to another and does not tackle design in the neat, linear fashion suggested by most textbook design processes. The log book forms the basis for the report but is not assessed directly.

The *project summary report* should be compiled in conjunction with the log book, and reviewed and edited as the project progresses. The report places all of the work that the student has done in a logical sequence, more akin to the linear design process and reflective of the assessment scheme. It identifies key stages of the project development and should explain the process followed, providing justification for the decisions taken. It is not merely a neat version of the log book but should highlight the key stages and findings at each stage of the design process. For example, in gathering research material, the bulk of the information obtained will be recorded in the log book as it is collected. The student will then place the key conclusions as they apply to the project in the report, cross-referencing the log book as appropriate. Another example might be in testing and evaluation. The student may have conducted a series of performance tests that are written up in the log book along with feedback from potential users and expert opinion. The results of these tests and other feedback would be used to write the product evaluation that would appear in the report. These are just a couple of examples to help distinguish between the log book and the report.

The report should also contain evidence of the outcome of the project (prototypes, models and so on) using good-quality photographs.

Choosing a project title

DT teachers will know that getting students to identify a problem to solve for a major project is a headache. To access the full marks available for Pl (a), the students must identify their own problem and formulate their own brief and specification. The best projects are those that answer a 'real life' need rather than being based on some hypothetical situation. The tackling of a genuine problem also focuses on the potential user(s) and links to expert opinion, which helps students to gather and analyse data and ideas and ultimately to evaluate solutions. The DP course, with its inherent CAS programme, provides a rich source of potential project ideas. Students should be encouraged to examine their various activities, local and global service projects and trips/expeditions to generate topics for their project. Teachers should check the following when approving a project title:

- Will the title allow the student to fully address all assessment criteria?
- What is the expected outcome? Prototype? Model?
- Can the outcome be achieved in the time available?
- Is the project challenging to the student and appropriate for the level?
- Does the student possess the necessary skills and knowledge?
- What facilities are required, in particular to realize the solution to a problem?
- Are there sufficient sources of research material available to the student? Clearly a student needs easy access to sources of data for problem analysis, research, evaluation of ideas and the like.

Some example project titles:

- A portable, solar powered battery charger for use in remote areas.
- A cheap, portable water filter for use in a disaster situation or while camping.
- A device to clip onto the top of a soft drinks can for more hygienic usage.
- Redesigning an existing garden for a wheelchair-bound user.
- An improved aircraft meal tray.

6.5 Awarding the final internal assessment grade

For the other sciences the two best scores in each of the eight criteria are added together to get a total out of 48 marks. This total is then halved by the IBO to scale the score to the 24% IA weighting. As mentioned earlier, DT is slightly different. The design project is a compulsory part of the course that must be assessed against all eight criteria and is allocated its own 12% weighting. But since each of the criteria is already assessed once in the design project, you can put forward your *best* mark (rather than the best two) for each criterion in the 'investigations' component (the other 24%). Thus, when your school sends its marks to the IBO, it will send two marks for DT: one for the design project and one for the other IA work. Each will be a score out of 24 but the IBO will subsequently scale the design project score to a total out of 12%. This explains why figure 15.34 has spaces for both investigations and design project final total scores.

7 Environmental systems (SL)

This subject follows the common group 4 curriculum model as described in section 1.1, but it also shares elements of a humanities course due to the substantial consideration of how environmental issues directly affect society and vice versa. For example, the issue of global warming is not just a matter of science but involves economics, politics and sociology. The manner in which these and many other disciplines are integrated and delivered through this course is known as the *systems approach*. This teaching methodology is used commonly in subjects such as geography. Indeed the package combination of environmental systems and geography works very well. On the other hand, the package combination of biology (SL or HL) with environmental systems is not allowed due to their significant curriculum overlap.

As with all group 4 SL courses, the duration of all theory should be 110 hours, leaving 40 hours for internal assessment. As in biology, many schools run residential field courses (field trips where students stay out of class for several days).

While this is often the terminal science for students who are not intending to take the sciences further, it is not an easy option within group 4. If anything, it demands higher-order skills than some of the other group 4 SL courses. It does give teachers an opportunity to bring real global and local issues to the attention of students and many animated discussions can ensue. The topical nature of the course probably explains why it has one of the fastest-growing candidatures of all DP subjects.

Selection of resources is not easy for this course as there is so much available and no one textbook covers the entire course. This and the inter-disciplinary nature of the subject also means that it can be taught successfully by teachers with a variety of backgrounds, biology and geography being the most common but not the only ones. A series of booklets published by the IBO has gone some way to helping expand on less familiar areas of the syllabus and one of these covers ecology in urban environments for those schools that have difficulty taking students into the field. Again the Online Curriculum Centre (OCC) provides support in a variety of ways, including help with internal assessment.

The pilot course 'Ecosystems and societies' which was first examined in selected schools in May 2003 is a modification and extension of environmental systems to allow it to fulfil group 3 and group 4 aims as one of the new trans-disciplinary SL subjects (see Chapter 18 in this book). It is most likely to be available as a mainstream subject around 2005 and is generally expected to replace environmental systems (although no official decision has been made at the time of writing). Administrators of new schools should bear this in mind when considering which course to implement.

Figure 15.36 Environmental systems (SL) course outline

Core	Options
1. Systems and models	A. Analysing ecosystems
2. The ecosystem	B. Impacts of resource exploitation
3. Global cycles and physical systems	C. Conservation and biodiversity
4. Human population and carrying capacity	D. Pollution management
	Students must study option A and one other option from B–D. As in all group 4 SL subjects, the duration of each option is 15 hours

8 Schemes of work: biology, chemistry and physics

The HL schemes of work in figures 15.37–15.42 are meant to give teachers who are new to the DP a good idea of what the course scheme *could* look like. There are a myriad different educational systems around the world, running on vastly differing timetables and, obviously, no scheme could possibly cover the many possible formats for teaching this course: the schemes need to be adapted to your own timetable and requirements. These schedules are based on a school that runs an annual academic calendar of 36 weeks, with classes lasting for 1 hour 20 minutes, meeting three times a week for an HL class. Year 2 will be considerably shortened due to the date of the final examination – assumed to be 27 weeks, giving a total of 63 weeks. This works out to a total of 252 hours for the entire course. Included are possible dates for the group 4 project and practice examinations. Times given on these schemes of work correspond more or less to those suggested by the IBO in the subject guide (which we have found to be fairly accurate) and should easily fulfil the requirements of 60 hours of IA time.

Schools teaching SL/HL combined classes should be able to adapt the given HL schemes to SL. Note, however, that the schemes are not suitable for anticipated students since they assume a full two-year schedule.

We have included example practical titles to give an idea of the breadth and depth required for the IA experimental work. SL practicals can be selected from this list as well.

8.1 Scheme of work: biology

Figure 15.37 Scheme of work: HL biology, year 1

Week no.	Subject area	Topic no.	Possible experimental investigations	Time allocation (hrs)	Comments
1–3	Cells	1	Microscopy of animal and plant cells Osmosis in potatoes Determining the relative stages of mitosis *or* Virtual practical (The Biology Project – see section 10 for further details) The permeability of membranes (beetroot)	9 + 3	Debatably the best unit to start with. It covers basics that may have been covered before, and leads students to the most important organelles and their functions. Cell membranes. Mitosis may be included here.
4–7	Biochemistry	2 6.5–6	Catalase and hydrogen peroxide Paper chromatography to separate amino acids Food testing	12 + 4	Possibly the most obvious second unit, because it covers the important biochemicals and chemical reactions.
8–13	Molecular genetics	2.4, 6 3.4 6.1–5	Extraction of DNA from onion Gel electrophoresis – crime scene DNA fingerprinting	18 + 6	Builds on the biochemistry already learned, although might be a bit of 'chemistry overload' for some. Introduces the 'here and now' element that the DP encourages. Electrophoresis is very expensive and many schools will not have the resources.

Topics 1–5 are core, 6–13 are AHL and lettered options are option topics.

Figure 15.37 Scheme of work: HL biology, year 1 (continued)

Week no.	Subject area	Topic no.	Possible experimental investigations	Time allocation (hrs)	Comments
14–17	Nutrition and ecology	4.1–5.1	Plan diagram of intestinal wall/villi Estimating population size using a quadrat (simulation) Ecological study of rice 'populations' Beach transect Field course? Full investigation into an aspect of a habitat.	12 + 4	A relief from all the chemistry! The digestion part of the course is so reduced as to be hardly worth it. The ecology should be included with a field course whenever possible to allow a true 'hands-on' approach. Ideal for full investigations (by now the criteria should be well understood).
18–21	Photosynthesis	2.8 7.2	Chromatography to separate pigments Floating leaf discs and light intensity Hill reaction *Elodea* rate of reaction – O_2 production data-logging	12 + 4	Adds some meat to the more discursive nature of ecology. Loads of practical opportunities here, especially using data logging.
24–26	Group 4 project			10–15	Up to 15 IA hours can be claimed for the group 4 project.
22–23 and 27–28	Coordination and response	11.1–2	'Twinkle toes' dissection – looking at chicken claws Reaction times and reflexes	9 + 3	A simple investigation into how tendons attach to muscles and their effect makes an otherwise dry unit more interesting.
29–36	Behaviour option	Option E	Mapping of the visual field Aggressive behaviour in Siamese fighting fish Eye dissection and retina interpretation Animal behaviour record in baboons	24 + 8	It is a good idea to have one of the options completed in the first year, or at least before the mock exams, so that it can be included in the internal end of year exam. This one allows a lot of practical work to be done.

Figure 15.38 Scheme of work: HL biology, year 2

Week no.	Subject area	Topic no.	Possible experimental investigations	Time allocation (hrs)	Comments
1–3	Plant science	13	Leaf adaptations Flower dissection Microscopy of vascular bundles in shoot and root	7 + 5	Fieldwork is recommended here. Allows the internationalism aspect to be discussed in adaptations of different plants to different climates. May be better in year 1, in order to be useful for extended essay work.
4–7	Mendelian genetics	3 8.1	Virtual *Drosophila* investigation (internet practical) Analysis of maize	13 + 3	This is a very theoretical unit, but can be completed quite quickly.
8–9	Homeostasis	5.5–6 12.1–2		10 + 2	Covers regulation and the kidney. Not many practicals in this one – kidney dissections are not very rewarding in my opinion!
10–12	Respiration	7.1	Respirometer using woodlice – data logging experiment Anaerobic respiration investigation	5 + 5	This may be quite late on for this important unit, but it separates out the heavily biochemical units if used here.

Figure 15.38 Scheme of work: HL biology, year 2 (continued)

Week no.	Subject area	Topic no.	Possible experimental investigations	Time allocation (hrs)	Comments
13–15	Reproduction	5.7 9.1–2	Microscopy diagram of ovary and testis	10 + 1	Some good video support available here.
16–17	Revision and mock exam			8	
17–20	Transport and defence	5.3–4 10.1	Heart dissection Microscopy analysis of veins and arteries	11 + 4	The heart and circulation is fairly basic, but the defence system is much harder – one of the most difficult topics, hence its late appearance.
21–27	Evolution option	Option D	Cystic fibrosis: a case for gene therapy Human evolution presentation	22 + 2	Very little practical work in this unit, but it provokes a lot of interest. Can be supplemented by good videos, particularly the human evolution section.

8.2 Scheme of work: chemistry

The schedule in figures 15.39 and 15.40 includes the modern analytical and further organic options; these are popular choices.

Figure 15.39 Scheme of work: HL chemistry, year 1

Week no.	Subject area	Topic no.	Possible experimental investigations	Time allocation (theory + practical) (hrs)	Comments
1	Introduction		Introduction to lab techniques	+ 1	Review course requirements and safety. Discuss IA criteria.
1–5	Stoichiometry, oxidation and reduction	1 + 10/19 (teach 10.1 and 19.1)	Determination of the Avogadro constant Formula of a hydrated salt Standardizing sodium hydroxide solution Analysis of supermarket vinegar by titration Determining the formula of a metal hydroxide What's an eggshell made of? *Percentage of iron in an iron tablet *Determination of hydrogen peroxide strength	14 + 5	Complete three or four practicals from these. *Practicals marked with an asterisk require redox stoichiometry. Complete both of these. I like to teach this section of redox early, as oxidation numbers and redox titrations are fundamental.
5–8	Atomic structure	2/12	Wavelengths of Na and Li emissions Investigating flame colours	8 + 1	Some people prefer to teach atomic structure at the very beginning to grab the students' interest. Stoichiometry can be rather dull, so you may want to consider this.

Topics 1–11 are core, 12–20 are AHL and lettered options are option topics.

Figure 15.39 Scheme of work: HL chemistry, year 1 (continued)

Week no.	Subject area	Topic no.	Possible experimental investigations	Time allocation (theory + practical) (hrs)	Comments
8–11	Periodicity	3/13	Investigating the properties of period 3 oxides Investigating the properties of period 3 chlorides Investigating aqueous halogens Illustrating the oxidation states of vanadium *or* *Elucidating the formulae of two complex ions by colorimetry	9 + 5	There is some overlap between atomic structure and periodicity which will help you to save some time. *This practical requires a colorimeter.
11–16	Bonding	4/14	Investigating structure and bonding and determination of unknown structure Investigation: bond polarity	17 + 3	By now, your students should be familiar with the IA criteria and should be scoring some 3s.
16–18	States of matter	5	Investigation: molar volume Molar mass of gases by direct weighing *or* Molar mass of a volatile liquid	5 + 2.5	
18–24	Organic chemistry 1	11/20/ H	Introduction to organic laboratory techniques Comparing the properties of hydrocarbons Investigating alcohols Preparation of ethyl ethanoate	18.5 + 5	If you choose further organic as an option, you can integrate it nicely with the core and AHL. It is too large, however, to teach all in one go. If you choose modern analytical, then you can further integrate this with the spectroscopy of the organic AHL.
24–26	Group 4 project			8	Other hours are needed for meetings and presentations. You could use up to 15 hours IA for this.
26–33	Modern analytical chemistry option	G	Identification of an unknown compound by chemical and spectroscopic analysis Extraction and identification of the pharmaceutically active chemical in willow bark *or* Investigation of local fruits and vegetables by thin layer and paper chromatography *or* Identifying over-the-counter pain-relieving drugs by thin layer chromatography. *Concentration of an unknown solution by application of Beer-Lambert Law	22 + 5	Ensure you have covered the organic AHL spectroscopy before teaching this – or integrate all spectroscopic techniques together. However, you must ensure that students are fully aware of which material is option work and which is not. I tend to dissect the material fully when revising, hopefully enabling them to compartment-alize the different assessment areas. *Colorimeter or spectrophotometer required. If you have contacts with local industries or universities which have spectroscopic instrumentation, then plan a day out for the students to visit.
34–36	Revision and end-of-year 1 practice exam. Start energetics with remaining time			7	It's good to have covered an option before the first practice exam, as you can then test the students on a genuine Paper 3

Figure 15.40 Scheme of work: HL chemistry, year 2

Week no.	Subject area	Topic no.	Possible experimental investigations	Time allocation (theory + practical) (hrs)	Comments
1–4	Energetics	6/15	Investigation: solubility of salts To determine an energy change by an indirect method (Hess's Law) Heat of combustion of alcohols Investigation: heat of neutralization *or* A thermometric titration	13 + 5 (incl. 3 from week 36)	Plenty of scope to cover all the IA criteria here and in the next three areas.
4–8	Kinetics	7/16	Investigation: rates of reaction Determining the order of reaction – HCl and CaCO₃ *or* The study of a reaction by the colorimetric method – iodination of propanone* Investigation: activation energy of a reaction	10 + 4	*Requires a colorimeter or spectrophotometer.
8–11	Equilibrium	8/17	Boiling point determination and vapour pressure curves Iodine distribution *or* Ammonia distribution The effect of concentration on equilibrium (iron (III) ions and thiocyanate ions) Determining an equilibrium constant (ethyl ethanoate esterification)	9 + 5	Teaching energetics, kinetics, equilibrium and then acids and bases amounts to a lot of physical chemistry together. I find that their interconnected-ness outweighs the tedium of calculations – but if I had chosen a different option that didn't have much integration with the core and AHL, I would have placed it in here so as to split up all the physical chemistry.
11–16	Acids and bases	9/18	pH curves for acid-alkali titrations Determination of dissociation constants of weak acids Hydrolysis of salts Investigation: buffers	14 + 6	Good opportunity for using ICT, with a variety of pH probes and software. The Texas Instrument CBL system is versatile and students may already use this calculator in their mathematics courses.
16–17	Revision and mock exam			4	
17–21	Oxidation and reduction 2	10/19	To determine a redox series for some metal/metal ion half-cells Investigation: electrochemistry Investigation: electrolysis	10 + 4	Teach the remainder of redox here: reactivity and electrochemistry. Good opportunities for planning investigations.
21–26	Organic chemistry 2	11/20/H	The chemical properties of carboxylic acids Fats and oils – degree of unsaturation by titration with permanganate ions The reactions of aldehydes and ketones The identification of a carbonyl compound	18 + 4	Cover the second section of your large organic chunk. When revising at the end of this subject area, revise all the organic and ensure the students know *exactly* which material is option work and which is not.
26–27+	Revision and final exam			6	

8.3 Scheme of work: physics

Figure 15.41 Scheme of work: HL physics, year 1

Week no.	Subject area	Topic no.	Possible experimental investigations	Time allocation (hrs)	Comments
1–4	Introduction and physical measurement	01	Introduction to errors and rule of propagation of errors	13 + 3	Can be done as a paper exercise and/or as a practical. Suitable experiment: density of regular objects.
5–16	Mechanics	02/08	1. Determination of g by free fall 2. Verification of $F = ma$ 3. Investigating the conservation of momentum 4. Investigating friction 5. Investigating stopping distances 6. Investigating circular motion 7. Factors affecting the range of a projectile	39 + 10	Practicals 5 and 7 are suitable for Planning (a) and (b) exercises. Practical 4 could be used to practise these skills (the IBO deems this practical unsuitable for assessment as it is readily available from textbooks). If time is short, planning can be done without carrying out the practical, although this is not recommended. Planning could be set for homework and the experimental work carried out in the next lesson.
17–23	Thermal physics	03/09	1. Measurement of specific heat capacity by method of mixtures 2. Measurement of specific heat capacity by electrical method 3. Measurement of specific latent heat of fusion of ice 4. Measurement of specific latent heat of vaporization of a liquid 5. Factors affecting the rate of evaporation	17 + 7	1 – 4 are standard textbook experiments that are good for the development of DC, DPP and CE skills. 5 can be used as a Planning (a) and (b) exercise.
24–30	Waves	04/10	1. Measurement of wavelength of coloured light using Young's fringes 2. Measuring the speed of sound with an electronic timer 3. Investigating the speed of waves in a string 4. Finding the refractive index of Perspex 5. Speed of sound using resonance 6. Investigating wave phenomena with a microwave kit	18 + 7	1 could be done with filter, single and double slit on an optical bench, or a laser could be fired directly at a double slit. DPP skills for graphs really develop here (practicals 1–5). All can incorporate use of maximum and minimum gradients.
31–36	Group 4 project, revision, internal exam			30	Start electricity and magnetism with remaining time.

Figure 15.42 Scheme of work: HL physics, year 2

Week no.	Subject area	Topic no.	Possible experimental investigations	Time allocation (hrs)	Comments
1–6	Electricity and magnetism	05/11	1. Current/voltage characteristics for a resistor and lamp 2. Investigating the relationship between resistance and length/cross-sectional area of a conductor 3. Verification of Joule's Law of electrical heating 4. Measuring the flux density of a magnet 5. Investigation of field due to solenoid 6. Factors affecting the efficiency of a transformer 7. Factors affecting strength of an electromagnet	22 + 8	For 4, use a U-shaped magnet and measure the force on a conductor in its field. 5 and 6 are Planning (a) and (b) exercises.
7–12	Atomic and nuclear physics	06/12	1. Measurement of e/m 2. Determination of Planck's constant 3. Dice analogue of radioactive decay 4. Measurement of atomic spacing	22 + 5	Equipment expensive so centres may only have one or two pieces of each equipment. Do as a circus.
13–19	Astrophysics option	F	1. Experiment to estimate the temperature of the sun (using a black body) 2. How the intensity of light radiated from a small source varies with distance 3. Power radiated from a black body 4. Elements in the sun – investigating Fraunhofer lines	22 + 5	For 1, use a 12V filament lamp as your black body. Use high voltages and assume resistance proportional to temperature. For 4, use spectrometer and diffraction grating. Not on syllabus but relatively easy to set up.
19–25	Relativity option	G	1. Curved space: analogy of light deflecting as it passes a massive object 2. Muon decay	22 + 3	Practical work is difficult for this option! Muon decay requires published data showing numbers of muons detected at different heights and is a useful DPP exercise.
25–27	Revision and final exam			5	

9 Future directions

Syllabus content will vary slightly with the regular review process that is central to the IBO's philosophy. The next review is due to start sometime in 2004, but most people do not envisage huge changes since the current curriculum model is popular with teachers. We would certainly welcome greater emphasis on topics such as internationalism in science and scientific ethics, as these are areas close to the overall IB ethos. Likewise, one would expect the IBO to rectify at some stage the present inconsistency in the extended essay rules, which insist on a single subject focus and thereby prevent students from taking a more holistic view. The hot topic is that of trans-disciplinary subjects like the currently piloted

'Ecosystems and society' course, which covers areas such as ecology and the relationship between science and society. The advantage of such trans-disciplinary subjects is that they cover the demands for both group 4 science and group 3 humanities, thus freeing up a subject slot in the otherwise constrained DP hexagon. In terms of educational philosophy and practice, trans-disciplinary teaching is very much within the spirit of the IBO, so one would expect to see continued development in this area in the future. See Chapter 18 for more details on the trans-disciplinary courses.

10 Resources

10.1 IB science workshops

The uptake of the IB DP throughout the world – an annual growth rate of about 10% worldwide – has placed a great strain on the demand for workshops to cater for both new and experienced teachers. One solution that the IBO has used is to combine both groups of educators in one workshop. However, this is generally regarded as ineffective; new teachers require a more basic introduction and experienced teachers are generally not stimulated enough. Nevertheless, the opportunity to network with other IB teachers and exchange useful resources make them a very worthwhile experience, particularly to the novice IB teacher. It should also be noted that the IBO requires all schools to be firmly committed to supporting its workshops, and that not only new teachers, but also the experienced will participate on a regular basis.

10.2 Essential reading

The IB documentation, including relevant forms and a sample PSOW form, can all be found in section 4, 'Group 4 sciences' and section F, 'Internal assessment' of the *Vade Mecum*. The group 4 assessment framework and internal assessment criteria are included in all group 4 subject guides. Extended essay criteria are in the extended essay guide. All of these publications are available from the OCC (see section 10.3).

The IBO supplies past papers and mark schemes in PDF format which are supplied on CD-ROMs. Ask your IB coordinator to purchase them for you.

10.3 IB Online Curriculum Centre

The Online Curriculum Centre (OCC) gives access to almost all relevant IBO publications, including:

- subject guides
- extended essay guide and subject criteria
- sample IA assessment material and marking guidelines
- relevant material from the *Vade Mecum* as outlined in section 10.2.

There is also an excellent electronic forum. Many teachers use this to query their group 4 project implementation or IA marking with other teachers in similar situations. The OCC can be found by going to the IBO website at www.ibo.org

and following the extranet link. Navigate by selecting 'diploma programme' then the relevant curriculum area that you wish to access. Note that extended essay advice is found in the extended essay section and not in individual subject areas. Ensure that your IB coordinator has enrolled your school as a member for this valuable resource.

10.4 Subject-specific resources

There are a myriad texts available for biology, chemistry and physics at pre-university level. The list of recommended publications below is in no way definitive and any preferences expressed are purely personal. I have tried to include most of the IB-specific publications available at the present time.

Biology

There is a huge variety of excellent textbooks available for biology. Some of the better ones are listed here.

Allott, A. (2001) *Biology for the IB Diploma*, Oxford University Press. This is useful for both HL and SL students. It covers all of the topic areas in sufficient detail, and is an excellent revision book. It is recommended that the students buy this book so that they can write in it.

Jones, M. and Jones, G. (1997) *Advanced Biology*, Cambridge University Press. This is a reasonable text with sufficient depth in most areas. Its main strength is its accessibility. It is highly readable, and very well presented, with past A-level questions.

Clegg, C. J. and Mackean D. G. (2000) *Advanced Biology Principles and Applications*, John Murray (International Student Edition). This is an excellent all-round textbook. It has clear and useful diagrams, and is accessible to all levels. Particularly useful for HL students.

Toole, S. and Toole, G. (1995) *Understanding Biology for the Advanced Level*, 3rd edition, Stanley Thornes. Another easy-to-read textbook. Very accessible, with past A-level examination questions at the end of every section.

Campbell, N. A. and Reece, J. B. (2002) *Biology*, 6th edition, The Benjamin Cummings Publishing Co. Inc. A brilliant resource for teachers, although quite high level for students. Its main attraction is the fantastic CD-ROM that gives you access to their website, and provides all the diagrams within the book, as well as many detailed animations of biological processes such as meiosis, protein synthesis and respiration. Incidentally, the website can be subscribed to without purchasing the book. Highly recommended! Look up www.campbellbiology.com for further details.

Senior Biology 1 and 2 (2002), Biozone International Ltd. These workbooks are designed to be bought and written in by students, and cover IB topics as outlined on the front. There are spaces for answers, as well as data analysis style questions. A useful companion for students. There is an answer book available for teachers as well. Different versions exist for different countries. There is also a supporting website. See www.biozone.co.uk/products.html for more information.

Some excellent websites provide teaching materials or ideas for topics. A particularly good one is The Biology Project by the University of Arizona (www.biology.arizona.edu/default.html). It provides some excellent virtual practicals, such as determining the phases of mitosis, and is a mine of information.

Chemistry

All of the publications listed below are certainly worth purchasing for personal or departmental use. The decision to buy one or more as student texts will depend on the balance between the strain on your budget and the possible benefits for your students. If you already use a set text for your existing pre-university system you should be able to use it with the DP, although it may have only limited coverage of some of the option topics.

Green, John and Damji, Sadru (1998) *Chemistry for Use with the International Baccalaureate*, IBID Press. This was the first IB-specific chemistry publication and as such garnered a lot of attention. Responses have been varied. Certainly, it doesn't match up to the quality of some of the impressive texts listed below, but it covers exactly what you need to know when teaching the IB syllabus. Indeed, for many IB teachers it has been an invaluable source of information, particularly with regard to the teaching of the options. The authors are experienced IB teachers and the text is designed to be straightforward and concise. Many students like the way it relates exactly to the IB objectives and they find it easy to use for independent study.

Neuss, Geoff (2001) *Chemistry for the IB Diploma – Standard and Higher Level*, Oxford University Press. This is an IB-specific revision guide and is really an excellent piece of work. Its brevity means that it can't take the place of standard student texts, but as a revision guide it works magnificently. Chapters are clearly separated into SL and HL sections and the intelligent use of diagrams enables the entire syllabus to be covered in an impressively small number of pages – just what students want for revision.

Ramsden, E. N. (2000) *A-level Chemistry*, 4th edition, Nelson Thornes Ltd. A thorough, well-written textbook with clear explanations and a comprehensive coverage of pre-university chemistry material, although no specific treatment of much of the IB option topics.

Zumdahl, S. S. and S. L. (2003) *Chemistry*, 6th edition, Houghton-Mifflin. This text, popular in the USA, is of a very high standard indeed. The authors' passion for chemistry comes across clearly. The explanations and worked examples are clear and easy to understand and the book has a very user-friendly feel. The text is certainly advanced enough for HL, but won't cover the options in a specific manner.

Fullick, A. and Fullick, P. (1994) *Heinemann Advanced Science: Chemistry*, Heinemann. A great student book, well written and easy to use, although possibly not quite advanced enough for HL. A good SL book.

Lainchbury, A. Stephens, J. and Thompson, A. (1996) *ILPAC: Independent Learning Project for Advanced Chemistry*, 2nd edition, John Murray. A really excellent set of teaching booklets which take the students through chemistry with good worked examples, detailed solutions to problems and well-designed experiments. The practicals included are first-rate but need to be amended to fit the IA criteria. Not specific to the DP so you would find it hard to justify buying a student set, but well worth buying a copy for the department as you'll get a lot of good ideas from it. The set of experiments are available independently.

Herron, J. *et al* (1993) *Heath Chemistry*, D C Heath & Co. A whole range of teaching publications for chemistry. This series is very popular in the USA. The experiments are comprehensive and detailed but must be amended for use with the IB IA system.

CLEAPSS Laboratory Handbook and Hazcards (2000 edition). CLEAPSS stands for the Consortium of Local Education Authorities for the Provision of Science Services. This service is mainly for schools and colleges in the UK but international schools are usually able to gain membership. Their safety publications are excellent and are designed to be used in schools, by teachers and provide essential safety information. Although it is designed for UK schools and with UK safety regulations in mind, it would be of great use with any system. Electronic versions of the publications are available. The 'hazcards' containing safety issues relating to specific chemicals are particularly useful for classroom teachers. See their website, www.cleapss.org.uk for how to purchase publications and for membership information.

Croner's Manual for Heads of Science, Croner Publications, London. Another very useful safety manual for any school science department, although not as comprehensive as the CLEAPSS range of publications.

Physics

Kerr, G., Kerr, N. and Ruth, P. (1998) *Physics for Use with the International Baccalaureate*, IBID Press. This text is not endorsed by the IBO but, nevertheless, covers all course content for SL and HL students, and includes chapters on each option. Syllabus statements are given throughout followed by topic material pertaining to a particular statement. The book is most suitable for SL students, its strengths being its conciseness, accessibility to students of all abilities and relevant worked examples. On the other hand, it does not contain the depth required for full and complete understanding. HL students, particularly the most able (and teachers), would benefit from …

Giancoli, D. C. (2001) *Physics Principles with Applications*, 5th edition, Prentice-Hall, Inc. This book meets the challenge of the more difficult concepts in the course and, as the title implies, refers to many applications of the relevant physics principles. It also contains questions at the end of each chapter of increasing difficulty. An excellent website accompanies the text and can be viewed at http://cwx.prenhall.com/giancoli/. Although more advanced-level textbooks like this one contain material relevant to the DP, they are probably best used by teachers and students for reference only.

Kirk, T. (2001) *Physics for the IB Diploma*, Oxford University Press. A handy revision book for both SL and HL.

Roby, P. (2003) *IB Physics Revision Guide*, Oxford Study Courses (OSC) Limited. A new revision book for the IB. OSC also cover chemistry and biology material, including some interesting work on the options. Visit www.osc-ib.com for further details.

www.harcourtcollege.com/physics/pse is the website companion to the editor's all-time favourite physics book by Serway and Beichner (2000) *Physics for Scientists and Engineers with Modern Physics*, 5th edition, Saunders College Publishing. This book combines the enthusiasm and far-sightedness of

Feynman's three famous textbooks, but consistently caters to weaker students as well. It has interesting historical anecdotes and takes great care to explain why the topics at hand are of interest to physicists, both at a basic application level and at an advanced post-doc level. It manages to do so without ever trivializing things or going over students' heads. Exercises start with the very basic and end with really fun and challenging problems. While officially designated a first-year university book, teachers and students will find it an endless source of inspiration – a must-have text.

Lederman, L. (1994) *The God Particle: If the universe is the answer, what is the question?*, Delta Publishers. While there are many great popular texts on physics, notably by Feynman and by Weinberg, many of these are of an inspirational metaphysical kind, or deal with physics on a level too high for school students. In the opinion of the editor, Leon Lederman's book is a prime example of an authoritative book that inspires but also engages in exciting physics in commendable and accessible detail. It explains the scientific history of the search for the smallest particles, starting with molecules and atoms, through to the hunt for the elusive Higgs Boson, the ultimate focus of this book. Motivated students will find this a page-turner!

Chapter 16

Group 5: Mathematics and computer science

Marc van Loo, MSc, PhD
and Peter Joseph, MA
with Bruce Love, BSc, MSc

Peter Joseph and Marc van Loo both started teaching the IB Diploma Programme (DP) at the United World College of South East Asia (UWCSEA) in 1995, and taught all four DP mathematics courses there. Both were at different times in charge of the further mathematics programme. Peter went on to explore his interest in IT and piloted the IBO's intended 'two-tier examination paper approach', and trained the faculty in the use of new IT components. He is now teaching at Ardingly College, a recently accredited DP school in the UK. Marc went on to develop his passion for experiential learning, through an educational resort he owns in nearby Indonesia (LooLa Adventure Resort), by taking up the position of coordinator of Critical Thinking at Nanyang Technological University, and by taking up the position of Professor of Mathematics and Physics at Overseas Family College, a college at the forefront of educational innovation in Singapore.

In this chapter, they discuss all four mathematics courses of group 5 in detail, with an emphasis on the components that make IB mathematics different: the use of IT and coursework.

The remaining subject in group 5, computer science, is discussed in section 10 by Bruce Love. Bruce has taught mathematics and computer courses for many years, mostly in New Zealand. He joined the Overseas Family School in Singapore in 2001 to take over the computer science DP course as an IB novice. He has been asked by the IBO to become a moderator for the internal assessment component. Armed with a fresh perspective (and a traditionally no-nonsense Kiwi attitude), Bruce takes the reader on a whirlwind tour of the subject.

1 Introduction

1.1 Overview of group 5

Group 5 consists of five subjects, listed in figure 16.1 and briefly summarized below.

Figure 16.1 Group 5 subjects

	HL or SL	Remarks
MSSL (Mathematics Studies Standard Level)	SL	Students must take
MMSL (Mathematics Methods Standard Level)	SL	one (and only one) of
MHL (Mathematics Higher Level)	HL	these three courses.
FM (Further Mathematics)	SL	Students can choose
Computer science	SL or HL	these as free electives.

MSSL is the least demanding and until recently the most popular course; it consists of a core and three option topics, of which students must study one. Schools need to be aware that not all universities recognize it – see details in section 1.5.

MMSL is an introduction-to-calculus type course for students who need a fairly rigorous mathematics foundation for their chosen field of study, typically in life sciences or business-type studies. It has recently narrowly overtaken MSSL as the most popular mathematics course. It consists of a core and two option topics, of which the students must study one.

MHL is a demanding course for students with a great interest in mathematics or who wish to pursue university studies in engineering, natural sciences or mathematics. It consists of a core and five option topics, of which the students must take one.

While it is in theory possible to take further mathematics (FM) to satisfy the group 5 requirement, in practice it is taken as a free elective *in addition* to the MHL course. FM simply consists of *all* the MHL options, and is offered at SL only, meaning it requires 150 contact hours (and not 240, as an HL course does). Most of the students taking this course wish to preserve the breadth of their DP package and thus prefer to take FM as an extra seventh subject outside of their DP package, which is possible if the school supports it.

Computer science can only be taken as a free elective, and is discussed separately in section 10 of this chapter.

1.2 Assessment outline

All mathematics subjects are examined in a similar manner, as illustrated in figure 16.2. To teachers who are familiar with programmes such as the American AP or British A-levels, the syllabuses offer few surprises in terms of mathematical content, but the coursework component, the relative emphasis on skill over content, and the prominent role of IT may well mark a difference with national education systems.

Note that the percentage next to each item in figure 16.2 indicates its weight in the final assessment, but that the percentages for the papers are rounded to

Figure 16.2 Assessment outline

Subject	Exam papers (80%)		Coursework (20%)
MSSL	Paper 1 1 hour, 15 questions, 4 marks per question	30%	One extended project
	Paper 2 2 hours, 6 long questions including option question worth 30 marks (15%); total mark for paper = 100	50%	
MMSL	Paper 1 1 hour, 15 questions, 3 marks per question	25%	A portfolio of short tasks – the best three of which count
	Paper 2 2 hours, 6 long questions including option question worth 30 marks (15%); total mark for paper = 100	55%	
MHL	Paper 1 2 hours, 20 questions, 3 marks per question	30%	As MMSL
	Paper 2 3 hours, 6 long questions including option question worth 30 marks (15%); total mark for paper = 100	50%	
FM	Paper 1 1 hour, 10 questions, 5 marks per question	25%	As MMSL, but only the best two tasks count
	Paper 2 2 hours, 5 questions; total = 100 marks	55%	

the nearest 5%. We are not aware of any rationale underlying the small differences in weighting.

Note that the most recent IB mark schemes for Paper 1 in MSSL, MMSL and MHL actually allocate 8, 6 and 6 marks respectively per question; the 4, 3 and 3 marks mentioned in figure 16.2 represent the *weighting* relative to the overall external paper mark. This is a welcome response to teacher criticism that the 4, 3, 3 mark allocation previously used was too coarse to allow for accurate grading.

1.3 Language, culture and global issues

Of all DP subjects, the mathematics courses pose the least problems for students whose first language is not the language of instruction. Nevertheless, there is one important issue. MSSL, created for students whose interest lies squarely outside mathematics, is much harder in language terms than the more technical MMSL course. The difference is so stark that schools working with weak-language students often find themselves forced to advise these students to take the latter course, even though this may not suit their interest.

On a general language note, IB DP examination questions, especially for Paper 2, can be quite wordy or require careful interpretation. The usual remedy for examination-specific problems – administering liberal doses of past examination papers – is therefore necessary for success. The need to practise repetitive past papers, however, is perhaps surprising as it seems contradictory to the central IBO objective of imparting thinking skills. In section 4.2, however, we will suggest ways of enriching the process of reviewing past papers to assist with the objective of developing thinking skills.

Turning to global issues, national mathematics curricula tend to cover a fairly similar body of knowledge in the pre-DP school years. The few truly notable differences are as follows. In South Asia and Eastern Europe, Euclidean geometry receives a lot of attention whereas in most of the rest of the world, it is rarely taught. In North America, conic sections and discrete mathematics feature prominently in early college years, whereas the rest of the world accords these little if any attention. Some Asian students are far ahead with algebraic skills but may never have seen graphs, a topic that features prominently in all DP mathematics courses (fortunately, hard-working students usually face few difficulties catching up in this area).

The MHL syllabus attempts to reflect the international differences through its palette of options, amongst which we find *discrete mathematics and graphs* and *Euclidean geometry and conic sections*. These options allow the national groups mentioned above to take credit for what they have built up earlier or to prepare them for what is expected later.

Finally, there is the issue of IT. While many national systems in the developed world can count on the presence of computers in schools, in the developing world this is not so. As a consequence, the IBO cannot enforce the use of computers, and thus opts for the GDC (graphical display calculator). This decision is not universally applauded. The division in the mathematics community is reflected in the opinions of the two principal authors of this chapter. Both of us believe that IT is a great tool to impart thinking skills in mathematics, but one of us feels that the GDC is user-clumsy dead-end technology and thus not the best way forward, while the other believes that the GDC has several unique and worthwhile benefits. Section 4 of this chapter is devoted to a more detailed discussion of the role of IT within DP mathematics.

1.4 What IBO materials do you need for reading this chapter?

Actually, not many. There is the *Vade Mecum* and the subject guide, but these are needed mostly to learn more about the specific guidelines for assessment of the extended essay in mathematics and about the precise syllabus requirements (although the requirements for MHL are implicitly also listed in our scheme of work in section 9). The most useful IB materials for mathematics teachers are past papers and mark schemes, the latter occasionally containing useful pointers to the range of problem-solving strategies of which students should be aware. Also very useful are sample coursework tasks: the *project* for MSSL and the *portfolio tasks* for MMSL, MHL and FM (all discussed in detail in section 3).

We now present a summary of each of the four mathematics courses of group 5.

1.5 MSSL: Mathematical Studies SL

This is an easy course by most national standards, not much deeper in content than a typical extended-level pre-DP course (with the earlier noted exception of its language demands). It is thus an ideal course for students whose interests lie squarely elsewhere and who need to free up time to pursue those interests to the fullest extent.

There are three options available – (easy) *calculus, statistics* and *graphs and matrices* – of which schools must choose one. Calculus is a common choice in view of the calculus entry demands of many universities, especially those in Europe. However, it must be stressed that MSSL is not an acceptable mathematics course for some universities, notably those in Germany, the Netherlands and Australia. To give students proper advice, schools must carefully research this issue with their target universities.

There is a project, which counts for 20% of the grade and which is quite rigorously assessed. This project should be based on an option topic of the syllabus or on an open investigation, and typically takes a few months to complete. Although students do not have to show evidence of truly independent work to score highly in the project, a full and coherent use of a wide range of appropriate techniques must be demonstrated. It is easy for a hard-working student to score a high mark in the project provided suitable teacher assistance is available. See section 3.1 for details.

Because the use of GDCs (graphical display calculators) is now permitted in the course, the emphasis in teaching and learning has shifted from the pure acquisition of basic techniques to the development of students' ability to choose between alternative strategies for solving problems. See sections 3 and 4 for details.

1.6 MMSL: Mathematical Methods SL

This is currently a quite well-balanced course, which covers about 60–70% of the mathematics HL course, discussed in section 1.7. In addition to a core component comprising *calculus, analytical geometry* and *probability and statistics*, the course also features the two options (of which schools must choose one): *statistical methods* and *further calculus*. These options are tackled at a level of difficulty found in a typical US college *Statistics* course and in the introductory chapters of a *Calculus I* course respectively. The emphasis in the course is on the application and use of techniques, rather than on their derivation, validity and possible generalization. The ability to use GDCs efficiently is as a rule a requisite for a high grade.

Traditionally, grades are not very high in this course. The course is very demanding for an SL course, especially in view of the time constraints, and it is difficult to score a 6 or a 7 without a solid background in mathematics.

There is a coursework component consisting of short investigative or modelling tasks, called *portfolio tasks*, which are best integrated with the teaching of topics. A selection of the best three of these tasks go towards 20% of the final examination mark. The type of work required will be fairly uncharted terrain to many mathematics departments, and is discussed in detail in section 3.

1.7 MHL: Mathematics HL

This course compares in level of difficulty with a typical British A-level course or a combination of the US college courses *Statistics, Algebra and Trigonometry*, and *Calculus I*. Nevertheless, the examination style, the yearly varying examination difficulty, the emphasis on GDC-related questions, and the option topics might well be unfamiliar to both students and teachers. The course includes as a core *algebra and functions, calculus, probability and statistics, complex numbers, vectors* and *matrices and transformations*, and features an additional five option topics (of which a school must choose one): *analysis, discrete mathematics, further statistics, group theory* and *plane geometry*. Of the option topics, probably only *further statistics* will be familiar to most teachers from other education systems, while American educators will recognize *analysis* as a (substantial) subset of a typical *Calculus II* college course. The other three option topics may well pose significant challenges for mathematics departments around the world.

As with MMSL, there is a portfolio consisting of at least three pieces of work relating to the syllabus – the best three of which count towards 20% of the overall grade.

Students must have done very well in mathematics in their previous years to pass this course, let alone gain the higher grades required by some of the more selective university courses requiring MHL. Success in the examination depends on a thorough grasp of topics as well as the ability to solve problems in a variety of ways. In particular, resourceful use of the GDC can sometimes reduce an otherwise difficult problem to a one-liner, while other questions can only be solved using a GDC. The examples below highlight such cases.

November 2000, MHL Paper 1 Question 5

Calculate the area bounded by the graph of $y = \sin(x^2)$ and the x-axis between $x = 0$ and the smallest positive x-intercept.

November 2001, MHL Paper 1 Question 14

A point $P(x, x^2)$ lies on the curve $y = x^2$. Calculate the minimum distance from the point $A\left(2, -\frac{1}{2}\right)$ to the point P.

Some students have little difficulty in spotting an opportunity to solve a question efficiently using a GDC. However, students and teachers raised on traditional pencil and paper techniques tend to need more explicit encouragement and examples to help them develop an increased GDC-aware outlook. Section 4 has the details.

With the possible exception of the GDC issue, examination preparation should be relatively straightforward work for experienced mathematics teachers new to the DP, but departments will need to develop a bank of appropriate portfolio tasks, and students will need considerable practice to get used to these – see section 3.

1.8 FM: Further Mathematics SL

This is for the most part a beautiful and well-balanced course, highly regarded by top-rated universities throughout the world. It simply consists of all the option topics of the MHL course. Interested and motivated students can easily obtain high scores in FM, provided the teachers are comfortable teaching what is really a university-level course. In fact, the heavy emphasis on proof would almost certainly entail sending teachers for mathematical refresher courses. Teachers' unease is one of the main reasons why each year fewer than 100 students sit the examination worldwide. The associated perceived elitist character of the course, in turn, invites pressure from within the IB community to abandon it. However, a well-qualified teacher with a passion for mathematics can really make this course shine: the topics invite digression and the syllabus provides more than enough time to indulge in those. Further mathematics students frequently describe it as the most satisfying and nourishing course in their entire diploma package.

Suggestions have been made to reintroduce as an extra option topic the previously offered *logic and proof* module, which made the course a lot more coherent, and would allow instructors a degree of choice (five out of six options rather than the current no-choice regime). *Euclidean geometry* (largely introduced under pressure from Eastern European countries) is attractive in the sense that it offers a closed unit with concrete results that can all be proved by the student. Students with prior exposure to the topic do very well at it. On the flipside, a serious drawback is that it is virtually impossible for a student new to the topic to master it within the recommended time. The *group theory* option, on the other hand, could easily be extended to include classification of all groups up to order 10, thus enlivening this abstract topic with concrete examples, and providing another closed unit where all results can be proved by the students. On account of FM's limited popularity, we do not discuss this course further in this book, but anyone wishing to know more is referred to our website www.dp-help.com, where materials are posted for downloading.

1.9 What this chapter concentrates on and why

As noted above, in terms of mathematical content there are no big surprises in the mathematics courses, apart from some of the option topics in MHL – which teachers can choose to avoid. To assist with the academic content, an example of a detailed scheme of work for the MHL course is included in section 9.

The aspects in which the DP courses really differ from mathematics courses in most national systems are the following:

- the use of practical coursework
- the use of IT (although American audiences will find fewer surprises here)
- the effects of the 'IB philosophy' on the subject
- the extended essay in mathematics
- the emphasis on proof in MHL and especially FM.

The last aspect is a purely academic skill that features centrally in any university mathematics course, so it can be taught using the well-established techniques in this field (which are outside the scope of this book). The other items on the list above may well signify some profound changes in the classroom and in the administrative demands upon teachers and heads of department new to the DP – and thus they occupy the core of this chapter.

2 Mathematics and the IB philosophy: some way to go

2.1 The gap and why it needs bridging

The overall aims of the DP call for a demonstration of the interconnectivity of knowledge, and of the relation between each branch of knowledge and society. They also call specifically for the development of thinking skills within a student-centred framework. The IBO frequently laments that mathematics departments in schools do not display sufficient initiative in these areas despite the supposed opportunities made available for this by the inclusion of the coursework components. There are reasons for this limited display of initiative, though, and some of these relate to the DP's own syllabuses.

First of all, it is not easy for mathematics teachers to find published examples of the relation of their field to the rest of the world. School books habitually present applications involving ladders and shadows in order to 'apply' trigonometry (whereas anyone wishing to know the length of a ladder just takes a measuring tape – or looks on the factory label). The 'applications' in business are similarly irrelevant and uninspiring. Few textbook writers have taken the trouble to recount the experiences of successful mathematicians-turned-businesspeople, who actually emphasize mathematical skills over techniques. For such accounts one has to turn to business magazines. This is a great pity, because students relate to and are invariably enthused by stories of successful company chairmen and stock-market mathematicians, and by stories of the key role played by mathematics in last century's great scientific breakthroughs: anti-matter, the Big Bang, Einstein's theories and IT, to name a few. University textbooks are similarly narrowly focused. While the applications featured in these texts are usually at least relevant, they tend to involve high-powered mathematics in fields far removed from students' daily experiences, and therefore fail to inspire.

In short, mathematics as a subject suffers from a lack of good resources illustrating its connection to the rest of our world. In view of the fact that so much of our world is, indeed, built on mathematics and intimately connects to it, this is a bizarre state of affairs.

A second reason for the hesitance of mathematics departments to adopt a more encompassing approach towards mathematics lies in the IBO's formulation of its syllabuses and assessments. The content of the mathematics syllabuses is standard and mainstream, and does not invite experimentation; and with the exception of the project in MSSL, the assessment structure does not explicitly reward students for efforts towards personalization and experimentation with new ideas. However, the assessment criteria in all the internally assessed coursework *do* place great emphasis on evidence of *understanding*. It is here that DP mathematics is demonstrably different from most national curricula, and it is here that efforts to tie mathematics to the real world will pay dividends. With 'traditional' tasks, it is very difficult for students to score highly in this aspect because 'understanding' in such tasks narrowly measures *technical* insight. Well-designed applied tasks, however, can virtually ensure full marks for understanding. The trick is to design a task so that it is impossible for students to complete it *unless* they think about it and understand what they are doing. In section 2.2 we present examples of course and class work tasks that link mathematics to the outside world and have inspired and enthused our own students.

On the connection of mathematics with other subjects there is one last concrete item that needs mentioning. The statistics topic *normal distributions* features in all mathematics courses, but also in economics and to some extent in geography, while *Spearman's rank correlation coefficient* features in geography, but not in any mathematics course. The departments of mathematics, economics and geography thus have an obvious chance to highlight the interconnectedness of their subjects and to align their teaching of these topics. Sadly, few schools seem to take up this opportunity, thereby confusing the students rather than enriching them.

2.2 Bridging the gap: examples for lessons and coursework

Three mathematical areas that connect particularly well to the everyday outside world are statistics, probability and exponential functions. In these areas, it is relatively easy to find decent resources.

In the MSSL project, statistical research is very popular with students, and it inspires many to investigate matters close to their hearts. Do people with bigger feet swim faster? Does obesity – or smoking – affect average grade? Do taller people have better jobs? How do the most popular supermarkets in town compare for prices?, and so on. The initial success of this type of coursework, however, led to a rather mechanical approach in many instances, and the IBO examiners started to award lower grades for it as a result. Students can still do well in such projects but their passion for the investigation must be real and convincing, and they must probe their results much more critically and show a real understanding rather than the ability to follow well-worn mechanical steps. Anyone can draw a line of best fit – in fact students should use software to do it – but few students truly understand that in some cases a line of best fit is pointless, while a non-pointless line – together with the correlation coefficient – is a complete *summary* of the data. Any decent school survey will show the students that there is a correlation between smoking and average grades, and they can (and should!) compare their own data against those available on the internet. But many will subsequently elect to either simply disbelieve the data/statistics or jump to the unsubstantiated conclusion that smoking makes you stupid – and thus in both cases completely miss the point. The coursework mark schemes rightly award grades for thoughtful interpretation of results as well as for clever use of software to perform and display the tedious technical calculations.

Apart from good project opportunities, the statistical investigations outlined above also make for excellent portfolio tasks (the shorter coursework pieces featuring in MMSL, MHL and FM). Such tasks can be guided, structured or pushed as appropriate. Many such tasks can for instance be structured as class or group exercises, with different groups possibly having different data collection tasks, and discussions afterwards can yield fascinating and insight-promoting debates. The mark schemes for the coursework leave teachers plenty of freedom to conduct the investigations as they deem fit – and IBO examiners will be very sympathetic to any evidence of personal growth in students.

For probability, the standard examples in textbooks tend to be fairly stale, but this need not be so. Many students take offence when you tell them that there is no such thing as a 'winning streak' in sports (performance appears to be simply binomial!), and will take you up on the challenge to keep track of their favourite sports star for a term. Analysing the resulting data will surely captivate your class! Other good challenges can be found with the issues of 'bad luck'. Analyse by ongoing experiments students' claims such as 'my sister is always lucky with the dice'. Ask someone to throw a couple of series of 10 shots at a basketball net, predict on the basis of outcomes obtained how many times she will score 10 out of 10, and follow it through. You could follow through your earlier survey within the school community relating smoking and average grade: this time *predict* (thus linking statistics and probability) worldwide correlation levels together with error margins, and go on the internet to check. Finding real data on the internet that agree with their predictions surely drives home the power of statistics and probability to students. Passions can run high in such lessons, creating a very conducive learning environment. Once convinced of the predictive power of well-conducted surveys, students can reach internationally valid conclusions about the level of popularity of their favourite rock band through surveys in their backyard – and again consult the internet to check. Ideally, by the end of the course, they understand how much can ride on political polls and how pollsters must weigh between reliability and cost/time constraints. Much is made in the media of pollsters being a few percentage points off from time to time. But it would be wonderful if your students gained a true appreciation of the achievement of being off by *only* a few percentage points, and could talk coherently about the challenges of obtaining such accurate results.

Everyone is familiar with lines like 'there's lies, damn lies, and statistics'; and many students will come out of statistics courses still taking such claims at face value. It is formally required – but sadly not tested in the examination – that students can qualify such claims and that they recognize that good statistics is an extremely powerful and reliable tool used daily in politics, entertainment, advertising, engineering and the social sciences. A portfolio task asking students to comment on *all* aspects of any poll of recent interest (the difficulty of obtaining a reliable sample, the mathematical techniques used, and how to interpret those) followed by a class discussion afterwards can do the trick.

For exponential functions, both textbooks and the DP syllabuses put a somewhat unfortunate emphasis on issues relating to compound interest. In practice, after all, financial issues are usually analysed with spreadsheet software, and for a good reason. Much more interesting well-established investigations are the economist's 'rule of 70' (that the 'doubling time' for $x\%$ growth is approximately $70/x$), radioactive decay and carbon-dating. But there is much more that one could do in this area. The outbreak of SARS in 2003, for instance, grew exponentially at first. Understanding this, working out the rate of unimpeded growth from daily statistics collected from the internet, analysing the risks, understanding that exponential growth cannot last: all of this can make for a truly beautiful lesson touching on exponential functions, statistics, biology, and demography. In general, much more could be done addressing widely publicized claims based on bad extrapolation or misunderstanding of the limits of exponential growth. To mention just two examples here: consider the claim that China will be the world's most popular tourist destination by 2010; and the speculation in some business magazines the year before the recent stock market crash that the US economy had found the magic formula for sustaining permanent growth. One sees such basic errors every day, and it is important that mathematics courses educate students to recognize such claims as errors.

Many of the tasks above can be nicely integrated with IT, using for instance MS Excel spreadsheet software. Let Excel determine the curve of best fit to daily SARS data (students to discuss and decide on the appropriate curve). Once Excel produces the curve, what does that curve really mean, and what is its range of validity? Students often spend a great deal of time on mechanical tasks such as the production of a curve of best fit without realizing the point of doing so.

But applications do not stop with statistics, probability and exponential functions. Below, we list examples in other areas that have worked for us. These and others will be posted on our website www.dp-help.com and readers are invited to contribute to these resources.

We begin by drawing attention to a vital mathematical skill that receives little attention in most mathematics curricula, including those of the DP, but which opens up an endless reservoir of meaningful applications. We are talking about the concept of *estimation*. Students are often so transfixed on calculators and IT that they do not realize that most truly important numbers in life are not exact, but are based on estimations. The questions below can all initially be attempted in class with the help of pencil, paper, and brainpower alone.

- If we fill the whole school with cola cans and everyone can take one can a day, how long can we drink?
- If you are locked in an airtight classroom, how long will the air last you?
- How much water does our city need? And how much does it receive? Will there be problems in the near future?
- How many chickens does our community import every day? How big a farm do you need to sustain this rate of consumption?
- How many babies are born every second (assuming there are 6 billion of us now)?
- How much money does the state generate with its tax on cigarettes?
- How much turnover and profit does McDonald's make in your town?
- Same question, but now for your favourite disco?
- Present your own business plan, including how much money you expect to make. List and estimate main costs as well as expected turnover. The rest of the class should act as potential partners and must decide eventually whether to invest or not. Makes for great class presentations with fervent participation.
- If the polar ice caps melted, by how much would the sea level rise? How do you explain discrepancies with 'official' estimates?
- How much does a war cost every month?
- How many cakes should you bake for a fund-raising event in your school?
- How much petrol are we using? How much petrol do we have? How long will it last if we keep going at the current rate?
- How many animals have been killed so far in order to feed you? (For non-vegetarian students, the sheer number of chickens they have eaten will give reason for pause and reflection.)
- Based on initial data on the SARS disease, how rapidly would the disease have spread had governments not acted?

As is clear from this list of examples, the possibilities are endless, and if well chosen – preferably connected to areas of personal or community concern – students are very interested in discussing the outcome and each other's findings. By checking their assumptions and estimates versus the 'real' data found on the internet or otherwise, they automatically enhance their research skills. They feel elated and empowered when they notice how often they get the right answer; and they can get truly dug in trying to understand the occasions when they don't. This process of verifying assumptions, checking the consequences, and modifying the original assumptions if need be, is, of course, the essence of science, and has tremendous value. In our experience as teachers of both physics and mathematics, the question format above is ideal for teaching the scientific method. By listening to each other's contributions, students will learn that there are many different ways of arriving at the same answers; and that the more independent ways we have of arriving at the same answer, the more reliable our estimate is. This is also one area where teachers will learn as much as students: we often had to completely adjust our initial hunches on the basis of our students' careful analyses. Students realize this very quickly and the knowledge that they will teach both peers and teachers alike again empowers them and motivates them to put in their best efforts.

The 'purely' mathematical concept students learn here is the value of *logic*. List your assumptions. Explain clearly how you derive conclusions from them. If the final answer is wrong, one or more of your assumptions must be wrong. Which is it and why? Refine and try again. Another valuable skill picked up automatically in the process is that of (mathematical) *communication*. Students will very quickly catch on to the fact that if they wish to convince their peers of their position, the only way forward is a logical and lucid presentation of their assumptions, derivations, calculations and conclusions.

The subject that lends itself most naturally to address such estimation questions is mathematics, and we would dearly like to see it made an explicit syllabus topic rather than the implicit one it is now. In the meantime, however, teachers do not need to be afraid to spend time on such non-examined material: the time 'lost' on discussing estimation issues is in our experience more than made up by students' increased mathematical confidence and communication skills.

Imaginative teachers will have no problem integrating problems of the type listed above in the project for MSSL, in the portfolio tasks for the other mathematics courses, or in application problems for the statistical methods option of the MMSL course or the further statistics option of MHL. In section 3 we illustrate on the basis of the mark schemes how one could structure the coursework to address an estimation problem.

We finish this section with some examples that bring algebra, trigonometry and calculus to life.

A great way to (re)introduce triangle trigonometry and algebra is through a lesson and/or project on the concept of the horizon. As it happens, students can figure out the size of the earth through a visit to the beach!

You could begin this exercise by asking students to guess what is the distance to the horizon. Since answers usually vary from 200 metres to 20,000 km, students are keen to see who made the best guess right from the start. One can put all of this in the historic perspective of the momentous clash between the 'flat earth' theory versus the 'round earth' theory. Once having conceived the idea that the earth might well be round, the concept of horizon follows naturally. The distance to the horizon is easy to measure (ask your students how they would do it if you gave them a little boat and a bit of money), so Pythagoras together with circle theorems immediately predicts the size of the earth (which was subsequently verified by sea voyages). This exercise goes a long way to demonstrate the power of mathematics: how it can turn a simple qualitative hypothesis into a strong quantitative prediction with real consequences. There are many meaningful extensions which involve rearranging formulas. If a pirate sits up twice as high in the mast, how much further can he see? If he wants to see *n* times further, how much higher does he need to go? Can you give approximated linear or quadratic approximations to your answer? For what ranges are these valid? (Use IT or otherwise.) Can you verify what you've found by climbing up a high building in your town? How do you verify the distance you can see, how do you correct for possible errors (hills and such)? Link back to students' original guesses in relation to estimations. Why is 1,000 km or 200 metres surely wrong?

Clearly, a project like this rapidly embraces a wide spectrum of knowledge, while addressing many 'hidden' mathematics skills, such as reading maps and using scales, and the use of logic to derive practical conclusions from the data obtained.

For our final example of how to bridge the gap between classroom mathematics and real life, we turn to calculus. Ask your students how *fast* they can throw a baseball, i.e. what is the speed of a baseball as it leaves their hand? Usually, a few students will remember the answers for professional baseball players. But what about their own achievements? Initial guesses usually range from 10 km/hour to 200 km/hour. How to find out? The key is that most students have a fair idea of how *far* they can throw a baseball – and if they haven't, you could take them to the sports field first. Using the fact that the gravitational acceleration vector in the (x, z) plane is $(0, -10)$ m/s^2, integrate twice to obtain the equations of motion. Using graphical software and/or calculus optimization techniques, verify that the 'optimal' angle (for furthest throw) is 45 degrees (to generate interest, it is better to ask your students to guess first!). By rearranging your formula or using IT, find the initial speed as a function of the distance thrown. Answers are typically between 50 and 90 km/hour.

Ask students now how fast they can run. They will quickly realize they can throw much faster than they can run. How is this possible? Is your arm so much faster than your leg? Ask them to estimate the speed of their rigid arm if they bring it round in an arc as quickly as possible. This is far short of the required speed. So what is happening? Give the class time and they will find out that it is the superposition of rotations at the waist, the shoulder, the elbow, the wrist, and the fingers that allows for this great speed. You can then immediately apply the insight gained to soccer, tennis, golf, karate, and so on. We have tried this exercise at the MSSL level with a group of mathematically challenged students. Of course in this case you need to start with a specific angle of, say, 30 degrees, and a given speed. But it is remarkable that the *desire* to find the answers leads students naturally to work with a variable angle and speed, to optimize the angle, and to rearrange when necessary. In our experience, students are amazed by their own achievements and findings, and you have a marvellous chance to boost their confidence by complimenting them on their results … and never again will you face questions on why one should worry about variables, rearranging, or calculus!

For a group of able MHL students at an advanced stage of the course, a portfolio task could simply be: 'Find out how fast you can throw a baseball and explain your result physiologically'. Then just sit back and enjoy the different approaches of your students. With financially affluent students, sooner or later you will receive some carefully analysed home-video footage, which makes for a fantastic class presentation matching theory and experiment. Others come in with catapults mounted on planks to control angles and speeds … there are great opportunities for personal expression here!

3 The internal assessment

In line with the general aim of the IBO to allow students to take ownership of their studies through internally assessed practical work, the DP mathematics courses all feature an internal coursework contributing 20% towards the overall grade. The IBO would not have minded increasing that percentage further, but is held back by the fact that many universities insist on mostly externally assessed work for mathematics.

The MSSL course features a *project* while the other mathematics courses all feature a *portfolio*, a set of mini projects.

3.1 The project for MSSL

The MSSL course features a single piece of coursework called *the project*. It should be based on an option topic of the syllabus (i.e. *calculus, statistics,* or *graphs and matrices*) or on an open investigation (i.e. outcome and/or methodology is not fixed), and typically takes from one to six months to complete. Apart from some of the easier estimation questions, all the examples in section 2.2 above could make for good projects since all are open investigations and some in addition address an option topic. Teachers could elect to integrate the project within the option topic of the syllabus or let the students propose a topic of their own choice, or mix these 'extremes'. You could introduce the project orally or through starter sheets – it is all completely up to you.

The project is quite rigorously assessed against the criteria shown in figure 16.3. In our experience, for a student to gain 20 or more marks (out of the maximum of 25), tight monitoring, supervising and moderation are necessary.

The criteria A, E and F basically reward effort and clarity and are fairly independent of the technical level of mathematics achieved. The student must include an introductory abstract outlining the purpose, structure, development and conclusions of the project. In the text, each method employed must be *explained* and *its use must be justified*. In the final conclusion all methods and results must be summarized and, if necessary, contrasted: the student should compare the ease of use, accuracy and *validity* of solutions obtained via various approaches. (The italicized parts in this paragraph are again rewarded in criterion D, stressing the importance of a true understanding of the work.) As discussed in section 2.2, a number of lessons on estimation problems serves as an excellent tool to prepare students for the required clarity in mathematical communication.

Figure 16.3 MSSL project assessment criteria (maximum total mark 25)

Criterion (max. mark)	Brief description of requirements
A Statement of task (3)	Clear statement of the task and the methodology to be employed.
B Data collection (4)	Collection and systematic organization of appropriate data.
C Analysis (6)	Accurate use of a wide and appropriate range of mathematical techniques (tabulation, graphing and algebra, trigonometry and mensuration, statistical computations, and so on); in our experience appropriate use of IT or calculus is needed to gain the highest marks.
D Evaluation (5)	Thorough discussion of the validity of answers and techniques.
E Structure and communication (4)	Overall structure should be coherent and methods used must be systematically discussed.
F Commitment (3)	Essentially there to reward students who tackle the project conscientiously.

The following paragraphs describe some projects that illustrate how students can succeed with the more mathematical criteria B, C and D.

Returning to the baseball project of section 2.2, you could give this as a class task within the calculus option, and build in even more variety and individuality by telling students they can choose from baseball, soccer, hockey, golf, or whatever interests them. You could start this project after having discussed differentiation (and perhaps integration) of polynomials. First guide the class quickly through a derivation of the equations of motion by integrating the acceleration vector twice – using concrete and easy initial conditions. (Following a 'base jumper' in free fall, for instance, generates lots of enthusiasm and allows for comparison with internet data.) It also makes for a great story on the origins of calculus, which was after all invented by Newton to solve problems in physics. Active participation can further be expected from examples involving sharp-shooting. From easy problems (how far does a bullet travel if fired horizontally?) you could go all the way to quite involved problems with a MHL class (shooting at a target board 100 metres away and 20 metres down the hill, how many centimetres do you need to aim above the bull's eye in order to hit it?). The easier problems needed to prepare MSSL students, however, can easily be completed within one lesson.

Now you are in a position to introduce the baseball project. You could open with a few questions on distance thrown using various easy initial speeds and angles. Once this is understood, you can ask for a proof of the general equation of baseball motion expressed in terms of an arbitrary initial angle and speed. Next, you may wish to hint that students might optimize the angle, showing them first what graphing software such as Omnigraph (see section 4.1) can do. You could leave it up to the students to work out the initial speed knowing the distance thrown, by using IT or rearranging or both. This whole main programme can be finished within a few weeks (but making sure your students write down their insights coherently while they are still fresh will be your biggest challenge). Finally, asking students to explain their results physiologically (as discussed in section 2.2) and apply them to other sports introduces an open end that can be pursued as far as you or the student wishes. Another few weeks should be enough to ensure all projects are on your desk.

Having worked with equations of motion and compound trigonometric functions (neither is on the syllabus) and having applied IT significantly and usefully, full marks for mathematical sophistication in criterion C should be assured. If your students fully understand what they have done (which is likely because they are interested in the results) they should score highly for criterion D as well. Any decent physiological extension should ensure full marks for D. Criterion B (data collection) is automatic if students include a few data from their efforts on the sports field, print the relevant graphs, and explain clearly where the equations of motions come from.

A more 'traditional' task used successfully at UWCSEA within the calculus option is set out in figure 16.4.

Note that the various surface area formulas are given to the students on their examination papers. None but the most able students will be able to handle the problems using calculus only, but the use of IT opens up a lot of possibilities. Students who are good at rearranging could express the area A in one variable, say r, and then use IT to graph $A(r)$ and subsequently read off the minimum area. Alternatively, they could find a number of points (r, h), use their calculators or MS Excel to plot A against r for each, and subsequently estimate the minimum. Students tend to refine their estimations to a state of ludicrous precision, far beyond what is relevant to this real-world problem, but note that all this extra but useless work will cost them marks in criterion D! If all goes well, however, by this stage much of the requirements of criteria B, C and D will have been met. At the point when you have covered the calculus option sufficiently far, students could verify their results once more using calculus.

Clearly, this exercise will also make it easy for students to fulfil all the assessment criteria, and it offers a wide range of options to obtain the relevant answers. However, since it is difficult to get excited about a problem like this, teachers will spend a lot more time prodding students to do the work.

Figure 16.4 The 'popcorn containers' project

(a) The management of a major popcorn supplier to cinemas wants to determine the best type of containers to use to hold a volume of 1500 cm³ of popcorn. Three basic containers are under investigation:

(i) cylinder   (ii) cone   (iii) cylinder surmounted by hemisphere

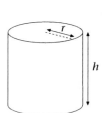 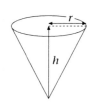 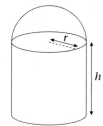

Find the minimum surface area for each container and the radius and height needed to produce the minimum surface area in each case.

(b) What conclusions can be drawn regarding the best packaging to adopt? Should any other factors be taken into account?

The statistics option offers many good opportunities to enthuse the students. You could base a project on understanding (and possibly re-enacting through a community survey) a recent poll that holds the interest of your class. You could ask students to perform various surveys relating smoking to (any kind of) performance, or leave them free to propose their own project (see section 2.2 for more examples and comments).

Students frequently propose projects linking arts and mathematics, but these may be short on mathematical content, so forethought and careful advice is needed (however, see the example in section 4.1 for an 'art' source that can be tapped many times). A similar warning applies for estimation problems. But any complex estimation problem, such as a full understanding of the water crisis your city may be facing, will involve a lot of tabulation and refining of assumptions. If the project is done well, and the student has kept a careful log of which assumptions were adopted, rejected and refined (and why), you can make a strong case for full marks for criteria C and especially D.

In the ideal world, students would all find projects that they are really enthusiastic about. In practice, this is not going to happen, and steering your students away from hopeless projects or prodding them through more viable individual ones can be a lot of work. On an administrative note, since MSSL students will tend to put mathematics relatively low on their priority scale, regular deadlines and individual feedback sessions must be built into the coursework schedule, especially if you administer it over a long period of time.

A well-chosen class project may well be the best option. Alternatively, you could make, say, the baseball problem the default problem but allow truly motivated students to propose their own projects. You then finish the whole enterprise within two months, reserving a number of lessons and half lessons exclusively for project work. Either way, you would have a focused and motivated class, you could weave the project into your lessons, and with just a few weeks allocated to cover the main body of work it is much easier to keep up momentum.

3.2 The portfolio for MMSL and MHL

The portfolio consists of a minimum of three short tasks, for both MMSL and MHL students, but many teachers elect to ask for five to eight tasks altogether. Each task needs to be completed within a week; the recommended timeframe is one lesson and two homework sessions. Out of all the tasks done, the officially assessed portfolio will consist of the best three tasks, one in each of the following three types:

Type I: Open investigation (methods and/or final result not prescribed).

Type II: Closed investigation (obtain a result with assistance of standard methods).

Type III: Modelling task (addresses a real-life problem).

Roughly speaking, an open investigation (type I task) is an investigation in which the methods and/or the final result are not prescribed; in other words, there is a significant opportunity for personal interpretation and expression. All investigations discussed so far in this chapter are examples of open problems. A closed investigation (type II task), on the other hand, is a more traditional mathematics task in which the student needs to achieve a set result through standard techniques. There is little scope for individuality here, but the tasks are easy to construct and moderate. To give an example: lead the student through the usual graphical introduction to differentiation using chords, followed by the standard steps to prove that $(x^n)' = nx^{n-1}$. Another example: lead students through a discovery of the rules for logarithms. Finally, a modelling task (type III) should address a real-life problem where the final result of the mathematical analysis needs to be translated back into language appropriate for the original problem.

Type III tasks can be simultaneously type I or type II tasks, providing welcome flexibility to choose the task's type at the end of a student's course (this flexibility can boost a student's grade, as we will see shortly). All problems discussed in section 2 are both type I and type III, since each deals with real life and each leaves significant scope for personal interpretation. An example of a task that is both type II and type III is a guided investigation into compound interest leading to the multiplier formula $e^{x/100}$ for continual interest at $x\%$. Another one is a guided investigation leading to the discovery of the popular result that the most economical shape of a cylindrical can (in terms of the area/volume ratio) is that where the diameter equals the height. In each of these examples, the tasks can be structured to suit the level of your (MMSL or MHL) students. The tasks can be summative *or* introductory in nature, so they do not have to be mathematically profound; the portfolio's purpose is rather to let students take meaningful ownership of their studies.

As noted earlier, it makes sense to strive to structure tasks as type III ('real life') tasks, dividing them evenly between type I and type II modelling tasks. This incentive for departments to create modelling tasks is in line with the DP's overall aim of emphasizing a subject's connection with the outside world.

The portfolio may very well signify the aspect of mathematics that marks the greatest change for teachers new to the DP. The nature and number of tasks that are officially assessed have been altered and reduced significantly due to pressure from DP teachers in recent years. The main current complaints levelled by teachers against these tasks concern the level of administration they necessitate – especially for internal moderation – and the increased overall coursework load they appear to impose on students. However, in our opinion and experience, illustrated with the examples so far and those below, effectively managed portfolio tasks can be used to enhance the quality of teaching and learning with no significant increase in the workload of staff or students. If properly designed – and this is the key – tasks can be integrated into the scheme of work, done during lessons under teacher supervision, continued for homework as usual, and marked and moderated relatively easily. They can further be used to introduce, reinforce and develop concepts, insights, and mathematical communication skills, by way of open or structured investigations or extended problems that cannot be effectively assessed under normal examination conditions. Sample portfolio tasks can be found later in this section and on the IBO Online Curriculum Centre (OCC). Readers of this book are further invited to download (and add!) successful portfolio tasks from our website: www.dp-help.com.

In our experience, it is easy for students to obtain high marks if the tasks are properly designed and used. To illustrate this, we turn to the portfolio assessment criteria – which are identical for MMSL and MHL except for a small difference in criterion E. These criteria are shown in figure 16.5.

Figure 16.5 Portfolio task assessment criteria for MMSL and MHL (maximum total mark 20)

Criterion (max. mark)	Brief description of requirements
A Notation (2)	Correct notation and terminology – relative to the state of progress in the course at time of task.
B Communication (3)	Coherent structure with introduction, conclusion and explanatory commentary linking individual sections.
C Mathematical content (5)	Accurate solution of all given tasks with insightful strategy or commentary necessary for full marks.
D Results and conclusions (3)	Correct results and conclusions, briefly discussed.
E Making conjectures (4)	Systematic derivation of a conjecture with clear justification (formal in MHL and informal in MMSL).
F Use of technology (3)	Appropriate use of technology to derive or check results.

Criteria A and B are the communication marks, which are fairly independent of the level of mathematics achieved. As mentioned earlier, communication skills can be effectively developed through class presentations on estimation problems, as well as through estimation portfolio tasks – see the examples below.

Criteria C and D relate to mathematical content, but note that both insist on the display of full *understanding* of the mathematics for maximum marks, in line with the DP's emphasis on developing thinking skills.

Criteria E and F need to be assessed *only once*, but for both mathematical reasons and reasons of flexibility, it makes sense to structure your portfolio tasks so that they address these criteria as often as possible. Criterion F is fairly straightforward and all remarks on IT in this chapter apply. In view of the emphasis on GDCs (graphical display calculators) in both MMSL and MHL, it is wise to encourage your students to use their calculators, and ask students who used their GDC effectively to tell the class afterwards how they did it.

For criterion E, the official IBO guidelines give a very narrow definition of conjecture, not reflective of habits in the professional field of mathematics. Conjectures can supposedly only be proven through the use of mathematical induction. In practice, however, it is our experience that examiners adopt a more realistic way of interpreting criterion E. You can award full marks if the student displays *a clear sequence of examples leading systematically to the formulation of a general hypothesis*. MHL students should then prove these conjectures mathematically or test them for more complicated examples using IT or otherwise. MMSL students, on the other hand, are only expected to make some reasonable attempts to discuss or validate their conjectures to achieve full marks for E.

The process of selecting the three tasks to go forward as the official component of the final student portfolio is a mathematical exercise in itself, and you should seriously consider asking your students to determine their own selection if you have more than three tasks. In fact, it would be a worthy portfolio task asking your students to program their GDCs or spreadsheet software to find the three tasks that optimize their grade within the constraints!

- Select three tasks, one of each type.
- Criteria E and F need to be addressed at least once.
- For criteria A–D take the *average* of the three tasks; for E and F, take the best.
- Add up the resulting marks and round to the nearest integer.

Figure 16.6 Optimizing grades

Name of student:	Type			Portfolio criteria						
Task	I	II	III	A	B	C	D	E	F	Total
1. Throwing baseballs	x		x	1	2	4	3		3	
2. Compound interest	x	x	x	2	3	5	2	2	3	
3. Water in our city	x		x	1	3	3	3			
4. Smoking and grades	x		x	2	2	5	4		3	
5. Transforming data	x	x		1	2	4	3	3	2	
6. The path of light		x	x	2	3	4	4			
Final score				1.7	2.7	4.3	3	3	3	18

In the example in figure 16.6, the student selected task 2 (as type III), task 5 (as type II), and task 6 (as type I) to gain a total of 18 points (out of a maximum of 20). In our experience, serious students should be able to gain at least 17 marks.

Below, we give examples of possible starter sheets for each of the tasks in figure 16.6. Two teaching models are featured. In tasks 1, 3 and 4, the instructions are deliberately concise to encourage thinking skills, while the other tasks are a bit more structured. The purpose of these six examples is to give teachers an idea of the freedom of design the portfolio affords. It really does provide a wonderful chance to experiment with teaching!

Task 1: Throwing baseballs (types I and III, assessing criteria A–D and potentially F)

- At what angle should you throw a baseball to maximize the distance?
- Find out how *fast* you throw, doing experiments as necessary.
- Explain your results physiologically, and apply your insights to a few other sports.

Introduce the task through a chat on the equations of motion, as outlined in section 2.2. Clever use of GDC or Omnigraph software (see section 4.1) allows for a display of the trajectory depending on adjustable initial values for angle and speed; be sure to discuss both non-IT and IT solutions afterwards. MMSL students could be given a few hints in class time.

Task 2: Compound interest (types I, II and III, assessing all criteria)

- You give A dollars to the bank at an interest rate of 3% a year. Express the amount of money you have after one year as mA, where m is called the *multiplier*.
- Suppose the bank pays out interest twice a year (1.5% each time), or once every month (0.25% each time), or every week, or every day. In each case, find a formula for the multiplier m and simplify m as much as you can.
- Express m generally as a function of n (the number of times interest is paid out per year) and x (the interest rate).

- When interest is paid out continually, $m(x)$ is of the form $e^{y(x)}$. Find out what $y(x)$ is and demonstrate that your answer is correct.
- Give sound financial advice to banking clients. Is it worth visiting many different banks to have interest computed every month or every second?

The meat of this exercise is of course in the formulation of $y(x)$, which will necessitate the use of IT. The systematic development towards general non-specified formulas qualifies the task for assessment under E. Since the questions lead the students through the mathematical process, this task is probably best described as a type II task, although the derivation of $y(x)$ can be achieved in so many different ways that one could also qualify it as a type I task; if one skips the first three guiding questions, the task is definitely best described as a type I task. This goes to illustrate that the definition of type is not cast in stone – so long as you can argue your choice, you should be fine. For a strong MHL class, you could add a second exercise guiding students towards discovery of the formulas for arithmetic and/or geometric progressions, also assessable under E.

> *Task 3: Water in our city* (types I and III, assessing criteria A–D, and potentially F)
>
> Singapore is worried about the availability of water in the near future. Estimate how much the city consumes and how much water it can retrieve through rainfall. How justified is the concern?

Such a fairly advanced estimation exercise should only be attempted after completing a number of easier estimation problems, discussed through presentations to improve communication skills – refer to section 2.2. This exercise works well if students begin in class by listing all assumptions and calculations using only pen and paper. In the homework sessions students should refine their assumptions through research on the internet or otherwise, and keep a log of all useful sites. A final concise and convincing report with appropriate references to relevant websites should earn full IT marks, and since it takes considerable mathematical skills (in logic, tabulation, and organization) to produce such a report, one can easily defend full marks for criterion C for a good report.

> *Task 4: Smoking and grades* (types I and III, assessing criteria A–D, and potentially F)
>
> Conduct a survey in school to see whether there is a significant correlation between smoking and average grade (GPA). Carefully address questions about relevancy of your sample, definitions, methods and conclusions. On the basis of your findings, make predictions on worldwide correlation levels. Compare your figures with publicly available figures from the internet, and comment. You may find it easiest to classify people in two categories: smokers and non-smokers. How do you define each category? (Even though many schools do not condone smoking on campus, students' private life is another matter and this task could meaningfully add to the discussion.)

Although one could also survey the number of cigarettes smoked against GPA, publicly available surveys tend to concentrate on surveys focusing on GPA of non-smokers versus those of smokers, so it is worth while steering your students in that direction. When one of the authors tried this exercise for the first time, it was with the intention of showing the class an example of non-correlated data. The unmistakable correlation emerging from a survey of just 50 students thus made for a very interesting lesson! It is a good idea not to give the game away beforehand, and maybe even to pretend you expect no correlation. If you want to, you can turn this task into a type II task by giving more guidance, but in our experience statistical understanding increases faster if students have to think through the entire exercise in the same way as pollsters have to.

Task 5: Transforming data (types I and II, assessing all criteria)

Assumed knowledge: Mean, median, mode, standard deviation, interquartile range.
Assessment criteria: All. The extensive use of a spreadsheet or GDC is expected in this task.

The table below shows the heights in cm of 60 students.

177	175	137	155	150	166	132	146	179	140
169	177	141	148	130	176	135	130	157	172
178	143	143	136	132	166	130	151	145	178
131	171	160	140	179	166	145	142	177	176
132	135	164	179	161	145	134	179	139	149
135	142	172	148	159	160	137	130	130	164

Calculate the mean and standard deviation of the heights of the students.

1. Investigate how the mean and standard deviation change when:
   (a) 5 cm is added to each height (b) 12 cm is subtracted from each height.
   How does adding a constant a to each score in any set of data change the mean and standard deviation?

2. Investigate how the mean and standard deviation change when each height is multiplied by (a) 5 (b) 0.2.
   How does multiplying each score in any set of data by a constant a change the mean and standard deviation? What happens in the case $a < 0$? (Note: this exercise is relevant when you wish to convert the height into inches, for instance. What multiplier would you use then? How do you expect the mean and standard deviation to change? Does your intuition match your results?)

3. Group the data into intervals and construct a cumulative frequency table from this grouped data. Draw a cumulative frequency diagram and use it to find the median and interquartile range of the heights.

4. Investigate how the median and interquartile range change when:
   (a) 5 cm is added to each height (b) 12 cm is subtracted from each height.
   How does adding a constant a to each score in any set of data change the median and interquartile range?

5. Investigate how the median and interquartile range change when each height is multiplied by (a) 5 (b) 0.2.
   How does multiplying each score in any set of data by a constant a change the median and interquartile range? What happens in the case $a < 0$?

6. Summarize your results and discuss their significance.

7. Use the results of your investigation to:
   (a) transform the given set of data so that it has a mean of 0
   (b) transform the given set of data so that it has a standard deviation of 1
   (c) transform the given set of data so that it has a mean of 0 and a standard deviation of 1.

This MMSL portfolio task, adapted from the IBO website, is fondly used by DP schools from Shanghai to Boston, typically after a short introduction to statistical calculations. The series of questions are clear, reasonably easy to complete correctly, and each encourages students to discuss their findings, thus making it easy for students to satisfy the requirements of criteria B, C, D and F. To obtain full marks for criterion C, one would expect a student to demonstrate full understanding of negative and fractional values of a. Full marks for criterion F, however, are virtually guaranteed by the structure of the task. Again, as in task 2, criterion E can be assessed because there is systematic development towards a general result not stated in the text. MHL students would be expected to find the final transformation formula and coherently argue why it is correct to qualify for full marks under E. The IBO website lists this task as type I but you could also count it as a type II task. It is type II in the sense that there is systematic guidance, but it is type I in the sense that it leaves the students free to choose their methods.

Task 6: The path of light (types II and III, assessing criteria A–D)

Fermat's principle states that when light travels from one point to another it takes the path of minimum time. Below, this principle is applied twice to understand two profound physical laws.

The law of reflection

Suppose light travels from A to B by bouncing off a mirror, as in the picture below.

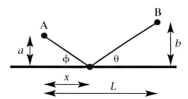

Suppose $a = 15$, $b = 24$, and $L = 52$, and let the speed of light be c.
- If the light hits the mirror at the midpoint, find the time taken for the journey in terms of c.
- If the beam of light hits the mirror at $x = 10$, find the time taken for the journey.
- Now find the travel time for arbitrary x, in terms of c and x.
- Using calculus, find the value for x for which the travel time is minimized, showing that this value is indeed a minimum. Show that the angles ϕ and θ are equal in that case (the law of reflection).

The law of refraction

Light travels again from A to B, but this time it passes through two media:

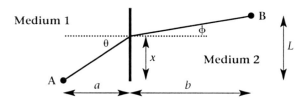

- Suppose the speed of light through medium 1 is c, and the speed through medium 2 is less than c. Argue convincingly why, to minimize time, the path must 'break' and we must have that $\phi < \theta$.

- Formalizing this, let the speed of light through medium 2 be kc, where $0 < k < 1$. Find an expression for the travel time in terms of x, a, b, L and c, and write down an equation in x for the minimum. Express the equation in terms of $\sin \phi$ and $\sin \theta$ and show that travel time is minimized precisely when $(\sin \phi) / (\sin \theta) = k$.

On to oil and gas now

This time, it is not light that travels from A to B, but oil, and the intention is to have it flow through a pipe (do you know the length of the longest such pipeline?). As so often happens, medium 1 is land and medium 2 is sea. The price of laying a pipe at sea is twice the price on land. Formulate a 'refraction law' for this case.

- Can you apply your insights to propose a pipeline from Amsterdam to London? If yes, do so with a sketch and comment; if no, explain why not.

A hot day on the road

Ever been on the highway on a really hot day? Remember occasionally seeing the image of the cars before you reflected in what looks like a momentary water puddle on the road? In this case, Fermat tells us there must be two paths of local minimum time: one direct and one 'mirrored' in the road. Sketch the two paths from the car to your eye and use Fermat's original law to draw a conclusion about the speed of light in hot air (just above the road).

This task is adapted from an original task designed by Peter Blythe at the UWCSEA. Since the formulation of the task leaves the student no choice but to use calculus and potentially hard algebra (if they do not find the easy way out), it is an MHL task. If you would leave the methodology completely open, the whole exercise could be solved with Geometer's Sketchpad, Omnigraph, a spreadsheet or the GDC, to mention just a few IT options (see section 4.1). You could then also give it to MMSL students (as a type I or type III task). For the oil and gas section, it is worthwhile hinting to your students that this part is a straight application of the second if they think hard enough. The Amsterdam-London pipeline (or any pipeline you can think of in your area) should yield interesting responses. Ideally, students understand that they can take great liberties recasting Britain's coastline with a few straight lines, and then use their mathematical results to pinpoint Britain's pipe exit point correct to within 100 km or so. From there onward, city planners and environmentalists would need to be consulted about the most economical way to get close to the exit point respecting the various local constraints along the way. Students should understand that because of such local constraints, it makes no sense to pinpoint the exit point too accurately!

We could not resist putting in the last question 'a hot day on the road'. Some may feel it is physics, but the ability to explore the logical consequences of a statement is mathematical in nature, and this example will give students something interesting to talk about next time they're on a highway on a long hot day. Perhaps include it as a bonus question. You could tell your class afterwards that the *reason* for the correct answer – light moves faster in hot air – is that there are fewer collisions of photons with particles in the lower-density medium (in this case, the hot air). This argument also explains why light moves more slowly in glass and water.

We include here one final MHL portfolio task to illustrate how one can encourage students to develop their GDC skills (in this case, the TI-83).

Task 7: The vector product (type II, addressing all criteria)

Assumed knowledge: matrix multiplication, scalar (inner, dot) product, calculation of vector product.

Define vectors **a**, **b**, **c**, **d** as **a** = $(1, 2, 4)$, **b** = $(-2, 3, -1)$, c = $(0, 2, 3)$, **d** = $(1, -3, 1)$, and let a or $|\mathbf{a}|$ denote the magnitude of **a**, and so on.

1. Ask your GDC for answers of all combinations **a** × **a**, **a** × **b**, **b** × **a**, **a** × **c**, and so on.

2. On the basis of this list, formulate two general laws which allow you to state that 'all combinations' actually means only six non-zero combinations. Which six are those?

3. What happens if you multiply any of the vectors by a constant and then evaluate the vector product? Considering unit vectors $\underline{\mathbf{a}}$ = **a** / a, and so on, use your result to write a general formula for **a** × **b** in terms of a, b, and $\underline{\mathbf{a}}$ × $\underline{\mathbf{b}}$. Next, store $\underline{\mathbf{a}}$, $\underline{\mathbf{b}}$, $\underline{\mathbf{c}}$, $\underline{\mathbf{d}}$ in the memory of your calculator.

4. Fact: if we denote the image of $\underline{\mathbf{a}}$ under a rotation transformation **R** as **R**$\underline{\mathbf{a}}$, then, for all rotations **R**, $|\mathbf{R}\underline{\mathbf{a}} \times \mathbf{R}\underline{\mathbf{b}}| = |\underline{\mathbf{a}} \times \underline{\mathbf{b}}|$. (Note: you don't have to verify this yourself.)

5. Can you now explain why the fact stated in (4) implies that the magnitude of the vector product between two unit vectors only depends on the angle θ between them?

6. For all six combinations ($\underline{\mathbf{a}}$, $\underline{\mathbf{b}}$) etc. calculate vector product magnitudes $|\underline{\mathbf{a}} \times \underline{\mathbf{b}}|$ and the angle between $\underline{\mathbf{a}}$ and $\underline{\mathbf{b}}$. Put the vector product magnitudes in L1 of your list editor and put the corresponding angles in list L2.

7. Obtain a scatter diagram of L1 (magnitude) against L2 (angle). What happens when the angle is 0? Fit a curve to the points, using the regression tools in the STAT CALC menu of the TI-83. Hence formulate your conjecture for the value of $|\underline{\mathbf{a}} \times \underline{\mathbf{b}}|$. Using your previous results, formulate a general conjecture for the value of $|\mathbf{a} \times \mathbf{b}|$.

8. Now prove your conjecture! Remember how to express the scalar product **a.b** in terms of the angle θ? So if your conjecture is correct, then for any pair of vectors **a** and **b** the term $|\mathbf{a} \times \mathbf{b}|^2 + (\mathbf{a.b})^2 = \ldots$? With **a** = (a_1, a_2, a_3) etc, prove your formula by expressing all terms in a_i and b_i's. Does this completely prove your conjecture?

Even though scatter diagrams are more conveniently done with spreadsheets, MS Excel for instance can fit polynomial and exponential curves but not trigonometric ones. It also does not calculate vector products (although you could very easily 'teach' it to do so). In this way tasks like this help to drive home the potential of a GDC to students. The task is so constructed that it is hard not to gain full marks for criterion F. The last question clearly illustrates the single assessment difference for MMSL and MHL: for full marks in criterion E, MHL students are expected to *prove* their conjectures if the proofs are feasible within the MHL syllabus (whereas MMSL students are only expected to make some reasonable attempts to validate their conjectures).

This task – like task 4 – requires that students use regression analysis to help formulate their conjecture. Regression analysis is not on the MHL or MMSL syllabuses (while it is part of the MSSL course). Such journeys outside the syllabus are strictly speaking not encouraged by the IBO, which does not wish to see the workload increased as a result of portfolios. However, all teachers involved felt that in this case it was worth while. The students scored highly in all aspects of the task, acquired a deeper grasp of vector product properties than a traditional lesson would have afforded them, and got to apply and critically evaluate a powerful modelling tool in the form of regression analysis.

3.3 Internal moderation

The internal moderation process is a source of frustration for many departments around the world, yet we believe that good organization can address the concerns effectively. Let us list the aspects relevant to moderation.

1. For each type of coursework your school has administered, the IBO will ask for a random sample set of graded student works (10 samples for a large school or all students for a small school; the list is sent to the DP coordinator, and schools submit the samples two months before the examination). Based on this sample, the *entire* school cohort of courseworks for that subject will be marked up or down by the same amount, in one instance in our experience down by 5 points. Thus, to be fair to students:
2. Departments need to develop *consistent* internal moderation.
3. Internal moderation should conform to IBO standards so as not to disappoint students.
4. For portfolio tasks to be effective teaching tools, it is necessary that they be graded and passed back to the students very quickly.

Clearly, the whole process begins with good design of the coursework. Well-designed coursework starters in which all criteria can be assessed over the full range are a prerequisite to successful moderation. We hope that the example starters in this chapter have provided sufficient ideas to tackle this part. There is no need to design many starters, nor do they have to be original, certainly for a school new to the DP; if you like the examples in our book, feel free to use them. It is more important that your students can grow through the coursework, so it is worth your while to adapt tasks so that they address your students' personal or community interests. A bank of half a dozen well-chosen portfolio tasks and project ideas can do the trick, and once department confidence increases, you can always add more tasks. Having only five or six tasks each for MMSL and MHL, you can address problem 4 (quick moderation) easily. The very first time a portfolio task is attempted, call a department meeting immediately after completion, and grade the work together. It works well if one person grades the work using a moderation sheet such as the one displayed in figure 16.7, and the next person then grades it again, after which both discuss each other's assessment interpretations. In our experience, a few such rounds in which you discuss low, average and good coursework suffice to achieve a common understanding. In this manner, concern 2 (consistent moderation) is automatically addressed. As to concern 3 (moderation consistent with the IBO), schools could attempt to enlist the help of experienced teachers from other schools if they wish to get it right the first time around. If there are no DP schools near you, you could try using email – it is easy to obtain the email addresses of other DP schools through the IBO website.

As soon as a task has been attempted once, all you need to do is keep a varied set of samples of moderated work, and do this for all the coursework adminis-tered by your department. Then, some time at the beginning of the year, you could call a single department meeting repeating the process outlined above with a few randomly selected pieces of coursework. For bigger departments, it may be a good idea to assign each new teacher a mentor (see the Mara College Banting case study described in Chapter 7), who will spend an hour or two during the year helping the new colleagues to grade their tasks.

Figure 16.7 is a cover template sheet for the MSSL project that has served us well (a similar template could be used for the portfolio). Note that the marks given are accompanied by an appropriate explanation. This piece was submitted as an example of a high scoring coursework and survived the internal and external moderation processes.

Criterion F for the MSSL project is the only criterion in all of the mathematics coursework which cannot be checked by the external moderators; it is ultimately up to the discretion of the teacher. Nevertheless, it is wise to justify your grade as in the example in figure 16.7. In our experience, using forms like this helps to form a quick and clear understanding of the assessment criteria in your own mind, and it subsequently goes a long way towards convincing the moderators of the validity of your grades.

Figure 16.7 Sample internal assessment cover sheet for MSSL

International Baccalaureate
Individual assessment cover sheet: Mathematical Studies SL

SUBMIT TO: MODERATOR   ARRIVAL DATE: 20 APR (20 NOV)   SESSION: May 2002
SCHOOL CODE: SCHOOL NAME:

Type or write legibly using black ink and retain a copy of this form
Complete one copy of this form to accompany each project submitted

SUBJECT: Mathematical Studies   LEVEL: Standard

CANDIDATE NAME: CAND. NO:

TITLE OF PROJECT: Playground Area and Perimeter Optimization

ASSESSMENT CRITERIA: Achievement level

	CRITERION	COMMENTS	
A	Statement of task	Aim and plan are clearly stated at outset	3 / 3
B	Data collection	Data systematically organized and of appropriate range	4 / 4
C	Analysis	Wide range of appropriate and sophisticated techniques used including Excel and calculus with negative powers	6 / 6
D	Evaluation	Appropriate domain and practicality of calculations and methods considered, but validity of calculus methods not understood	3 / 5
E	Structure and communication	Overall structure coherent with methods used; exception already penalized in D	4 / 4
F	Commitment	All deadlines met, and initiative and determination was shown in following advice	3 / 3
	TOTAL		**23** / 25

4 The role of IT in IB mathematics

4.1 What to use and how to use it

The role of IT in education continues to be a topic of debate. Its benefits are by no means assured: a major UK government-sponsored school survey in 60 schools found no positive correlation between use of IT and learning outcomes (see the original statistics on www.becta.org.uk/research/impact2, not the unwarranted conclusions). Just as any other tool, IT has to be used wisely, and just as any other tool, it is a means to solve mathematical problems, not an end. One has to consider how long it takes to gain mastery of educational software, and ask if that time is well spent in view of the overall learning objectives. Moving from software to hardware, a common picture in (IB) schools throughout the world is this: classrooms with one or two moderately aged computers each; on the side, an over-booked and/or under-maintained computer lab. This picture is unlikely to change in the medium or even long term – hardly an ideal environment to explore mathematics through technology!

But no matter how you feel about IT or what the practical constraints are, one option you do not have as a teacher in IB mathematics is to neglect IT. It is needed in the coursework component, typically in the form of PC software, and it is needed in the examinations in the form of graphical display calculators (GDCs). We therefore begin by commenting here on a few pieces of software whose benefits seem uncontested amongst those who have tried them.

Omnigraph

The only disadvantage of Omnigraph graphing software is that it is only available for the PC (search the web to find the free one-month demo). It is very easy to use (within 2 minutes you're up and running), it can do an awful lot, it has great interactive exercises, it is small (1 MB), it runs on all Windows versions, and it is very cheap. You can introduce variables (as many as you like) by typing for instance $n=1$, $c=1$, and subsequently type $y = \sin(nx) + c$. To see the effect of changing n and c on the graph, simply use the 'dynamic editor' button, which also allows you to control the speed of the changes.

Particularly nice features you should not miss are the exercises and sample files (go to *file* and click *open*: should the samples not come up, you can browse to find them in the Omnigraph folder on the C drive). Amongst many other examples, there are graphs of lines, quadratics, cubics and trigonometric functions, and students have to find the correct equations for these graphs. Your students could first play with the values of m and c in $y = mx + c$ (the opening exercise in the lines folder) to discover the meaning of these constants, and then test the quality of their insights by trying the other line exercises. This is an effective and enjoyable way of letting your students teach themselves about lines. Likewise you can revise quadratics (in factorized or completed square form). For MHL students, the cubic curves offer a brilliant learning opportunity. There are a number of ways in which students could find the equations of the cubic graphs. They could look at the intercepts or the stationary points. They could ask the software to graph the gradient first, use their knowledge of parabolas to find the equation of the gradient, and then integrate. Letting a class discover the various methods for themselves and communicate their insights to each other makes for an enriching lesson. The comparison of various methods all leading to the same result encourages the students to develop a wide range of problem-solving skills, which is exactly what they need in order to do well in the examination. Going beyond cubics with MHL students, finding the formulas for the so-called *composed functions* exercise can generate profound insights. Omnigraph software comes with just a single page containing all the answers to the self-help exercises, yet this single page can keep your class busy for many weeks!

Omnigraph's parametric graphing utility is great to graph projectile motions, and students can display the trajectory of our famous baseball easily as a function of two parameters (initial speed and angle). In the course of our classes, we further stumbled on a method to create beautiful parametric 'flower' curves. Write the parametric equations for the orbit of a point on a circle of radius r that is rolling along the edge of the unit disc (this exercise will challenge even a good MHL class). Then graph the orbit (take large values for the Omnigraph's parameter t), adjust r (be sure to look at $r = 1, 0.5, 0.8$), and enjoy the show. Save your equation because there is surely room for many a mathematics and arts project in MSSL here! Does the curve always close? Can you tell how many times the circle needs to roll around the disc to close the curve for $r = 0.85$? How many flower petals do we have for various values of r? What happens when the curves do not close? And so on.

Omnigraph is not only a great tool for the students; it also makes for a powerful teaching instrument. Especially if you have a projector or TV hooked to your PC, you may very well quickly find yourself using it in every lesson to illustrate your points, even if it is for only a few minutes. You could draw a graph of $\sin x$ and a number of its Taylor approximations on the same screen. The time you save in terms of imparting understanding of Taylor polynomials and Taylor error theory (part of the analysis option of MHL) is huge, and the pictures are beautiful and compelling. A graphical demonstration of how the concept of chords lead to tangent lines and differentiation is, in fact, easier to present with Omnigraph than with a board marker on a white board. Not only is it easier, but it is also much clearer – at least for those teachers whose drawing skills resemble those of the authors – and you can use the zooming tool to illustrate the concepts forcefully. You can save your examples easily (on the hard drive or the school server if you have one) so that you have them available anywhere anytime. The possibilities with Omnigraph are endless, they enthuse the students, and they require no extra work – in fact they save everyone time and effort. Once hooked on Omnigraph, you might find it difficult to teach without it!

Spreadsheet software: Microsoft Excel

A second recommendation we can make unreservedly is for spreadsheet software such as Microsoft Excel. In contrast to Omnigraph, there is a little learning to do here before one can make use of it. However, spreadsheets are rapidly entrenching themselves in virtually all areas of professional life. There is no doubt that they are here to stay, and schools should recognize this. One can thus make a strong case for taking out half a school day to introduce all students to spreadsheets. No great fans of Microsoft (MS) ourselves, the authors nevertheless acknowledge that MS Excel has educational advantages over its major competitors. One of the authors of this book was lucky enough to be able to introduce Excel college-wide, a move welcomed by instructors of business, social sciences, science and mathematics. Two to three interactive hours are enough to familiarize students with features such as making a colour-coded term-long diary showing weekends and timetable; comparing and editing mortgage schemes; producing graphs to illustrate data; producing curves of best fit to data (including a display of the curve's equation); and 'programming' Excel to calculate the mean of an (x, f) frequency distribution.

Particularly useful in mathematics is to follow up such an introduction with some statistics lessons. Using (x, f) frequency distributions, you could ask students to program the standard deviation using the two different textbook formulas, to verify that these give the same result. Teach the students that once they have programmed Excel, they can save their work on the school server, or they can send themselves an email. After that, all they ever need to do is to change the data to immediately obtain the statistics. Following this, you could do lessons on correlation and scatter diagrams. To further enhance Excel skills, you could ask students to 'program' in the formula for the correlation coefficient in terms of the X and Y data. There are some clever ways of doing this so that the result changes correctly with any change in the data or in the number of data entries; to help students in this respect you could introduce them to the COUNT function which can be used to count the number of data. Of course Excel has a special function CORREL that calculates the correlation coefficient directly, but it is amazing to see how students will not give up until 'their' formula gives the same result as Excel's. The process by which they eliminate their own errors one by one conveys skills important to all problem solving. By the time you have come this far with Excel, many of your students will have become better than you (at least this is true for us) and if you need any technical help from there on, you can just ask your class. (One important little technical trick you will need often: the dollar signs in $B3 and B$3 respectively ensure that the B remains a B and the 3 remains a 3 when you 'drag' a formula containing the cell B3, and B3 locks the cell B3 completely under dragging.)

One can also use Excel to impart important thinking skills, particularly in statistics. Ask students to *estimate* the mean, median and standard deviation of data in their head and then ask Excel to *calculate* it. That way, your students obtain a real understanding of what these terms mean, and they can easily generate their own examples to become even better. You could give 10 series of real-life (X, Y) data to your students, ask Excel for scatter diagrams and then ask your students again to estimate the correlation coefficient before asking Excel for the exact answer. Next, ask Excel for a line of best fit – ask the students first if this makes sense – and then ask the students what this line of best fit means in words. Should we force the line to go through the origin? (You can ask Excel to do this.) What does the intercept mean? Does extrapolation make sense? What does the gradient mean? The line of best fit of a price comparison between two shopping malls A and B may reveal that for cheap items, centre A is cheaper whereas it tends to be 10% more expensive for expensive items. It is this sort of interpretation of mathematics that is rightly important in IB mathematics (at least in the coursework); the calculations are of little importance as they require no insight and can be done electronically.

One of us always has his students drop stones from various floors and measure heights and times (using stopwatches or hand phones or whatever is available). Theory says height h and time t should be related as $h = at^2$ where

$a = 5$. Now fit the data of the various groups and the class with Excel to a quadratic curve forced to go through the origin. Can you explain the departures from $a = 5$? Why did some groups do better than others? And so on. You could also graph h against t^2 and ask for the *line* of best fit, which should theoretically have a gradient of 5. Which method do the students prefer? A lesson like this reinforces knowledge on quadratics and lines, and demonstrates that statistical concepts such as lines of best fit also have an important role in exact sciences. It will certainly teach your students respect for those people who measured g correct to two significant figures two centuries ago!

The formal derivation that diameter equals height for a cylindrical can of given volume and minimum area is too difficult for many a student. Yet students may have little trouble finding specific values for r and h given a specific volume V (using Omnigraph, for instance). Ask them to keep a log of a few of these paired values, make scatter diagrams and ask Excel for various curves of best fit. After Excel suggests the algebraic relations between r and h and r and V, you could ask your students to attempt to prove these formulas.

Geometer's Sketchpad

As a final piece of software before moving on to GDCs, we should mention Geometer's Sketchpad (GSP) here. In terms of geometry use, it is brilliant for plane geometry issues, and no teacher who wishes to do the plane geometry option in MHL or analytical geometry in MMSL should go without it. With a little experience, teachers will find that an amazing number of problems can be worked through with GSP, even those that don't seem related to geometry at all. A calculus problem like the Fermat portfolio task (task 6 in section 3.2), for instance, can be easily modelled and solved with GSP. Similarly, problems like finding the optimum position for viewing a cinema screen, or how to best place crops in a rectangular field as part of an efficient irrigation system, can be represented dynamically and solved accurately using GSP. Students quickly come to grips with the modelling features of this highly intuitive piece of software and many come to choose it as a first line of attack (if given an open choice) when dealing with optimization problems of the type sketched above.

GSP also has graphing facilities which, along with variables called *sliders*, allow students to investigate properties of Cartesian and polar graphs in a similar way to Omnigraph. As with Omnigraph, GSP also has a comprehensive folder of examples and online suggestions that can be integrated with the teaching of course material. For instance, the Vectors.gsp file allows students to interactively investigate the properties of vectors including vector products. The Leastsq.gsp file provides a novel geometric way of introducing the idea of the 'least squares' regression line. Students could be asked to use this as a starting point for a formal justification for the equation of the line of best fit.

Since GSP offers very few tools but an amazing number of different ways of combining and using them, it is great software for encouraging thinking skills.

In our opinion and to the best of our knowledge, no other PC software merits special recommendation. There is a whole lot of software on the internet, but it is either too complicated for school students, too limited in its use, too unintuitive, too slow, too expensive, or generally simply not worth the trouble. Naturally, we would love to hear from you, our reader, if you feel we have wrongfully omitted software in our short list above.

Graphical display calculators

Having discussed the potential of the PC, we now turn to the GDC (graphical display calculator), whose use is required in the DP examinations. The GDC was first introduced in DP mathematics examinations in May 2000, and the signs are that it is there to stay for the foreseeable future. The IBO does not enforce the use of a specific model but the Texas Instruments TI-86 and TI-83 plus are without doubt the most popular calculators in use. The former has many in-built functions such as programs that solve polynomial equations or system of equations. However, the TI-83 plus is the calculator we favour as it has a wide range of statistical tools and can be easily upgraded to include new functions.

In the opinion of one of the authors, GDCs are not spectacularly user-friendly (his view is that it's like using a handphone screen to look at the internet, and he keeps forgetting how to navigate the tiny buttons), and working mathematicians, scientists and engineers hardly use GDCs since they favour professional and dedicated software. Nevertheless, the good news comes in many forms. The first bit of good news is that a GDC like the TI-83 can do all of the tasks described above and much more. The second bit of good news is that many students will catch on faster to the GDCs than their teachers. Aim to let your students teach each other and look over their shoulders to pick up some tricks yourself. The happy side-effect of students realizing that they can teach the teacher is empowerment and increased motivation, especially if you can invite students to display their latest GDC insights through an LCD projector. The third bit of good news is that every student has one, and that they can thus use it quickly and independently to test out various approaches to problems. For instance the inflexion points of $y = e^{2x}\cos x$ on the interval $(-\pi, \pi)$ can be found using algebra throughout, or by looking at the stationary points of y' on the GDC screen, or by looking at the zeros of y'' on the GDC screen. Students can thus readily contrast and learn from each option for themselves.

Another way you can enhance the quality of mathematics education using the TI-83 is through programming. Many programs exist (those doing for instance binomial expansions, partial fraction decompositions or vector products are often passed between students without teacher instigation), and can be downloaded from websites such as www.ticalc.org using the graphlink cables that now ship with the TI-83 plus. However, while the TI-83 programming language is simple, some of these programs could be better written and made more user-friendly. You could ask your MHL students to analyse and improve these codes – leaving the programming enthusiasts free to redesign the programs from scratch. In this way the student's grasp of the underlying mathematical principles can be assessed and developed without spending much time and effort on programming. An additional benefit of this process is that students automatically develop the ability to write their own TI-83 programs to perform particular tasks they like to see automated, which can be very handy for their examinations.

Compared with the three PC software packages described above, it will take a bit more effort to generate full class enthusiasm for the GDC. However, as usual, the effect applies that when students are good at something, they like it; and it is in our opinion a good idea to capitalize on this very early on in the course. There is no escaping the GDC, so it is better to build in GDC questions on every test you give. This will drive home the message to the more GDC-stubborn students that they will lose marks if they cannot use their calculators effectively. Not too much time should go into teaching GDC skills, however; simply stress where appropriate (e.g. at the end of a topic or when going over tests and past examinations) what the GDC is able to do and let the students work out the technicalities for themselves. It won't be long before your students know more about their calculator than you do, and you can then leave any GDC-specific teaching to them. Appointing (rotating) 'GDC masters', for instance, boosts confidence, motivation and pride amongst the masters and encourages class collaboration. Students should continually be encouraged to compare (and contrast) their strategies for tackling GDC as well as non-GDC related questions. In this way learning can be made more student-oriented, and a broader understanding of the underlying mathematics and the pros and cons of different approaches can be established.

In the ideal scenario, students have GDCs on their desks as well as a few PCs in the classroom. At each moment in time during class, they are able to use the tool they think is best for solving a problem. In this happy scenario all that teachers sometimes have to do is ask students to highlight successful approaches to each other.

In the following section, we discuss the specific GDC demands that the DP mathematics examinations makes on teachers and students, and give tips on how to deal with those. As we will see, the DP examination questions illustrate that the IBO itself is still struggling with the issue of IT. In some instances questions are mathematically barren, although the IBO, as always, is responding to criticism in this regard and seems intent to use IT to better assess true mathematical knowledge and understanding.

4.2 Examination preparation and IT

Ideas for teaching the students (and yourself) how to use the GDC are discussed in section 4.1. Here we discuss the GDC in specific relation to examination issues. The emphasis on GDC skills in DP examinations varies from year to year, and it is therefore difficult to say how much GDC knowledge is needed (make sure your students know this too, since this wisdom adds extra motivation for them to go the extra mile to get to know their calculator). To our mind a good balance was struck in the November 2002 MHL papers between questions necessitating some GDC use and those where GDC use was either non-essential or inappropriate. However, there have been a good number of cases in the last few years where questions could be rendered trivial with a GDC without any need to understand the mathematics. An example is the following MHL November 2000 question:

Calculate the area bounded by the graph of $y = \sin(x^2)$ and the x-axis between $x = 0$ and the smallest positive x-intercept.

Solving this question is just a matter of button pressing, as shown in the TI-83 screenshots that follow.

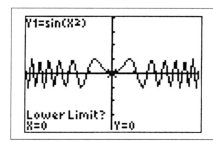
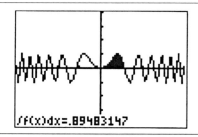

As indicated in the IBO's notes on 'Solutions Using a Graphical Display Calculator', a sketched copy of the graph and a final answer correct to three significant figures would guarantee full marks even in Paper 2 (where answers must be supported by appropriate working). Thus no mathematical knowledge or insight is required beyond spotting a trivial GDC question and responding accordingly.

The question below can be solved with pen and paper, but again, it is completely trivial with a GDC, as the GDC print indicates.

November 2001, MMSL Paper 1 Question 8

The diagram below shows the graph of $y = x \sin\left(\dfrac{x}{3}\right)$, for $0 \le x < m$, and $0 \le y < n$, where x is in radians and m and n are integers.

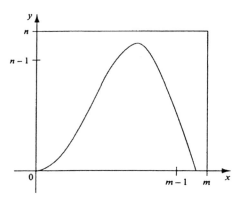

Find the value of

(a) m;

(b) n.

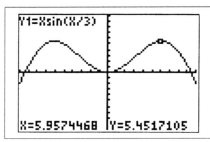

However, if, say, $y = x \sin(x/30)$ or $y = e^{10x} \sin(x/3)$ were used instead, the problem would become one where the only advantage provided by the GDC would be the opportunity to check one's reasoning, since a first graph would not display enough information. In that case, an understanding of the properties of the sine function would be required for solving this version of the problem, i.e. unlike the actual question it would in fact test mathematical knowledge and understanding. Subtle modification of actual examination questions such as this is a useful and time-efficient way of preparing students for the examinations, and it helps develop their insight into both the mathematics and the limitations and advantages of GDCs.

A better type of question used sometimes in MHL and MMSL examinations is given here:

Find to 3 d.p. the real number $k > 0$ such that $_0\int^k dx / (x^2 + 2x + 7) = 0.1$

The typical approach here would be to do the integration first and then decide on a suitable point at which to use the GDC to obtain the final solution. There are no doubt non-trivial strategies that a resourceful student could use to solve this particular problem entirely using the GDC. In either case, a definite mathematical insight or ingenuity is required to solve this problem.

The calculus questions for MHL have become a lot easier over the last few years, especially for students who are good with the GDC. The MHL question below can be solved entirely with pen and paper, but with the exception of part (c) it can also be solved using a GDC only. It is thus in our opinion an ideal IT question. Students must understand the mathematics but it is *advantageous* to know the capabilities of the GDC. In such cases, IT is used to develop the ability to pick tools within a range of problem-solving strategies. In other words, true problem-solving skills are being taught, which is surely why one wants to teach IT in the first place.

May 2000, MHL Paper 2 Question 3

Let $f(x) = 1n|x^5 - 3x^2|$, $-0.5 < x < 2$, $x \neq a$, $x \neq b$; (a, b are values of x for which $f(x)$ is not defined).

(a) (i)   Sketch the graph of $f(x)$, indicating on your sketch the number of zeros of $f(x)$. Show also the position of any asymptotes.

   (ii)   Find all the zeros of $f(x)$ (that is, solve $f(x) = 0$).

(b) Find the **exact** values of a and b.

(c) Find $f'(x)$, and indicate clearly where $f'(x)$ is not defined.

(d) Find the **exact** value of the x-coordinate of the local maximum of $f(x)$, for $0 < x < 1.5$. (You may assume that there is no point of reflexion.)

(e) **Write down** the definite integral that represents the area of the region **enclosed** by $f(x)$ and the x-axis. (Do **not** evaluate the integral.)

© IBO 2000

Parts (a) and (b) can be read off from the calculator display, and full marks are awarded for a sketched copy of the graph, indicating how all answers can be found on the sketch. According to IBO regulations GDCs *must not* be equipped to do symbolic differentiation (although this is technically possible) so the student will have to do part (c) by hand. In part (d) the student could guess the value from the graph of $f(x)$ and then verify that this value makes $f'(x)$ zero, but obviously, in this case it is faster to just do the mathematics with pen and paper.

Previously hard trigonometric questions such as 'solve the equation $\tan^{-1}(3x) + \tan^{-1}(x) = \pi/4$' are rendered trivial with the permission to read the answers off the GDC graph. The solutions given by the GDC may be in decimals, but there are programs available that can convert decimal solutions to simple surds and multiples of π. However, the examinations sometimes require students to give exact answers that are not simple surds, which is why teachers should continue to contrast both algebraic and purely GDC solutions to such problems.

As a final example of a good question, which allows students the *option* to work with the GDC, we look at the following algebra question:

November 2001, MHL Paper 2 Question 1

(a) Solve the following system of linear equations

$$\begin{aligned}
x + 3y - 2z &= -6 \\
2x + y + 3z &= 7 \\
3x - y + z &= 6.
\end{aligned}$$

(b) Find the vector $v = (i + 3j - 2k) \times (2i + j + 3k)$.

(c) If $a = i + 3j - 2k$, $b = 2i + j + 3k$ and $u = ma + nb$ where m, n are scalars, and $u \neq 0$, show that v is perpendicular to u for all m and n.

(d) The line l lies in the plane $3x - y + z = 6$, passes through the point $(1, -1, 2)$ and is perpendicular to v. Find the equation of l.

© IBO 2001

It is worth noting that the system of equations in (a) can be solved in under three minutes using a GDC, and that students could have downloaded or written programs to ask the calculator for the answer to (b). The time gain of using the GDC may not be significant here, but students could decide to use the GDC to *verify* that their previously obtained 'pen and paper' answer is correct. Parts (c) and (d) are most easily done by hand.

In summary, it seems safe to say that for the MMSL and especially the MHL course, the GDC is occasionally indispensable for examination questions on calculus or equations. Students therefore need to be very familiar with the GDC facilities for graphs, their derivatives and integrals, as well as the calculator techniques to solve equations. Calculators are further of great help in computing all kinds of statistics. In general, as the sample examination questions above demonstrated, a GDC can render certain questions trivial or much easier – a major benefit under examination conditions. In areas such as the core MSSL course, GDCs have so far not been essential, but they can make life easier in questions involving graphs and equations or trigonometry since they give the student the opportunity to verify their 'pen and paper' answer, or to answer the question entirely using a downloaded program.

4.3 The future of IT in IB mathematics

The IBO is currently studying examination formats that will further shift the emphasis in teaching and learning towards developing problem-solving skills, in particular the ability to choose effectively between a range of available strategies. Based on feedback from the Curriculum Review Committee (ultimately responsible for devising the DP mathematics syllabuses of 2004), the considered model for the examination of mathematics courses has two-tiered papers. One paper would not permit the use of any calculators while the other would permit the use of CSAs (calculator-based symbolic algebra systems).

One of the authors has been pioneering such a two-tiered approach at the UWCSEA in a test case for the IBO. This involved using TI-89 calculator algebra systems (on loan from Texas Instruments) with two groups of mixed-ability pre-DP students over one year. Screenshots showing some of the capabilities of this calculator are displayed below:

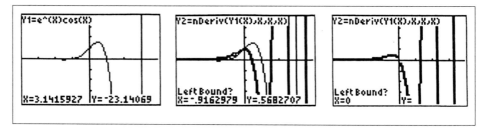

The decision to use the TI-89 was a controversial one as some staff felt that developing familiarity with the TI-89 would waste an opportunity to develop competence with the TI-83, which is compulsory at UWCSEA. These problems were addressed through the addition of TI-83 emulating software. We then attempted to develop students' problem-solving skills (particularly their strategy selection skills) with an emphasis on getting students to check their algebraic working, which the TI-89 can do but the TI-83 cannot.

The course was only partially successful. There were a few students across the ability range who succeeded in developing basic competence together with the desired greater ability to choose appropriate strategies. However, many students from more traditional mathematical backgrounds felt throughout that the TI-89 compromised their development of basic skills and stubbornly (or ignorantly) avoided using it even under examination conditions when its use would have been to their benefit. Many weaker students became overly reliant on the TI-89 and as such did not really develop their grasp of basic techniques, a concern that needs careful addressing before any decision is made to introduce the TI-89 in the MSSL or MMSL courses. Such introduction is unlikely in the near future, however; it is only seriously considered for the MHL course at the moment.

The TI-89 is an incredible piece of technology, and it is a requisite part of many university level courses in engineering and mathematics. However, such courses clearly attract mathematically very able students who typically acquire the necessary technological competence quickly anyway, so some more thought may need to go into the added benefits of CSAs for MHL students.

The experiment at UWCSEA only ran for a year and possibly with more experience on the part of staff could have been developed into a course that could produce more algebraically and technologically aware students. Or maybe not. It seems clear that four things need to happen:

1. The MHL course content needs careful rethinking to reflect the presence of CSAs, to avoid a re-run of the introduction of the TI-83 where the IBO examiners frequently seemed less than fully aware of the capabilities of the calculator.
2. It must be demonstrated that the inclusion of CSAs will mean much more than simply adding a fancy tool, and will improve overall mathematical competence for all participating students.
3. Students moving on to university courses requiring the TI-89 should have real benefits from their inclusion in the MHL course.
4. The IBO should provide staff with considerably more support than it did with the TI-83. It should provide a large set of examples of CSA-oriented examination questions that demand understanding and insight rather than the ability to press buttons.

The discussion within the IBO community on the role of IT in mathematics is ongoing. Many teachers feel that the welcome ultimate aim of developing true mathematical understanding can simultaneously be pursued in other ways, notably by shifting the emphasis from the current quantitative examination format into a more qualitative one. Significantly, the IBO has not published a timeline for implementation of the two-tiered system, which means it will not be implemented before 2010, if it happens at all.

5 External assessment

As a way of trying to ensure the worldwide relevance and freshness of the IB curriculum, subject syllabuses are reviewed and revamped every five years. This process includes changing the chief examiners. Teachers are also involved in this review process as they are invited to send back the G2 feedback forms (found in the *Vade Mecum* and submitted to the IBO immediately after the examinations with individual teacher's comments and criticisms on the examination papers). In fact, as is emphasized in Chapter 2, the IBO encourages schools to more actively take advantage of this avenue to help shape the curriculum.

This review process, combined with the advent of the TI-83 (first examined in May 2000), has led to some significant shifts in the content and style of DP mathematics examination questions over the years, particularly in MHL. We saw in the previous section that the examination of calculus has become less demanding as a result of the GDC, but also partly by design, as is illustrated by the non-GDC question from the November 1999 paper on page 468. Therefore, many of the pre-1999 calculus examination questions may needlessly scare your students. More generally, one definitely finds very hard questions such as the one from May 1995 (which also strains language skills) much less frequently now:

Consider the function $f_k(x) = \begin{cases} x \ln x - kx, & x > 0 \\ 0, & x = 0 \end{cases}$, where $k \in \mathbb{N}$

(a) Find the derivative of $f_k(x)$, $x > 0$.

(b) Find the interval over which $f_0(x)$ is increasing.

The graph of $f_k(x)$ is shown below.

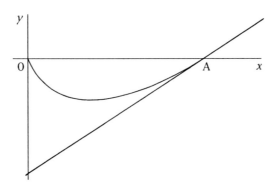

(c) (i) Show that the stationary point of $f_k(x)$ is at $x = e^{k-1}$.

   (ii) One x-intercept is at $(0,0)$. Find the coordinates of the other x-intercept.

(d) Find the area enclosed by the curve and the x-axis.

(e) Find the equation of the tangent to the curve at A.

(f) Show that the area of the triangular region created by the tangent and the coordinate axes is twice the area enclosed by the curve and the x-axis.

(g) Show that the x-intercepts of $f_k(x)$ for consecutive values of k form a geometric sequence.

An aeroplane approaches the end of the runway from the west with an angle of descent of 24°. A tower is 18 metres high and is situated 135 metres north and 250 metres west of the end of the runway.

(a) Write down the position vector of the top of the tower relative to an origin at the end of the runway, and a vector in the direction of the line of descent of the aeroplane.

(b) Hence or otherwise, calculate how close, to the nearest metre, the aeroplane comes to a warning light that is at the top of the tower.
(Note: the distance between a point with position vector $\vec{a}$ and a line through the origin and in the direction $\vec{u}$ is given by $\dfrac{|\vec{a} \times \vec{u}|}{|\vec{u}|}$).

This is not to say that hard (and bad) questions do not occur at all any more, as is illustrated by the following MHL question from 2001:

In a game, the probability of a player scoring with a shot is $1/4$. Let X be the number of shots the player takes to score including the scoring shot. (You can assume that each shot is independent of the others.)

(a) Find $P(X = 3)$

(b) Find the probability that the player will have at least three misses before scoring twice.

(c) Prove that the expected value of X is 4. (You may use the result $(1-x)^{-2} = 1 + 2x + 3x^2 + 4x^3 + \dots$)

© IBO 2001

Not only is the language in part (b) not clear, but students must also link their knowledge of discrete probability distributions with an unfamiliar algebraic expansion, and all of this under examination conditions. This question attracted a lot of criticism through the G2 feedback forms, but then so did other such questions over the years. Clearly, there is room for the IBO to improve its examination design: surely a few proofreading teachers should be able to weed out this type of question. Until that time, however, it remains a useful exercise to include pre-2000 examination questions (and bad post-2000 questions!) as part of the revision and familiarization process for students. In fact, to score highly in the final examination, students still need to be able to deal with the harder questions more typical of a pre-2000 paper. The reason for this is that – due to examination moderation – the generally easier papers of the last few years have not led to any significant increase in the allocation of high final grades.

Moving on to another issue, the choice of option is also worth a note. In all mathematics courses (with the exception of FM) the students need to study one option. Time constraints mean that most schools will teach only one option in each course, so that the student effectively has no choice during the examination. Since the option counts for more than 15% of the final grade, it is worth while to think carefully as a teacher which option to choose within each course.

In MSSL, most teachers settle for the calculus or statistics option, and avoid the option (discrete mathematical) graphs and matrices. Both calculus and statistics can be taught fruitfully, and the examination questions in these options tend to be equally difficult.

In MMSL, there are only two options – further calculus and further statistics – and both are taken frequently. Again, there are no irrefutable patterns in comparative difficulty of the examination questions, and both can be enjoyable courses.

In MHL, there are five options: further statistics, groups, discrete mathematics, analysis (i.e. further calculus) and plane geometry. Here, schools tend to choose amongst the first three and avoid the last two. A problem particularly evident in MHL is that the comparative difficulties of the questions are so different. Discrete mathematics tends to be easy (which does not mean the teaching of it has to be so), while groups and further statistics can vary between the easy and the very hard. While the moderation process tries to ensure that students do not suffer from such differences in terms of grade, a nasty examination question of course does little good for the nerves. The IBO has acknowledged the problem of unequal difficulty and is working on resolving it, so it is not wise to assume that the current patterns will continue.

Naturally, the choice of option for many teachers is inspired by expertise. Teaching something new, however, can be a great stimulus, and enrich the teaching experience.

In our view, the IB mathematics curriculum is special in that it tries to encourage students to embrace a wide variety of methods as well as a wider view of the role of mathematics in the world around us. The tools it uses to meet these aims are the coursework, the use of IT, and the increasing emphasis on modelling tasks in both coursework and syllabus. While it is work in progress, including the flaws that come with such work, there is little reason to expect that things will ever roll back to a more traditional curriculum, and every reason to expect the contrary. While traditional teaching techniques can still determine the greater part of the final grade, an ever-increasing part of the grade depends on the willingness of the teacher to experiment with new ideas and new methods. This will occasionally mean stepping into the unknown, but this is what the IB is all about: growth for every stakeholder by challenging the boundaries.

6 Extended essay

Few students choose to do their extended essay in mathematics: about 2–3% every year. The grades obtained are quite good, however. This could be partly due to the fact that mathematics teachers get fewer requests for extended essays and hence consider them less of a chore than some of their colleagues in other departments. For students, however, extended essays in mathematics – just like science – can easily become a lot of work, more so than in many other subjects. The reason for this is that the extended essay formally requires students to go beyond their subject syllabus. In mathematics, many teachers take that to mean the student must research university type texts, which are extremely hard to read for high school students. It should be kept in mind, however (refer to Chapter 11), that the key to a successful extended essay lies mostly in the correct implementation of the general – rather than subject-specific – criteria. No-one expects evidence of a new Euler rearing his head, and the grade weighting for mathematical sophistication is quite low.

As such, many of the examples listed in this chapter so far could easily be turned into extended essays. To give an example, the horizon problem sketched out in section 2.2 allows the student to do quite a bit of practical, historical and mathematical research. *Practical:* test out the formulas yourself, describing your methods. *Historical:* find out about other ways of measuring the size of the earth, for instance Gauss's geodesic triangle method, and research what role mathematics played in ending the controversy surrounding the flat earth versus the round earth paradigms. *Mathematical:* you'd go beyond the syllabus of any DP mathematics course by touching upon the subject of linear approximations of complicated algebraic functions and the numerical issue of their validity.

Other avenues worth exploring for the extended essay concern the obvious gaps in the MHL syllabus. The absence of any coverage of mechanics is considered by many to be a gross disservice to mathematics and to students (hence also our suggestion in previous sections to put it back through the coursework). Not only is a chance to apply and develop powerful mathematical models denied, but students intending to follow engineering courses at university are put at a disadvantage. However, a good extended essay could address, say, the use of vector calculus in circular motion, or differential equations in simple harmonic motion. This helps to address the gaps without forcing students and teachers to study a completely new and abstract area of mathematics from scratch.

7 Streaming and advising; combining classes?

Smaller schools won't have the luxury of separating the three different mathematics courses over different classes. If one has to combine classes, it probably makes most sense to combine MHL with MMSL, since the latter syllabus is part of the former. It would be an unfortunate teacher who had to teach MHL and MSSL in one class. In fact, it is hard to imagine that either group could possibly achieve decent grades in this scenario. Not only are the syllabuses totally different, but the coursework components are completely different as well (unlike HML and MMSL courses, which both include portfolio tasks). Most schools that teach joint MMSL/MHL classes tend to work with the MMSL syllabus in the first year then do the specific MHL parts in year 2.

If a school has the luxury of splitting the courses along class lines, it may have the additional luxury of streaming the students within each course. Whether this is a good thing or not is a well-known debate within education, and the IB offers no new perspective here.

Which mathematics course should one advise the students to take?

There are two issues to consider here: a student's ability, and university requirements. We have already mentioned that, apart from those who struggle with the English language, every student should be able to do well in MSSL with appropriate guidance from the teacher. MMSL and MHL are both hard courses where the syllabus exerts a lot of (in our opinion, too much) pressure on the timetable, especially in MMSL. Students signing up for these courses must be very able and very committed – the pace is relentless.

As for university requirements, there are still a number of universities that frown on MSSL and feel the course is too light to satisfy their entry requirements despite the welcome addition of the calculus option to MSSL. For best advice in this area, it is imperative that schools check with the universities to which their students will apply.

8 Resources for mathematics

Unfortunately there are no DP-specific textbooks for either MHL, MMSL or MSSL that we can recommend unequivocally as a complete student resource. None of the IBID books listed below adequately covers the core syllabus of the respective subject. However, each one provides useful examples (particularly GDC-related ones) that warrant at least one copy of each being held as a departmental resource. The other texts listed have been used successfully in at least one large mathematics department. However, none provides complete coverage of the option topics (and some provide none at all); all need to be supplemented with additional texts or home-grown resources when covering the core syllabuses.

8.1 Books for MHL

Sadler, A. J. and Thorning, D. W. S. (1995) *Understanding Pure Mathematics*, Oxford University Press. This is an accessible student text that covers the core MHL syllabus comprehensively. The examples and exercises are broad-ranging and the miscellaneous exercises offer a challenging range of examination-type questions. The downside, however, is that vector products, core-level statistics and GDC issues are not addressed in this text.

Perkins, M. and Perkins, P. (1998) *Advanced Mathematics: A Pure Course*, Collins Educational, Harper Collins Publishers. This older text again does not address vector products, statistics or GDC use. Otherwise, it is a useful student text that does cover much of the core MHL syllabus quite comprehensively and rigorously.

Perkins, M. and Perkins, P. (1983) *Advanced Maths Book 2*, Collins Educational, Harper Collins Publishers. Another older text (soon if not already out of print) that contains a selection of chapters from Perkins and Perkins, *Advanced Mathematics: A Pure Course* with the addition of some quite thorough chapters on binary operations and groups, and probability and statistics.

Cirrito, F. (ed.) (1999) *Mathematics Higher Level (Core)*, 2nd edition, IBID Press. See the introductory comments to section 8.

Stewart, J. (2004) *Calculus*, 5th edition, Brooks, Cole. This is more of a teacher resource that includes useful work on series and vectors in addition to the obvious coverage of calculus from the basics to the level required for the analysis option (and beyond!). It is a very popular text for first-year university programmes in the USA, and it is supported by the brilliant website www.hotmath.com, which goes step by step (controlled by the student) through every odd-numbered question!

Crashaw, J. and Chambers, J. (2001) *A Concise Course in A Level Statistics with worked examples*, 4th edition, Nelson Thornes. This book covers the core and the probability and statistics options quite thoroughly but very traditionally. However, the *t*-statistic and GDC issues are not addressed.

Crashaw, J. and Chambers, J. (1997) *A-Level Statistics Study Guide (Concise Course)*, Nelson Thornes. This is a more concise and student-friendly version of the statistics text above. It similarly lacks any GDC tips but the examples are very thorough and the exercises with full solutions at the end of the text provide good examination preparation.

Morgan, L. (1997) *Statistics Handbook for the TI-83*, Texas Instruments Inc. This is the definitive teacher resource covering the use of the TI-83 GDC for the core and the probability and statistics options. The full range of core and option concepts are thoughtfully linked with the efficient use of technology.

Bostock, L., Chandler, S. and Rourke, C. (1993) *Further Pure Mathematics*, Nelson Thornes. This probably contains too much excess material to be a user-friendly student text, but it is a good teacher resource rigorously covering core topics such as vectors, transformations, differential equations and complex numbers. Also includes sections on group theory, infinite series and conics – useful for option topics.

8.2 Books for MMSL

Bostock, L. and Chandler, S. (2000) *Core Maths for 'A' Level*, Nelson Thornes. This student text covers the core MMSL course quite comprehensively but arguably the exercises do not provide enough challenge for able students.

Thong, Hon Soo and Hiong, Khor Nyak (2001) *New Additional Mathematics*, Pan Pacific Publishing. This text also covers the core syllabus reasonably well but many of the exercises are not particularly accessible to less able students.

Cirrito, F. (ed.) (1998) *Mathematical Methods*, 2nd edition, IBID Press (see introductory comments to section 8).

8.3 Books for MSSL

Cirrito, F. (ed.) and Strid, V. (1998) *Mathematical Studies*, IBID Press. This text covers logic reasonably effectively and some of the main features of the different MSSL option topics, but lacks enough practice exercises for students to be a viable whole-class resource. However, there is some attempt made in the text to show how the GDC can be used to enhance the teaching of graphing and functions.

8.4 Hardware and software

See section 4.1 for software recommendations: Omnigraph, spreadsheets, Geometer's Sketchpad. These can be found on the internet with a simple Google search (or accessed through our website www.dp-help.com), and can be bought online.

For hardware recommendations, we would argue very strongly for a PC plus LCD projector in every teaching room. Only when materials are easily available will people readily experiment with them. If LCD projectors are too expensive, you could hook up a TV to your PC for classroom demonstrations as a good substitute.

8.5 IBO workshops

As there are three different mainline mathematics courses, parallel workshops are run for these. Recent IB workshops have tended to concentrate on the coursework components and the integration of technology into the different mathematics courses (especially the use of graphical display calculators, in teaching and examinations). The general feeling is that such sessions have been of some benefit to new teachers but are of more use to experienced IB teachers.

9 Scheme of work for MHL

Figure 16.8 shows the scheme of work for a 57-week MHL course, based on one followed by UWCSEA students who start MHL with a strong algebraic background including introductory calculus (note: 1 week = three × 1 hr 10 minute lessons). The texts used are listed in full in section 8 of this chapter. It goes without saying there are many other ways to cover the syllabus, but we hope that this scheme will provide some insight into the level at which to pitch the course, the relative weight each topic deserves, and the typical pitfalls one might face with certain topics. The set of portfolios mentioned here, and others, will be posted on www.dp-help.com as MS doc files.

Note that this is a scheme of work for a strong MHL group. A notable consequence of this is that we cover two option topics rather than the customary single one, and that the portfolio tasks indicated in the scheme are deliberately more summative (and demanding) in nature than those (often introductory) tasks that would be given to MHL students with less background experience. Clearly it would not be appropriate to give students who already possess a good background in calculus a task introducing differentiation as a limiting process for chord gradients for polynomials. However, this does not mean that some other more appropriate introductory task could not be assigned for such strong students, such as an investigation of limits of chord gradients for exponential functions. None the less, the summative use of portfolio tasks does allow ordinary lessons to proceed largely independently of the given task. The 14-day optimal turnaround period designated at UWCSEA between giving out a portfolio task, marking it and having it finally moderated is then followed by a feedback session that reviews students' performance in the portfolio task and the key issues the assignment was intended to address (see also section 3.3, internal moderation).

Figure 16.8 Scheme of work for mathematics HL

Topic	No. of weeks	Content/general notes	Suggested resources
		1 ALGEBRAIC TECHNIQUES	
1.1 Roots of quadratics and polynomials	1	• Review quadratics, applications of the discriminant and inequalities – stress nature of discriminant • Review factor and remainder theorems and extend to double roots occurring in the derivative – link to curve sketching and solving inequalities	• Sadler & Thorning p145–152 Sadler & Thorning p153–156 Perkins & Perkins Book 2 p30–39
1.2 Introduction to complex numbers	1	• Sum and product of roots of quadratics; addition, subtraction, square roots of complex numbers – stress use of GDC; the Argand plane	• Sadler & Thorning p460–464 Perkins & Perkins Book 2 p391–403 • *Portfolio task 'Complex valued functions' – type I –* used to introduce portfolios and review and extend concepts of function and differentiation

Figure 16.8 Scheme of work for mathematics HL (continued)

Topic	No. of weeks	Content/general notes	Suggested resources
		1 ALGEBRAIC TECHNIQUES (continued)	
1.3 Partial fractions and series	2	• The usual three forms of partial fractions. Link to differentiation of rational functions and also to integration techniques • Review APs and GPs; $\Sigma\, r$, $\Sigma\, r^2$, $\Sigma\, r^3$, summing via differences $(\Sigma\, 1/(r(r-1)) = \Sigma\, 1/(r-1) - \Sigma\, 1/r$, etc.)	• Sadler & Thorning p451–460 Sadler & Thorning p217–222, 456–460 Perkins & Perkins Book 2 p251–256
1.4 Inequalities	1	• Review quadratic inequalities and extend to rational inequalities of the form: $\dfrac{3-x}{x+1} \le 3$ Stress use of alternative strategies esp. use of GDC	• Sadler & Thorning p344–349
1.5 Proof by induction	2	• Applications to sums of series, matrices results, divisibility results (divisibility by 3, etc.)	• Sadler & Thorning p217–222 Perkins & Perkins Book 2 p9–16 • *Portfolio task 'Finding sums of series' – type I –* used summatively to assess grasp of induction for series
1.6 The binomial expansion	1	• Include proof	• Sadler & Thorning p222–231, 455–456
1.7 Permutations and combinations	1	• Link to binomial expansion and probability	• Sadler & Thorning p188–207
		2 TRIGONOMETRY	
2.1 Trig graphs	1	• Review properties of $\sin x$, $\cos x$, $\sec x$, reciprocal graphs; transformations of trig and polynomial graphs esp. $af(bx + c) + d$ form	• Sadler & Thorning p99–109, 284–288
2.2 Review of simple trig equations	0.5	• Extend to general solutions and review radian measure	• Sadler & Thorning p110–114, p362–365
2.3 Review Pythagorean identities, and double, half and compound angle formulae	1	• Can use matrix rotation as basis of proof of compound angle formula–link to transformations and matrices; application to finding distances between parallel lines	• Sadler & Thorning p114–123 • *Portfolio task 'Distances between lines' – type II –* used summatively as application of trig techniques and formulas
2.4 $a\cos x + b\sin x$ formula	0.5	• Link to transformations and rational functions	• Sadler & Thorning p353–356
2.5 Inverse trig functions	1	• Link to solutions of quadratics e.g. $\tan^{-1}(2x) + \tan^{-1}(x) = \pi/4$	• Sadler & Thorning p356–361
2.6 Small angles and limits	0.5	• Link to trig differentiation and first principles	• Sadler & Thorning p365–367

(continues overleaf)

Figure 16.8 Scheme of work for mathematics HL (continued)

Topic	No. of weeks	Content/general notes	Suggested resources
		3 CALCULUS	
3.1 Techniques of differentiation: polynomials and rational functions	1.5	• Differentiation from first principles; chain, product and quotient rules. Link differentiation to induction (i.e. proof of $(x^n)' = n\,x^{n-1}$ using first principles and product rule). Implicit and parametric differentiation. Applications and binomial expansions should be used to formalize the idea of the gradient function	• Sadler & Thorning p225–272, 317–334 • *Portfolio task 'The path of light' – type III* (see task 6 in section 3.2) – used summatively as application of differential calculus
3.2 Curve sketching	1	• Include rearranging rational functions into quadratics to find the range of y values (e.g. $y = (x + 2)/(x^2 - 1)$ rearranged to $x^2 y - y - x - 2 = 0$ and use discriminant); include finding oblique asymptotes – link to dividing polynomials	• Sadler & Thorning p335–351
3.3 Trig differentiation	1	• Radians; derivatives from first principles	• Sadler & Thorning p367–377
3.4 Logarithms and exponentials	1	• Include differentiation of log and exp – link to first principles	• Sadler & Thorning p477–488 • *Portfolio task 'Compound interest' – type I, II or III* (see task 2 in section 3.2) – used to introduce properties and applications of e
3.5 Integration techniques	2.5	• Reverse of chain rule. Substitution. Inverse trig functions. Partial fractions. Integration by parts. Applications	• Sadler & Thorning p496–508 Perkins & Perkins Book 2 p69–98 • *Portfolio task 'The spread of SARS' – type I, II or III* (see section 2.2) – used as opportunity to apply work on functions (esp. exponentials) to real life
3.6 Differential equations	1	• Formation, variables separable, homogeneous form using substitution $y = vx$	• Sadler & Thorning p509–523 Perkins & Perkins Book 2 p313–318 • *Portfolio task 'Throwing a baseball' – type I or III* (discussed in sections 2.2, 3.1 and mentioned as portfolio task 1 in section 3.2) – used as opportunity to apply broad range of already familiar concepts to an open modelling scenario

Figure 16.8 Scheme of work for mathematics HL (continued)

Topic	No. of weeks	Content/general notes	Suggested resources
		FIRST YEAR INTERNAL EXAMINATION	
		4 COMPLEX NUMBERS	
4.1 Review of algebraic form (see 1.2)	0.5		• Sadler & Thorning p460–476 Perkins & Perkins Book 2 p391–426
4.2 Polar form	0.5	• Link to geometric significance of multiplying and dividing complex numbers	• Sadler & Thorning p460–476 Perkins & Perkins Book 2 p391–426
4.3 De Moivre's theorem with applications	1	• Proof by induction; roots of complex numbers, with geometric interpretation; cube and nth roots of unity in polar and Cartesian form • Trig identities – expansions of $\sin(nx)$ and $\cos(nx)$ in terms of powers and vice versa – link to integration	• Sadler & Thorning p460–476 Perkins & Perkins Book 2 p391–426
		5 VECTORS AND MATRICES	
5.1 Vectors and lines in two and three dimensions	1.5	• Position and unit vectors in 2D and vector geometry – link to complex numbers • Scalar product for 2D • Vector equation of line in 3D • Applications of scalar product in 3D: finding angles and orthogonal vectors • Intersecting lines in 3D, skew lines, distance between lines, distance from point to line, reflection of point in a line	• Sadler & Thorning p47–68, 415–422
5.2 The vector product	1	• Link to scalar product to find orthogonal 3D vectors • Applications to finding distances between lines, areas of triangles, volumes of parallelepipeds, coplanarity of vectors, torque of forces	• Stewart, *Calculus* p702–709 • *Portfolio task 'Modulus of vector product'- type II* (portfolio task 7 in section 3.2) – used to introduce vector product by linking it with scalar product
5.3 Planes in 3D	1.5	• Vector equations of planes, normals to planes, distance to origin, Cartesian form, parallel planes, angles and distances between planes, intersection of planes, intersection of planes and lines, link to use of vector product for finding normals to planes	• Sadler & Thorning p423–433 • *Portfolio task 'Lines and planes' – type II* – used summatively to review properties of lines and planes
5.4 Matrices and determinants	1.5	• Link matrices to base vectors • General transformations with and without origin invariant • Significance of determinant and finding inverses • Solutions of simultaneous equations in 2D – link with 3D case (see 5.5)	• Sadler & Thorning p159–188

(continues overleaf)

Figure 16.8 Scheme of work for mathematics HL (continued)

Topic	No. of weeks	Content/general notes	Suggested resources
5.5 Systems of plane equations	1	• Cartesian form and systems of equations • Determinant of 3D matrix • Geometric interpretation of solutions or no solutions of systems • Use of GDC	• Sadler & Thorning p435–447
6 STATISTICS AND PROBABILITY (CORE)			
6.1 Descriptive statistics	0.5	• Box and whisker plots, histograms • Measures of location and dispersion • Biased and unbiased estimators of population mean and variance	• Crashaw and Chambers, *A-Level Study Guide*, p1–11 • *Portfolio task 'Water in our city' – type I or III* (portfolio task 3 in section 3.2) – used as opportunity to apply statistical and estimation techniques to real life
6.2 Probability	1.5	• Link to permutations and combinations • Venn diagrams, addition rule, conditional probability, independent events, tree diagrams • Bayes' Theorem for two events	• Crashaw and Chambers, *Study Guide*, p22–34 • Sadler & Thorning, p188–207, 235–254 • Crashaw and Chambers, *A Concise Course in A-Level Statistics* p169–174
6.4 Discrete random variables, esp. the binomial distribution	1	• Expectation and variance • Uniform, geometric, binomial distributions and Poisson distribution • Expectation algebra to link with option	• Crashaw and Chambers *Study Guide* p35–48, 49–60 • Perkins and Perkins Book 2 p434–441
6.5 Continuous probability distributions, esp. the normal distribution	1.5	• Link to discrete random variables and calculus • Expectation, variance, median and mode • The normal distribution – use of tables and GDC • Normal approximation to the binomial and Poisson distributions (with continuity correction)	• Crashaw and Chambers *Study Guide*, p38–48, 61–77 • Perkins and Perkins Book 2 p442–457
7 STATISTICS AND PROBABILITY (OPTION)			
7.1 Linear combinations of random variables	1.5	• Linear combinations of independent random variables (see 6.4) – include sums of normal and Poisson distributions and link to sample means	• Crashaw and Chambers *Study Guide* p78–84 • Crashaw and Chambers *A Level Statistics* p416–433
7.2 Estimation of population parameters	1	• Unbiased estimators and pooled estimators • Distribution of the sample mean • The central limit theorem	• Crashaw and Chambers *Study Guide*, p85–93 • Crashaw and Chambers *A Level Statistics* p447–451, p476–487

Figure 16.8 Scheme of work for mathematics HL (continued)

Topic	No. of weeks	Content/general notes	Suggested resources
7.3 Confidence intervals for mean of normal population	1.5	• z and t intervals for known and unknown population variance – stress use of TI-83	• Crashaw and Chambers *Study Guide* p88–93 • Crashaw and Chambers *A Level Statistics* p487–496
7.4 The chi-squared distribution	1	• H_0, H_1, significance levels, degrees of freedom and critical regions for chi-squared distribution • Goodness of fit for discrete and continuous distributions • Contingency tables • Use of TI-83	• Crashaw and Chambers *Study Guide* p119–133 • Crashaw and Chambers *A Level Statistics*, p573–627
7.5 Significance testing	2	• One- and two-tailed tests • Testing means and differences between means based on samples • Use of normal and t-distributions – stress use of TI-83 • Link to 7.4	• Crashaw and Chambers *Study Guide* p94–118 • Crashaw and Chambers *A Level Statistics*, p507–538
8 SETS, GROUPS AND RELATIONS (OPTION)			
8.1 Sets	1	• Venn diagrams, set equality and inclusion, finite sets and cardinality of infinite sets – link to injective functions • De Morgan's Laws • Cartesian products	• School-generated notes
8.2 Relations and equivalence relations	1.5	• Binary relations • Reflexive, symmetric and transitive relations • Partitions of sets	• School-generated notes
8.3 Functions	1.5	• Injections, surjections, inverses and composition	• School-generated notes
8.4 Groups	3	• Group axioms esp. commutativity, inverse and identity • Cayley tables • Examples of finite and infinite groups including groups of functions and matrix groups – link to core topics • Subgroups, cyclic groups, order of groups and Lagrange's theorem and corollary • Isomorphisms for finite and infinite groups – link to 8.3 • Direct product groups – link to Cartesian products	• Bostock and Chandler *Further Pure Maths* p566–623 Perkins & Perkins Book 2 p464–494
MOCK EXAM PREPARATION (2 WEEKS)			
MOCK EXAMINATION			
REVISION AND PAST EXAM PAPERS (8 WEEKS)			

10 Computer science

The computer science syllabus is similar in many respects to the British A-level syllabus and both skills and content material will spring no surprises for experienced teachers. The assessment consists of external examinations and internal assessment, the latter usually posing the greatest challenges in teaching the course.

10.1 Prerequisites

Computer science is available at HL and SL, and the HL course contains the SL. The SL course requires no previous experience by the students in the subject. At a recent IB workshop it was stated that only students doing mathematics HL would be able to handle computer science at HL. However, my best student this year was one who studied mathematical studies (SL). He didn't understand data representation very well but in all other aspects of programming he excelled.

10.2 Course overview (SL and HL)

It is convenient to think of the syllabus (both HL and SL) as divided into three parts. Part A deals with what students have to know and understand, part B deals with what students must be able to do, and part C is internal assessment. This section deals with parts A and B – see section 10.4 for internal assessment.

Part A: Knowledge and understanding (including case study)

The first part is devoted to the acquisition of knowledge and understanding of computers and computer systems. The level of knowledge required of SL students is not very high. To give an idea, students must know that a mouse is an input device (one of many) and when and why it is useful, but do not need to understand how it works. They must have a general knowledge of binary representation of numbers and how it applies to analog/digital conversions. That is as difficult as it gets. Apart from an understanding of binary representation, this part of the course is completely non-mathematical and does not require the student to 'think' at all (in the mathematical sense) – just to remember and understand.

HL students need to know all of this too, but HL requires a much deeper knowledge of computer systems. For example, the machine instruction cycle must be examined in detail, to the extent that the student understands what the function is of each different part of the processor (ALU, program counter, etc.). Boolean logic and circuit diagrams are developed to the depth of a *full adder* (a circuit diagram that combines three binary digits together to give an answer and carry). Binary representation is covered to the depth of floating point representation. Evaluating algorithm efficiency is covered, with use of the 'big O' notation.

An emphasis in this section of the syllabus (and also in the internal assessment) is on system analysis and design. The stages include investigation and analysis of existing systems, requirements specification, system design, software design construction, testing, implementation and evaluation. The syllabus is not too fussy about the stages. So if you want to put in feasibility study as one of the stages then feel happy to do so. The important thing is for students to realize that software has both a design and a purpose.

In Paper 2, for both HL and SL, there is one question based on a *case study*, published about six months before the examination. To give an example, a recent case study focused on human evolution research. It explained how CT scans (used to diagnose brain tumours amongst other things) are used to digitize information about fossils. The resulting scans can be stored and compared. The questions pertaining to the case study are never deep but draw on the concepts it raises. To give two examples, one question was 'Identify one situation in the case study where data integrity is important' and another one was 'Explain why such high-power workstations are needed to process the image files.'

The initial idea was for the case study to be available at the start of the course so that the teacher could continually refer to it during the course. This aim fits in beautifully with the IBO's philosophy of integrating an area of knowledge with the real world rather than treating it as an abstract body of knowledge on its own. However, such early availability proved impossible in the current system of one different case study each year, so the proposal is that in the near future there should be only one case study for every *two-year* period, which will hopefully bring the original aim back to life.

Part B: Programming

The second part is the practical aspect of the subject. SL students need to learn how to program in a high-level language. At the time of writing, the language chosen can be one of the following: Pascal, Delphi, C, C++, Modula 2, Ada, Structured Basic, Java. However, from 2004 (examination in 2006) onwards, Java will be the only accepted language. The level of programming expertise includes arrays, 2D arrays (very popular in examination questions), branching with **if** and **case**, looping using **while** and **for**, records and user defined types, and finally, subprograms with emphasis on passing variables by value and passing by reference. Students' programs must be able to read data and write data to a disk text file. All these skills need to be mastered before starting the internal assessment. The SL students never have to use their programming ability as a tool for solving difficult problems although the teacher may choose to implement the teaching of programming in this fashion. Examination problems in SL usually give an algorithm and the students have to explain it first, make modifications to one or two lines in the second stage and finally create their own algorithm for a different situation.

HL students need to understand and use much more complicated constructs such as pointers, static and dynamic data structures including queues and stacks (using arrays and linked lists), trees, objects, and recursion (another examination favourite). They have to extract data and write data to the middle of a text file. There is a much greater demand on thinking skills in HL programming (as well as in the internal assessment) and the student must have proven mathematical ability or a great interest to cope successfully with this part.

10.3 Assessment outline

In the syllabus four objective levels are clearly described and action verbs that identify them are detailed. These are important because they tell the teacher the depth of the work.

Objective 1 – remember terms, define words

Objective 2 – know all relevant information about

Objective 3 – analyse and compare

Objective 4 – plan and create.

In the examination papers all algorithms are presented in a standard pseudo code called PURE. The subject guide contains a detailed definition of this code. The examination board is forced to include this common programming language because students are allowed to be taught a variety of programming languages. The students need to be able to read PURE but do not need to write algorithms using it. For the examination and for their dossier they may use the language of their choice. After 2004 this pseudo code will be removed and replaced with Java.

Figure 16.9 Objectives for assessment

Component	Objectives 1 + 2	3 + 4	Time	Details
Paper 1 (30%)	18%	12%	SL: 1 hr 15 mins HL: 2 hrs	Section A: several short answer questions Section B: choose three longer structured questions from a choice of four (HL: four out of five)
Paper 2 (35%)	15%	20%	SL: 1 hr 45 mins HL: 2 hrs 30 mins	Three (SL) or five (HL) compulsory questions, including an extended response question involving the construction of an algorithm, a structured question based on the case study, and one (SL) or three (HL) structured questions
Internal assessment: dossier (35%)	20%	15%	SL 25 hrs HL 35 hrs	One in-depth project containing a single program that enables the candidate to demonstrate mastery of the required aspects

10.4 Internal assessment (the dossier)

The internal assessment is called the *program dossier*. It can only be done when the student has completed most of the course since it draws on ideas from throughout the syllabus. Also, the students are expected to program their solution and this can only be done when the students have sufficient programming experience. The dossier is usually completed in one closed session lasting two months in the second year.

The student chooses a problem that lends itself to an IT solution and processes this problem through the design cycle to produce a complete program that actually works and solves the initial problem. The emphasis is on the design and evaluation of the project: almost all marks are attributed to these aspects. An example of a suitable dossier project could be the local dry-cleaning shop that processes everything through a ledger and does not have a computer. They accept clothes from their customers, tag them, and then send them away to a large commercial dry-cleaning place. Naturally, the shop must keep track of the customers and their clothes. This situation is analysed, a program design is proposed, and the final result is a program that keeps track of both customers and their clothes. The differences between HL and SL are illustrated at the end of this section.

Invariably when students start to program they find their proposed design is inadequate. They will then change their design based on their program and so their design ceases to be a design. To prevent this situation, it is a good idea to require students to complete and hand in the initial paper stages of the dossier (analysis, design of algorithm, data structures, program general design, testing strategy) *before* they start to write their program. It is important to realize that a program that does not exactly match the design is not a problem, and the marking will only penalize students if their final product is really completely unrelated to the design.

There are two parts to marking the dossier. First there are 12 criteria, each of which is broken into achievement levels, which are openly shared with the students. For new teachers these achievement levels are very difficult to apply. The natural inclination is to award the top level of achievement to the top work in a class. A new teacher must put a lot of time into reading the notes in the subject guide and even then some aspects are not clear until the third reading. In fact, I would very strongly recommend that you work through an example with an experienced teacher or at the very least ask some colleagues from other schools to send you copies of their graded work. To illustrate the kind of difficulties I faced, consider criterion A. This tests the quality of the student's *analysis* of the problem, and the highest achievement level is 3. The tricky bit is the unconventional use of the word *analysis*. In the notes preceding the level descriptors it is stated that 'a good analysis includes sample data, information and requests from the intended user'. Teachers must take care to use *this* definition of analysis and not their own. I initially used my own definition of analysis, which is 'the ability to break up a problem into detailed steps'. To my mind this is what analysis is all about. At a recent computer in-service course the matter was explained and I had to change my ideas.

All of the criteria are applied and a mark out of 35 is obtained. I will call this the *criteria total*. Note that SL and HL work are subjected to exactly the same criteria. The second part of the marking is using the so-called *mastery factor*. In SL there are seven aspects of programming ability that the pupil must have demonstrated in their program, one of which for instance is 'parameter passing'. If students miss one of these aspects their mastery factor is 0.75, and if they miss two or three aspects the mastery factor is 0.50, if they miss four or more then the mastery factor is 0.25. The mastery factor is then multiplied by the criteria total to obtain the final mark. The HL is similar except that there are eleven mastery aspects (all different from the SL) and HL students must include nine of these. Students are not free to explore a problem of their choosing unless it contains the potential to satisfy these mastery aspects. This is a rigid and harsh system. It is proposed that it be replaced after 2004 with a system that is more flexible (offering more criteria, and mastery aspects shown in a smaller fraction) and less harsh (when an aspect is not shown in one criterion the mastery factor is 0.9 rather than 0.75).

Returning to the dry-cleaning example, we can now illustrate the differences between HL and SL for the dossier. It would be sufficient for the SL student to read all the customer data from a file into an array, do all the processing on this array, then at the end of the program write the data back to the file. This is one mastery aspect for SL. For the HL student there are three possible mastery aspects here: searching for a record in a file, deleting directly a record from a file, and adding directly a new record to a file. For the HL student to show mastery in all three they must consider the customers as a random access file. They must process the file by accessing each separate record. For example if a customer changed their phone number, the customer's record would be searched in the file, the record (and only this record) read into the program, changes made and then the record (and only this record) stored back in the file. This would of course only be necessary if the database were too big to be read into the computer, but HL students simply need to do it to satisfy requirements.

10.5 Teaching strategies, also for combined HL/SL classes

The fun in teaching this course is of course the programming. Very few subjects have this hands-on approach. What makes programming so nice is that if a student is stuck working on a program or makes an error in it, a few well-placed print statements will demonstrate what is happening. The student can quickly (in minutes) see what is wrong, then quickly (in hours) fix it, and then learn this technique of placing prints in their program really quickly (in years).

The syllabus emphasizes a top-down approach. This means that the problem is considered as a whole first, and is then broken into two or more smaller problems. For example, one part may be concerned only with the input and ensuring that correct input is received, another part may be concerned with the organization and storage of the data. Then each of these parts is again broken into smaller parts. This process continues until the part is small enough to understand and to translate into a programming language. This is of course the best approach for solving large and more complex problems. However, some schools have had great success in emphasizing a bottom-up approach in the first year (a 10-line program scarcely needs a top-down approach) and then considering system analysis and modularity and a top-down approach in the second year.

It is important that a student can put in homework time on the programming part of the course and on the internal assessment. This means that they must have the same compiler at home as at school. Although some teachers believe in the virtue of the academic approach (theory first, practice later), I firmly believe that it is important that students start to program early on. If they have to wait weeks before writing their first program then their enthusiasm may evaporate. First-lesson-first-program has worked well for me.

It would be a delight to have a class of only HL students but in reality most schools do not have sufficient students and must teach HL and SL students in one class. Fortunately the syllabus does lend itself to multi-level teaching. Generally a school will timetable HL students to have an extra period during the school week. This is the opportunity for the teacher to teach them their special work. I would recommend that you acquire or design self-help resources that will allow the student to learn their programming skills. There are many books on different computer languages and some of these provide a slow-paced, hands-on introduction to the language. I personally use worksheets that are divided into 15 chapters. The students must complete all the problems in each worksheet before I give them the next one. I provide general guidelines for completion of the material to the class. The students then work through such materials at their own pace, and also for homework, which frees up my time to help individual students.

10.6 Extended essay

This is a popular choice for students but it is often confused with ITGS (information technology in the global society, see section 6 in Chapter 14). In the computer science extended essay the student must take care not to be merely descriptive. For example, talking about one method of data compression is descriptive but comparing two methods becomes analysis (which is required in a computer science essay). As with all extended essays, the student must come up with a focused research question. The student must further analyse and conclude. It is possible to write a program for an extended essay although this only works if the student is very strong in programming. The extended essay will – just like the program dossier – consist of the problem analysis and the design. The output of the resulting program can be used to justify arguments and conclusions. What makes the extended essay different from the dossier is that it must explain relevant computer science theory and directly relate a computer system to the research question.

10.7 Future directions

Major changes were proposed in the last curriculum review report (February 2003).

1. Programming language: it is proposed that only one programming language is used in the course – Java. This will simplify the setting of examination questions on algorithms and it will be no longer necessary to learn the pseudo code PURE.
2. Case study: it is proposed that the case study is released every two years instead of once every year.
3. Program dossier: the criteria have been considerably modified. They have been organized into stages. Part of the first stage is to create a prototype (a simple version of the program which is used as part of the design process). A new criterion is introduced (holistic approach to the dossier) to assess the degree to which a student participated; understood; showed initiative, perseverance and insight; and met deadlines. The other major change is in the mastery aspects. It is proposed that SL and HL both have 15 (although different) aspects and that the student must include 10 of these in their project. If they only include nine then the mastery factor would be 0.9. This is a very welcome step as it will free up the constraint that a student must build their project around the mastery aspects.

10.8 **Resources**

Books

Meyenn, Andrew and Jones, Richard (2002) *Computer Science*, IBID Press. A very recent book with an excellent coverage of the syllabus although thin in many places. A must-have book.

Bradley, Ray (1999) *Understanding Computer Science for Advanced Level*, 4th edition, Stanley Thornes. This is a massive book that contains very comprehensive material. Goes far deeper than necessary, so guidance is needed.

Barnes, David and Kolling, Michael (2003) *Objects First with Java: A Practical Introduction Using BlueJ*, Prentice Hall. A book about BlueJ, which is an integrated Java environment designed for introductory teaching. The environment BlueJ is available free of charge for PC and Mac systems.

Websites

www.uwcsea.edu.sg/comp/ib.html
United World College of South East Asia Computer Science Department. Contains detailed notes of the theory topics and detailed help for Java programming. The programs are explained and the source code is available; they can be run from within the browser.

www.wollum.net/Disc.htm
Computer science at Shanghai American School, discussion web. This website allows students from throughout the world to post questions on their dossier. Other students or teachers around the world can read and answer.

www.bluej.org
The website for the last book in the list above. It features the Java compiler which had enormous support from teachers at a recent computer science course.

Chapter 17
Group 6: The arts

Robert Walker, PhD, BMus

Professor Walker was chief examiner for music, coordinator for the IB diploma arts programme, and a member of the IBO Bureau from 1987 to 1994. He instigated a major revision of the IB diploma's music syllabus resulting in its current basic structure. Theatre arts became a full subject on his watch, and the group 6 arts programmes developed more affinity with each other in terms of structure and assessment. He has conducted workshops in every IB region, most notably in the Asia-Pacific – where he set a speed record in agreeing to conduct one in Bali. With the support of the IBO and the group 6 chief examiners, Professor Walker was instrumental in organizing a major conference on the arts and culture in Singapore in 1995. A film was made of this event and is distributed by the IBO. In his academic work, Professor Walker has published 7 books and over 100 research articles on his main interests, which are cultural theory and aesthetics, musical acoustics and performance practices across cultures, and associated pedagogy. He moved to the University of New South Wales in 1998 to be Head of the School of Music and Music Education, until January 2003 when he returned to his duties as a researcher and academic.

This chapter not only details the nature of the IB diploma arts programme, but it also reflects Professor Walker's long commitment to the IBO and its philosophy.

The author wishes to thank the following for their invaluable comments: Professor Sergio Espinosa, Chief Examiner for Music; Peter Wilkins (Deputy Chief Examiner for Visual Arts), Rowley Moore, Miles Tranter, Jonathan Carter, Sarah Brown, and others who looked over the text.

1 The IB diploma arts programme: general issues

1.1 Nature of the arts subjects

The subjects in group 6 – music, visual arts, and theatre arts – are the areas of expression, knowledge and experience which touch the most secret, the most personal, and the most human of all human activities. They are found in all cultures and in all historical times. The IB diploma arts programmes expect students to be able to express themselves in an artistic medium: the production of *original* art work is considered an essential way of knowing the medium. But artistic expression never occurs in a socio-cultural vacuum; it is always embedded within a context of powerful social, cultural, economic and political forces. The individual artists are sensitive to these forces and their expressions show their reactions, their commentary, and their insights into contemporary events. In recognition of this, the IB diploma arts programmes also require the student to reflect on and become critically involved in discussion about the effects of art, its meaning, and its relationship to life, both in the student's own culture and in other cultures. This dual commitment to original creative expression in – and reflection and critical thinking on – the arts of one's own and other cultures is what sets the Diploma Programme (DP) apart from most other high school arts curricula. It is clearly reflected in the content and assessment of the individual DP arts programmes; the differences are merely in the individual nature of each medium of expression.

In my experience in conducting over 40 workshops worldwide, for experienced teachers new to the DP the most surprising component of the DP arts is the element of critical thought and reflection, assessed through a written paper or a portfolio. Teachers, especially in music, are more used to written papers which focus on replication of factual knowledge, technical understanding of established forms, and sometimes historical detail. When they first undertake DP preparation with their students they often request help to deal with the new requirements. How to teach the students to analyse and reflect on the artistic products of other cultures is a particular concern. However, once they see samples of previous students' work and the type of questions asked in assessment, feedback is virtually unanimous that this is a desirable educational requirement. The infusion of critical reflective thought on the nature of artistic expression can actually improve standards of performance and help ensure that they are not just replications of what a teacher might believe to be the definitive performance. Nevertheless, some teachers more used to performance-only programmes worry that the extra intellectual requirements in the IB diploma arts programmes may compromise the standards of performance. They may be concerned about tertiary admissions, imagining that these demand a high level of technical competence and knowledge of historical facts, and little else. But tertiary institutions have moved away from this narrow focus for quite some time in the visual and theatre arts, and somewhat more recently in music as well. As a result, the additional familiarity with critical analysis actually gives students a distinct advantage with their study at tertiary level. In summary, teachers and parents can rest assured that the IB diploma arts programmes have been carefully structured to meet with the demands of even the most selective arts institutes.

Many national arts curricula place emphasis on the traditionally important arts of their culture. In music, for instance, Western music often features as the most important, if not the only, component of the music curriculum. While fully acknowledging the importance of 'local' arts that people can identify with, the DP arts curriculum takes a resolutely global perspective, in line with its overall aims. The practising artists, musicians, and actors in today's world are becoming more and more international and intercultural in their content, their technical demands, and their aesthetic views. Composers, playwrights, and visual artists now commonly fuse ideas and expressive devices from different cultural traditions in their work. The DP expects its arts students to be critically aware of these trends and to be able to practise them.

The expectation that students recognize the importance of arts across all cultures and times is not rooted in a principle of relativism. Quite the contrary, the student is required to address the issue of the *integrity* of an artistic expression, in terms of its technical qualities, its expressive qualities, its cultural relevance, its underlying belief system, and its aesthetic focus. The students are examined on these issues through written works and through their performance. No style or genre is prohibited; what counts is that students meet the criteria and required levels of competence applicable to that particular genre or style.

The overall IBO aims state a commitment to a holistic education, i.e. one that examines the interconnectedness of all knowledge and human enterprise (see Chapter 2). The specific vehicle the IBO uses to further its holistic aims is the TOK (Theory of Knowledge) course, which enables students to examine such issues as relativism, positivism, and the origin of aesthetic responses as well as their relation to other subjects. (Beauty is not the exclusive domain of the arts. The following sentiments are widely shared in the scientific community. One of the 20th century's great mathematicians, G. H. Hardy, said: 'A mathematician, like a painter or a poet, is a maker of patterns. If his patterns are more permanent than theirs, it is because they are made with ideas. … The mathematician's patterns, like the painter's or the poet's, must be beautiful: the ideas, like the colours or words, must fit together in a harmonious way. Beauty is the first test: there is no place in this world for ugly mathematics. … It may be very hard to define mathematical beauty, but … that does not prevent us from recognizing [it].' Albert Einstein put it this way: 'The most beautiful thing we can experience is the mysterious. It is the source of all true art and science.' Such quotes would make for excellent discussion items in DP arts classes, see section 1.3 below.) All IB subjects are expected to encourage the holistic view, but the IB arts courses make it explicit in their expectations for assessment, as we shall see. To illustrate how art connects with the world around it, this introductory section explores some examples of relationships between arts and science, arts and culture, and arts and politics, with the aim to give teachers the inspiration to add more examples of their own.

Figures 17.1 to 17.3 set out the outlines of the assessment process in the arts, which indicate how the IBO assesses the curriculum expectations listed above. These outlines are further clarified in the subsequent sections and in the individual arts sections.

1.2 Assessment outlines

Figure 17.1 Assessment outline for theatre arts

Theatre arts (HL or SL)		
	External assessment	**Internal assessment**
HL	**Research commission 25%** Written study (2,500 words). Candidate imagines he/she has been commissioned by an actor, designer etc. to contribute to a production of an unfamiliar theatrical tradition. Requires reflection, originality and critical analysis.	**Performance skills and theatre production 25%** Original performance and production work requiring reflection and critical analysis. Internally assessed, externally moderated.
	Practical play analysis 25% Oral presentation (20–30 mins). Application of social, intellectual, cultural contexts to the expression of a directorial vision for the prescribed text. Requires knowledge of social and intellectual context, plus reflection.	**Portfolio 15%** Written paper (4,500 words) Reflection on and critical analysis of performance and production. **Individual project (HL only) 10%** Reflection on candidate's development and responses.
SL	Identical except that the written study is 1,750 words, and the oral presentation is 15–20 mins.	Identical except that the portfolio written work is 3,000 words and SL candidates *do not* do an individual project. Both components count for 25%.

Figure 17.2 Assessment outline for music

Music (HL or SL)		
	External assessment	**Internal assessment**
HL	**Listening paper (2.5 hours) 30%** Five musical extracts and five compulsory questions, based on recorded examples on CD, requiring critical reflection and discussion of the socio-historical-cultural context. More than one cultural practice will be presented, but one question will be on a major set work.	**Solo performance 25%** 20 minutes (SL: 15 mins) approximately. Presented in one or more live performances and recorded for external moderation.
	Musical investigation 20% Written *media script* (explained in section 3.4) (1,200–1,500 words) to 'engage an audience'. Self-directed, independent study involving two distinct musical genres. Investigating cross-cultural relationships. Involves critical and analytic comment.	**Composition 25%** Three contrasting compositions (SL: two) to be presented. Original work in any genre or style. To be performed and recorded.
SL	Identical: HL and SL candidates even sit the same paper.	Students choose **one** of the above **or** they can do a **Group performance** 15–20 minutes long. Two or more public performances must be used (an option especially for those without prior experience). **50%**

Figure 17.3 Assessment outline for visual arts

Visual arts (HL or SL option A or SL option B)	
External assessment (by visiting examiner)	**Internal assessment** (externally moderated)
HL **Studio work 70%** Original art work plus a viva voce (live chat) component with a visiting examiner involving reflection and critical analysis.	**Research workbooks 30%** A journal tracking the student's progress during the course. Should contain independent critical research and analysis on artistic theories and practices, and comment on intellectual, emotional, cultural, historical and social dimensions of the visual arts.
SLA Identical to HL, while option SL B swaps external and internal components:	
SLB **Research workbooks 70%**	**Studio work 30%**

Note: even though the assessment content in HL and SL is identical, the greater amount of time spent in HL is expected to result in more sustained growth and commitment.

The similar structure of the HL and SL courses provides the school with welcome timetable flexibility: it is quite straightforward to teach HL and SL together in one class. To study SL does not necessarily mean a lower attainment, since many talented students study SL arts because of timetable constraints. In fact the standard expected of SL work is the same as that of HL – it is just that there is less of it. One does expect to see more growth and a more sustained commitment at HL though.

The standard of performance expected is consistent with the highest levels of attainment required on entry to tertiary-level institutions for those students aiming at that route. (Most tertiary institutions, especially in music, however, insist on HL for entry – to find out whether SL is acceptable, it is recommended to check directly with the target institution.) However, not all students may wish to become professional artists or performers, and so the DP arts courses cater to various levels of attainment, interest and involvement. Deficiencies in performing should be no barrier to any student, certainly not at SL.

The sections below illustrate in greater detail how one can teach the assessment components that raise regular questions at workshops. Section 1.3, on arts and science, aims to help understanding of how to promote a holistic view and historical awareness. Such awareness, in turn, will help students in their reflections and critical analysis.

1.3 The arts and science

Technology enjoys a vital presence in all the arts, and while the DP arts do not explicitly demand that students become involved in technology, those who do are awarded for it in the assessment. In the theatre, for example, staging requirements are heavily reliant on technology: think of scenery change, lighting, and amplification. While it is perfectly possible to make music with acoustic instruments without direct involvement of technology, there are implied scientific matters of acoustics, tuning, and possibly amplification. And then there are recordings, where technological issues are often paramount in such things as location (the acoustics of space; placements of microphones and speakers) and the quality of recording. Electronic music can be the medium of production in composition and performance. In the visual arts, computer-generated art work is permissible.

It is, however, mostly in music that science (rather than technology) becomes an important factor, since it intermingles with historical awareness. From the very earliest beginnings of Western music, science has played an integral part in musical thinking. From the proportional theory of the Pythagoreans, Plato listed the ratios that are thought to produce the most perfect and suitable musical sounds: 2:1 the octave; 3:2 the perfect 5th; and 4:3 the perfect 4th, are at the very foundation of Western harmonic and melodic structure. Such facts are important to the IB music programme: the beginnings of Western music in Ancient Greek thinking and its amazing development over more than 2,000 years, especially from the High Renaissance to the present. So powerful has this musical theory become in the West, especially because of its mathematical underpinning, that Western thinking has historically assumed an air of cultural superiority. However, it is important to realize that this is the result of a cultural way of thinking and arguing. It is not the musical truth for all time and all people.

For DP students, it is important to understand something of the nature of the Pythagorean theory, its development and dissemination, and its role as the cultural context of Western music. They should realize that the music inspiring the theory came from Ancient China, as did some of the Western tuning systems. A critical analysis and reflection on such issues helps students understand how interdependent cultures can be, and also how belief systems can emerge and become socially and politically important to a culture. The IBO firmly holds the view that no culture is privileged over another. But it is no good just saying that; it is important to examine why this is so, and to be able to argue convincingly for cultural parity.

Many cultures believe their music and visual art comes from the heavens. This is the case with the Balinese, the Australian Aborigines, and many cultural groups among the indigenous Americans. This fact affords a great opportunity for reflection on the ways in which these people receive their music, in dreams or trances, from the lips of long-dead ancestors. To a purely objective mind such things might seem fanciful; Western traditions emphasize objectivity, and many people will claim that such a mode of reception is unverifiable and therefore suspect. But the DP student should go further to question to what extent the experience of music is open to scientific enquiry. Do attempts at objectivity belie the true function and role of the arts in human life? Do we respond to music as we do because of the 'objective' acoustic content of the sounds, or because we have developed the habit and believe in the responses we make? There is a very rich historical context of this debate from Plato to the French encyclopaedists to current-day psychology, and students and teachers are encouraged to explore such history as well as current developments. Psychologists today study the effects of music in our everyday life by asking people to explain how they use music to construct their sense of reality, or to confirm it, or to support their sense of identity. Others experiment with certain types of music to see how it affects our purchasing habits. One such study recently found that when Italian music was played in a wine store in parts of the UK, people purchased more

Italian wine than before. For the DP music students, the effects of music on people are a crucial part of the critical and reflective aspects of the programme. They are required to develop some understanding of the kind of issues sketched above (though not necessarily of the particular examples listed above), and are assessed on it in both the listening paper and the musical investigation (see figure 17.2). Interested students could take any of these examples further and develop it in the musical investigation component.

It is the same with visual arts. During the European Enlightenment, for example, the theory of colour claimed that because of its physical properties, blue was a cold colour. Gainsborough proved this wrong by painting 'The Blue Boy', a very 'warm' product to the eye. Today however, you still find that old beliefs die hard when you discuss the decoration of a house or apartment! Certain colours are believed to engender specific moods and atmospheres. DP students are expected to have some knowledge of the issues involving colour and mood: is it entirely socially generated, or is there something to the physics of the colour spectrum? Likewise, consider the fact that computer programs (defining beauty in terms of symmetry) do an excellent job in predicting the outcomes of beauty contests. A worldwide survey involving a series of carefully chosen abstract paintings elicited the same overall responses, independent of culture and education. What does this tell us about visual perception? And how does this tally with the fact that all cultures still have their own beliefs and interpretations of visual phenomena? One could also talk about the more dramatic impact of visual arts on society. The gruesome photographs of the Vietnam War are still etched in many people's memories; and these had arguably more impact on public opinion than 'scientific' statistical casualty reports. Students are assessed on their ability to deal with such matters in their studio work, in their research workbooks, and in their interview with the visiting examiner.

In theatre arts, there are important connections with the social and human sciences. Important developments include the emergence of the psycho-dramatist and the socio-political work of Bertolt Brecht, and more recently Augusto Boal, who construct social realities that will encourage performers and audiences to create judgement in role. This is integral to Brecht's 'Verfremdungs-effekt' (Alienation Technique) and to Boal's Theatre of the Oppressed. A classic example of how theatre spawned new science is the radio show *The War of the Worlds* in October 1938 by Orson Welles and his Mercury Theater, which told of an invasion by Martians which reportedly led to mass panic (although some claim the media grossly exaggerated the panic). Some gems from this time that would make for great discussions in theatre classes: in the *New York Tribune*, Dorothy Thompson foresaw that the broadcast would alert politicians on how to use the power of mass communications to manipulate the public. 'All unwittingly, Mr Orson Welles and the Mercury Theater of the Air have made one of the most fascinating and important demonstrations of all time,' she wrote. 'They have proved that a few effective voices, accompanied by sound-effects, can convince masses of people of a totally unreasonable, completely fantastic proposition.' The events were adopted by the new science of social psychology after Hadley Cantril, a professor at Princeton, published one of the classics of mass communication research, *The Invasion From Mars: A Study in the Psychology of Panic*.

It should certainly come as no surprise that many politicians these days are taking speech coaching to sound more sincere and convincing. The way we say things is as important as what we are saying.

1.4 Culture and the arts

The IB arts programmes encourage a study of local indigenous arts, so that the student can actually see and communicate with nearby artists and thus experience living art work. The syllabus component on culture in the DP arts is not very prescriptive, enabling teachers to combine the DP and existing local school programmes effectively.

It is not at all expected that DP arts students have an encyclopaedic knowledge of all the different practices across the world's cultures; that is impossible in any case. Also, it is not necessary to have a wide-ranging knowledge in order to understand the concept of cultural differences in artistic production and reception. It is the *nature* of the diversity that is the point, not its extent or extensive detail. One could consider the following examples as indicative of the kind of variety that students should be exposed to (an experience that can be bewildering to a student with a previously monocultural viewpoint and experience!).

The Indonesian theatre, in which the Balinese Hindu express their being through the Ramayana epics, involves the expressive use of elaborate masks and dance movements requiring extensive toe and eye movement as well as the use of fingers bent backwards at impossible angles. These have no equivalent in other cultures, but are understandable in terms of their dissemination across the entire Hindu world. The all-male Kabuki rituals and Noh plays of Japan, where inscrutable masks hide the human face and voices are in falsetto mode throughout, makes for another interesting example. One might think at first glance that it has few equivalents outside Japan. However, the practice of all-male productions in the theatre is very common in Western history where boys played the parts of women, and castrati sang women's parts in opera. The DP student is expected to develop some understanding of the nature of different cultural practices, though not necessarily those cited above.

The *different elements* used in different cultural practices can also be a focus, and can figure in the written question papers in both music and theatre arts, as well as in the portfolio in the visual arts programmes. For example, music students could examine the type of sounds found in different cultures: the exploitation of the frequency spectrum of the didgeridoo by the Australian Aborigines using tongue and mouth movements as well as circular breathing techniques; a traditional flute of the Hawaiians played through the nose; the throat music (or *katajak*) of the Arctic Inuit which is voiceless in the technical sense of using the vocal folds; the gamelan ensembles of the Javanese or Balinese with their unique tuning systems; the symphony orchestra of Europe with their Pythagorean tunings; and the various sounds of the drums and guitars of rock music world-wide with their extensive use of noise. Music in every society has its own special sounds and its own special meanings. To give an example, note how often movies involving dramatic chases in wild landscapes play horn music, which can be traced back to the use of horns in hunts in ancient Europe. Although the specific elements above are not compulsory knowledge, what is compulsory (and examined in the written paper) is an understanding of the general principles of how one examines the nature of the elements making up the production.

It is similar with the visual arts. From the sand paintings of the indigenous people of the American Southwest, the decorated blankets and masks of the Kwakiutl people of western Canada, the stone carvings of ancient Maya, or the still-life paintings and drawings of 18th- and 19th-century Europeans, each visual shape and pattern has its own special cultural meaning, role and function in society.

Artistic products are known by the people of the culture to touch something deep inside their being, something so intensely personal that words are inadequate to express it. Today, many young people across the world find meaning and relevance to their lives in the music of popular culture. The IB invites its students to critically explore and experience such contemporary trends.

The intention is not just to learn about what cultures have to offer; students should also critically examine it. Is there a place in current-day society for all-male theatre? Is Chinese theatre in Singapore worth exploring when hardly anyone shows up? More generally, is it worth maintaining artistic traditions when the new generation doesn't care? How come that Balinese dance and music is still alive today while some other local art expressions struggle to survive? How is it that Mozart is still being played all over the world? What will happen with the music of Madonna and the Rolling Stones? What do they say about the world or the region of origin at that time? How did they change the human landscape? Should society move to resist the more controversial forms of rap music? What value does it have and what does it say about society? And so on. Whichever cultural product the DP students study, they should understand its backgrounds and feel comfortable discussing questions such as these.

1.5 Production of art works

Production of original artistic works is essential in the DP arts. Students can produce work in whatever medium they choose, provided it displays originality and personal commitment. The use of imitation or pastiche is not acceptable in any DP artistic production. The originality of the student's work must be demonstrated in workbooks, in comments supplied to examiners accompanying art works, and in response to questions asked in face-to-face interviews with the external examiner in the visual arts. As far as music is concerned, this marks a significant departure from the requirements of many national programmes where imitation and pastiche are required in examination.

DP students will find that tertiary institutions all over the world share the IBO's commitment to breadth as well as its focus on the role of arts in society, both historical and geographical. The days when, say, in music, students studied just the music of the European traditions of the last few centuries and nothing else are gone. Even the most traditional of the tertiary institutions in music now have popular music in their syllabuses, as well as the music of many different cultures across the world. The same applies to the visual arts and theatre arts. To this extent, the DP is both an ideal preparation for tertiary study in the arts and a rewarding and meaningful study for students aiming at other futures.

1.6 Using one's own experiences in art production

Sometimes the events or personal feelings that inspire a work of art lie so deep in the psyche as to be almost impossible to unravel – you just know! That is the power of the arts for the human experience.

Ideas of links between art expression and social or political context have inspired many DP students in the past. I remember in particular marking the work of a group of students who had lived in Sarajevo during the terrible bombing and atrocities of the 1990s war in the Balkans. They produced a combination of visual art and music for their expressive productions at HL in both music and visual arts. Their work was clearly a form of catharsis for them, but it also contained clear political and social comment in both the music, much of which was electronically generated, and the visual arts. This is the point: to produce an expression that goes beyond mere technique and which involves a commentary on the life around you through art; to take risks and be as creative and original as you dare to be.

This need not always be concerned with events of such magnitude as a world-shattering regional war; it can also be concerned with a more personal situation. Students often use their experience of falling in love as a basis for their compositions. Lost love, and current love, are popular themes, and even adoration from afar, 'a young man wanting to know a particular girl but hasn't yet made the move', occurs quite frequently. Other interesting compositions have been offered based on existing popular songs, where students produce not just a 'cover' version, but a genuinely new work with alterations, even electronic distortion.

The point is that as students attempt to find expression for themselves in any of the arts, they will relate more closely to the work of other artists from different times and different cultures and the work these artists have produced in response to their environment.

1.7 Combining the DP and local demands

It is often the case with the DP that the school has to juggle demands of local school-leaving examinations with the demands of the DP, and the two may not be all that compatible. A most likely commonality is the need for performance or composition for the student in both the local examination and the DP. A most likely difference will be found in the DP demands for critical thinking and reflection, rather than just performance or composition and the study of set works. However, many aspects of both the DP and local programmes might overlap, making it easier to teach both the DP group and those taking just the local examination in one class. In such a case the teacher will need to decide whether or not there is the time and desire to involve non-DP students in the essential DP component of critical analysis and reflection. Some schools insist that their students take both the DP and the local examination, in which case it becomes essential that common components are identified early to avoid timetable mishaps. In particular, we recommend that the teacher examine the suggested number of hours of teaching required for both DP (both levels) and the local programme as well as the number of hours of overlap. Each component must be planned carefully to ensure that all demands of either programme are met successfully. Deadlines are important in this respect, particularly those involving the submission of work.

1.8 End-note

The above sections highlight some important features of the assessment requirements of the DP arts subjects. Although specific examples are described here, it is important to emphasize the open nature of the *content* requirements in the DP arts. This should be distinguished from the compulsory *skills* requirements in assessment involving reflection, critical analysis, understanding of cultural and historical embedding, as well as the demands for originality in art work submitted for assessment. Full details of syllabus content can be found in the *Vade Mecum*, and more details on the individual arts subject can be found in the relevant subject guides. What follows in section 2 and 4 are brief summaries of the theatre arts and the visual arts programmes, based on the subject guides of 1999 (meant for programmes to start in 2002) and interviews with some current chief examiners and deputy chief examiners. Section 3 features a more detailed account of the music programme that includes comments from current DP teachers, students, and ex-students.

2 Theatre arts

2.1 Nature of the subject

The theatre arts subject guide makes the following observations:

- Theatre is one of the oldest, most universal and most profound human activities.
- Theatre has its own ends, its own means and must be taught on its own terms.
- Theatre's work begins in playfulness, and in this formless and directionless play lies work of the most rigorous and valuable kind.
- As Alfred Hitchcock said, 'Theatre is life without the boring parts'.
- But theatre is not life any more than landscape painting is nature.
- The truth of the theatre lies in its artifice.
- In its essence all theatre requires is an actor, two planks and a passion, but at a pinch it does not need the two planks.

The above succinctly reflects the nature of theatre and its conception as an IB diploma programme subject. It is live communication, and it requires a large variety of different skills. These range from actors, directors, playwrights, designers, carpenters, painters, costumiers, musicians, visual artists and electricians, as well as accountants and publicity agents. It is this complex variety of skills and techniques that come together as a production in front of an audience in the modern theatre. But in some cultures it all works differently and is sometimes inspired by other motivations as well as by different emotional and spiritual needs.

2.2 Course content

The aims of the programme in theatre arts are to help students in the following:

- to understand the nature of the theatre
- to understand it by making it as well as studying it

- to understand it not only with their minds but with their senses, their bodies and their emotions
- to understand the forms it takes in cultures other than their own
- and through this understanding better to understand themselves, their society and their world.

There are five major parts to the syllabus:

- performance skills
- world theatre studies
- practical play analysis
- theatre production
- individual project.

HL candidates cover all five parts while SL candidates cover the first four only. All these parts are related by strong links that were explored in the previous sections. It is important to realize that theatre arts is not an acting course. Students will need to develop their knowledge of major developments and techniques of theatre in more than one culture, and develop an ability to interpret and illuminate playscripts and texts analytically and imaginatively. The ability to perform before an audience is essential, as are demonstrations of acting techniques although the course places similar emphasis upon all aspects of theatre practice. Knowledge of production is equally essential, as is the ability to research topics imaginatively in theatre history and current practice. The focus is on imaginative, creative and original contributions, not mere replication. Below, we discuss the five syllabus components in a little more detail.

Performance skills

It is essential that teachers encourage students to take risks in performance, but in an imaginative and controlled way, through appropriate research into the characters they play, appropriate use of physical and technical resources, and through working cooperatively with others. Every student must perform before an audience.

World theatre studies

The basis of this part is a practical exploration of theatre from different cultures. Here teachers are encouraged to use local resources as much as possible. Different theatre conventions, traditions and practices are to be explored through action and involvement. HL candidates are expected to study in detail at least three texts from different traditions and cultures which reflect three contrasting theatrical practices. At SL, only two are required. The theatre arts subject guide provides examples of texts and practices, as well as suggesting approaches which may be creatively incorporated into a school programme as a whole.

Practical play analysis

This part requires the student to go much further than merely studying texts. The expectation is that students will apply their knowledge of theatre practices from the perspective of a *director*. The aim is to develop the ability and understanding required for turning a text into a theatrical production. The process of bringing the play to life is the focus, and should include demonstrating an understanding of the relationship between the themes of the play, actions of characters, expected effects on an audience, and the directorial concept for realization on stage. The student-director needs to learn to imagine the play on stage, even though they may not be required to actually direct a complete play. In other words, the practical play analysis is an imaginative exercise in direction, encouraging the student to see a script as a 'blueprint for action'. There is no specification that the ideas must incorporate different cultural perspectives, or that the student has to impose a cultural tradition upon a script. The practicalities are quite simple. The Board specifies three plays; the student chooses one and then can present an entirely individual concept. The play analysis rewards *practical imagination* and not reproduction of a studied tradition.

Theatre production

Students should be involved in at least two productions themselves at HL, and one at SL. They may create an original piece or use an established text. This part puts into practice the work required in the previous parts, and provides a practical demonstration of the links between the other parts of the syllabus although it cannot be a duplication of other parts of the course, i.e. the individual project cannot be counted as part of the student's involvement in theatre production. The aim is that the student acquires the necessary skills of the theatre practitioner's craft and an understanding of how to deal with the multi-faceted elements of creating a production for public performance, including methods of organizing and developing ideas. Suggested methods and approaches include workshops, character-building exercises, acting exercises, play-writing and script creation, choreography or musical direction, design, and technical aspects of stage management, as well as administration and promotion.

Individual project (HL only)

This must not be a duplication of work done elsewhere in the programme. It provides the student with an opportunity to heighten knowledge and skill in a specific aspect of performance and production in greater depth than is possible in the four parts above. It might include devising and presenting a solo performance, creating a major role in a performance, even writing an original play or directing a piece. The project provides the opportunity for students to display a high level of creativity, originality, ability and commitment to challenging and risk-taking in order to demonstrate their passion in theatre arts.

It is important to stress that the study should be a practical undertaking. The subject guide states: 'As far as possible, the teacher should assess the merit of the work itself, rather than merely evaluating the record of this work' (page 26). In other words, where possible, performance and direction work should result in a public production, design work should result in a model, costume work should result in an article of clothing.

2.3 Assessment

The assessment outline was presented in figure 17.1. Below, we provide some clarification.

External assessment

HL and SL both feature the *research commission* and the *practical play analysis* in their external assessment. The research commission is presented in the form of a personal letter to the hypothetical actor, designer, or director (approximately 2,500 words at HL and 1,750 words at SL). The practical play analysis is in the form of an oral presentation of a directorial vision for a prescribed text lasting 20–30 minutes for HL and 15–20 minutes for SL. Each is assessed using a given set of criteria, with descriptors for each attainment level. The subject guide has details of the criteria and descriptors of levels of attainment. It should be noted, however, that there continues to be heated debate about the research commission. Schools report that the information in the guide and advice from both the Board and the Online Curriculum Centre (OCC) still fail to define the exact nature of the task and how it is crucially and evidentially different from the play analysis component. 'The point, purpose and nature of this component are somewhat muddled in their conception, and certainly vague in specific direction. Students are often at a loss as to what is exactly expected of them as theatre artists. Many colleagues are equally confused,' reports Jonathan Carter, Head of Drama at the United World College of South East Asia. The research commission as it stands is the subject of a possible syllabus review. In view of this, we elect not to elaborate on it here.

Internal assessment

This involves *performance skills and theatre production* as well as a *portfolio* (both HL and SL), while HL students in addition need to do an *individual project*. The first of these assessment components is carried out by the teacher and concerns the candidate's work in class activities and theatre productions during the course. The assessment criteria include commitment, technical skills, working with others, and practical understanding of theatre techniques. The assessment is summative, taking account of evidence gathered over a period of time from a variety of activities. It cannot be moderated by the IBO in view of the fact that it is carried out throughout the course. The *portfolio* should be a selective record of the candidate's learning and experiences throughout the course. 'It should be neither a scrapbook nor a record of triumphs' (subject guide, page 25), but rather a review of the work done during the course, and it should include personal reflection and various stages of development. The portfolio should be well organized, legible and literate. The assessment criteria include range and quality of work, ability to select and edit, and quality of reflection. The *individual project* (HL only) should be documented in written form and should include problems and difficulties encountered, as well as future possibilities for further development. Assessment criteria for the individual project include independent research, and technical skill. The subject guide has the details.

3 Music

3.1 Nature of the subject

In the commercial world of entertainment, one will be hard pressed to find a performance without music. In movies, television commercials, even on news bulletins, music is present. Music is one of the most important things in life to many people, especially to the young. The very ubiquity of music presents challenges for educational institutions (such as, how much attention should be accorded to popular music?) and the DP music programme tackles them in the context of its commitment to intellectual rigour, breadth and depth, and the world community of different cultures and beliefs (details in section 3.7).

The subject guide poses the question: How might the intelligent and sensitive performer, composer and listener prepare to hear 'the music of the universe seeking to be heard'? This particular reference is an attribute to the many world cultures that believe music is present in the universe and humans receive it as a gift, either in trances or in dreams, or through visitations by long-dead ancestors. The study of music, the guide goes on, allows for exploration of the shared human perceptions and emotions across different socio-cultural environments. Moreover, a 'vibrant musical education fosters curiosity in, and sensitivity to, the musical worlds which surround us'. It is in such statements that the tone and focus of the IB diploma music programme can be caught and understood.

3.2 Course content

The aims of the music programme are to help students to:

- explore and enjoy the diversity of music throughout the world
- develop skills to recognize, speculate, analyse, identify, hypothesize and discriminate
- develop creativity, knowledge, skills, and understanding through performance and composition
- develop their individual potential as musicians, and explore their own preferences and style
- use appropriate terminology to describe and reflect critical understanding of music
- develop acute auditory perceptual skills in response to music
- develop knowledge and understanding of socio-cultural aspects of music.

HL students are further expected to

- develop performance skills through solo music making
- develop compositional skills

while SL students need to

- develop *either* performance skills (in solo or in ensemble) *or* compositional skills.

The externally assessed part of the syllabus is called *musical perception and analysis* (assessed identically for SL and HL in the listening paper and the musical investigation), while the internally assessed part involves a *solo performance* in voice or instrument (assessed in one or more recitals before an audience), a *composition* (assessed in three contrasting compositions which are to be performed and recorded), or a *group performance* as a member of an ensemble (assessed in two or more public performances). HL needs to do the first two of the internal components, while SL must choose one of the three. All the internally assessed parts will be discussed in detail in the sections below, but we begin with a clarification of the externally assessed part of the syllabus: the *musical perception and analysis*.

3.3 Musical perception and analysis (HL and SL)

This component comprises a study of a major set work (MSW) set by the IBO as well as a study of different musical genres and styles, focusing on socio-historical and cultural context and musical characteristics such as melodic structure, form, use of improvisation, rhythm, etc. The student is expected to use not only the score of the MSW in the examination, but also some previously unseen scores provided in the examination. A compact disc (CD) containing an excerpt from the MSW as well as four other works provide the material on which questions are asked. Students are expected to be able to notate parts of the extract for which they might not have the score, as well as comment on such matters as style, use of instruments, formal structure, socio-cultural or historical context, and manner of performance practice.

Students are expected to have some understanding of historical Western musical practices as exemplified, for example, in the contrast between a 16th-century motet and an 18th-century string quartet, or in the difference between the essentially modal contrapuntal style of compositions during the 16th and early 17th centuries, as compared with the diatonically based harmonic and melodic styles which evolved during the 18th and 19th centuries. Examination questions will expect such knowledge as well as recognition of different styles from Western musical history. For example, candidates may be asked to identify the stylistic content of arrangements of a well-known song, which might be quite different in style or genre from the original. Candidates are expected to be able to comment on the arrangement and its relationship with the context of the original song.

At least one example of extracts on the CD set for the examination will be from some world culture. The students are expected to extrapolate from their studies of different musical cultures, rather than be an expert in every one. The study of two or three different world cultures in music should provide the necessary tools to analyse, comment on and critically evaluate other pieces of world music, even if the student has never heard such music before.

The choice of cultures or musical practices to be studied for the world music component is left entirely up to the individual school. The IBO encourages schools to make use of local practices so that students can gain experience of live performance and, perhaps, interact with the performers. In North America, for example, the local indigenous music-making of any type might include native Americans as well as music from the early Spanish settler traditions. If teachers decide to study such music with their classes, they should focus on such things as use of instruments, ways of playing instruments, use of the voice, melodic and rhythmic constructions, formal attributes of the music, as well as its socio-cultural contexts.

However, it is advisable to introduce students to a variety of different cultural practices from across the world, since a major objective of the music programme is to encourage students to be aware of the variety and complexity of different musical practices worldwide. The type of questions asked in the listening paper regarding world music may require the student to comment on what they have heard, and to relate this to any appropriate socio-cultural context and musical structure. Madonna, for example, can be placed in the context of early feminism since she attracted many millions of young girls to awake to their sexuality in her song 'Like a Virgin' (which came in for special criticism in the US Congress in the 1980s). Specific knowledge of the culture involved is not necessarily required, but candidates would do well to recognize some specific instruments from among those used in world music, for example the gamelan, or the tabla, or the shakuhachi flute, and so on. At the very least, candidates should be able to distinguish between stringed and blown instruments, or between different types of percussion instruments.

Assessment of the questions on the four examples of music outside the major set work in the listening paper is based on specific criteria and descriptors of levels of achievement. The four criteria are: *aural perception*, *technical language*, *structural analysis* and *context*. These criteria provide a good sense of the major areas of study required for both Western musical history and world music. In each there are six levels of attainment ranging from a mark of 0 (for an answer that displays no knowledge at all), to level 5 (for an excellent answer). For example, if the candidate mentions nothing at all about the cultural context of an extract, then the mark allocated for that criterion will be zero. For instance, if a modern popular song has been arranged for a baroque ensemble in the style of a concerto grosso, and the candidate does not recognize the concerto grosso style, and does not realize that it is an arrangement for this specific instrumental ensemble of a song normally sung by a popular singer in a popular style, then clearly no sense of context is present. The ideal answer in this case would be to recognize the original popular song and its context, which is almost certainly to be named in the question paper, and to explain the arrangement in terminology appropriate to the baroque form of concerto grosso, commenting on how the arrangement has utilized the musical elements of the popular song in the arrangement. Obviously, if the candidate knows nothing about the concerto grosso, this would be a difficult question to answer. But such a lack of knowledge would not preclude candidates from obtaining a reasonable mark purely by making intelligent comments about the musical elements, even if they do not know the appropriate terminology. Such an answer would be unlikely to gain full marks, but it could easily be awarded high marks for intelligent perception and accurate description of contents. This is the point: the IBO does not require encyclopaedic knowledge, but rather intelligent and critical comment based on previous study and applied with care and accuracy.

3.4 Musical investigation (HL and SL)

The basic idea of the musical investigation is to encourage the student to carry out an independent investigation into the relationship between two *different* identifiable musical genres from any traditions, cultures or regions of the world, with a focus on one or more pieces of music from each. The investigation must be presented in the form of a 1,200–1,500-word *media script*, which is like a potential magazine, radio or TV script for a public presentation.

The musical investigation is the equivalent of the research commission in theatre arts and the research workbook in the visual arts. However, it is a component new to the music assessment procedures, introduced only in 2002, and the IBO reports that the purpose of this investigation is not yet fully understood by schools. Notably the concept of genre (versus that of style) and the concept of media script have given rise to confusion. It should be noted that the idea of the media script is still under development and that significant changes cannot be ruled out, so it is important to study the latest editions of the subject guide and to keep an eye out for curriculum reviews. The following is based on some observations by the current chief examiner, expressly for this chapter, on which I have elaborated a bit.

The intention of the musical investigation is that the student has an opportunity to learn about and become involved in musical traditions that are different from the student's own time and place. One example given in the subject guide tells of a Chilean who grew up hearing indigenous Andean music but learns to play the electric guitar from listening to heavy metal music. His investigation involved two pieces featuring Jimi Hendrix as compared with computer-generated sounds of another composition and the candidate's own experimentation with this electronic medium. Another example cited is where a pianist from the UK investigated the use of indigenous music from Central Europe in the compositions of Béla Bartók. When deciding on suitable titles for the musical investigation, Miles Tranter from the United World College of South East Asia reports that the department found it helpful to simply insist that the music be chosen from two different *cultures* (focusing the official requirement which talks about two different *genres*). So to give another example, one successful musical investigation might be the use of voice in Western pop and Indian folk dance songs with an analysis of one piece from each genre. One title that would *not* be successful is 'A comparison of Western Opera (*Don Giovanni*) and The Musical (*Les Miserables*)'.

Students often confuse *genre* with *style* and more generally misunderstand the term genre. As a result, it will be very difficult to successfully engage all the assessment criteria, so even at the risk of repeating things, it may be worthwhile to elaborate the issue here. Genre, as defined in the music subject guide, refers to socio-historical context and/or geographic region. Indonesia's gamelan music is a different genre from Western symphonic music, and hard rock is different from soul, for example. Style refers to such musical features as melodic structure, form, harmony, rhythm, and use of instruments. Style may change within genre, as has been the case with the development of Western music over the last 400 years: Mozart and Tchaikovsky come from the Western Classical genre but they represent two different styles. Another common mistake for students is to equate genre with performer. Again, distinctions between different popular music artists are generally distinctions in style, not in genre – think of Frank Zappa (a unique style in the rock and jazz genre), Prince (a unique style in the pop genre) or Astor Piazolla (a unique style within the tango genre). The point of an investigation considering two different genres is really, as stressed above, to make comparisons between different *cultural* practices.

It is advisable not to make the genre too broad nor too abstract, and to make sure that the two genres have a musical link. For example, Western opera as compared with Chinese opera provides far too broad a task for comparison. A comparison of the use of solo voice in performances in Western and Chinese operas is better. Popular music is another far too complex genre to consider as a whole; the 'disco movement of the eighties' may be more appropriate. The teacher should advise students carefully to ensure that a candidate can realistically cope with the chosen genres within the 1,200–1,500 word limit.

There is much discussion on the IBO website forum with regard to the interpretation of the style and genre issue. The site also features a lot more examples of suitable musical investigation titles.

The media script could be a straightforward narration or a conversation or an interview. It could also be in the form of a dramatic presentation. One impressive music investigation reported by the chief examiner was presented in the form of a literary drama. Candidates should imagine the audience, and how they might best engage their interest. Some schools report that they have successfully interpreted the media script as 'an article for a specialist music magazine'. This interpretation enables the students to use musical and technical language, and therefore ensures that issues of presentation do not override the musical content and depth of the investigation.

The investigation is externally assessed through descriptors which categorize levels of achievement from *very poor* (for example, only one genre has been mentioned) to *excellent* where two clear genres are described, excellent comparisons are made, similarities and differences have been explored 'with intelligence and ingenuity, resulting in an investigation which is articulate, convincing and engaging, showing excellent command of technical language' (music subject guide). The descriptors are clear for experienced music instructors and allow teachers to give sound advice to the students.

Care needs to be taken over the use of websites. Apart from potential problems with plagiarism, the information on some websites may not be reliable or the website might be a form of advertising masquerading as research information. The teacher should provide as much help as possible to the student during the drafting period, short of editing the work for the student or making suggestions for content which should rightly be made by the student only.

3.5 Performance

There are two types of performance that count towards assessment: the *solo performance* (mandatory for HL and optional for SL) and *group performance* (optional for SL only).

Solo performance

Candidates should prepare one or more solo recitals for the solo performance. A single instrument or voice is required, and although candidates are able to perform on more than one instrument or on instrument and voice, it is advisable to present the best performance possible rather than to attempt to stretch the capabilities of the candidate too broadly. No extra reward is given for performance on more than one instrument. The performance is to be given before an audience, but the recording for assessment may contain items recorded on different occasions. The candidate should present their best work for assessment, and this should be based on two years of sustained practice and rehearsal time. Assessment of the solo performance will be by criteria and descriptions of levels of attainment. There are four criteria: *overall impression, technical competence, style and interpretation*, and *repertoire*. In each case the descriptors range from 0 (no achievement) to 5 (excellence achieved in technical competence, control, and mastery of technical challenge).

Group performance

The optionally available group performance at SL provides an opportunity for students who are not primarily performers or composers to participate in the IB music programme. The group performance is ideal for students who are relative beginners but who play in an ensemble or in a rock band or aspire to do so. Doing what they like will count towards their assessment! No wonder schools and many students have responded enthusiastically to this opportunity.

It should be made clear that the ensemble is assessed as a whole and not the individual performer within the ensemble. Therefore each member of a particular ensemble will receive the same mark. This strikes many teachers as unfair, but the IBO's response is that if one performer is markedly weaker then he or she shouldn't be in the ensemble, while one that is markedly stronger could opt for the solo performance instead. Interpreted like this, schools report that this option is working very well.

Assessment of the group performance is based on holistic descriptors with five levels of attainment. The assessment criteria are not unusual and should be familiar to music teachers used to other educational systems.

3.6 Composition

Composition for both HL and SL requires a notated score and recordings of each work. HL requires three works, and SL two. The works may use any media, including home-made instruments, electronics or computer-generated sounds, and of course more traditional instruments and voice. Notations of any type can be utilized provided they are appropriate for the piece. An audio recording of the pieces must be supplied, unless there are special circumstances, in which case permission must be obtained beforehand from the IBO. Candidates should also provide an explanation of the content of the piece, so that the external moderator may have some idea what the candidate is aiming at.

There are no real constraints on the style or genre of the compositions, except the time length, which should be strictly between 5 and 15 minutes. Assessment is by criteria (and descriptors of the corresponding achievement levels). These are: *overall impression, structural and stylistic integrity, technical knowledge of the medium or media, control and development of musical elements* and *notation*. Achievement levels range from zero to excellent.

The compositions offered for assessment should be original works composed by the student. Over the years, there have been some memorable compositions produced by DP students, which overall demonstrate an incredible range of musical creative thought and action. They range widely over media, content, performance practice, and technical production. At one extreme, I remember as chief examiner receiving a composition from one young man which comprised a single sheet of paper with the word 'Guitar' in large letters at the top, and a square shape in the middle with the words 'My composition'. This was probably an attempt to emulate John Cage's famous piece *4' 33"*, which is usually performed on the piano, where the pianist closes the lid for the first movement, and opens it at the end, and so on. Needless to say, the candidate earned zero for this piece of nonsense. Cage was emulating the visual artist Robert Rauschenberg in his range of white paintings, where the visual experience was provided by the perceiver. This candidate obviously knew nothing at all about the provenance of Cage's piece, thinking it was merely a piece of silence. If students wish to emulate such works they should know a great deal about the work in question and be able to provide the same complex perceptual background which underpinned the Cage work.

I also remember a most creative composition which arranged a Beatles song utilizing various electronic means of manipulation. This was extremely well done, and earned very high marks. Another very fine piece was a complete first movement of a symphony, fully orchestrated, complete with recording of the school orchestra performing it. This was a tour de force indeed, and while it was not very creative (as the arrangement of the Beatles song was), it was a very fine piece of technical writing and scoring. Another very creative piece was by two young women from Bosnia who wrote compositions, including some electronics, illustrating their responses to the bombing around them during the Bosnian war, and allied these with paintings they submitted for the visual arts programme. These were not only very moving, for obvious reasons, but they were very personal, very creative and expressive, and highly competent works technically. There seems to be no limit to the potential range of ideas and creative expressions which young people are capable of, given the freedom to compose in their own style. This is the strength of the IBO composition component in music, and what makes it such an exciting part of the DP music experience.

3.7 DP music and Western historical technical expertise

Of all the arts subjects, music has the most historical baggage. This exerts considerable influence over curricula in music in every country where formal education is in place. The enormous weight of Western historical traditions in music, stemming especially from the 16th-century High Renaissance in Italy to our 21st century, presents serious problems of choice and selection for all music curricula in any school or university. How much historical knowledge is enough, since obviously one cannot cover everything that happened in 400 years of musical activity and development? The rise of various electronic media of dissemination during the 20th century, and especially the commercial entertainment media, has presented formal music education with considerable problems as well. To what extent should we include popular music in all its genres and styles in any formal music education? Virtually all young people today have an interest in or are involved with popular music, which means that any music programme which excludes it faces real problems of credibility in the eyes of many potential students. Yet, can one be considered educated in music with only a knowledge and experience of popular music? The answer must be no. Furthermore, considering the international character of the DP, there has to be a substantial component of music from different cultures. The IB diploma music programme is a compromise between all these competing demands. It seeks to develop understanding in breadth and depth across cultures and times, but at the same time it allows for sufficient choice to enable students to continue a musical specialization or emphasis on what they like best.

It is a problem in some IB schools that the music departments still focus too much on (Western-style) performance only. This won't gain high grades in the assessment, leading some teachers to confide that they feel the DP music programme is a 'soft option'. We have already said in the introduction that teachers need not be concerned about tertiary admissions: the IB diploma music programme's philosophy is fully in line with that of leading tertiary institutions. The DP music programme's rationale is further based on the fact that many very fine young performers will, and should, already have reached a very high standard of performance by the age of 16, before they start the DP. The enriching nature of the DP music programme will thus supply a necessary breadth of understanding. A performer who is technically very proficient but little else has small chance of success. Technique is not enough on its own, and in the Western traditions it never has been.

Music is not the sole preserve of the West. Just as the students who are obsessed by the world of popular music must extend their knowledge, expertise and experience beyond such narrow confines, so a student who is expert in any cultural tradition must do the same. In view of this, the IB music programme can accommodate the highest levels of technical accomplishment in performance in any genre or style, but at the same time it is intended to ensure that the student enjoys a broad-based musical experience across different cultures and different times.

4 Visual arts

4.1 Nature of the subject

First and foremost, the IBO regards the practices and theories of visual art as essentially cultural manifestations. Expression in the visual arts 'is characterized by forms of visual representation which reflect the cultures of different societies … and which are embedded in particular societies and cultures'. The visual arts subject guide goes on to state that 'artistic learning requires a high level of cognitive activity that is both intellectual and emotional … and for students to communicate visually they must locate themselves within a cultural context, or contexts, from which to discover and develop appropriate techniques'. It is important that both students and teachers are very clear about what is meant by 'culture'. Teachers have found it helpful here to refer to the description of culture in the trans-disciplinary subject world cultures (see Chapter 18).

The subject guide further states that 'engagement in the arts promotes a sense of identity and makes a unique contribution to the development of each student … and provides students with the opportunity to develop a critical and intensely personal view of themselves in relation to the world' (1999 subject guide, for the examination starting in 2002, page 3). A related aim is to enable students to learn about themselves and others through individual and (where appropriate) collaborative engagement with the visual arts.

The above statements illustrate the extent to which visual art education has moved from a purely technical affair concentrating on acquiring various techniques of representation in visual media to a much broader-based experience requiring reflection and critical analysis. The visual arts programme requires the student to be self-examining, self-critical and self-aware in more overt and intrusive ways than the other arts programmes. Students taking the visual arts should be aware of these demands at the outset.

There are three possible courses for the student to follow: in the HL course candidates are required to demonstrate their abilities in both studio work and research; in Standard Level option A (SLA) the emphasis is more on studio work

Figure 17.4 Recommended hours of teaching for the visual arts courses

	HL	SL A	SL B
Studio work	168 hours (70%)	105 hours (70%)	45 hours (30%)
Research workbook	72 hours (30%)	45 hours (30%)	105 hours (70%)

than on research; and in Standard Level option B (SLB) the emphasis is reversed. Figure 17.4 illustrates this (note that the number of hours correspond exactly to the assessment weights of 30% and 70% displayed in figure 17.3).

The SLB option allows students with perhaps less experience in the production of practical art, or with outstanding analytical/critical skills, to pursue a course with an emphasis on the historical/cultural/contextual aspects. Naturally, the studio work component is still there because this is a vital element in fully understanding how their studies are linked to the experiences of artists and the creative processes involved.

Candidates at all three levels are expected to cover the core elements which include:

- introduction to art concepts, criticism, and analysis
- acquisition of studio technical and media skills
- relation of art to socio-cultural and historical contexts.

One remarkable point is that the visual arts programme does not have specific units, modules or items of study from which the teacher constructs the course. Instead, the programme provides a framework from which the teachers choose content and activities appropriate to their own and their students' interests and experience. Teachers should design their courses according to three main factors:

- the cultural background and personal needs of the student
- the situation of the school and the influences of local culture
- the teacher's own training and special skills (subject guide, page 7).

Flexibility is thus one of the distinguishing features of the visual arts programme, which is further evidenced by the fact that there is no specified amount of work required for each level. The quality and even the quantity of work produced by a talented SL student may well be superior to that of an HL student. What counts is *growth* and commitment: examiners expect to see a more sustained growth with HL students, corresponding to the longer exposure afforded by HL. The way growth is assessed is through the research workbook, which acts as a journal detailing the developments in critical awareness over the two years of study. Entries from the student plus comments of the teachers should be dated and kept in chronological order and should not be edited by cutting out what may be considered weaker material. The content of the research workbooks, some selected studio work, and the relationship between these two will form the basis of the discussions between candidate and external examiner.

4.2 Studio work

All students should be introduced to art concepts and techniques through practical work in the studio. They are expected to produce works of art with imagination and creativity through individual and, where appropriate, collaborative work. Each candidate should eventually prepare an exhibition which should comprise artistic products and research work, sketches, notes, and other preliminary work. The actual selection of these materials will have significance in the assessment. No specific quantity of work is prescribed, but below are the main factors to consider:

- technical characteristics of the media and production processes (candidates are expected to solve formal and technical problems they encounter)
- the nature of the images and the process of their development
- appropriate use of a variety of media
- technical skills
- complexity
- scale
- imagination and creativity
- synthesis of conceptual content, knowledge of form, and technical skills in works that are personally, socio-culturally, and aesthetically meaningful
- purposeful exploration demonstrating an enquiring and integrative approach to a variety of visual phenomena (refer to the psychology of visual perception)
- the time available at each level of the programme – in this case assessment will take account of the time available for either HL or SLA or SLB work.

Selection of an appropriate exhibition space is important. It should be quiet, well-lit, and have no other activities taking place there. The role of the external examiner is to draw out the candidates' views and encourage them to talk about their work, its origins and its development.

In order to prepare their candidates for this assessment, teachers should support students in efforts to express themselves meaningfully and they should provide structured opportunities for the students to learn to appreciate the aesthetic qualities of visual arts, the relationships between form and meaning, and its social and cultural functions. Students should be encouraged and helped to use their individual strengths. The main aim is to produce work demonstrating maturity of artistic understanding, rather than superficial work showing acquaintance with a large number of techniques. Students should be encouraged to embark on a wide-ranging personal experimental journey through the arts that includes an exploration of local arts. Encourage them to share their visions and work collaboratively, but their own work must show evidence of individual achievement utilizing several different techniques and media, 'ranging from painting to puppetry, calligraphy to computer graphics, and sculpture to conceptual art' (subject guide).

4.3 Research workbooks

The main purpose of the research workbooks is to encourage personal research and discovery, at all levels. The workbooks should incorporate the following:

- analytical research
- discovery
- interpretation
- media experiments.

They should contain both visual and written information, including the student's own original works in the form of sketches and diagrams, and should function as working journals of the student's journey through the programme. There should be a balance between analytical research and open-ended enquiry, illustrating the 'creative processes' of the student.

All candidates will be expected to:

- demonstrate clearly in visual and written terms how personal research has led to an understanding of the topics or concepts being investigated
- analyse critically the meaning and aesthetic qualities of art forms using an informed vocabulary
- show some historical and social dimensions of themes in more than one cultural context
- examine the visual and functional qualities of art from their own and other cultures for meaning and significance.

The content can vary considerably from student to student, but there must be evidence of research into the socio-cultural and historical contexts of more than one culture. The use of the vocabulary of art criticism should be encouraged. The following suggestions provide an idea of the scope and extent allowed and expected in the content, a fuller version of which is in the subject guide.

- Personal reports of visits to museums and galleries, local artists and designers should be included. Photographs, copies, cut-outs from magazines are allowed if relevant and accompanied by commentary. Relevant information from other disciplines can also be included.
- Evidence of teacher–student dialogue should be included, and pertinent questions and comments of either teacher or student should be recorded; students should not edit out the teacher's input to their work.
- Information may be recorded by any means, e.g. drawing, painting, word processing.
- Workbooks are journals which should reflect a personal approach. Entries should be dated and kept in chronological order and should *not* be edited by cutting out what may be considered weaker material.
- Formal papers should not be included; long essays should be avoided.
- It is recommended that workbooks be bound, with unlined pages, rather than loose-leaf.
- Legibility is always important.

4.4 Assessment details

At all three levels of the programme, the candidate's body of work *as a whole* is assessed. This includes both the finished products in the studio work and the processes of artistic research and development. There are two general criteria used in the assessment: *growth* (primarily in studio work) and *integration* (of research and studio work). The content of the research workbooks will form the basis of the discussions between candidate and external examiner. The emphasis in discussion of these workbooks will be on issues of art criticism and cultural understanding. The external examiner will draw out the student's views on relevant matters through questions designed to open up the discussion as far as possible so that the candidates feel they have adequate opportunity to articulate their views and experiences.

A *Candidate Record Booklet* is to be prepared by the candidate to facilitate moderation of the internal grade awarded for the research workbooks. Full details of this booklet are contained in the *Vade Mecum*, but it should contain the following:

- a personal statement by the candidate about their work (300 words) describing briefly their growth and development as an artist
- a representative set of photographs of their work; candidates should select 12 photographs for HL and SLA, and fewer for SLB
- some suitable pages (20 pages in all) photocopied from the research workbooks which show how all assessment criteria are covered.

This booklet has become a vital part of the assessment process. Moderation has affected grades considerably in recent years, and this booklet is the *only* evidence that moderators have at their disposal. An increasing emphasis is being placed on the quality of the photographs used to document studio work. Poor photographs can penalize students. Also, it is no easy task to select 20 pages for photocopying from a huge body of work in the research workbooks, simultaneously making sure they show how a student's enquiry has covered the four assessment criteria. Since the moderator only has these photocopies to work with, however, it is vital that the photocopied pages show the best work for the four assessment criteria in equal measure.

Internal assessment of both studio work (SLB) and research workbooks (HL and SLA) will follow similar procedures to those of externally assessed work, except that they will be carried out by the teacher in the school. This work must be made available to the external examiner, who will view it for external moderation.

All assessment is done through specific assessment criteria, with descriptors of each level of attainment. The point of this type of assessment by criterion referencing is to make judgements appropriate to each individual candidate, not according to some normative marking scheme. Full details are contained in the subject guide.

4.5 Visual arts: pedagogical leader?

The visual arts programme attempts to ensure that the candidate is fully engaged in development as a visual artist, both on a level of personal involvement and in terms of being able to make informed critical comments about art work across different cultures and times. Both a candidate's artistic products and their growth and development through the processes of making art are integral and equally important components in the assessment. Candidates are really a part of the assessment process in that they are judged on their ability to judge themselves and their work. The practices of studio work in the visual arts have long been concerned with self-criticism and re-evaluation of both the art work and the processes of its evolution and development. These activities are carried out as part of a group, so that the individuals make judgements not only about themselves and their work, but also about others in the group, who will return the favour. Thus it becomes a process of critical self-examination, submission to the processes of group examination and criticism, and participation in the group criticism of each individual. This process is somewhat unique to the education of visual artists (but vital for students who wish to do well). It does not occur in music, nor does it occur to the same extent in theatre arts. Some, including this writer, feel that the arts in general would benefit enormously by adopting such procedures instead of allowing each individual to work in isolation, immune from peer criticism, and lacking in support or critical analysis from peers. When artists work in society, they have little option but to submit to group analysis and comment, so there is a lot to be said for starting this process during educational development. In this sense, the visual arts educators are pedagogical leaders in the arts.

5 Pilot programmes in dance, film, and 'text and performance'

The IBO is developing a number of additional programmes in the arts as pilot programmes, and trials are taking place in some selected schools. These include dance, film, and a new trans-disciplinary subject called 'text and performance' (see Chapter 18). Details of these exciting new ventures are not yet available, but note should be taken of these developments for future reference.

Chapter 18
The school based syllabus and trans-disciplinary subjects

Ellie Alchin, BA
with Gautam Sen

Ellie Alchin was coordinator of the school based syllabus (SBS) course 'Science, technology, and society' at the United World College of South East Asia (UWCSEA) from 1997 to 2000, and coordinator of the trans-disciplinary course 'Ecosystems and societies' at the International School of Geneva until July 2003. She is an IB examiner for geography and a member of the IB steering committee for 'Ecosystems and societies', for which course she is also one of the IBO-appointed external paper setters. In this chapter she details the challenges, rewards and future potential of the SBSs (school based syllabus subjects) and the trans-disciplinary subjects.

The case study 'Turkish social studies' in section 1.2 is provided with the help of Gautam Sen, a teacher at the Koc School in Istanbul, Turkey.

1 The school based syllabus

In addition to the regular courses a school may offer its students as part of their Diploma Programme (DP), some IB schools offer what are known as school based syllabus subjects (SBSs, only offered at Standard Level). These are courses written and developed by schools and which have been approved by the IBO. A few examples of the approximately 20 SBSs currently offered in IB schools are:

- human rights
- Greek and Roman studies
- electronic music
- historical and contemporary Brazilian studies
- science, technology and society (see case study in section 1.1)
- Turkish social studies (see case study in section 1.2).

Recognizing the value and potential of curriculum innovation within schools, the IBO encourages schools or groups of interested educators to submit proposals for potential SBSs to the IBO curriculum and assessment centre for approval. Proposals are then subject to rigorous assessment by the IBO to ensure that academic standards are appropriate, overlap with existing courses is minimal, and the integrity of the DP is maintained. All SBSs are Standard Level (SL) courses and can be substituted for a subject in groups 2, 3, 4 or 6. Full details about the submission process can be found in the *Vade Mecum*.

For schools new to the DP, submitting a proposal for a new SBS is not an option allowed by the IBO for a few years, but nevertheless they do represent an exciting opportunity for teachers and curriculum planners who wish to develop specific programmes in the longer term. Collaborating with the IBO on a joint curriculum project such as a new SBS can be an extremely positive professional experience for teachers. Another key advantage is that the SBS can enable schools to meet their national educational requirements without imposing an additional workload on DP students. However, attempting to balance the examination requirements of the national universities, the demands of Ministries of Education and the spirit and style of the IB in a coherent approach is often a major challenge.

SBSs can become hugely popular among students. 'Brazilian studies', now offered in a number of Brazilian schools, is a favourite among students who see it as a real opportunity to study and discuss local and current issues in their own language. It is the only course in the British School of Rio in which the teaching and most of the resources used are in Portuguese and the language of assessment is English, which has contributed very positively to the development of integrated language skills.

In some cases an SBS can evolve into a mainstream course: environmental systems, for instance, developed from an SBS in marine biology. Schools wishing to offer an SBS that has been developed by another school may apply to the IBO to be allowed to do this.

1.1 Case study: 'Science, technology and society'

This SBS was introduced by a group of teachers at the UWCSEA in the early 1980s. The course was originally entitled: 'Science, technology and social change', and it focused on exploring the ways in which science and technology could be a positive or negative force for societal change in the process of economic development. A key feature of the course involved an exploration of the ideas of appropriate technology, pioneered by E. F. Schumacher, and the study of these principles in local contexts in South East Asia. As might be inferred from the title, the course was a cross-curricular initiative, involving teachers from the technology, science and geography departments. It was approved by the IBO, and was taught successfully at UWCSEA for almost 15 years.

During this time the course underwent syllabus revisions: the role of information technologies and modern scientific innovations in changing modern societies was increasingly pertinent and these issues were therefore built into the course content. New units on how social institutions attempt to control science and technology were also added. The course became known as 'Science, technology and society' (STS) but the central conceptual heart of the subject remained the same.

The advantages of offering STS as one of the DP course options were considerable. Pedagogically, a cross-curricular course is immensely beneficial for students. The emphasis on case studies (such as the industrial revolution, the internet, and technology and warfare) gave the course a sense of cohesion and afforded the student the opportunity to approach the same issues from a variety of angles. Conceptually it required students to think more holistically. The assessment models were designed to ensure that skills in all areas were assessed – and therefore involved lab work, technical design projects, research, data response and essays. To do well students had to be able to integrate these skills to respond to broader questions which addressed the central theme of the course: that of the interaction between societies and technology.

As a United World College located in Asia, issues of economic development, and the sensitive use of technology in the economically less developed world, were particularly relevant to our students. The extensive opportunities for local fieldwork in Malaysia and Indonesia were a distinct advantage, and the emphasis on learning 'in the field' was a particularly strong element of the course.

Much of the content for the course was extremely contemporary, and the course represented a new area of study for many students, which made it a popular option choice. As a cross-curricular course STS could be taken as a group 4 (Experimental sciences) or group 3 (Individuals and societies) subject. It had particular appeal for students interested in careers in development and aid, economics, engineering, scientific research, management, design and IT, and many felt it gave them the opportunity to talk about something original in their interviews at tertiary institutions. For their part, many institutions were impressed that a course undertaken by students aged 16–19 was so inter-disciplinary – a feature that mirrored trends in many of their own courses.

The process of developing and teaching STS afforded huge opportunities for the professional enrichment of the staff involved. Working together to debate the conceptual basis for the course, to develop new units, to moderate internal assessment, write examinations, lead residential field trips, and to resource and teach the course, was extremely rewarding. The course built on existing expertise within the staff body, but also ensured that new teachers had a chance to broaden the spectrum of their teaching and develop new teaching skills.

It was not, however, without its difficulties. With any new course there may be some initial suspicion from parents and students (and sometimes colleagues) to be overcome. Is it a 'proper' course? Will it be recognized by universities? More fundamental was the concern that as a cross-curricular course STS could not hope to be of the same standard as its contemporaries in groups 3 and 4. All these questions were asked frequently. The responses were of course that STS had been officially endorsed by the IBO and was indeed a proper course subject to the same process of evaluation and review as other IB courses. It was explained that most universities looked on the course very favourably (though sometimes required clarification of what it had involved). To answer the third question required an acknowledgement that clearly the amount of content could not be the same as in the 'pure' subjects, but that conceptually the cross-curricular approach contained many unique features and enabled students to develop essential new academic and intellectual skills which were not present in the 'pure' subjects.

As the course was taught by non-specialists, the demands on staff were considerable. Several units required teaching outside the subject areas, a challenge that required a strong commitment to personal reading, research and preparation. The need for collaboration, though rewarding, was time-consuming, and many staff found lesson preparation for STS took much longer than for their mainstream subjects. Experience built up over many years of teaching the course was invaluable for teachers, but of course this did lead to problems with staff turnover and deciding who would teach it from year to year. To a huge extent, the success of an SBS depends on the staff who develop it and are able to teach it. Resourcing a course with no recognized textbooks was another challenge – one shared by coordinators of other SBSs around the world – and therefore centralized support from a course coordinator was vital.

Examination papers must be written and marked by the teachers themselves, and of course are subject to rigorous standards of security. They are externally moderated to ensure fairness, but it was a burden on staff to have to deal with these administrative elements in addition to their normal teaching commitments.

The dynamic nature of the SBS is a key attraction (schools are free to lead changes to the syllabus without reference to other schools) but can also be challenging. The establishment of Information Technology in a Global Society (ITGS) (see Chapter 14) as a mainstream IB course posed a new dilemma as it contained considerable content overlap with units in STS. The development of the radical new trans-disciplinary subjects within the IB – with their emphasis on cross-curricular approaches to learning – have stolen the thunder somewhat from courses such as STS.

More generally, an advantage of the trans-disciplinary subjects over the SBSs is their external assessment. As students are not allowed to opt for both a trans-disciplinary subject and an SBS the numbers opting for the SBS may decline.

1.2 Case study: 'Turkish social studies' by Gautam Sen

The 'Professor' is not a machine for giving lectures, but is a resource to the students – one who inspires them to investigate and question, one who guides them and one who is able to sustain their enthusiasm for study and research. The real professor is himself a life-long student.

Minister of Education for Turkey at a speech at Istanbul University, 1933

It is often assumed that all IB schools introducing an SBS share a common curricular and pedagogical culture where teachers have some degree of autonomy for setting priorities, selecting resources, and defining assessment standards, subject to well-understood norms of accountability.

In Turkey, however, teachers teach a syllabus that is essentially set by the Ministry of Education, whose objective in teaching the social sciences is to impart a particular view of Turkish culture and history that conforms to the national ideology implicit in an officially codified set of principles based on the ideas of Mustafa Kemal Atatürk. Until we introduced the SBS, the teaching of social studies was regarded as imparting a body of uncontested facts about the geography, history and sociology of Turkey. The assessment consisted either of multiple choice or short answer questions that tested recall much more than the understanding and application of concepts and principles. Teachers were expected neither to be familiar with developments in their subject or in their pedagogy, nor to provide different perspectives, beyond what was presented in government-approved textbooks. The only international perspective appeared in topics such as the Ottoman conquest of south-eastern Europe and west Asia, or in the role of the Great Powers in the policies of the Ottoman empire in the 19th century. Significantly, no history is taught in the high school curriculum that covers events after the death of Atatürk in 1938. Finally, apart from exceptions such as business and management, economics, ITGS and psychology, no IB group 3 subject can be taught by a Turkish IB school (i.e. where Turkish citizens are educated and one that is subject to the supervision of the Ministry of Education) in a language other than Turkish or by a teacher other than a Turk.

Not surprisingly then, my proposal to introduce an SBS syllabus 'Turkish social studies' was met with a mixture of enthusiasm and trepidation: enthusiasm over the possibilities it offered for the autonomous design of a curriculum, trepidation about the degree to which we could depart from the content and spirit of the Ministry curriculum. My initial proposal of a thematic structure and inter-disciplinary approach was rejected as being too radical to pass the approval process at the Ministry.

We eventually settled on a curriculum that consisted of two parts: one part that re-ordered the topics in the Ministry curricula for history, geography and sociology under the broad heading 'Turkey and the Aegean region' (in order to conform to IB requirements for greater internationalism) while including certain topics from Greek history, culture and geography as well; the other part retained the more traditional topics in Turkish history but with a greater emphasis on the 19th and 20th centuries up to 1938 under 'History of Modern Turkey'. The assessment followed the standard IB practices (criterion-based marking of a variety of written work, one examination paper for each part, based on short, structured responses to data or documentary extracts, as well as extended essay-type answers).

Uniquely, the course is the only SBS to be taught and assessed in Turkish, i.e., in a language that is not one of the working languages of the IBO. The fact that this was allowed by the IBO is an indication of the flexibility with which the IBO can adapt to a national requirement. Likewise, the process of approval of the course by the Turkish Ministry of Education seemed to indicate that there was greater interest in curricular innovation than we had at first suspected.

Although the SBS involved two years of preparation and numerous meetings between teachers from several schools, the outcome was not very satisfactory.

Student evaluations of the course in its first two years showed that they felt they were better off under the previous system, partly because their teachers seemed more confident about teaching that, and partly because they were denied the advantage of a textbook and were forced to rely on large numbers of class handouts, or books to which they referred only for certain details. Moreover, the changes in the syllabus were not accompanied initially by changes in the style of teaching that the syllabus required, because many teachers tended to mitigate their discomfort with the new syllabus by teaching it in their accustomed fashion. In informal interviews, students often made a clear distinction between their other IB courses (including Turkish A1) and the SBS, which they felt was 'not really an IB course'.

This persuaded me to initiate an early review of the syllabus, with the support and consent of the assessor and the IB Curriculum Centre, this time with a thematic organization and more properly inter-disciplinary method. The syllabus (possibly with the new title 'Turkey in a globalizing world') aims to integrate analytical concepts and tools from history, sociology, geography and religious studies (all compulsory parts of the national curriculum), and will be organized along the following themes:

A Growth of human settlements (cities, villages and urbanization, nomads)

B Industrialization and trade contacts

C Encounters with West and East

D Modernization, republicanism, and democracy

E Religion, politics and the nation state.

The process of review includes a weekly seminar with a professor of history at a local university who inspires our teachers with ideas about the social sciences and how to teach them. The other schools will be invited to participate in the review process upon completion of the first draft of the revised syllabus.

The process of working with other schools 'sharing' an SBS has led in some cases to a certain amount of professional rivalry, but also an appreciation of the intellectual challenges of designing a curriculum. Teachers often felt exhausted by the amount of effort that the syllabus demands, and by the sheer frequency of inter-school meetings, often ending with issues unresolved.

The enthusiasm for the course, especially in its new form, seems to have waned somewhat among the other participating schools, since they are more concerned about the coverage of topics in the Ministry curriculum than we are (the fact that most of our IB students can afford to go abroad relieves them from the obligation of sitting the Turkish university entrance examination which includes topics from the Ministry's social studies courses). This affords us a greater freedom to take risks and innovate, a freedom that is increasingly explored by our teachers as a result of the culture of experimentation that the introduction of an SBS has brought.

2 The trans-disciplinary subjects

The importance of students making connections in their learning and accessing new knowledge across the curriculum and between separate disciplines is evident in the elements of the design of each of our (IB) programmes. Making connections is essential in an international curriculum which focuses on questions of global significance in areas such as sustainable development and the global environment, human rights, and peace and security.

Helen Drennen, former Academic Director of the IBO

A number of schools around the world are currently in the pilot phase for a new kind of course developed by the IBO called the *trans-disciplinary subject*. The name for these subjects has been chosen because of the inclusive sense of the prefix 'trans' which suggests an area of academic study which *includes* methodologies from more than one diploma subject group. To be credible, of course, these new subjects must retain their own academic integrity and autonomy as well as fulfilling the aims of the two groups they represent. At this stage three such syllabuses have been developed:

Ecosystems and Societies (groups 3 and 4)

Text and Performance (groups 1 and 6)

World Cultures (groups 3 and 6).

It is hoped that trans-disciplinary subjects will enhance the flexibility of the diploma hexagon (see Chapter 1), improving access to different options for students. The idea is that each of these courses satisfies the aims of two groups *at the same time*. So, unlike the SBS course STS, described in section 1.1, which could be taken as *either* a group 3 *or* a group 4 subject, 'Ecosystems and societies', for example, can be taken as *both* group 3 *and* group 4. The benefits to students of such an option are evident. Someone who has fulfilled the requirements of groups 3 and 4 with a single subject is now able to take, say, two subjects from group 6, or an additional language. In short the trans-disciplinary option allows students greater specialization within their package, whilst not sacrificing the breadth that is one of the hallmarks of the DP.

Whilst the study of discrete subject areas is still the central framework of the DP, it is hoped that the trans-disciplinary subjects will enhance the holistic inter-disciplinary ways of learning that are already encouraged in the DP through the Theory of Knowledge and the group 4 science project. The IBO also hope that contemporary themes such as 'Global environmental issues' and 'World cultures' will symbolize and reflect the international spirit of its diploma.

In terms of professional development, trans-disciplinary subjects offer exciting opportunities for different subject specialists to collaborate on a shared course. Arguably the preferred method of delivery should be for individual teachers to assume responsibility for the teaching of the whole syllabus, but to work in mixed specialist teams to ensure adequate support in their weaker areas. In this way the holism of the course is preserved and the students are less likely to compartmentalize the subject matter. Not only is it professionally enriching to teach new subject material, but it can also be very rewarding personally to learn new material and to be exposed to assessment models from a different discipline.

Having said this, teaching a trans-disciplinary subject can be a huge undertaking as it involves a willingness to keep abreast of new material that may be outside the teacher's main subject area. This means that supporting the team with adequate resources is particularly important, requiring considerable investment in training, texts and other resources by the school. Schools must ensure that adequate collaboration takes place; that funding is equally shared; and that members of different subject areas are willing to be involved. The school's management needs to provide a clear lead in asserting the equal merit of trans-disciplinary courses to counter the inevitable claims of lower standards that will be levelled at them.

The quality of support provided by the IBO is considerable, however, and makes the decision for a school to offer a trans-disciplinary a less daunting one. The syllabus for 'Ecosystems and societies', briefly discussed below, is particularly detailed to ensure that non-specialists know exactly what is expected. Flexibility is retained with choices for illustrative case studies so that teachers can teach to their strengths and make the most of local opportunities for fieldwork. The community of support provided through the Online Curriculum Centre (OCC) and IB workshops is excellent.

Should the pilot phases prove successful, the three trans-disciplinary courses will become mainstream subjects available to all DP schools soon after 2005.

In the descriptions of the three individual trans-disciplinary courses below, it must be remembered that each is currently a pilot course; the information here reflects the current thinking but is still subject to change.

2.1 Ecosystems and societies

The syllabus of 'Ecosystems and societies' (groups 3 and 4) is based on the already highly successful group 4 'Environmental systems' SL course, but to meet the aims of group 3 the balance of content has shifted markedly and now includes much more emphasis on social systems and environmental ethics.

The main purpose of this course is to give students a coherent perspective on the interrelationships between ecosystems and societies. To fully understand the causes and effects of environmental problems and how societies try to manage them, students are required to look at issues such as global warming, pollution, famine, and soil degradation holistically, from scientific, ethical, historical, economic, cultural and socio-political perspectives. The systems approach, familiar to both geographers and biologists, is a fundamental and unifying aspect of the course. Not only do ecosystems function as a whole, which is illustrated by the systems approach, but this same approach is also common to many humanities subjects, such as economics, geography, sociology and politics. The course aims to enable students to adopt an informed personal response to current environmental issues and to understand the impact of their own choices and decisions on the environment. Comparing the course description above with the overall DP aims set out in Chapter 2, it is evident that this subject is a 'model citizen' of the DP family.

The syllabus is being piloted in a handful of schools around the world and is expected to be an extremely popular trans-disciplinary subject once the review and evaluation process has been completed and the IBO launches it worldwide.

The advantages of offering this course are numerous. Apart from the very real benefits it provides for students in terms of package selection, it is an exciting and contemporary course to teach. Environmental issues have an increasingly high profile politically and, for students wishing to pursue careers in this or related fields, 'Ecosystems and societies' is a great place to start. The approach of studying ecosystems together with their relation to society is mirrored in the approach of international organizations such as the UNEP (United Nations Environmental Programme) and in a great deal of current environmental thinking in tertiary institutions.

2.2 Text and performance

This course is a synthesis of language A1 and theatre arts. It incorporates the essential elements of literature and theatre and aims to explore the dynamic relationship between the two. At the heart of the course is the interaction between a conventional literary emphasis on close reading, critical writing and discussion on the one hand, and the practical, aesthetic and symbolic elements of theatre on the other.

The course seeks to broaden the perspectives of students through the exploration of texts from diverse cultures, periods and genres, and to foster a personal and passionate engagement with literature and the theatre, and by so doing to guide students towards a better understanding of themselves and the world.

Candidates will be expected to demonstrate:

- knowledge and understanding of texts of different genres, cultures and periods
- an appreciation of the literary techniques and theatrical potential in the texts studied
- an ability to speak and write about the texts and theatrical traditions studied
- performance skills, both as individuals and in collaboration with others
- an understanding of the principles and practices involved in the realization of theatre from different cultural traditions
- an ability to reflect on and respond to the processes of reading and performance.

2.3 World cultures

At the heart of 'World cultures' (groups 3 and 6) is a three-stage engagement by the student with a work of art or cultural phenomenon:

1. The student's direct encounter with the object or performance (the cultural phenomenon).
2. The student's research into the literature and body of knowledge about this particular cultural phenomenon.
3. The student's continuous informed personal interaction with the cultural phenomenon, linking it to a range of concrete examples of other works of art and cultural phenomena.

Other essential features of 'World cultures' are:

- an international cultural perspective across space and time
- an understanding of the student's own and other cultures
- the placing of cultural phenomena in their social and economic context
- an exploration of universal concepts of existence/systems of belief
- an appreciation of different aesthetic frameworks
- a study of the effect of international exchange – creative and positive

- an examination of the culture of consumption and its effects
- an examination of phenomena with defined limits and defining characteristics that are representations of a particular culture
- the study of a body of recognized literature about the phenomena
- an investigation of the place of works of art in society.

As a tool to exploring cultural objects and phenomena, 'World cultures' draws on the methodologies of historical investigation, art history, ethno-musicology, anthropology and sociology. In this way, it genuinely is a trans-disciplinary subject.

Chapter 19
Closing thoughts

John Goodban

The aim of this book has been to focus on the Diploma Programme (DP) from the pre-application stage, through the authorization procedures, the development of the school's DP, the specific hexagon groups and subjects and their teaching, assessment and resourcing. The book is not in any way geared to be competitive with the wealth of diploma materials published by the IBO. Indeed its objective has been to provide a reference companion to complement the existing materials and to give school administrators and teachers a greater insight (and encouragement) into what the IBO expects of them and how best they can serve the interests of their students in the classroom, the laboratory and in the field. Furthermore, the importance of teacher-training workshops should not be underestimated, and no book, no matter how well written and expansive, can ever be considered an adequate substitute for first-class professional training.

The DP that is taught today would be immediately recognizable by the programme's early founders of the 1960s. The hexagon, the extended essay, the Theory of Knowledge and CAS retain their central positions, and students are still required to study a broad range of six subjects chosen in line with the IBO's guidelines. The Mission Statement is expressed in greater detail, but its aims are essentially unchanged. It is interesting to observe that the global issues extant at the time when the aims were originally spawned and nurtured were not all so different from the issues extant at the beginning of the Second Millennium. The north–south divide, the economic and political importance of major oil reserves, the threats from the proliferation of weapons and armed conflicts around the globe, overpopulation, the debasement of human values, and the occurrence of conflict at the intercultural interface are no less a problem now than they were 35 years ago. None is a national issue that can find national solutions. They are international problems that can only be solved in the global parliament of debate and consensus. As a consequence, the need to foster in young minds a strong sense of the importance of international understanding, intercultural awareness, tolerance and compassion has never been greater than it is today. While national curricula inevitably lean towards national perspectives, the DP's strict non-allegiance to any government policies, political theory and religious doctrines has been of significant advantage to the IBO throughout its history in its claim to offer the world's only truly international curriculum.

The ultimate justification and test of all curricula are in the academic, intellectual and personal development of the students who receive them. It was the aim of the founders of the DP that its students are able to demonstrate that they:

- are able to function successfully across the entire curriculum
- have achieved high levels of literacy and numeracy

- have a sound grasp of scientific and technological principles
- are able to articulate ideas clearly and accurately
- have a strong sense of their own national identity and an understanding and respect for other cultures
- are able to select and analyse information efficiently
- are able to work and think independently and creatively
- have learned how to learn.

DP students who have acquired these specific skills and values are increasingly welcomed by universities which recognize the programme as an excellent preparation for successful tertiary careers. The attrition rate of DP students at university appears to be low. However, it has to be acknowledged that, to date, much of what the IBO has claimed for many years in terms of the derived benefits for its DP students is axiomatic rather than research based. Though many would assert that these benefits are self-evident, to leave it at that is not acceptable. Consequently, at its May 2003 meeting, the Council of Foundation agreed that this unsatisfactory situation would be addressed through the launching of a longitudinal study that will, in particular, be brought to bear on DP graduates' careers, especially their performance at tertiary education level.

There is little doubt in my mind that the outcome of the study will confirm the reality of many of those benefits. Having been involved personally with the IB in several roles since 1972 as a teacher, a DP coordinator, a curriculum writer, an IBO regional representative and, finally, as the IBO regional director of the Asia-Pacific for 11 years, I have witnessed first-hand how DP students change during their two-year programme. Particularly notable is their rapid growth in self-confidence, their ability to manage time efficiently and to work independently and in groups, their genuine respect for learning and discovering, their increased community awareness and compassion for the disadvantaged, and their awareness of their own identity against the backdrop of an international environment, coupled with a tolerance towards those who look, think, and believe differently. While it could be said that these developments are an inherent part of the maturation process of all senior high school students, I am convinced that the DP does more than any other programme at this level to encourage the growth and development of a very wide range of skills, humane values and a genuine love of learning from the experience of its whole curriculum.

From 1968 until 1994 the IB was the diploma. However, in 1994 this was to change with the introduction of the Middle Years Programme (MYP) which, having successfully completed its pilot stage, became available to schools worldwide. The MYP is a five-year programme designed for young people aged 11–16 years. In 1997 the Primary Years Programme (PYP) likewise became available. The IBO was now in the unique position of being able to offer an international curriculum that comprised three programmes, covering the entire span of formal education from the ages of 3 to 19 years. Each programme could stand alone in its own right with no requirement to teach either of the other two or, where a school wished and had the necessary age range of students, it could also be taught as a curriculum continuum linking directly with one or two of the other programmes.

The MYP, like the DP, was originally created by the International Schools Association (ISA) and was known as the International Schools Association Curriculum (ISAC). The development process began in the early 1980s and it was

Figure 19.1 The MYP octagon

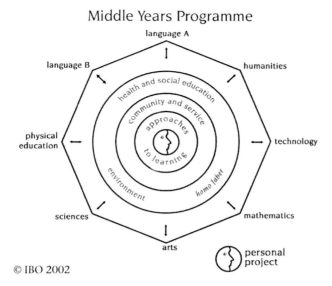

Middle Years Programme

language A

language B

humanities

health and social education

community and service

approaches

physical
education

to learning

technology

environment

homo faber

sciences

mathematics

arts

personal
project

© IBO 2002

largely a response to the growing demand by DP schools that wanted to have some sort of 'pre-IB' programme that would prepare their students well for future DP studies.

However, the aims of the ISA went well beyond the pragmatic creation of a formal curriculum designed for students aged between 11 and 16 years. From the start the ideals of the IBO's DP were recognized as being equally important to the ISAC programme. Great emphasis was placed on the student around whom the whole curriculum was constructed. Thus the MYP is a child-centred curriculum and its development has been firmly based on the personal and intellectual needs of the child as seen by the child, the parents and the school. Unsurprisingly, the list of skills and values that appears earlier in this chapter applies as much to the MYP as it does to the DP. The difference is merely in the level of expected achievement and the maturity of thought and expression.

The geometry of the MYP curriculum is an octagon with eight groups of subjects, six as for the DP, and the additional two accommodating technology and physical education (figure 19.1). As in the DP, the emphasis is on concept and process. The curriculum is broad and balanced. The student, whose development is the focus of the MYP, is at the centre of the curriculum model.

Surrounding the individual subjects are the *areas of interaction*. These are not subjects but are common themes embedded in the subjects that bind the MYP into a holistic curriculum. The areas of interaction are as follows:

- *Approaches to learning (ATL):* this provides the students with the various study skills that are essential for them to take an increasing responsibility for their own learning.

- *Community and service:* students are encouraged through a range of activities from the classroom to the community at large to develop an understanding of the nature of 'community', a concern for its well-being and a personal sense of responsibility to contribute to it.

- *Homo faber* (literally 'man the maker'): students learn through this area about the nature of the products manufactured by people, and to recognize that genius has both its creative and destructive features, and that the impacts on society are directly related to these. Students also learn about the relationship between science, technology and society and the ethics of technological development, change and decision-making.

- *Environment:* 'aims to develop the students' awareness of their inter-dependence with the environment so that they understand and accept their responsibilities' (*MYP Monograph*, IBO, 2002). A wide range of environments and environmental issues is the focus of much of this area; the challenges of solving the grave problems of environmental hazards and ensuring a sustainable future are two of the major issues for students to address.

- *Health and social education:* this area relates directly to the students' personal development and welfare in terms of physical, social and emotional health. 'Integrating health and social education throughout the curriculum and school life aims to prepare students for life by developing the ability to make choices for alternatives and to evaluate and make decisions about the health hazards they may face' (*MYP Monograph*, IBO, 2002).

Whereas it may be argued that the uniqueness of the DP is to be found at the hexagon's centre – the extended essay, the Theory of Knowledge and CAS – it is the areas of interaction that make for the uniqueness of the MYP. Not only are the areas most effective when integrated seamlessly into the courses of the eight subject areas, it is a strict IBO requirement that this should be the case in all authorized and aspiring MYP schools. Many schools initially find this to be the most difficult aspect of introducing and developing the programme.

It could be said that the MYP is more international than the DP in the sense that the curriculum materials are available in Chinese as well as English, French and Spanish. Chinese is the first non-European language to be adopted by the IBO for any of its publications. Students wishing to achieve the IBO MYP certificate can have their work moderated in any of the four languages. There is no external assessment of student achievement in the MYP. All of the students' work is assessed by teachers and measured critically against a specific set of assessment criteria listed in all subject guides. Students who wish to receive the MYP certificate, however, must have their internally awarded grades moderated externally and validated by the IBO.

The three IB programmes share an overarching philosophy and dominant common aims. Effectively, this means that where schools teach more than one of the programmes there will be no major curriculum paradigm shift at the programme interface(s). The MYP leads directly into the DP and, in similar fashion, the PYP interlinks with the MYP that follows it.

Returning to the DP and to conclude, it is hoped that authorized and implementing schools and individual teachers have found the wealth of information and advice in this book of considerable assistance in furthering their knowledge and understanding of the programme. However, as repeatedly mentioned in this book, this text should not be seen as a quick fix. There are no short cuts. The introduction and maintenance of a quality programme demand time, investment and an ongoing commitment including the full support of the school's governance, administration, teachers and parents. As for the contributors to this book, we all believe this is a price worth paying for the ultimate rewards and benefits that students and schools will derive from it.

Glossary

A1	a group 1 literature course taken in the student's mother tongue or best language
A2	a group 2 language and literature second language course for bilingual students
ab initio	a group 2 language course for beginners
A-levels	the collective term for the standard British high school (pre-university) curriculum
AP	Advanced Placement courses offered by US schools; they can enable direct credit towards some university courses
B	a group 2 language course for students developing competence in a second or a foreign language
CAS	creativity, action and service – one of the three core DP components
CEO	chief executive officer
Certificate	qualification awarded to students who do not take the full Diploma Programme, but just a few subjects
CIS	Canadian International School (Singapore)
CLEAPSS	Consortium of Local Education Authorities for the Provision of Science Services – it produces safety data for use in schools
DfES	Department for Education and Skills (UK)
DP	Diploma Programme of the International Baccalaureate Organization
DPC	DP coordinator
ECIS	European Council of International Schools
EE	extended essay – one of the three core DP components
ESL	English as a second language
ESOL	English for speakers of other languages
FM	further mathematics
GCE	General Certificate of Education (UK) (see A-levels)
GCSE	General Certificate of Secondary Education (UK)
GDC	graphical display calculator
GNVQ	General National Vocational Qualification
GPA	Grade Point Average
Group 1	language A1, the student's first language
Group 2	second language, for which there are three different levels of study: *ab initio* (beginner's course); language B (second language level); and A2 (bilingual level)
Group 3	individuals and societies – the humanities group
Group 4	experimental sciences – the science group
Group 5	mathematics and computer science
Group 6	the arts (and free electives)
hexagon	name of the curriculum structure of the DP
HL	Higher Level: one of two typical levels (see SL) at which one can study an academic subject in the DP. It requires a minimum of 240 hours of contact time spread out over two years. Students must take three (maximum four) of the six group subjects at HL.
IA	internal assessment
IB	International Baccalaureate
IBAEM	International Baccalaureate Africa, Europe and Middle East

IBAP	International Baccalaureate Asia-Pacific
IBCA	International Baccalaureate Curriculum and Assessment Centre in Cardiff, UK
IBHQ	International Baccalaureate Headquarters, in Geneva
IBLA	International Baccalaureate Latin America
IBNA	International Baccalaureate North America and Caribbean
IBNET	a collection of electronic services for IB coordinators. The latest version uses the global power of the internet and the world wide web. It is only available to Diploma, Middle Years and Primary Years programme coordinators in IBO member schools. The system currently works in English, French and Spanish. It can be accessed via the IB website: www.ibo.org
IBO	International Baccalaureate Organization
IB World	the IBO's quarterly magazine, which contains articles relating to the three IB programmes, and showcases what IB schools and students around the world are doing
ICT	information communication technology
IGCSE	International General Certificate of Secondary Education
IHRC	International Heads of School Representative Committee
IRP	intensive revision programme
ISA	International Schools Association
ISAC	International Schools Association Curriculum
ISB	International School, Brunei
ISI	Independent Schools Inspectorate (UK)
ISS	International School, Singapore
ITGS	information technology in a global society
LSC	Learning and Skills Council
MARA	Council of Trust for the People (acronym of Malay terms)
MCB	Mara College Banting (Malaysia)
MHL	mathematics Higher Level
MMSL	mathematics methods Standard Level
MNC	multi-national corporation
MSSL	mathematics studies Standard Level
MUN	Model United Nations club
MYP	IB Middle Years Programme
OCC	IB Online Curriculum Centre
Ofsted	Office for Standards in Education (UK)
OSD	Ontario Secondary Diploma
PALMS	Pan-Asia Librarians and Media Association
PBL	prescribed book list for A1 languages
PCF	Programme Completion Form
PHSE	personal, health and social education
PSOW	practical scheme of work
PWL	prescribed World Literature list for A1 languages
PYP	IB Primary Years Programme
QPT	Quick Placement Test
RAC	Regional Advisory Committee
RHRC	Regional Heads of School Representative Committee
SAT	Scholastic Assessment Test (UK)
SBS	school based syllabus (subjects)
SL	Standard Level: one of two typical levels (see HL) at which one can study an academic subject in the DP. It requires a minimum of 150 hours of contact time spread out over two years.
SMT	senior management team
SPM	Malaysian equivalent of the UK's GCSE
subject guide	each subject in the DP has its own subject guide, which details the aims and objectives of that subject, the content material, the skills that need to be taught, and notes on how the subject is assessed.

subject report	produced by the examiners after each examination session. The report highlights how candidates performed in each of the assessment components.
TDS	trans-disciplinary subjects – subjects that satisfy the criteria of two of the IB hexagon groups
TNC	trans-national corporation
TOK	Theory of Knowledge – one of the three core DP components
TSM	teacher support material
UCAS	Universities and Colleges Admissions Service (UK)
USP	undergraduate scholar programme
UWCSEA	United World College of South East Asia
Vade Mecum	the IBO's coordinators' handbook for the DP. It lists general and subject-specific regulations and procedures.
WL	World Literature

Printed in the United Kingdom
by Lightning Source UK Ltd.
132857UK00001BA/100/P